CONSUMER GUIDE®

New COMPLETE HOME REPAIR MANUAL

Consultant and Contributing Editor:
Dan Ramsey

Publications International, Ltd.

Dan Ramsey is a freelance writer who has written over 50 how-to books for consumers, including *Small Engine Repair Made Easy*, *Small Appliance Repair Made Easy*, and *Home Improvements: 52 Easy Weekend Projects*. He is a member of the National Association of Home & Workshop Writers.

Contributing Writer: James Hufnagle

Illustrations: Clarence A. Moberg (chapters 1, 2, 3, 4, 5, 7, 8, 9); Tim Kilian (chapters 6, 10); Marty Smith (chapter 6).
Contributing Illustrators: Jeff LeVan, Paul Pearson.

Photography: Dave Szarzak/White Eagle Studio.

Models: Andrew Newman/McBlaine and Assoc.; Kevin Langle/McBlaine and Assoc.

Special acknowledgments to Stanley Tools, Division of the Stanley Works, New Britain, CT, and Skokie Ace Hardware, Skokie, IL, for supplying photography props.

TABLE OF CONTENTS

INTRODUCTION...6

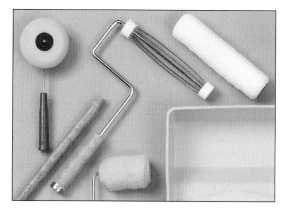

CHAPTER 1
WORKING SMART...10
Tools for the Do-it-Yourselfer • Working Safely

CHAPTER 2
INSIDE JOBS...34
Walls and Ceilings • Floors and Stairs • Windows • Doors

CHAPTER 3
INTERIOR DECORATING...68
Painting • Special Painting Effects • Wall Coverings • Understanding Wood Furniture •
Furniture Repairs • Furniture Refinishing

CHAPTER 4
ELECTRICITY...113
How the System Works • Repairing and Replacing Electrical Components • Installing
Other Electrical Components

TABLE OF CONTENTS

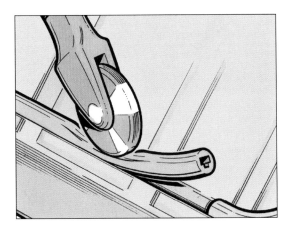

CHAPTER 5
MAJOR APPLIANCE REPAIR...146

Understanding Major Appliances • Repairing Gas Ranges and Ovens • Repairing Refrigerators and Freezers • Repairing Dishwashers • Repairing Washers and Dryers

CHAPTER 6
SMALL APPLIANCE REPAIR...204

Understanding Small Appliances • Troubleshooting Small Appliances • Repairing Toasters, Toaster Ovens, Coffee Makers, Food Mixers, Food Blenders, Electric Can Openers, Garbage Disposers, Vacuum Cleaners, and Hair Dryers

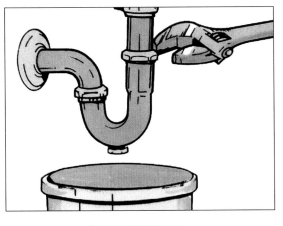

CHAPTER 7
PLUMBING...232

How the Plumbing System Works • Repairing Sinks, Tubs, and Drains • Repairing Toilets • Solving Pipe Problems

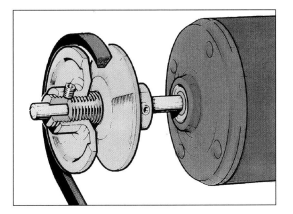

CHAPTER 8
HEATING AND COOLING SYSTEMS...260
How Heating and Cooling Systems Work • Maintenance Procedures • Troubleshooting
Heating Plants, Distribution Systems, and Cooling Systems • Conserving Energy

CHAPTER 9
OUTSIDE JOBS...316
Yard Work • Fences • Other Outside Jobs • Exterior Painting

CHAPTER 10
SMALL ENGINE REPAIR...351
Understanding Small Engines • Servicing Small Engines • Troubleshooting
Small Engines

INDEX...370

Congratulations! By purchasing the *New Complete Home Repair Manual*, you've taken the first big step on the road to becoming an accomplished home handyperson— now you can do much of your own home repair yourself. Of course, there's lots to learn along the way. This book is your definitive guide, so make sure to keep it nearby whenever you start a new project!

The *New Complete Home Repair Manual* is designed to save you time and money. It can make difficult jobs easier and tough jobs fun. It will help you around the house or apartment, offering clear step-by-step instructions on how to safely perform jobs you may have been putting off, leading you to a greater sense of accomplishment as you complete these jobs yourself. The easy-to-follow directions are designed to guide you through the repair process, telling you what to watch for and alerting you to possible pitfalls along the way.

Perhaps you're eager to flip the pages and tackle a do-it-yourself job or two that urgently need doing at your home. Great! Have at it! First, however, please take a few minutes to learn how the *New Complete Home Repair Manual* is organized and why it's organized the way it is. By familiarizing yourself with the contents of each chapter, you can quickly turn to the right place when you need help.

We'll begin with a short overview of your new manual.

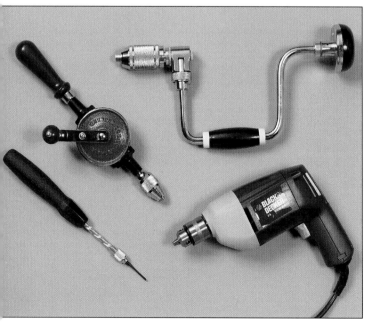

Chapter 1 includes practical information on selecting and using tools.

Working Smart

Tools can make any job easier or more difficult. The first chapter puts tools in your hands and safety on your mind. It includes practical information on selecting and using tools, abrasives, materials, fasteners, and adhesives to solve household problems. It also offers proven tips for making jobs around the home safer. Before you tackle your first home repair, make sure you at least browse this first chapter to get a better understanding of the tools you'll be using. In fact, the time you spend learning about tools can save you much valuable time later. Chapter 1 also tells about an extremely important issue: safety. Choose safe tools, learn how to correctly use them, and employ safety equipment at all times to avoid injuries. If you follow safety guidelines, the home repairs explained in the book can be done easily and safely—if you use shortcuts, you can be risking danger. Think safe and be safe.

Inside Jobs

Now that you know about working smart and working safely, the next likely question is: Where to start? Chapter 2 helps you where you live: on the inside of your home. It features step-by-step instructions and professional tips on making common repairs to walls, floors, stairs, windows, and doors. The instructions are clear, concise, and practical. They will guide you through many common jobs within your home, offering techniques used by professional remodelers and

Chapter 2 helps you where you live: on the inside of your home.

handypersons. Look around your home right now and you'll probably see many opportunities for repairs that are covered in this chapter. They include hanging things on walls, replacing moldings, installing paneling, repairing ceramic tile, installing and finishing a new wall, upgrading a ceiling, installing a new floor, and much more.

Interior Decorating

Is your home tired? Would you like to spruce it up for just a few dollars and a few hours of your time? Here's how: To improve the livability of your home, Chapter 3 helps you decorate the interior with fresh paint and wall coverings. It shows you how to plan and prepare for painting, how to select and use painting equipment, and how to clean up. It covers techniques for painting walls, ceilings, and woodwork as well. Chapter 3 also offers proven techniques for selecting, installing, repairing, and removing wall coverings. It also helps you repair and refinish wood furniture—refinishing wood furniture is much cheaper and usually much more attractive than buying new things. After you complete these projects, your home will reflect your good taste as well as your creativity and drive!

Chapter 3 helps you decorate the interior of your home.

Electricity

Your home is powered by electricity. You knew that! Chapter 4 includes uncomplicated explanations and easy-to-follow instructions for understanding and repairing your home's electrical system. If electricity is a scary thing to you, you're not alone! This chapter can help make it a little less intimidating. Topics include electrical service, overload protection, circuits, safety, and grounding.

You will also find information on restoring a circuit, coping with a power outage, and checking polarity. Step-by-step instructions for rewiring a

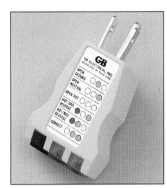
Chapter 4 shows you how to repair your home's electrical system.

lamp, replacing fixtures, replacing a switch, repairing a doorbell, and much more, will help you take care of commonplace electrical problems without having to rely on the neighborhood electrician. Chapter 4 also covers installing other electrical components such as ceiling fans, a home security system, an intercom system, a built-in sound system, and a garage door opener.

Major Appliance Repair

Chapter 5 applies what you've learned about electricity to the job of troubleshooting and repairing major appliances. This chapter alone can save you hundreds of dollars as you repair ranges, refrigerators, freezers, dishwashers, washers, dryers, and other major appliances. You'll learn how to disassemble the appliance, locate the

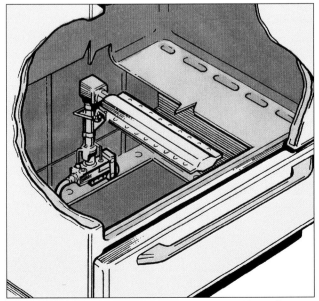
Learn how to troubleshoot and repair major appliances in Chapter 5.

problem, and replace parts, and also how to reassemble that major appliance without ending up with lots of leftover parts laying around! You'll learn how to fix cords, switches, thermostats, controls, heating elements, timers, thermocouples, motors, and more. You'll be given complete instructions for finding and fixing just about any problem that your major appliance can get into.

Small Appliance Repair

Chapter 6 can save you a few bucks, too, with step-by-step instructions for repairing common small appliances. Included are toasters, toaster ovens, coffee makers, food mixers and blenders, electric can openers, garbage disposers, vacuum cleaners, and hair dryers. Don't throw a malfunctioning small appliance away: Fix it! You'll learn the difference between heating, motor, and combination appliances. Comprehensive troubleshooting guides will help you pinpoint the cause of nearly any small appliance problem, and logical step-by-step instructions will guide you safely through the repair. You'll see how your small appliances work and what you should check if they don't. You'll also learn how to identify when an appliance is fixable and when to get a new one. Don't throw that hair dryer away before checking to find out if something simple just needs a small bit of attention.

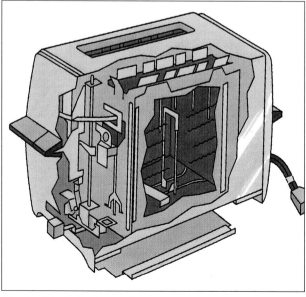

Chapter 6 includes instructions for repairing common small appliances.

Plumbing

Plumbing is your home's forgotten friend—until it begins acting up. Chapter 7 offers specific instructions on how to repair your home's plumbing system, including information on solving sink, tub, drain, toilet, and pipe problems. That probably doesn't sound like much fun, and as a matter of fact, it usually isn't. But it can be tolerable as well as rewarding if you know how to find and fix the problem fast. Besides, it is never fun writing a check to a plumber when you can easily do the job yourself. Learn how to clear

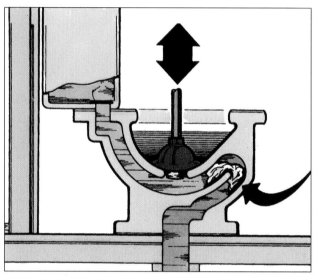

Chapter 7 tells how to repair your home's plumbing system.

clogged drains, stop faucet drips and leaks, replace a faucet, repair a spray hose or shower head, replace a trap, or work on a toilet. Also learn all about pipes: what to do if they become troublesome and—even better—how to keep them trouble-free from the start.

Heating and Cooling Systems

The level of comfort in your home depends on your heating and cooling systems. Chapter 8 shows you how to maintain and repair heating plants, distribution systems, and cooling systems. It goes a step farther with tips on conserving energy in your home to make it more comfortable and at the same time making it more efficient. Learn about forced air, gravity, radiant heat, and other heat distribution systems. Understand how controls work and what to do when they don't. Learn how to replace filters, maintain motors, and perform other seasonal maintenance tasks that can add years to the life of your system. Unclear on how air conditioners work? This chapter describes how they do their magic and what can happen to prevent an air conditioner from working effectively. In addition, you'll find

Learn about heating and cooling systems in Chapter 8.

valuable tips on improving heating and cooling efficiency. You will save money on your heating and cooling bills by keeping your systems maintained and working efficiently.

Outside Jobs

A spring or fall day invites you to spend time outdoors working in the yard. Chapter 9 offers tips on how to maximize enjoyment and minimize work time in your yard. It includes step-by-step instructions on basic yard work, fence repairs, and various other outside jobs necessary for maintaining an attractive and orderly home. This chapter explains how to mow, edge, and water lawns more efficiently and presents techniques for managing weeds and insects. You'll find out how professional landscapers plant new lawns and shrubs and how they prune trees. You've heard that good fences make good neighbors, and Chapter 9 covers topics such as how to select, install, and repair fences. The repair of siding, shakes, shingles, roofs,

Chapter 9 tells how to maintain and beautify the outside of your home.

garage doors, and porches are also detailed in this chapter. And don't forget those gutters—they are also covered in this chapter.

If you still have some energy left from these outside jobs, you can master the steps for painting the outside of your home: Learn about everything from removing old paint to selecting and applying the most suitable paint for your home's particular conditions. You'll be impressed with your knowledge and how attractive your home will look—and so will your friends and neighbors. Your home is sure to be a showplace at your next barbeque or get-together!

Small Engine Repair

Many of the tools and toys you use outside your home are powered by small engines. Chapter 10 will guide you through servicing and trouble-shooting lawn mowers, tillers, cultivators, and other two-stroke engines. Step-by-step instructions are offered for maintaining and repairing these time-saving tools. This chapter includes instructions for servicing an air cleaner, crankcase breather, and cooling system, plus muffler repair, lubrication, and tune-ups. Useful illustrations will guide you through the steps to keep your tools and toys doing their jobs better and longer.

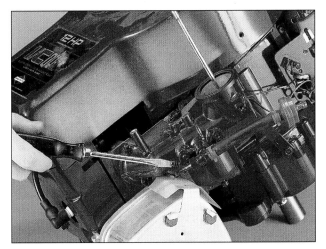

Learn how to service and repair small engines in Chapter 10.

We hope you find the *New Complete Home Repair Manual* to be a comprehensive and useful book you will refer to again and again. Use it to help make your home a more enjoyable, efficient, attractive, and well-run place to live.

Work smart. Be safe. Save money. Have fun!

CHAPTER 1

WORKING SMART

Working safely is working smart. For the do-it-yourselfer, working smart means having the right tools and materials for the job. That's what this first chapter is about. In it, you will learn or be reminded of the basic tools that are necessary for common home repairs. You don't have to spend lots of money on these tools. In fact, the money you save on your very first do-it-yourself repair may pay for the tools you needed. And after that, these tools are yours to keep. You'll also learn how to select and use the materials used in common repairs. Most important, you'll read about easy-to-apply rules for working safely and learn techniques for using tools and materials without injuring yourself or others.

Tools for the Do-It-Yourselfer

Useful tools for common home maintenance and repairs include measuring tools, saws, drills, and fastener tools. Next come tools for specific tasks: electrical, plumbing, small engine, and other jobs.

The smartest rule about tools is to buy good ones. Quality tools are safe and easy to use, and most will last a lifetime if you take care of them. You can spot a quality tool by its machining: The metal parts are smooth and shiny, and the tool is well balanced. Inexpensive tools are often painted to hide defects or rough metal parts, and the machining is crude. You can often tell quality by the price tag as well. You'll typically pay an average of 25 percent more for quality equipment. But cheap tools are no bargain—you frequently get what you pay for.

Measuring Tools

Just about every project calls for accurate measurements. Not only do you have to know precisely how many feet and inches are involved, you also usually have to ensure that everything comes out plumb, level, and square. The following are the basic devices for measuring and marking.

Tape Measures

Flexible tape measures are available in lengths of up to 50 feet; a tape that is 16 to 24 feet is usually considered to be adequate. You should buy a tape at least ⅝-inch wide, so it will stay rigid when extended. Many rules have an automatic power return that is useful but not necessary.

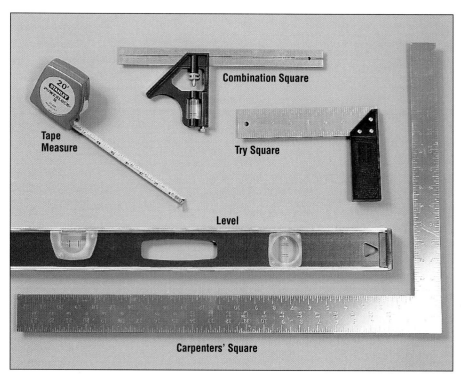

Common measuring tools for do-it-yourselfers.

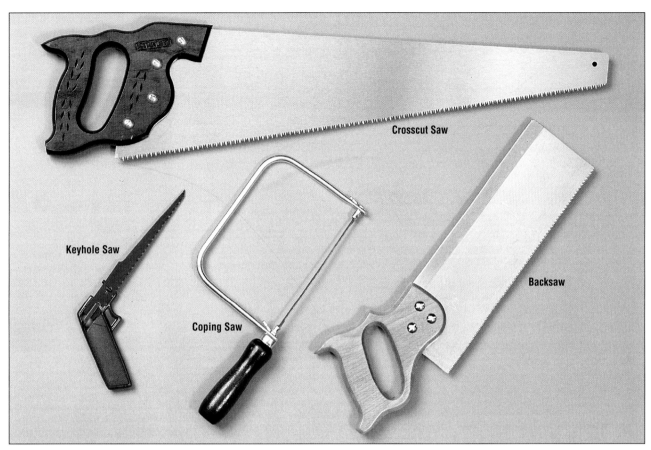

Common types of handsaws.

Squares

The standard sizes for carpenters' squares are 18 to 24 inches (body) by 12 or 18 inches (tongue). The size is important for laying out projects on plywood and hardboard. Carpenters' squares are steel or aluminum; they have multiple scales for figuring board-foot requirements, brace (rafter) height, stair-step stringer angles, and rafter cuts.

For small jobs, a combination square is easier to use than a carpenters' square because the combination square is smaller—typically only 12 inches long. The body of the square slides along the blade and can be fixed at any point with a thumbscrew. The body of the square may incorporate a small bubble level or a scratch awl, which can be used for leveling and marking your work. This square can also be used as a depth gauge, a miter square, and, with the blade removed, as a straightedge and ruler.

The try square looks like a small carpenters' square with a wood or plastic handle. The measurements go across the metal blade, not the handle. The try square is used to test the squareness of edges in planing and sawing work. It can also be used to check right-angle layouts. The tongue has a maximum length of 12 inches; it is wide, but it can be used as a straightedge, ruler, and depth gauge.

Levels

Two- and three-bubble levels are standard for most leveling needs. Some of the bubbles are in vials that can be moved for angle leveling; these vials can be replaced if they are damaged or broken. The edges of a level can be used as a straightedge. Laid flat against a vertical surface, the level can determine both horizontal and vertical levels—often needed when installing cabinets, hanging wallpaper, or hanging pictures. Level frames are made of either wood or lightweight metal such as aluminum. Lengths range to 6 feet, with 30 inches being the most popular size.

Saws

Once measurements are made, materials can be cut using a saw. There are many types of handsaws and power saws offered to match the needs of a variety of cutting jobs.

Crosscut Saw

The crosscut saw, as its name implies, cuts across the grain of the wood. Crosscut saws have from five to ten or more teeth per inch to produce a smooth cut in the wood. They are used for cutting plywood and hardboard panels, and for cutting miters. They can be used for ripping but aren't as fast as the ripsaw.

Ripsaw

The ripsaw cuts along the grain of the wood, called "ripping." Its teeth are spaced from three to five teeth per inch. Because the ripsaw's teeth are wider-set than those of the crosscut saw, they can slice through wood like a chisel. The final cut of a ripsaw is rough, and the wood usually has to be planed or sanded to its final measurement.

Backsaw

A backsaw has a reinforced back to stiffen the blade. Its teeth are closely spaced—like those of a crosscut saw—so the cut is smooth. A backsaw is used for making miter cuts and for trimming molding. It's designed for use in a miter box; the reinforced back serves as a guide.

Keyhole Saw

The keyhole saw has a 10- to 12-inch tapered blade. It's used to cut openings for pipes, electrical boxes, and almost any straight or curved internal cuts that are too large for an auger bit, drill, or hole saw. Quality keyhole saws have removable blades with a variety of tooth spacings for cutting various materials such as wood, plastic, metal, and hardboard. Similar to the keyhole saw is the compass saw, which has a blade 12 to 14 inches long. A compass saw is used like a keyhole saw, but the keyhole saw can make a tighter turn.

Coping Saw

The coping saw looks like a C-clamp with a handle. The blade is thin and replaceable. It is secured with two pins at the ends of the saw, and the handle turns to put the proper tension on the blade. A variety of blades are available, with both ripsaw and crosscut tooth spacing. Blades can be inserted into the frame to cut on the forward or backward stroke, depending on the sawing project; the pins can also be turned to set the blade at an angle for special cuts.

Circular Saw

Power saws can be intimidating at first, and they should be. Improperly used, any power tool can do a lot of damage in a hurry. You should always observe the proper safety precautions. Once you make a few practice cuts, however, you'll soon overcome normal fears.

A portable electric tool, the circular saw is the power version of a crosscut or ripsaw. The guide on the saw can be adjusted to cut miters and pockets in almost any building material. Several blades are available: crosscut, rip, masonry, metal, and plastic. A table is among the accessories available for the circular saw, so the saw can be mounted to work as a small table saw.

Saber Saw

The saber saw, also called a jigsaw, consists of a four-inch blade driven in an up-and-down reciprocating motion. This portable power tool uses many blade designs for a variety of materials, including wood, metal, plastic, masonry, ceramic, and high-pressure laminate. This is the power counterpart to the keyhole and the coping saw; it will make smooth fine-line or contour cuts either with or across the grain.

Drills

Hole-cutters are two-part tools: A drill or brace applies rotating force to a bit that makes the hole. The following are some of the drills and the jobs each do best.

Hand Drills

The hand drill is similar to an eggbeater in both design and execution. A drive handle moves bevel gears to turn a chuck in which a drill has been locked. This drill can't make large holes, but it can make small-diameter, shallow holes in wood and soft metals. The two main types of hand drills used are the push drill and the hand brace.

The push drill requires only one hand to use; as you push down on the handle, the shank turns a chuck into which a small bit fits. This is a limited-capacity tool, but it's excellent for making pilot holes and is handy for setting hinges and similar jobs. The bits are usually stored in the handle of the drill; sizes are available up to $\frac{1}{4}$ inch.

The hand brace has a rotating offset handle that turns a chuck with a ratcheting mechanism; auger bits, countersinks, and screwdriver attachments are available, and the ratchet is particularly handy because it also lets you work in restricted areas. The large-capacity chuck accommodates bits that will cut holes up to $1\frac{1}{2}$ inches in diameter.

Power Drills

Three sizes of chucks are available for power drills: $\frac{1}{4}$-inch, $\frac{3}{8}$-inch, and $\frac{1}{2}$-inch capacity. The two most popular sizes are $\frac{1}{4}$ and $\frac{3}{8}$ inch. The $\frac{1}{4}$-inch chuck has a capacity of $\frac{1}{4}$-inch drills in metal and $\frac{1}{2}$-inch drills in wood. It can handle only a limited range of drilling

BITS		
Drill Bit	**Drill Type**	**Use**
Twist Drill	Hand, power, or drill press	Small-diameter holes in wood and metal.
Spade Bit	Power or drill press	Holes up to 1½ inches in wood.
Auger Bit	Brace	Holes up to 1½ inches in wood.
Expansion Bit	Brace	Holes up to 3 inches in wood.
Fly Cutter	Drill press	Holes up to 6 inches in wood; smaller holes in other materials.
Hole Saw	Power or drill press	Holes up to 3 inches.

operations and shouldn't be used for difficult jobs, but it's the least expensive type of electric drill.

The ⅜-inch drill can make ⅜-inch holes in metal and ¾-inch holes in wood; a hole saw can also be used with this tool to cut holes up to three inches in diameter. Many ⅜-inch drills have a hammer mode that permits drilling in concrete, along with a reversing feature that is handy for removing screws. A variable-speed drill is also a handy tool to own; this type can be started slowly and then sped up. A variety of attachments and accessories are available, including wire brushes, paint mixers, and

even a circular saw attachment.

The most common drill bits include those shown in the table above.

Fastener Tools

Fastener tools are often the first to be selected for the do-it-yourselfer's toolbox. They are simply tools that help you apply fasteners such as nails, screws, bolts, and adhesives. Fastener tools include hammers, screwdrivers, wrenches, pliers, and clamps.

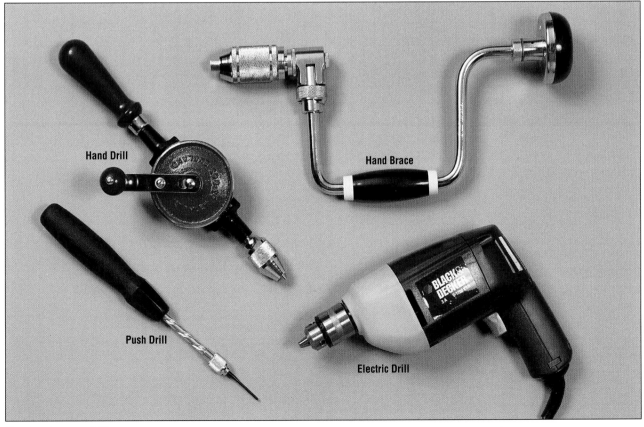

Hand Drill

Hand Brace

Push Drill

Electric Drill

Hand and power drills.

Hammers

The most popular hammer is the carpenters' curved-claw nail hammer. It is steel-headed, wood- or steel-handled, and is used for driving nails, wedges, and dowels. The claw at one end of the head is a two-pronged arch used to pull nails out of wood. The other parts of the head are the eye and the face. A flat-faced, or plane face, hammer is easier for beginners to use, but it is more difficult to drive a nail flush to the work surface using the hammer. A convex, or bell-faced, hammer is preferred by experienced deck builders because it allows the nail to be driven flush.

Screwdrivers

Contrary to popular use, screwdrivers are designed to tighten and loosen screws. They are frequently misused to open paint cans, chisel wood, counterpunch nails, and to accomplish various other creative tasks. Fortunately, screwdrivers are inexpensive to replace. However, a toolbox should have one set of high-quality screwdrivers that are used appropriately.

There are many types of screwdrivers, which vary depending on the screw head each is designed to fit. The most popular screw heads are standard, Phillips, and Torx.

- **Standard Head.** The standard head (also known as flat or straight) screwdriver is the most common type. Make sure the tip is the correct width and thickness to snugly fit the screw-head slot.
- **Phillips Head.** Phillips head (also called cross or X-head) screwdrivers fit into a cross-shaped recess in the screw or bolt head.
- **Torx Head.** Torx head (or similar designs called Robertson) screwdrivers fit into a square or hexagonal hole in the screw. This design allows more torque to be used either for tightening or loosening the fastener.

Wrenches

The function of a wrench is to turn a bolt head or nut. Selecting the appropriate wrench depends on the fastener's design and size. It can also depend on how difficult the fastener is to reach.

Wrenches include open end, box—or closed—end, combination, adjustable, socket, and Allen wrenches. When using a wrench, pull the wrench toward you rather than push it away. Besides giving you more control, it normally reduces the chance of injury if the wrench slips.

- **Box End Wrench.** A box, or closed, end wrench is used where there is room to place the wrench mouth around the fastener. Box end wrenches are available in 6- and 12-point versions to match the number of sides on the fastener. Hexagon fasteners have six sides or points and are the most popular.
- **Open End Wrench.** An open end wrench is used for turning fasteners in locations where a box end wrench cannot encompass the fastener.
- **Combination Wrench.** A combination wrench has ends that perform individual tasks. One end may be open and the other closed; one may be offset and the other straight; or the two ends might be of fractionally different sizes.
- **Adjustable Wrench**. An adjustable wrench can be used on a variety of fastener sizes. The disadvantage is that it is less stable than a fixed-size wrench and can more easily injure you or damage the fastener. An adjustable wrench should be used only if the correct size wrench is not available.
- **Socket Wrench.** A socket wrench fits over the fastener, making removal easier and safer than with other wrenches. Sockets are available in standard depth and extended depth. Extensions are available to make removing fasteners easier. Socket wrenches are typically purchased in sets by drive size.
- **Allen Wrench**. Some fasteners have a hexagonal hole in the head. These fasteners are tightened or loosened with an Allen wrench that fits into the hole. Allen wrenches are available with L- or T-shaped handles.

Pliers

Pliers are an extension of your fingers. They are used to grasp and hold a part. Pliers should not be used as wrenches to tighten or loosen fasteners. Common pliers include slip-joint, groove-joint, needle-nose, and locking pliers.

- **Slip-Joint Pliers.** Slip-joint pliers have two connected holes in the handle to allow for two widths. Once the correct width is selected, the handles are closed together to force the jaw around the part and hold it securely.
- **Groove-Joint Pliers.** Groove-joint pliers are similar to slip joint except that they use an elongated hole in the handle with grooves that allow multiple widths.
- **Needle-Nose Pliers.** Needle-nose pliers have jaws that come to a point for securely grasping small parts or wires, especially in tight locations.
- **Locking Pliers.** Locking pliers, known under the brand name of Vise Grip 7®, are adjustable pliers that can be locked to hold a part in place.

Clamps

Clamps are essential for many jobs. The do-it-yourselfer should start with several C-clamps and a set of bar clamps. If you plan to repair wood furniture, you should get strap clamps too.

- **C-clamp.** C-clamps are made from cast iron or aluminum and have a C-shaped body. A screw with a metal pad applies the tension on the material being clamped. Because C-clamps can exert lots of pressure, buffer blocks of scrap wood should be inserted between the jaws of the clamps and the material being clamped. C-clamps are available in a wide range of sizes.
- **Screw clamp**. Screw clamps have parallel wood jaws; they are the basic woodworking clamps. Tension is applied by hand with two threaded wood spindles, and the clamps can be adjusted to angles by moving the spindles. Screw clamps are expensive.

- **Bar clamp.** Bar clamps are made to fit on long metal rods or pieces of pipe; tension is applied by tightening a screw. Bar clamps are used for gluing boards together and on wide surfaces where the throats of C-clamps are too shallow to accept the work.
- **Strap clamp**. Strap, or web, clamps are simply webbing straps, usually nylon, with a sliding tension clamp. The clamp is used for four-way tensioning on odd-shaped or four-cornered pieces. Because the clamps are fabric, the pressure won't damage the material being clamped.
- **Spring clamp.** Spring clamps look like large metal clothespins. They're used for clamping small jobs, such as veneers glued to core material. Spring clamps are inexpensive and also come in handy.

Clamps for do-it-yourselfers.

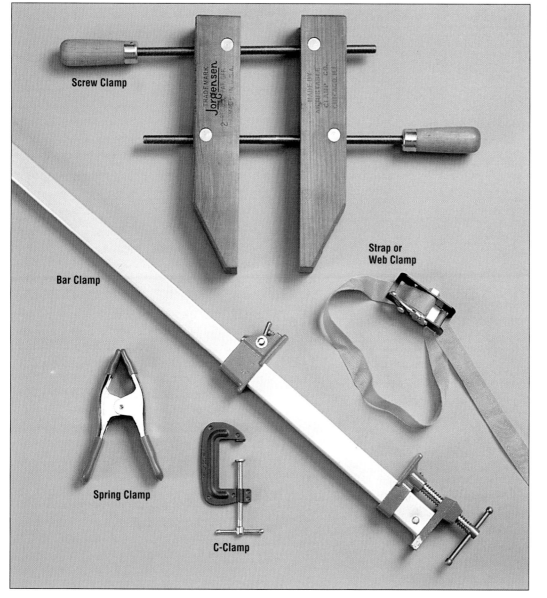

Screw Clamp

Bar Clamp

Strap or Web Clamp

Spring Clamp

C-Clamp

Painting Tools

A good interior paint job depends as much on selecting the right tools as on selecting the right paint. With the proper equipment, even inexperienced do-it-yourselfers can do a professional-quality job. At the paint store, you may well be confronted with a dizzying assortment of paintbrushes, a selection that probably varies more in regard to quality and price than to specific job requirements. But with few exceptions, paintbrushes fall into two camps: natural-bristle brushes made of animal hair and synthetic-bristle brushes, usually made of nylon. At one time, the naturals were considered the best of the lot, but today the synthetics are every bit as good. Besides, you can't use a natural-bristle brush with water-based latex paints because water makes the bristles limp. Consequently, if you're painting with a water-thinned paint, your brush selection is already 50 percent easier.

Buy the best brushes for your money. Regardless of price, you can distinguish between a good brush and a bad one by examining them closely at the store. Here's what to look for:

- Split-ends, called "flags," on the ends of the bristles. Spread the bristles and inspect the tips. The more "flags," the better the brush and its paint-spreading capabilities.
- Tapered bristles. With square-cut bristles you won't be able to paint as fine a line or as smooth a finish.
- Relatively little shedding. Rap the brush on the edge of a counter. A good brush may lose a few bristles, but a bad one will lose many. A brush that sheds in the store will shed even more when you load it with paint and drag it across your wall at home.
- Long bristles, particularly on narrow brushes. Short bristles will be stiff and difficult to paint with. As a general rule, the bristle length should be about one and a half times as long as the width of the brush. A 1½-inch-wide brush, for example, should have bristles about 2¼ inches long. Bristle length gives you flexibility to paint into corners and around trim.

The exception is with wider brushes, often called wall brushes. A wall brush that is four inches wide and has four-inch bristles will produce a good painted finish.

- Smooth, well-shaped handles of wood or plastic that fit in your hand comfortably. There are four basic handle types. Beaver-tail handles, common on wide brushes, allow you to cradle the handle in the palm of your hand for wide-stroke spreading. Pencil- and flat-handled varieties are usually found on narrow brushes and promote fine-line accuracy. The kaiser handle gives you an easy-to-hold grip and good control.

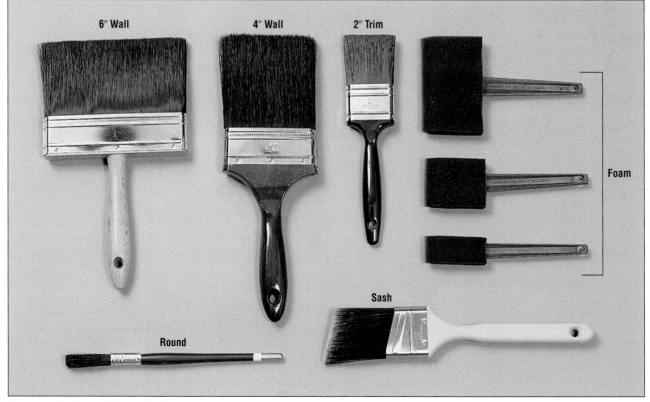

Common bristle and foam paintbrushes.

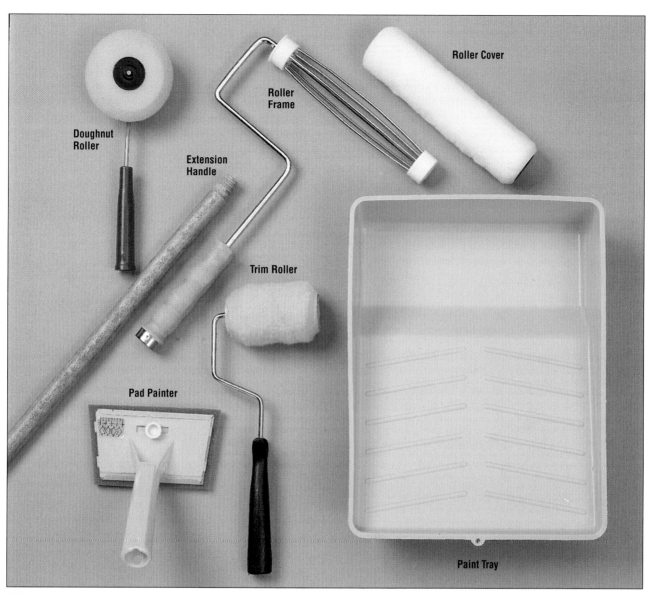

Paint rollers, pad, and tray.

How many different brushes do you need? That depends on what kind of painter you are, what kind of paint you're using, and how many different colors you'll be using. Unless you're meticulous about cleaning a brush, you run the risk of contaminating a second color with residue of the first color or with water or paint cleaner. To avoid color contamination (which may not show up until the paint dries), it's best to buy one brush of several basic types for each color of paint you'll be using. The basic three-brush inventory for most interior jobs includes:

- **Wall brush.** This is the one that spreads the most paint over the most surface. For ordinary purposes, a 4-inch-wide brush is a good choice, though 3½-inch and 3-inch wall brushes may be easier to use,

especially for people with small hands. If you're doing a big masonry job, you may want to move up to a 6-inch-wide wall brush.

- **Trim brush.** The 2-inch-wide trim brush is ideal for woodwork and for "cutting in" around windows and doors before painting walls with a roller.
- **Sash brush.** The sash brush has an angled bristle end. Available in 1-inch, 1½-inch, or 2-inch widths, the angled sash brush makes close work easier—especially when you're painting around windows. Used carefully, it reduces the need to scrape dried paint off window panes.

The same size brushes are also available in foamed urethane. Instead of bristles, they have spongelike heads. They are increasingly popular among do-it-yourselfers, particularly in smaller sizes used for interior or exterior trim painting. Disposable foam brushes come in widths up to 3 inches and are cheap enough to toss out after one use.

For large, flat surface areas like walls and ceilings, paint rollers will help you get the job done in about half the amount of time it would take with a paintbrush. Most painters use brushes for trim work and for "cutting in" around windows and doors and then turn to rollers to fill in the big blank spaces. Rollers for painting flat areas come in varying widths—from 4 to 18 inches—but the two most common sizes for interior jobs are 9 inches and 7 inches wide. For trim work and small spaces, there are specially designed rollers—some miniaturized versions of the basic wall roller, others cone- or doughnut-shaped—that range in width from 1 to 4 inches.

Paint rollers intended for wall or ceiling painting have handles made of plastic or wood that may have been hollowed out and machined to accept an extension handle. They also have a cylindrical frame—either a solid metal tube or a series of metal ribs—that is slipped inside a roller cover. Of the two types, the metal-rib version (also known as a "bird cage" or spring-metal frame) is best because it's easier to clean and is less likely to stick to the inside of the roller cover.

The type of roller cover you should buy is largely determined by the kind of paint you'll be using, but they are all fiber- or urethane foam-covered cylinders that soak up paint from a tray and then release it when rolled over a flat surface. The rolling action creates a vacuum that actually pulls the paint off the roller. Made of lamb's wool, mohair, Dynel, acetate, or polyurethane foam, most rollers are labeled with the kind of paint for which they are intended to be used. Choose your roller cover accordingly.

The roller package will also identify the length of the roller cover's nap or pile, which can vary from $\frac{1}{16}$ to $1\frac{1}{2}$ inches. For rough surfaces, use the long naps. For smooth surfaces, choose the short ones. The pile is attached to a tube (which slips over the roller's frame) made of plastic or cardboard. Unless you intend to use the cover just once and then toss it out, buy the plastic type because it will stand up to repeated cleanings with solvents or water.

Paint trays are made of aluminum or plastic and come in standard 7-inch and 9-inch versions. The 9-inch size is best because you can then use either a 7-inch or 9-inch roller. Some trays come with hooks that allow you to attach them directly to a ladder. The trays, of course, are washable and durable. But to make cleanup even easier, buy some disposable plastic tray liners or line the tray with aluminum foil.

Electrical Tools

To make simple electrical repairs, you'll need a few simple tools. The more extensive and complex your repair work, the more tools you'll need. Most, however, are inexpensive and can be found in your local hardware store. Besides the hand tools covered earlier, you'll need tools for testing electrical circuits and some cans of compressed air and electrical contact cleaner.

Electricity must have a continuous path, or circuit, in order to flow. Think of it as a two-lane road from point A to point B and return. If one or both lanes are blocked, traffic stops. The flow of auto traffic over a highway is measured with a traffic counter placed across the road. The flow of electrical current is measured by placing an electrical tester at two points in the circuit. Most electrical problems can be solved by using a voltage tester, a continuity tester, or a volt-ohm-milliammeter (VOM), also known as a multimeter or multitester.

Voltage Tester

The voltage tester is the simplest of these tools. It consists of a small neon bulb with two insulated wires attached to the bottom of the bulb housing; each wire ends in a metal test probe. The voltage tester is always used with the current turned *on*, to determine whether there is current flowing through a wire and to test for proper grounding. It is also used to determine whether adequate voltage is present in a wire. Look for a tester rated for up to 500 volts.

To use a voltage tester, touch one probe to one wire or connection and the other probe to the opposite wire or connection. If the component is receiving electricity, the light in the housing will glow. If the light doesn't glow, the trouble is at this point. For example, if you suspect that an electrical outlet is faulty, insert one probe of the tester into one slot in the outlet, and the other probe into the other slot. The light in the tester should light. If it doesn't, the outlet may be bad. To further test the outlet, pull it out of the wall. Place one probe of the tester on one terminal screw connection and the other probe on the other terminal screw. If the tester bulb lights, you know the outlet is malfunctioning—there is current flowing to the outlet, but it isn't flowing *through* the outlet to provide power to the appliance plugged into it. If the test bulb doesn't light, there is no current coming into the outlet. The problem may be a blown fuse or tripped circuit breaker, or the wire may be disconnected or broken behind the outlet.

Continuity Tester

The continuity tester consists of a battery in a housing, with a test probe connected to one end of the battery

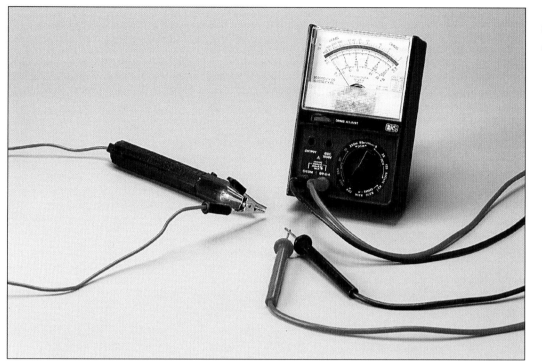

housing and a test wire with an alligator clip connected to the other end. The continuity tester is used with the current turned *off*, to determine whether a particular electrical component is carrying electricity and to pinpoint the cause of a malfunction.

To use a continuity tester, unplug the appliance and disassemble it to get at the component to be tested. Fasten the clip of the tester to one wire or connection of the component and touch the probe to the other wire or connection. If the component is receiving electricity and transmitting it, the tester will light or buzz; this indicates that the circuit is continuous. If the tester doesn't light or buzz, or if it reacts only slightly, the component is faulty. ***Caution:*** *Do not use a continuity tester unless the appliance is unplugged or the power to the circuit is turned off.*

Volt-Ohm Meter (VOM)

The voltage tester and the continuity tester are adequate for many diagnostic jobs, and they're relatively inexpensive. But for serious electrical and appliance troubleshooting and repairs, invest in a volt-ohm-milliammeter, or volt-ohm meter (VOM), also known as a multitester. VOMs range in price from $10 to more than $100; you can buy one that's adequate for appliance testing for about $30. The VOM is battery-powered and is used with the current turned *off*. It's used to check continuity in a wire or component and to measure the electrical current—from 0 to 250 volts, AC or DC—flowing through the wire or component. The

VOM is used with plug-in test leads, which may have probes at both ends or a probe at one end and an alligator clip at the other. An adjustment knob or switch is set to measure current on the scale desired, usually ohms; the dial indicates the current flowing through the item being tested. ***Caution:*** *Do not use a VOM unless the appliance is unplugged or the power to the circuit is turned off.*

The VOM is useful for appliance testing because it is used while the power is turned off, so there's no danger of electric shock while you're using it. It provides more precise information than the continuity tester, and therefore is preferable for testing many components. Learning to read a VOM is very easy, and manufacturers provide complete operating instructions with the meters. You can also buy information sheets on test readings of various electrical components used in appliances and in other applications such as lights, switches, and outlets.

Compressed Air

A can of compressed air, sold under a variety of names and brands, is very useful for cleaning appliances and electrical fixtures. Compressed air can remove particles of food or even help dislodge loose parts. Some compressed air cans come with an extension tube that fits in the can's nozzle to precisely direct the air. If you don't find canned compressed air at your hardware or building-supply store, try a computer shop where it's sold as a dust remover for keyboards and other electronics.

Electrical Contact Cleaner

Electrical contact cleaner is simply compressed air with a cleaning agent that evaporates, such as isopropyl alcohol. It is useful for cleaning electric components that have food, grease, or oils on them. It can dislodge foreign elements and clean components. Several brands of electrical contact cleaner are available at larger hardware stores, electronics dealers, and hobby shops.

Plumbing Tools

You may already have many of the tools necessary for most plumbing jobs. They are the same tools used for other do-it-yourself projects. Other special tools include pipe wrenches and various plumbing aids.

Pipe Wrenches

You'll need a medium-size adjustable pipe wrench to tighten and loosen pipes and other plumbing connections. You can purchase adjustable pipe wrenches at hardware stores and plumbing-supply houses.

A basin wrench is a specialized tool that allows you to reach tight spots under sinks and basins. The jaws of a basin wrench not only adjust to accommodate nuts of different sizes, but also flip over to the opposite side, so that you can keep turning without removing the wrench.

A socket wrench set is useful for removing recessed packing nuts and also on tub and shower fixtures as well as other do-it-yourself household repairs.

For changing a toilet seat, you'll need a wrench, or perhaps a deep socket wrench or a hacksaw. If you need

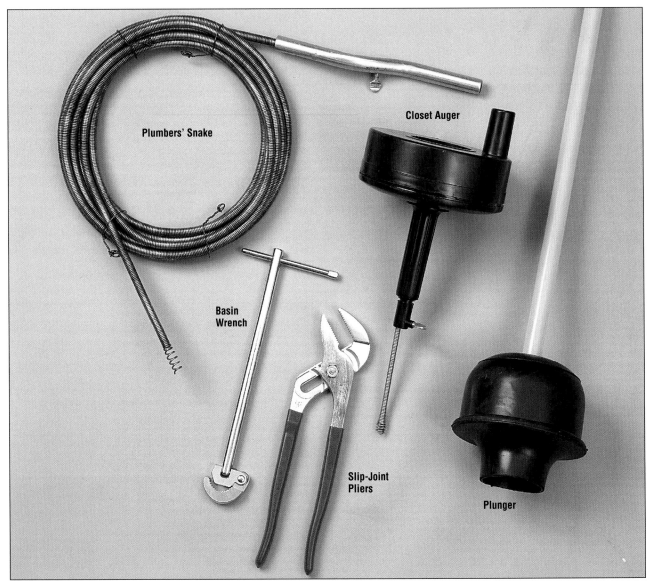

Plumbers' Snake

Closet Auger

Basin Wrench

Slip-Joint Pliers

Plunger

Common plumbing tools for do-it-yourselfers.

to remove a toilet for replacement or repair, you may need a spudwrench. Older toilets frequently have a large pipe—called a spud—that connects the tank to the bowl. The spud is held to the bowl and tank by extra-large hexagonal slip nuts. A spudwrench is designed to remove these slip nuts. The adjustable type of spudwrench is far more versatile than the nonadjustable type, which has a fixed opening at each end.

Plumbing Aids

Plumbers' snakes, or drain-and-trap augers, come in various lengths. A short snake is all that's necessary for most plumbing repairs. A closet auger is a version of the plumbers' snake designed specifically for clearing clogs in toilets. The closet auger is shorter than a regular snake, and it comes encased in a plastic or metal housing with an easy-to-use crank.

The most frequently used plumbing aid is the plumbers' friend, also known as a plunger or a force cup. Get one with a long handle, and be sure the suction cup is large enough to cover the toilet's drain opening.

Small Engine Tools

Most small engine service procedures can be performed using basic tools covered earlier this chapter: screwdrivers, wrenches, and pliers. However, many small engines require wrenches and drivers of metric rather than standard sizes.

Standard vs. Metric

Because much of the rest of the world uses metric or SI measurements, small engine parts and tools commonly use these measurements. However, the metric standard has not been fully accepted by U.S. manufacturers and consumers. Therefore, many parts and tools continue to be made and identified in standard or SAE sizes by fractions or decimal inches. What's the difference?

A millimeter (mm) is about $1/25$th of an inch. So a $1/2$-inch bolt is about the same size as a 13mm bolt—but not exactly. Wrenches are available in fractions of an inch as well as millimeters. Unfortunately, this means a toolbox should have both SAE and metric tools. If you're certain that all of your service and repairs will be on equipment that is either standard or metric, you can buy tools for one or the other. But even finding a tool set that uses only one measurement system is difficult. Never use standard tools on metric fasteners or vice versa.

Abrasives

Choosing the proper abrasive for a given job usually means the difference between mediocre results and a truly professional appearance. Depending on the job, you'll choose between sandpaper, steel wool, or a file.

SELECTING SANDPAPER				
Grit	Number	Grade	Coating Available[1]	Common Uses
Very Coarse	30 36	2½ 2	F,G,S F,G,S	Rust removal on rough finished metal.
Coarse	40 50 60	1½ 1 ½	F,G,S F,G,S F,G,A,S	Rough sanding of wood; paint removal.
Medium	80 100 120	0(1/0) 00(2/0) 3/0	F,G,A,S F,G,A,S F,G,A,S	General wood sanding; plaster smoothing; preliminary smoothing of previously painted surface.
Fine	150 180	4/0 5/0	F,G,A,S F,G,A,S	Final sanding of bare wood or previously painted surface.
Very Fine	220 240 280	6/0 7/0 8/0	F,G,A,S F,A,S F,A,S	Light sanding between finish coats; dry sanding.
Extra Fine	320 360 600	9/0 —[2] —[2]	F,A,S S S	High finish on lacquer, varnish, or shellac; wet sanding. High-satinized finishes; wet sanding.

[1] F = flint; G = garnet; A = aluminum oxide; S = silicon carbide. Silicon carbide is used dry or wet, with water or oil.
[2] No grade designation.

SELECTING STEEL WOOL		
Grade	**Number**	**Common Uses**
Coarse	3	Paint and varnish removal; removing paint spots from resilient floors.
Medium Coarse	2	Removing scratches from brass; removing paint spots from ceramic tile; rubbing floors between finish coats.
Medium	1	Rust removal; cleaning glazed tiles; removing marks from wood floors; with paint and varnish remover, removing finishes.
Medium Fine	0	Brass finishing; cleaning tile; with paint and varnish remover, removing stubborn finishes.
Fine	00	With linseed oil, satinizing high-gloss finishes.
Extra Fine	000	Removing paint spots or stains from wood; cleaning polished metals; rubbing between finish coats.
Superfine	0000	Final rubbing of finish; stain removal.

Sandpaper

Most do-it-yourselfers still refer to various grades of "sandpaper," but the proper term for these sanding sheets is "coated abrasives." There are four primary factors to consider when selecting any coated abrasive: the abrasive mineral, or which type of rough material; the grade, or the coarseness or fineness of the mineral; the backing, paper or cloth; and the coating, or the nature and extent of the mineral on the surface.

Paper backing for coated abrasives comes in four weights: "A," "C," "D," and "E." "A" (also referred to as "Finishing") is the lightest weight for the lightest sanding work. "C" and "D" (also called "Cabinet") are for heavier work, while "E" is for the toughest jobs.

The coating can either be open-coated or closed-coated. Open-coated means that the grains are spaced so as only to cover a portion of the surface. An open-coated abrasive is best used on gummy or soft woods, soft metals, or on painted surfaces. Closed-coated means that the abrasive covers the entire area. Closed-coated abrasives provide maximum cutting, but they also clog faster and are best used on hard woods and metals.

There are three popular ways to grade coated abrasives. Simplified markings (fine, very fine, etc.) provide a general description of the grade. "Grit" actually refers to the number of mineral grains that, when set end to end, equal one inch. The commonly used "O" symbols are more or less arbitrary. The coarsest grading under this system is 4½, and the finest is 10/0, or 0000000000.

Steel Wool

Steel wool comes in many grades of coarseness. Always apply the correct grade of steel wool to the work you have at hand, as shown in the chart above.

Files

A wood rasp, with a rasp and/or curved-tooth cut, is used to remove excess wood. The piece of wood is final-smoothed with a single-cut or double-cut file. To start off your set, buy an assortment of flat files—wood rasp, bastard, second-cut, and smooth files.

Materials

Selecting the right materials is vital to any do-it-yourself job. This section offers basic information on selecting lumber, plywood, drywall, fasteners, and other materials for common do-it-yourself projects.

Lumber

Lumber sizes are somewhat misleading. The nominal cross-section dimensions of a piece of lumber, such as 2×4 or 1×6, are always larger than the actual, or dressed, dimensions. The reason for this is that dressed lumber has been surfaced or planed smooth on four sides (called S4S).

Board measure is a method of measuring lumber in which the basic unit is 1 foot long $\times$ 1 foot wide by 1 inch thick, called a board foot. Board measure is calculated by nominal, not actual, dimensions of lumber. The easiest formula for figuring nominal board feet is:

$$\frac{\text{Thickness (inches)} \times \text{Width (inches)} \times \text{Length (feet)}}{12}$$

The answer is stated in board feet. Lumber is often priced in board feet. However, most building material retailers and lumberyards also price lumber by the running foot for easier calculation. That is, a $2 \times 4 \times 8''$ is priced at eight times the running foot cost rather than as 5.333 board feet.

One-by (1×) lumber is called boards:

Nominal Size	Dressed Dimensions (inches)
2×2	1½×1½
2×4	1½×3½
2×6	1½×5½
2×8	1½×7¼
2×10	1½×9¼
2×12	1½×11¼
4×4	3½×3½

Two-by (2×) and four-by (4×) lumber is called dimension lumber:

Nominal Size	Dressed Dimensions (inches)
1×6	¾×5½
1×8	¾×7¼
1×10	¾×9¼

Plywood

Knowing about plywood can save you money and may mean the difference between a successful project and one that fails. For example, you don't need to buy an expensive piece of plywood that's perfect on both sides if only one side will ever be seen. Similarly, there's no sense in paying for ⅝-inch thickness when ¼-inch plywood is really all you need. Plywood also comes with different glues, different veneers, and different degrees of finish. By knowing these characteristics you may be able to save money as well as do a better job.

Plywood is often better than lumber for some jobs. It is strong, lightweight, and rigid. Its high impact resistance means that plywood doesn't split, chip, crack all the way through, or crumble; the cross-laminated construction restricts expansion and contraction within the individual plies. Moreover, you never get "green" wood with plywood. Plywood is available at home centers, hardware stores, and lumberyards.

When you buy a sheet of plywood, you know exactly what size you're getting. A 4×8-foot sheet of ¾-inch

PLYWOOD GRADES

Interior Grade				
A-A	A	A	D	Cabinet doors, built-ins, and furniture where both sides show.
A-B	A	B	D	Alternate for A-A. Face is finish grade; back is solid and smooth.
A-D	A	D	D	Finish grade face for paneling, built-ins, and backing.
B-D	B	D	D	Utility grade. One paintable side. For backing, cabinet sides, etc.
C-D	C	D	D	Sheathing and structural uses such as temporary enclosures, subfloor. Unsanded.
Underlayment	C-Plugged	D	C,D	For underlayment or combination subfloor-underlayment under tile and carpeting.
Exterior Grade				
A-A	A	A	C	Outdoors, where appearance of both sides is important.
A-B	A	B	C	Alternate for A-A, where appearance of one side is less important. Face is finish grade.
A-C	A	C	C	Soffits, fences, base for coatings.
B-C	B	C	C	For utility uses such as farm buildings, some kinds of fences, base for coatings.
C-C (Plugged)	C-Plugged	C	C	Excellent base for tile, backing for wall coverings, high-performance coatings.
C-C	C	C	C	Unsanded, for backing and rough construction exposed to weather.

plywood measures exactly 4 by 8 feet and is exactly ¾ inch thick. This contrasts with the distinction between nominal and actual measurements that affects other types of lumber.

When you buy plywood, look for a back-stamp or edge-marking bearing the initials APA or DFPA. APA stands for American Plywood Association, while DFPA is the Douglas Fir Plywood Association. These two organizations represent most of the plywood manufacturers, and they inspect and test all plywood to ensure that quality is high and grading is accurate. Their stamp is your assurance that what you see is what you get.

Plywood is broadly categorized into two types: exterior and interior. Exterior plywood is made with nothing but waterproof glue, and you should always select exterior plywood for any exposed application. Interior plywood, made with highly resistant glues, can actually withstand quite a bit of moisture. There is interior plywood made with IMG (intermediate glue), which is resistant to bacteria, mold, and moisture, but no interior plywood is made for use outdoors.

The most critical plywood grading category for most home projects is the appearance grade of the panel faces. Check the accompanying "Plywood Grades" table before you buy any plywood. The table indicates the various uses for each grade. The first letter indicates the face grade, while the second indicates the back grade.

Drywall Materials

Drywall, also known as gypsum wallboard, has all but replaced plaster as a wall surface in modern-day homes. Rocklike gypsum core makes drywall as fire-resistant as plaster, and its heavy paper facing eliminates the cracking problems that plague plaster walls. Best of all, drywall is far easier to work with than plaster.

Though they are heavy, big sheets of drywall go up fast to finish off framed walls, and you can cut them easily with a utility knife or handsaw. Once up, drywall can be paneled, wallpapered, or painted.

The standard-size sheets for walls measure 4×8 feet. All drywall sheets are 4 feet wide, but many building material outlets offer 10-foot and even 12-foot lengths. The most popular thicknesses of drywall are ½ and ⅝ inch. Your building materials retailer can suggest the number of nails, rolls of tape, and the amount of joint compound you will need for the job.

Fasteners

Nails, screws, and bolts are fasteners that every do-it-yourselfer uses. But very few know about all the different types and their specific uses. The following are many of the most common types of fasteners.

Nails

The easiest way to fasten two pieces of wood together is with nails. Nails are manufactured in a variety of shapes, sizes, and metals to do almost any fastening job. Most commonly, nails are made of steel, but other types—aluminum, brass, nickel, bronze, copper, and stainless steel—are available for use where corrosion could occur. Nails are also manufactured with coatings—galvanized, blued, or cemented—to prevent rusting and to add holding power.

Nail size is designated by penny size, originally the price per hundred nails. Penny size, almost always referred to as "d," ranges from 2-penny, or 2d—1 inch long—to 60 penny, or 60d—6 inches long. Nails shorter than 1 inch are called "brads"; nails longer than 6 inches are called "spikes."

The length of the nail is important, because at least two-thirds of the nail should be driven into the base, or thicker, material. For example, a 1×3 nailed to a 4×4 beam should be fastened with an 8-penny, or 8d, nail. An 8d nail is 2½ inches long; ¾ inch of its length will go through the 1×3, and the remaining 1¾ inches will go into the beam.

Nails are usually sold by the pound; the smaller the nail, the more nails to the pound. You can buy bulk nails out of a nail keg; the nails are weighed and then priced by the retailer. Or, you can buy packaged nails, sold in boxes ranging from 1 pound to 50 pounds.

There are several types of nails:

- **Common Nails.** Common nails are made from wire and are cut to the proper length. They have thick heads and can be driven into tough materials. They're used for most medium-to-heavy construction work. Common nails are available in sizes 2d through 60d.
- **Box Nails.** Box nails are similar to common nails, but they are lighter and smaller in diameter. Box nails are designed for light construction and household use.
- **Finishing Nails.** Finishing nails are lighter than common nails and have a small head. They're often used for installing paneling and trim where the nail head shouldn't show.
- **Roofing Nails.** Roofing nails, usually galvanized, have a much larger head than common nails, to prevent damage to asphalt shingles.
- **Drywall Nails.** Annular-ring nails have sharp ridges all along the nail shaft. Their holding power is much greater than that of regular nails. Nails made for drywall installation are often ringed and have an indented head.
- **Masonry Nails.** There are three types of masonry nails designed for use with concrete and concrete block: round, square, and fluted. Masonry nails should

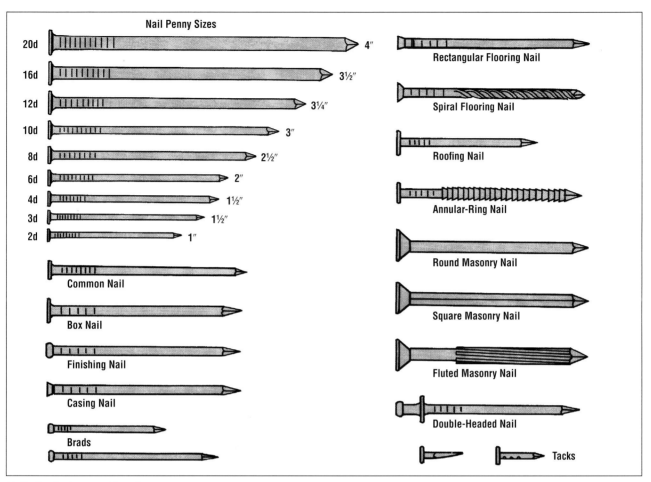

Nail Penny Sizes

20d		4″
16d		3½″
12d		3¼″
10d		3″
8d		2½″
6d		2″
4d		1½″
3d		1½″
2d		1″

Common Nail

Box Nail

Finishing Nail

Casing Nail

Brads

Rectangular Flooring Nail

Spiral Flooring Nail

Roofing Nail

Annular-Ring Nail

Round Masonry Nail

Square Masonry Nail

Fluted Masonry Nail

Double-Headed Nail

Tacks

Nails for do-it-yourself projects.

not be used where high strength is required. Fastening to brick, stone, or reinforced concrete should be made with screws or lag bolts.

- **Tacks.** Tacks, made in both round and cut forms, are used to hold carpet or fabric to wood. Upholstery tacks have decorative heads.
- **Corrugated Fasteners.** Corrugated fasteners, also called "wiggly nails," are used for light-duty joints where strength isn't important. The fasteners are set at right angles to the joint.

Screws

Screws provide more strength and holding power than nails do; and, if the work will ever be disassembled, screws can be removed and reinserted without damage. For these reasons, screws should be used instead of nails for most woodworking.

Screws are manufactured with four types of heads, and also with different types of slots. Flathead screws are always countersunk into the material being fastened, so that the screw head is flush with the surface. Oval-head screws are partially countersunk so that about half the

screw head lies above the surface. Round-head screws are not countersunk; the entire screw head lies above the surface. Fillister-head screws are raised above the surface on a flat base to keep the screwdriver from damaging the surface as the screw is tightened.

Straight-slot screws have plain slots and are driven with regular-blade screwdrivers. Phillips-head screws have crossed slots and are driven with Phillips-head screwdrivers. Stopped-slot screws are less common; they're driven with special screwdrivers.

Screw size is measured in two dimensions: length and diameter at the shank. Shank diameter is stated by gauge number, from 0 to 24. Length is measured in inches: in ⅛-inch increments from ¼ to 1 inch, in ¼-inch increments from 1 to 3 inches, and in ½-inch increments from 3 to 5 inches. Not all lengths are available for all gauges, but special sizes can be ordered.

The length of screws is important. In most cases, at least half the length of the screw should extend into the base material. For example, if a piece of ¾-inch plywood is being fastened, the screws that hold it should be 1½ inches long.

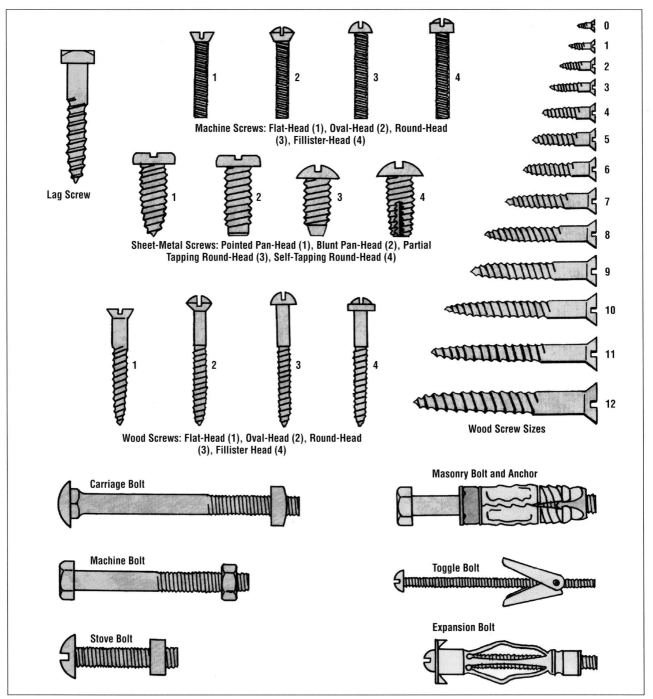

Machine Screws: Flat-Head (1), Oval-Head (2), Round-Head (3), Fillister-Head (4)

Lag Screw

Sheet-Metal Screws: Pointed Pan-Head (1), Blunt Pan-Head (2), Partial Tapping Round-Head (3), Self-Tapping Round-Head (4)

Wood Screws: Flat-Head (1), Oval-Head (2), Round-Head (3), Fillister Head (4)

Wood Screw Sizes

0 1 2 3 4 5 6 7 8 9 10 11 12

Carriage Bolt

Machine Bolt

Stove Bolt

Masonry Bolt and Anchor

Toggle Bolt

Expansion Bolt

Screws and bolts for do-it-yourself projects.

To prevent the screws from splitting the materials being fastened, pilot holes must be made before the screws are driven. For small screws, pilot holes can be punched with an awl or ice pick. For larger pilot holes, use a small drill or a combination drill/countersink.

- **Wood Screws.** Most commonly, wood screws are made of steel, but other metals—brass, nickel, bronze, and copper—are used where corrosion could occur.

Like nails, screws are also made with coatings—zinc, chromium, or cadmium—to deter rust.

- **Sheet-Metal Screws.** Sheet-metal screws, used to fasten pieces of metal together, form threads in the metal as they are installed. There are several different types of sheet-metal screws. Pointed pan-head screws are coarse-threaded; they are available in gauges from 4 to 14 and lengths from ¼ inch to 2 inches. Pointed pan-heads are used in light sheet metal. Blunt pan-head screws are used for heavier sheet metal; they are available in gauges from 4 to 14 and lengths from ¼ inch to 2 inches. Both types of pan-head screws are available with either plain or Phillips-head slots.

Partial-tapping round-head screws have finer threads; they can be used in soft or hard metals. They are available in diameters from ³⁄₁₆ inch to 1¼ inches. Self-tapping round-head screws are used for heavy-duty work with thick sheet metal; they are available in diameters from gauge 2 to ¼ inch and in lengths from ⅛ inch to ¾ inch. Both types of round-head screws are available with either plain or Phillips-head slots.

- **Machine Screws.** Machine screws are blunt-ended screws used to fasten metal parts together. They are commonly made of steel or brass. Like other fasteners, they are also made with coatings—brass, copper, nickel, zinc, cadmium, and galvanized—that help deter rust. Machine screws are manufactured with each of the four basic types of heads—flat-head, oval-head, round-head, and fillister-head—and with both plain and Phillips-head slots. They are typically available in gauges 2 to 12 and diameters from ¼ inch to ½ inch, and in lengths from ¼ inch to 3 inches.
- **Lag Screws.** Lag screws are heavy-duty fasteners. They are driven with a wrench and are used primarily

DRILLING FOR WOOD SCREWS

Gauge Number	Decimal Diameter	Fractional Diameter	Shank Hole		Pilot Hole								Auger Bit Number	Threads Per Inch
					Hardwood				Softwood					
			Twist Bit	Drill Gauge	Twist Bit		Drill Gauge		Twist Bit		Drill Gauge			
					s	p	s	p	s	p	s	p		
0	.060	¹⁄₁₆−	¹⁄₁₆	52	¹⁄₃₂	–	70	–	¹⁄₆₄	–	75	–	–	32
1	.073	⁵⁄₆₄−	⁵⁄₆₄	47	¹⁄₃₂	–	66	–	¹⁄₃₂	–	71	–	–	28
2	.086	⁵⁄₆₄+	³⁄₃₂	42	³⁄₆₄	¹⁄₃₂	56	70	¹⁄₃₂	¹⁄₆₄	65	75	3	26
3	.099	³⁄₃₂+	⁷⁄₆₄	37	¹⁄₁₆	¹⁄₃₂	54	66	³⁄₆₄	¹⁄₃₂	58	71	4	24
4	.112	⁶⁄₆₄+	⁷⁄₆₄	32	¹⁄₁₆	³⁄₆₄	52	56	³⁄₆₄	¹⁄₃₂	55	65	4	22
5	.125	⅛−	⅛	30	⁵⁄₆₄	¹⁄₁₆	49	54	¹⁄₁₆	³⁄₆₄	53	58	4	20
6	.138	⁹⁄₆₄−	⁹⁄₆₄	27	⁵⁄₆₄	¹⁄₁₆	47	52	¹⁄₁₆	³⁄₆₄	52	55	5	18
7	.151	⁵⁄₃₂−	⁵⁄₃₂	22	³⁄₃₂	⁵⁄₆₄	44	49	¹⁄₁₆	³⁄₆₄	51	53	5	16
8	.164	⁵⁄₃₂+	¹¹⁄₆₄	18	³⁄₃₂	⁵⁄₆₄	40	47	⁵⁄₆₄	¹⁄₁₆	48	52	6	15
9	.177	¹¹⁄₆₄+	³⁄₁₆	14	⁷⁄₆₄	³⁄₃₂	37	44	⁵⁄₆₄	¹⁄₁₆	45	51	6	14
10	.190	³⁄₁₆+	³⁄₁₆	10	⁷⁄₆₄	³⁄₃₂	33	40	³⁄₃₂	⁵⁄₆₄	43	48	6	13
11	.203	¹³⁄₆₄−	¹³⁄₆₄	4	⅛	⁷⁄₆₄	31	37	³⁄₃₂	⁵⁄₆₄	40	45	7	12
12	.216	⁷⁄₃₂−	⁷⁄₃₂	2	⅛	⁷⁄₆₄	30	33	⁷⁄₆₄	³⁄₃₂	38	43	7	11
14	.242	¹⁵⁄₆₄+	¼	D	⁹⁄₆₄	⅛	25	31	⁷⁄₆₄	³⁄₃₂	32	40	8	10
16	.268	¹⁷⁄₆₄+	¹⁷⁄₆₄	I	⁵⁄₃₂	⅛	18	30	⁹⁄₆₄	⁷⁄₆₄	29	38	9	9
18	.294	¹⁹⁄₆₄−	¹⁹⁄₆₄	N	³⁄₁₆	⁹⁄₆₄	13	25	⁹⁄₆₄	⁷⁄₆₄	26	32	10	8
20	.320	²¹⁄₆₄−	²¹⁄₆₄	P	¹³⁄₆₄	⁵⁄₃₂	4	18	¹⁄₆₄	⁹⁄₆₄	19	29	11	8
24	.372	⅜	⅜	V	⁷⁄₃₂	³⁄₁₆	1	13	³⁄₁₆	⁹⁄₆₄	15	26	12	7

s = Slotted head   p = Phillips-head

for fastening to masonry or wood framing. For light work, lead, plastic, or fiber plugs (called anchors) can be used to hold large screws. For larger jobs and more holding power, lead expansion anchors and lag screws are used. The anchors are inserted into holes drilled in the masonry, and the lag screws are driven firmly into the anchors.

Bolts

Bolts are used with nuts or locknuts, and often with washers. The three basic types are carriage bolts, stove bolts, and machine bolts. Other types include the masonry bolt and anchor, and toggle and expansion bolts, used to distribute weight when fastening something to a hollow wall.

Machine bolts are manufactured in two gauges, fine-threaded and coarse. Carriage and stove bolts are coarse-threaded. Bolt size is measured by shank diameter and by threads per inch, expressed as diameter × threads—for example, as $1/4 \times 20$. Carriage bolts are available up to 10 inches long, stove bolts up to 6 inches, and machine bolts up to 30 inches. Larger sizes usually must be special-ordered.

- **Carriage Bolts.** Carriage bolts, used mainly in making furniture, have a round head with a square collar and are driven with a wrench. When the bolt is tightened, the collar fits into a prebored hole or twists into the wood, preventing the bolt from turning. Carriage bolts are coarse-threaded and are available in diameters from $3/16$ to $3/4$ inch and lengths from $1/2$ inch to 10 inches.
- **Stove Bolts.** Stove bolts are available in a wide range of sizes. They have a slotted head—flat, oval, or round, like screws—and are driven with a screwdriver or a wrench. Most stove bolts are completely threaded, but the larger ones may have a smooth shank near the bolt head. Stove bolts are coarse-threaded and are available in diameters from $5/32$ to $1/2$ inch and lengths from $3/8$ inch to 6 inches. Stove bolts are quite versatile and can be used for almost any fastening job.
- **Machine Bolts.** Machine bolts have either a square head or a hexagonal head. They are fastened with square nuts or hex nuts and are wrench-driven. Machine bolts are manufactured in very large sizes; the bolt diameter increases with length. They are either coarse-threaded or fine-threaded and are available in diameters from $1/4$ inch to 2 inches and lengths from $1/2$ inch to 30 inches.
- **Masonry Bolts and Anchors.** These bolts work on the same principle as the lag bolt or screw; a plastic sleeve expands inside a predrilled hole as the bolt is tightened.

- **Hollow-Wall Bolts.** Toggle bolts and expansion bolts are used for fastening lightweight objects to hollow walls. Toggle bolt wings are opened inside the wall by a spring. Expansion bolts are inserted into an expansion jacket, which expands as the bolt is tightened. The bolts are available in diameters from $1/8$ to $1/2$ inch and lengths up to 8 inches for walls as thick as $1 3/4$ inches.

Adhesives

Adhesives chemically attach two or more surfaces. The right adhesive can make any job easier and longer-lasting. Here's some information on adhesives frequently used by do-it-yourselfers.
- **Multipurpose Adhesives.** If you keep a small assortment of multipurpose adhesives in stock you will be able to make a wide variety of repairs. The following are the most common types of multipurpose adhesives.
- **White Glue (Polyvinyl Acetate).** PVA glue is a white liquid, usually sold in plastic squeeze bottles. It is recommended for use on porous materials—wood, paper, cloth, porous pottery, and nonstructural wood-to-wood bonds. It isn't water-resistant. Clamping is required for 30 minutes to one hour, until the glue sets; curing time is 18 to 24 hours. School glue, a type of white glue, dries more slowly. PVA glue dries clear. It is inexpensive and nonflammable.
- **Epoxy.** Epoxies are sold in tubes or in cans. They consist of two parts—resin and hardener—which must be thoroughly mixed just before use. They are very strong, very durable, and very water-resistant. Epoxies are recommended for use on metal, ceramics, some plastics, and rubber; they aren't recommended for flexible surfaces. Clamping is required for about two hours for most epoxies. Drying time is about 12 hours; curing time is one to two days. Epoxy dries clear or amber. It is more expensive than other adhesives.
- **Cyanoacrylate (Instant Glue).** Cyanoacrylates are similar to epoxy, but are one-part glues. They form a very strong bond and are recommended for use on materials such as metal, ceramics, glass, some plastics, and rubber; they aren't recommended for flexible surfaces. Apply sparingly. Clamping is not required; curing time is one to two days. Cyanoacrylates dry clear. They deteriorate gradually when exposed to weather and weaken in temperatures above 150°F.
- **Contact Cement.** A rubber-based liquid sold in bottles and cans, contact cement is recommended for bonding laminates, veneers, and other large areas, and for repairs. It can also be used on paper, leather, cloth,

rubber, metal, glass, and some plastics because it remains flexible when it dries. It isn't recommended for repairs where strength is necessary. Contact cement should be applied to both surfaces and allowed to set, and the surfaces then pressed together for an instant bond. Because no repositioning is possible once contact has been made, a sheet of paper can be used to prevent contact between surfaces until positioning is correct. Clamping isn't required; curing is complete on drying. Contact cement is usually very flammable.

- **Polyurethane Glue.** This high-strength glue is an amber paste, sold in tubes. It forms a very strong bond similar to that of epoxy. Polyurethane glue is recommended for use on wood, metal, ceramics, glass, most plastics, and fiberglass. It dries flexible, and can also be used on leather, cloth, rubber, and vinyl. Clamping is required for about two hours; curing time is about 24 hours. Polyurethane glue dries translucent and can be painted or stained. Its shelf life is short, and it is expensive.

- **Silicone Rubber Adhesive or Sealant.** Silicone rubber glues and sealants are sold in tubes and are similar to silicone rubber caulk. They form very strong, very durable, waterproof bonds, with excellent resistance to high and low temperatures. They're recommended for use on gutters and on building materials, including metal, glass, fiberglass, rubber, and wood. They can also be used on fabrics, some plastics, and ceramics. Clamping is usually not required; curing time is about 24 hours, but the adhesive skins over in less than one hour. Silicone rubber adhesives dry flexible and are available in clear, black, and metal-colored forms.

- **Household Cement.** The various adhesives sold in tubes as household cement are fast-setting, low-strength glues. They are recommended for use on wood, ceramics, glass, paper, and some plastics. Some household cements dry flexible and can be used on fabric, leather, and vinyl. Clamping is usually not required; setting time is 10 to 20 minutes, curing time is up to 24 hours.

- **Hot-Melt Adhesive.** Hot-melt glues are sold in stick form and are used with glue guns. A glue gun heats the adhesive above 200°F. For the best bond, the surfaces to be joined should also be preheated. Because hot-melt adhesives are only moderately strong, and bonds will come apart if exposed to high temperatures, this type of glue is recommended for temporary bonds of wood, metal, paper, and some plastics and composition materials. Clamping isn't required; setting time is 10 to 45 seconds, and curing time is 24 hours.

Wood Glues

Wood glues are specifically made for wood repair projects. Here are your main choices.

- **Yellow Glue (Aliphatic Resin, Carpenters' Glue).** Aliphatic resin glue is a yellow liquid, usually sold in plastic squeeze bottles, and often labeled as carpenters' glue. Yellow glue is very similar to white glue, but forms a slightly stronger bond. It is also slightly more water-resistant than white glue. Clamping is required for about 30 minutes until the glue sets; curing time is 12 to 18 hours. Yellow glue dries clear and does not accept wood stains.

- **Plastic Resin Glue (Urea Formaldehyde).** Plastic resin glues are recommended for laminating layers of wood and for gluing structural joints. Plastic resin glue is water-resistant but not waterproof, and isn't recommended for use on outdoor furniture. It is resistant to paint and lacquer thinner. Clamping is required for up to eight hours; curing time is 18 to 24 hours. Apply plastic resin glue only at air temperatures above 70°F.

- **Resorcinol Glue.** This glue is waterproof and forms strong and durable bonds. It is recommended for use on outdoor furniture, kitchen counters, structural bonding, and boats and sporting gear. It can also be used on concrete, cork, fabrics, leather, and some plastics. Resorcinol glue has excellent resistance to temperature extremes, chemicals, and fungus. Clamping is required; curing time is 8 to 24 hours, depending on humidity and temperature.

Adhesives for Glass and Ceramics

Most multipurpose adhesives will bond glass and ceramics, but specialized versions often bond more securely.

- **China and Glass Cement.** Many cements are sold for mending china and glass. These cements usually come in tubes. Acrylic latex-based cements have good resistance to water and heat—other types are not recommended. Clamping is usually required.

- **Silicone Rubber Adhesives.** Only silicone adhesives made specifically for glass and china are recommended. They form very strong bonds, with excellent resistance to water and temperature extremes. Clamping is usually required.

Metal Adhesives and Fillers

Need to make a repair in metal? Here are some popular adhesives that can make a strong bond with metal.

- **Steel Epoxy.** Steel epoxy is a two-part compound sold in tubes. It is quite similar to regular epoxy. It forms a very strong, durable, heat- and water-resistant bond, and is recommended for patching gutters and gas tanks, sealing pipes, and filling rust holes. Drying time is about 12 hours; curing time is one to two days.

- **Steel Putty.** This metal putty consists of two putty-consistency parts that are kneaded together before use. It forms a strong, water-resistant bond, and is recommended for patching and for sealing pipes that aren't under pressure. It can also be used for ceramic and masonry. Curing time is about 30 minutes; when dry, it can be sanded or painted.
- **Plastic Metal Cement.** Plastic metal is a one-part adhesive and filler. It is moisture-resistant but cannot withstand temperature extremes. It is recommended for use on metal, glass, concrete, and wood, where strength is not required. Curing time is about four hours; when dry, plastic metal cement can be sanded or painted.

Plastic Adhesives

Plastics present a special problem with some adhesives because solvents in the adhesives can dissolve plastic. Here are some popular plastic adhesives.

- **Model Cement.** Model cements are usually sold in tubes as "model maker" glues. They form a strong bond on acrylics and polystyrenes, and can be used on most plastics, except plastic foam. Clamping is usually required until the cement has set (about ten minutes); curing time is about 24 hours. Model cement dries clear.
- **Vinyl Adhesive.** Vinyl adhesives, sold in tubes, form a strong, waterproof bond on vinyl and on many plastics, but don't use them on plastic foam. Clamping is usually not required. Vinyl adhesive dries flexible and clear; curing time is ten to 20 minutes.
- **Acrylic Solvent.** Solvents are not adhesives as such; they act by melting the acrylic bonding surfaces, fusing them together at the joint. They are recommended for use on acrylics and polycarbonates. Clamping is required; the bonding surfaces are clamped or taped together, and the solvent is injected into the joint with a syringe. Setting time is about five minutes.

Working Safely

Working smart means working safely. Choose safe tools, learn how to correctly use them, and employ safety equipment to avoid injuries. Think safe and be safe.

Tool Safety

Tools are used to shape and fasten wood and metal. Unfortunately, tools can also shape and fasten you, albeit painfully. The key to using tools safely is to choose tools that aren't inherently dangerous, learn how to use them, and to select and use safety equipment—just in case.

Choosing Safe Tools

The most dangerous tool is one that isn't well maintained. A dull saw is less safe than a sharp one. A hammer with a loose handle can certainly do more damage than one in good repair. A power tool with a frayed cord can electrocute you.

The first rule of safe tools is: Don't buy cheap. You don't necessarily have to buy the best, but lowest cost can often mean lowest value. The best value is typically higher-quality tools and equipment purchased at a nominal discount.

The second rule of safe tools is: Use them wisely. That sounds like common sense, but it isn't. It's tempting to use a screwdriver as a chisel or a wrench as a hammer. Doing so can damage the tool and, more important, damage you.

The third rule of safe tools is: Maintain. Tighten loose parts, fix damaged cords, sharpen dull blades, and don't use unsafe tools.

Following these three simple rules can ensure that you will enjoy being a do-it-yourselfer.

Using Safety Equipment

Protective safety goggles or safety glasses should be worn when working with power tools or equipment. Safety glasses should also be worn when sanding, filing, or doing any other job that produces flying particles. Make sure your safety glasses wrap around the sides to keep deflected particles from reaching your eyes from any angle.

Ladder Safety

More do-it-yourselfers are injured on ladders than any other household tool. Why? Because ladders add a dimension that is sometimes forgotten or ignored: height. It's difficult to always remember that you're off the ground. A misstep or off-balance reach can accidentally remind you how far you are off the ground by eliminating the distance.

Choosing Safe Ladders

If you don't already own a stepladder, get one. Maybe you can change light bulbs and hang curtains by teetering on a stool or an old chair, but you can't paint a room without a ladder—not safely anyway. So, invest in a good one and use it for all those out-of-reach projects.

Most home-use ladders are made of wood or aluminum. Depending on quality, both are reliable. Aluminum, however, weighs only 20 to 50 percent as much as wood, which means it's easier to take it in and out of storage or move it around. On most good ladders you'll find labels that indicate a rated strength. A Type I industrial-grade, rated at 250 pounds, is the strongest. A Type II commercial-grade is rated at 225 pounds. A

Tips for ladder safety.

Type III household-grade is rated at 200 pounds. Each type has actually been successfully tested at four times its rated load. For around-the-house purposes, invest in security and durability and buy a Type II ladder. One that's 6 feet tall will do for most homeowners, but taller ones—8, 10, 12, and all the way up to 16 feet—are available. For an extra measure of safety, get one with rubber feet so your ladder won't skid on hard floors.

If you're painting a ceiling from a single stepladder, you'll find yourself going up and down like a yo-yo, constantly moving the ladder to reach unpainted areas. An alternative is to buy a second ladder of the same size. Then, using a pair of 2×8 boards, make a scaffold between them, a platform from which you can paint for longer periods of time by moving from one end of the bridge to the other. For stability, don't make your scaffold higher than is absolutely necessary, nor longer than six to eight feet in length. Use C-clamps to fasten each end of the 2×8s to a rung of each ladder.

Using Ladders Safely

There's no such thing as an absolutely safe ladder. Gravity is always an unrelenting enemy. However, there are ways to greatly reduce your risk of accidents and injury.

• Inspect a rented, borrowed, or old ladder for defects—loose rungs, rivets, or screws, cracks or splits in the rails.
• For stability, always open a stepladder to its fullest position, lock the spreader braces on each side in place, and pull down the bucket shelf.
• Whether you are going up or coming down, always face the ladder head-on and use both hands to hold on to the side rails or rungs.
• Don't climb higher than two rungs from the top; don't sit or stand on the top or the bucket shelf.
• To keep yourself from overreaching and getting off balance, never let your navel go beyond either of the ladder's side rails.
• If you must work on a ladder in front of a door, lock the door.
• Put the paint can or tray on the bucket shelf before you climb the ladder. And don't go up the ladder with tools in your hand or in your pockets.

Electrical Safety

Electricity can help you—or it can hurt you. An appliance can make your coffee in the morning. A bare cord can electrocute you. Here are some simple rules for working safely with electricity.

• Never work on an electrical circuit that is live or attached to an electrical source. Unplug the circuit, trip the circuit breaker, or unscrew the fuse before you begin working.
• Use only equivalent replacement parts. That is, replace a controller with one that has the same function and rating. Don't replace a 10-amp appliance cord with one that is rated for 5 amps.
• Some appliances use capacitors, electrical components that store high voltage. Touching a charged capacitor,

such as those in a microwave oven, can electrocute or burn you.

- Most important, think before you act. Electricity follows strict laws. You must follow the same laws in order to repair electrical systems safely.

Circuit Breaker and Fuses

An electrical circuit is a complete circle that allows the electrical voltage to flow through an electrical appliance and return. A break in the circuit stops the flow. How can you protect the appliance on a circuit from being damaged by excessive current? By applying the principle of "the weakest link in a chain breaks first." If the appliance would be damaged by a current of more than 25 amps, then you simply place something in the same circuit that will fail at 25 amps and thus open the circuit.

In newer homes, the weakest link in the chain is a circuit breaker that trips, or turns the circuit off, if specified amperage is exceeded. That is, a 15-amp circuit breaker will open and shut off a circuit if more than 15 amps of current pass through it. In older homes, the weakest link is a fuse. This fuse includes a piece of metal calculated to melt and thus open the circuit if the amperage is exceeded.

Knowing this, make sure that the total amperage of appliances on a circuit doesn't exceed the rating of the circuit breaker or fuse. The amperage of an appliance is typically written on the bottom near model numbers. If the amperage isn't listed, but the wattage is, divide the wattage by 120 (volts) to estimate the amperage. So a 900-watt toaster draws about 7.5 amps.

You may be tempted to simply increase the breaker's or fuse's amp rating, replacing a 15-amp breaker or fuse with one rated at 20 amps, for example. Don't! If you do, the weakest link in the chain may become the wiring. Then, when the design amperage is exceeded, the wiring will get hot and potentially cause a fire. If you must increase the amperage on a circuit, have a licensed electrician make the modification.

Switches and Receptacles

Switches and receptacles simply complete a circuit. A switch opens and closes the circuit. An open circuit is off and a closed one is on.

An electrical receptacle—called a plug-in—receives an electrical cord. Once the cord is plugged into the receptacle, the circuit is closed and electricity flows through the cord to the appliance.

Grounding and Discharging

For safety, all electrical appliances, switches, and receptacles should be grounded. That is, a wire connected eventually to the ground or zero voltage

reference point should be included. An appliance may be grounded to its own chassis. An electrical receptacle will have a third prong receptacle to receive grounded cords. If your appliance has a grounded cord, don't break off the grounding prong or replace it with an ungrounded cord.

Loose Wires

A loose wire can not only break an electrical circuit, it can also injure you if you touch it while it is energized or hot. Loose wires are caused by vibration or other factors. Carefully check all loose wires for related damage or stress and reconnect them using electrical tape, wire nuts, or other enclosing fasteners.

Fire Safety

Electricity can cause fires. A home with electrical appliances should have a dry-chemical fire extinguisher rated at least a C. Even better is a utility extinguisher rated A-B-C for flammable solids (wood and fabric), flammable liquids (grease and paint), and electrical fires.

Small Engine Safety

The final chapter of this book will cover small engines. Whether you are operating a small gas engine, servicing it, or repairing it, safety is important. Engines are machines powered by hundreds of internal ignitions every second. Parts are revolving thousands of times per minute. Blades, chains, belts, and other devices are moving at blurring speeds. Gasoline is an explosive fuel. Lubricants can burn. Carbon monoxide can poison.

Fortunately, common sense can help you remain safe as you work on and around small gas engines.

Working with Fuels and Hazardous Materials

Gasoline, solvents, lubricants, and other flammable liquids should be stored in closed, leakproof containers. Gas vapors are even more flammable than liquid gasoline, so gas should be stored in containers that eliminate any chance of gas vapors escaping. Never fill a gas tank on or near an engine that is running. The gas vapors can be ignited by heat or spark from the engine.

Shop rags that have been used to clean up spilt fuel and lubricants are highly flammable. Keep all such rags in a closed metal container, such as a coffee can, away from any source of spark or flame.

Ventilation and Carbon Monoxide

Carbon monoxide is a by-product of gas-powered internal combustion engine operation. A small dose of carbon monoxide can make you drowsy. A larger dose can kill you, others around you, or pets. Always make sure there is sufficient ventilation when operating a gas engine. Indoors, make sure an operating engine has a sufficient supply of fresh air to dissipate carbon monoxide in the exhaust. Even outdoors, a low fog can trap carbon monoxide gas into a pocket and possibly suffocate you.

Hearing Protectors

Small gas engines are noisy, especially when operated in a shop or garage. Engine noise can damage hearing if the machine is operated without a muffler. To avoid hearing loss, wear hearing protectors or earplugs to reduce noise levels that reach your sensitive eardrums.

Other Safety Tips

To prevent an engine from starting during service or repair, remove the lead wire from the spark plug and attach, or ground, the lead wire to the frame.

Some small gas engines use batteries to provide voltage for spark, starting, lights, or other functions.

Batteries create electricity using a chemical reaction between lead and acid. Flammable hydrogen gas is produced when a battery is charging or discharging. If the hydrogen gas is ignited, the battery can explode, spraying acid and fragments. Always keep sparks and flames away from batteries.

Don't wear loose-fitting clothing or jewelry when working on or around engine-powered tools or toys. A loose sleeve or long hair can quickly become entangled in rotating parts, pulling you into the equipment.

Coils can produce up to 30,000 volts of electricity. Current is low, but the electrical power in a coil is still sufficient to damage or burn internal organs. Always use insulated wire pliers to remove a wire from an operating spark plug or coil.

Keep your shop, garage, or storage shed floor clean and free of gas or lubricants. Not only are lubricants a fire hazard, they can also cause you to slip and injure yourself.

Work smart!

CHAPTER 2

INSIDE JOBS

The inside of your home is made up of surfaces: walls, ceilings, floors, windows, and doors. Before you decorate the inside of your home (see Chapter 3), you should make any necessary repairs, including repairing drywall, replacing molding, repairing carpeting, fixing a broken window, or replacing an interior door. This chapter describes common repairs and improvements you can make to surfaces inside your home.

Walls and Ceilings

Walls and ceilings constitute about five-sixths of a home's interior surfaces, so it's hardly surprising that they get a lot of attention from do-it-yourselfers. This fact shows up on the shelves at home centers and hardware stores, which offer a wide array of products that can make wall and ceiling jobs much easier than you might think.

Hanging Things on Walls

Pictures, mirrors, shelves, lamps, tools, sports equipment—the list of items you can hang on walls is almost endless. To keep them hanging where they belong, you need to choose the proper fastener and install it in the proper way.

Most wall framing is covered with drywall that typically measures ½ or ⅝ inch thick. To hang light-weight and medium-weight objects, you need only pierce this covering with a nail or expandable plastic screw anchor. Heavier objects, such as a large mirror, should be supported by hardware that either attaches to the wall framing or clamps securely to the wall surface from behind.

The wooden framing in walls, called studs, are typically spaced 16 inches apart. You can locate studs with a magnetic stud finder that detects the nails that hold the wall covering to the studs. If you don't own this handy device, you can measure 16 inches from a corner of the room and begin knocking the wall with your knuckles. If the wall sounds more solid at a point exactly 16 inches from the corner, there's a stud there; you'll most likely find other studs, spaced in increments of 16 inches from the first, along the length of the wall. If you hear a hollow sound at a point 16 inches from the corner, go to the opposite end of the wall, measure 16 inches, and knock. You'll probably find a stud there, because carpenters always space studs from one end of the wall or the other.

Hanging Light Objects

To hang most lightweight objects, such as small pictures:

Step 1: Place a small piece of cellophane tape over the spot where the nail will be driven. This prevents the wall's drywall or plaster from crumbling.

Step 2: Place a picture hanger flat against the wall and drive a nail through the hanger.

Picture hangers are handy for hanging lightweight objects on walls.

To hang medium-weight objects, such as large pictures:

Step 1: Buy plastic or nylon wall anchors made for the size screws you have, and examine the package to find out what size drill bit to use for the holes.

Step 2: Drill a hole in the wall to accommodate the plastic anchor.

Step 3: Tap the anchor all the way in with a hammer.

Step 4: Insert the screw through the item it is to hold, and then turn it into the anchor. The screw will expand the anchor to make it grip the sides of the hole.

Hanging Heavy Objects

When hanging heavy objects, such as shelves and mirrors, the best device is the expansion anchor, or bolt. This type of fastener comes in different sizes to accommodate differences in wall thickness and in the

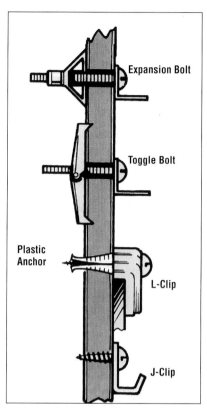

Fasteners for hanging heavier objects from walls.

- Expansion Bolt
- Toggle Bolt
- Plastic Anchor
- L-Clip
- J-Clip

weight of the things they are to hold. Once you get the right fastener, here is how to install it:

Step 1: Check the package to see what size drill bit you must use, and then drill a hole in the wall.

Step 2: Lightly tap the fastener in place with a hammer.

Step 3: Turn the slotted bolt clockwise. When you can't turn it any more, back it out. The fastener is then secure against the inside of the wall, and you are ready to hang the object.

Step 4: Put the bolt through the object or its hanger, then reinsert the bolt in the expansion anchor.

For very heavy objects, such as cabinets or a bookshelf unit, use toggle bolts. Available in several sizes, toggle bolts require you to drill holes in the wall. Here is how to install them:

Step 1: Drill the proper-size hole.

Step 2: Remove the bolt from the toggle.

Step 3: Put the bolt through the object to be hung, or through its hanger, before you insert it into the wall. (You can't remove the bolt after the device is in the wall without the toggle falling down behind the wall.) Reinsert the bolt in the toggle.

Step 4: Squeeze together the toggle with your thumb and forefinger and push it into the hole.

Step 5: Hold the object you are hanging right next to the wall as you insert the toggle. When it goes through, pull the bolt back toward you until you feel the toggle open and hit the back of the wall.

Step 6: Turn the bolt clockwise until the hanger or the item itself is flat and secure against the wall.

Replacing Moldings

Because baseboards are down at floor level where they can be struck by all sorts of objects, they are the most easily damaged moldings. The following procedures guide you on how to replace baseboard molding, but you can apply the same techniques to other types of moldings as well.

Removing a Molding

The first task in replacing molding is to remove the old molding. Here's how:

Step 1: Remove any shoe molding, the quarter-round piece that fits against both the baseboard and the floor. Because it's nailed to the subfloor, apply gentle prying pressure with a putty knife at one end of the shoe molding to get it started. Then, use a short pry bar and a wood block for leverage. Once started, the shoe molding should come up easily.

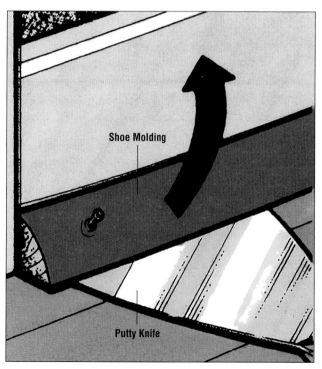

- Shoe Molding
- Putty Knife

To remove a shoe molding, first pry it gently with a putty knife, then use a small pry bar.

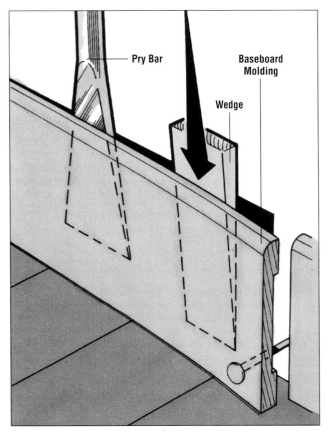

To remove a baseboard, pry it with a pry bar, then use a wedge.

Step 2: Pry off the damaged baseboard. Start at one end, inserting a small, flat pry bar between the baseboard and the wall. Pry gently, and move farther down the molding whenever you can, slipping small cedar shingle wedges into the gaps. Work all the way along the baseboard, prying and wedging. Then work back between the wedges, tapping the wedges in deeper as the baseboard comes out further. Continue until the molding comes off.

Step 3: Check to see if any nails have been pulled through either the shoe molding or the baseboard. If so, pull out the nails completely.

Using a Miter Box

If the old baseboard came off intact, you can use it as a pattern for cutting the new one. If part of it is missing or if it is badly damaged, however, you will have to cut the new moldings to fit without the aid of a pattern. You will need a miter box to cut the moldings. An inexpensive wooden or plastic miter box is adequate for this work. Slots in the box allow you to cut molding at 45-degree angles. Use either a backsaw or a fine-toothed blade in a hacksaw to do the sawing. Before sawing, place the molding you are about to cut next to the molding against which it will rest to make certain that the cut you plan to make is the correct one. The following steps instruct you on how to make two 45-degree cuts, joining two pieces of molding so they form a right angle:

Step 1: Place a length of molding in the miter box, making sure that the lip of the miter box presses against the edge of a table or bench so that you can keep it steady.

Step 2: Hold the molding tightly against the side of the miter box to prevent it from slipping as you saw a 45-degree cut at one end.

Step 3: Repeat the procedure for the other length of molding. The two lengths should form a perfect right angle.

Installing Molding

When you finish all the mitered joints, you are ready to install the new baseboard molding and reinstall the shoe molding.

Step 1: Fit all the pieces together before nailing to make sure that you cut them correctly.

Step 2: Locate the wall studs. If you're replacing a molding, they'll be at the points where the old one was nailed. If the molding is brand-new, locate the wall studs (see "Hanging Things on Walls" on page 34.)

Step 3: Nail the baseboard in place with finishing nails, then use a nail set to drive the nail heads below the surface of the molding.

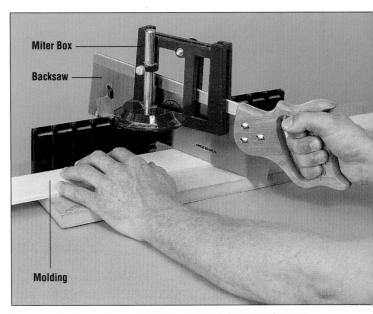

Use a miter box and a backsaw to make 45-degree miter cuts.

Step 4: Install the shoe molding with finishing nails as well. Shoe molding, however, must be nailed to the floor and not to the baseboard. Drive the nail heads below the surface of the shoe molding with a nail set.

Step 5: Paint or stain the moldings to match your walls.

Installing Paneling

If you want a way to cover up badly deteriorated walls, finish off a basement room, or give any area a new look, consider wall paneling. You can buy plywood paneling that is either finished or ready-to-finish. Or, you can buy hardboard panels that simulate various finishes.

You can apply panels directly to the wall studs where you have new construction, but because the panels are thin and not soundproof, it is best to provide a drywall

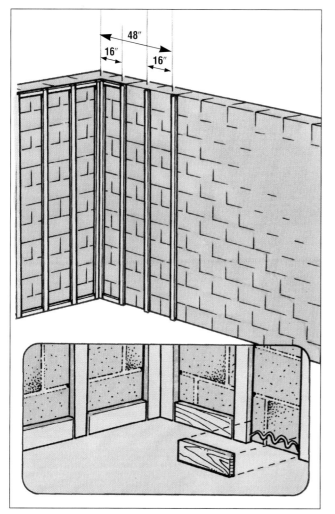

To install furring on relatively smooth walls, put up vertical strips, spaced 16 inches apart, then cut short horizontals to fit at top and bottom.

backing. Many building codes require a drywall backing, especially in basements. If you decide to apply paneling directly to the studs, make sure that the studs are free of high or low spots. To install paneling on existing walls:

Step 1: Remove the molding and trim and check for high or low spots by moving a long, straight board against the wall and watching for any gaps as you draw it along.

Step 2: Build up any low spots with drywall joint compound, and sand down any high spots. *Note: If the walls are cracked or very uneven, attach paneling to furring strips. Masonry walls must always be furred and waterproofed. See "Installing Furring Strips" on page 38.*

Step 3: Stack the panels in the room to be paneled with strips of boards between each one. Leave them there for at least 48 hours before installing them to allow the panels to adjust to the moisture content of the room.

Step 4: Once the panels are stabilized, lean them against the walls, matching the wood graining in the most pleasing manner. When you have the panels arranged the way you want them, number the panels on the back side.

Step 5: As necessary, cut the panels to fit their position on the wall. If you are using trim molding, the fit at the floor and ceiling doesn't have to be as tight as for panels without trim molding. Also, make sure that panels at room corners are cut to fit well, as most corners aren't perfectly plumb (vertically level).

Estimating Wall Paneling

It's easy to estimate how many 4×8-foot panels you need, if you know the dimensions of the room you plan to panel. Use this table:

Perimeter of Room	Panels Needed
20 Feet	5
24 Feet	6
28 Feet	7
32 Feet	8
60 Feet	15
64 Feet	16
68 Feet	17
72 Feet	18
92 Feet	23

Step 6: If you plan to nail the panels, use 3d finishing nails to attach the panels to furring strips or wall studs. Drive nails about every 6 inches along the edges of the panel and about every 12 inches through the center. If you are using panel adhesive, run a ribbon of adhesive across all furring strips or in a similar pattern on the wall surface. Place the panel against the wall or furring strips and press it down, then pull it away from the wall and reset it to distribute the adhesive for a better bond.

Step 7: To cut paneling out for a door or window, use a large sheet of paper to make a pattern. Tape the paper in place, press it against the door or window frame, mark it with a pencil, and use scissors to cut it to size. Use this pattern to transfer the marks to the panel.

Step 8: To make cutouts for electrical outlets or switches, trace the outline of the switch or outlet box on the panel and drill pilot holes at opposite corners. Then use a keyhole saw to connect the corners with a saw cut.

Step 9: Finally, apply finish molding as described earlier in this chapter. Be sure to countersink the nails and fill the holes with matching wood putty.

Installing Furring Strips

Furring strips are 1×2s or 1×3s that are nailed or glued to the wall, with pieces of cedar shingle under them to even up low spots. Use 1×3s because they provide a better bearing surface and are easy to install.

The amount of furring depends on how uneven your walls are. If they're smooth, with a variation of only ½ inch or so between high and low spots, you need only put up vertical strips, nailing or gluing them over studs and compensating for low spots by wedging shingles under the strips. Then cut short horizontal pieces to fit between them at floor and ceiling level.

If your walls are very uneven, you may need to double-fur them. With double-furring, you create a grid with two layers of strips. Start by nailing up vertical strips, spaced 16 inches on center from floor to ceiling. Even these up as best you can with shims and note any problem spots. Next, install horizontal strips, spaced 16 inches from center to center. Nail these to the vertical strips, further shimming as necessary to smooth the grid.

At electrical wall switches and outlets, you'll need to compensate for the increased thickness of the wall. Remove the cover plates and reset the electrical boxes out the necessary distance. *Caution: Turn off the electrical power to the circuits you are working on before removing the cover plates.*

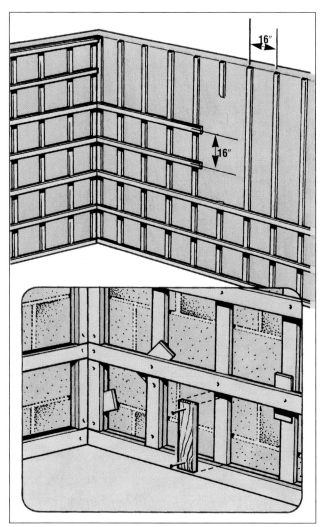

Double-fur uneven walls with a second layer of horizontal strips. Shim as necessary to smooth the grid.

Repairing Ceramic Tile

Ceramic tile is very durable, but it can eventually show signs of wear. Tiles crack or loosen, and the grout between tiles wears down and crumbles out. These are more than simple cosmetic problems, because unless you repair the damage, water can seep behind the tiles and cause more serious trouble. To keep the problem from getting worse, make the repairs as soon as you can.

Replacing a Tile

The hardest part of this job is finding a tile to match the broken one. If you can't find a new tile that matches, try salvage yards for an old tile. To replace a tile:

Step 1: Remove the old tile. To do so, put a piece of masking tape at the center of the tile. Then, wearing safety goggles, drill a hole into the

Remove the damaged ceramic tile by drilling a hole in the center and cutting it with a glass cutter. Chisel out the pieces.

Step 6: Let the grout set for 15 minutes, then wipe the wall with a clean damp sponge or towel to remove any excess grout. Be careful not to disturb the grout around the new tile. After removing the excess, let the grout dry completely—at least 12 hours. Do not let the tile get wet during this drying period.

Step 7: Once the grout is dry, rub the tile firmly with a damp towel to remove any remaining grout from the wall.

Loose ceramic tiles can be removed and then reattached with the same procedure. Scrape out the old grout around the loose tile with the corner of a putty knife, and carefully pry out the tile. If it cracks, it will have to be replaced by a new one, as explained above. You can locate loose tiles by tapping across the wall with the handle of the putty knife.

Regrouting Tile

Crumbling grout should be replaced as soon as possible to prevent mildew and water damage. To regrout tile:

Step 1: Scrub the tile thoroughly with a strong household cleaner. Rinse well. If the old grout is

taped spot with an electric drill and a carbide bit. Peel off the tape and score an X across the tile with a glass cutter. Then break up the tile with a cold chisel and hammer and remove the pieces.

Step 2: Use a scraper or a chisel to remove old adhesive and grout from the wall where the old tile was. Make sure there's no loose grout around the opening.

Step 3: Spread ceramic mastic on the back of the new tile with a putty knife or a notched spreader, leaving the tile edges clean.

Step 4: Carefully set the new tile into the opening on the wall. Press the tile in firmly, moving it slightly from side to side to distribute the mastic, until it's flush with the surrounding tile surface. The space around the tile should be even, and the tile should be perfectly aligned. Tape the tile in place with masking tape or adhesive tape. Let the mastic cure as directed by the manufacturer.

Step 5: Remove the tape holding the tile in place. Wear rubber gloves as you mix ceramic tile grout to fill the joints around the tile, following the manufacturer's instructions. Use a damp sponge to apply the grout all around the new tile, filling the gaps completely.

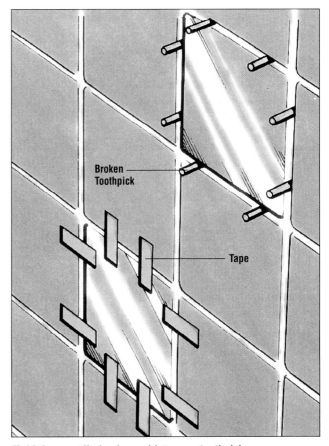

Broken Toothpick

Tape

Hold the new tile in place with tape or toothpicks.

Estimating Ceramic Tile

Most ceramic tile is 4¼ square inches. You can use the table below to estimate how many of these tiles you need per linear foot.

Length of Row	Tiles Required
5 Feet	15
6 Feet	17
7 Feet	20
8 Feet	23
9 Feet	26
10 Feet	29
11 Feet	32
12 Feet	34

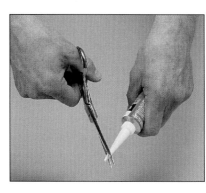

Cut the nozzle of a caulk tube at an angle.

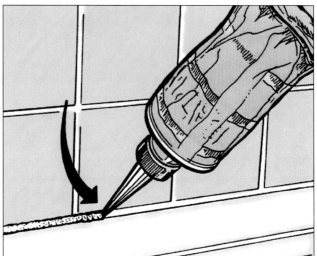

Squeeze caulk evenly along the joint to waterproof it.

mildewed, you must remove the mildew before you regrout. Scrub the tile joints with a toothbrush dipped in chlorine bleach, then rinse the wall thoroughly.

Step 2: Remove all the crumbling grout you can with the edge of a putty knife, then vacuum.

Step 3: Rinse the wall to make sure it's absolutely clean, but don't dry it. It should be damp when the new grout is applied.

Step 4: Wearing rubber gloves, mix ceramic tile grout according to the manufacturer's instructions. Apply the grout with a damp sponge, wiping it firmly in the wall areas that need grouting to fill the joints. Smooth the newly grouted joints with a clean damp sponge. As necessary, add more grout and smooth it again, filling the tile joints completely.

Step 5: Let the grout dry for at least 12 hours. Don't let the wall get wet during this period. Then scrub the wall firmly with a clean dry towel to remove any grout that's left on the tiles.

Step 6: To protect the new grout, seal the tile joints with a silicone tile grout spray.

Recaulking Fixtures

Because tubs and sinks are used practically every day, caulking between the fixture and the wall often cracks or pulls loose. When this happens, water seeps into the opening and damages the joint and the surrounding wall. Use silicone caulk or bathtub caulk to make the repair. To recaulk kitchen and bathroom fixtures:

Step 1: Use a putty knife or a utility knife to remove all the old caulk from the joint.

Step 2: Clean the joint thoroughly with a strong household cleaner. If the joint is mildewed, scrub it out with chlorine bleach. Dry the joint thoroughly with a clean rag wrapped over the blade of a putty knife.

Step 3: Apply caulk to the joint. Cut the nozzle of a caulk tube at an angle, so that the opening is a little larger than the open joint. If you're caulking several joints, start with the smallest joint and work up, recutting the nozzle of the tube as necessary for the larger joints.

Step 4: Let the new caulk dry for several hours. Don't let it get wet during the drying period. Let the caulk cure completely (see manufacturer's instructions) before using the fixture.

Installing New Ceramic Tile

Installing ceramic tile is easy with modern fast-setting mastics, sealants, and grout. Many styles of ceramic tile are available pregrouted with flexible latex grout. Whatever style or size you choose to install, the principles are the same.

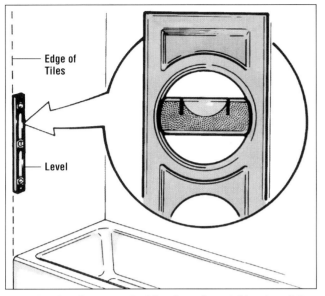

Use a level to draw a vertical line from the outside edge of the tub to mark the end of the tiles.

Before you begin, you'll need a hammer, chalk line, level, saber saw with carbide blade (helpful but not necessary), rubber gloves, tile mastic, tile grout sealer, tiles, (edging cap and two outside corner edge caps for ceramic tile), and a paint stirring stick or old toothbrush to use for forcing grout deeply into the tile joints. You can also rent a grooved trowel, tile nippers, tile cutter, and rubber squeegee.

Inspect the walls. They must be smooth and free of loose plaster, dust, or peeling paint. Read the mastic instructions; on new plaster or unfinished drywall, a primer may be necessary. To install ceramic tile:

Step 1: Start at the back wall (the wall opposite the faucet end of the tub). Using a level, draw a vertical line from the outside edge of the tub up as high as you want the tile on the wall. Check

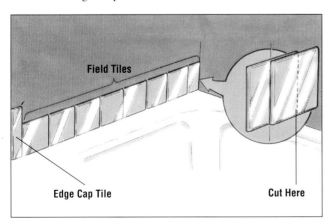

Temporarily place the starter row to mark the end pieces for cutting.

the tub for level: If one side is higher or lower by more than 1/8 inch, adjust the starter row of tiles.

Step 2: Temporarily place the starter row of tiles (start with an edge cap tile) along the top edge of the tub. The tile next to the corner wall will have to be cut to fit. Adjust the run slightly so that not less than half a tile will have to be cut. Remove the tile.

Step 3: Spread as much mastic along the wall of the tub as you'll be able to cover with tiles in a half hour. As you progress, spread more mastic as needed.

Step 4: Place the first row of tiles in position. Push each tile with a slight twisting motion to spread the mastic, but don't slide the tile around or the mastic will rise in the grout line. Leave a 1/8-inch gap between the tub and the first row of tiles.

Apply mastic, then place the tiles in a stair-step pattern.

Step 5: Put the edge cap and first two tiles of the next row in place. Then put the edge cap and first tile of the third row in place. You now have the beginning of a stair-step pattern.

Step 6: Continue placing tiles in a stair-step pattern until all except the top row of cap tiles are in place. Finish by placing the row of cap tiles along the top of the tiled area, starting with an outside corner cap.

Step 7: Place the tiles on the long wall in the same stair-step fashion. Start by placing a row temporarily along the top of the tub to determine how much must be trimmed off the tile. Spread the mastic as you did for the first wall, and install a row of tiles along the edge of the tub. Then place the tiles of the next two rows to start a stair-step pattern. Fill in the rest of the wall, and finish the top with a row of cap tiles.

Step 8: The procedure for the faucet wall is the same as it is for the other two walls. Use a saber saw equipped with a carbide blade or use tile nippers to cut the openings for the spout, faucets, and shower arm. The openings don't have to be exact, because the chrome trim rings (escutcheons) will cover minor imperfections.

Step 9: Clean up any excess mastic and clean the tools. Allow the mastic at least 24 hours to dry thoroughly.

Grouting Ceramic Tiles

Grout can be applied to the ceramic once the mastic is completely dry. To grout ceramic tiles:

Step 1: Mix the grout to a creamy consistency and set it aside. Wet the tiles so that they do not remove moisture from the grout. Wear gloves and spread grout evenly over half of the back wall, then use a rubber squeegee to work the grout well into the tile. Wipe the excess away with a wet sponge.

Spread grout evenly over the wall using a rubber squeegee to work the grout into the areas between the tiles.

Step 2: Use a blunt stick to force the grout deep into the tile joints. Remove the excess grout with a sponge and continue in the same manner for the remaining area.

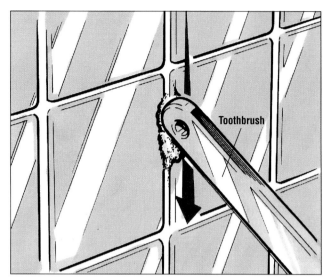

Use the end of an old toothbrush to force the grout into the tile joints.

Step 3: Allow the grout to dry overnight. Polish off the thin film of grout that has dried on the tile. Run a bead of tub caulk around the ⅛-inch gap between the tub and the first row of tiles. If you have tiled around a window, be sure to caulk it carefully.

Step 4: Apply a grout sealer according to the manufacturer's directions.

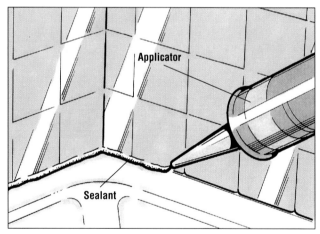

Run a bead of sealing caulk along the tub and the first row of tiles.

Framing a Partition

Converting a basement or attached garage into more usable living space requires building a partition wall. Framing a wall is easy. The components of a partition wall include the top plate; the sole, or floor, plate; and the wall studs. The studs are usually on 16-inch centers,

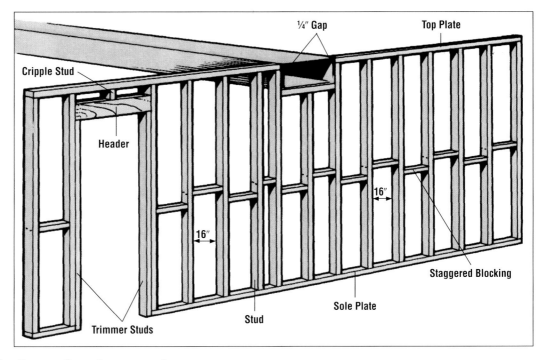

Components of a partition wall.

which means that the distance from the center of one stud to the center of the next measures 16 inches. All framing lumber for a project is of the same size, usually 2×4s.

The framing described here is for a nonload-bearing partition wall. Because it isn't designed to support the ceiling or the floor above, you need not worry about the roof caving in. Just make the finished wall look as attractive as possible. Remember that minor cosmetic faults in the framing will be covered by drywall or paneling.

In planning a wall, consider all the uses of the room and what furniture or equipment will go into it. Think about the best place for a door. To get an idea of how a new wall will affect existing space, put tape or 2×4s on the floor to mark the spot for the proposed new wall. Shift these around until you're satisfied with your plan. To frame a partition:

Step 1: Cut the top plate and sole plate for the wall. Use long lengths of lumber (10-, 12-, or 16-foot lengths) to make the plates all one piece, if possible. Remember that the sole plate doesn't run through a doorway. Mark the top and sole plates for stud locations. The studs may be 16 (recommended) or 24 inches on center.

Step 2: Snap a chalk line on the floor where the sole plate is to go to guide you as you install it. Nail the sole plate in position.

Step 3: With the sole plate in place, use a long, straight 2×4 to position the top plate directly above the

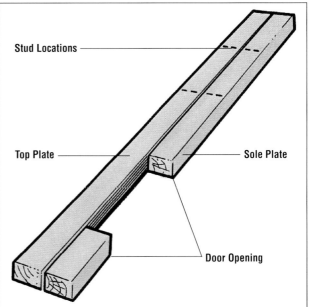

Lay the top and sole plates side by side to mark them for stud locations.

sole plate. Place the straightedge against the 2×4, and use a level to make it vertically level, or plumb.

Step 4: Install the top plate. If the wall runs across the joists in the ceiling above, nail the top plate to each joist. If the wall runs parallel to the joists and cannot be positioned so that the top plate can be nailed to a joist, install bridging of 2×4s between the joists to provide solid nailing for the top plate. Space the bridging pieces on 16-inch centers and nail them to the joists with two nails through each end of each bridging piece.

Step 5: Assemble the studs and top plate on the floor as a unit, which will be raised as an assembly. This allows you to nail through the top plate and straight into the top of each stud. If the studs must vary in length, however, install the top plate, cut each stud to fit, and then toenail each stud in place. Toenailing means driving 16d nails into the side of the stud at about a 45-degree angle so that the nails penetrate the plate. Drive two nails into each stud.

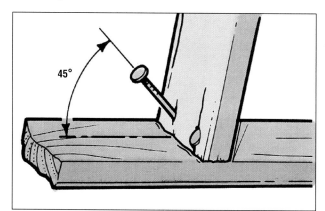

Toenailing means driving a nail into the side of a stud at about a 45-degree angle.

Step 6: Toenail the studs to the sole plate. Openings for doors in the framing must be about 3 inches wider and 1½ inches higher than the actual size of the door. Nail extra 2×4s on both sides of the door opening, and nail a header at the top. Then place a short cripple stud between the header and the top plate and nail it in place.

Step 7: Nail 2×4s horizontally between studs at the midpoint of the wall. This blocking may be staggered so the pieces can be end-nailed.

Step 8: Cover the stud partition with paneling or drywall.

Installing Drywall

Installing drywall is easy, but taping the joints between panels requires some practice. Some do-it-yourselfers install the drywall themselves, then call an experienced drywall taper to finish the job.

Although it's easy to figure how much drywall to buy (just compute the square footage of the walls and ceiling), it takes some planning to end up with as few joints as possible. The standard-size sheets for walls measure 4×8 feet. They are usually installed with the long side running from floor to ceiling, but if you can eliminate a joint by placing them horizontally, do so. All drywall sheets are 4 feet wide, but many building-material outlets offer 10-foot and even 12-foot lengths. The most popular thicknesses of drywall are ½ and ⅝ inch, but check your local building code for requirements.

Consult a dealer to learn how many nails, rolls of tape, and how much joint compound you will need. As a general rule, 1,000 square feet of drywall requires about seven pounds of coated drywall nails, a five-gallon pail of joint compound in mixed form, and a 500-foot roll of tape. Each outside corner requires one metal cornerbead. Drywall tape is used for inside corners.

Placing Drywall

To install drywall on the ceiling and walls of a framed room, you'll probably need an assistant, especially for the ceiling. Here's how to cut and install panels:

Step 1: Construct a pair of T-braces from 2×4s about an inch longer than the distance from floor to ceiling. Nail 2×4s about 3 feet long to one end of each longer 2×4 to form the Ts.

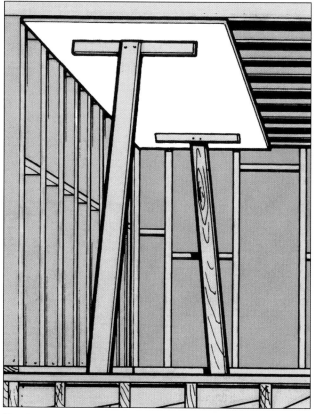

Use T-braces to install drywall on a new ceiling.

Step 2: Cut drywall panels to size. Use a sharp utility knife along a straightedge to cut drywall. After you make the cut through the face paper, place the board over a length of 2×4 laid flat on the floor, or some other type of support, and snap the scored section down. The gypsum core will break along the line you cut. Then turn the panel over, cut the paper on the other side, and smooth the rough edges with very coarse sandpaper on a sanding block.

Step 3: Install drywall panels on the ceiling. If possible, try to span the entire width with a single sheet of wallboard to reduce the number of joints. Position and wedge the T-braces against the drywall sheet to hold it in place until you finish nailing it.

Step 4: Drive nails at 6-inch intervals into all the joists covered by the sheet. Start in the center of the drywall panel and work out. Give each nail an extra hammer blow to dimple the surface slightly without breaking the face paper.

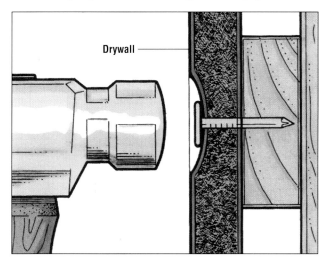

After you drive each nail in, give it an extra blow to dimple the surface without breaking the drywall face paper.

Step 5: When the ceiling is finished, cut and install wall panels. Carefully measure for any cutouts in the drywall, including electrical outlets, switches, or light fixtures. To make cutouts, draw a pattern of the cutout on the wallboard, drill a hole on the pattern line, and then use a keyhole saw to follow the pattern.

Step 6: Space the nails 6 inches apart, but start nailing 4 inches from the ceiling. Butt the wall panels against the ceiling sheets. Dimple all nails. Nail metal outside cornerbeads to cover any outside corners.

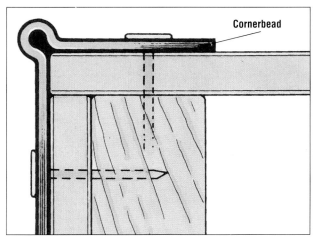

It's not necessary to dimple the nails of outside cornerbead, because the surface will be covered with drywall putty.

Taping Drywall

The next step in installing drywall is covering the nails and joints, called taping.

Step 1: Use a 5-inch-wide drywall taping knife to spread joint compound into the slight recess created by the tapered edges of the drywall

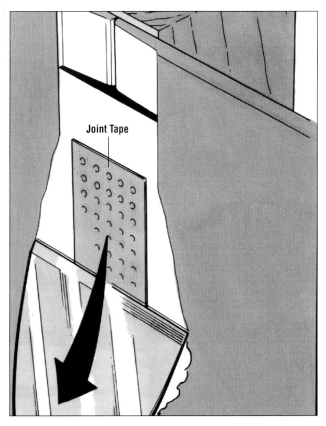

Taping a joint means applying joint compound followed by a strip of drywall tape, then two thin coats of joint compound.

sheets. Smooth the compound until it is even with the rest of the board surface.

Step 2: Center the drywall tape over the joint and press it firmly into the compound. Because some compound will squeeze out, make sure that there is still a good bed underneath. When you get the tape embedded into the compound all along the joint, smooth it with the taping knife. At the same time, fill all the nail dimples with compound.

Step 3: When the compound is completely dry (usually 24 hours later) apply a very thin second coat of compound that extends out a few inches to either side of the first coat. After the second coat dries completely, apply a third coat, this time with a 10-inch-wide taping knife, extending the compound about 6 inches to either side. When the third coat is dry, feather all the edges with a sanding block covered with medium-grit sandpaper.

To tape inside corners, including the spots where the walls and ceiling meet, cut the tape to length and fold it in half. After laying the bed of compound, press the folded tape into the compound and feather the compound out at least 1½ inches to each side. The corners require three coats, and the last coat should extend about 8 inches to each side. Sanding is required here, too.

To finish the outside corners, install a metal corner (from your building-supply store), then apply three coats of compound that taper up to the bead. The last coat should extend the compound on each wall to about eight inches wide. Sand as with other drywall joints.

Let the walls dry for five days. Give the surface of the drywall a coat of primer made for paint or wallpaper. When the primer is dry, sand the drywall surface lightly with fine-grit sandpaper on a sanding block. Be sure to sand between each additional coat of paint with fine-grit sandpaper. New drywall should receive at least three coats: a sealer, primer, and finish coat.

Replacing Damaged Ceiling Tiles

To remove and replace one or more damaged interlocking ceiling tiles, follow this procedure.

Step 1: If the tile is applied to furring, use a keyhole saw to cut a hole large enough to stick your hand through in the center of the damaged tile. Carefully remove the damaged tile with your fingers. If the tile is glued directly to a plaster or drywall ceiling, make a hole in the tile with a sharp tool and carefully pry off the pieces.

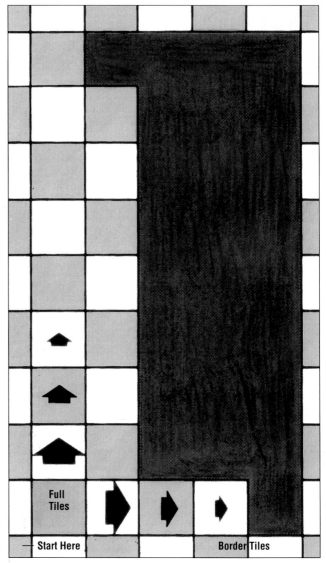

When setting new tile, set corner and border tiles first.

Step 2: Cut the tongue or grooved edges from the replacement tile with a utility knife. The edges you should remove can be determined by holding the tile in position over the opening in the ceiling. Match the cut tile to the opening. It may need trimming to fit. Remove any old staples or adhesive from the furring strips or ceiling. Be careful not to damage the edges of adjoining tiles.

Step 3: Place ceiling tile adhesive at each corner of the new tile, and press the tile into the opening. If it is not aligned with the surrounding tiles, you can slip it into the proper position before the adhesive dries. Then hold the tile in position for several minutes until the adhesive sets enough to support the tile.

Tiling a Ceiling

The fastest way to get a new ceiling is to install ceiling tiles directly to an existing drywall ceiling. If the ceiling surface isn't sound or has open joists, staple the tiles to furring strips. Alternately, you may be able to lower the ceiling with a suspended ceiling system if the ceiling is high enough. The procedure for installing a suspended ceiling is covered later in this chapter.

To determine how much tile you need, multiply the room's length by its width to get the square footage, then add about 10 percent for trimming and errors. To figure how many boxes of tile you need, divide the square footage by the number of square feet of tile in a box. If the room is not square or rectangular, draw a sketch of the room on graph paper, using each square on the paper to represent one square foot. Then count the squares to determine how many tiles you need.

Installing Tile With Adhesive

To apply tile directly to the existing ceiling surface with adhesive:

Step 1: To find the center of the ceiling, measure and mark the midpoint of each wall. Stretch a chalk-box line between opposite midpoints and snap the chalk line. Repeat in the other direction. The center is where the lines cross. Use a carpenters' square to make sure the lines form 90-degree angles.

Step 2: Measure the ceiling to determine the width of the tiles that will go around the edges of the room. To calculate the width of the border tiles, note the inches measured past the last full foot in each direction—5 inches, for example, from 17 feet 5 inches. Add 12 inches—the width of one full tile—and divide by 2. The result is the width of the border tiles at each end of each row of tile laid in that direction. For example, if the inch measurement is 5, border tiles in rows across the direction measured will be 8½ inches wide. Calculate the width of border tiles along both directions.

Step 3: Start in one corner of the room, measuring out the width of the border tiles in each direction and marking these points on the ceiling. Snap a chalk line on the ceiling at a right angle through each of these points, making sure each of the two new lines is parallel to one of the chalk lines across the center of the ceiling.

Step 4: Set the corner tile first. Mark it to the measured size with a pencil. Cut the first tile, face up, with a sharp utility knife and a straightedge. Ceiling tiles are made to lock together, with two grooved edges and two tongued edges. The tongued edges of the starter tile must face toward the center of the room, so cut the grooved edges to trim the corner tile to size. The border tiles along the two starter walls will be trimmed along a grooved edge. The tiles bordering the two far walls will be cut along the tongued edges.

Step 5: Apply adhesive to the back of the trimmed corner tile with a putty knife, putting daubs of adhesive in the center of the tile and about 1½ inches in front of each corner. Place the tile into the corner, tongued edges out, and slide it into position exactly within the two chalked lines. Press it firmly into place.

Step 6: Cut border tiles to work out from the corner tile along the two corner walls. As you work, slide the grooved edges of each tile over the exposed tongues of the last tiles to lock the tiles firmly together. Fill in between the border tiles with full-size tiles in an expanding wedge pattern, gradually extending the rows of border tiles and fanning tiles out to cover the entire ceiling. *Note: To work around light fixtures, hold the tile up to the ceiling before applying adhesive. Mark and cut off the portion to be removed, then apply adhesive and slide the tile into place.*

Step 7: Continue setting tiles until you reach the far corner of the room. Before cutting border tiles for the two far walls, measure the gap left beyond the last full tile. Mark and cut border tiles along these walls one by one to make sure they fit the gap.

Step 8: Install cove molding along the edges of the ceiling.

Installing Tile on Furring Strips

To install tile over an uneven or badly damaged ceiling, nail furring strips across the ceiling.

Step 1: Locate each ceiling joist in the room, and mark them on the ceiling. Nail 1×2 or 1×3 furring strips at right angles across the joists and along the edges of the ceiling with 6d common nails, 12 inches apart from center to center. Use a carpenters' square to make sure the strips are even and properly angled. Cut the strips to fit.

Step 2: To mark the lines from the starting corner for the corner tile and the first two border rows, carefully snap a chalk line each way on the furring strips. Trim tiles to this dimension.

Step 3: Attach tiles to the furring strips using a heavy-duty stapler and staples of a length specified by the tile manufacturer. Staple through each tile's grooved edges, then slide in the next tile's tongued edge to interlock the tiles.

Step 4: Cut the corner tile and set it into place, grooved side toward the center of the room and centered on the furring strips. Staple it to the furring strips, setting three staples along each exposed grooved edge. Nail the other two sides firmly into place with 4d common nails, as close to the walls as possible.

Step 5: Continue across the room, setting border tiles and then filling in with full tiles, sliding new tiles in to lock over old ones as you go. Staple each new tile with three staples along each grooved edge.

Step 6: Fasten border tiles into place at the wall, driving three nails along each trimmed tongued edge, as close to the wall as possible. These nails will be covered by molding. Trim and set border tiles for the far walls one by one as you work.

Step 7: Install cove molding along the edges of the ceiling.

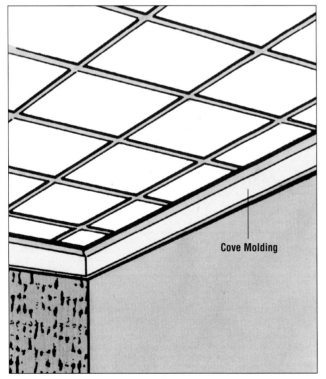

Cove Molding

Finish the ceiling with cove molding along the edges.

Installing a Suspended Ceiling

A suspended ceiling can cover a lot of flaws and obstructions, including pipes, wiring, and ductwork. It works, however, only where you can afford to lose some ceiling height. Suspended ceiling panels are sold in 2×2-foot and 2×4-foot sizes. Use the smaller size for smaller rooms. To install a suspended ceiling:

Step 1: Measure the ceiling and plot it out on graph paper, marking the exact locations of all windows and doors. Mark the direction of ceiling joists. Mark the joists on the ceiling itself, using a pencil or chalk to draw the joist lines across the ceiling.

Step 2: Take the diagram with you when you buy the ceiling materials. With the dealer, plan the layout for the ceiling, figuring full panels across the main ceiling and evenly trimmed partial panels at the edges. To calculate the width of the border panels in each direction, determine the width of the gap left after full panels are placed all across the dimension; divide this number by two. The dealer should help you calculate how many panels you'll need, and should tell you how many wall angles (in 10-foot lengths), main runners (in 12-foot lengths), and cross tees (in 4-foot or 2-foot lengths) you'll need, and how much 12-gauge hanger wire to buy.

Step 3: Mark the level the new ceiling will hang at, allowing at least 4 inches clearance between the panels and the old ceiling. Snap a chalk line at this height across each wall, using a level to keep it straight. Make sure the lines meet exactly at the corners of the room. Nail wall angle brackets along the chalk line all around the room, with the bottom leg of the L-angle facing into the room and flush along the chalk line. Use 6d common nails to fasten the brackets, setting them every $1\frac{1}{2}$ to 2 feet. Cut the bracket to the required lengths with tin snips or a hacksaw.

Step 4: Install screw eyes following the ceiling layout diagram. The long panels of the ceiling grid are set parallel to the ceiling joists, so the T-shaped main runner must be attached at right angles to the joists, every 4 feet across the ceiling. Hanger wire threaded through screw eyes in the joists suspends the main runners of the grid system.

Step 5: For each screw eye, cut a length of hanger wire that is long enough to fasten securely through

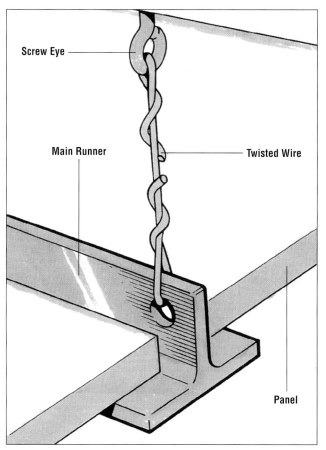

Screw Eye

Main Runner

Twisted Wire

Panel

Suspended ceiling panels are supported by a grid of main runners and cross tees attached to the ceiling with wire and screw eyes.

the screw eye. Extend the wire down to the stretched runner string, and fasten the runner. Thread a wire through each screw eye and twist the end firmly around the dangling wire. Exactly at the point where the wire crosses the string beneath it, bend the wire sharply with pliers to a 90-degree angle.

Step 6: Set the main runners into place. Cut T-shaped main runner sections to required lengths with tin snips or a hacksaw. Lift each long main runner and set one end into place on the wall angle bracket at one side of the ceiling, with the single leg of the "T" facing up. Swing the other end up and position the runner exactly along the marker string and under the screw eyes in the joists. Thread the bent end of each hanging wire through a hole in the runner leg; bend the end of the wire up and secure it. Check each runner with a level, and adjust the length of the hangers if necessary. Repeat until all main runners have been installed.

Step 7: Install the cross tee sections of the ceiling grid. Snap the sections into place every 2 feet along the main runners. If you're using 2×2-foot ceiling panels, use 2-foot cross tees to divide each 2×4-foot panel in half.

Step 8: Install the panels. Tilt each panel to angle it through a grid opening, then carefully lower it until it rests on the bracket edges of the grid sections. Measure border panels carefully and cut them to size with a utility knife.

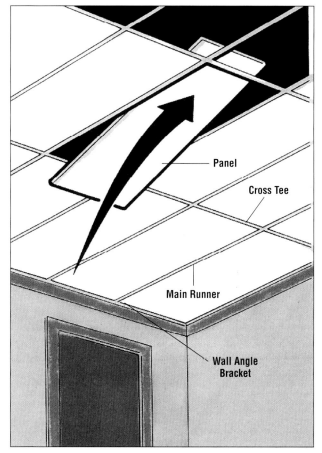

Panel

Cross Tee

Main Runner

Wall Angle Bracket

To install a panel, tilt it through the grid opening, then carefully lower it to rest on the grid.

To fit a panel around a post, carefully measure across the opening to the post in both directions; sketch the opening and mark the post. Measure the diameter of the post. Mark the panel lightly where the post will go through it, then cut the panel in two exactly through the center of the post, across the shorter dimension. Carve an opening for the post on the inside cut edge of each panel, forming two semicircular or rectangular cutouts. Cut only a little at a time, holding the cut sections up to the post frequently to fit them exactly. Set the two sections into place in the suspension grid.

Floors and Stairs

W hen you consider the punishment caused by everyday foot traffic, it's surprising that floors and stairs hold up as well as they do. Eventually, though, wear and tear take their toll. Squeaks develop, minor damage afflicts resilient tile and sheet flooring, or the entire surface begins to show its age and needs replacing or refinishing. The following pages offer techniques for solving common floor and stair problems.

Removing Floor Squeaks

Squeaky floors and stairs aren't serious structural problems, but they can be annoying. If your floors are exposed hardwood, you may be able to stop the squeak by sprinkling talcum powder over the noisy boards and sweeping it back and forth to force it down into the cracks. On stairs, use packaged graphite powder or talcum powder in a squeeze bottle; apply the lubricant along all the joints in the problem area. The powder will lubricate the edges of the boards, eliminating the noise. For a more permanent repair, here are steps to solving squeaky problems.

Squeaky Floors

If there's a basement or crawl space under the noisy floor, work from this area to locate the problem. You'll need a helper upstairs to walk on the squeaky spot while you work. Watch the subfloor under the noisy boards while your helper steps on the floor above. If the subfloor moves visibly, or if you can pinpoint the noise, outline the affected areas with chalk. At the joists closest to your outlines, look for gaps between the joist and the subfloor; wherever there's a gap, the floorboards can move. To stop squeaks here, install shingles or wood shims into the gaps to reduce movement.

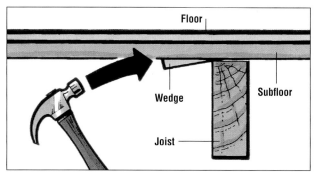

From under the floor, drive wedges into gaps between the subflooring and the joists to stop squeaks.

If there are no gaps along the joists, or if the squeaks are coming from an area between joists, there's probably a gap between the floorboards and the subfloor. To pull the two layers together, install wood screws up through the subflooring in the squeaky areas. Make sure you drill pilot holes before inserting the screws. The wood screws must be long enough to penetrate into the floor above you, but not so long that they go all the way through the boards and stick up through your floor.

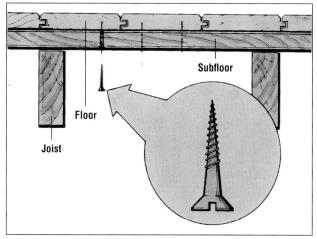

Squeaks between subflooring and flooring can often be eliminated using wood screws to pull the layers together.

If you can't get at the floor from underneath, you'll have to work from the top, with spiral flooring nails. First, locate the squeak and try to determine whether it's at a joist or between joists. To eliminate the squeak, drive two spiral flooring nails, angled toward each other in a V, through the floorboards and the subfloor. If the squeak is at a joist, use longer spiral flooring nails, driving them through the floorboards and the subfloor and into the joist. Drill pilot holes first to keep the boards from splitting.

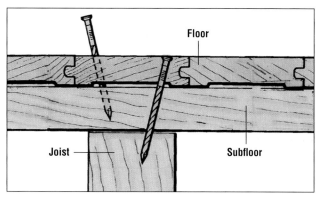

If you cannot access the underside of the floor, toenail flooring nails from above into a joist, then fill the nail hole with wood putty.

If the floor is tiled or carpeted and you can't get at the floorboards from above or below, you probably won't be able to eliminate the squeak without removing the floor covering. Before you do this, try to reset the loose boards by pounding. Using a hammer and a block of scrap wood as a buffer, pound the floor firmly over the squeaky boards, in an area about 2 or 3 feet square. The pressure of the pounding may force loose nails back into place.

Squeaky Stairs

Stairs are put together with three basic components: the tread, the riser, and the stringer (the side piece). In most cases, squeaks are caused by the tread rubbing against the riser or the stringer. If you can, work from under the stairs to fix the squeak. You'll need a helper to walk up and down the stairs while you work.

While your helper walks on the stairs, watch them from below, looking for movement and for cracks in the wood, loose nails, or other problems. The simplest way to fix a squeak is to wedge the components that are moving. Cut small wedges from wood shingles or shims. To install a wedge, apply carpenters' glue to the side that will lie against the stairs. Drive the wedge into the squeaking joint, either tread-riser or tread-stringer. When the wedge is tight, secure it with small nails, being careful not to split the wedge. The nails must be long enough to hold the wedge securely, but make sure they don't go all the way through the stair component and stick out on the other side.

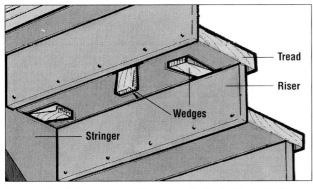

Squeaks in stairs can sometimes be eliminated by installing wedges between the moving components.

If the joints aren't wide enough to take wedges, use 1×2 wood braces to stop the movement of the boards. Use one long or two or more short 1×2 blocks for each stair-width joint. Apply carpenters' glue to the sides of the block that will lie against the stairs, then set the block into the squeaking joint and nail it into place.

If you can't get at the stairs from underneath, work from the top. For squeaks at the front of a tread, where

it meets the riser below it, drive pairs of spiral flooring nails, angled toward each other in a V, across the tread and into the top of the riser. Countersink the nail heads with a nail set, and cover them with wood filler. For squeaks at the back of a tread, where it meets the riser above, drive thin wedges into the joint at the back of the tread. Coat the wedges with carpenters' glue, and use a hammer and a wood buffer block to pound them in. Then carefully trim the wide ends of the wedges flush with the riser. If the wedges are noticeable, cover the joint with quarter round or other trim molding; treat all other joints the same way so that they match.

Repairing Resilient Flooring

Today's resilient floors are a real boon, but they can lose their attraction very quickly when they're damaged. Fortunately, even the worst-looking damage is easy to repair, whether the resilient flooring is tile or sheet vinyl.

Tile Floors

Tile repairs are very simple, because only the affected tiles must be repaired. If a tile is loose, it can be reglued with floor tile adhesive; if it's just loose at one edge or corner, there may be enough old adhesive left on the tile to reattach it. Cover the tile with aluminum foil, and then with a clean cloth. Heat the loose edges with an iron, set to medium heat, to soften the old adhesive and rebond it. When the adhesive has softened, weight the entire tile and let the adhesive cure for several hours or overnight.

If the old adhesive isn't strong enough to reattach the tile, use a floor tile adhesive made for that type of tile. Heat the tile as described above, and carefully lift the loose edges with a paint scraper or a putty knife. Scrape the old adhesive off the edges of the tile and apply a thin coat of new adhesive, using a notched spreader or trowel. Then smooth the tile firmly from center to edges and weight the entire tile. Let the adhesive cure as directed by the manufacturer before removing the weights.

If a tile is damaged, you can easily replace it. To remove the tile, heat it with a propane torch with a flame-spreader nozzle, taking care not to damage the surrounding tiles. Pry the damaged tile up with a paint scraper or a putty knife. Or, instead of heating the tile, cover it with dry ice. (Make sure you wear work gloves to protect your hands when working with dry ice.) Let the dry ice stand for about ten minutes and remove any remaining ice; then carefully chisel out the tile, from the center to the edges. The cold will make the tile very brittle, so that it shatters easily. After removing the tile, scrape all the old adhesive off the floor to make a clean base for the new tile. Fill any gouges in the tile base with spackling compound or wood filler, and let the filler dry completely.

Check the fit of the new tile in the prepared opening, even if you are using the same standard size as the old tile. If the new tile doesn't fit exactly, sand the edges or carefully slice off the excess with a sharp utility knife and a straightedge. When the tile fits perfectly, spread a thin coat of floor tile adhesive in the opening, using a notched trowel or spreader. Warm the new tile with an iron to make it flexible, and then carefully set it into place in the opening, pressing it firmly onto the adhesive. Weight the entire tile firmly, and let the adhesive cure as directed by the manufacturer. Remove the weights when the adhesive is completely cured.

Sheet Floors

When the floor is badly worn or damaged, use scrap flooring to patch it. You'll need a piece of flooring a little bigger than the bad spot, with the same pattern.

Step 1: Position the scrap over the bad spot so that it covers the damage completely, and align the pattern exactly with the floor pattern.

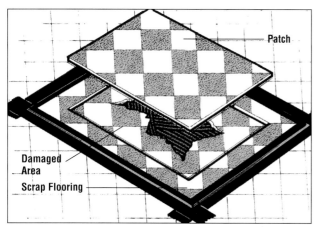

Use a piece of scrap flooring to cut a patch for damaged flooring.

Step 2: Tape the patch firmly in place on the floor, using package sealing tape all around the edges. Then, with a straightedge and a sharp utility knife, cut a rectangle through the scrap piece and through the flooring below it, to make a patch bigger than the damaged area. Cut along joints or lines in the pattern, if possible, to make the patch harder to see. Be sure the corners are cleanly cut.

Step 3: Once the flooring is cut through, untape the scrap piece and push out the rectangular patch.

Soften the old flooring inside the cut lines by heating it with an iron, set to medium heat. First, cover the patch area with aluminum foil and then with a clean cloth; press until the adhesive holding the flooring has softened. Carefully pry up the damaged piece with a paint scraper or putty knife. Scrape all the old adhesive off the floor to make a clean base for the patch. If there are any gouges in the floor, fill them with water putty and let it dry completely.

Step 4: Install the patch in the opening. If it binds a little, you can sand the edges slightly with medium-grit or fine-grit paper to adjust the fit. When the patch fits exactly, spread a thin coat of floor tile adhesive in the opening with a notched trowel or spreader. Then set the patch into the gap, press it firmly in, and wipe off any excess adhesive around the edges.

Step 5: Heat-seal the edges to the main sheet of flooring. Protect the floor with aluminum foil and a clean cloth, as above; press the edges firmly but quickly with a hot iron.

Step 6: After bonding the edges, weight the entire patch firmly and let the adhesive cure as directed by the manufacturer. Remove the weights when the adhesive is completely cured. Don't wash the floor for at least a week.

Repairing Burns in Carpeting

Professional carpet repair can be expensive. But what else can you do when your carpeting is damaged by cigarette burns? Actually, with a little patience, you can usually repair the damage just as well yourself. Here are some ideas.

When only the tips of the carpet fibers are burned, carefully cut off the charred fiber with a pair of small, sharp scissors. Sponge the area lightly with a mild detergent solution, and again with clean water. The low spot won't be noticeable when the carpet dries.

Use a pair of small, sharp scissors to cut off burnt carpet fibers.

If a large area of carpet is damaged, you'll have to replace the burned area with a patch cut from a piece of scrap carpet. Here's how:

Step 1: From scraps, cut out a rectangle or square of carpet a little larger than the burned area. In order for the patch to blend in with the existing carpet without being highly noticeable, it must match any pattern in the carpet, and if it's pile, the pile must run in the same direction as the damaged pile.

Step 2: Press the patch firmly over the damaged area. Holding it carefully in place, use a utility knife to cut around its edges and through the carpet under it. Cut completely through the backing, but don't cut into the carpet padding.

Step 3: When the entire damaged area is cut out, lift the burned piece out of the hole. Check the patch for fit, and, if necessary, trim the edges slightly so that it fits the opening exactly.

Step 4: To install the patch, use double-faced carpet tape or latex carpet adhesive. On each side of the hole, stick a piece of tape to the padding or apply adhesive. Position the patch and press the edges firmly onto the padding. Let the adhesive dry for several hours before walking on the patch.

Repairing a Hardwood Floor

If you are tired of floor coverings and want to restore the natural warmth and beauty of hardwood under the carpet, the job is difficult, but it can be done. You will have to remove the old finish and strip the floor down to the bare wood. Only then can you apply the new finish.

You'll need a drum sander with a dust bag attachment and a disk sander or edger, available at a tool rental store. The store can supply or recommend sandpaper. Buy open-coat sandpaper in 20, 40, and 100 grits.

Before you start, move everything out of the room. This includes curtains and draperies, pictures—everything. Floor refinishing is messy, especially during the sanding operation.

Step 1: Seal off all heating and cooling outlets with masking tape, and seal around all doorways except the one you will use (seal that one, too, when you are ready to start). Some sanding dust will get into the rest of the house, but sealing doorways and duct outlets will help reduce the mess.

Step 2: Carefully remove all quarter round, baseboard, and other molding at the floor. Check the entire floor for nails, and countersink any that protrude. Open the windows.

Step 3: For the first sanding, use 20-grit paper in the drum sander. Go back and forth over the entire floor, with the grain, overlapping each pass about three inches. At the end of each pass, you will have to lift the sander and move it over—but be careful in doing this to avoid digging into the floor. Go slowly. Use the disk sander or a sanding block in areas near the walls where the drum sander cannot reach.

Step 4: Repeat the procedure with 40-grit paper, and then again with 100 grit. When you are satisfied that you have removed the old finishes, you can return the rental equipment.

Step 5: Vacuum the room thoroughly, including the walls and around windows, to remove all the dust. If you do not remove all the dust, you will obtain an inferior finish.

Step 6: If your floor is pine, use a pine floor primer to seal the wood. Give the primer an hour to dry before applying your finish. If your floor is oak, rub some turpentine on a small section to see what the wood would look like with a natural finish. If you like the way the floor looks, you

To sand a hardwood floor, you can rent a floor sander.

need not stain it. If you decide to stain the wood, apply the stain evenly and let it dry thoroughly according to the directions.

Step 7: Apply the finish. Clear-finish polyurethane varnish is ideal. The first coat will tack-dry in about 15 minutes and will be ready for the second coat in about an hour. When the second coat dries, wax and buff the floor. For a high gloss, wait overnight and apply a third coat using a mixture of one part reducer to four parts finish. Let this coat dry overnight before use. After the third coat, the floor will not require waxing and can be shined with a dry mop. If you prefer, natural varnish is a traditional finish coat that requires more care to apply. It is slower drying, and there is more chance for dust to foul the finish. It is subject to checking as it grows older, though when applied properly it dries water-clear for a beautiful finish. Follow it with a coat of wax and buff.

Windows

• •

Windows are often trouble spots. Along with doors, windows are the major heat-loss areas in most homes; they may stick shut when they're painted or swell shut from humidity. Inside, shades and venetian blinds may not work right; outside, glass gets broken and screens get torn. Both inside and out, there's a lot you can do to keep your windows working right.

Unsticking a Window

Double-hung wood-frame windows, especially in older homes, often stick. The most common cause of this problem is that the window has been painted shut, and the paint has sealed it closed. The solution is usually simple: Break the seal and clear and lubricate the sash tracks. Unsticking a window takes strength, but it isn't difficult. Here's how:

Step 1: Before you start to work, make sure the window is unlocked.

Step 2: Look for evidence of a paint seal between the sash and the window frame. To break the seal, push the blade of a stiff putty knife or paint scraper into the joint, cutting straight in through the paint. If necessary, tap the knife lightly with a hammer to force the blade in. If the window was painted on the outside, repeat the procedure to break the seal on the outside.

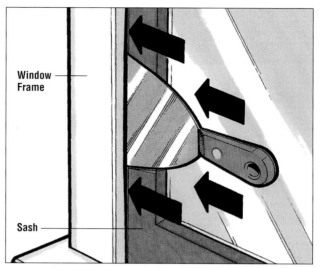

Use a putty knife to free a window that's been painted shut.

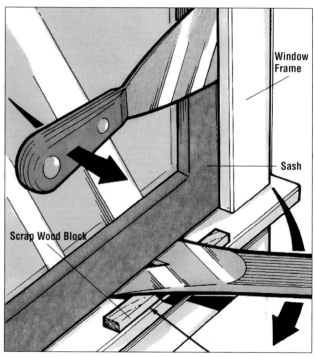

A really stuck window may require using a small pry bar to open it.

Step 3: If the window still doesn't open, check the tracks in the window frame above the sash; they're probably blocked with built-up paint. Using a hammer and chisel, carefully clean the excess paint out of the tracks. Cut out the thickened paint, but be careful not to gouge the wood of the tracks. Smooth the cleaned-out tracks with medium-grit sandpaper on a narrow sanding block, and then spray them with silicone lubricant.

Step 4: If the window still sticks, paint in the lower part of the tracks is probably holding it. Set a block of scrap wood against the sash at the window frame. Gently tap the block of wood with a hammer to force the sash back from the frame. Move the block of wood all around the window sash, tapping the sash back from the frame; then try the window again. If it opens, clean and sand the tracks, and lubricate them with silicone spray.

Step 5: If the window *still* doesn't open, use a small pry bar on it, preferably from the outside. Insert the flat end of the pry bar under the sash; set a block of scrap wood under it for better leverage. Pry gently at the corners of the sash and then from the corners in toward the center. Use the pry bar very carefully; too much pressure could damage both the sash and the frame. If the window opens, clean and lubricate the tracks with silicone spray. If it doesn't open, the sticking may be caused by extreme humidity, poor construction, or uneven settling. Call a carpenter to fix the window rather than trying to force it open.

Replacing Broken Glass

A broken windowpane not only allows the weather into your home, it is also a security hazard. Luckily, broken glass is one of the easiest problems to fix. You can buy replacement glass, cut to measure, at lumberyards and hardware stores. Here's how to replace a broken pane:

Step 1: Remove the broken glass from the window frame. Wearing heavy gloves, work the pieces of glass back and forth until they're loose enough to pull out. Knock out any stubborn pieces with a hammer.

Step 2: Remove all the old putty from the frame, using a chisel or a scraper to pry it out. As you work, look for the fasteners that held the glass in place—metal tabs called glaziers' points in wood-frame windows; spring clips in metal frames. If the putty doesn't come out easily, paint it with linseed oil and let the oil soak in. Then scrape out the softened putty, being careful not to gouge out the window frame. Use a wire brush on the frame to take off the last traces of putty.

Step 3: Paint the raw wood around the pane with linseed oil to prevent the new putty from drying out too fast. If the frame is metal and susceptible to rust, paint it to prevent rusting.

Measure the window frame from inside edge to inside edge, then have the new glass cut 1/16 to 1/8 inch smaller each way.

Step 4: Measure the frame for the new glass. The glass should be just enough smaller than the opening to allow for expansion and contraction, and to allow for imperfections in the frame or the glass. Measure both ways across the opening, from inside edge to inside edge, and subtract 1/16 to 1/8 inch each way. Have double-strength glass cut to these precise dimensions. Purchase enough new glaziers' points or clips to be installed every 6 inches or so around the pane.

Step 5: Install the new glass using glaziers' compound or putty. Roll a large chunk of compound between your palms to make a long string about

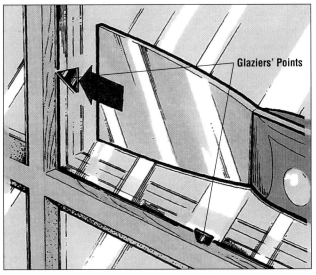

Glaziers' points hold the glass in place in a wood-frame window. Push the points in with a putty knife.

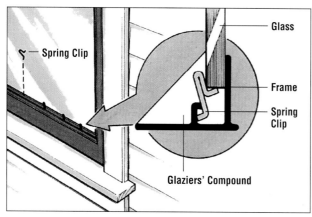

Metal-frame windows often use clips to hold glass in place.

Labels on figure: Spring Clip, Glass, Frame, Spring Clip, Glaziers' Compound

the diameter of a pencil. Starting at a corner, press the cord into the outside corner of the window frame, where the glass will rest. Cover the entire diameter of the frame. With the compound in place, carefully set the new pane of glass into the frame, pressing it firmly against the cord of compound. Press hard enough to flatten the compound, squeezing out air bubbles and forcing some of the compound out around the frame. Then, to hold the glass in place, install new glaziers' points or spring clips every 6 inches or so around the pane. Push the points partway into the wood with the blade of a putty knife held flat against the glass; or, if the frame is metal, snap the spring clips into the holes in the frame.

Step 6: To seal the new pane with glaziers' compound all around the outside edge, roll another cord of glaziers' compound and press it firmly into the

Seal the pane with glaziers' compound. Use a putty knife to smoothly spread it.

glass-frame joint, all around the pane. Use a putty knife to smooth the compound all along the joint around the pane, matching the putty to other nearby windows. Hold the putty knife at an angle to the lip of the frame, so that the knife cuts the compound off cleanly and evenly along the glass. If the putty knife sticks or pulls at the glaziers' compound, dip the blade into linseed oil and shake off the excess. Use long, smooth strokes to keep the joint even around the pane.

Step 7: With a razor blade or a glass scraper, carefully remove excess glaziers' compound from both sides of the new glass and the frame. Let the compound dry for about three days.

Step 8: Paint the new compound and the frame to match the rest of the frame. Lap the paint slightly over the edge of the compound and onto the glass to seal the pane completely. Make sure the paint is dry before you clean the glass.

Repairing or Replacing Screens

Screens are essential in summer to let air in and keep bugs out. When your screens develop holes, from abuse or just old age, it's time to take action. It isn't hard to repair the holes, or, when the screen is badly damaged, to install new screening.

Patching Holes

Pinholes in screening are very simple to fix. If the screening is metal, use an ice pick or a similar sharp tool to push the strands of wire back toward the hole; you may be able to close the hole completely. If there's still a hole, apply clear nail polish or household cement over it. Let the sealer dry. Apply additional coats until the opening is filled.

If the screening is fiberglass, move the threads back into place. Otherwise, fill tiny holes with clear nail polish or household cement. Be careful not to let any sealer run down the screen.

To close a large hole, cut a patch from a scrap piece of screening, the same type (fiberglass or metal) as the damaged screening. Don't use metal screening made of a different metal; placing two metals together—steel to copper, for instance—can cause corrosion.

A fiberglass patch is very easy to install, if you can lay the screen flat. Cut a patch about ½-inch bigger all around than the hole, and set it over the hole. Place a sheet of aluminum foil over the patch area, shiny side down, and press the patch firmly with a hot iron, being careful not to touch the screen directly with the iron. The heat will fuse the patch onto the screening. If you

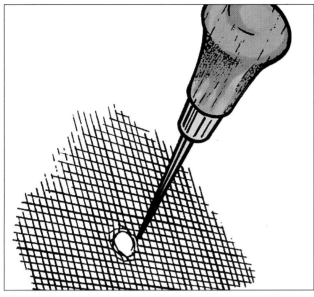

Use an awl or other pointed tool to repair a small hole in a metal screen.

can't lay the screen flat, sew the patch into place with a needle and nylon thread using a firm running stitch, but don't pull the thread too tight. Apply clear nail polish over the edges of the patch to keep it from fraying.

To patch metal screening, cut a square or rectangular patch about 1 inch bigger all around than the hole. Pull out the wires on all four sides to make a wire fringe about ½ inch deep around the patch. Bend the fringe wires down sharply at a right angle; use a block of scrap wood to make a clean bend on each side of the patch. When the fringe wires are evenly bent, set the patch over the hole in the screen and press it to insert the bend fringe wires through the screening around the hole. The patch should be flat against the screen, covering the hole completely. When it's properly positioned, fold the fringe wires down flat toward the center of the patch on the other side of the screen. Then stitch around the entire patch with a needle and nylon thread, or with fine wire.

Replacing Screening

When a screen has many holes or when metal screening becomes bulged and rusted, consider replacing the screening entirely. As long as the frame is in good condition, this isn't as difficult as it sounds. You may be able to buy the screening cut to size. If not, use scissors to cut it about 1½ inches larger all around than the opening. An aluminum-framed screen will require plastic splining, a few inches longer than the diameter of the screen, to replace the old spline. To replace a screen in a wood frame:

Step 1: Use a stiff putty knife to carefully pry up the molding around the edges. Pry out the tacks or staples that held the screening in place, and remove the screening. Pull out any staples or tacks left in the frame.

Step 2: Lay the new screen fabric over the frame and trace the outline of the opening on it with chalk. Then cut the screening to size, 1½ inches larger all around than the traced outline.

Step 3: Bow or arch the frame for easier installation. There are two ways to do this, by weighting or clamping. To use the weight method, set the frame the long way across two sawhorses, and hang a heavy weight from a rope around the

Patch a larger hole in a metal screen using a small piece of screening.

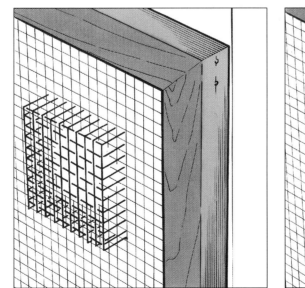

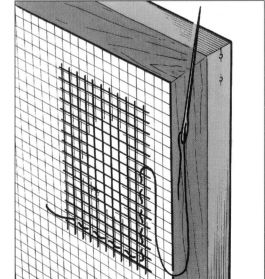

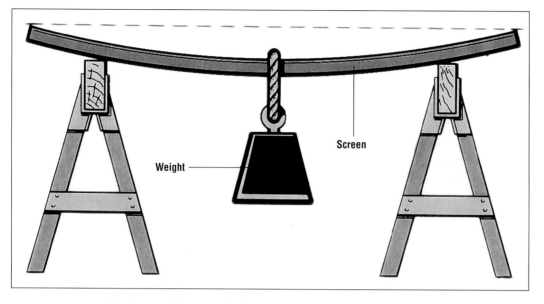

Bow the screen frame using two sawhorses and a weight.

Weight

Screen

center of the frame. To clamp the frame into a bow, set it on a workbench or on a wide board across two sawhorses. Place a C-clamp at the center of each long side, holding the frame to the work surface, and set a long piece of scrap wood, such as a 2×4, between the frame and the work surface at each end. As you tighten the C-clamps, the frame will bow.

Step 4: Set the screening across the frame, aligned along one unclamped end. Use a staple gun loaded with heavy-duty staples to attach the

screening to the wooden frame, placing the staples at right angles to the frame, about 2 to 3 inches apart. If you're using fiberglass screening, turn the cut edge under about 1 inch before stapling it down. When the first end is securely stapled, pull the loose screening over the clamped frame and stretch it firmly and evenly across to the opposite end. Holding it firmly as you work, staple the second end into place, setting the staples 2 to 3 inches apart at right angles to the frame. Then unclamp or unweight the frame; the screening should be

Use a C-clamp, a table, and two 2×4s to bow a screen frame.

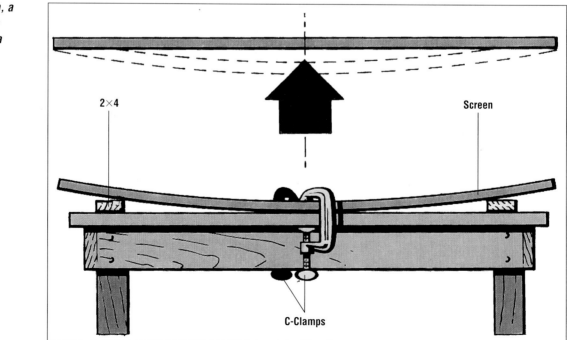

2×4

Screen

C-Clamps

pulled very tight as it straightens out. Staple the two sides into place; trim off any excess screening.

Step 5: Replace the molding to cover the stapled edges of the screening.

To replace a screen in an aluminum frame:

Step 1: With a screwdriver or putty knife, pry up the plastic spline that holds the old screening in place; remove the old screening.

Step 2: Lay the frame flat and position the new screening over it. Trim the edges so that the screening extends just to the outside edges of the frame. If necessary, set scrap boards the same thickness as the frame under the screening to help keep them on the same level.

Step 3: Position the screening so that one end and one side are lined up on the outside edge of the splining groove in the frame. Hold the screening carefully in place and, with the convex roller of a splining tool, force the edge of the screening into the splining groove. Secure the other two sides the same way, stretching the screening taut as you work.

Step 4: When all four sides of the screening are in place, cut off any excess screening with snips. Using the concave end of the splining tool, drive the spline into the groove to hold the screening in place. Start installing the spline at a corner and work around the frame. Cut off the excess splining where the ends meet.

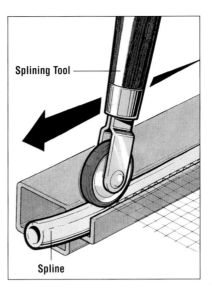

On metal-framed screens, a plastic spline holds the screening in a groove. To install the screening; roll the spline into the groove with a splining tool.

Splining Tool

Spline

Repairing Window Shades

Every homeowner and apartment-dweller who's ever used window shades is familiar with the many problems that beset them. There's the shade that's so tightly wound it snaps all the way up, the one that's so loose it won't go up at all, the one that binds at the edges or falls out of its brackets. In most cases, only a simple adjustment is needed to get shades working properly.

A shade that binds is being pinched by brackets set too close together. If the brackets are mounted on the wall or on the outside of the window frame, this is easy to remedy: Tap the brackets slightly outward with a hammer. This technique also may work on brackets mounted inside the window frame. If the shade still sticks, take it down. You'll have to remove some wood from the roller. Remove the round pin and the metal cap on the round-pin end of the roller. Then sand the end of the roller down with medium-grit sandpaper. Badly binding shades may require further adjustment. If the

brackets are outside-mounted, you can move one bracket out slightly. Fill the old screw holes with wood plastic. If the brackets are inside-mounted, the shade will have to be cut down professionally to fit the frame or replaced.

The opposite problem occurs when the mounting brackets are set too far apart. In extreme cases, the shade

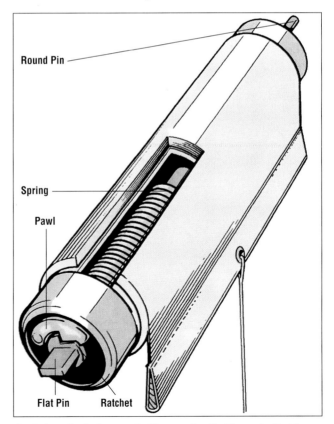

Round Pin

Spring

Pawl

Flat Pin   Ratchet

A window shade is operated by a spring that is controlled by a pawl and ratchet.

may even fall when you try to use it. If the brackets are mounted outside the frame, tap them gently together with a hammer or move one bracket in closer to the other. If the brackets are mounted inside the frame, you'll have to adjust the space with shims. Take the shade down and cut a piece of thin cardboard a little smaller than one bracket. Unscrew the bracket, set the shim behind it, and screw the bracket on over the shim. If necessary, add one or more shims to both brackets.

When the shade won't go up or down properly, the roller mechanism is probably at fault. Shades are operated by a strong coil spring inside one end of the roller. The pin that holds the shade up at this end of the roller is flat; this flat pin tightens or loosens the spring when you roll the shade up or down. At the flat-pin end of the roller, the spring is controlled by a pawl and ratchet that stop the movement of the spring when the shade is released. If the shade is too tight or too loose, or if it doesn't stay in place when you release it, there is usually a problem with the spring or with the pawl-and-ratchet mechanism. Unless the spring is broken, this is easy to fix.

If the shade won't stay up, the spring is too loose. Pull the shade down enough to turn the roller a few times; if it's extremely loose, pull it down about halfway. Lift the flat-pin end of the roller out of its bracket. Then roll the shade up by hand, keeping it tightly rolled. Set the roller back on the bracket and try the shade again. If it still doesn't stay up, repeat the procedure.

If the shade snaps up and is hard to pull down, the spring is too tight. With the shade rolled up, lift the flat-pin end of the roller out of its bracket and unroll the shade two or three turns by hand. Replace the roller on the bracket and test its operation. Adjust it further if necessary.

If the shade won't stay down, the pawl-and-ratchet mechanism may need cleaning. Take the shade down and remove the cap at the flat-pin end of the roller. Vacuum out any obvious dust, and clean the mechanism with a soft cloth. Spray silicone lubricant into the mechanism. Replace the metal cap and rehang the shade.

Repairing Venetian Blinds

Venetian blinds are one of the most practical and long-lasting window treatments around, but they can eventually develop problems. When the cords break or the tapes look frayed and shabby, you can give your blinds new life by installing replacement cords and tapes, often sold in kits.

If the blind is clean and otherwise in good condition, and the old lift cord is not broken, you can install a new lift cord without removing the unit from the window. Here's how:

Step 1: With the blinds down, tilt the slats horizontally. The ends of the cord are secured to the bottom of the bottom rail. If the bottom rail is wood,

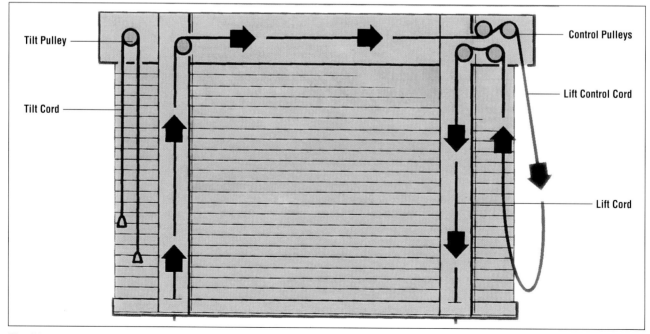

The lift cord is threaded up one side of the blind, over a pulley, across the top and through the control pulleys, and then down the other side. A loop of cord from the control pulleys forms the lift control.

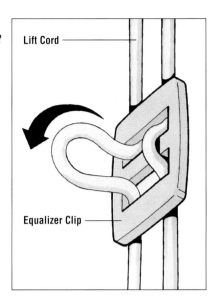

An equalizer clip allows for adjustment of the lift cord.

Lift Cord

Equalizer Clip

the knotted ends of the cord are simply stapled under the ends of the tapes. If the bottom rail is metal, remove the end caps and the clamps from the rail to expose the knotted cords. Untie the knot on the side opposite the lift cord, and butt the end of the new cord to this end. Tape the two ends firmly together with light adhesive tape.

Step 2: Pull gently on the old cord to draw the new cord up through the slats on this side, across the top, and through the control pulleys. Leave a loop of excess cord for the new lift cord, and continue to draw the cord down through the slats on the lift cord side.

Step 3: When the taped end of the new cord reaches the bottom rail, untape the old cord, discard it, and cut off any excess cord at the starting end. Knot both ends of the new cord and secure them the same way the old cord was secured. Replace the end caps on the bottom rail and slide the equalizer clip off the old lift cord and onto the new one. Adjust the cord with the equalizer until the blind works smoothly.

To replace the tilt cord:

Step 1: Untie the knots at the ends of the tilt cord and remove the pulls. The tilt cord is simply threaded over a pulley and out again; it doesn't connect with the lift cord. Remove the old tilt cord by pulling it out. Then thread one end of the new cord over the pulley and feed it in until it comes out over the other side of the pulley.

Step 2: Slip the cord pulls over the ends of the cord and knot the ends to hold the pulls on.

When the lift cord is broken, the slats need cleaning or painting, or you want to replace the ladder tapes:

Step 1: Take the blind down.

Step 2: Lay the blind out flat, all the way open, and untie both ends of the lift cord, as above. Pull the cord entirely out of the blind and set the equalizer clip aside.

Step 3: Remove the blind's slats one by one, stacking them in order. If they're dirty, soak them in a mild solution of liquid detergent, then rinse and dry them thoroughly.

Step 4: Pull out the hooks that hold the tapes in place at the top of the blind. (One hook holds the tapes on each side.) Position the new tapes in the top box and slide the hook into each pair of tapes, front and back, at the sides of the box. Slide the slats into place between the tapes; make sure they're all right side up, facing the right way. Fold the ends of the tapes under and fasten them to the bottom rail under the last slat.

Step 5: Thread a new lift cord into the blind, starting at the tilt cord side and working up that side, across the top, through the control pulley, and down the other side. The tapes have woven strips, or ladders, connecting the front and back pieces on alternating sides. Insert the new cord right at the center of the tapes, so that these ladders are placed on alternate sides of the cord. At the control pulley, leave a long loop of cord for the new lift cord and keep threading the cord down through the slats on that side.

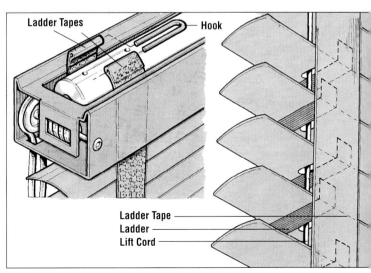

Ladder Tapes — Hook

Ladder Tape
Ladder
Lift Cord

Removing slats from a venetian blind system requires removing the lift cord and dismantling the ladder.

Step 6: Cut off any excess cord, knot both ends of the cord, and secure the ends to the bottom rail.

Step 7: Slide the equalizer clip onto the lift cord and install a new tilt cord, as above.

Before rehanging the blind, check the control pulley mechanism to make sure it's working properly. If you can see dirt or lint in the pulleys, vacuum it out and wipe the mechanism clean with a soft cloth. Then spray a little silicone lubricant into the pulleys to keep them working smoothly.

Doors

• •

Doors are great—when they work. But what if a door is sticking or won't entirely close? Or perhaps you want to replace a door with a different style or type. Repairing or replacing a door is relatively easy and requires only a few common tools and a couple hours of your time.

Unsticking a Door

Doors, like windows, stick for a number of reasons— from poor construction to extreme humidity. In most cases, it's easy to unstick the stubborn door. To diagnose the problem, close the door, watching it carefully to locate the binding point. If there's a gap between the door and the frame opposite the binding edge, the hinges probably need adjustment. If you can't see a gap anywhere between the door and the frame, and you had to slam the door to close it, the wood has probably swollen from extreme humidity. If the hinges and the wood are both all right, the door frame itself may be out of alignment; check the frame with a carpenters' square. If the binding is caused by poorly adjusted hinges:

Step 1: Examine the hinges for loose screws, both on the door and on the frame. Tighten any loose screws securely.

Step 2: If a screw doesn't tighten, the screw hole has become enlarged. When the hole is only slightly enlarged, you may be able to correct the problem by replacing the screw with a longer one, but make sure the head is the same size. Another option is to use a hollow fiber plug with the old screw. To do this, spread carpenters' glue on the outside of the plug and insert the plug into the screw hole. Then drive the screw into the hole. If the screw hole is badly enlarged, use wood toothpicks to fill it in.

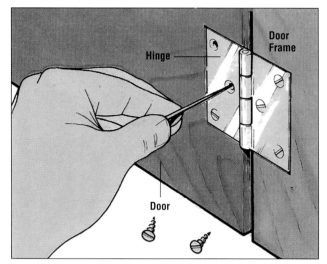

Loose hinge screws can be tightened by filling the hole with wooden toothpicks dipped in glue and trimmed flush.

Dip the toothpicks into carpenters' glue and insert them around the screw hole; let the glue dry and then trim the toothpicks flush with the surface. When you drive the screw into the filled-in hole, it should hold securely.

Step 3: If the screws are not loose, the hinges may have to be readjusted on the door frame. Close the door, watching to see where it sticks and where it gaps. If the door is tilted in the frame, it will stick at the top on one side and at the bottom on the other and there will be a gap between the door and the frame opposite each binding point.

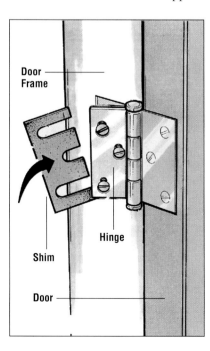

A hinge shim can be cut from a piece of cardboard and installed behind the door hinge.

Step 4: If the door hinges need shimming, open the door as far as it will go. Push a wedge under it to hold it firmly. At the hinge to be adjusted, loosen the screws from the hinge leaf on the door frame but don't touch the screws in the door itself. Cut a piece of thin cardboard to the same size as the hinge leaf and mark the location of the hinge screws on it. Cut horizontal slots in the shim to fit over the screws; slide the shim over the screws behind the loosened hinge leaf. Keeping the shim in place, tighten the screws to resecure the hinge. Remove the wedge holding the door and close the door. If the door still sticks, but not as much as it did before, add another shim under the hinge.

Once the door edge is planed, carefully bevel the corner with a plane.

against the frame and give it several firm hammer blows. This may move the frame just enough to solve the problem. If this doesn't work, you'll have to adjust the hinges or plane the edges to allow for the unevenness of the frame. The door may end up slightly crooked, but it won't stick.

Hanging an Interior Door

Hanging or installing a door isn't as difficult as it may seem. Replacing an existing door is easy if the new door core is the same size. Installing a door in a new partition wall is also very easy if you buy a prehung door so you don't have to build the door frame yourself.

Installing Prehung Doors

Prehung doors are the easiest to install. These doors come already set in a frame, and one side of the frame has been trimmed with molding. Usually, the hardware has been installed, too, making installation even easier. To buy a prehung door, you need to know the size of the rough door opening. There are approximately 3 inches at the side jambs and 1½ inches at the head jamb for fitting purposes. To install a prehung door:

Step 1: Set the door into the rough opening, and vertically level or plumb the jamb sides, filling any gaps at the top and sides with cedar shingle shims.

Step 2: Nail the head and side jambs to the rough framing, using 16d finishing nails. Countersink the nail heads into the face of the jambs. Fill the holes with wood putty.

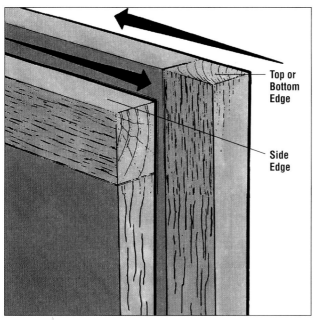

Top or
Bottom
Edge

Side
Edge

A plane can remove excess wood to free a door.

Step 5: If the door sticks even after shimming, or if there is no gap anywhere around the frame, you'll have to remove some wood at the binding points. Use a block plane on the top or bottom of the door, or a jack plane to work on the side. If the door sticks at the sides, try to plane only on the hinge side; the latch side is beveled slightly, and planing could damage the bevel. Use the plane carefully, removing only a little wood at a time. Keep your cuts even across the entire binding edge.

Step 6: If the door sticks because the frame is out of alignment, there's not much you can do to fix it. At the binding point, set a piece of 2×4 flat

Measure the old door and opening before buying a new door or prehung door system.

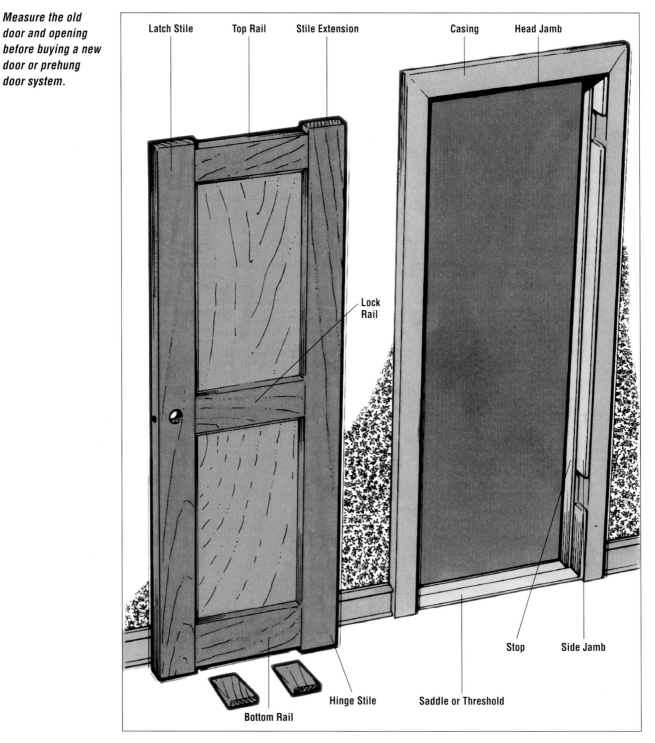

Latch Stile   Top Rail   Stile Extension   Casing   Head Jamb

Lock Rail

Stop   Side Jamb

Hinge Stile   Saddle or Threshold

Bottom Rail

Step 3: Nail the finished casing or molding to the doorway with 10d finishing nails. Countersink the nail heads. Fill the heads with wood putty.

Step 4: Apply wood sealer to both sides of the door and the top, bottom, and side edges. Seal the casing and door moldings, too.

Installing Folding Doors

If you need a door where there just isn't room for it to open, consider installing a folding door. A bifold door uses only half the space of a regular door. Bifold doors are available with two to eight panels; two panels fit a standard door opening. To install a bifold folding door:

Step 1: Measure the inside of the door opening. Subtract 1¼ inches for vertical clearance and ½ inch (or, for a four-panel door, ¾ inch) for horizontal clearance. Buy a door cut to fit this size opening; make sure the panels are already hinged together and the necessary pivots are included.

Step 2: Insert the top pivot bracket into the metal track that guides the door, as directed by the manufacturer. If you're installing a four-panel door, insert the second top pivot bracket into the other end of the track as directed. Set the track in position across the inside top of the door opening, with the edge of the track flush with the edges of the jambs. Mark the location for screw holes along the track and set it aside.

Step 3: Drill pilot holes for screws as directed by the manufacturer, and fasten the track into place. For a two-panel door, from the top pivot bracket at the corner of the opening where the door will fold together, drop a plumb bob from the center of the pivot bracket to the floor. Set the bottom pivot bracket on the floor at this point, so that the holes in the two brackets line up exactly. Mark the screw holes for the bottom

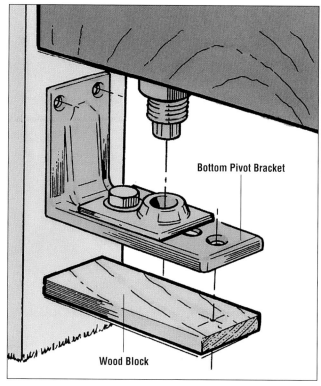

Bottom Pivot Bracket

Wood Block

To ensure door clearance over carpeting, set a wood block under the bottom pivot bracket.

pivot bracket. Drill pilot holes for the screws and screw the bracket into position on both the floor and door frame. For a four-panel door, install the second bottom pivot bracket in the same way, aligning it exactly under the top pivot bracket at the other side of the door frame.

Step 4: Determine the position of the bottom pivot bracket or brackets as before, but don't attach them. If you're installing the door in a carpeted area, allow adequate clearance over the carpeting. Trace the outline of each bracket exactly on a block of scrap wood that is the same thickness as the carpeting. With a handsaw, cut the block of wood to the same size as the bracket. Cut out a similar size section of carpet, set the block in place, and screw the bottom pivot bracket into the block and the door frame.

Step 5: Fold the door panels together. The pivot panel has pivot pins at top and bottom to fit into the pivot brackets; the guide panel has a wheel that moves along the track. Set the bottom pivot pin into place in the bottom pivot bracket and tilt the folded-together door into the door frame. Slide the top pivot bracket over to the top of the tilted door and insert the top pivot pin into the bracket. Tilt the door slowly into position, sliding the top bracket back toward the pivot corner. Insert the guide wheel in the track as soon as the angle of the door allows. Open the door to bring it firmly upright. If you're installing a four-panel door, repeat this procedure to install the second pair of panels on the other side of the door frame.

Step 6: Test the door for proper operation. If it sticks or doesn't hang evenly, adjust it according to the manufacturer's instructions.

Step 7: Attach doorknobs provided on both sides of the hinge joint. Mark and drill pilot screw holes, if necessary, then screw in the knobs with the screws provided. If you're installing a four-panel door, attach doorknobs to each set of panels. Close the door and attach the aligner plates provided to hold the panels firmly together.

Installing a Lockset

Once you've hung a new door, you need to fit it with a lockset. Some doors come predrilled for standard-size locksets. Other doors require you to drill the holes yourself, using a template provided by the lock manufacturer. With any door, you need to cut mortises, or holes, in the door edge for the lockset and in the frame for the strike plate that engages the lock's bolt. Here's how to install a lockset.

Step 1: Wrap the paper or cardboard template that comes with the new lockset around the edge of the door, according to the manufacturer's directions. Use tape to secure the template if necessary. The template will be used to locate two holes: One hole is for the lock cylinder, and the other goes into the edge of the door for the bolt. Mark the centers for these two holes on the door.

Use the template furnished with the lockset to cut a hole in the door.

Step 2: Use a power drill with a hole-saw attachment to drill a hole of the size specified for the lock cylinder. Be careful not to damage the veneer on the opposite side of the door. When you see the point of the drill coming through, stop and finish boring from the other side.

Step 3: Drill a hole of the appropriate size for the bolt into the edge of the door until you reach the cylinder hole. Use a combination square against the edge of the door and the drill bit to keep the bit at a right angle to the door. Smooth the edges of the holes with sandpaper.

Step 4: Insert the bolt into the hole, and place the bolt plate in position over it. Trace the bolt plate's

Drill a hole for the lock cylinder, then the door bolt.

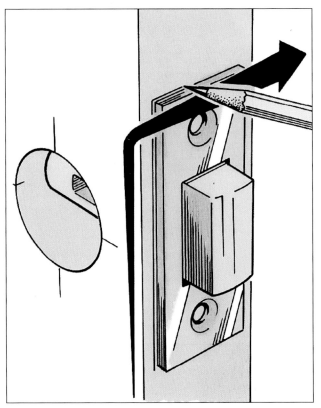

Insert the bolt assembly and trace its outline over the edge of the door; remove excess wood to mount the assembly.

*Install the outside
lock cylinder so that
the stems or
connecting bar fits
into the bolt
assembly.*

outline on the edge of the door. Remove the bolt, and mortise the edge for the bolt plate so it will be flush with the surface.

Step 5: Use a chisel to cut the mortise.

Step 6: Insert the bolt and plate in the mortise, and drill pilot holes for the mounting screws. Install the screws to secure the bolt in place.

Step 7: Insert the outside lock cylinder so that the stems or the connecting bar fits into the bolt assembly. Attach the interior lock cylinder and secure it with screws.

Step 8: Locate the proper spot for the strike plate on the jamb and drill a proper-size hole in the jamb. Using the strike plate as a pattern, mark the jamb for mortising, and cut the mortise. Install the strike plate with screws so that it fits flush with the jamb.

Step 9: Test the operation of the lock.

CHAPTER 3

INTERIOR DECORATING

The interior of your home or apartment serves many functions. Besides providing shelter and keeping you warm and dry, it reflects your tastes in colors, fixtures, and furniture. If you're not happy with this reflection, you can always paint, decorate, repair, and refinish. That's what this chapter is all about.

The first section of this chapter discusses painting: planning, preparation, selecting tools and materials, and making the job easier. The next section offers a decorative alternative to paint: wallpaper. The third and final section of this chapter includes easy-to-use instructions on repairing wood furniture. Within this chapter are literally dozens of ideas and tips on how to make any house or apartment feel more like home.

Planning to Paint

Before you pop the top on a fresh can of paint, even before you venture out to your local paint dealer to pore over color chips, there are things you should know about the liquid coatings called paint and how to use them successfully. An experienced dealer can be of enormous help to the novice, but there's really no substitute for first-hand knowledge.

Selecting Paint

Though there are paints for every possible surface, there is no such thing as an all-surface paint. Because the wrong paint can damage a wall surface and often not adhere well, it's crucial to know in advance what goes where and when. Fortunately, modern paint technology has taken a lot of the risk out of choosing the proper paint. Formulas for the so-called "latex paints" have been improved to withstand dirt, moisture, and daily wear and tear, and are no longer reserved exclusively for low-traffic areas. They are as washable and durable as the old oil-base paints. This means you no longer have to think in terms of latex paints for walls and oil-base enamels for woodwork, windows, and doors.

Still, an important factor in paint selection—aside from personal color preference—is its gloss. Regardless of the type of coating you choose, the gloss of the one you buy will affect both its appearance and its durability. High-gloss paints are the most durable because they contain more resin than either semigloss or flat paints. Resin is an ingredient that hardens as the paint dries. The more resin, the harder the surface. Consequently,

for kitchens, bathrooms, utility rooms, doors, windows, and trim, high-gloss paints are ideal. Semigloss paints, with less resin and a reduced surface shine, are slightly less wear-resistant but still suitable for most woodwork. Finally, flat paints are the coatings of choice for most interior walls and ceilings because they provide an attractive, low-glare finish for surfaces that take little abuse and require only infrequent washings.

Here's a paint primer to help you decide what kind of paint you need for the project at hand.

Latex Paint

The word "latex" originally stemmed from the use of rubber in one form or another as the resin, or solid, in paint. The solvent or thinner, called the "vehicle," was water. Today, many paints are made with water as the thinner but with resins that are not latex, and the industry is leaning toward terms such as "water-thinned" or "water-reducible." If the paints are called latex at all, the term often used is "acrylic latex" because they contain a plastic resin made of acrylics or polyvinyls rather than rubber.

In addition to the speed of drying, new opacity (the ability to completely cover one color with another), and washability of acrylic latex paints, the greatest advantage of water-thinned paints is that you can clean up with water. The higher expense—as well as the potential fire hazard—of volatile thinners and brush cleaners is gone. If you wash the brush or roller immediately after the painting session is over, it comes clean in a few minutes.

Latex paint works well on surfaces previously painted with latex or flat oil-base paints. It can even be used on unprimed drywall or unpainted masonry. However, latex usually does not adhere well to high-gloss finishes and, even though it can be used on wallpaper, there is a risk that the water in the paint may cause the paper to peel away from the wall. Because of its water content, latex will cause bare steel to rust and will raise the grain on raw wood.

Alkyd Resin Paint

The use of synthetic alkyd resin for solvent-thinned (oil-base) paints has brought several advantages. One of the most useful is a special formulation that makes the paint yogurt-thick. A brush dipped in it carries more paint to the surface than previous versions. Yet, under the friction of application, the paint spreads and smooths readily.

In most gloss and semigloss (or satin) paints, alkyd materials are still preferred for trim, doors, and even heavy-traffic hallways. Many homeowners still like them best for bathrooms and kitchens, where they feel more confident of washability despite the availability of water-thinned enamels in satin or gloss that can be safely cleaned with standard household cleaners.

The opacity of alkyd paints has been improved through the addition of a new ingredient. When the paint is manufactured, a portion of the white pigment particles (titanium dioxide) is replaced with a material that diffuses and evaporates, leaving minute bubbles. These "microvids" reflect and scatter light, giving the paint the effect of more thickness than it really has. With paints of this formula, one coat of white will cover black completely. It will even cover bright yellow.

While alkyds should not be used on unprimed drywall (they can raise the nap of its paper coating) or unprimed masonry, they are suitable for raw wood and almost any previously painted or papered surface. The most durable of interior paints, alkyds are dry enough for a second coat within four to six hours. Solvents must be used for thinning and cleanup. Check the label to find out which solvent is recommended by the manufacturer. And, while the solvents may be almost odorless, they're still toxic and flammable, so you should work in a well-ventilated room.

Estimating Painting Jobs

Estimating the paint you'll need for a job is easy. Take a few minutes at home to measure the area to be painted.

A gallon of paint will typically cover 450 square feet according to the manufacturer's calculations. It's safer to figure 400 square feet of coverage per gallon of paint. If you're buying two or more gallons of the same color, it's a good idea to mix them all together at home so that color variations don't show up in the middle of a wall.

To determine the amount of paint required to cover a wall, multiply the height of the wall by its length, then divide by 400. This means a gallon of paint will cover a 10×15-foot room with one coat. Two coats will take two gallons. However, there are other factors you should consider when calculating coverage.

When a wall is textured or rough-troweled, it will require more paint than if it were a smooth wall. This is because the texture represents added surface to be covered, even though it does not contribute to the size of the area. Just how much more surface area there is depends on just how textured the surface is, but for medium-rough, porous, or previously unpainted walls, you can safely estimate 300 to 350 square feet of coverage from a gallon of paint.

Most walls have doors or windows or other areas that are not painted. If the nonpaint area is a single window or door, ignore it in your calculations. Two or three windows, a door and a window, multiple sliding doors, or a fireplace reduce the paint you'll need. By how much? Multiply the lengths by the widths of these non-paint areas to get the total square footage that you can subtract from your overall surface figures, or you can subtract about 15 square feet for typical windows and 21 square feet for typical doors. (These figures also can be used to estimate the paint you'll need for each if you plan to use a different color or surface finish.) If you're painting the ceiling, figure its square foot area at width times length too.

Estimating the time you'll have to put in on any given paint project is less precise. Some people work faster than others, so there's no way to estimate individual differences in speed. On the average, you should be able to cover about 120 square feet of flat surface in about an hour. For bare wood or plaster, figure about 100 square feet. In a typical 12×15-foot room, you're likely to spend four or five hours on the job, including trim work, for the first coat. The second coat, if it's necessary, will go faster, but you'll have to wait for the first coat to dry, anywhere from two to 36 hours.

INTERIOR PAINTS		
Type	**Characteristics/Use**	**Application**
Acoustic	For acoustic ceiling tile. Water-thinned, water cleanup.	Spray (preferable), or roller.
Alkyd	Solvent-thinned, solvent cleanup. Don't apply over unprimed drywall.	Brush, roller, pad.
Cement	For concrete, brick, stucco. Some contain waterproofing agents. Must be mixed just before use.	Brush.
Dripless	For ceilings. More costly than ordinary paints.	Brush or roller.
Epoxy	For metal, glass, tile, floors, woodwork: high-stress areas. Expensive. May require special mixing; tricky to use.	Brush.
Latex	Most popular. Water-thinned, water cleanup. Gloss, semigloss, flat. May be used over most surfaces, but not on wallpaper, wood, or metal.	Brush, roller, pad.
Metal	For bare or primed metal, or as a primer for other types of paint. Some water-thinned, most solvent-thinned.	Brush or spray.
Oil	Slow-drying, strong odor. Coverage may not be as good as synthetic paints. Solvent-thinned, solvent cleanup.	Brush, roller, spray.
One-Coat	Water- or solvent-thinned. Costs more than regular latex or alkyd. Surface must be sealed first. Excellent covering power.	Brush, roller, pad.
Polyurethane/Urethane	Expensive. Can be used over most finishes, porous surfaces. Extreme durability. Solvents, primers vary.	Brush.
Texture	Good for covering surface defects. Premixed or mix-at-home types. Application slow. Permits surface design of choice.	Brush, roller, pad, trowel, sponge.

Rubber-Base Paint

Containing a liquified rubber, this paint is available only in a limited number of colors and in flat or low-gloss finishes. It's expensive and has a potent aroma. But, because rubber-base paint is waterproof and durable, it's an excellent coating for concrete. It can be applied directly to unprimed masonry. When it's used on brick, rubber-based paint should be preceded by a sealing coat of clear varnish. Before putting it on new concrete, wash the concrete with a ten percent solution of muriatic acid, rinse thoroughly, and allow it to dry completely. (Wear goggles and gloves when working with muriatic acid and make sure you are in a well-ventilated space.) Like alkyds, rubber-base paints require special solvents; check the label for specifications.

Textured Paint

If you're after a finish that looks like stucco, or if you simply want an effective cover-up for flawed surfaces, textured-surface paint will do the job. Some varieties come premixed with sandlike particles suspended in the paint. Because of their sandy grittiness, their use is usually reserved for ceilings. With other varieties, you have to add the particles and stir thoroughly. Another form of textured paint has no granules. Thick and smooth, it's applied to the surface then textured with special tools.

Textured paints are available in either flat-finish latex or alkyd formulations. Latex versions are frequently used on bare drywall ceilings because they can be used without a primer and they help to camouflage the seams between sheets of drywall.

One of the special problems with textured paint becomes evident when the time comes to paint over it. All those peaks and valleys created by the texturing actually increase the surface area of the wall. The rough surface will require 15 to 25 percent more paint the second time around.

Dripless Paint

Quite a bit more expensive than conventional alkyd paint, dripless paint is ideal for ceilings because it's so thick it won't run off a roller or a brush. It will usually cover any surface in a single coat, but, because of its very dense consistency, it won't go as far as its more spreadable relatives.

One-Coat Paint

With additional pigment to improve their covering capabilities, true one-coats are otherwise just more expensive versions of ordinary latex or alkyd paints. For best results, reserve them for use on flawless, same-color surfaces that have been previously sealed. Not all paints advertised as "one-coat" really are.

Acoustic Paint

Designed for use on acoustic ceiling tile, it covers without impairing the tile's acoustic qualities. It can be applied with a roller, but a paint sprayer is more efficient and less likely to affect the sound-deadening properties of the tile.

Primers

Primers are inexpensive undercoatings that smooth out uneven surfaces, provide a barrier between porous surfaces and certain finishing coats, and allow you to use an otherwise incompatible paint on a bare or previously painted surface. For flat paint finishes, the primer can be a thinned-out version of the paint itself. But that's often more expensive than using a premixed primer, which contains less expensive pigment, dries quickly, and provides a firm foundation or "tooth" for the final coat of paint. Latex primer has all the advantages of latex paint—almost odor-free, quick drying, and easy to clean up—and is the best undercoat for drywall, plaster, and concrete. Don't use it on bare wood, though, because the water in it will raise the grain. For raw wood, it's best to use an alkyd primer that won't raise the grain but will create a good base for most other paints, including latex.

Preparing to Paint

Even the best of paints, applied with the best of tools by the best of painters, won't result in a job well done if you fail to fix the flaws in the surfaces that are to be painted. When used properly, paint is a marvelous material, but don't expect it to hide a multitude of surface sins. Chances are, it will make them even more noticeable. Peeling or "alligatored" old paint, cracks in plaster, dents and popped nail heads in drywall, and splits in woodwork all have to be dealt with first.

To find flaws in surfaces to be painted, remove all the furniture from the room, if possible. If not, cluster it in one area and cover it and the floors with drop cloths. Take down the draperies and the drapery hardware. Loosen the light fixtures; let them hang and wrap them

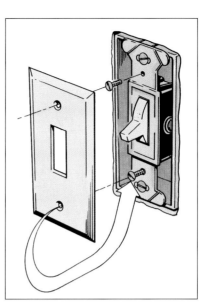

Before you begin painting, remove the wall plates from electrical outlets and switch plates from switches. Paint them separately, even if you intend to paint them the same color as the wall.

with plastic bags. Remove the wall plates from electrical outlets and switches (if you intend to paint them the same color as the wall, do so while they're off the wall).

If you found flaws, now is the time to fix them. You needn't feel compelled to take care of the whole project in one weekend and shouldn't try. Make the surface mends and otherwise prepare the to-be-painted surfaces one weekend and paint the next.

Preparing Walls

Two of the most common defects you'll find are damaged drywall (newer homes) and damaged plaster (older homes). Age, settling, temperature swings, variations in humidity, and, of course, everyday wear and tear take their toll on walls. Fortunately, these problems can easily be corrected by the do-it-yourselfer.

Repairing Popped Nails

In most newer homes, the walls are surfaced with gypsum wallboard, also known as drywall. Drywall, like all building materials, has its own characteristics and problems. One of the most common problems results from shrinking or warping in the framing behind the drywall. As the wood studs age and shrink, nails loosen and pop out of the wood, producing an unsightly bump or hole in the surface. No matter how many times you drive the nails back in, the problem is likely to recur, so it's better to fix it permanently the first time around.

The first step is to redrive the popped nails. If the nails are sticking out far enough to get the claw of a hammer around, you can pull them out first. To redrive them, hold a nail set over the nail head and hammer the nail as far as you can into the stud. The nail head will

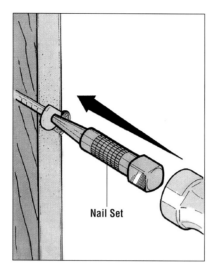

Nail pops in drywall are easy to eliminate. First drive the popped nail with a nail set as far as possible into the stud; then drive another nail about two inches above or below it.

Nail Set

punch through the drywall's outside layer of paper and into the drywall itself.

To make sure the nail stays there (and to take the pressure off it), drive another drywall nail through the wall into the stud about two inches above or below the old nail. Pound the nail flush with the wall and then give it one more light hammer whack to "dimple" the drywall surface around the nail head. Using a putty knife, cover the new nail head and fill the hole over the old one with spackling compound. Let it dry, sand it lightly, and, if necessary, repeat the process once or twice more. Touch up the patches with paint or primer.

You can find more information on drywall installation and repair in Chapter 2.

Repairing Holes in Drywall

Tough as it is, drywall can withstand only limited abuse. A door flung open with too much force can produce a doorknob-size hole in the wall. This kind of damage looks bad, but even large holes are easy to repair. For small holes you may use a tin can lid to back a plaster patch; for large ones, cut a patch from scrap drywall of the same thickness. To fix a small hole:

Step 1: Remove any loose paper or plaster around the edges.

Step 2: Apply a drywall patch, available from a building-material retailer, following instructions on the package. Alternately, use a clean tin can lid, at least 1½ inches more in diameter than the hole, for a backer. Measure the diameter of the lid and use a keyhole saw to cut out a narrow slit in the wall on each side of the hole. The measurement of the hole, plus both slits, should equal the diameter of the lid so that you can insert the lid sideways into the hole. Punch two holes in

the center of the lid and thread a 12-inch piece of string or thin wire through the holes. Then, holding the ends of the string or wire, slide the lid through the slit. Pull the lid flat against the inside of the wall. To hold it in place, set a stick of scrap wood over the hole on the outside of the wall and tie the string or twist the wire tightly over the stick. The tin can lid should be firmly held against the inside of the wall.

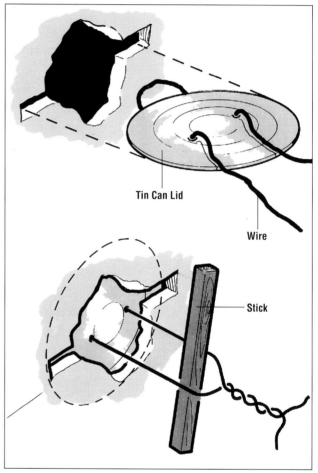

Tin Can Lid

Wire

Stick

Cut slits out from the sides of the hole, then thread a wire through a tin can lid and slide it in. Pull the lid flat on the inside of the wall, and hold it in place with a stick.

Step 3: Purchase a premixed drywall patch compound and apply the compound over the patch following instructions on the container. Don't use spackling compound, as it shrinks as it dries. Alternately, mix plaster of paris with water to make a thick paste, and pack the plaster into the hole against the backer and behind the stick. Keep the plaster inside the hole, cover the backer, and fill the slits, but don't spread the plaster on the wall surface. Leave the patch slightly low. Don't try to level it yet. Let the patch dry until the plaster turns bright white, typically at least 24 hours. When the plaster is dry, cut the string or wire and remove the stick.

Step 4: To finish the patch, fill it completely with more plaster of paris to make the patch level with the wall surface. Let it dry, sand it lightly, and prime.

To fix a large hole:

Step 1: Cut a scrap piece of drywall into a square or rectangle a little bigger than the hole or damaged area. Set the patch against the damaged area and trace around it lightly with a pencil. Cut out the outlined area with a keyhole saw. Keep the saw cut on the inside of the traced line so that the hole will be exactly the same size as the patch.

Step 2: To hold the wallboard patch in place, install a board about six inches longer than the long dimension of the hole. Insert this backing into the hole and hold it firmly against the inside of the wallboard. To keep it there, fasten the ends of the board to the drywall with flathead screws driven through the wall at the sides of the hole; countersink the screws below the surface of the drywall.

Step 3: Use spackling compound or wallboard joint compound as a glue to hold the patch in place. Spread compound on the back of the drywall patch and around the edges. Set the patch into the hole and adjust it so it's exactly even with the surrounding wall. Hold it in place until the compound starts to set. Let the compound dry at least overnight.

Step 4: Once the compound is dry, fill the patch outline and cover the exposed screw heads with spackling or joint compound. Let it dry, sand it lightly, and prime.

Repairing Cracked Plaster

Paint will hide hairline cracks in plaster, at least temporarily. The cover-up, though, may last only a few hours or a few months. Small plaster cracks have an annoying way of showing up again and again. It may be smarter to enlarge them and repair them properly once and for all. Making a small flaw bigger may sound like reverse logic, but it's easier to fix big cracks in plaster than small ones. Use plaster of paris, which doesn't shrink as it dries. To repair a large crack in a plaster wall:

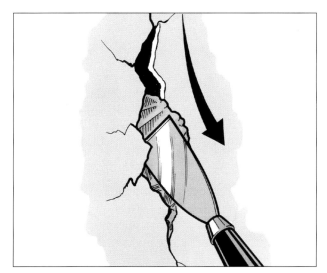

To fill a large crack in a plaster wall, remove loose plaster, then wet the crack and pack plaster of paris in to its full depth. Smooth the surface with a scraper.

Step 1: Use the pointed end of a can opener to cut out the loose plaster. Turn the opener to undercut and widen the opening. Remove debris while preserving the structural integrity of the surface

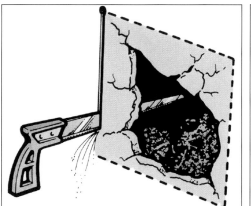

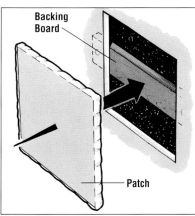

Backing Board

Patch

Far left: *To mend a large hole in drywall, cut a square or rectangular patch piece; then cut out the damaged area to exactly the same size and shape as the patch.*

Left: *Secure a backing board on the inside of the wall to brace the patch; then coat the edges of the patch with spackling compound and set it into place in the hole.*

around it. Clean the loose plaster and dust from the crack with a vacuum cleaner.

Step 2: Mix a thick paste of plaster of paris and water (or purchase premixed plaster repair compound) and wet the crack thoroughly with a paintbrush dipped in water. Pack the plaster of paris into the wet crack to its full depth and smooth the surface with a scraper or trowel. Let the filled crack dry at least 24 hours.

Step 3: Sand the patch lightly when the plaster is dry, using a medium-grade or fine-grade sandpaper wrapped around a wood block. If the crack was wide, replaster it at least once more to make the surface smooth, rewetting the plastered area each time. Let it dry for at least 24 hours after the final plastering.

Step 4: Sand the patch lightly and prime it with a thinned coat of paint or primer. When the primer is dry, you can paint the entire wall.

Preparing Surfaces

Once surface repairs are made, final preparation for painting can begin. Cleaning the surfaces to be painted requires just as much patience as the other steps. Washing down walls, ceilings, and woodwork that are about to get a new coat of paint anyway may sound like a waste of time, but it's not. Cleaning ensures that the new paint will stay where you put it so you'll be happy with the final result. Good paint needs a good, clean surface foundation to bite into. Otherwise, you risk peeling or chipping or, later, the bleed-through of grease spots, all of which will mar the new paint.

Scrubbing and Sanding

If you're painting over a new, primed wall, you can safely skip this step. But if you're painting over a previously painted surface, look for rough, peeling, or chipped areas; sand them smooth, then give the entire wall a thorough washing. Use warm water and a good household detergent or wall-cleaning soap to remove soot, grease, cigarette smoke, and airborne dirt. New paint will cover all of these soils, of course, but not for long.

Approach wall washing the same way you approach floor washing, with a sponge or a sponge mop. With the mop just slightly less than dripping wet, go over a vertical strip of wall about two feet wide. Squeeze the dirty water out of the sponge into a separate pail or down the drain. Go over the wall with the squeezed out sponge to pick up as much of the remaining dirt as possible. Squeeze out the mop again and then rinse it in

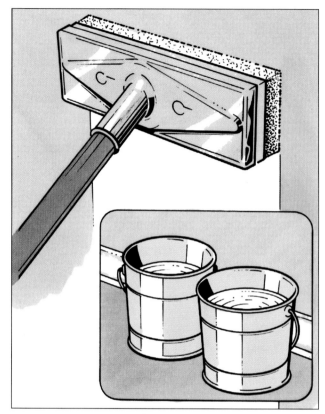

Scrub walls with a sponge mop. Squeeze dirty water out of the mop into a separate pail or down the drain.

clean water. Then, sponge-mop the same area once more to remove the last of the dirt and detergent residue.

This routine sounds tedious, but it actually goes fast, and you'll end up with a wall that is clean and provides a good surface for a new coat of paint.

Don't attempt to paint over a surface that already has a glossy finish, even if it is clean. Glossy surfaces don't provide enough adhesion. And even if the paint goes on, it may not stay on. To cut the gloss on an entire wall, wash it down with a strong solution of trisodium phosphate (available at hardware or paint stores). Mix the TSP powder into hot water until no more will dissolve. Swab it on the wall and sponge it dry. Rinse with clear water and sponge-dry again. If TSP is not available (in many communities it has been banned because of its tendency to pollute water sources), you can use a commercial deglosser, a solution that you swab on glossy surfaces before painting.

You can use deglossing solutions on woodwork too, or you can give woodwork a light sanding with medium-grit and fine-grit sandpaper. Wipe off or vacuum off the resulting powder before you paint.

On baseboards, remove accumulations of floor wax or acrylic floor finish with a wax remover or finish remover.

Scraping

The older your house, the greater the chances there's an area that needs scraping. A previous paint job may have begun to peel or crack in some places. Or window sills and sash frames may have chipped, or the old paint may have "alligatored" into a maze of cracks. If you find these conditions, scrape them gently to remove the loose particles and then sand them smooth to blend with the area around them. If you get down to bare wood on woodwork, prime the spots before you apply the final coat of paint. If it's impossible to blend the scraped areas with the nonscraped areas on walls, go over them with a light coat of drywall joint compound. When it dries, sand them smooth, prime, and paint.

Masking Basics

Where two new paint colors come together on a single surface, it's practically impossible to keep a straight line between them while painting freehand with either a brush or a roller. To get a straight line, use a carpenters' level and a pencil to draw a faint line on the wall. Then, align masking tape with the line across the wall. Peel the tape off the roll a little at a time and press it to the wall with your thumb. Don't pull the tape too tightly as you go, or it may stretch and retract once it's in place. To keep the paint from seeping under the masking tape, use the bowl of a spoon to press the tape tightly to the surface.

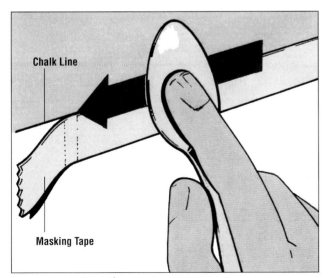

Chalk Line

Masking Tape

To keep paint from seeping under masking tape, use the bowl of a spoon to press the tape tightly to the surface.

Don't leave the tape on until the paint is dry. If you do, it may pull the paint away from the surface. With latex paint, you only need to wait a half hour or so before peeling off the tape. With alkyds, two or three hours is enough. The paint can's label will tell you how long it takes for the paint to set completely.

Masking tape is useful for protecting trim around doors, windows, built-ins, baseboards, or bookshelves. When you're brushing or rolling new paint on the wall, you won't have to slow down or worry about sideswiping the trim.

Using Painting Equipment

• •

The selection of painting tools was covered in Chapter 1. Once you have assembled the materials and completed the prep work, you're ready to resuscitate those old, drab walls with clean, new paint. You'll soon discover how easy and natural it is to use brushes and rollers competently. Even so, there are a few techniques that will help postpone fatigue and provide a neater job.

Using a Brush

The grip you get depends on the brush you're using. Trim and sash brushes with pencil handles are grasped much as you would a pencil, with the thumb and the first two fingers of the hand. This technique gives you excellent control for intricate painting. With beaver-tail handles on larger brushes, you'll need a stronger grip because the brushes are wider and heavier. Hold a beaver-tail handle with the entire hand, letting the handle span the width of your palm as you would hold a tennis racket. This technique works best when you're painting large, flat surfaces.

The goal of loading a brush is to get as much paint on the wall as possible without dribbling it all over the floor and yourself in the process. It will take you only a few minutes to be able to gauge accurately how much paint your brush will hold along the way.

Meanwhile, start the job by dampening the bristles of the brush (with water for latex, with the appropriate thinner for other types of paint) to condition them and make them more efficient. Remove excess moisture by gently striking the metal band around the handle's base against the edge of your palm and into a sink or a mop pail.

Never dip the brush more than about one-third the length of the bristles into the paint. If you do, the heel of the brush will gradually fill with paint and become next to impossible to clean.

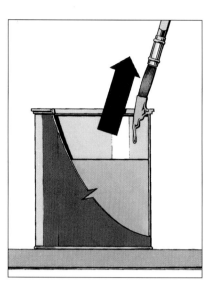

To remove excess paint, gently slap the brush against the inside of the paint can or lightly drag it across the inside edge of the lip of the can.

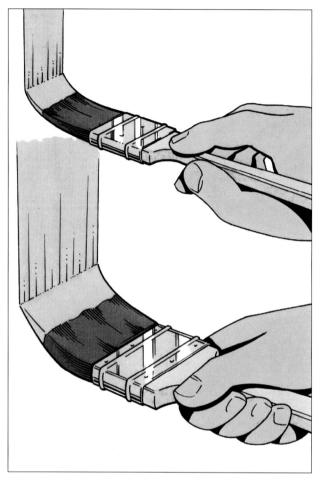

Grasp sash and trim brushes as you would a pencil (top). Hold a wall brush with your entire hand (bottom).

Never dip a brush more than about one-third the length of the bristles into the paint. If you do, the brush will become next to impossible to clean.

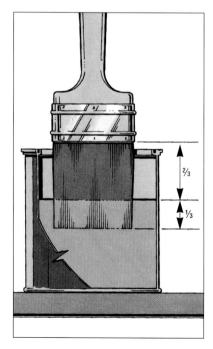

With the first dip, move the brush around a bit in the paint to open the bristles and let the brush fill completely. It will be easier to pick up a full load if you jab the brush gently into the paint with each dip. With most latex paints, you can simply dip the brush and let the excess drip off for a few seconds before moving the brush to the wall. With thinner coatings, however, you may have to gently slap the brush against the inside of the paint can or lightly drag it across the inside edge of the lip to remove excess.

Using a Roller

Working with a roller is even less exacting than working with a brush. Even a novice painter can get the feel of it in just a few minutes. As with brushes, moisten the roller first in the appropriate thinner. Roll out the excess moisture on a piece of scrap lumber, craft paper, or even on paper grocery bags. Don't use newspapers because the roller may pick up the ink. Fill the well of the roller pan about half full and set the roller into the middle of the well. Lift the roller and roll it down the slope of the pan, stopping just short of the well. Do this two or three times to allow the paint to work into the roller. Then, dip the roller into the well once more and roll it on the slope until the pile is well saturated. You'll know immediately when you've overloaded the roller. It will drip en route to the wall and have a tendency to slide and smear instead of roll across the surface.

The most effective method of painting with a roller is to paint two- or three-square-foot areas at a time. Roll the paint on in a zigzag pattern without lifting the roller from the wall, as if you're painting a large M, W, or a backward N. Then, still without lifting the roller, fill in the blanks of the letters with more horizontal or vertical zigzag strokes. Finish the area with light strokes that

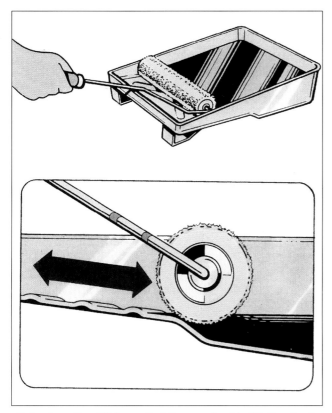

To load a roller, fill the well of the pan about half full and set the roller into the well. Then lift the roller and roll it down the slope of the pan two or three times to work paint into the roller.

Using an Airless Sprayer

For larger painting jobs, an airless sprayer is the most efficient way to apply paint. An airless sprayer uses an electrically run hydraulic pump to move paint from a bucket or container, through a tube, into a high-pressure hose, to a spray gun, and, finally, to the surface. Once you get the knack of it, an airless sprayer is easy to use, but if you rent one, make sure you get a set of written instructions.

The instructions will tell you how to flush the system with solvent (usually water or mineral spirits, depending on the paint you'll be using) and how to pump the paint through the hose to the spray gun. For cleanup, the procedure is reversed: Pump the leftover paint out and flush with solvent.

You'll only need the spray rig for a day or two, but plan to spend at least another day beforehand to thoroughly mask off everything you *don't* want to paint. Tape drop cloths to every floor surface. Drape windows, the fireplace, and doors. Remove all hardware or cover it with masking tape. Mask switches and outlets. Paint from a sprayer travels on the tiniest of air currents and settles a fine mist of overspray on just about every surface in a room.

Plan to keep at least one window in each room open and set up an exhaust fan to draw paint vapor out of the room. Be sure, too, to wear a painters' mask, hat, and old clothes with long sleeves to protect your arms.

Airless sprayers are equipped with several filters to keep paint particles and foreign matter from clogging the spray tip, but it's a good idea to filter the paint yourself through a nylon stocking or paint filter before you pump the paint through the hose.

Using an airless sprayer effectively takes some getting used to, so plan to practice on some scrap plywood or an inconspicuous part of the room or the house. The object is to cover the surface with a uniform coating of paint. Hold the spray gun a constant 6 to 12 inches from the surface and maintain this distance with each pass of the gun. Keep the gun precisely parallel to the wall. Don't sweep it back and forth or you'll end up with a wide arc of paint on the wall; the paint will be concentrated in the middle of the arc and almost transparent at each end.

Paint about a three-foot horizontal strip at one time, then release the trigger and drop down to paint another strip of the same length, overlapping the first strip by one-third to one-half. Once you've covered a three-foot-wide area from the top of the wall to the bottom, go back to the top and start another three-foot section adjacent to the first, overlapping the edge of the first painted area by several inches as you work your way down the wall again.

start in the unpainted area and roll into the paint. At the end of the stroke, raise the roller slowly so that it leaves no mark. Go to the next unpainted area and repeat the zigzag technique, ending it just below or next to the first painted patch. Finally, smooth the new application and blend it into the previously finished area.

Be careful not to run the roller so rapidly that centrifugal force causes it to spray droplets of paint.

Here are two more useful tips from professional painters. First, always start with a roller stroke that moves away from you. On walls, that means the first stroke should be up. If you roll down on the first stroke, the paint may puddle under the roller and run down the wall. Second, be careful not to run the roller so rapidly across the wall that centrifugal force causes it to spray.

To use a sprayer, hold the gun a constant 6 to 12 inches from the surface. Maintain this distance with each pass of the gun, and keep the gun precisely parallel to the wall. Don't sweep it back and forth or paint will end up concentrated in the middle of the arc and almost transparent at the ends.

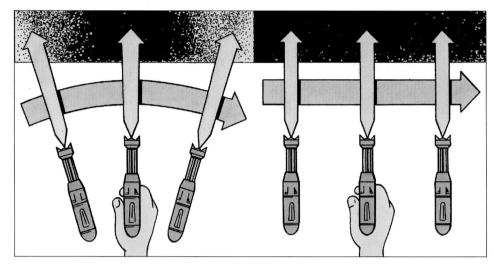

Examine the painted areas to make sure the entire surface is receiving a uniform coat of paint. Too much will run or sag; too little will let the old paint show through. If you notice these flaws, it means you are not keeping the spray gun a uniform distance from the wall at all times, or that you are tilting it. An upward tilt will deliver excess paint to the bottom of the painted strip. A downward tilt will concentrate paint at the top of the strip.

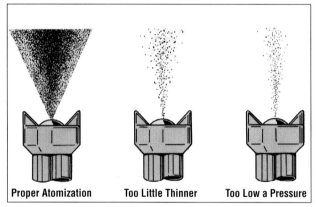

Proper Atomization   Too Little Thinner   Too Low a Pressure

Too much or too little thinner, too high or too low a pressure, and the paint won't atomize properly. Follow the manufacturer's instructions for thinning and adjusting pressure.

To prevent paint buildup at the end of each strip, release the trigger on the gun a fraction of a second before the spray gun stops moving at the end of your stroke. When beginning a new strip, start moving the gun a fraction of a second before compressing the trigger. Always keep the gun moving when it's spraying.

Be sure, too, that you've properly thinned the paint and adjusted the pressure control according to the manufacturer's instructions. If there is too much or too little thinner or too high or too low a pressure, the spray of paint won't atomize properly.

Painting Precautions

Except for the danger of falling off a ladder or scaffold, painting may not seem to pose much risk to the painter or other members of the family, but paint itself is a substance that can be hazardous to health. It is a combination of chemicals and requires careful handling and proper precautions.

- Water-thinned or solvent-thinned, paint ingredients are poisonous and should be kept away from children and pets. Antidotes are listed on can labels.

- Work in well-ventilated areas at all times, even if you're using odorless paints. They still contain fumes that may be harmful if inhaled. Wear a paper painters' mask when painting indoors. Also wear one outdoors if you're using an airless sprayer. Do not sleep in a room until the odor has dissipated.

- Do not smoke while painting and, if possible, extinguish pilot lights on gas appliances. Shut off gas to the unit first.

- Toxic paint chemicals can be absorbed through the skin. Wash up as soon as possible.

- When painting overhead, wear goggles to keep paint out of your eyes. Chemical ingredients can cause burns to sensitive eye tissue.

- Never drink alcohol while you're painting. Combined with paint fumes it can be deadly.

Using an Airless Sprayer Safely

Airless sprayers are fast and efficient because they supply pressures of up to 3,000 pounds per square inch. This force moves the paint at 100 to 200 miles an hour through the spray tip. All that power can be dangerous. Consequently, treat an airless sprayer with lots of respect, follow the manufacturer's instructions to the letter, and take the following precautions to prevent accident or injury:

- As you would with a firearm, keep the safety lock on when you're not painting.

- Make sure the spray gun has a trigger guard and a safety shield around its tip.

- If the spray tip becomes clogged, do not try to clear it by pressing your finger on it while the paint is being sprayed. Keep your fingers away from the tip when the sprayer is operating.

- Never point the gun at anyone else or allow anyone to point it at you.

- Always turn the sprayer off and disconnect it from its electrical source before you clean out the gun or the sprayer's filters. Even then, if you have to clean the tip, squeeze the trigger to release any built-up pressure in the hose.

- Only work in a well-ventilated area, wear a painters' mask to avoid inhaling fumes, and don't smoke or work around open flames. If you're working outside, don't leave containers of solvents sitting in the hot sun; put them in the garage or another shady spot.

- Never leave the sprayer within reach of children or pets.

Painting Walls and Ceilings

Whether you're using one, two, or more colors of paint in a single room, paint the ceiling before painting the walls. Not only does this top-down approach eliminate the risk of spattering ceiling paint on newly painted walls, it gets the most arduous overhead work out of the way first, so the job gets easier, not harder, when your energy begins to diminish.

Brush Work

Rollers make quick work of vast expanses of flat surfaces, but they are not effective for painting in wall-to-wall or wall-to-ceiling corners or even around woodwork. At these junctions, you'll need a trim brush to paint a two-inch-wide border around the ceiling, the walls, windows, doors, and baseboards. This border painting technique is called "cutting in," and there are two ways of doing it.

Where Same-Color Surfaces Meet

Using a trim brush with beveled bristles (the end of the brush resembles a chisel), paint five or six strokes perpendicular to the edge of the ceiling or the wall. Next, smooth over these strokes with a single, long

stroke. Where two walls meet, this means painting out from the corner first, then vertically. Where the wall and ceiling come together, use downward strokes on the wall first, followed by smoothing horizontal strokes. On the ceiling itself, cut in strokes toward the center of the room, away from the wall. Then paint a smoothing horizontal stroke on the ceiling that follows the direction of the wall. Even if you're using the same color of paint on adjoining surfaces, follow this method of cutting in with two-inch-wide borders rather than just plopping a loaded brush directly into a corner so you don't end up with drips, sags, and runs.

Use a brush to paint along the edge of the ceiling next to moldings and to paint next to corners. This technique is called "cutting in."

79

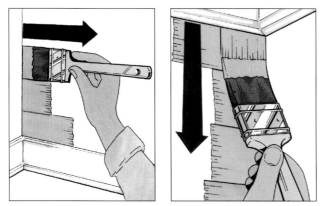

To cut in at a corner, paint out from the corner for five or six strokes, then smooth over them with a single, long, smoothing stroke.

Where Different-Color Surfaces Meet

This cutting-in approach, also known as beading, can practically eliminate the need to use masking tape to protect one painted area from another. Use a beveled trim brush with nice long bristles. Hold the brush so that your thumb is on one side of the metal ferrule and your fingers on the other. Press the brush lightly against the surface, then, as you move the brush, add just enough pressure to make the bristles bend away from the direction of your brush stroke. Keep the brush about $\frac{1}{16}$ inch away from the other colored surface. The bent bristles and the pressure will release a fine bead of paint that will spread into the gap. With both methods of cutting in, but especially when you're dealing with two colors, it's better to have a brush that's too dry than one that's too wet. This is detail work. To do it effectively, go slowly and only cut in four or five inches at a time. It will seem tedious at first, but your speed and accuracy will improve with practice, and even one ordinary-size room will give you lots of practice.

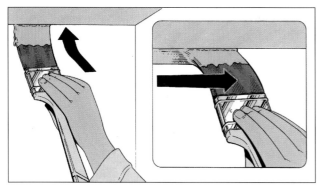

Where different-color surfaces meet, use a technique called beading. Press the brush lightly against the surface, then, as you move the brush, add just enough pressure to bend the bristles away from the direction of your brush stroke.

Roller Work

If this is your first venture with a roller, you'll be amazed at how fast the job goes and what an efficient device a roller really is. Still, there are a few variations in technique, depending on what surface you're dealing with.

Ceilings

When rolling paint on the ceiling, maintain a wet edge at all times to avoid creating lines and ridges. If you're using fast-drying paint, you may have to work faster than you anticipated and without taking a break. Both speed and ease can be achieved by using an extension handle so you can paint from the floor instead of from a stepladder that has to be moved around the room. Many roller handles are made to accept a screw-in extension that you can buy at the paint store, but you may want to see if the threaded end of your broom or mop handle will work.

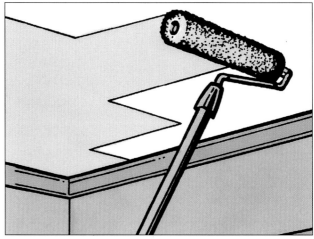

When using a roller, work in strips across, always working over the wet edge of previously painted strips.

You can paint in a series of strips or by using the zigzag technique mentioned on page 76 to put the paint on the ceiling. In either case, fill in the blanks with a crisscross motion and paint from the dry areas into the wet areas, smoothing as you go. Don't worry about keeping your roller strokes all the same length. The lines won't show when the paint dries. If you paint in strips, do so across the narrow dimension of the room to maintain the wet edges previously mentioned. If you choose to use the zigzag method, start about three feet out from one corner and paint toward the corner. Make an M, backward N, or W pattern about three feet square and fill it in. Then, working across the narrow dimension of the room again, roll on another three-

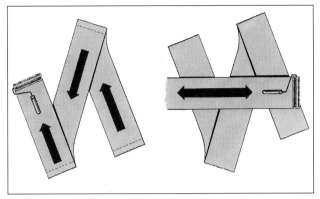

With a roller, begin by making an M, backward N, or W pattern about three feet square. Always start with an upstroke so paint won't run down the wall. Next, fill in the pattern with crosswise strokes. You should be able to paint each three-square-foot area with one dip of the roller.

square-foot area. You should be able to paint each three-square-foot area with just one dip of the roller in the paint pan.

Walls

As with the ceiling, paint an entire wall before taking a break so that the painted portions won't lose their wet edges. Then stand back, scan the wall, and cover any missed spots or smears. Whether you paint in sections from top to bottom or from side to side across the room is up to you. But if you're using an extension handle, you may find it more convenient to start at one high corner and go all the way across the room with a series of completed zigzag patterns. That way you won't have to constantly change the handle on your roller as you would if you painted in sections from the ceiling down to the floor. If you're right-handed, start in the room's left-hand corner; if you're left-handed, start in the room's right-hand corner.

Tight Spots

Over and under windows and above doors and doorways, you probably won't have enough room to use the zigzag technique. Instead, just roll the paint on horizontally. For areas that are narrower than the standard 7- or 9-inch roller you're already using, use a 4-inch roller or resort to a paintbrush. Between the two, the little roller is best because it will give you the same surface finish as the rest of the wall. Brushes apply paint less evenly and tend to leave telltale trails.

Minimizing Drips and Spatters

Even if you have already cut in around the room, avoid bumping the roller into the walls as you paint the ceiling

or into the ceiling as you paint the walls, even if you're using the same color paint on both surfaces. The roller may deposit a visible ridge of paint each time it touches the ceiling or the wall.

No matter how slowly and steadily you move the roller across a surface, it will emit a fine spray of paint. So wear a scarf or cap (inexpensive painters' caps are available at paint stores) and make sure the floor and furniture are covered with drop cloths. Canvas drop cloths are best because they're durable, washable, and reusable. Plastic drop cloths, though, are far less expensive and, if you tape them down so they won't slide around, just as effective.

If you choose not to mask around windows, doors, and woodwork, minimize the risk of spatters by using a paint shield, either homemade or purchased from a paint dealer. The store-bought shields come in several sizes and materials (plastic or aluminum). Do-it-yourself shields can be made from thin cardboard or the slats of an old venetian blind. The paint shield works like a moving masker. Holding the shield in one hand, place it perpendicular to the surface being painted. Then, with the other hand, apply the paint. Paint shields are ideal for painting window frames because they can be used to keep paint off the glass, eliminating the need to scrape off dried paint later.

Because some spatters and spills are inevitable, keep a moist sponge and a pail of water handy when you're using latex paints. If you're using a solvent-thinned paint, keep some thinner and a supply of rags nearby to wipe up spatters and drips before they dry into bumps.

Painting Woodwork

● ●

Should you paint woodwork first or last? There is wide disagreement even among veteran painters about whether to paint woodwork before or after painting walls. It comes down to personal preference. The argument for painting the trim first is that any stray drips or spatters that end up on the wall only need to be feathered out, not removed, since the wall's going to get a new coat of paint anyway. If you get all of the slow, detail work out of the way first you'll feel as if you're flying right along when it's time to fill in the big, flat areas.

On the other hand, rollers always emit a powder-fine spray of paint into the room. No matter how careful you are, some of it is going to end up on the woodwork. Consequently, if you paint the trim first, mask it off when you paint the ceiling and walls.

A third option, if you're using only one color and one finish on all surfaces, is to paint the trim as you come to it in the process of painting the walls. Of course, you'll have to keep alternating between brush and roller if you use this technique, but this shouldn't be difficult in rooms that have only a couple of windows and a single door.

No matter when you decide to paint woodwork, inspect all the woodwork in the room for defects and make the necessary repairs before you actually get down to painting. If you'll be painting over already-glossy woodwork, sand it lightly with sandpaper or steel wool first to give it adhesion. Or, give it a coat of deglosser.

Painting trim progresses even more slowly than cutting in walls and ceilings, and there's more room for error. If, however, you learn to paint freehand and eliminate the time-consuming step of applying masking tape, the job goes faster.

Baseboards and Wainscoting

Use the cutting in or beading technique discussed on page 80 to paint the top of the baseboard. Then, using a painting shield or a thin piece of cardboard as a movable masker, cut in along the floor. After that, you can fill the unpainted space between with long brush strokes. Paint only two or three feet of baseboard at a time. Examine the surface for drips, spatters, and overlapped edges and clean them up immediately. Do not wait until the entire baseboard is painted, or else the paint flaws will have already set.

Painting wainscoting or paneling requires a similar approach. Cut in along the top and bottom edges where the wainscoting meets the wall and the floor, just as you did with the baseboard. Next, paint the indented panels and the molding around them. Paint tends to collect in the corners of these panels, so your brush strokes should be toward the center of the panel. On the raised surfaces around and between panels, work from the top down and use up-and-down strokes on the verticals, back-and-forth strokes on the horizontals.

Windows, Doors, and Shutters

Flush doors—those with smooth, flat surfaces—are easy to paint with either a brush or a roller, but doors with inset panels can be tricky. No matter what type of door you're dealing with, paint the entire door without stopping. Otherwise the lap marks may show. Before you start, remove the doorknobs, the plates behind them, and the latch plate on the edge of the door.

For ornate doors, start by painting the inset panels at the top of the door. As with wainscoting, paint all the panels and the molding around them. Then work your way down from the top to the bottom, painting the top rail, middle rail, and bottom rail (the horizontals) with back-and-forth strokes. Next, paint the vertical stiles (the sides) with up-and-down strokes. If you're painting both sides of the door, repeat this procedure. If you're painting only one side, paint the top edge of the door with a light coat. Over time, paint can build up on the top edge and cause the door to stick. Finally, paint the door's hinge edge and latch edge.

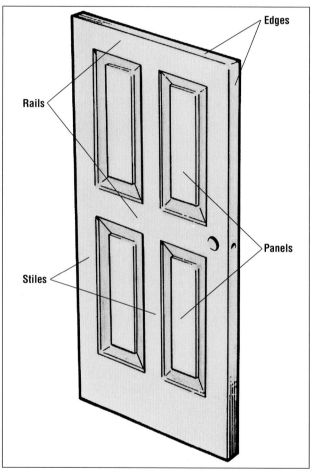

When painting a door, paint the panels first. Then paint the rails, the stiles, and finally the edges, working from the top to the bottom.

The job of painting windows will go faster if you purchase a 2- or 2½-inch sash-trim brush, angled slightly across the bottom to make it easier to get into 90-degree corners and tight spaces.

To paint wood-frame windows, first raise the bottom sash more than halfway up and lower the top sash until its bottom rail is several inches below the bottom sash. Paint the bottom rail of the top sash and on up the stiles as far as you can go. Paint all the surfaces of the bottom

Paint double-hung windows in the sequence shown, moving the top and bottom sashes for access to all surfaces.

sash except the top edge. Reverse the position of the sashes: top sash up to within an inch of the window frame, bottom sash down to within an inch of the sill. Then, paint the formerly obstructed surfaces of the top sash and the top edges of both sashes.

Don't paint the wood channels (jambs) in which the sashes move up and down yet. Instead, paint the window frame, working from top to bottom, including the sill. When the paint on the sashes is dry to the touch, move them both down as far as they will go. Paint the exposed jambs. Let the paint dry, raise both sashes all the way, and paint the lower jambs. To keep the sashes from sticking in the jambs, put on only as much paint as is necessary to cover the old coat. Wait for the paint to dry, then lubricate the channels with paraffin or a silicone spray.

The best way to paint shutters, both interior and exterior types, is to spray them, using either canned spray paint or an airless power sprayer. But, because that's not always possible, you can still get a quality finish on old shutters by using a brush. Take them down and scrape, sand, and clean them as needed. Then if you can hang them from an open ceiling joist—in the garage, for example—you can paint both sides at the same time. Otherwise, stand them upright or lay them out on the floor and paint one side at a time.

Keep your brush on the dry side. An excessively wet brush will result in runs and sags and, if the louvers are adjustable, sticking problems. Paint the window side of the shutter first. That way, if you do miss a sag or run, it won't show. On adjustable shutters, put a wooden matchstick or a little wood wedge between the adjusting rod and one or two of its staples to keep the rod away from the louvers, making both of them easier to paint. Paint the louvers first with a ½-inch or 1-inch trim brush. Then paint the frame with a 2-inch brush. Leave the shutter edges until last so you can periodically turn the shutter over to check for runs. If you find any, smooth them out with an almost-dry brush before they set. When the front is dry, paint the back.

....

Cabinets

Painting cabinets and cupboards will be easier if you remove all obstructions first, including shelves, drawers, handles, pulls, knobs, and latches. If the hinges on the doors have pins that you can remove easily, take off the doors until the cabinet and cupboard interiors and surfaces have been painted.

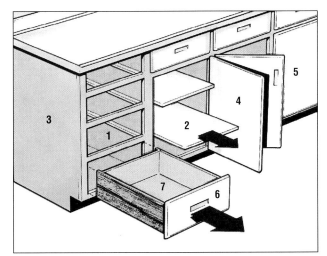

With cabinets, paint in this sequence, starting inside and working out. Paint drawers last. Don't be in too much of a rush to put everything back together again; doors and drawers can stick to tacky surfaces.

The most difficult part of painting cabinets is reaching the barely accessible interior surfaces. Consider shortening the handles on your trim brushes to make things easier. Paint the inside back walls, inside top, side walls, and bottoms, tops, and edges of shelves. Then paint all the exterior surfaces, working from the top down. If the doors are still in place, swing them open and paint the inside surfaces. Then close them partway and paint the outsides. Finally, stand the drawers up on newspapers and paint only their fronts. Do not paint the exterior sides or bottoms of the drawers.

Don't be in too much of a rush to put the cabinets and cupboards back together again. Doors and drawers have an annoying tendency to stick to still-tacky surfaces.

Floors

Once reserved for porches, paint is turning up on wood floors with increasing frequency, particularly in vacation homes. The techniques for painting floors are the same as for painting any other large, flat surface. Be sure to remove all traces of wax and sand the floor lightly to roughen its surface, improving its paint-holding ability. You can use ordinary porch and deck paint, but the color selections may be limited. You can also use a good-quality oil-base enamel. In either case, follow up with two to four coats of clear polyurethane to protect the painted finish.

First, remove all the furniture from the area and cut in the paint around the baseboards with a brush. Then you can use either a wide wall brush or a medium-pile roller for the rest of the floor. If you use an extension handle on a roller you will be able to do the job standing up. Paint your way out of the room. On most wood floors, plan on applying at least two coats of paint, then two, three, or four coats of polyurethane. Let each coat dry to absolute hardness before reentering the room, and wear rubber soled shoes until after the very last coat to avoid marring or scarring the surface.

Painting masonry floors is easier, faster, less expensive, and more common than painting wood floors. Moisture is a major cause of masonry painting problems. Most masonry is porous, and water that comes through it pushes at the paint, causing small particles to come off. In addition, the alkalinity in masonry affects the adhesiveness of some paints and attacks the pigments in others. Paint designed for masonry surfaces can handle rough treatment.

There are a number of latex-based masonry paints that offer the advantages of easy application and easy cleanup. They can be used in damp conditions without adhesion problems. Cement-based paints are frequently used on previously unpainted concrete where very low-pressure moisture is a problem. Epoxy paints are often applied where a hard finish that resists moisture and chemicals is needed. Just make sure that the paint you use is compatible with any existing paint and with the type of masonry you'll be covering. A paint dealer can help you select the appropriate coating.

Before you get down to painting, repair and patch all cracks and holes and allow the patch compounds to cure fully. Then, wearing rubber gloves and goggles, use a ten percent muriatic acid solution to remove efflorescence, the whitish powder that appears in spots on concrete. Mop up the solution, let the area dry, rinse it thoroughly, and let it dry again. Wash the entire floor with a strong detergent or a concrete degreaser. Then, once the floor is dry, and just before painting, vacuum it to get rid of any leftover dirt.

On most masonry floors you can paint with a long-napped roller fitted with an extension handle so you can paint standing up, but you may need a brush for very rough areas. Depending on the surface conditions and the kind of paint you use, you may have to apply a second coat. If so, read the label on the paint can to find out how long you should wait between coats.

Cleaning Up

If you used drop cloths, and you wiped up drips and spatters during the paint job, most of your cleanup work is done. Now all you have to do is clean your tools, track down and remove any stray paint, and put the room back together again.

Cleaning Painting Equipment

Cleaning painting equipment includes not only brushes and rollers, but also reusable drop cloths, paint cans, containers, and roller pans. Don't delay cleaning your equipment one minute longer than necessary. Fresh paint comes out of brushes, rollers, and pans easily; let paint dry for a while and you'll have to put a lot more time and effort into getting it out.

Rollers don't respond well to even thorough cleaning. Some paint residue will remain in the nap of the roller cover. When the roller is exposed to fresh paint later, the dried-in paint can soften and cause streaks in the new finish. Since roller covers are inexpensive, buy a new one for each new job and save yourself the time and effort of trying to clean them. If the ones you bought are too costly to toss out, clean them as best you can, but use them only on projects using the same colors.

When the brush is clean, shake out the excess solvent or water and comb out the bristles.

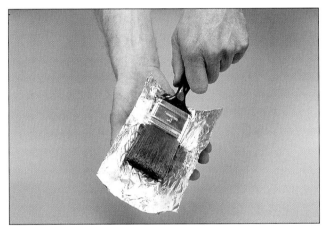

If you must stop painting temporarily, wrap the paintbrush in aluminum foil or put it in a plastic sandwich bag.

If you used latex paint, drag the brushes across the lip of the paint can to remove most of the paint. Then rinse the brushes and rollers under warm tap water and wash with dishwashing detergent. A paintbrush comb can help remove paint residue from the bristles. To get out the excess water, gently squeeze the bristles or take the brush outside and give it a few vigorous flicks. Squeeze the water out of the roller covers. Use paper towels to soak up any remaining water in both brushes and rollers.

With solvent-thinned paints, use the appropriate solvent as identified on the paint can's label. Agitate brushes and rollers in a container of the solvent. Repeat this process to get out all the paint. To clean brushes, pour the solvent into an old coffee can. For rollers, use an inexpensive aluminum foil loaf pan or a clean roller pan. Solvents are toxic and flammable, so don't smoke or work near a water heater or furnace, and make sure there's plenty of ventilation. Use paper towels to blot out the excess solvent from brushes and rollers, then wash everything in warm, soapy water. Hang brushes up until they're dry; set roller covers on end.

Wipe out, wash, and dry roller pans and paint containers. Wipe off the lips of paint cans and hammer down the lids to preserve leftover paint. Store the paint and solvent cans away from extreme heat or cold and out of the reach of children. If you have less than a quart of paint left, store it in a tightly capped glass jar and save it for touch-ups. Brushes and rollers that have been cleaned and dried should be wrapped up before they're stored away. Brushes can go back in the plastic or paper packages they came in, or you can wrap them in aluminum foil. Rollers can be wrapped in kraft paper, foil, or perforated plastic sandwich bags.

For reusable drop cloths of heavy-duty plastic or canvas, wipe off major paint splotches with soap and water and paper towels. Don't use solvent on drop cloths, as it may cause them to dissolve. Let them dry thoroughly, fold them up, and store them with your other equipment for the next project.

Cleaning Windowpanes, Spatters, and Drips

The best time to clean up paint drips and spatters is when they're still wet. If you do miss them, you can clean them up later with some extra effort.

If you used masking tape around windows, peel it off right after painting. Otherwise it may pull off some of the paint. If you painted with a painting shield or freehand, there will most likely be a few errant drops or smudges on the glass. A razor-blade scraper, available at paint and hardware stores, will scrape the paint off the

Use a razor-blade scraper to remove dry paint from glass. Avoid breaking the seal between the paint and windowpane.

glass easily. Avoid breaking the seal between the new paint and the windowpane when you're cleaning up ragged edges around the sash.

Cleaning up drips and spatters on most other surfaces is easier and less time consuming. For latex paint, a soft cloth combined with household detergent and warm water should do the trick. Don't scrub a freshly painted finish, though, even if it is dry to the touch. Many paints don't cure for 30 days or more. For solvent-thinned paints, use a soft cloth and turpentine or mineral spirits to soften and remove dried-on paint droplets. Then, go over the area again with warm water and detergent.

To get paint drips off hardwood, ceramic tile, or resilient flooring, wrap a cloth around a putty knife and gently scrape them up. Then wash the areas with warm, soapy water. Don't use solvent if you can avoid it, as it can damage the finish on the floor.

Finally, put everything in the room back where it was. Replace the caps on ceiling fixtures and rehang drapery hardware and draperies and/or blinds. Put the electrical outlet and switch plates back on. Remount doorknobs and latch plates on doors. Slide the drawers back into the cabinets and replace the pulls, handles, and knobs. Restore and arrange the furniture.

Special Painting Effects

Sometimes extraordinary measures are required to deal with extraordinary conditions, such as a seriously marred wall surface. Or you may want to produce a more decorative painted finish than can be achieved with just a new coat of paint. In either case, several special techniques can fulfill your requirements. The materials and tools are readily available at most retail paint stores.

Texture Painting

What can you do if you have a wall with flaws so serious that ordinary paint won't cover them up? Or what if you want a surface with a more tactile quality? Or maybe you want to try for a weathered or stucco look. For any of these, texturing is a good option. Paints specifically designed for texture work are as thick as pancake batter or wet plaster. Some are gritty and some are not. All are ideal for flawed surfaces and for creating a rustic look. You should still wash the surface, scrape off flaking

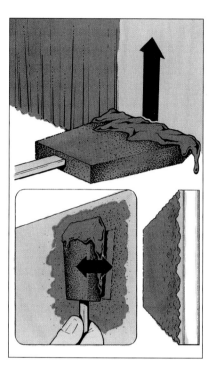

To texture paint with a foam brush, slather it on, then go over the surface with the flat of the brush, patting the paint.

paint, and patch major holes, but you don't need to make the surface perfectly smooth. Texture paints will camouflage most surface blemishes.

Texture paint without granules in it can be applied with special texturing rollers, a wide brush, a urethane foam brush, or even a trowel. Whatever tool you use, smear the paint onto the surface, about 1/16 inch thick. As with regular wall paint, work with sections approximately three feet square.

Create the surface design in one section at a time. A long-napped texturing roller will give you a uniform stippled effect all over. Similar but less regular stippling can be achieved with a foam brush. Apply the paint, then go over the surface with the flat of the brush, patting the paint to create little peaks and valleys. You can use less conventional texturing tools once the paint is on the wall, such as crumpled wax paper or a big sponge. With a coarse brush you can create circles or swirls in the paint. Keep the thickness and the texture uniform from one section to another, overlapping their borders as you go along.

For applying grit-textured paint to ceilings, buy a special long-napped roller or use a synthetic-bristle brush. Instructions on the can explain how to apply the paint.

Striping

You can paint stripes on walls or furniture using some easy techniques.

For medium-wide stripes of one to four or more inches, use a carpenters' level to draw two parallel lines on the wall. Follow the lines with masking tape, pressing the tape down carefully with your thumb or the bowl of a spoon so that paint doesn't seep under its edges. Use a trim brush to paint between the masking tape lines. Wait until the paint is just barely dry to the touch, then slowly peel the tape away from the wall.

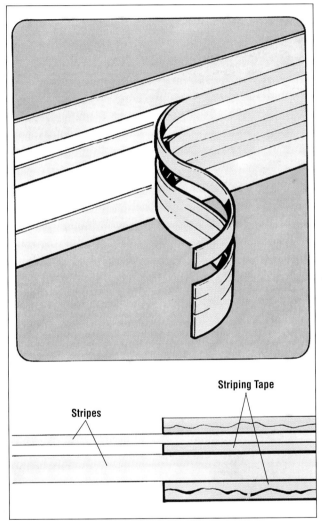

To paint a series of thin, parallel stripes all at one time, use special striping tape, the kind used to paint racing stripes on cars.

A series of thin, parallel stripes can be painted all at one time if you use special striping tape, the kind used to paint racing stripes on cars, available at automobile supply stores. The tape is one inch wide overall, but it has up to eight $\frac{1}{16}$-inch peel-off strips down its length. Again, use a carpenters' level to create a straight line. Follow the line with striping tape. Then peel as many of the removable strips off the roll as you like, automatically exposing what will soon be stripes. Because you're dealing with more tape edges here than before, go back over the tape again, carefully pressing down all the edges to keep the paint from seeping under them. Finally, working with a dry brush, paint over the tape. (A $\frac{1}{2}$-inch trim brush is best for delicate work.) Let the paint dry to the touch, then slowly peel away the tape.

....

Stenciling

Stenciling is one of the oldest and easiest decorative painting techniques. Use it to create borders of various patterns on walls, ceilings, floors, and around windows and doors. Stencils look like the reverse of a coloring book page, with spaces where the pattern would ordinarily be. About the size of a sheet of typewriter paper, reusable stencils are made of thin plastic or heavy paper. They're available at art supply stores or retail paint outlets.

You can make your own stencils, too. Use thin cardboard—shirt cardboard is fine. Sketch a design, transfer it to tracing paper, and cut it out with scissors or a craft knife. Lay the pattern on a piece of cardboard slightly larger than the pattern itself, trace around it, then cut it out.

To transfer your design to the wall, tape up the stencil at all four corners. Use a special stenciling brush—usually round in shape, but flat across the bristles—to apply latex or alkyd paint to the cutout. Pour paint into an old saucer or pie tin. Dab the brush lightly into the paint, then dab it lightly on kraft paper to remove excess paint. You should be working with an almost dry brush. Don't stroke the paint on the stencil. If you do, you'll force the paint under its edges. Instead, use a light up-and-down dabbing motion. Let the paint dry to the touch, peel the stencil slowly away from the wall, and move on to the next area.

If you want to create a border using the same pattern over and over again, it makes sense to buy or make extra stencils so you can continue to work on other areas as the paint dries on the first ones. If your stencil requires two or more colors, paint with only one color at a time and let the first dry before adding the second.

Plastic ready-made stencils are washable and reusable. Those made of heavy paper or cardboard, however, will only last so long before the paint saturates the fibers and weakens the stencil. When that happens, buy or make new ones so that the stencil stays flat against the wall as you paint.

Selecting a Wall Covering

••••••••••••••••••••••••••••••••••••••

With the wide assortment of wall coverings available today, choosing among them can be a challenge equal to putting them up. Notice that they're referred to here as wall *coverings*, rather than wall*paper*. That's because, in addition to regular printed paper, you'll find coverings made of fabric, fiber, plastic, or a combination of materials.

The newer wall coverings have several important advantages over old-fashioned papers. Besides being easier to handle and more rip-resistant, they're also more durable. Many are prepasted at the factory and come with pre-trimmed edges. Combined, these features make installing wall coverings easier and more attractive to do-it-yourselfers than ever before. In fact, over half of all wall coverings sold today are put up by the people who purchase them.

Though color, pattern, and texture will undoubtedly influence your choice of which covering to buy, durability is a crucial factor. Some wall coverings, like some paints, are simply tougher than others, a characteristic that makes them particularly suitable for areas like a child's room, bath, or kitchen. Among commonly used wall coverings, fabric-backed vinyls tolerate the most abuse. Not only are they more washable than painted surfaces, they're more resistant to scuffs and scratches. Next on the scale of durability comes unbacked vinyls, then vinyl-coated paper.

Other wall coverings that are not as strong are more suited for rooms that are subjected to little wear and tear. Among them are regular printed papers, flocked papers, foils, and grass cloths.

Adhesives vary widely as well. Many, if not most, commonly used wall coverings are available prepasted. The dry, factory-applied adhesive on the back becomes sticky when moistened with warm water. After that, it's ready to hang. Use an appropriate premixed or mix-it-yourself adhesive with other wall coverings. For example, paper-backed burlaps, flocks, hand prints, foils, murals, and vinyls should be hung with vinyl adhesive. Regular papers and unbacked burlaps require wheat paste or stainless adhesive. For strippable wall coverings, use strippable adhesive or wheat paste. Some adhesives, especially the wheat pastes, come in mildew-resistant formulas that should be used in high-humidity situations or with any vinyl-coated paper. Vinyl can trap moisture

behind the covering and promote the growth of mildew, which can lead to problems.

Another factor that may influence your choice of coverings is the pattern and whether it was printed by machine or silk-screened by hand. Of the two, machine prints are more common and less expensive. Intricate patterns are more difficult to hang than large patterns because of the time needed to make sure the patterns from one strip are perfectly matched with the strip that follows it.

In silk-screened or hand-printed papers, color can vary slightly from roll to roll. Consequently, instead of just cutting off a strip and pasting it to the wall, minimize variations in shading by matching strips from the same or different rolls as closely as possible before hanging them.

Color is uniform on machine-printed rolls cut from one continuous run, but it may differ slightly from previous or subsequent runs. Because of this, wallpaper manufacturers assign lot or run numbers to each roll. When you buy machine-printed paper, make sure to get rolls that have the same lot number on them or exchange odd-lot numbered rolls for matching-lot rolls.

Color variations can also be found in certain fabric wall coverings, too, and in grass cloth. The fibers in these don't always absorb dyes evenly. The shadings can contribute to the appeal of fabric wall coverings, but try to prevent abrupt color changes by hanging every other strip upside down. The light edges will be adjacent to light edges and dark edges adjacent to dark edges.

Many retail dealers have lending libraries of wall covering books with pages of samples that you can take home for a day or two. This lets you compare the colors of a prospective purchase to the colors of your furniture, carpeting, and painted woodwork. Also, by propping the open book against the wall you can get a good idea of how a covering will look in the room. If your dealer doesn't lend sample books, ask for cuttings of several coverings that you can take home and tape to the wall before making a purchase.

If you plan to paint the ceiling or the woodwork in a room, do it before hanging your new paper. And though it's not absolutely necessary, it's a good idea before papering a previously painted wall to give it a coat of wall sizing, a solution that will roughen the surface slightly. Sizing, which you can apply with a paint roller, makes sliding a strip of wall covering into position on the wall easier and aids in removing the wall covering the next time around.

All the tools you'll need for installing wallpaper typically come prepackaged. If not, buy a trimming knife, cutting wheel, a paper stripper, plumb bob, paste bucket (unless the adhesive comes premixed), sponge,

Vinyl Smoothing
Brush

Artists' Brush

Utility
Knife

Non-Vinyl
Smoothing Brush

Scissors

Seam
Roller

Paste Brush

Sponge

Paper-hanging tools are often sold prepackaged. If an entire kit isn't available, plan on buying a paste bucket, water tray, sponge, paste brush, smoothing brush, artists' brush, utility knife, scissors, and seam roller.

Paste Bucket

Water Tray

paste brush, smoothing brush, seam roller, triangular trimming guide, metal straightedge, and, if you're using prepasted paper, a water tray. For cutting and trimming, a utility knife and scissors will come in handy. You may have use for a putty knife and wall scraper.

How much time a wall covering project takes depends in part on the kind of covering and adhesive you buy and the surface it's intended for. Naturally, if you have to do a lot of patching beforehand, or if you have to remove one or more previous layers of paper, the preparation alone could take a weekend. Otherwise, even a first-time paper hanger can expect to finish a typical 12×15-foot bedroom in a single day. Whatever you do, however, don't rush the job. Establishing straight lines, matching patterns, and trimming and cutting around windows, doors, woodwork, and light switches is time consuming, but doing those things slowly and carefully makes the difference between a professional-looking job and a

botched one. Besides, who says you have to finish the job in one day or even a weekend? You can stop whenever you have to and pick up hours or even days later without jeopardizing a successful job.

Repairing and Removing Wallpaper

• •

D espite the remarkable durability of today's wall coverings, they are not indestructible. When damage occurs or flaws turn up, it's best to fix them as soon as possible. Defects have an annoying way of enlarging themselves. The longer you wait, the larger they get; and the larger the defect, the tougher the repair job.

Repairing Blisters, Seams, and Torn Sections

Blisters, which result from excess adhesive or air trapped in bubbles between the wall and the backside of the wall covering, can show up within minutes, days, weeks, or even years after the project is finished. The easiest way

89

to deal with them is to prevent them in the first place. Smooth out a newly applied strip of paper thoroughly with a smoothing brush, a straightedge, or a sponge. If you encounter blisters, work them toward the nearest edge of the strip to release trapped air or excess adhesive.

Blisters located in inconspicuous places won't be noticed. If you're using an untreated printed paper, small blisters may go away by themselves as the paste dries and the paper contracts. However, if a blister is still there an hour after the strip has been applied to the wall, it's not likely that it will disappear on its own.

Blisters that are only an hour or two old can often be repaired following these steps:

Step 1: Use a straight pin to puncture the blister.

Step 2: With your thumbs, gently squeeze out the trapped blob of still-wet adhesive or trapped air through the hole, being careful not to rip the paper.

Step 3: If that doesn't work, use a single-edge razor blade or utility knife to slit a small "X" in the wall covering and peel back the tips of the slit.

Step 4: If there's a lump of adhesive underneath, gently scrape it out. If air was the cause, use an artists' brush to apply a small amount of adhesive behind the flaps, then press the flaps back down. The edges may overlap a little, but this overlapping is seldom detectable later.

To repair a blister in wallpaper, slit it twice to form an "X." Peel back the tips of the slit, brush paste into the blister, and smooth the paper down.

Loose seams are even easier to repair:

Step 1: Lift the seam slightly, use an artists' brush to work some paste under the seam, then just press it back down and go over it with a seam roller.

Step 2: If the seam shows any tendency to pull away, tack it in place with two or three straight pins stuck through the paper and into the wall until the adhesive is dry. The tiny holes won't show.

Step 3: If you find a loose seam in overlapped vinyl wall covering, use a vinyl-to-vinyl adhesive to stick it back down.

Holes and tears in wall coverings require more effort to repair, but if done with care the repairs will be nearly invisible. Here's how:

Step 1: Use a single-edge razor blade to trim off any ragged edges around the damaged area.

Step 2: Tear out a slightly bigger patch from a piece of scrap wall covering. Hold the scrap faceup with one hand, and rotate the scrap as you gently tear out a round patch. With practice, you'll have a patch with an intact design on the printed side of the paper and a slightly feathered edge on the backside.

Step 3: Spread a thin coating of adhesive on the back of the patch and place it over the damaged area.

Step 4: Line up the pattern on the patch with the pattern on the wall as best you can. A perfect pattern alignment may not be possible, but the match will be close enough to escape detection.

Another technique for repairing holes is called double cutting. With this method you create a patch that is perfectly sized to fit the damaged area.

Step 1: Cut a square scrap of wall covering about an inch larger all the way around than the damaged section.

Step 2: Place the scrap over the hole and align the pattern with the pattern on the wall.

Step 3: Hold it in place with masking tape or thumbtacks, whichever is the least likely to damage the wall covering.

Step 4: Using a metal ruler held firmly against the wall over the scrap, take a very sharp utility knife and cut a square slightly bigger than the hole itself through both layers of wall covering.

Step 5: Remove the scrap and the square patch you've just made and set them aside. Use the end of the utility knife to lift one corner of the original wallpaper square with the hole, and peel this square off the wall.

Step 6: Paste the back of the new patch and press it into the cleaned-out area on the wall, making sure the patterns are once again aligned.

Removing Wallpaper

You can successfully paper over old wall coverings, but it's not always a good idea because the moisture in adhesives can cause both the old and new coverings to peel away from the wall. Also, if previous strips of wall covering have been lapped at the seams, these lap marks will show through the new covering. As necessary, sand the seams smooth, tear away any loose strips, and re-paste loose edges around butt seams or defects before applying the new covering. If you're papering over foil or vinyl wall coverings, go over the shiny areas lightly with coarse sandpaper and then vacuum or wipe the sanding dust off the wall.

Stripping off the old wall covering is usually wiser than leaving it on. New coverings adhere better to stripped-down surfaces. Depending on the wall covering and the kind of wall it's on, there are several ways to approach the job.

Strippable Papers

Though most strippable wall coverings are characterized by smooth, plasticlike textures (including vinyl, fabric-backed vinyl, or fabric-backed paper), the only way to find out if a covering is really strippable is to try peeling it off the wall. Here's how:

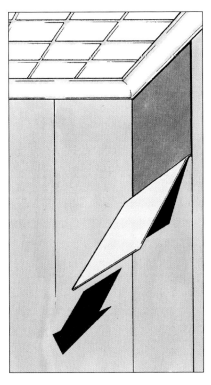

To remove strippable paper, lift up one corner and pull the paper down the wall, keeping it as close to the wall as possible to minimize the possibility of tearing.

Step 1: Pry the paper up in an inconspicuous corner at the top of a wall with the tip of a utility knife.

Step 2: Grasp the tip of the corner and, keeping it as close to the wall as possible, try to pull it down the surface of the wall. Pulling it toward you and away from the wall increases the likelihood of tearing it. If a covering is strippable, it should peel away from the wall when you apply steady, moderate pressure. If not, you're probably dealing with a nonstrippable paper that you will have to soak, steam, or dry-strip off the wall. Do not soak or use steam-stripping methods on drywall, though. The moisture can soften the wall's kraft-paper surface and its gypsum core. Instead, use a dry-strip method.

Slitting and Soaking

With this technique, you make horizontal slits in the surface of the old wall covering with a razor blade or a special tool called a paper stripper, available at wall covering stores. The slits, made eight or ten inches apart, allow warm, soapy water or a liquid paper remover to get behind the paper and soften the adhesive so you can pull or scrape the paper off plaster walls. You can apply either solution with a sponge or a spray bottle. *Caution: If you spray on a liquid paper remover, use a painters' mask to keep from inhaling chemical vapors.*

Step 1: Apply the water or the paper remover and let it soak in for a few minutes.

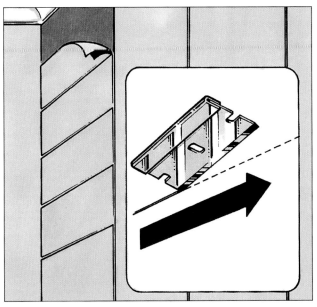

One way to remove non-strippable paper is to slit and soak it. Make slits at eight- or ten-inch intervals; allow soapy water or a liquid paper remover to get behind the paper and soften the adhesive.

Step 2: Do the same thing on the next strip, then go back to the first and wet it again top to bottom.

Step 3: Use a 3½-inch-wide wall scraper with a flexible blade to begin stripping. Slide the blade under the top edge of one of the horizontal slits and, holding it at about a 30-degree angle, push up on the wet paper. A scraper-width section should rip along the sides of the blade and wrinkle up above it as you push.

Step 4: Continue pushing as long as the paper comes off. If the strip of scraped paper breaks, resoak that area and start scraping at another slit. If, after repeated soaking and scraping attempts, the adhesive is clearly not yielding, you'll have to use another method.

On walls made of drywall, use a paper stripper to make the horizontal slits as before, but don't wet the paper. Just slowly scrape or peel it away from the wall.

Steaming

Many tool rental and wallpaper outlets rent electrical steamers to do-it-yourselfers. These appliances typically consist of an electrically heated water tank connected by a long hose to a steamer plate with a perforated face. Here's how they're used:

Step 1: Once the water is hot, hold the plate against the wall until you see the wall covering darken with moisture around the edges of the plate. Start on a single strip and work from the top down.

Step 2: After about half of the strip has been steamed, lift a top corner with a fingernail or a utility knife and attempt to peel the paper downward. If that doesn't work, resort to a wall scraper. You may have to steam the same areas two or three times to loosen the adhesive behind the paper.

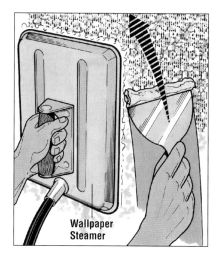

Removing old wallpaper is no easy job. You can rent a steamer, but you still have to scrape off most of the covering with a wide-blade putty knife.

Wallpaper Steamer

Estimating Wall Coverings

Smart do-it-yourselfers calculate precisely how much wall covering materials are needed, then buy it all at once.

Wall coverings are sold in rolls that are 15 to 54 inches wide. Regardless of the width, a single roll contains about 36 square feet; with trimming and waste, figure on getting only about 30 square feet of coverage per roll.

To calculate how many rolls you'll need for a given room, find its perimeter by measuring the length of each wall and adding all four measurements together. For example, in a 9×12-foot room, the perimeter equals 42 feet (9 + 9 + 12 + 12). Now measure the room's height—8 feet, say—and multiply your first figure (42) by the second (8) to get the total square footage of the walls (336 square feet). Divide this figure by 30—the average usable number of square feet in a typical roll of wall covering—to find out how many rolls you'll need. In this case, 11 rolls will do the job.

If there is only one door and one window, ignore them in your calculations; if you have multiple doors and windows, calculate their square foot totals by multiplying the height by the width of each and adding them together to get a square foot total you can subtract from your overall total. For instance, if there was a 3×7-foot entrance door and two 3×7-foot sliding doors in our 9×12-foot room, we would subtract 63 square feet from our previous total of 336 square feet, giving us a final figure of 273 square feet. Dividing by 30, then, we'd need 10 rolls instead of 11.

If you're papering a ceiling, multiply its width by its length (9×12) to determine the surface area in square feet (108). Again, divide the total by 30 to determine how many rolls of wall covering will be required (4).

Wallpaper borders are sold by the yard, not by the roll. If you plan to put up a border all the way around the room, add up the distance around the room in feet, then divide by three to find out how many yards of border to buy.

SELECTING WALL COVERINGS

Types	Uses	Adhesives	Installation
Lining Paper	As base over rough surfaces, especially for murals, foils, burlaps.	Pre-sized wheat paste.	Butt seams.
Printed Papers Vinyl-coated Fabric-backed Untreated	Living and dining rooms, master bedrooms.	Wheat or stainless.	Butt or lap seams; paper fragile when wet.
Vinyl Coverings Paper-backed Fabric-backed	Kitchen, bathroom, children's bedrooms, halls, laundry room.	Vinyl paste, mildew-resistant.	Butt pre-trimmed seams; use plenty of paste to cover backing.
Flocked Coverings Paper-backed Vinyl-backed Foil-backed	Entranceways, halls, dining rooms, formal areas.	Vinyl for foil- or vinyl-backed; wheat for paper-backed.	Keep paste off flocked surface; blot spots, don't rub.
Foil Coverings Paper-backed Fabric-backed	Halls, alcoves, breakfast nooks.	Mildew-resistant vinyl paste.	Use lining paper and avoid creases. Use caution around outlets and switches.
Prepasted Coverings Paper Vinyl Flock Foil	Same as non-pasted coverings of same type.	Factory-applied, water-activated.	Use water tray, follow soaking instructions.
Textured Coverings Vinyl Silk Grass Cloth Burlap Paper	Living and dining rooms, bedroom, den.	Vinyl for vinyl-backed, otherwise wheat or stainless.	Use paste sparingly (covering sensitive to moisture). Butt seams. Use over lining paper.
Cork Paper-backed Fabric-backed	Dens, family rooms.	Wheat paste for paper-backed; vinyl for vinyl-backed or fabric-backed.	Use lining paper. Roll seams immediately.
Murals Paper-backed Vinyl-backed	Living, dining, and family rooms, bedroom.	Wheat paste for paper-backed; vinyl for vinyl-backed or fabric-backed.	Requires precise pattern matching. Use lining paper, roll seams.

Papering Walls

Putting up a wall covering is something you can master within a very short period of time. The materials and techniques are simply repeated all the way around the room. After the first strip is up, you'll be amazed at how fast the job goes.

Cut the first strip of wall covering four to six inches longer than the height of the room. Place it pattern side up on the pasting table. Cut the second piece and all subsequent pieces for the same wall to match the pattern and length of the first strip. Then paste and hang them in order.

Using Prepasted Wallpaper

The advantages of prepasted wall covering should be evident from the name. Because the water-activated adhesive is applied at the factory, you don't have to bother with paste brushes, rollers, or adhesive mixes. Consequently, you can paper a room faster than with other wall coverings.

To activate the adhesive, soak sheets of wall covering briefly in a special water box available from the wallpaper store. Here's how:

Step 1: Place the box on the floor directly next to the wall where the paper will go, then pour water into the box until it is about two-thirds full. Position a stepladder in front of the box.

Step 2: Cut a strip of paper to length, reroll it loosely so the pattern is on the inside, and dunk it in the water-filled box. The manufacturer's directions will tell you how long to let the paper soak, anywhere from ten seconds to one minute. If the roll floats in the water, slip a mixing spoon inside to weigh it down for the specified amount of time.

Step 3: Grasp the top end of the strip at both corners and let it unroll as you climb the ladder. Take your time at this point, letting the water cascade off the strip and back into the box.

Step 4: Apply paper to the wall as described below in "Placing the First Strip."

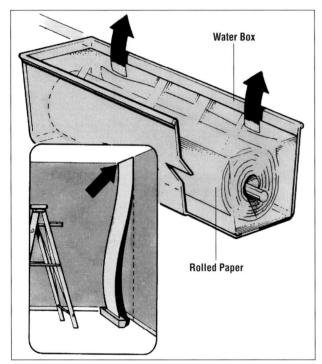

To activate the adhesive on prepasted wall coverings, soak them briefly in a special water box. After the paper is soaked, grasp the top end of the strip at both corners and let it unroll as you climb the ladder.

Applying Paste to Paper

Applying paste to wallpaper can be very messy, so keep a container of clean water close by, along with clean rags and a sponge. To keep the paste off the patterned side of the paper, wash your hands frequently and wipe off the handles of brushes, seam rollers, and cutting tools as you go along.

Knowing how to paste a strip of wallpaper properly will keep the paste in its place. Follow this guide and you'll have a lot less cleaning up to do both during and after the job.

Step 1: Cut a strip of paper to length and place it pattern side down on the table. Let the top edge hang over the edge of the table. The bottom edge and one side of the paper should hang over the tabletop by only about ¼ inch.

Step 2: Brush paste on the bottom quarter of the strip, the quarter that extends slightly beyond the tabletop.

Step 3: Still working from the bottom, slide the strip over the other edge of the table and again let the bottom and the edge of the paper go beyond the tabletop by ¼ inch. Paste the other bottom quarter of the strip. Slightly less than half the length of the strip should have paste on it at this time.

Step 4: Fold the pasted portion of the strip on top of itself so that paste meets paste. Do not crease the fold.

Step 5: Pull the strip toward you so that the top of the strip is in the position the bottom was when you began. Paste one top quarter of the strip, shift the paper to the other edge of the table, and paste the last quarter.

Step 6: Fold the strip so that paste meets paste and the top edge of the strip meets the bottom edge. Again, do not crease the fold. Now the strip is pattern side up with the pasted surfaces inside. There's no paste on the table to be wiped off before pasting another strip.

Placing the First Strip

It's vital to establish a straight, vertical line down the wall and to align the outside edge of the first strip of wall covering with that line. That way, all the following strips (and the pattern on them) will fall into line almost automatically. Start off with a tilt, however, and the problem will compound itself with each successive strip.

Because there is no such thing as a perfectly plumb wall or a perfectly level floor or ceiling, you can't just align the edge of the paper with a corner of the room and keep going. By the time you work your way around to the starting point, the last strip may be seriously out of whack. Therefore, you must establish a plumb line for the first strip.

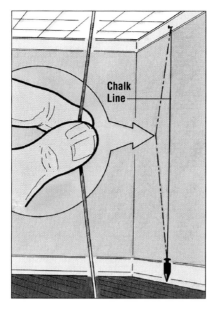

To place the first strip of wallpaper, measure the paper's width from a corner, less one inch. Then snap a chalk line. Check the chalk line with a level to make sure it's accurate.

Chalk Line

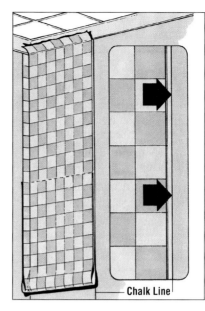

Align the first strip of paper with the chalk line and press the paper to the wall. Let the excess paper at the top, bottom, and side lap onto adjacent surfaces.

Chalk Line

Step 1: In an inconspicuous corner, mount a stepladder to measure out the width of a roll of wall covering minus one inch. Drive a nail into the wall near the ceiling at this point.

Step 2: On the nail, hang the looped end of the plumb bob, unreel the chalked string, and let the bob hang to within about an inch of the floor. When the bob stops swinging, pull the string taut, hold it against the bottom of the wall with the thumb of one hand, and reach up and pinch the string with the other. Pull it out from the wall an inch or so and let it snap back. The chalk from the string will give you a perfectly plumb line on the wall. Take down the plumb bob, reel in the chalked string, and remove the nail. Check the chalk line with a level to make sure it's accurate.

Step 3: Align the outside edge of the first strip of pasted paper with your chalk line. Press the paper to the wall using a smoothing brush or sponge. Let the excess at the top and bottom of the strip lap onto the ceiling or the baseboard. You will trim the excess after all of the strips have been pasted up. Smooth the overlap down on the adjoining wall.

Step 4: Place the second strip of wall covering as near as possible to the outside edge of the first strip. Slide it toward the edge of the first strip until the edges of both strips butt. Slide it up or down slightly to match the pattern. Smooth it with a brush or a sponge, working air bubbles and excess adhesive out from the middle of the strip toward the edges.

Step 5: Repeat the process around the room. Except for papering around corners, doors or windows, the procedure remains basically the same for the rest of the project.

....

Seaming

A seam is the joint between any two strips of wall covering. There are three basic kinds of seams: lapped, wire-edge, and butt. In the past, the lap seam was the most common. It's rarely used anymore because it leaves an unsightly ridge where one strip of paper overlaps another by ¼ to ½ inch. The wire-edge seam is also a lap seam, but much smaller, about 1/16 inch. It's still used with wall coverings that don't butt smoothly and those

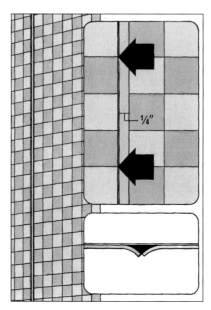

¼"

To make a butt seam, lightly stick up the second strip about ¼ inch from the first, slide the second strip until it bumps into the first and slightly buckles both strips, and align the patterns.

that have a tendency to shrink and leave a gap between strips. The butt seam, however, is by far the most popular today because it produces a joint between strips of wall covering that is all but invisible. To make a butt seam:

Step 1: Lightly stick up the second strip about ¼ inch from the first and align the patterns.

Step 2: Slide the second strip of paper over until it bumps into the first. The edges of both strips should buckle slightly when this collision occurs.

Step 3: Install several strips of paper in this manner before finishing off the first seam. As the adhesive dries, the paper will contract just enough to make the buckle in the joint flatten out against the wall.

Step 4: Fifteen or 20 minutes after you've made a butt joint, go over it with a seam roller to press the edges together and to the wall. *Caution: Don't use a seam roller on flocked, foil, or textured wall coverings, because it can damage the paper. Instead, use a sponge or your hands to finish the seams.*

If you must lap the seams, make the laps as small as possible to create a wire-edge joint. To do this, lap the edge of the second strip over the first by about ½ inch. Then slide the second strip away from the first until the lap measures only about ¹⁄₁₆ inch. If the wall covering is patterned, be sure the patterns match from strip to strip.

Because vinyl wall covering will not stick to itself, its seams should be butted. Where that's not possible, the

Fifteen or 20 minutes after you've made a butt joint, go over it with a seam roller to press the edges to the wall. Don't roll flocked, foil, or textured wall coverings.

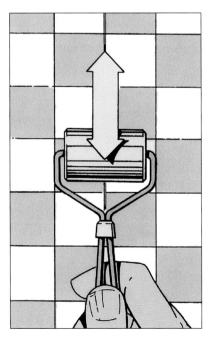

second-best solution is to double-cut them. To double-cut vinyl wall covering:

Step 1: Overlap the first strip with the second by about ½ inch. Smooth the lap seam down lightly.

Step 2: Using a metal straightedge to guide your utility knife, cut through both layers of the lap, slicing downward through the middle of the overlap.

Step 3: Peel off the top layer of the overlap, pull back the edge of the strip of wall covering you just put up, and peel off the cut-through edge of the first strip.

Step 4: Press both new edges together with a sponge and seam roller.

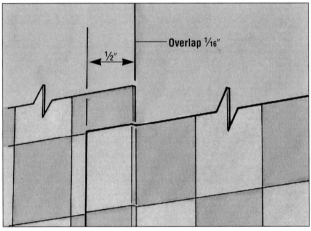

If you must lap seams, lap the edge of the second strip over the first by about ½ inch, then slide the second strip away from the first until the lap measures about ¹⁄₁₆ inch.

Papering Around Corners

The last strip of paper you put up on a wall should be made to turn any corner it encounters. Because perfectly straight walls and perfectly plumb corners are rare, never start or stop a strip of paper at or in a corner. If you do, there will be a noticeable gap in the seam, or the pattern will be out of alignment. Instead, plan to run the final strip of paper on the wall into or around the corner and then master the double-cutting technique outlined before. Here's how to successfully negotiate a turn:

Step 1: On inside corners, measure the distance from the edge of the last strip of paper you put up to the corner of the room. Do this at the top as well as at the bottom of the strip. Then take the wider of those two measurements and add ½ inch. Cut the next strip of paper vertically to make a strip that is as wide as your final measurement.

At an inside corner, measure—both top and bottom—from the edge of the last strip of paper. Take the wider of these measurements, add ½ inch, and cut a strip to this dimension.

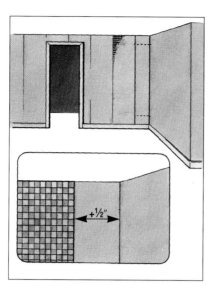

Step 2: Paste and hang this strip, butting it to the edge of the previous strip and running it into and out of the corner. Smooth it on both walls and trim at top and bottom as necessary.

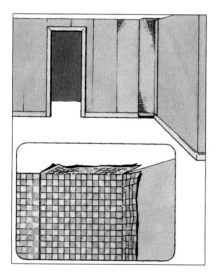

Paste and hang the corner strip, butting it to the edge of the previous strip and running it into and out of the corner. Trim at top and bottom as necessary.

Step 3: Establish a plumb line on the adjacent and as-yet-unpapered wall, as you did when you put up the first strip. Subtract one inch from the roll's width, measure out this distance from the corner of the room, and snap a chalk line from ceiling to floor. Align the outside edge of the first strip on the unpapered wall with the chalk line. You have now overlapped the corner in both directions.

Step 4: Use a sharp utility knife and a straightedge to double-cut both thicknesses on one of the two walls, getting as close to the corner as you can. Peel away the top layer of paper, lift the new

edge of the top strip, and peel off the inner layer of the paper. Smooth both edges together and use a seam roller to flatten them to the wall.

Step 5: When you get to an outside corner, wrap the wall covering an inch or two around the bend. A wrap of much more than that may wrinkle or buckle when you try to smooth it out. Overlap the next strip on the unpapered wall. Then double-cut the overlap as before, but about an inch away from the corner.

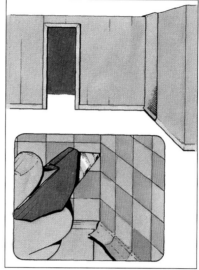

Again, establish a chalk line the width of the roll minus one or two inches from the corner. Cut and hang a strip here, aligning it with the chalk line, then double-cut at the corner.

Cutting In Around Woodwork, Switches, and Outlets

Papering around windows, doors, built-ins, and woodwork is time consuming but relatively easy. To make the work easier, use a sharp utility knife and change the blade as soon as it shows any signs of pulling or tearing the wall covering.

Step 1: Use a smoothing brush or a sponge to make a snug fit around obstacles, pounding lightly against the paper with the bristles of the brush. Let the paper overlap the window or door frame, then run the tip of your utility knife into the joint. Around windows and doors, you may be able to slide the blade of the knife behind the frame while trimming the paper to fit.

Step 2: Around large openings or obstacles, make the longest cuts first. At a door, for example, slice the paper from the top of the frame to the baseboard and discard or set aside this strip. Next, crease the flap of paper at the top of the frame and make a horizontal cut, using the frame as a guide. Most such cuts can be done freehand, but you can use a metal straightedge if you desire. Force the knife into the junction between wall and woodwork and guide the tip of the knife along the edge.

At door and window frames, let the paper overlap the frame, then run the tip of your utility knife into the joint. You may be able to slide the knife blade behind the frame.

Step 3: For outlets and switches, just remove the faceplates and paper right over the recessed electrical boxes. With your utility knife, trim away the overlap, cutting a rectangle in the paper the same size as the box itself. *Caution: Wall covering paste is a superb conductor of electricity, so plan on cutting off the power to the circuits you're working on at the circuit breaker box. If you need additional light, run an extension cord to a "live" outlet in another room.*

Paper right over switches and outlets. Turn off the power, then cut around the box. You can also paper the faceplates.

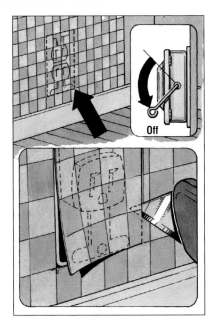

Step 4: To paper the faceplates, loosely remount the plate on the wall. Cut a rectangle of wallpaper slightly larger than the plate. Place the paper over the plate, folding the top edge over the top edge of the plate so that the pattern on the plate will match the pattern on the wall. Once you've matched the pattern at the top, make a crease in the paper and repeat the procedure to get a match at the sides. Remove the creased paper and the plate. Position the plate facedown on the pasted side of the paper. Trim off the corners of the paper diagonally so that you can then fold the four edges over the back of the plate without overlapping them. Cut an "X" in the paper where the toggle switch will go through, pull the flaps through the hole, and paste them down.

For best results around both wall-mounted and ceiling-mounted light fixtures, take them down completely. Then you can paper right over the electrical box. Afterward, use the inside of the box as a guide for your knife and cut away the paper covering the opening.

Applying Specialty Coverings

●●●●●●●●●●●●●●●●●●●●●●●●●●●●●●●●●●●●●●

There are two popular reasons for using an out-of-the-ordinary wall covering: Either the wall surface is rough or your taste in decoration dictates something special. In either case, applying specialty coverings can be as easy as applying standard coverings.

Vinyl

Washable, durable, and heavier than regular printed papers, vinyl wall coverings are available in extra-wide rolls that can reduce the number of seams and trims. They are usually more strippable than ordinary papers. Perhaps their greatest value, though, is that vinyl wall coverings can cover up defects that paint or thinner wall coverings can't begin to hide.

Because vinyl is not as fragile as printed paper, you don't have to worry about punctures or ripped edges.

Vinyl wall coverings work best if the seams are butted and rolled. Vinyl will not stick to itself, so if you have to resort to a lap seam you'll need to have some vinyl-to-vinyl adhesive on hand.

Most vinyl-to-wall adhesives come premixed, another advantage over paper and mix-it-yourself wheat pastes.

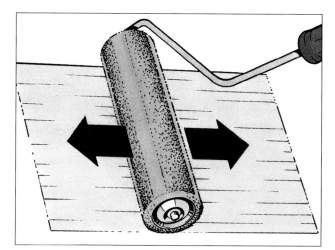

Most vinyl-to-wall adhesives come premixed, and you can spread them onto the vinyl with a paint roller equipped with a mohair cover.

You can spread the adhesive on the vinyl with a paint roller equipped with a mohair roller cover. Afterward, apply the vinyl strips to the wall as you would any other wall covering, but use a smoothing brush with ¾-inch bristles, which are shorter and sturdier than the longer-bristled brushes used on paper. With really heavy-weight vinyl, even a short-bristle brush may not do an adequate job of smoothing. If that's the case, use a straightedge, such as a strip of hardboard or a yardstick.

Smooth three or four vinyl strips on the wall and then go back to make the trims and look for blisters. Puncture blisters with a needle or the tip of a single-edge razor blade and then squeeze out the trapped air or excess adhesive.

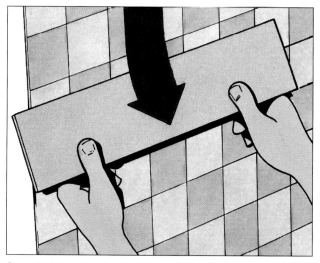

Smoothing brushes for vinyl have short, sturdy ¾-inch bristles. With really heavy-weight vinyl, you may need to smooth with a straightedge, such as a strip of hardboard.

Fabric

Ordinarily, fabric wall coverings are seen more in offices and business settings than in homes, even though they are good at giving texture and imparting a cozy look to walls. Fabric wall covering, which is quite expensive compared to more common papers, is usually sold by the yard instead of by the roll. But one of its chief advantages is that it's available in 45-, 54-, and 60-inch widths.

Most of the fabric coverings designed to be used on walls are backed with paper. With these you can use either wheat paste or a stainless cellulose paste. Unbacked fabric is far more difficult to deal with and is not recommended, especially for do-it-yourself paperhangers. If you do purchase an unbacked fabric, however, use a powdered vinyl adhesive and brush it on the wall, not on the back of the fabric. No matter which kind of fabric covering you decide to use, be sure to put lining paper on the walls first so you are able to get a good bond between wall and fabric.

Paper-backed fabric can be smoothed either with your hands or with a smoothing brush. Unbacked fabric requires that you trim off the selvages with scissors before pasting the fabric to the wall. Another disadvantage to unbacked fabric is that fabric will often absorb moisture from the adhesive on the wall. The extra weight makes it heavy and gives it a tendency to droop. Moisture also may allow the fabric to stretch, which can be hazardous because as the adhesive dries and the moisture evaporates, the fabric may shrink and seams may open. If possible, pat and smooth the fabric on the wall with your hands, pulling it taut but not out of shape.

Foil

Both expensive and very delicate, foil coverings are often used to add dramatic sparkle to entire rooms, entries, or alcoves. Foil coverings must be carefully applied in order to avoid imparting just the wrong kind of drama to a space. Most foil coverings are backed with either paper or fabric and should be used with a vinyl adhesive, since water in wheat paste can't evaporate through the foil.

Install foil wall coverings over a lining paper; because of the reflective surface, foil wall coverings tend to emphasize the tiniest bumps or pockmarks in a wall. Be very careful when you put it up, as it is easy to wrinkle or crease the foil. And instead of a smoothing brush, which may scratch the foil, smooth it on the wall with a sponge or a folded towel. Bond the seams the same way, because it's possible that a wooden seam roller may dent the foil.

Understanding Wood Furniture

• •

Unlike most of the other components that make up your home, your furniture is movable. It goes with you when you move, it's rearranged or shifted periodically, and it may be handed down for generations. You add to your furniture collection gradually, and you may end up with more old pieces than new. Because it gets moved around, and because it takes a lot of abuse over years of service, your wood furniture needs regular care to keep it looking good. And when it needs repairing, you should know how to do the job yourself.

Furniture Construction

Like all the other components of your home, furniture is easy to work with when you know how it's put together. Essentially, all furniture is made to provide comfort and convenience and is judged on the basis of how well it succeeds in providing them. To function well, all wood furniture—no matter what type and age—must be sturdy, steady, and securely joined. Of course, there's more to good furniture than sturdy legs. Good wood and workmanship make good furniture, age enhances its value, and style is also important. All of these factors affect the quality and usefulness of your furniture as well as the techniques you need to know.

Furniture Finishes

Furniture finishes can be classified into several basic types: varnish, penetrating resin, shellac, lacquer, wax, and oil. All of these finishes are designed to protect the wood and to bring out its natural beauty, and all of them can be assessed in terms of how well they accomplish these objectives. Choosing a finish comes down to two essential factors: how you want the wood to look and how durable you want the finished surface to be.

Of the six most common finishes, all can be beautiful, but when it comes to durability, two types outperform all the others: varnish and penetrating resin. Varnish, the most durable of all finishes, is available in high-gloss, satin, and flat forms, for whatever surface shine you want. Applying varnish can be difficult, but the results are worth the work. Penetrating resin sinks into the wood to give it a natural look and feel; it is easy to apply and durable. The other furniture finishes do have their advantages. Oil produces a very natural finish, and shellac dries fast and is easy to use. But for most refinishing, varnish or penetrating resin is often the best choice.

Whatever finish you choose, it's important to know exactly what you're working with. Some finishes can be mixed and some cannot. Each finish has its own preferred application techniques, and each finish requires different tools and materials. Before you buy and apply a finish, always read the ingredient and application information on the container. And always follow the manufacturer's instructions and recommendations.

The one requirement common to all finishes is a dust-free environment during application. Providing this environment isn't easy, but it can be done. Consider using a finish that dries with a matte or flat surface. This type of finish gives you the opportunity to remove dirt and lint with rubbing abrasives. Before starting to work, clean your working area thoroughly and let the dust settle for about 24 hours. Keep doors and windows closed. Don't work near heating/cooling registers or next to open windows, and never work outside. Wear lint-free clothes, and don't wear gloves.

Before applying any finish, make sure you have all the materials you need. Set up the working space so that the piece of furniture will be between you and the light to make it easy to see dust and lint on the newly finished surfaces. Work with clean tools and new finishing materials, and make sure you have adequate light and ventilation. Clean all surfaces carefully with a tack cloth before applying the finish; if necessary, give the piece of furniture a final going-over with mineral spirits to remove dirt and fingerprints. Let the wood dry thoroughly before applying the finish. To keep the new finish smooth, remove specks of dust and lint from wet surfaces with an artists' brush or lint picker.

In most cases, how a piece of furniture stands up to wear is as important as how it looks, and durability is a primary consideration in choosing a finish. The most durable finishes, varnish and penetrating resin, are thus the two basic finishes for refinishing. Varnish is the more protective of the two because it is a surface coat; damage to the varnish does not always extend to the wood. Penetrating resin hardens in the wood itself; although it doesn't protect the surface from damage as effectively as varnish, it may stand up to heavy use better because it's easy to reapply and doesn't chip or craze.

Furniture Repairs

The first step in giving wood furniture long life is to take care of needed repairs. This means repairing veneer and hardware. After this is done, surfaces can be refinished to enhance the function and beauty of wood furniture.

Repairing Veneer

Most wood furniture is constructed using veneer rather than solid woods to keep costs down. Because veneer is only a thin layer of wood attached with glue to a solid base, it is very vulnerable to damage. On old furniture, the glue that holds the veneer is often not water-resistant. Prolonged humidity or exposure to water can soften the glue, letting the veneer blister, crack, or peel. Veneer is easily damaged from the surface, and old veneers are often cracked, buckled, or broken, with chips or entire pieces missing.

In most cases, as long as the veneer layer is in good shape, the thinness that makes it damage-prone also makes it easy to repair. Undamaged veneer can be re-glued; chips and bare spots can be filled with matching veneer. If you're careful to match the grain, the repairs will hardly show.

Blisters

Small blisters in veneer can usually be flattened with heat. Here's how:

Step 1: Set a sheet of smooth cardboard on the surface to protect it, and cover the cardboard with a clean cloth.

Step 2: Press the blistered area firmly with a medium-hot iron; if there are several blisters, move the iron slowly and evenly back and forth. Be careful not to touch the exposed surface with the iron. Check the surface every few minutes or so as you work, and stop pressing as soon as the blisters have flattened.

Step 3: Once done, put a weight on the cardboard for 24 hours. Then remove the cardbord, and wax and polish the surface.

Large blisters must usually be slit because the veneer has swelled. To repair a large blister:

Step 1: Using a sharp craft knife or a single-edge razor blade, carefully cut the blister open down the

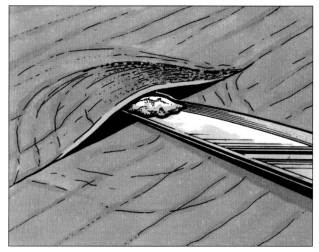

To repair a large blister in veneer, slit it and insert a little glue under the edges; then flatten it with heat.

middle, along the grain of the wood. Be very careful not to cut into or damage the base wood.

Step 2: Cover the surface and apply heat, checking every few seconds to see if the glue has softened. If the glue has deteriorated and does not soften, carefully scrape it out and insert a small amount of carpenters' glue under the slit edges of the bubble with the tip of the knife. Be careful not to use too much glue; if necessary, wipe off any excess as the blister flattens.

Step 3: As soon as one edge of the slit bubble overlaps the other, carefully shave off the overlapping edge with a craft knife or razor blade.

Step 4: Heat the blister again. If the edges overlap further, shave the overlapping edge again.

Step 5: When the blister is completely flattened, weight the repair area solidly for 24 hours.

Step 6: Wax and polish the entire surface.

Loose Veneer

Lifted veneer occurs most often at the corners of tabletops and on cabinet and dresser edges, legs, and drawer fronts. If the loose veneer is undamaged, it can be re-glued. Here's how:

Step 1: Remove the residue of old glue left on the back of the veneer and on the base wood. With a sharp craft knife or razor blade, carefully scrape out as much of the old glue as possible. Don't lift the veneer any further; if you bend it up, you'll damage it.

Loose veneer can be re-glued. Apply glue to the base wood, press the veneer into place, and clamp it firmly.

Step 2: Clean the bonding surfaces with mineral spirits or benzene to remove any residue; glue left under the loose area will interfere with the new adhesive. If any glue still remains, sand the bonding surfaces lightly with fine-grit sandpaper, and then wipe them clean with a soft cloth moistened with mineral spirits. If more than one veneer layer is loose, clean each layer the same way.

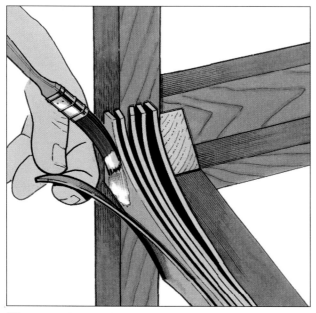

When more than one layer has separated, work from the bottom up and from the inside out to re-glue each layer.

Step 3: To re-glue the veneer, apply contact cement or carpenters' glue to both bonding surfaces and let it set as directed by the manufacturer; if necessary, set a small tack or two between the layers to keep them from touching. Or apply carpenters' glue to the base wood, spreading it on along the grain with a small brush. Then, starting at the solidly attached veneer and working out toward the loose edge, smooth the loose veneer carefully into place. Contact cement bonds immediately, so make sure the veneer is exactly matched; if you're using carpenters' glue, press from the center out to force out any excess, and wipe the excess off immediately. If more than one veneer layer is loose, work from the bottom up to re-glue each layer.

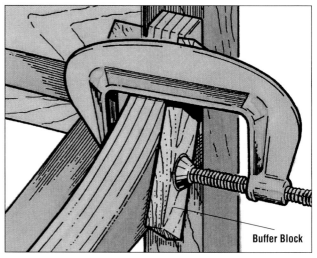

Buffer Block

Press the re-glued layers together to align them properly, wipe off excess glue, and clamp the mended part securely.

Step 4: Clamp or weight down the veneer. To protect the surface, cover it with a sheet of wax paper after all excess glue is removed. Set a buffer block of scrap wood over the newly glued area, and use another block or a soft cloth to protect the opposite edge or side of the surface. Clamp the glued and protected surface firmly with C-clamps or hand screws, for one to two days.

Step 5: Remove the clamps and the buffers, then wax and polish the entire surface.

Cracked or Broken Veneer

If the veneer is lifted and cracked, but not broken completely through, it can be re-glued; large areas may be easier to repair if you break the veneer off along the cracks. Broken veneer can be re-glued, but you must be very careful not to damage the edges of the break. Do not trim ragged edges; an irregular mend line will not be as visible as a perfectly straight line.

Before applying glue to the veneer, clean the bonding surfaces carefully. Fit the broken edges carefully together to make sure they match perfectly. Then apply contact cement to both surfaces, or spread carpenters' glue on the base wood. Set the broken veneer carefully into place, matching the edges together. Clamp the mended area. Refinishing may be necessary when the mend is complete.

Chipped or Missing Veneer

Replacing veneer is easy, but finding a new piece to replace it may not be. If the piece of furniture is not valuable, you may be able to take the patch from a part of it that won't show. The patch area must be along an edge so that you can lift the veneer with a craft knife or a stiff-bladed putty knife.

In cases in which patch veneer should not be taken from the same piece of furniture, you'll have to buy matching veneer to make the repair. If only a small piece is missing, you may be able to fill in the hole with veneer edging tape, sold at many home centers and lumberyards. Or, if you have access to junk furniture, you may be able to salvage a similar veneer from another piece of furniture. For larger patches, or if you can't find a scrap piece of matching veneer, buy a sheet of matching veneer from a specialized wood supplier, locally or by mail. To fit a chip or very small patch:

Step 1: Set a sheet of bond paper over the damaged veneer. Rub a very soft, dull lead pencil gently over the paper; the edges of the damaged area will be exactly marked on the paper. Use this pattern as a template to cut the veneer patch.

Step 2: Tape the pattern to the patching wood, matching the grain of the new veneer to the grain of the damaged area. Cut the patch firmly and carefully with a sharp craft knife; it's better to make it too big than too small.

To make a larger patch:

Step 1: Tape the patching veneer firmly over the damaged area with masking tape, with the grain and pattern of the patch matching the grain and pattern of the damaged veneer. Make sure the patch is flat against the surface and secure.

Step 2: Cut the patch in an irregular shape or in a boat or shield shape; these shapes will be less visible than a square or rectangular patch would be. Cut the patch carefully with a craft knife, scoring through the patching veneer and through the damaged veneer layer below it.

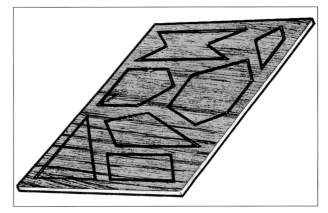

To mend veneer, cut a patch in an irregular shape; any of these shapes will be less visible than a square.

Step 3: Untape the patching sheet and pop out the patch. With the tip of the craft knife, remove the cut-out patch of damaged veneer. If necessary, score it and remove it in pieces. Be very careful not to damage the edges of the patch area. Remove only the top veneer layer; do not cut into the base wood. Remove any old glue, and clean the base wood.

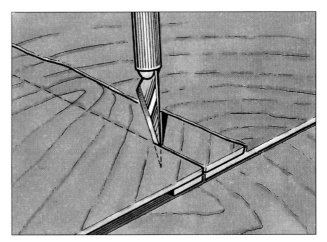

With the patch veneer held firmly to the surface, cut through the patching sheet and the veneer below it.

Step 4: Test the fit of the patch in the hole. It should fit exactly, flush with the surrounding surface, with no gaps or overlaps. If the patch is too big or too thick, do not force it in. Carefully sand the edges or the back with fine-grit sandpaper to fit it to the hole.

Step 5: Glue the fitted patch into place with contact cement or carpenters' glue and clamp or weight it solidly. Let the repair dry for one to two days; then very lightly sand the patch and the surrounding veneer.

Before gluing the patch in, test it for fit. It should fit flush with the surrounding surface with no gaps.

Step 6: Refinish the damaged area or, if necessary, the entire surface or piece of furniture.

Repairing Hardware

Drawer pulls, handles, hinges, locks, protective corners, decorative bands and escutcheons, and other furniture hardware often begin to show signs of long, hard use. Sometimes hardware is missing; sometimes it's loose, broken, or bent. Loose hardware can be repaired; missing or damaged pieces should be replaced. Replacement is also the solution if you don't like the existing hardware.

Many pieces of furniture are made with very common types of hardware; matching these basic designs is simple. If the hardware is more distinctive or unusual, it may be easier to replace all the hardware than to find a matching piece. In this case, make sure the new hardware's bases are at least as large as the old bases. If the piece of furniture is very valuable or antique, however, or if the hardware is very attractive, the old hardware should not be removed. In this case, missing parts should be replaced with matching or similar hardware; a slight difference in design usually doesn't look bad.

Hardware stores, home centers, and similar stores offer a wide selection of furniture hardware. Specialty hardware outlets and craft suppliers are also good sources.

Drawer Pulls and Handles

To tighten a loosely attached drawer pull, remove the pull and replace the screw with a longer one. If the screw is part of the pull, you'll have to make the hole in the wood smaller. When the hole is only slightly enlarged, you can tighten the pull by using a hollow fiber plug with the screw; for metal pulls, fit a piece of solid-core solder into the hole and then replace the screw. When the hole is much too big:

Step 1: Insert wood toothpicks or thin shavings of wood, dipped in glue, into the hole.

Step 2: Let the glue dry, then carefully trim the shavings flush with the wood surface.

Step 3: Dip the pull's screw into glue, replace the pull, and tighten the screw firmly.

For a more substantial repair, enlarge the hole, glue a piece of dowel into it, and drill a new screw hole in the dowel.

Hinges

Hinges that don't work properly usually have bent hinge pins that should be replaced. If the hinges are loose, try using slightly longer screws to attach them. When the screw holes are greatly enlarged, adjust them using one of the methods detailed before. If the hinge leaves are damaged and the hinges cannot be replaced, glue the hinges into position with epoxy or a rubber- or silicone-base adhesive.

Locks

Locks on old pieces are often damaged, and keys are often missing. If the piece of furniture is antique, or the lock is very unusual, have it repaired by a professional. Otherwise, remove the damaged lock and take it to a locksmith so they can order a matching or similar lock to replace it. Install the new lock the same way the old one was secured.

Loose Metal Bands and Escutcheons

Old bands and escutcheons often have an attractive design and patina. If this is the case, don't replace them unless they're badly damaged. To secure a loose band or escutcheon, squeeze adhesive caulking compound under the metal and press it down to bond it to the wood. If this doesn't work, fasten the band or escutcheon with tiny metal screws of the same metal as the hardware. You must match the metals—brass to brass, copper to copper, steel to steel, etc. If you don't match the screws to the metal plate, the metal will corrode. Use several screws, placing them to form a pattern, and drill pilot holes before inserting them.

Cover-up Hardware

If old hardware holes are impossible to repair, or if you want to change the look of a piece entirely, the damage can be covered with new wood or metal escutcheon plates. Escutcheons are mostly used under drawer pulls or handles; many handles are made with escutcheon-type backers. Attach the escutcheons with adhesive or with screws, matched metal to metal. If you're using escutcheon-type handles, no other treatment is necessary. If you're using an escutcheon under other hardware, drill new mounting holes as required. Keep your design simple.

Furniture Refinishing

T he most common furniture problems involve the finish—the coating that protects the wood and gives it its glossy surface. Most furniture finishes are surface coatings; they protect the wood by forming a solid layer on top of it. Shellac, lacquer, and varnish, the most common furniture finishes, are all surface coatings. Other finishes, such as oil and penetrating resin, sink into the wood; they don't form a surface coating, but protect the wood by hardening inside the fibers. A damaged finish coating can be repaired easily when the damage doesn't extend into the wood underneath it. When the damage goes all the way through the finish and into the wood, repairs will involve spot refinishing— an unpredictable technique, and not always a successful one, especially when the wood is stained. The less finish you remove, the better your results are likely to be. If the surface is badly damaged, consider refinishing.

Many repair jobs, and most restoration projects, require a knowledge of the finish you're working with. If you don't know what the finish is, you could end up damaging a perfectly good finish or wasting your time on a technique that won't work. This knowledge is also essential when you have to match one finish to another.

In most cases, the only distinction that really matters is the difference among the three natural, or clear, finishes: shellac, lacquer, and varnish. The pigmented finishes, such as paint or enamel, are easy to identify. The only other finishes you may encounter are oil, wax, and penetrating sealers, identifiable by touch and by the absence of a high gloss.

Modern furniture is often lacquered, but the finish on a piece made before about 1860 is usually shellac, because lacquer and varnish were not developed until the mid-1800s. A varnish finish is rare on factory-finished pieces, because varnish is hard to apply and requires a long drying period in a dust-free environment. Very old furniture may be finished with oil, wax, or milk paint, and many fine furniture pieces are French-polished, a variation of the shellac finish. In general, old finishes are natural products; brand-new finishes, such as the polyurethanes, may be synthetics.

Before you make any extensive repairs to a finish, take a minute to identify it. First, test the finish with denatured alcohol; rub a little alcohol onto an inconspicuous finished area. If the finish dissolves, it's shellac. If it partially dissolves, it's probably a combination of shellac and lacquer. If this is the case, test it again with a mixture of denatured alcohol and lacquer thinner; this should completely dissolve the finish.

If alcohol doesn't affect the finish, rub a little lacquer thinner on an inconspicuous finished spot. If the area turns rough and then smooth again, the finish is lacquer; if the finish crinkles and doesn't get smooth again, it's some type of varnish. If neither alcohol nor lacquer thinner affects it, the finish is varnish.

If the piece of furniture is painted, test the finish with ammonia. Very old pieces may be finished with milk paint, which is dissolved only by ammonia. If the piece of furniture is very dirty or encrusted with wax, clean it first with a mixture of denatured alcohol, white vinegar, and kerosene, in equal parts. Then test it with the various solvents.

Stains and Discoloration

Old or new, furniture often shows evidence of hard service: stains, scratches, burns, and all the other signs of use and abuse. Veneer may be loose or broken; hardware may be missing; the wood may be discolored. Unless the damage is severe or extensive, most of these problems are easy to deal with. Surface repairs aren't difficult, but it can be hard to tell what you're getting into. If only the surface is affected, the damage is usually easy to repair. If the wood is damaged too, you may have to refinish part or all of the piece. In this case, consider refinishing.

White Spots

Shellac and lacquer finishes are not resistant to water and alcohol. Spills and condensation from glasses can leave permanent white spots or rings on these finishes. To remove these white spots, first try polishing the surface with liquid furniture polish, buffing the surface firmly. If this doesn't work, lightly wipe the stained surface with denatured alcohol. Use as little alcohol as possible; too much will damage the finish.

If neither polishing nor alcohol treatment removes the white spots, the damaged finish must be treated with abrasives. Gentle wood abrasive pastes are available at larger building-supply stores and woodworker's shops. Rub the paste over the stained area, along the grain of

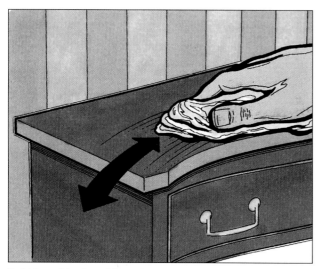

Rubbing with oil and fine abrasives is often effective in removing spots and blushing. Rub along the grain of the wood, then wipe the surface clean.

the wood, and then wipe the surface clean with a soft cloth. If necessary, repeat the procedure. Stubborn spots may require several applications. Then wax and polish the entire surface.

If this doesn't work, use a coarser abrasive paste, rubbing carefully to control the removal. As soon as the white spots disappear, stop rubbing and wipe the wood clean with a soft cloth. Then apply two coats of hard furniture wax and buff the wood to a shine.

Blushing

Blushing, a white haze over a large surface or an entire piece of furniture, is a common problem with old shellac and lacquer finishes. The discoloration is caused by moisture, and it can be removed following these steps:

Step 1: Buff the surface slightly and evenly with No. 0000 steel wool dipped in boiled linseed oil; work with the grain of the wood, rubbing evenly on the entire surface, until the white haze disappears.

Step 2: Wipe the wood clean with a soft cloth.

Step 3: Apply two coats of hard furniture wax and buff the surface to a shine.

Black Spots

Black spots are caused by water that has penetrated the finish completely and entered the wood. They cannot be removed without damage to the finish. If the spots are on a clearly defined surface, you may be able to remove the finish from this surface only; otherwise, the entire piece of furniture will have to be refinished. When the finish has been removed, bleach the entire stained

surface with a solution of oxalic acid, as directed by the manufacturer. Then refinish the piece.

Ink Stains

Ink stains that have penetrated the finish, like black water spots, cannot be removed without refinishing. Less serious ink stains can be removed following these steps:

Step 1: Lightly buff the stained area with a cloth moistened with mineral spirits.

Step 2: Rinse the wood with clean water on a soft cloth.

Step 3: Dry the surface thoroughly, and then wax and polish it.

Step 4: If this does not work, lightly rub the stained area along the grain of the wood with No. 0000 steel wool moistened with mineral spirits. Wipe the surface clean and wax and polish it.

The last step may damage the finish. If necessary, refinish the damaged spot (see Spot Refinishing on page 107). If the area is badly damaged, the entire surface or piece of furniture will have to be refinished.

Grease, Tar, Paint, Crayon, and Lipstick Spots

These spots usually affect only the surface of the finish. To remove wet paint, use the appropriate solvent on a soft cloth—mineral spirits for oil-base paint, water for latex paint. To remove dry paint or other materials, very carefully lift the surface residue with the edge of a putty knife. Do not scrape the wood, or you'll scratch the finish. When the surface material has been removed, buff the area very lightly along the grain of the wood with No. 0000 steel wool moistened with mineral spirits. Then wax and polish the entire surface.

Wax and Gum Spots

Wax and gum usually come off quickly, but they must be removed carefully to prevent damage to the finish. To remove wax or gum:

Step 1: Press the spot with a packet of ice wrapped in a towel or paper towel until the deposit hardens.

Step 2: Lift it off with your thumbnail. The hardened wax or gum should pop off the surface with very little pressure. If necessary, repeat the ice application. Do not scrape the deposit off, or you'll scratch the finish.

Step 3: When the wax or gum is completely removed, buff the area very lightly along the grain of the wood with No. 0000 steel wool moistened with mineral spirits.

Step 4: Wax and polish the entire surface.

Spot Refinishing

Deep scratches, gouges, burns, or any other surface damage requires refinishing the repair area. Spot refinishing is not always easy, and it's not always successful, especially on stained surfaces. But, if the damage isn't too bad, it's worth trying. If you have to touch up several areas on one surface, consider completely refinishing the surface or the piece of furniture. Here's how to refinish a spot:

Spot-staining is tricky, but it is sometimes successful. Apply stain to the repair area with an artists' brush or a clean cloth.

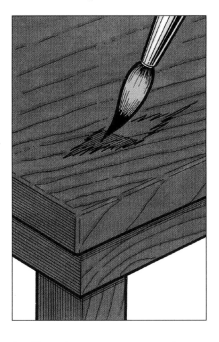

Step 1: Select the stain. To stain one area on a surface, use an oil-base stain that matches the surrounding stain. You may have to mix stains to get a good match. Test the stain on an inconspicuous unfinished part of the wood before working on the finished surface.

Step 2: Sand the damaged area smooth with fine-grit sandpaper, and wipe the surface clean.

Step 3: Apply the stain to the damaged area with an artists' brush or a clean cloth, covering the entire bare area.

Step 4: Let the stain set for 15 minutes and then wipe it off with a clean cloth. If the color is too light, apply another coat of stain, wait 15 minutes, and wipe again. Repeat this procedure until you're satisfied with the color; then let the stain dry according to the manufacturer's instructions.

Step 5: Lightly buff the stained surface with No. 0000 steel wool and wipe it clean with a tack cloth.

Step 6: Apply a new coat of the same finish (varnish, penetrating resin, shellac, or lacquer) over the newly stained area, feathering out the new finish into the surrounding old finish.

Step 7: Let the new finish dry for one or two days, then lightly buff the patched area with No. 0000 steel wool.

Step 8: Wax the entire surface with hard paste wax and polish it to a shine.

Surface Damage

Scratches, dings, dents, cracks and gouges, burns, and other maladies can also mar furniture surfaces. Here's how to treat these afflictions:

Scratches

To hide a small scratch, rub oil from the meat of a walnut, pecan, or Brazil nut along the scratch. The oil in the nut meat will darken the raw scratch, making it less conspicuous. These oils are available at woodworker's stores or from the nut itself. They're the main ingredient in many scratch-removal products.

When many shallow scratches are present, apply hard paste wax to the surface with No. 0000 steel wool, stroking very lightly along the grain of the wood. Then buff the surface with a soft cloth. If the scratches still show, apply one or two more coats of hard paste wax to the surface. Let each coat dry thoroughly and buff it to a shine before applying the next coat.

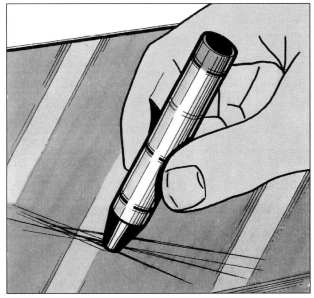

Wax patching sticks can be used to hide fairly deep scratches. Press firmly to fill the scratch. Level with the edge of a piece of thin plastic or a credit card.

For one or two deeper scratches, wax furniture-patching sticks are usually effective. These retouching sticks, made in several wood colors, are available at hardware and, sometimes, grocery stores. Choose a stick to match the finish. To use the wax stick, run it firmly along the scratch, applying enough pressure to fill the scratch with wax. Remove any excess wax with the edge of a credit card or other thin plastic card. Let the wax dry; then buff the surface with a soft cloth.

Badly scratched surfaces should usually be refinished, but to hide one or two very deep scratches, you may be able to stain the raw area to match. Apply oil-base stain with an artists' brush, drawing it carefully along the scratch; let it stand for 15 minutes, then wipe it off. If necessary, repeat this procedure until the scratch matches the rest of the wood. Let the area dry completely, as directed by the stain manufacturer; then apply hard paste wax and buff the waxed surface to a shine.

Dings

Dings are tiny chips in the finish, usually caused by a sharp blow. The wood may not be affected. To repair a ding:

Step 1: Use a craft knife to remove any loose finish in or around the ding. Work carefully, scraping the damaged spot with the flat, sharp edge of the knife blade; do not scratch the spot.

Step 2: Carefully feather the edges of the ding with No. 0000 steel wool.

Step 3: Clean the ding area with a soft cloth moistened in mineral spirits. Let it dry completely.

Step 4: Apply new finish to the spot using an artist's brush to match the rest of the finish. The spot will be very noticeable at first. Let the finish dry; it will be glossy.

Step 5: Lightly buff the spot with No. 0000 steel wool; then wax and polish the entire piece of furniture. The ding should blend perfectly when the job is complete.

Dents

Small, shallow dents in pine and other soft woods are usually easy to remove; large and deep dents, especially in hard wood, are harder to repair. Dents are easiest to remove from bare wood. Very large, shallow dents are probably best left untreated. Very deep dents should be filled, as detailed later for cracks and gouges.

Step 1: Using fine-grit sandpaper, carefully remove the finish for about ½ inch around the damage.

Step 2: Raise the wood in the dent by applying a few drops of water to the dent. Do not wet the entire surface. Let the water penetrate the wood for a day or so. This treatment may be enough to raise the dent, especially if the dent is shallow and the wood is soft.

Step 3: If this doesn't raise the dent, soak a cloth in water and wring it out. Place the damp cloth, folded in several layers, over the dent; then press the cloth firmly with a warm iron. Be careful not to touch the iron directly to the wood. This moist heat may be enough to swell the wood and raise the dent. If it isn't, apply a commercial wood-swelling liquid to the area and give it time to work—about a day or so, as directed by the manufacturer.

Step 4: For deep dents that can't be raised with water, heat, or wood sweller, use a fine straight pin or needle to drive a series of holes in the dent. Pound the straight pin in about ¼ inch and carefully pull it out with pliers. The holes should be as small as possible. Then treat the dent as previously described. The pinholes help the water penetrate the wood's surface.

Use a fine pin or needle to drive a series of small holes in a stubborn dent, then swell the wood to raise the dent.

Step 5: After the dent has been raised, let the wood dry for about a week. Refinish the damaged area as previously described. Let the finish dry completely. Lightly buff the new finish with No. 0000 steel wool, then wax and polish the entire surface.

Cracks and Gouges

Cracks and gouges should be filled so that they're level with the surface of the wood. For very small holes, like

Fill deep cracks and gouges with wood plastic or water putty; leave the filler slightly high to allow for shrinkage as it dries. When the patch is dry, sand it smooth.

staple holes, wood-tone putty sticks can be used. If you can't match the wood, several colors can be mixed together. To use a putty stick, wipe it across the hole and smooth the surface with your finger. If you plan to finish or refinish the wood, let the putty dry for at least a week before proceeding further.

For larger holes, wood plastic and water putty are the easiest fillers. These fillers can be used on bare or finished wood; wood plastic is available in several colors, and water putty can be tinted with oil or water stain. However, wood plastic and water putty patches are usually noticeable, and may look darker than the wood. For the best results, test the patch on an inconspicuous surface to make sure the color is right. To use wood plastic:

Step 1: Clean the crack or gouge with the tip of a craft knife.

Step 2: Press the plastic firmly in with the tip of a craft knife or the edge of a putty knife. Wood plastic shrinks slightly as it dries, so press it in tightly and leave it mounded slightly above the surface of the wood. Let the wood plastic set for at least two days.

Step 3: Smooth the patch lightly with fine-grit sandpaper and buff the area with No. 0000 steel wool. If surrounding finish is involved, feather

the edges so that the new patch blends in with the rest of the finish.

Step 4: If necessary, stain the patch and buff it lightly with No. 0000 steel wool. Apply finish to match the rest of the surface, using an artists' brush and feathering the edges. Let the finish dry and then lightly buff it with No. 0000 steel wool.

Step 5: Clean the area of any residue and wax, and polish the surface.

Water putty dries flint-hard, usually harder than the wood being patched. It's best used on bare wood. Water putty can be toned with oil and water stains, but you'll have to experiment to come up with a perfect match. To use water putty, mix the powder with water to the consistency of putty; then trowel it into the break with a putty knife, leaving the patch slightly high. Let the patch dry completely; then sand and steel-wool the area smooth and level with the surrounding surface. Finish the patch area as mentioned before, or finish the entire piece of furniture.

Heat the shellac stick over an alcohol lamp or a propane torch; hold a palette or putty knife between the stick and the flame to keep it from dripping.

For the most professional patching job, use shellac sticks to fill cracks and gouges. Shellac sticks leave the least conspicuous patch and are very effective on finished wood that's in good condition. Shellac sticks are available in several wood-tone colors; use a stick that matches the finish as closely as possible. Practice on scrap wood before working on a piece of furniture.

Carefully clean the crack or gouge with the tip of a craft knife. Shellac sticks must be heated and melted to fill the crack. The best heat source for this is an alcohol lamp or a propane torch turned to a low setting. Do not use a match to soften the stick; the smoke from the match may discolor the shellac. Do not use a range burner; liquid shellac could damage either gas or electric ranges. Hold the stick over the blade of a palette knife or a putty knife to prevent it from dripping. To use a shellac stick:

Step 1: Hold the stick to the heat source above the knife until it has softened to about the consistency of glazing compound or putty. Then quickly press the softened shellac into the crack and smooth it with the hot knife. Make sure the soft shellac fills the break completely; it hardens quickly, so you'll have to work fast. Leave the patch slightly high.

Step 2: Use the heated putty knife blade to trowel the shellac smooth.

When the shellac has softened to the consistency of putty, quickly press it into the crack, smoothing it in with the hot knife. Leave the patch slightly high.

Step 3: Let the patch set for one to two hours. When the shellac is hard, plane or sand the surface smooth and level. The finish surrounding the break usually doesn't have to be retouched, but the surface can be coated with shellac, if desired.

Step 4: Rub the surface smooth with No. 0000 steel wool and linseed oil.

To fill very deep holes, use wood plastic or water putty to fill the hole almost level. Let the filler dry completely; then fill the indentation with a shellac stick. If a hole or split is very large, consider filling it with a piece of wood cut and trimmed to fit perfectly. If the patching wood can be taken from the piece of furniture in a spot that won't show, the repair may be almost impossible to detect.

Fit the wood patch into the hole or split; use carpenters' glue to bond it to the surrounding wood. Leave the patch slightly high. When the glue is completely dry, sand the plug smoothly level with the surface of the surrounding wood. Then refinish the piece of furniture.

Burns

Burns on furniture can range from scorches to deep char, but the usual problem is cigarette burns. Scorches from cigarettes or cigars are usually very easy to remove. Buff the scorched area with a fine steel wool pad moistened with mineral spirits until the scorch disappears. Then wipe it clean and wax and polish the surface.

More serious burns require the removal of the charred wood. Shallow burns, when repaired, will always leave a slight indentation in the wood, but this depression will be inconspicuous. To repair a burn hole:

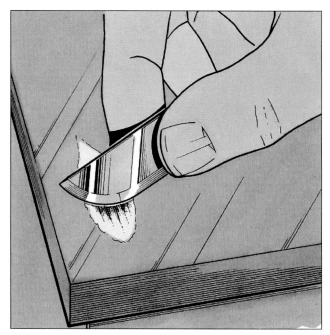

To remove a burn spot, scrape away the charred wood with a craft knife; feather the edges of the depression.

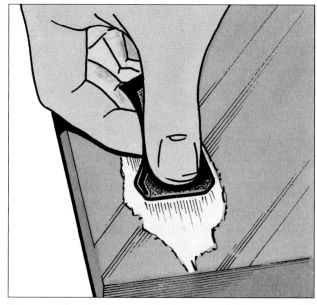

After removing the char, sand the burn area lightly to smooth it and level it out to the surrounding surface.

Step 1: Remove the damaged wood. With the flat, sharp edge of a craft knife, very carefully scrape away the charred wood. For deep burns, it's best to use a curved blade. Do not scratch the burn area. Scrape away the char right to the bare wood, feathering out the edges. Any burned or scorched spots will show, so all the burn crust must be removed. Work carefully to avoid scratching the wood with the point of the knife.

Step 2: Lightly sand the edges of the groove or trench to level it with the surrounding surface as much as possible. Press lightly into the groove with fine-grit sandpaper, removing only the char from the burned area. Be careful not to damage the surrounding finish. If you're not sure all the burn has been removed, wet the sanded area. If water makes the burned area look burned again, you haven't removed all the char.

Step 3: Level the groove as much as possible with fine-grit sandpaper, but stay close to the edges of the groove. If you sand too far out from the burn area, the damaged area will be very visible as a wide saucer-shaped indentation. If the depression isn't too deep, try swelling the wood as detailed before for dents. If you're left with a deep gouge, the burn area can be filled with wood plastic or stick shellac.

Step 4: Refinish the damaged area. Let the new finish dry for one or two days, then lightly buff the patch with No. 0000 steel wool to blend the edges into the old finish.

Step 5: Wax and polish the entire piece of furniture.

Reviving an Old Finish

Refinishing is a long, slow, messy job. Before you strip the old finish off any piece of furniture, take a good look at it. A complete refinishing job may not be necessary. Instead, you can use a few simple restoration techniques to revive the old finish. Restoration doesn't always work, but it's well worth trying before you resort to more drastic means. Start with the simplest techniques and work up; the easiest way is often best.

After identifying the finish (see page 105), you're ready to restore it. Whether the problem is dirt, cracks, discoloration, or overall wear, it can often be solved by these restoration techniques.

The easiest restoration process is cleaning. What first appears to be a beat-up finish may be just dirt. Over a period of years, even well-cared-for furniture can acquire a dull, sticky coating of wax and dust. In many cases, this coating can be removed with an oil-based commercial wood cleaner/conditioner, which can often dig through layers of dirt and wax. They are available at furniture stores, some supermarkets, and paint stores. Here's how to restore a surface by cleaning it:

Step 1: Apply the cleaner generously with a soft cloth and let it stand for an hour or two.

Step 2: Wipe off the cleaner with another cloth. Repeat the process, using plenty of cleaner, until the wood is clean and lustrous. This may take up to four or five applications.

Step 3: Buff the clean wood *lightly* to remove excess oil. Let the wood dry completely. If there's a haze on the finish, you may be able to remove it with steel wool. Buff the surface lightly along the grain of the wood with No. 0000 steel wool. Then apply a commercial cleaner/conditioner and buff the wood gently again.

If detergent cleaning doesn't work, use a solvent to clean the wood. Solvent cleaning is the last resort to consider, because it may damage the finish, but it is worth a try. Use mineral spirits or turpentine on any finish; use denatured alcohol on varnish or lacquer. Do not use alcohol on shellac or on a shellac/lacquer mixture. Working in a well-ventilated area or outdoors, apply the solvent with a rough cloth, such as burlap or an old towel. Then wipe the wood clean with another cloth. Finally, apply a commercial cleaner/conditioner and buff the wood lightly.

Professional Furniture Strippers

Professional furniture strippers can help you reduce the labor of refinishing wood furniture. These services use huge tubs of methylene chloride or other wash-away chemicals. Your chest of drawers, table, or chair is dipped into the solution, which eats off the old finish right down to the bare wood. The furniture item is then dipped into a neutralizing chemical and/or sprayed with water to remove the chemicals.

The cost of commercial finish removal usually depends on the size of the item to be cleaned. A chair, for example, would cost less to clean than a dresser. The cost for most items, however, is not prohibitive. Professional strippers will remove the finish from almost any item, including woodwork or railings; their work isn't limited to furniture.

There are some advantages and some disadvantages to professional strippers.

Pros: The item you have stripped comes out extremely clean. If there are several layers of finish on the item, a commercial stripper can definitely save you hours of labor. It is probably less expensive to have the piece stripped than to buy the remover to strip it yourself.

Cons: The chemicals used by commercial strippers are thought by some furniture buffs to take the "life" or "oil" out of the wood and render it "deadwood." Moreover, the chemicals sometimes soften or destroy the adhesive that holds the furniture together.

Professional strippers are a good investment for most projects, but you will want to make sure the service is bonded in case your antique furniture is damaged in the process. Better yet, strip antiques yourself by hand.

Covering a Worn Finish

All materials wear down over a period of time, and furniture is no exception. Sometimes the entire finish is worn, sometimes only heavy-use spots. Worn spots are most common around doors and drawers. On an antique, wear is part of the patina of the piece and is used to date and determine the value of the furniture. It should not be covered or restored. The same consideration applies to almost any piece of furniture: Wear and tear adds a certain character. But a thin, old finish can be recoated. And where refinishing is the only alternative, you may be able to repair the worn spots. Here's how to cover a worn finish:

Step 1: Clean the surface carefully with mineral spirits or, for lacquer or varnish, denatured alcohol. If the entire finish is worn, clean the whole piece of furniture; you must remove all dirt and grease.

Step 2: Apply a new coat of the finish already on the wood.

If you're touching up worn spots rather than recoating an entire finish:

Step 1: Clean the entire worn surface, then sand the worn spots very lightly with fine-grit sandpaper. Be careful not to exert much pressure.

Step 2: To touch up the worn spot, use an oil-base stain that matches the stain on the piece of furniture. You may have to mix stains to get a good match. Test the stain on an inconspicuous unfinished part of the wood before working on the worn spots. Apply the stain to the damaged area with an artists' brush or a clean cloth, covering the entire bare area.

Step 3: Let the stain set for 15 minutes and then wipe it off with a clean cloth. If the color is too light, apply another coat of stain, wait 15 minutes, and wipe again. Repeat this procedure until you're satisfied with the color. Let the stain dry according to the manufacturer's instructions.

Step 4: Lightly buff the stained surface with No. 0000 steel wool and wipe it clean with a tack cloth.

Step 5: Apply a new coat of the same finish already on the surface (lacquer, shellac, penetrating resin, or varnish) over the newly stained areas, feathering out the new finish into the surrounding old finish.

Step 6: Let the new finish dry for one or two days; then lightly buff the patched areas with No. 0000 steel wool.

Step 7: Wax the entire surface with hard paste wax, and polish it to a shine.

CHAPTER 4

ELECTRICITY

Reading this chapter won't qualify you for an electrician's license. However, you will learn about the workings of your home's electrical system, how to make simple repairs, and how to make safe electrical improvements easily. Any electrical work beyond the basics typically requires a thorough understanding of local building codes and safe, standard electrical practices. What's more, some codes require that these tasks be performed only by a licensed person, and insurance policies often don't cover fires that result from illegal wiring.

Consequently, this chapter is limited strictly to electrical repair and improvement projects that require no license or special expertise. First, let's look at what happens when you flip on a light switch or activate an electrical appliance.

How the System Works

Your home's plumbing and electrical systems may seem as different as any two things could be. But there are significant parallels. Water enters your home through a pipe, under pressure (hydraulic pressure, measured in pounds per square inch), and when you turn on a tap, the water flows at a certain rate (gallons per minute). Electricity enters your home through wires (copper or aluminum, and sometimes both), also under pressure (electrical pressure, called electromotive force or voltage, measured in volts). When you turn on an electrical device, the electricity flows at a certain rate; this is current, measured in amperes, or amps. But unlike water, which is used as it comes from the tap, electricity is meant to do work; it is converted from energy to power, measured in watts. Since household electrical consumption is relatively high, the unit of measure most often used is the kilowatt, which is equal to 1,000 watts. The total amount of electrical energy that you use in any period is measured in terms of kilowatt-hours (kwh).

The instrument that records how much electricity you use is called an electric meter. This meter also determines how high your electric bill will be.

There are two types of electric meters in general use. One type displays on its face a row of small dials with individual indicators. Each meter dial registers a certain number of kilowatt-hours of electrical energy. For example, if you leave a 100-watt bulb burning for 10

hours, the meter will register 1 kilowatt-hour (10×100 = 1,000 watt-hours, or 1 kwh). Each dial registers a certain number of kilowatt-hours of electrical energy. From right to left on most meter faces, the far right is the one that counts individual kilowatt-hours from 1 to 10; the next one counts the electricity from 10 to 100 kilowatt-hours; the third dial counts up to 1,000; the fourth counts up to 10,000; and the dial at the extreme left counts kilowatt-hours up to 100,000. If the arrow on the dial is between two numbers, the lower number should always be read.

One common type of electric meter displays a series of dials that register the number of kilowatt-hours used. Some dials run clockwise, some counterclockwise.

The second type of electric meter performs the same function, but instead of having individual dials, it has numerals in slots on the meter face, much like the odometer in your car. This meter is read from left to right, and the numbers indicate total electrical consumption. Some meters also use a multiplying factor—the number that appears must be multiplied by 10, for instance, for a true figure in kilowatt-hours. Once you know how to read your meter, you can verify the charges on your electric bill and become a better watchdog of electrical energy consumption in your home.

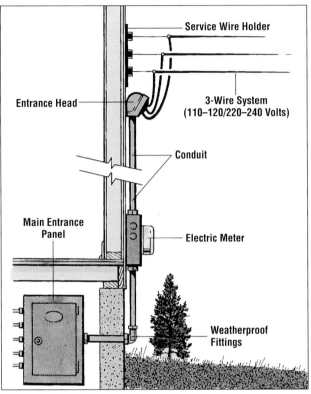

The electrical service drop, or supply line, and the meter are as far as the local utility company is involved in your home's electrical system. From that point on, the system is your responsibility.

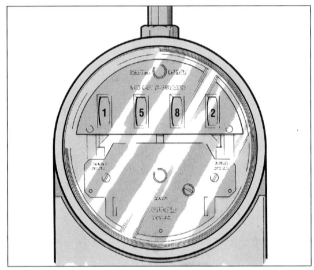

Another type of electric meter works like a car's odometer; numerals in a series of slots register the kilowatt-hours used. This type of meter reads from left to right.

The electrical service drop, or supply line, and the meter are as far as the local utility company is involved in your home's electrical system. From that point on, the system is the homeowner's responsibility. Electricity passes from the meter to the service equipment by means of three lines (older houses may have two) that supply 110–120/220–240 volts AC (alternating current). The exact voltage varies depending on several external factors. This three-wire system gives you 110–120-volt power for lighting, outlets, and small appliances, as well as 220–240-volt power for air conditioning, an electric range, a clothes dryer, a water heater, and, in some homes, electric heating.

Electrical Service Entrance

Electricity enters your home through the power company's service equipment. By definition, the service equipment is simply a disconnect device mounted in a suitable approved enclosure. Its purpose is to disconnect

the service from the interior wiring system. This disconnect might be a set of pull-out fuses, a circuit breaker, or a large switch. The disconnect device is usually called a main fuse, main breaker, main disconnect, or often just "the main." It can be in a separate enclosure, and though it's usually installed inside the building, it can be mounted outdoors in a weatherproof box.

In practice, main disconnects are nearly always inside the house, in a large enclosure that also contains the fuses or circuit breakers, which handle the distribution of power throughout the house. This is called a main entrance panel, main box, or entrance box. The three wires from the meter enter this box. Two of them—the heavily insulated black and red lines—are secured in lugs to the tops of a parallel pair of exposed heavy copper bars, called buses, that are positioned vertically toward the center of the box. These two lines are the "live," or "hot," wires. The third wire, generally bare, is the "neutral." It is attached to a separate grounding bar or bus, a silver-colored strip usually found at the bottom or to one side of the main box. In most homes this ground bus is actually connected to the ground—the earth—by a heavy solid copper wire that is clamped to a cold-water pipe or to an underground bar or plate.

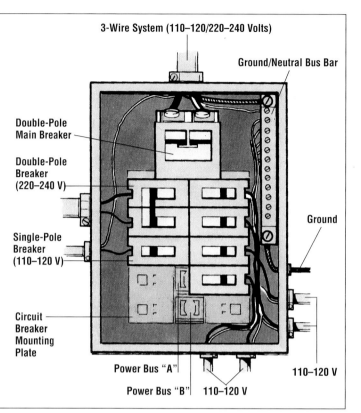

3-Wire System (110–120/220–240 Volts)

Ground/Neutral Bus Bar

Double-Pole Main Breaker

Double-Pole Breaker (220–240 V)

Single-Pole Breaker (110–120 V)

Ground

Circuit Breaker Mounting Plate

Power Bus "A"

Power Bus "B"   110–120 V

110–120 V

A main disconnect is nearly always located inside the house in the top part of a large enclosure also containing the fuses or circuit breakers. This is called the main entrance panel, main box, or entrance box.

Overload Protection

Power is distributed through your house through various electrical circuits that originate in the main entrance panel. The 110–120-volt circuits have two conductors—one neutral (white) wire and one hot (black) wire. The 220–240-volt circuits may consist of two hot wires alone, or a third, neutral wire may be added. In all cases, the hot lines are attached directly to the hot main buses. The neutral wire is always connected to the ground bus, and never, under any circumstances, passes through a fuse or circuit breaker.

Fuses and circuit breakers are safety devices built into your electrical system. If there were no fuses or circuit breakers, and if you operated too many appliances on a single circuit, the cable carrying the power for that circuit would get extremely hot, short-circuit, and, quite possibly, start a fire.

To prevent electrical overloads, fuses and circuit breakers are designed to blow or trip, stopping the flow of current to the overloaded cable. For example, a 15-ampere fuse should blow when the current through it exceeds 15 amperes; a 20-ampere circuit breaker should

Fuse Panel

In addition to screw-in fuses, a typical main fuse panel has a main disconnect and other pull-out blocks with cartridge-type fuses. To reach cartridge fuses, simply pull the fuse blocks out of the main entrance panel.

trip when the current through it exceeds 20 amperes. A fuse that blows or a circuit breaker that trips is not faulty; it is doing its job properly, indicating that there is trouble somewhere in the circuit. When a fuse blows or a circuit breaker trips, either there are too many appliances plugged in, or some malfunctioning device, like an appliance with an internal short, is connected to the circuit.

A blown fuse or a tripped circuit breaker is the signal that you should look for trouble. It makes no sense to replace a blown fuse or reset a tripped circuit breaker until you've located and eliminated the cause of the trouble. *Caution: Never try to defeat this built-in safety system by replacing a fuse with one of a larger current-carrying capacity.* The fuse or circuit breaker capacity

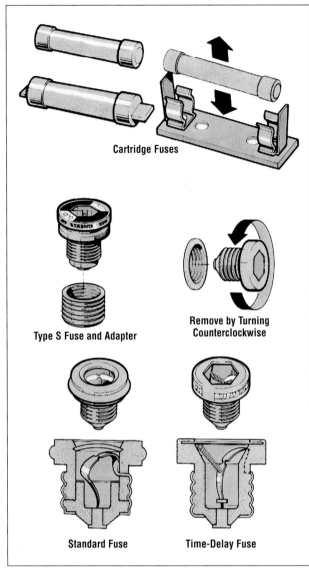

Cartridge Fuses

Type S Fuse and Adapter

Remove by Turning Counterclockwise

Standard Fuse

Time-Delay Fuse

To protect against serious overloads, fuses and circuit breakers are designed to blow or trip, stopping the flow of current to the overloaded cable. A 15-ampere fuse, for example, should blow when the current passing through it exceeds 15 amperes.

should be equal to or less than the current-carrying capacity (or ampacity) of the conductors. The older Edison-base type of plug fuses can be interchanged in certain sizes, as can some cartridge fuses. But if you replaced a 15-ampere fuse with a 25-ampere version, you could be placing yourself in a highly dangerous situation. The once-common practice of placing a copper penny behind a blown fuse can also lead to disaster. Some types of circuit breakers can be interchanged, but like fuses, they never should be. The newer Type S fuses are not interchangeable. You should replace fuses and breakers only with ones of the same size and amperage.

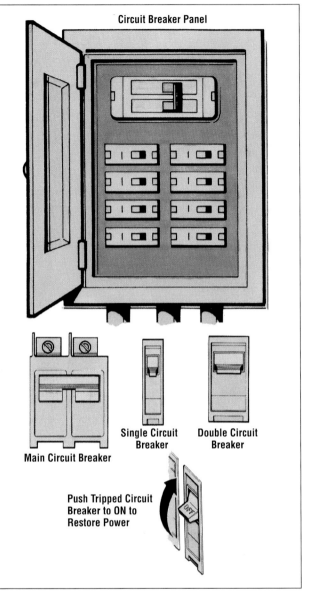

Circuit Breaker Panel

Main Circuit Breaker

Single Circuit Breaker

Double Circuit Breaker

Push Tripped Circuit Breaker to ON to Restore Power

Circuit breakers do not blow like fuses; they are switches that automatically trip open to interrupt the flow of electrical current when it overloads the circuit.

Branch and Feeder Circuits

From the fuses or circuit breakers, circuits go to all the devices in your home that require electrical power. There are two types of circuits: feeder and branch. Feeder circuits are relatively heavy cables that travel from the main entrance panel to other, smaller distribution panels called subpanels or load centers. These auxiliary panels are located in remote parts of the house or in outbuildings, and they are used for redistribution of power, such as in a garage. Feeder circuits aren't found in all houses.

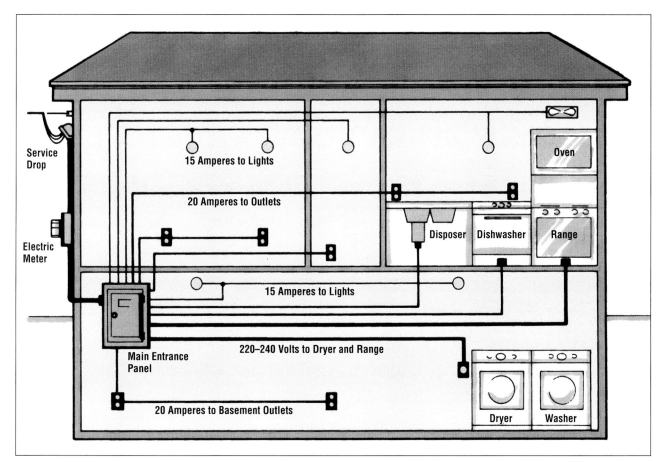

Newer homes have three incoming power lines that supply 110–120/220–240 volts AC. This provides 110–120 volts for lighting, outlets, and small appliances, and 220–240 volts for heavier appliances.

All of the circuits that run from either the main entrance panel or other, smaller panels to the various points of use are branch circuits. For 110–120-volt needs, a circuit branches out through a circuit breaker from one of the main buses and from the ground bus. For 220–240 volts, many circuits use only the two main buses. But all three wires are needed for devices that operate on both 110–120 and 220–240 volts.

The 110–120-volt branch circuits go through fuses or circuit breakers, which are labeled either 15 amperes or 20 amperes. The 15-amp branches go to ceiling lamps and wall outlets in rooms where less energy-demanding devices, such as floor and table lamps, are found. The larger, 20-amp branch circuits go to outlets in the kitchen, dining, and laundry areas where heavy-duty appliances are used. Every home should have at least two 20-amp circuits.

A 15-amp circuit can handle a total of 1,800 watts, while a 20-amp circuit can handle a total of 2,400 watts; but these figures represent circuits that are fully loaded. In practice, you should limit the load on a 15-amp circuit to no more than 1,440 watts, and the load on a

20-amp line should be limited to no more than 1,920 watts. How can you know the load on a circuit? Add up the individual wattages for all lamps and appliances plugged into each circuit.

When computing the load on each branch circuit, allow for motor-driven appliances that draw more current when the motor is just starting up than when it's running. A refrigerator, for example, might draw up to 15 amps initially, but will quickly settle down to around 4 amps. Suppose the refrigerator is plugged into a 20-amp branch circuit, and a 1,000-watt electric toaster (which draws a little more than 8 amps) is also plugged into that circuit. If the refrigerator motor starts while the toaster is toasting, the total current load will exceed the current-carrying capacity of the circuit, and the fuse will blow or the circuit breaker will trip.

Electrical Safety

Basic tips for electrical safety were offered in Chapter 1, but there are other things you should know about working safely around electricity.

that you can't easily disconnect for signs (or smells) of malfunction.

Replace the fuse or reset the breaker. If the circuit holds, it's possible that something you disconnected is faulty. Check for short circuits or other problems. If there's no evidence of electrical fault in the fixtures, the problem may be too much current draw for the circuit to handle. In this case, remove some of the load from the circuit.

If the new fuse blows or the circuit breaker refuses to reset, the problem lies in either the equipment that's still connected or in the circuit cable itself. Check the still-connected items, examining each for faults until you find the offending equipment. If the circuit still goes out when there are no loads connected to it, the wiring is faulty, probably due to a short in a junction or outlet box, or in the cable itself. If you suspect faulty wiring, call an electrician.

A circuit breaker is a remarkably trouble-free device, but once in a while a breaker does fail. The result is that the circuit will not energize, even when it's fault-free. When a circuit goes out, if the circuit breaker itself has a distinctive, burnt-plastic smell, if the trip handle is loose and wobbly, or if the breaker rattles when you move it, it has probably failed. Check it with a continuity tester, and replace the breaker as needed.

Coping With a Power Outage

What do you do when all the power in the house goes off? Usually this is due to a general power outage in the entire neighborhood or district, but sometimes the problem lies in the individual residential wiring system.

The first step is to see whether the outage is a general power outage or restricted to your home. If it's night, look around the neighborhood to see if everyone else's lights are off. During the day, call a neighbor to see if others are affected. Or, if you have a circuit breaker main disconnect, check to see whether it has tripped to the OFF position. If the main entrance is wired with fuses, pull the fuse block out and slip the fuses free. Check them with a continuity tester to see if they are still good. With a probe lead touched to each end of the fuse, the tester light will come on if the fuse is good.

If the trouble is a general power outage, all you can do is call the power company. If your main breaker is still in the ON position or both main fuses are good, but your neighbors have power and you don't, the fault lies between your main entrance panel and the power transmission lines. The reason could be a downed service drop, a faulty or overloaded pole transformer, or some similar problem. Call the power company; this part of your system is their responsibility.

If you find a tripped main breaker or blown main fuses in your main entrance panel, the problem lies within the house and may be serious. Do not attempt to reset the breaker or replace the fuses. The difficulty may be a system overload, using more total current than the main breaker can pass. Or there may be a dead short somewhere in the house.

The first step is to go back through the house and turn off everything you can. Then, if you have a circuit breaker panel, flip all the breakers to the OFF position. Once the breakers are off, reset the main breaker to the ON position. One by one, trip the branch circuit breakers back on. If one of them fails to reset, or if the main breaker again trips off as you trip the branch breaker on, the source of the trouble lies in that circuit. The circuit will have to be cleared of the fault.

If all the breakers go back on and the main breaker stays on, you're faced with two possibilities. One is that something you disconnected earlier is faulty. Go back along the line, inspect each item for possible fault, and plug each one back in. Sooner or later you'll discover which one is causing the problem, either visually or by noticing that a breaker trips off when you reconnect it. The other possibility is system-wide overloading. This is characterized by recurrent tripping-out of the main breaker when practically everything in the house is running, but there are no electrical faults to be found. There are two remedies for this problem. One is to lessen the total electrical load. The other remedy is to install a new, larger main entrance panel, with new branch circuits to serve areas of heavy electrical usage and help share the total load. This job requires a licensed electrician.

The troubleshooting approach is similar if the main panel has fuses, except that you'll need a supply of fuses on hand. First, pull all the cartridge fuses and unscrew all the plug fuses in the panel. Replace the main fuses and put the fuse block back into place. Then, one by one, replace each fuse or set of fuses until the one that's causing the outage blows out again. This is the circuit that must be cleared. General overloading, however, will cause the main fuses to go out again. If this happens, call in an electrician, who can test for overloading and suggest remedies.

Checking Outlet Polarity

Residential wiring systems installed in older homes use a two-wire system in the 110–120-volt branch circuits. One conductor is hot and the other is neutral. The neutral may also serve as a ground, but, unfortunately, it usually does not. When this is the case, the system is ungrounded, and the situation is potentially hazardous.

You can easily tell if your circuits are of this type by looking at outlets. There are only two slots for each plug in ungrounded outlets. Modern wiring calls for the installation of a third conductor, a bare wire called the equipment grounding conductor. Outlets used with this system have three openings: two vertical slots and a third, rounded hole centered above them. Either two-prong or three-prong plugs can be plugged into these outlets, but only the three-prong kind will carry the equipment grounding line to the electrical equipment. Also, one of the vertical slots is different in size from the other, so the newer types of two-pronged plugs can be inserted in only one direction. This ensures that the equipment being connected will be properly polarized, hot side to hot side and neutral to neutral.

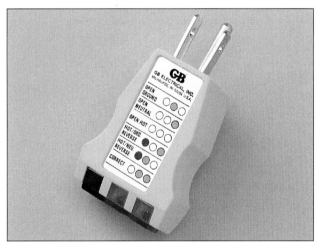

To make sure outlets are installed properly—with the individual conductors going to the correct terminals—you can use a plug-in analyzer to check polarity.

For proper operation and safety, it is essential that all outlets on each circuit be installed with the individual conductors going to the correct terminals so that there are no polarity reversals along the line. Unfortunately, outlets are not always connected this way, even in new wiring systems installed by professional electricians. Check out your outlets with a small, inexpensive tester called a polarity checker, designed for this purpose. It looks like a fancy three-pronged plug and contains three neon bulb indicators. Here's how to check your outlets for polarity and fix reversed polarity if necessary.

Step 1: Plug the polarity checker into an outlet. The lights will tell you if the polarity is correct and, if not, which lines are reversed.

Step 2: If there is a reversal, turn the circuit off, pull the outlet out of the electrical box, and switch the wires to the proper terminals. (This will be discussed in greater detail later in the chapter.)

Step 3: If the equipment-grounding circuit is open (discontinuous), trace the circuit with a continuity tester until you find the disconnection or missing link; reconnect it to restore the effectiveness of the circuit.

Rewiring a Lamp

You can easily repair household lamps that don't work properly. The plug and cord are simple and inexpensive to replace. You can get them at any well-stocked hardware or electrical store. You can install a new socket as easily. Replacement sockets come in various finishes so you should be able to find a socket that is similar to the color tone of the existing socket.

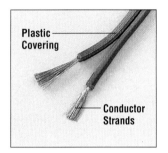

The most common lamp and small appliance cord is Type SPT, often called zip cord. The conductor sheath is plastic; it splits easily along a molded groove.

Lamp cord is known as Type SPT, also known as zip cord. The #18 size is satisfactory for most lamp applications. Zip cord is available in many colors, the most common being black, brown, white, and transparent. Match the cord color to the lamp. The customary length is six feet, but you can use as much cord as you need to reach from the lamp to the outlet. To figure out how much cord to buy, calculate the length of the cord (including a cord that is hidden in the lamp), and add one foot for attachments to socket and plug, and for some slack. In terms of safety and appearance, it's better to have an adequate length of cord than to compensate for a short one with an extension cord. To rewire a lamp:

Step 1: Pull the plug out of the wall socket. You should never do any work while the lamp is connected.

Step 2: Remove the shade, unscrew the bulb, and squeeze the socket shell at the switch to separate the shell and the cardboard insulator from the socket cap. If you plan to reuse the socket, do not use a screwdriver to pry the socket apart. Pull the socket out of the shell as far as the attached wire permits. If this doesn't give you enough wire to work with, push some of the cord up from the bottom of the lamp for additional slack.

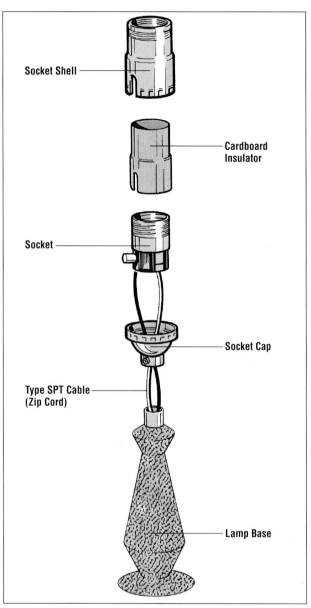

Socket Shell

Cardboard
Insulator

Socket

Socket Cap

Type SPT Cable
(Zip Cord)

Lamp Base

Fixing a lamp is not difficult; the electrical components are inexpensive and easy to replace. The parts that are most often responsible for lamp failure are the socket, the cord, and the plug.

Step 3: Loosen the socket's terminal screws and remove the cord wires from under them. If the lamp is a small one and the cord goes through in a straight path, slide the old wire out and feed the new wire through from either end to the other. If the old cord offers any resistance at all, don't tug on it. Check to see if you can disassemble the lamp to make removal easier. Also make sure the cord is tied in a knot to keep it from being pulled out at its base.

Step 4: To remove a tight cord, cut the wire off about 12 inches from the lamp's base, slit the cord's two conductors apart, and strip about an inch of insulation off the ends. Do the same to one end of the new length of cord. Twist the bare new and old conductor ends together and fold the twists flat along the cord. Wrap plastic electricians' tape around the splice. Pull on the old cord from the top of the fixture and work the new cord through; at the same time, push on the new cord from the bottom to aid the process. When you have a sufficient length of new cord through the top, clip off the old cord.

Step 5: Once you pass the new cord through the lamp, split the end so that you have about three inches of separated conductors. Use a wire-stripper tool to strip about ¾ inch of insulation from the end of each conductor, then twist the strands of each together. Be very careful not to nick the strands when you strip the insulation.

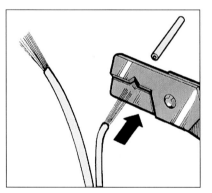

Before connecting the lamp cord, split the conductors apart for about 3 inches. Then, with a wire stripper, remove about ¾ inch of insulation from each conductor end. Do not use a knife for this job.

Step 6: Bend the twisted end of each wire into a clockwise loop, and place each loop under a terminal screw on the socket, with the loop curled clockwise around the screw.

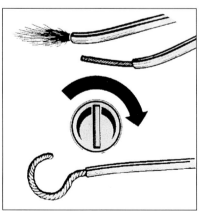

Twist the exposed conductor strands to form a solid prong; then loop the prong clockwise around the terminal screw. The loop is pulled tighter as the screw is tightened.

Step 7: Tighten the terminal screws. As each screw is tightened, the clockwise loop will pull the wire tighter under the screw head. (A counterclockwise loop would tend to loosen the wire.)

Step 8: Clip off excess bare wire with diagonal cutters. All the uninsulated wire must be under the screw heads, with no loose strands or exposed bare wire. If bare wire is visible beyond the screw heads, unscrew the terminals, remove the wires, and make the connection again.

Step 9: Slide the socket shell over the insulator, and slip the shell and insulator over the socket. Then snap the shell and socket into the cap.

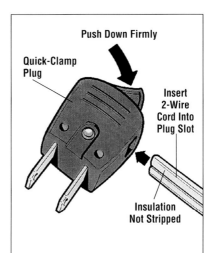

Push Down Firmly

Quick-Clamp Plug

Insert 2-Wire Cord Into Plug Slot

Insulation Not Stripped

A quick-clamp plug is very easy to install. Metal prongs inside the plug bite through the cord's insulation and pierce the copper wires inside to make the electrical connection.

LAMP TROUBLESHOOTING CHART		
Problem	**Possible Cause**	**Solution**
Lamp does not light	1. Lamp unplugged.	1. Plug lamp in.
	2. Circuit dead.	2. Restore circuit.
	3. Bulb loose.	3. Tighten bulb.
	4. Bulb burned out.	4. Replace bulb.
	5. Loose connection at plug or socket.	5. Trace and repair.
	6. Defective wall switch.	6. Replace switch.
	7. Defective socket switch.	7. Replace socket.
	8. Defective center contact in socket.	8. Pry contact up or replace socket.
	9. Broken conductor in line cord.	9. Replace line cord.
Lamp blows fuse or trips circuit breaker	1. Overloaded circuit.	1. Check total load on circuit. If overloaded, transfer some equipment to different circuit.
	2. Short circuit in socket, in cord, or in lamp wiring.	2. Replace socket and cord. Rewire carefully to make sure no bare wires touch each other or any metal parts of lamp.
Lamp flickers when moved or touched	1. Lamp bulb loose in socket.	1. Tighten bulb.
	2. Loose connection, usually where line cord wires are fastened under terminal screws on lamp socket.	2. First make sure lamp is unplugged; then take socket apart and inspect wire connections under screws. Tighten screws or, if necessary, cut off a short piece of cord and reattach wire ends.
	3. Defective contacts or faulty switch in socket.	3. First make sure lamp is unplugged; then remove socket and replace it with new one.
	4. Defective lamp cord.	4. Replace cord. Rewire so no bare wires touch each other or any metal parts of lamp.

Step 10: Install a quick-clamp plug on the other end of the cord. Stick the end of the cord into a slot on the side of the plug and push down on the lever at the top. Metal prongs inside the plug will bite through the cord's insulation, piercing the copper wires to make the electrical connection. If you use a screw-type plug, prepare the wire ends just as you did when making the socket screw connections, then knot them together. Loop each wire around a prong of the plug before tightening the bare end under the screw head. The knots and loops keep the wires from accidentally touching each other and also make it more difficult to loosen the connections by pulling on the cord.

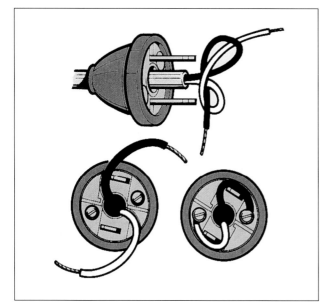

On screw-type plugs, insert the cord, tie the wires into a knot, and pull the knot down into the plug. Then loop each wire around a prong before tightening the bare end under the screw head. This helps keep the wires from touching each other accidentally and provides some resistance to stress.

Step 11: Tighten the wires under the screw heads, and clip off any excess uninsulated conductor before you plug in the lamp.

Replacing Incandescent Lighting Fixtures

Replacing a lighting fixture is relatively simple. In fact, the worst difficulties you'll probably encounter involve not the electrical connections but the mechanical complexities of attaching a new fixture to older mounting hardware. *Caution: Before you replace or repair*

any lighting fixture, de-energize the appropriate electrical circuit by pulling the appropriate fuse or tripping the proper circuit breaker. To replace an incandescent lighting fixture:

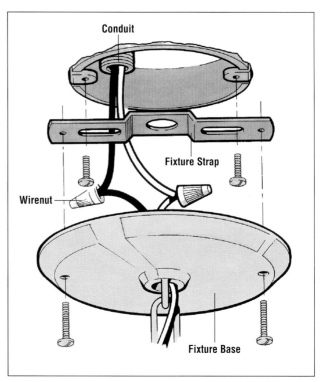

The simplest fixture installation uses a fixture strap secured to the electrical box. Connect white wire to white and black to black.

Step 1: Take off the light cover, unscrew the bulb(s), and disassemble all mounting hardware. Usually there are just screws holding the fixture against the wall or ceiling. If the lighting fixture has no visible mounting hardware, the fixture could have a decorative feature that doubles as a fastener. Take off the mounting hardware and withdraw the fixture from the electrical box.

Step 2: Disconnect the lamp fixture wires from the circuit wires. If the wire joint is fused together with old insulating tape, cut the wires close to the tape. *Caution: If the wires or insulation coming into the electrical box are brittle or frayed, that part of the circuit should be professionally rewired.*

Once you remove the old fixture, examine the electrical box and new fixture to determine which of the following installation procedures you should use for additional steps. For fixture installation in a standard electrical box:

Step 3: Make sure you have about ¾ inch of bare copper conductor on the end of each line wire before you start to connect the wires of your new lighting fixture. If necessary, remove enough insulation from the line wires so that you can twist each line wire end together with the end of each light fixture wire, white wire to white and black to black.

Step 4: Screw a wirenut tightly over each pair of twisted ends. Hold on to the fixture to support its weight until you attach the mounting screws; otherwise, you might break a connection or damage the fixture wires.

Step 5: If the fixture has more than one socket, connect the black wire from each socket to the black line wire, and the white wire from each socket to the white line wire. When three or four socket wires are joined to a line, use a larger wirenut.

Step 6: Mounting screws of the proper length are typically included with your new lamp fixture. Screws 2 or 2½ inches long are sufficient for most fixtures. Insert the screws into the attachment screw holes in the electrical box, and tighten each screw four or five turns to hold it in place. Mount the fixture by passing the fixture's keyhole slots over the screw heads. Then rotate the fixture enough so that the screws are forced into the narrow parts of the keyhole slots.

Step 7: Tighten the screws, being careful not to overtighten them; they should be just snug enough to hold the fixture firmly in place. If you tighten the mounting screws too much, you may distort and misalign the fixture. With the fixture mounted properly, screw in the bulbs and attach the globe or cover.

Step 8: Replace the fuse or trip the circuit breaker back on. Flip the wall switch. If the fixture lights, your job is finished. If nothing happens, go back and figure out which connection needs remaking.

Some fixtures are mounted with a short piece of threaded pipe, called a nipple. To mount this type of fixture, screw the nipple into the center hole of the strap and set the fixture onto the nipple. Screw a cap nut onto the nipple to hold the fixture in place.

Some light fixtures are not strap-mounted. Instead, a nipple is connected to the box stud with a reducing nut or an adapter called a hickey. A reducing nut is threaded at one end to fit the stud, and at the other end to fit the nipple. To mount a fixture that uses a reducing nut,

screw the nut onto the stud and the nipple onto the nut. Set the fixture onto the nipple, set the fixture into place, and screw a cap nut onto the nipple to hold the fixture in place. To mount a fixture with a hickey, screw the hickey onto the stud, and then mount the fixture the same way.

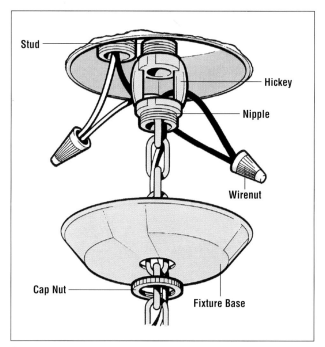

Some fixtures don't use a mounting strap; the fixture is secured to the stud with a hickey, or a reducing nut.

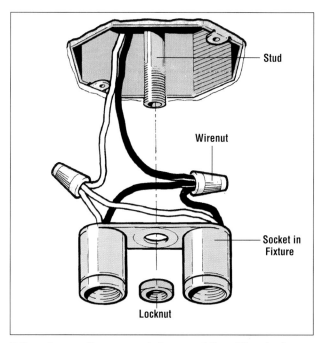

If there is more than one socket, connect the white wire from each socket to the white line wire, and the black wire to the black line wire.

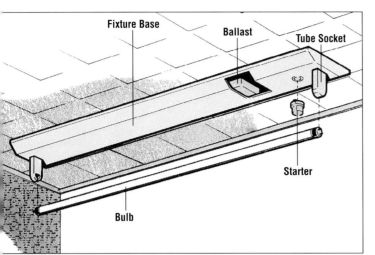

A fluorescent fixture has three main parts—bulb, ballast, and starter. When one of these components malfunctions, replacement is usually the answer.

Installing Fluorescent Lamps

You might consider replacing some of your old incandescent fixtures with fluorescent lamps. Fluorescent light provides even and shadow-free illumination, but best of all, fluorescent bulbs are more efficient than incandescent bulbs. In an incandescent bulb, much of the electric power is discharged as heat instead of light. The fluorescent bulb, in contrast, remains cool.

How does a fluorescent lamp work? In a fluorescent circuit, beginning at the left-hand prong of the plug, current goes through the ballast, then through one of the lamp filaments, through the closed switch in the starter, through the other filament in the lamp, and out the right-hand prong of the plug. The current heats the two small elements in the ends of the fluorescent tube; then the starter opens, and current flows through the lamp.

The ballast is a magnetic coil that adjusts the current through the tube. It makes a surge of current arc through the tube when the starter opens, and then it keeps the current flowing at the right rate once the tube is glowing. In most fluorescent fixtures, the starter is an automatic switch. Once it senses that the lamp is glowing, it stays open. The starter closes whenever you de-energize the fixture.

Many fluorescent fixtures have more than one tube in order to provide more light. These lamps must have individual starters and ballasts for each tube. The fixture may appear to have two tubes working off one ballast, but actually there are two ballasts built into one case. Fixtures with four tubes, similarly, have four starters and

four ballasts. In some kinds of fixtures, the starters are built in and cannot be individually replaced.

Since there are only three primary parts in a fluorescent lamp, you can usually take care of any repairs yourself. All fluorescent lamps grow dimmer with age, and they may even begin to flicker or flash on and off. These are warning signals, and you should make the necessary repairs as soon as you notice any change in the lamp's normal performance. A dim tube usually requires replacement, and failure to replace it can strain other parts of the fixture. Likewise, repeated flickering or flashing will wear out the starter, causing the insulation at the starter to deteriorate.

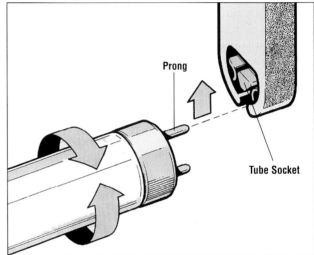

To install a new fluorescent tube, insert the tube's prongs into the holder and twist the tube to lock it into place. Change the tube when it dims, flickers, or flashes on and off.

Fluorescent fixtures can be serviced quite simply by the replacement method. If you suspect that a part may be defective, replace the part with a new one. Start with the fluorescent tube or bulb. You can either install a new one or, if you're not sure the tube is burned out, test the old tube in another fluorescent fixture. Doing both gives you double verification. Remove the old tube by twisting it out of its sockets in the fixture. Install the new tube the same way; insert the tube's prongs into the socket and twist the tube to lock it into place.

Caution: *Discard old fluorescent tubes carefully to avoid injury to yourself or others. Wrap an old tube in heavy paper such as a grocery bag, smash the tube with a hammer, and put the wrapped broken glass in another bag before disposing of it properly.*

If the problem is not in the tube, change the starter, if possible. Fluorescent lamp starters are rated according to wattage, and it's important that you use the right starter for the tube in your fixture. Remove the old starter the

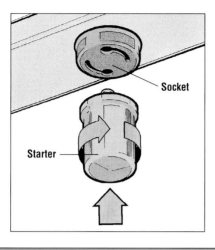

To install a starter in a fluorescent fixture, simply insert the starter and twist it to secure it in its socket.

Socket

Starter

same way you removed the old tube, by twisting it out of its socket in the fixture. Install the new one by inserting it into the socket and twisting it to lock it into place.

The ballast is also rated according to wattage, and a replacement ballast—like a replacement starter—must match the wattage of the tube and the type of fixture. The ballast is the least likely part to fail and most difficult to replace, so leave the ballast for last when you start replacing parts. If neither the tube nor the starter is defective, the problem must be the ballast. To replace a faulty ballast, de-energize the circuit, disassemble the fixture, transfer wires from the old ballast to the new one—one at a time, to avoid an incorrect connection—and, finally, reassemble the fixture.

FLUORESCENT LAMP TROUBLESHOOTING CHART

Problem	Possible Cause	Solution
Lamp will not light	1. Burned-out tube.	1. Replace with new fluorescent tube of correct dimensions and wattage.
	2. Defective starter.	2. Replace starter with new one of appropriate wattage.
	3. Defective ballast, sometimes accompanied by the odor of burning insulation.	3. Replace ballast; before replacing, consider cost of new ballast in comparison to value of lamp fixture.
	4. Defective switch.	4. Replace switch.
	5. Tube not seated correctly in sockets.	5. Reseat tube in sockets.
	6. No power to lamp.	6. Check power circuit.
Lamp glows dimly	1. Defective tube.	1. Replace tube. If lamp has been flashing on and off repeatedly for extended period, also replace starter.
	2. Defective starter.	2. Replace starter with one of correct wattage.
Tube ends lit but middle dim or dark	1. Wiring incorrect.	1. Check wiring.
	2. Shorted starter.	2. Replace starter with new one of appropriate wattage.
	3. Tube burned out.	3. Replace tube.
Spiraling or flickering lamp	1. Tube burned out.	1. Replace with new fluorescent tube of correct dimensions and wattage.
	2. Defective or wrong starter.	2. Replace starter with one of appropriate wattage.
	3. Low line voltage.	3. Check voltage; it must be within 10 percent of 120 volts.
	4. Wrong ballast.	4. Replace ballast.
Lamp flashes on and off repeatedly	1. Defective tube.	1. Replace tube and starter.
	2. Defective starter.	2. Replace starter with one of appropriate wattage.

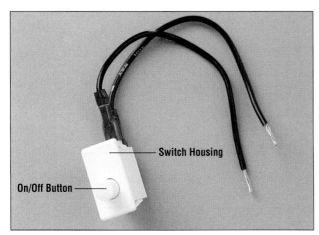

If the lamp is controlled by a push-button switch, the switch can also be replaced. Transfer the wires one at a time from the old switch to the new one.

Switch Housing

On/Off Button

If the tube, the starter, and the ballast are all working properly but the lamp still doesn't light, check for a defective switch. If the lamp is controlled by a wall switch, replace the switch, as detailed in the next section. If the lamp has a push-button switch, the old switch can be replaced by a new one of the same type. To de-energize the circuit before working on the switch, remove the circuit's fuse or trip the circuit breaker.

In most cases, the switch screws into a threaded mounting nut on the inside of the lamp. Two wires from the switch are connected, usually with wirenuts, to four wires from the fluorescent tube. Disassemble the fixture as far as necessary to gain access to the back of the switch, then screw in the new switch and transfer wires from the old switch to the new one, one at a time to avoid an incorrect connection. Finally, reassemble the fixture and re-energize the circuit.

If you're considering installing a new ballast or a new switch, consider putting in an entirely new fixture. An old fluorescent fixture suffers the same aging effects that an incandescent fixture does. Of course, you can also replace an old incandescent lamp with a new fluorescent model. Either replacement is well within the capabilities of the do-it-yourselfer. Here's how to install a new fluorescent fixture:

Step 1: De-energize the old fixture. Note that simply turning off the wall switch may not de-energize the fixture, so be sure to remove the circuit's fuse or trip the circuit breaker.

Step 2: Remove the old hardware that holds the existing lamp fixture in place, and disconnect the lamp wires from the circuit line wires. Then disassemble the new fluorescent lamp as far as necessary to gain access to the fixture wires.

Step 3: Connect the fixture wires to the line wires with wirenuts or crimp-type solderless connectors. Match the wires by color: white wire to white, black to black.

Step 4: Position the fixture against the ceiling and fasten it with the screws that are packaged with the new lamp. You may have to reassemble the fixture, either before or after mounting it; this depends on its style.

Step 5: Once you get the lamp back together, restore the power and turn on your new fluorescent lighting fixture.

Replacing a Wall Switch

Sometimes a lamp that's in perfect operating condition doesn't work because the wall switch is faulty. There are several primary symptoms of switch failure:

- When the switch loses its snap, when the handle hangs loosely in any position, or when there is no clear distinction between the OFF/ON positions.
- When flipping the switch no longer turns the light on or off.
- When flipping the switch makes the light flicker, but the light will not stay on or off.
- When the switch may work occasionally, but you have to jiggle the handle back and forth several times to keep the light on.

If you spot any of these symptoms of switch failure, install a replacement wall switch as soon as you can. Here's how:

Step 1: De-energize the electrical circuit that controls the switch.

Step 2: Remove the switch cover plate. If the cover plate doesn't come off easily, it is probably being held in place by several layers of paint. Use a razor blade or a craft or utility knife to cut the paint closely around the edge of the plate to free it.

Step 3: Inspect the old switch to determine the type of replacement model you must buy. (Replace cover until you return with new switch.) You must use the same type, but in most cases you can install a better grade of switch than the one you had before. All work on the same general principles, and you can usually choose a switch with the features you like best. The single-pole toggle switch is still the most popular. When the toggle switch is mounted properly, the words ON and OFF are upright on the toggle lever, and the light goes on when

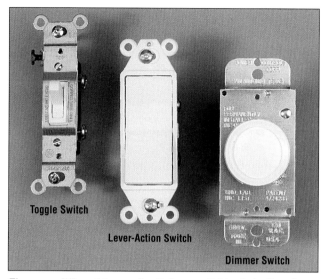

Toggle Switch

Lever-Action Switch

Dimmer Switch

There are different types of switches available, but all work on the same general principles. Usually, you can base your selection of a replacement switch on the features you like best.

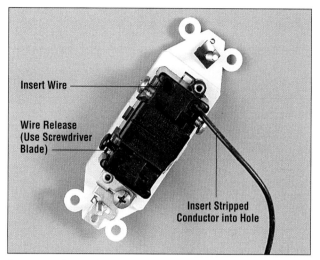

Insert Wire

Wire Release (Use Screwdriver Blade)

Insert Stripped Conductor into Hole

Some switches and receptacles don't have terminal screws. They have holes into which the stripped wire ends are inserted. Other types, like this one, have both holes and terminal screws.

you flip the switch up. A variation of the traditional toggle switch is the lever-action switch. The lever-action switch lies almost flush with the wall. It turns the fixture on when someone pushes the top of the switch in. The push-button switch has a single button that turns the light on when pressed, and off when pressed again. Some switches are available with the extra feature of a built-in neon lamp that glows when the switch is off, making it easy to locate the switch in the dark. Dimmer switches, with a dial to control the brightness, turn the light off when the dial is turned all the way down or pushed in. Some dimmer switches are like toggle types. Sliding the toggle upward increases the light's intensity; sliding it all the way down turns off the light. You can install these switches as replacements for nearly any type of switch.

Step 4: Prepare the new switch for installation. Some kinds of wall switches have no terminal screws for conductor attachments. Instead, the switch has small holes that are only slightly larger than the bare copper conductors. Remove about ½ inch of insulation from the ends of the wires, then push the bare ends into the holes. Locking tabs make the electrical connection and grip the wires so that they can't pull out. If necessary, release the wires from the old switch by inserting a narrow-blade screwdriver in the slots next to the wire-grip holes.

Step 5: Remove the mounting screws on the switch cover plate and take off the plate. With the plate removed, you'll see two screws holding the switch in the switch box. If necessary, remove the screws and carefully pull the switch out of the box as far as the attached wires allow. If there are two screws with wires attached, the switch is a simple on/off (single-pole) type. If there are three screws with wires

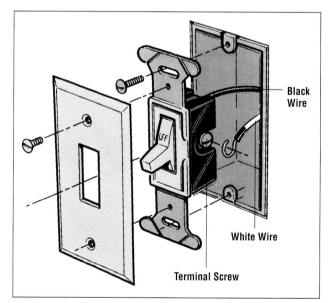

Black Wire

White Wire

Terminal Screw

If a switch has only two terminal screws with wires attached, it's a simple on/off (single-pole) switch. This type of switch is very easy to install. Connect the line wires to the screws, secure the switch, and replace the cover plate.

attached, you're working with a more complicated type called a three-way switch. The new switch must be the same type as the old one, either single-pole or three-way. Three-way switches allow you to turn a light on and off from two different locations, such as at the top and the bottom of a stairway. Look carefully at the three terminal screws; you'll see that two are one color, while the third is a different color. Do not disconnect any wires until you compare the old switch with the replacement switch so you know which wire goes to which terminal screw.

Step 6: Loosen one of the old terminal screws, remove the wire, and attach the wire to the corresponding terminal screw on the new switch. Then do the same with the remaining wires. Take care to connect the wires so that all the bare wire is safely under the screw heads; clip off any excess uninsulated wire. The procedure is the same whether you're working with a simple on/off switch or a three-way switch, but you must be more careful with the latter. Verify your wiring by comparing it with the manufacturer's diagram on the package of your new switch.

Step 7: If you're installing the modern wire-grip type of wall switch, cut off the end of each wire to leave only ½ inch of bare wire. Push one bare end of wire into each wire-grip hole, and

check that the wires have caught properly by tugging gently on them. ***Caution:*** *If the wires or insulation going into the electrical box are brittle or frayed, that part of the circuit should be professionally rewired.*

Step 8: Replace the switch in the wall electrical box. Push the switch into the box carefully, and make sure the wires fit neatly into the box behind the switch. There are small tabs extending from the switch's mounting bracket; these tabs are supposed to lie flat against the wall outside the electrical box. They hold the switch flush with the wall no matter how the electrical box is angled inside.

Step 9: Put the switch back into place, using the two mounting screws provided with the new switch. Oval holes in the mounting bracket allow you to fasten the switch so that it's straight up and down even when the screw holes in the electrical box are tilted.

Step 10: Attach the cover plate with the screws you took out earlier, and replace the circuit fuse or trip the circuit breaker back on. Then enjoy the convenience of a switch that works the way it should.

Replacing a Receptacle

Few people call an electrical outlet by its proper name, a receptacle, but nearly everyone has come across an outlet that doesn't work as well as it should or one that doesn't work at all. How does it happen that an outlet fails to do its job efficiently and safely? There are two possible explanations.

An electrical outlet can be permanently damaged through improper use. Sticking a hairpin or a paper clip in it, for example, can shorten an outlet's—and your—life. You may never do anything as foolish as sticking hairpins or paper clips in an outlet, but you can do the same damage when you plug in an appliance with a short circuit. Regardless of how the damage occurred, the damaged outlet must be replaced.

Another possible explanation for an outlet that doesn't work efficiently and safely is that it's just so old, and has been used so often, that it's worn out. There are two clear indications of a worn-out outlet: the cord's weight pulls the plug out of the outlet; or the plug blades do not make constant electrical contact within the outlet slots. At that point, the old outlet should be replaced. This is not difficult, but you must follow the correct installation procedures precisely. To replace an outlet:

Three-way switches allow you to turn a light on and off from two different locations—such as at the top or the bottom of a stairway.

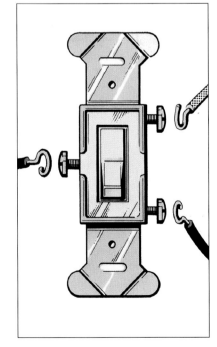

Step 1: Inspect the old outlet to see whether it can take a plug that has a round prong (for grounding) in addition to two flat blades. Buy a new outlet with a 20-amp rating of the same type—grounded or ungrounded—as the one you're replacing.

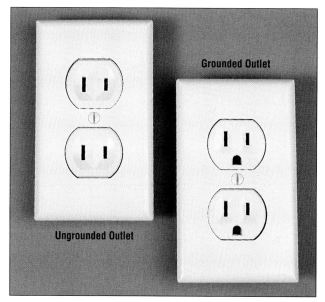

When replacing a receptacle, see whether it accepts only plugs with two flat blades or whether it can take plugs that have a rounded ground prong.

Step 2: Before working on the outlet, de-energize the circuit that controls it.

Step 3: Take off the plate that covers the outlet. This should be an easy task; the cover plate should fall off when you remove the center screw. If it doesn't, it's probably being held in place by several coats of paint. Cut the paint closely around the edge of the cover plate with a razor blade or a craft or utility knife.

Step 4: Remove the two screws holding the outlet in the electrical box. Carefully pull the outlet out of the box as far as the attached line wires allow. Loosen the terminal screws on the outlet and remove the line wires. If you find the wiring is quite old and the insulation is brittle, that part of the circuit should be professionally rewired.

Step 5: Connect the wires to the new outlet, with the white wire under the silver-colored screw and the black wire under the dark-colored screw. If there's a green or bare wire in the box, fasten it under the screw with the dab of green color on it, and then fasten it to the box with a grounding screw or clip. Be sure to loop the line wires

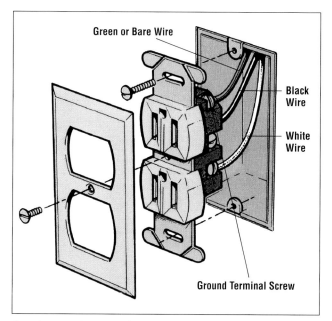

A replacement receptacle must match the one you are removing. If you have the grounded type, you must buy a receptacle that has a ground terminal screw and slots for three-prong grounded plugs.

in a clockwise direction under the heads of the terminal screws so that the screw heads will pull the wire loops tighter. Take care to connect the wires so that all the wire without insulation is safely under the screw heads. Clip off any excess uninsulated wire.

Step 6: Carefully fold the wires into the space in the electrical box behind the outlet, then push the outlet into the box. Although there's no such thing as right side up for a two-blade outlet, there is a correct position for outlets designed to handle three-prong grounding plugs. Grounding plugs often attach to their cords at a right angle, so you should position the outlet so that the cord will hang down without a loop.

Step 7: Tighten the two screws that hold the receptacle in the outlet box, replace the cover plate, and your work is done. Restore the fuse or trip the circuit breaker.

Slots in some outlets are not identical; one is wider than the other. The wider one connects to the white or neutral wire, while the narrower slot connects to the black or hot wire. Some plugs, in fact, are designed with one wide and one narrow blade, and these plugs will fit into the outlet in only one way. The idea behind such a polarized plug is to continue the hot and neutral wire identity from the circuit to the appliance.

131

Repairing a Doorbell

Many people consider a broken doorbell a repair that requires a professional, but at the same time, they don't consider it a repair that warrants immediate attention. Thus, some homeowners simply put up a sign to tell friends and neighbors that the doorbell doesn't work, and then settle down to wait until the electrician has to be called in for some other pressing task—at which time the doorbell finally gets fixed, too. There's no reason why you should follow this course. Repairing a broken doorbell is a job you can easily do yourself.

When your doorbell or door chime doesn't ring, the fault could be in any part of the circuitry—the button, the bell or chime, or the transformer. The transformer is the electrical component that steps down the 110–120-volt current to the 10 to 18 volts at which doorbells and chimes operate. You can work safely on all parts of the doorbell circuit except the transformer without disconnecting the power. If you don't know which part of the circuit is faulty:

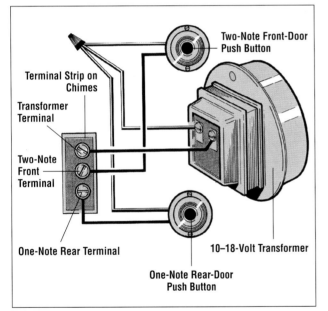

Terminal Strip on Chimes

Transformer Terminal

Two-Note Front Terminal

One-Note Rear Terminal

Two-Note Front-Door Push Button

10–18-Volt Transformer

One-Note Rear-Door Push Button

If your doorbell or chime doesn't work, the fault could be in any part of the circuitry—from a push button, to the bell or chimes, or to the transformer. Before removing any wires at the terminal strip, it's a good idea to tag them so that they can be replaced correctly.

Step 1: Remove the screws that hold the doorbell push button to your house.

Step 2: Pull the button as far out as the circuit wires allow, and then detach the wires by loosening the terminal screws on the button. Bring the two bare wire ends together. If the bell rings,

you know the fault is in the button. Install a new one by connecting the two wires to the terminal screws of the new button and reattaching the button to your house. The doorbell button is a single-pole switch (two wires attached), and you can place either wire under either screw.

Step 3: If the bell doesn't ring when you bring the two bare wire ends together, the fault lies elsewhere: in the bell or chime assembly, the wiring, or the transformer. Go to the bell or chime and remove the snap-on cover. Removal may be harder than you expect; there are several different types of covers, and you may have to try several procedures. Try lifting the cover upward slightly and then pulling it out. If this doesn't work, pull it straight out without first lifting it up. Or look to see whether the snap-on cover is held to the bell or chime assembly with prongs; if so, depress the prongs and then pull the cover to release it. Whatever you do, never pull so hard that you risk damaging the decorative cover.

Step 4: Once the cover is removed, look for two, three, or more terminals and wires, depending on how many tones ring in your doorbell system. A standard bell or buzzer has two wires. Detach the wires by loosening the terminal screws, then connect them to a 12-volt circuit tester or attach them to the terminal screws on a substitute bell or chime. An inexpensive bell or buzzer or a 12-volt car lamp bulb in a socket with two wires can be used for testing purposes. If the test bell or buzzer sounds or the bulb lights when you push the doorbell button, you will have to install a new bell or chime.

Step 5: If you have a chime assembly with three or more wires, tag them with masking tape: "T" for transformer, "2" for the front-door chime, and "1" for the back-door chime. Loosen the terminal screws, remove all the wires, and connect the wires labeled "T" and "2" to the screw terminals on the test bell or bulb. If the test bell rings or the bulb lights when you push the front-door button, your old chime set is faulty. To check this conclusion, connect the wires labeled "T" and "1" to the screw terminals on the test bell. If the bell rings when you push the back-door button, then you're doubly certain that the chimes must be replaced.

Step 6: If the bell doesn't ring or the bulb doesn't light at the button or at the bell box, both are okay. By process of elimination, you now know that the problem must be in the transformer or the wiring. You'll usually find the transformer mounted on an electrical junction box, a subpanel, or the main entrance panel. The bell wires are attached to exposed terminal screws on the transformer. Connect the test bell directly to the exposed low-voltage transformer terminals; don't touch any other screws. If the bell doesn't ring, the transformer is defective or not getting power. ***Caution:*** *The transformer is connected directly to the power supply, and it carries current that can hurt you. Before working on the transformer, de-energize the branch circuit that supplies power to the transformer. Remove the appropriate fuse or trip the correct circuit breaker, or throw the main switch to shut off all the electricity in your home.*

Step 7: Before replacing the transformer, check to make sure that it's getting power from the 110–120-volt circuit. With the circuit de-energized, disconnect the transformer from the line wires. Then turn the circuit back on again and touch the probes of a 110–120-volt circuit tester to the bare wire ends. If the tester light glows or the indicator reads 110–120 volts, the circuit is all right.

Step 8: If the transformer is defective, de-energize the circuit and remove the transformer. Buy a replacement transformer of the same voltage and wattage. You can find the electrical information stamped on the transformer, and you should find installation instructions on the package. Follow the instructions carefully. Use crimp-on connectors or wirenuts to attach the new transformer to the circuit line wires of your electrical system. Then connect the bell wires to the low-voltage screw terminals on the transformer, turn the power back on, and press the doorbell button. If you've installed the transformer properly, you should hear the bell or chime.

Step 9: If the transformer and its power circuit prove to be all right, the only possibility left is a break or a loose connection somewhere in the bell wiring. Trace the bell circuit from transformer to bell or chime to push buttons, searching for a loose terminal screw or wire joint. If this proves unsuccessful, you'll have to check each segment of the circuit with a continuity tester.

Step 10: To test each segment of the circuit, disconnect the bell wires at the transformer to de-energize the bell circuit. A continuity tester can never be used on an energized circuit. Disconnect the transformer wires at the bell or

DOORBELL OR CHIME TROUBLESHOOTING CHART		
Problem	**Possible Cause**	**Solution**
Bell or chime does not ring	1. Defective button.	1. Test by removing button and touching wires together. If bell rings, button is defective; replace button.
	2. Defective bell or chimes.	2. Detach wires from bell or chimes and connect them to a test bell or light. If bell rings or bulb lights when doorbell button is depressed, bell is defective; replace bell.
	3. Defective transformer.	3. Connect test bell to transformer and press door button. If bell does not ring, transformer is defective; replace transformer.
	4. Loose connection or break in circuit.	4. Trace and check all wiring; tighten loose connections or replace damaged wiring.
	5. No power at transformer.	5. Check to see that circuit is turned on; check for loose connection at transformer primary. If transformer is defective, replace.

chime, and twist them together so they make contact with one another. Go back to the transformer, and touch the probe leads of the continuity tester to the bare ends of the bell wires. If the tester lights up, or if you get a reading on the meter dial, the circuit has continuity and there are no breaks or loose connections in the line. That part of the circuit is all right. If the tester does not register, there's a break somewhere. If that segment is fault-free, go on to the next segment and check it the same way.

Step 11: If there is a break, you must try to locate it and make repairs. Sometimes, however, especially where much of the bell circuit wiring is hidden within walls or is otherwise inaccessible, the easiest course of action is to run a new segment of bell wire along whatever path is easiest and forget about the old wiring segment.

Installing Other Electrical Components

You are in for a pleasant surprise if you think that electrical repairs and replacements represent the limit of what you can do with the electrical system in your home. Many do-it-yourselfers with no prior experience install their own ceiling fan, alarm system, sound system, and garage door opener. The following pages will show you how to complete each of these tasks.

Installing a Ceiling Fan

Replacing a light fixture with a new ceiling fan is an easy process. With just a little more work you can add a new lighting fixture to the bottom of the fan unit. Only basic tools and skills are needed. Here's how:

Step 1: To de-energize the circuit, remove the appropriate fuse or trip the correct circuit breaker. Or you can throw the main switch to shut off all the electricity in your home.

Step 2: Remove the original light fixture from the ceiling. Most fixtures are bolted or screwed into

the ceiling and can be disconnected once the cover is removed.

Step 3: Lower the fixture and disconnect the wires. Mark each with a piece of masking tape to identify it later.

Step 4: Review the manufacturer's instructions on color coding of the wiring and recommended installation procedures. In most homes, there will be two wires in the circuit and three in the fixture. Connect the black wires together, the white wires together, and then connect the remaining ground (bare or green) wire to the metal junction box or other location suggested by the manufacturer. Use twist-on electrical nuts to make the connections and, once connected, check them for tightness.

Step 5: Check over the wiring, reviewing the manufacturer's instructions to make sure everything is correct. Then carefully push all wires into the junction box.

Step 6: Attach the fixture to the junction box or hangers as directed by the manufacturer.

Step 7: If you're installing a light below the fan, make sure the two parts are of the same brand and designed to work together (this will make the process much easier). Remove the bottom cover from the fan unit and pull out the ends of any loose wires. Follow the manufacturer's instructions for connection. Typically that means connect black to black, white to white, and ground to ground.

Step 8: Re-energize the circuit and test the system.

Installing a Home Security System

Some home security systems are complex and should be installed by a professional. However, there are many good home security systems sold in kit forms that can be installed by any do-it-yourselfer. Most simple systems use a bell, loud buzzer, or other sound source to note intrusion.

Installation involves mounting the sound source or sounder in a location where it can be easily heard. Then attach a circuit of switches to the sounder and connect a battery to the system. Since the sounder operates from the battery, it remains an effective alarm system even in the event of a power failure.

In electrical terminology, this alarm system is called a closed-circuit system. When the doors and windows are shut, the attached switches are closed. Because all the switches are in a wiring loop, opening any one of them

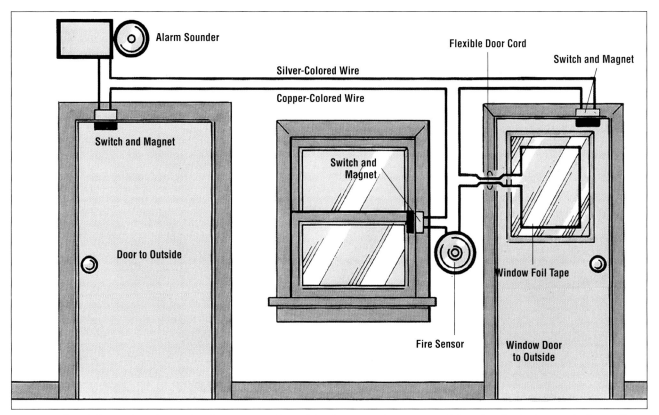

Because all switches in this closed-circuit system are in a wiring loop, opening any one of them breaks the loop and triggers the bell-ringing circuit.

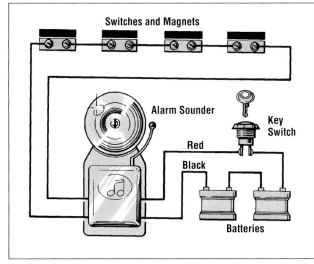

The diagram shows how the closed-circuit wiring loop is connected to a key switch, the alarm bell, and the batteries.

breaks the loop and triggers the sounder circuit. Simply closing the door or window, moreover, does not restore the switch loop circuit continuity and does not stop the sound until either the battery becomes exhausted or someone switches off the circuit from battery to sounder.

There is an electronic switch built into the sounder. This switch is turned on by breaking the magnetic-switch loop. A key-operated switch in the sounder circuit allows you to turn the alarm system completely off when it is not needed. Also, once the alarm goes on, operating the key switch is the only way to silence the sounder. Only someone who has a key to the switch can reset the system.

The switch device consists of two parts that look much alike: one small plastic box that contains a strong magnet, and another that contains the actual switch. When magnet and switch are not near each other, the switch contacts are separated and the switch is open. On the other hand, when the magnet and switch are near each other, the switch contacts move together and the switch closes. The magnet part of the device is screwed to a door or window, and the switch part is screwed to the door or window frame. Thus, opening a door or window separates magnet from switch, causing the switch to open and trigger the alarm.

The three electronic parts that comprise the solid-state switch of the alarm sounder are mounted on a circuit board. Under the circuit board are a solenoid coil and a plunger that strikes the bell or activates the electronic sounder. Below the coil is a set of breaker

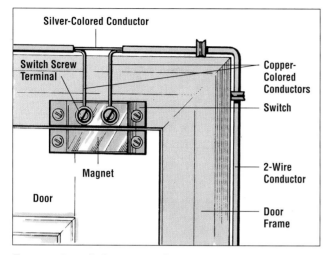

To connect a switch, cut apart the copper-colored wire only and bare the ends. The ends are connected to the terminal screws of the magnet switch.

points that causes the plunger to vibrate up and down, activating the sound source.

Install the sounder first. Decide where you want it located—either to attract the most attention for help or to scare away an intruder. If you decide to mount the sounder outdoors, you must drill a hole through the wall for the wires. To shield the sounder from the weather, you should install it in a protective metal box of the type made especially for alarm sounders. Inside the box is a bracket for mounting a tamper switch that sets off the alarm system if someone tries to open the alarm sounder box. Located in the side of the box is the key switch that allows a person with a key (but no one else) to activate, service, reset, or deactivate the alarm system.

If you want the sounder to be located indoors, you need not install it in a protective metal box. Mount the sounder on the wall in a place where it can be heard easily. Placing an indoor sounder in a closet or other confined space is not recommended.

The kit should include a mounting backplate attached to the sounder by a mounting screw. Remove the nut and separate the backplate from the sounder. You will see a pattern of holes in the backplate. Using wood screws, toggle bolts, or other suitable fasteners, attach the plate to the wall at the place you have chosen to position the sounder. Mount the backplate with enough fasteners to hold the sounder solidly in place. Make sure that the plate is mounted right side up, and that the correct side is forward. There is usually a tongue on the backplate that should be at the top when it is mounted properly. Do not connect the sounder to the backplate until later. You will find that the protective box for an outdoor installation already contains a built-in backplate. Mount the box in the desired location.

Next, install the door and window switches. The magnet part goes on the door or window, while the switch part goes on the window frame or door jamb. Use the mounting screws in the kit to attach the parts. Try to position the two parts of the switch so that they are close together—almost touching—when the window or door is closed, and widely separated when the door or window starts to open.

If you wish, you can include fire sensor switches in the loop of entry-detection switches. Use the kind of fire sensor switch that breaks the loop when the air temperature in its vicinity reaches 135°F. Since that is more than the air temperature is ever likely to reach normally—except in attics, furnace rooms, or over wood or coal stoves or other high-heat producers—you will never experience false alarms during hot weather. Install 190°F sensors in normally hot locations. You should mount the fire sensor switches in the spots where you feel they will be most effective. There is no reason why you cannot put one or more sensor in every room that is being wired for the security system.

Consider using current-conducting window foil tape for additional security. Silver foil with a self-adhesive backing is probably available where you purchase your alarm system. It is designed to trigger the alarm if an intruder breaks the glass in a door or a window. During installation, make sure there are no breaks in the foil that you stick on the glass; the tape must be continuous. Self-adhesive foil terminals or connectors at the ends of the foil tapes let you connect the loop circuit wiring, and a flexible door cord allows you to open a foil-taped door or window without setting off the alarm system.

Once you have mounted the sounder backplate and installed all the switches, fire sensors, and window foil, it is time to wire the system together. The wire for the entry-detection switch loop is a thin (nearly transparent) two-wire cord that is quite inconspicuous when you run it up the corner of a wall, down a door frame, or along the baseboard.

Start at the point farthest away from the sounder (the foil taped to a window or door glass, for example). Using a knife or wire stripper, bare about ¾ inch of the wire ends. Loop each wire under a separate terminal screw on the switch or door cord. Without cutting the two-wire cord, route it to the next device—a magnet switch, for example. Use small staples to keep the wire runs neat, but be careful not to damage the wire when you hammer in the staples. At the second device, use a knife to split apart the side-by-side conductors for a distance of a few inches. Cut apart the copper-colored wire only—do not cut apart both wires. Bare about ¾ inch of the copper wire ends and connect them to the switch's terminal screws.

Continue in this manner to the next switch, cutting apart only the copper-colored wire in the cord and attaching the bared ends of the cut wire under the terminal screws on the switch. One after the other, run the wire to all the entry-detection switches and fire sensors, finally running the two-wire cord to the sounder backplate location.

If you need more than the spool of wire included in security system kits, buy another spool and start the new length at the last switch reached by the first length of wire. Cut off what remains of the first length of wire at the switch, and bare the two conductors in both wires. Attach the copper-colored wires to the switch terminal screws. Twist together the two silver-colored wires, and affix a small, solderless connector. Continue the run back to the sounder with the new spool of wire, but do not connect the wire to the sounder yet.

You have just finished wiring the intruder-entry sensor switch loop. If you did it properly, the circuit of the copper-colored wire will go to and through all the switches, and the silver-colored wire will return from the farthest end with no breaks or interruptions.

Now it is time to install the battery circuit. Purchase two 6-volt lantern-type batteries or a suitable type of rechargeable battery pack. Decide where you are going to locate the batteries; they can be hidden in a closet or a cabinet or placed on a shelf you can install for that purpose. The security system kit should contain some lengths of single-conductor wire called bell wire. One should be covered with red insulation and the other with black. Use this wire for connecting the batteries to the sounder.

In the battery-to-sounder circuit, you must connect the positive (+) and negative (-) terminals of the battery

SECURITY SYSTEM TROUBLESHOOTING CHART		
Problem	**Possible Cause**	**Solution**
Key switch turns alarm off, but alarm sounds immediately when key switch is turned on	1. Faulty connection in switching unit loop.	1. Check each terminal screw in loop for satisfactory connection. Also check loop connection to bell. Test system for satisfactory reset.
	2. Defect in switching unit.	2. Place jumper across the terminals of each switching unit, one at a time, to test the system. Satisfactory reset indicates that the jumped switching unit is defective. Replace defective unit.
	3. Faulty conductor in two-wire loop cable.	3. Replace loop cable. Test system for satisfactory reset.
	4. Fault in solid-state switching circuit.	4. Replace entire bell assembly.
Alarm will not sound when door or window is opened	1. Batteries weak or exhausted.	1. Replace batteries; or recharge old batteries, if possible.
	2. Defective key switch.	2. Place jumper across the terminals of the key switch; then trigger system by opening a door or window. If alarm sounds, replace key switch.
	3. Defective solid-state switch.	3. Replace entire bell assembly.
False alarm occurs randomly	1. Door or window not fully closed.	1. Check to make sure doors and windows are fully closed.
	2. Loose connection in loop wiring.	2. Check each terminal location in loop. Jiggle wire at terminal to try to cause a false alarm. If alarm rings, repair loose connection.
	3. Faulty loop component.	3. Briskly tap each magnet switch and fire sensor. Replace unit that, when tapped, sets off false alarm.
	4. Defective solid-state switch.	4. Replace entire bell assembly.

to the sounder to make the solid-state switches operate properly. The bell wire ends are also black and red. Such color coding is helpful for wiring the battery to the sounder correctly. Run both a black and a red wire from the sounder location to the battery location. Connect the red wire to the positive (+) terminal of one of the cells, and connect the black wire to the negative (-) terminal of the other cell. Later, as a last step, you will connect a wire between the negative (-) terminal of the first cell and the positive (+) terminal of the other cell. Wait to do this, however, because while you are working on the installation you might accidentally touch the black and red wires together. Since that would quickly discharge the batteries, you should leave the between-the-cells section of wire out until last.

Now it is time to connect the sounder. Use solderless connectors to join the black wire from the battery to the black wire of the sounder, and the red wire from the battery to the red wire of the sounder. If your installation includes a key switch, however, run the red wire first to the key switch and then to the sounder. At the key switch, cut the red wire, strip insulation from the ends, and fasten each cut end under a separate screw terminal on the switch. Thus, operating the key switch will open and close the circuit in the red wire.

Connect the wire ends from the switch loop to the two smaller wires on the sounder. Fasten the sounder to its backplate, and tighten the attachment screw. Finally, with the key switch in the OFF position, attach the short wire between the two battery cells.

Close all the entry-detection switches by shutting all windows and doors in the loop. Turn the key switch on. The circuit should now be in operation. Test it by opening a door. If you installed everything correctly, the alarm should sound. When you close the door, the system should keep ringing. Turning off the key switch, however, should shut off the alarm. When you turn the key switch back on, the alarm should remain off until the loop circuit is again interrupted.

If the alarm sounds as soon as you turn the key switch on, check the loop circuit to make sure it is intact. All switches must be closed, all wires have to be attached properly to switches under terminal screws, and no break can exist in the window foil. On the other hand, if the alarm does not sound when you open the door, check to make sure that the key is on and that the wiring from the battery to the sounder is correct.

Once you get the system into operation, set it off deliberately about once a week just to make certain that the circuit is still in working condition and that the batteries still contain enough power to operate the system properly. Test the system only briefly; then turn it off and reset it.

You can usually leave the security system turned on in the sentry mode for a considerable period of time. Since the entry-detection switch circuit draws a standby current of only about one-thousandth of an ampere, the batteries should last for months when used only to supply the entry-detection switch loop. Using the sounder puts a heavy drain on the batteries. After the alarm has sounded for a few hours, the batteries become exhausted and the alarm stops sounding. Know how much use your batteries can stand, and replace or recharge them before their energy is depleted.

When you combine this intruder alarm system with a timer that switches on lights and a radio, you have a home security system that compares favorably with some of the more elaborate and expensive systems. In addition, you have a security system that you can easily keep in good operating condition and at little expense.

Installing a Home Intercom System

A home intercommunication system can be much more than just an easy way to call members of the family to dinner or to summon someone for a phone call. At a relatively modest cost, you can have a paging system that includes a radio to provide music throughout the house. Moreover, you can enhance home security with a front-door speaker that allows you to talk with a visitor before opening the door. Installing the system requires only moderate carpentry ability as well as some simple wiring tasks.

An intercom system has one major focal point: the master station. It contains the electronic circuitry for the voice communications. If it includes a music system, the master station will also contain a radio or tape player.

Intercom stations, at which you can only listen and reply, are called slave, remote, or substations. The typical substation contains a speaker (which doubles as a microphone during reply) and a switch to transfer from "listen" to "talk" modes of operation. A typical installation consists of a master station installed at a convenient location, several indoor substations, and an outdoor substation. The outdoor substation is usually located at the front door and includes the button for the doorbell or chimes.

In some intercom sets, all operations are controlled by the master station: power on/off, radio on/off, and call station selection. You can call only one substation at a time or all at one time from the master station, and the single station you call is the only one that can reply. Operating the push-to-talk button or lever cuts off the sound of the radio for the duration of your conversation. More elaborate systems allow communication with or monitoring of any substation, call initiation either from

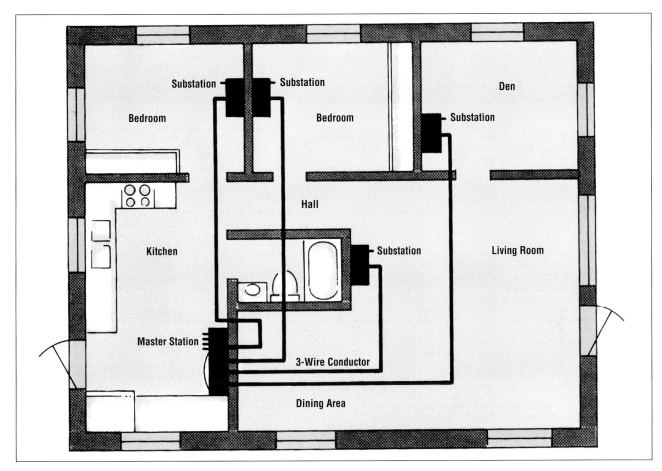

Begin the installation of the home intercom system by selecting the locations for the master station and substations. Often, the master station is located in the home's kitchen.

substation to substation or from substation to master station, or privacy at any substation without being monitored, plus music transmission to any or all substations.

All parts of the built-in system—even the master station—are sufficiently thin so you can install them flush on a wall in holes cut into the wall space. The master station will usually fit in the space between wall studs. All wiring can be hidden if you route it through the wall and along some of the underfloor joists. To illustrate the process, let's work through the installation of a system with one master and four substations. Although such a system would be adequate only for a small home, the same principles can be applied easily in a larger building.

Step 1: Begin the installation by inspecting the master station box or enclosure to determine how large an opening must be cut for it, and then select the location for the master station. Usually the manufacturer provides a bracket or flange, with holes for the mounting screws, for installing the

master station within a wall. After you make the necessary measurements to determine the size and shape of the hole for the master station and its mounting provisions, locate the studs inside the wall. The hole you cut should be located between the studs. Decide on a convenient height above the floor—five feet is a good compromise for both short and tall persons— and pencil the shape of the master station hole on the wall. Drill ⅜-inch holes into the wall at the four corners of your penciled outline, then use a keyhole or saber saw to cut out the hole for the master station. Set the master station box in place to make sure that it fits the hole, and trim the edges of the hole if necessary. Set the box aside until you finish installing the wiring.

Step 2: Cut similar holes in the walls at each substation location. Try the holes for size, trim as necessary, and then set the substations aside until after you install their wiring.

After drilling holes at each of the four corners of your penciled outline, use a keyhole or saber saw to cut out the opening for your master station.

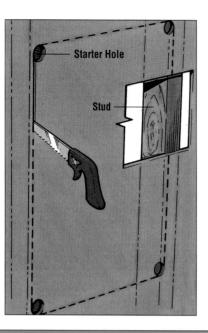

Starter Hole

Stud

Step 3: Check the wiring diagram. In the usual master station-substation installation, only the master station connects to the household's electrical system. Multiwire cable links the substations to the master station. If such cable is not supplied with your kit, or if you need additional cable, you can purchase it separately from a radio-electronics parts supplier. Ask for intercom cable with the required number of conductors, preferably with a jacket covering the conductors.

Step 4: Run a separate cable from each substation back to the master station. For neater installation, run the wire from the substation down inside the wall and into the basement or crawl space. Then, pass the wire through holes in the joists and alongside joists to a hole that leads up into the in-wall space below the master station.

INTERCOM TROUBLESHOOTING CHART

Problem	Possible Cause	Solution
System totally inoperative	1. Blown fuse or tripped circuit breaker; loose line connection, break in power circuit.	1. Inspect load center. Replace fuse or reset circuit breaker. Check power circuit and connections.
	2. Defective transformer. Output can be tested with a voltmeter.	2. Replace with new transformer of same power rating and voltage step-down ratio.
	3. Defect in master station.	3. Replace master station.
One substation only inoperative	1. Defective wiring to substation.	1. Verify wiring fault by temporarily interchanging inoperative substation with substation that operates satisfactorily. Replace intercom wiring to inoperative substation location.
	2. Defective substation.	2. Verify substation defect by interchanging. Replace defective unit.
	3. Defective selector switch in master station or other internal problem.	3. Repair master station.
Station can receive voice call, but cannot reply	1. Faulty "talk-listen" switch in substation.	1. Replace switch in substation or replace substation, whichever is more feasible.
	2. Faulty wiring to substation.	2. Verify wiring fault by temporarily interchanging inoperative substation with substation that operates satisfactorily. Replace intercom wiring to inoperative substation location.
Radio reception is erratic or totally inoperative at all substations, although voice calls can be sent and received	1. Faulty radio in master station.	1. Replace or repair radio unit or replace master station.

Since the cables from all the substations run to the master station, you need a larger entry hole through the floor space in the wall below the master station. Maneuver each cable up to the master station opening, and label it according to its substation location. Numbered pieces of pressure-sensitive tape work well to identify the wires.

Step 5: At each substation location, connect the three wires to the terminals on the substation unit, following the wire color or other identification code that you will find stamped alongside the terminal screws. Fasten the substation unit in the wall—preferably to a wall stud—and attach the trim molding that surrounds the perimeter of the unit to hide the edges of the opening cut in the wall.

Step 6: Run line power to the master station. *Caution: If the master station connects directly to your home's electrical system, be sure to de-energize the circuit involved and take precautions to prevent someone else from turning it back on while you are working on the circuit.* If a transformer is supplied with the master station to power the system, place the transformer on or near a junction box or the main entrance panel, and connect it to the electrical system (after you de-energize the circuit) according to the manufacturer's instructions.

Step 7: Attach all substation and power line wires to the master station, but be sure that you make the attachments according to the markings on the master station's terminal connections. Mount the master station in the wall, affix it firmly to the wall studs, and attach the trim molding. Then restore power to the circuit.

Step 8: Test the intercom system to see how well it performs. If any one of the substations fails to work, check the connections to terminals as well as the connections its wires make to the master station. If you suspect a defective substation unit, replace it with another. That should pinpoint the problem to either defects in the wiring or to a defect in the unit itself, thereby allowing you to make the necessary repairs.

Wiring Your Home for Sound

Have you ever wished that you could have music from your stereophonic sound system follow you throughout the house wherever you go? You could spend thousands of dollars having a special sound system designed and installed. Or you can install a simplified version yourself.

The typical home sound system has two speakers, one for each stereo channel. When you simply hook on additional speakers, you create an impedance mismatch, which not only degrades the tone quality but also may damage the electronic parts of your sound system. The impedance mismatch has fostered the blanket rule not to add more speakers to your system.

When you look at the rear of your stereo you will probably see two connections for the left channel and two for the right channel. One speaker is wired to the terminals for the left-channel output, and the other speaker is wired to the right-channel output. In high-quality stereos, each speaker is actually a combination of two or more speaker units—possibly a large-diameter woofer for low sounds and small-diameter tweeter for high sounds. The two units work together as a single wide-range speaker combination. Nevertheless, even in such units, all speaker leads connect back to the two-conductor cable between the speaker and the tuner/amplifier.

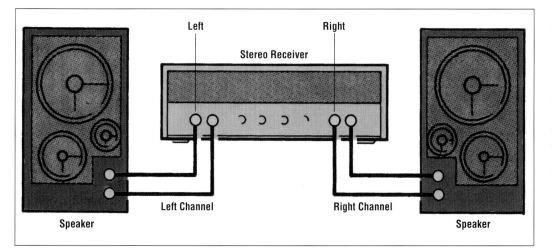

The typical home stereo system has two speakers—one for each stereo channel. Simply adding a speaker or two will result in impedance mismatch and degraded sound quality.

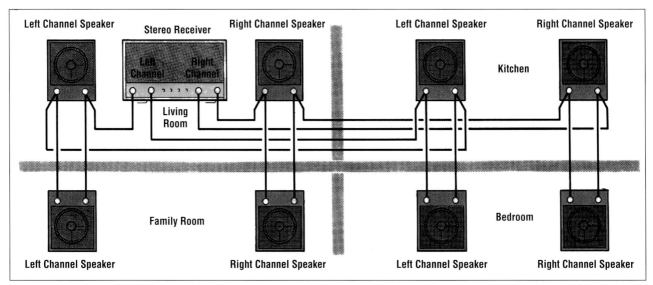

It is possible to obtain acceptable stereo sound throughout your home by adding three pairs of speakers to your present system by using series-parallel circuitry. The wiring arrangement is depicted here.

Two important speaker specifications, watts and ohms, are imprinted either on the speaker itself or on an attached label. The wattage rating tells you how much sound power or loudness the speaker can handle without damage. If your amplifier can deliver 60 watts, your speakers must be capable of handling that much power. Too much power to a speaker is called "overdriving" and results in distortion. Severe overdriving of a speaker can damage it. Even more important is the speaker ohms specification. Most systems are engineered for 8-ohm speakers, and most speakers sold today are 8-ohm speakers. Connecting a second speaker to either channel would result in unbalanced ohms, or impedance mismatch, and the sound performance would be degraded.

It is possible, nonetheless, to connect four speakers to one channel in an unusual wiring arrangement. With this wiring configuration, four 8-ohm speakers act like one 8-ohm speaker. There is some loss of sound quality, but your system will not be harmed. The arrangement is known as a series-parallel circuit, and with it you can install a pair of speakers in four different locations for a total of eight speakers. For example, you could install a pair of speakers in four rooms in your home. Any combination of four locations will work, but it must be only four speakers on each channel, wired together for each channel and expanded to two channels.

Although the only absolute requirement for all speakers is that they must have the same impedance, typically 8 ohms each, you will be more satisfied with the results if all speakers are the same model from the same manufacturer. Unless you are prepared to do some cabinetmaking, purchase speakers that are already

mounted in suitable enclosures. If you wish to conceal the speakers in a piece of furniture or if you want to build enclosures that fit a certain space, however, you should buy unmounted speakers of a quality comparable to the performance of those of your stereo system.

Lamp cord, Type SPT, in #16 gauge, is quite suitable for wiring the tuner-amplifier in your stereo to the extension speakers. Use lighter-gauge speaker cable only for runs of less than 25 feet. To keep the installation neat, route the extension wiring inside the walls or through the underfloor space. Unlike wiring for lights and receptacles, the speaker wire can run through small holes ($\frac{5}{16}$-inch diameter). Drill the floor hole near a corner where it will be inconspicuous, and run the wire to a predrilled hole along the baseboard. If your baseboards are dark, dark-colored cord is recommended. Of course, if your baseboards are white, use white cord. If all your wiring will be hidden inside the walls or in the underfloor space, however, consider using a different color cord for each channel. The different colors will help you install the wiring correctly. Drive small staples into the baseboards about every three feet of the run and at the corners to keep the installation neat, being careful not to damage the wire.

As far as the wiring itself is concerned, follow the diagram above to hook up the four pairs of speakers. After you have completed the wiring for all the speakers, turn on the system. If one channel fails to operate properly, turn off the system immediately and determine the cause of the trouble. In the four-speaker wiring circuit, a poor connection to any one speaker (or one faulty speaker) affects the entire channel, causing an imbalance in sound output.

Installing a Garage Door Opener

A garage door opener is one of the handiest gadgets you can install in your home. And you can install it yourself following these general instructions and the specific instructions that come with the unit.

The typical garage door opener consists of a reversible motor that drives a carriage along a rail above the door. Attached to the carriage is a drawbar to move the door between its opened and closed positions, with travel-limiting devices to stop the door's movement precisely at the fully opened and fully closed positions. A relay or reversing switch reverses the direction of drive from opening to closing and back again. Most modern garage door openers include a radio receiver that allows you to open the door by sending a signal from an electronic module in your car. Here's how to install a garage door opener:

Step 1: Determine the location for the mechanism. Use a tape measure to figure the width of the garage door. Half this distance is the center of the door. On the inside of the door, toward the top, draw a short vertical line down the center of the door. When you affix the drawbar (the mechanism for raising and lowering the door) at this line, the door weight will be evenly balanced at the lifting point.

Step 2: Raise and lower the door, observing the top point of its travel. Mark this location, because you must mount the opener so that the rail is higher than the peak of the door's travel. Otherwise, as the door opens, it could strike the rail.

Step 3: Inspect the area right above the garage door at your vertical dividing line; there must be a support in that location suitable for attaching the front end of the rail. If your garage lacks a structural member in that location, install a front mounting board. Center and fasten a length of 2×6-inch plank securely with lag

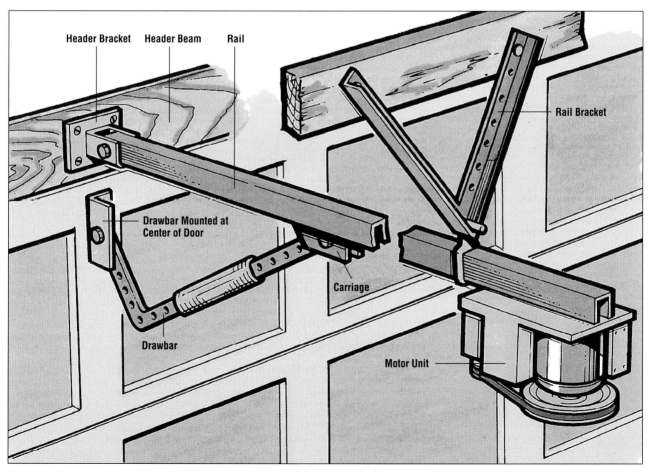

The typical garage door opener consists mainly of a reversible motor that drives a carriage along a rail above the door. Attached to the carriage is a drawbar to move the door between its opened and closed positions.

143

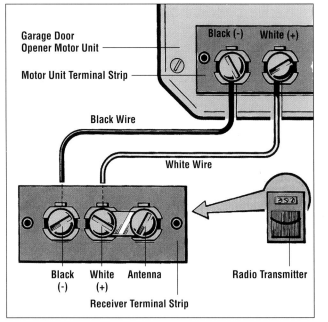

Garage Door
Opener Motor Unit

Motor Unit Terminal Strip

Black (-)   White (+)

Black Wire

White Wire

Radio Transmitter

Black   White   Antenna
(-)   (+)

Receiver Terminal Strip

Shown is a typical wiring arrangement for connecting a garage door opener's radio receiver to the motor unit.

screws across two wall studs over your mark of highest door travel. Transfer your high-point mark to this plank, and extend the vertical door center line onto the plank as well.

Step 4: Attach the rail to the motor unit on the garage floor, following the procedure outlined in the kit instructions. With the garage door down, lift and fasten the outermost end of the rail to the front mounting plank at a location about two inches above the intersecting marks you made for your door's high point and center line. The rail bracket provided for this purpose usually fastens to the front mounting plank with lag screws. If bolts and nuts are provided, however, you must drill suitable holes through the front mounting plank. Be sure to use washers under the heads of the bolts to keep them from pressing into the wood.

Step 5: Raise the motor assembly to the point where the rail is horizontal, or parallel with the door track. With the motor assembly held or supported in this position, raise and lower the garage door by hand to make sure that the rail location does not interfere with the door's movement. Once you establish the correct position and height for the motor assembly, fasten it to the garage joists with the metal brackets in the kit. If the position of the motor

assembly is between two joists, or if the garage joists run the same direction as the rail, you'll need to fasten a length of 2×4 across the joists, and then mount the brackets to the 2×4. If your garage ceiling is finished, you can mount a ¾-inch plywood panel overhead, fastening it to the joists with lag screws. Attach the mounting hardware to the plywood panel with heavy-duty toggle bolts.

Step 6: Attach the drawbar to the rail carriage, and move the carriage to its closed-door position. Mark the drawbar mounting-screw holes on the garage door, and drill the holes in the door. With the drawbar mounted and the holes drilled, insert and tighten the attaching hardware that fastens the drawbar to the door.

Step 7: Make all the necessary adjustments to the drive chain or lead screw, observing particularly the location of the bolts that limit the chain's travel.

Step 8: Install the radio receiver and manual push button. You can use ordinary bell wire for the push button, but be sure to place it where you can see the garage door opener in operation when you push the button. You can also install an optional key switch.

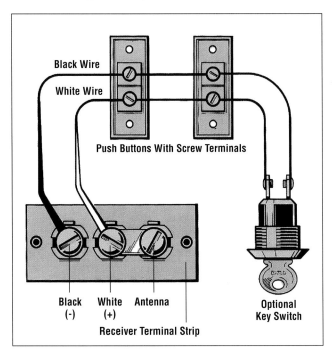

Black Wire

White Wire

Push Buttons With Screw Terminals

Black   White   Antenna
(-)   (+)

Receiver Terminal Strip

Optional
Key Switch

Shown is a typical wiring arrangement for connecting the radio receiver of a garage door opener to one or more manual push buttons and key switch.

Step 9: Plug the drive assembly cord into an extension cord, and plug the extension cord into a convenient receptacle. Set the garage door in motion, using the manual push button. During the door's first test rising, pull the plug from the extension cord several times so you can check to make sure that there is no binding anywhere and that the lifting action is satisfactory. Make any necessary corrections using the adjustment provisions built into the garage door opener system, and verify the operation of the radio remote module.

Step 10: Disconnect the extension cord, and plug the drive assembly line cord into its permanent outlet. If possible, connect the cord to the garage overhead light socket.

GARAGE DOOR OPENER TROUBLESHOOTING CHART

Problem	Possible Cause	Solution
Garage door opener totally inoperative	1. No line power.	1. Test garage receptacle with a different appliance for power. Check for blown fuse or tripped circuit breaker. Make necessary replacement or repairs.
	2. Defective motor.	2. Repair or replace motor.
	3. Motor overload tripped.	3. Reset or wait for automatic reset; check and remedy cause of overload.
Motor hums, but opener will not operate	1. Defective limit reversal operation.	1. Inspect trip mechanism for binding or broken parts. Repair or replace needed parts; relay or switch.
	2. Defective motor capacitor.	2. Replace capacitor.
	3. Damage in carriage drive.	3. Inspect for damage. Make suitable repairs.
Motor runs, but door opener will not operate	1. Broken belt or coupling.	1. Replace belt or coupling.
	2. Broken chain or worm drive.	2. Replace chain or repair worm drive.
	3. Loose setscrew on drive pulley.	3. Tighten setscrew.
Door operates from radio module, but not from push button	1. Defective push button.	1. Replace push button.
	2. Defective wiring.	2. Repair wiring to push button.
Door operates from push button, but not from radio module	1. Defective receiver.	1. Repair or replace receiver.
	2. Defective module.	2. Repair or replace module.
Door does not completely open or completely close	1. Incorrect adjustment of limit control device.	1. Adjust the limit control device according to kit instruction.
	2. Door binding.	2. Uncouple door from drawbar. Raise and lower by hand to verify binding. Correct as necessary.
Unit does not shut off when door meets an obstruction; e.g. rock, snow, etc.	1. Safety limit mechanism inoperative.	1. Inspect unit to determine how safety limit action occurs. Look for a defective component or an incorrect adjustment. Make necessary repairs or adjustments.

CHAPTER 5

MAJOR APPLIANCE REPAIR

Appliances are built to perform. They work hard, year after year, usually without too many problems. They're easy to take for granted. The result is that when an appliance breaks down, you may be completely at a loss—you don't know how it works, you have no idea why it stopped working, and you certainly don't know how to fix it.

What can you do? You can pay a professional to fix it, or you can fix it yourself and save money.

Understanding Major Appliances

Most appliances operate on your home's electrical system: They use AC current from the circuit wiring in your home. Small appliances work on 110–120-volt circuits, and the plugs on their cords have two blades. Large or major appliances, such as air conditioners, dryers, and ranges, usually require 220–240-volt wiring and cannot be operated on 110–120-volt circuits. Large appliances are wired with a grounding wire; their plugs have two blades and a prong. This type of appliance must be plugged into a grounded outlet—one with openings to accept both blades and grounding prong—or grounded with a special adapter plug. All appliances are labeled—either on a metal plate or on the appliance casing—with their power requirements in watts and volts, and sometimes in amps.

Small appliances are usually fairly simple machines. They may consist of a simple heating element, a fan, a set of blades, or rotating beaters attached to a drive shaft; or they may have two or three simple mechanical linkages. Repairs to these appliances are usually correspondingly simple, as you will learn in Chapter 6. Large appliances are more complex—one major appliance, such as a washing machine, may have a motor, a timer, and a pump, as well as various valves, switches, and solenoids. With this type of appliance, problems can occur in either the control devices or the mechanical/power components. Failure of a control device may affect one operation or the entire appliance; failure of a mechanical/power device usually affects only the functions that depend on that device. When a major appliance breaks down, knowing how to diagnose the problem is as important as knowing how to fix it.

Because major appliances are so complex, it usually isn't obvious where a malfunction is. The first step is to decide whether the problem is in a control device or a mechanical device. In a dryer, for example, the control devices govern the heat, and the mechanical components turn the drum. Which system is affected? If the drum turns, but the dryer doesn't heat, the problem is in the control system. If the dryer heats, but the drum doesn't turn, the problem is mechanical. This kind of analysis can be used to pinpoint the type of failure—control system or mechanical system—in all large appliances.

To find out exactly what the problem is, you must check each part of the affected system to find the malfunctioning part. This isn't as difficult as it sounds, because appliance components work together in a logical sequence. Starting with the simplest possibilities, you can test the components one by one to isolate the cause of the failure. The troubleshooting charts in this chapter will help you diagnose the problem. Each chart also describes the measures you should take to repair the appliance once you've found the problem.

Repairing Major Appliances

There are three very important rules you must follow when you attempt to make any type of appliance repair. Don't ever try to save time or money by ignoring these rules. You won't save anything at all, and you could end up hurting yourself or ruining the appliance.

- *Always* make sure the electric power and/or the gas supply to the appliance is disconnected *before* you test the appliance to diagnose the problem or make any repairs. If you turn the power on to check your work after making a repair, do not touch the appliance; just turn the power on and observe. If adjustments are needed, turn the power off before you make them.
- If the parts of an appliance are held together with screws, bolts, plugs, and other take-apart fasteners, you can probably make any necessary repairs. If the parts are held together with rivets or welds, don't try

to repair the appliance yourself. Call a professional service person.

- In most cases, broken or malfunctioning appliance parts can be replaced more quickly and inexpensively than they can be repaired by you or a professional. Replace any broken or malfunctioning parts with new parts made especially for that appliance. If you cannot find an exact replacement for the broken part, it's okay to substitute a similar part as long as it fits into the old space. In this case, refer to the manufacturer's instructions for installation.

Appliance parts are available from appliance service centers, appliance-repair dealers, and appliance-parts stores. You don't always have to go to a specific brand-name appliance parts center to obtain the parts and service you need for brand-name appliances, so you do have some shopping/service choices. If you can't locate a parts service center in your area, order the part you need directly from the manufacturer. The name and address of the appliance manufacturer are usually printed on the appliance. Be sure to give the manufacturer all the model and parts data possible for the appliance.

Before you make any appliance repair, make sure the appliance is receiving power. Lack of power is the most common cause of appliance failure. Before you start the testing and diagnosis process, take these preliminary steps:

- Check to make sure that the appliance is properly and firmly plugged in and that the cord, the plug, and the outlet are working properly. To determine whether an outlet is working, test it with a voltage tester, as detailed on page 18 of Chapter 1.
- Check to make sure the fuses and/or circuit breakers that control the circuit have not blown or tripped. There may be more than one electrical entrance panel for your home, especially for 220–240-volt appliances such as ranges and air conditioners. Check for blown fuses or tripped circuit breakers at both the main panel and the separate panel.
- Check to make sure fuses and/or breakers in the appliance itself are not blown or tripped. Push the reset buttons to restore power to appliances such as washers, dryers, and ranges. Some ranges have separate plug-type fuses for oven operation; make sure these fuses have not blown.
- If the appliance uses gas or water, check to make sure it is receiving an adequate supply.
- Check the owner's manual for the appliance. Many manufacturers include helpful problem/solution troubleshooting charts. If you don't have a manual for an appliance, you can probably get one—even for an old or obsolete appliance—from the manufacturer's customer service department.

Disassembling Major Appliances

Before you can repair a major appliance, you'll have to disassemble all or part of it. All major appliances are different, but the disassembly procedure is about the same: Remove the parts in reverse of the way the manufacturer put them together. Check your owner's manual for assembly diagrams and instructions. Remember that you'll have to put the appliance back together again, so lay the parts out in the order in which you remove them, with fasteners in hand. If you aren't sure you'll be able to put the appliance back together, take notes and make drawings as you work. Label all terminals and wires if you must disconnect more than one wire at a time.

To disassemble a major appliance, start with the obvious knobs and fasteners. Many knobs and dials are push-fit. Simply pull them off their control shafts. Knobs may also be held in place by setscrews, springs or spring clips, or pins; or they may be screwed on. All of these types of fasteners are easy to release. Housing panels are usually held by screws or bolts. They may also be held in place by tabs. Sometimes, parts are force-fitted and may be hard to remove. Never force parts apart; look for hidden fasteners. For instance, there may be no obvious fasteners holding the top of a washer in place. However, you can locate the clips that hold the top of the washer down by sticking the blade of a putty knife into the seam where the top panel meets the side panel. Run the knife along the seam until you hit an obstruction; this is a spring clip. To release the clip, push the blade of the knife directly into the clip, at a right angle to the seam, while pushing up on the top panel. Repeat this procedure to locate and remove any other spring clips holding the top panel in place. Then lift the panel off.

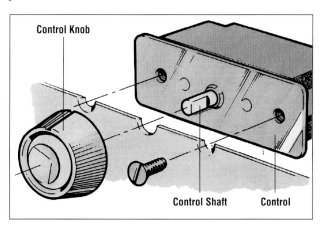

To disassemble an appliance, start with the obvious knobs and fasteners. Knobs and dials either pull right off or are held by setscrews, pins, or clips.

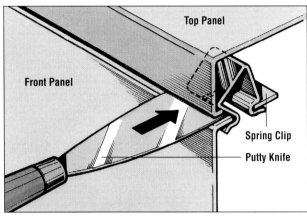

Spring clips are often hidden. To remove a panel held by spring clips, use a putty knife to find each clip; then push in against it to release the panel.

Fasteners may also be hidden under a nameplate or company logo, behind a scarcely visible plastic plug, under a cork pad on the bottom of the appliance, or under an attachment plate. Carefully pry up the part that is hiding the fastener. When you reassemble the appliance, snap the concealing part back over the fastener, or, if necessary, glue it into place. If you can't find hidden fasteners on force-fitted parts, warm the parts gently with a heating pad; the heat may make disassembly easier. Inside the appliance, watch for clips holding parts to the housing panel.

Before reassembling a major appliance, carefully vacuum inside the appliance to remove all dust and lint. Check for other problems and make any necessary repairs or adjustments. If the appliance has a motor, lubricate the motor. Check carbon brushes in universal motors for wear and replace them if necessary, as detailed on pages 155–156. Lubricate moving parts sparingly and make sure electrical contacts are clean.

Reassemble the appliance in reverse of the way you took it apart. Never force parts together or overtighten fasteners. Make sure moving parts, such as armatures or gears, don't bind. After reassembly, connect the power and turn it on. If it makes noise, smells, or overheats, turn it off and disconnect the power. Then go back over your repair.

Grounding Systems

Some major appliances (washers, dryers, ranges) are grounded by a wire that's attached to a cold-water pipe. The cold-water pipe runs into the ground outside your home and grounds the appliance so that any leaking electricity goes into the ground. Disconnect this grounding wire before you make repairs and be sure to reconnect it before you turn the power back on.

Many homes today are equipped with electrical outlets that have a three-wire system. The third wire is a grounding device and operates the same way as the grounding wire on stationary appliances. Large appliances, whose plugs have two blades and a prong, should be plugged into a grounded outlet or grounded with a special adapter plug. ***Caution:*** *Never remove the prong from a three-wire plug to make it fit an ungrounded outlet; always use an adapter plug.*

Proper grounding is vital for metal-framed appliances. If the insulation on the power cord of a metal-framed appliance (such as a washer or dryer) is broken or worn away at the point where the cord enters the frame, contact between the current conductor and the metal frame could charge the whole appliance with electricity. When this happens, dampness can cause a shock hazard even if the appliance is properly grounded. If you accidently touch a charged metal frame in a damp location or while touching a water faucet or radiator, the current would surge through you and could kill you.

There are three things you can do to eliminate this hazard. First, make sure your major appliances are properly grounded and follow the electrical safety rules presented in Chapter 4. Second, make sure that all appliance cords are in good repair, and that they are not chafing against burrs or rough spots where they enter the appliance frame. Third, add a ground-fault circuit interrupter (GFI or GFCI) to the circuit. GFIs are monitoring devices that instantly shut off a circuit when a current leak occurs. They are required by the National Electrical Code on all new 15-amp and 20-amp outdoor outlets and for wiring in bathrooms, where dampness is a common problem. GFIs are available to plug into existing outlets as adapters, to replace outlets, and to replace circuit breakers in the electrical entrance panel. A professional electrician should install the circuit-breaker type; you can install the other types yourself. Ground-fault circuit interrupters are available at electrical supply and home center stores.

Double-Insulated Appliances

In double-insulated appliances and power tools, the electrical components are isolated from any parts of the appliance that could carry electrical current. However, these appliances are not completely shock-safe. You should use caution with any electrical device. For example, never operate an electric drill while standing on a wet surface—and never drill into a wall where power lines may be present. Double-insulated appliances and tools should almost always be repaired by a professional, because the double insulation depends on a plastic housing and a plastic buffer between parts that carry electricity. If these plastic parts are not properly positioned, the appliance or tool could produce a harmful electrical shock. Appliances and tools that are double insulated are usually labeled as such.

Repairing and Replacing Appliance Components

Major appliances have many components in common, making repairs easier. For example, once you've learned to repair a power cord on a refrigerator, you can apply the same skills to repairing a washing machine's power cord.

The following section explains common devices that are used on major appliances and offers tips on how to repair them.

·······················

Power Cords and Plugs

Many appliance "breakdowns" are really due to worn, frayed power cords or plugs that no longer make proper electrical contact. To ensure safe operation, you should check all appliance cords for problems periodically and replace frayed or broken cords immediately. When you suspect a cord is faulty, remove it from the appliance and test it with a continuity tester. Clip the tester to one blade of the plug and touch the probe to one of the two wires—or, if it's a plug-in cord, insert the probe into one of the two holes—at the appliance end of the cord. If the tester lights or buzzes, move it to the other wire or hole and test again. Repeat this procedure to test the other blade of the plug. If the tester lights or buzzes at every test point, the cord is not faulty; if it fails to light or buzz at any point, the cord or the plug is faulty. You can pinpoint the defect by cutting off the plug and testing the cut end of the cord; if the tester lights or buzzes at all test points now, the plug is the defective part. The damaged component—cord, plug, or both—should be replaced.

Often, the hardest part of replacing an appliance cord is determining how the appliance comes apart so that you can remove the old cord and attach a new one. Sometimes all you have to do is remove the cover from a connection box. In other cases, as with a small hair dryer, the unit itself must be partially disassembled before you can reach the terminals. In nearly all cases, the cord is held in place by a clamp or by a fitted strain-relief device. To remove the cord, unscrew the terminal screws or pull the pressure connectors apart, loosen the clamp or remove the strain-relief device, and pull the cord out. Installation of the new cord is simply a reverse procedure. Be sure to save the strain-relief device and replace it on the new cord. If you damage the strain-relief device when you remove it, replace it with a new one of the same type.

In some equipment, the conductor ends are looped around terminal screws, making new connections easy. Carefully strip off the outer insulation (not the insulation on the inner wires) for about 2 inches at the end of the cord. Then, using a wire stripper, remove about ½ inch of insulation from the end of each conductor wire. Twist the exposed filaments of each wire clockwise into a solid prong. Loosen the terminal screws and loop each bare wire end clockwise around a screw. Tighten the screws firmly. Connect the wires at the appliance end of the new cord the same way the old wires were connected.

In some major appliances, solderless connection terminals may be clamped to the old cord, and you'll have to fit replacement terminals to the new cord. This requires terminals of a matching kind and a tool called a crimper. You can find this tool at automotive or electrical-supply stores. In a few cases, the terminals may be soldered to the conductor ends. You can replace them with solderless connectors.

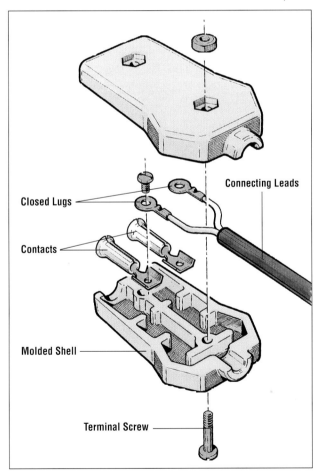

Closed Lugs

Connecting Leads

Contacts

Molded Shell

Terminal Screw

When a female plug malfunctions, open it and check the conductor wires. If the wires are loose, tighten the terminal screws. For other problems, replace the plug.

If only the plug on a major appliance is faulty, you can attach a new plug to the old cord. Male plugs, with two blades or with two blades and a grounding prong, plug into an outlet. Female plugs, often used at the appliance end of the cord, have terminal holes instead of blades. Male plugs can usually be taken apart so you can access the terminal screws. Female plugs may be held together by rivets or by screws. Screw-held plugs can be taken apart, but rivet-held plugs cannot be repaired.

When a plug malfunctions, open the plug, if possible, and check to make sure the conductor wires are properly attached to the plug's screw terminals. If the wires are loose, tighten the terminal screw. This may solve the problem; otherwise, the plug should be replaced. To attach a new male plug:

Step 1: Insert the cord end through the plug opening and pull it through for about five or six inches.

Step 2: Carefully strip off the outer insulation for about 2 inches. Then, using a wire stripper, remove about ½ inch of insulation from the end of each conductor wire.

Step 3: Twist the exposed filaments of each wire clockwise into a solid prong. After twisting the conductor ends, tie a tight knot with the inner wires of the cord. Then pull the plug down over the knot, leaving the exposed ends of the conductor wires sticking out. Loosen the terminal screws in the plug.

Step 4: On a two-wire plug, loop each wire around one prong and toward a screw terminal. Loop the bare wire end clockwise around the screw terminal and tighten the screw. If the screws are different colors, connect the white wire to the

On a two-wire plug, tie a tight underwriters' knot with the inner wires (top). If there is a grounding wire, tie the knot as shown (bottom).

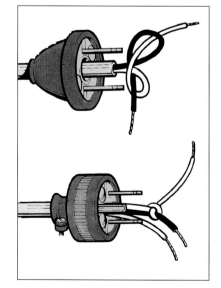

white screw and the black wire to the yellow screw. On a three-wire plug, use the same technique to connect each of the three wires to a terminal screw. Connect the green grounding wire to the green screw terminal.

Step 5: When the conductor wires are firmly secured to the terminal screws, slide the cardboard insulator over the blades of the plug. If the plug has a clamp-type sleeve, clamp it firmly around the cord.

Gaskets

Major appliances that use water, heat, or cold to do a job have gaskets, which are most commonly located on the door. Gaskets do two things: They prevent leaks of water and air, and they increase the efficiency of the appliance. When a gasket fails, it should be replaced as soon as possible. To determine whether a gasket is faulty, inspect it for cracks and tears. It should feel spongy. If the gasket has hardened, it should be replaced. Be sure to replace a faulty gasket with a new one made specifically for the appliance. Do not use a universal, fit-all gasket.

There are two common types of gaskets—flush-mounted and channel-mounted. A flush-mounted gasket is secured to the door by a series of screws or clips, or held in place by a retaining strip or a panel. A channel-mounted gasket is held in a retaining groove. A splining or gasket tool makes installation easier. Use gasket cement to install either type of gasket if specified by the manufacturer. To replace a gasket:

Step 1: Remove the old gasket. If it's channel-mounted, pull it carefully out of the channel. If it's flush-mounted, remove the fasteners, retaining strip, or panel to release the gasket.

Step 2: Clean the gasket area thoroughly with warm water and liquid detergent, or with mineral spirits, if necessary. Dry the door.

Step 3: Install the new gasket, smoothing it evenly into place and easing it around corners. Use gasket cement if specified by the manufacturer. If you're installing a channel-mounted gasket, press it into place with a splining tool. Make sure the gasket is properly and smoothly positioned, with no part sticking up or curled under.

Step 4: Replace the fasteners or the retaining strip or the panel and its fasteners. Remove any excess gasket cement with mineral spirits, but be very careful not to damage the appliance's finish.

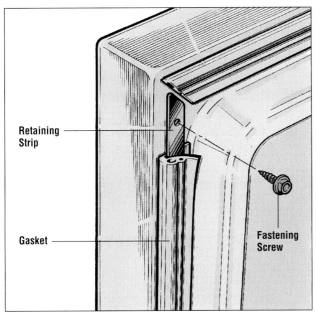

A flush-mounted gasket is held in place by a retaining strip, fastened by screws or clips.

Labels on image: Retaining Strip, Gasket, Fastening Screw

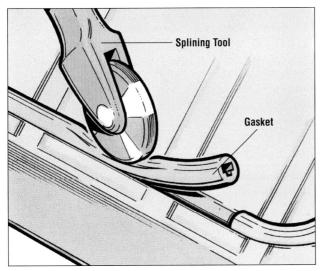

A channel-mounted gasket is held in a retaining groove.

Labels on image: Splining Tool, Gasket

Wiring

Many appliance repair tasks involve wiring or connecting wires to install a new electrical component. The electrical wires in appliances may be connected in one of several ways, including the basic screw-terminal connection, the push-in terminal, and sometimes the sleeve-type lug terminal. Wires may also be joined with the solderless connectors called wirenuts. Components that have many wires—washer timers, for instance, which control several operating cycles—are often connected in a wiring harness: a group of wires enclosed in a plastic sleeve. Each type of wire connection, for each individual wire and each wire of a harness, must be properly made when you install a new component. Before you disconnect any wiring in an appliance, make sure you know how it's attached. When you install the new component, attach its wires the same way.

Switches

Switches operate by making contact with the conductor of an electrical circuit. When an appliance is plugged in, it's connected to a circuit in your home. Power runs through the wires of the circuit to the appliance. When the appliance's on/off switch is turned on, the conductors of the appliance cord are moved into contact with the circuit conductors, and electricity flows through the switch to operate the appliance. The current flows in a loop through the appliance, making a complete circuit back through the switch to the line wires. Other basic appliance components are variations of switches. Rheostats, thermostats, solenoids, and timers, for example, are all switches or secondary switches. These components operate inside appliances to turn on motors, open and close valves, control heating elements, and turn on different parts of the appliance during different cycles, such as the rinse and spin cycles of a washer. There are several common types of switches—push buttons, toggles, rockers, slides, throw switches, and so on.

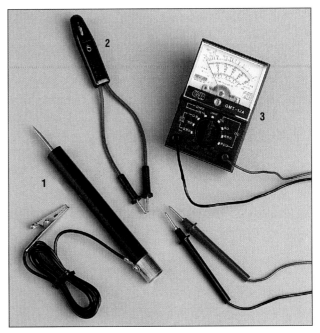

Testing devices you will need include (1) a continuity tester, (2) a voltage tester, and (3) a volt-ohm-milliammeter or volt-ohm meter (VOM).

All switches consist of electrical contacts in a mechanical housing. Switch failure can be caused by problems with either the contacts or the housing. When a switch malfunctions, turn it to the ON position and watch to see if the contacts are moved into position so that they touch. If the contacts are not operating properly, the switch housing is faulty, and the switch should be replaced. If the switch's mechanical operation is all right, its contacts may be dirty or misaligned. If the switch has terminal screws, they may be loose. If the contacts are dirty or corroded, rub them gently with a fine emery board and then with a soft cloth. If they're misaligned, bend them gently back into place. Tighten any loose terminal screws. If the contacts or screws are badly corroded, the switch should be replaced. To determine whether a switch is working properly:

Step 1: Disassemble the appliance to test the switch with a continuity tester or a VOM set to the RX1 scale.

Step 2: With the appliance unplugged, hook the clip of the continuity tester to one lead of the switch and touch the probe to the other; or touch one probe of the VOM to each terminal.

Step 3: Turn on the switch. If the switch is functioning, the continuity tester will light or buzz, and it will stop glowing or buzzing when the switch is turned off; or the VOM will read zero. If the tester doesn't light or buzz, or the VOM reads higher than zero, the switch is faulty and should be replaced. (Note that some switches should have a higher reading than zero, as detailed for each appliance.)

Step 4: Replace a defective switch with a new one of the same type, and connect it in exactly the same way the old switch was connected.

Thermostats

A thermostat is a switch that controls temperature in a heating element or a cooling device. Thermostats used in appliances may use a bimetal strip, bimetal thermodiscs, or a gas-filled bellows chamber to control the electrical contact. Faulty bimetal-strip and thermodisc thermostats should be replaced. Gas-filled thermostats can sometimes be professionally repaired. If repair is possible, it is much less expensive than replacement. To determine whether a thermostat is functioning:

Step 1: Disassemble the appliance to access the thermostat, and test it with a continuity tester or a VOM set to the RX1 scale.

Step 2: With the appliance unplugged, hook the clip of the continuity tester to one lead of the thermostat and touch the probe to the other; or touch one probe of the VOM to each terminal. The continuity tester should light or buzz; or the VOM should read zero.

Step 3: Turn down the temperature control dial; you'll see the contact points open at the thermostat. The tester should stop glowing or buzzing when the contacts open.

Step 4: If the thermostat is faulty, replace it with a new one. Follow the manufacturer's instructions.

Switch Control Devices

Many appliances perform several functions—for example, the various cycles of a washer or dishwasher. These appliances operate automatically; once the on/off switch is turned on, switch components inside the appliance take over to control heat, water or fuel flow, motor speed, and other variables. The most important of these devices—used to operate switches, levers, and valves automatically—are solenoids, relays, and sensor/responder pairs.

Heating Elements

Heating elements work very simply. Unlike conductors, they are made of metal with high electrical resistance. When current flows through the element, this high resistance prevents it from flowing easily. Current must work to get through the element, and this work is converted into heat. When the current is turned off, the element cools. There are three types of heating elements: wire, ribbon, and rigid. To determine whether a heating element is functioning:

Step 1: Disassemble the appliance to access the element and test it with a continuity tester or a VOM set to the RX1 scale.

Step 2: With the appliance unplugged, hook the clip of the continuity tester to one terminal of the heating element and touch the probe to the other terminal; or touch one probe of the VOM to each terminal. If the element is functioning, the tester will light or buzz; or the VOM will read from 15 to 30 ohms. If the tester doesn't light or buzz, or the VOM reads higher than 30 ohms, the element is faulty. Replace it.

Note: If you use a continuity tester, look closely at the tester, especially if it is the light-up type. Some heating elements have an extremely high resistance factor, and the light may produce only a dim glow or a faint buzz. This reaction does not mean that the element is faulty, but rather that it converts current to heat efficiently.

....

Timers

The operation of a major appliance that has several cycles (for example, a washer, dishwasher, dryer, frost-free refrigerator, or range) is controlled by a timer—a complex rotary switch powered by a small synchronous motor. The timer consists of a shaft, gears, and a series of notched cams, one for each circuit or cycle. The timer itself is powered by the timer motor; the appliance is powered by the much larger appliance motor. When the switch is turned on, electrical contact is made with the timer motor, and a spring on a trip arm is coiled. The arm trips when the spring is tight, releasing the spring and moving the cam of the switch to the next circuit. At the last cycle, contact with the motor is broken, and the timer turns the appliance off.

When a timer malfunctions, it should usually be replaced. Professional rebuilding is sometimes possible, but this is likely to be more expensive than replacement. Many timers are sealed units. Some timers have an adjustment shaft, which can be turned with a screwdriver blade. To determine whether a timer is functioning:

Step 1: Test the timer with a continuity tester or a VOM set to the RX1 scale. Make a sketch of the timer wires and then, with the appliance unplugged, disconnect all timer wires from their terminals. Make sure you'll be able to reconnect the wires exactly the same way.

Step 2: Touch or clip one probe of the tester or the VOM to the common terminal. Touch the other probe to each cycle terminal in turn. Rotate the timer control knob as you work. The continuity tester should light or buzz at each circuit; the VOM should read zero.

Step 3: If one or more circuits do not give these results, the timer is faulty and should be replaced. To replace a timer, disconnect its wires one at a time, connecting the corresponding wires of the new timer as you progress in order to avoid the chance of a misconnection.

....

Pilot Lights and Thermocouples

Gas-fired appliances often have pilot lights that provide instant ignition when the gas is turned on. The pilot light is a small open flame that is fed by a steady flow of gas.

Problems occur when the gas flow is obstructed or misdirected, or when the pilot is blown out. In newer appliances, ignition may be achieved by a sparking device or a glow bar instead of a pilot light. In furnaces and water heaters, and in some ranges and dryers, the pilot light is accompanied by a safety device called a thermocouple—a heat sensor that turns the gas off if the pilot flame is extinguished.

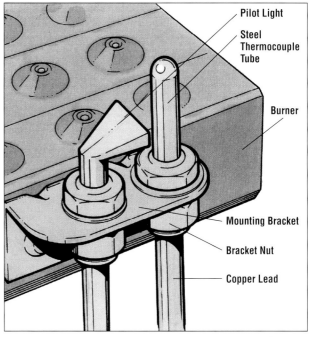

The thermocouple is a safety device; it shuts the gas off if the pilot light goes out. A faulty thermocouple should be replaced.

Caution: Some older appliances may not have a safety device to turn the gas off when the pilot is extinguished. With any gas-fired appliance, if a strong smell of gas is present, do not try to relight the pilot or turn the appliance on, or turn any lights on or off. Get out of the house, leaving the door open, and call the gas company or the fire department immediately to report a leak.

A correctly adjusted pilot flame is steady and blue, and stands between ¼ and ½ inch high. If the flame goes out repeatedly, it may be getting too little air; if it's yellow at the tip, it's getting too much air. To correct either condition, turn the pilot adjustment screw slightly, as directed by the manufacturer. When a pilot goes out, relighting it is simple:

Step 1: If there is a gas valve at the pilot, turn the valve to the OFF position and wait at least three minutes to let any built-up gas dissipate. After three minutes, turn the valve to the PILOT position. If there is a safety or reset button, push the button, and keep it depressed.

153

Step 2: Hold a lighted match to the pilot orifice and turn the gas valve to the ON position. Then, when the pilot is burning brightly, release the reset button. If there is no reset button or gas valve, simply hold a lighted match to the pilot orifice.

Step 3: If the pilot flame won't stay lit after several tries, it should be adjusted by a professional. Don't try to adjust the mechanism or tamper with the gas line.

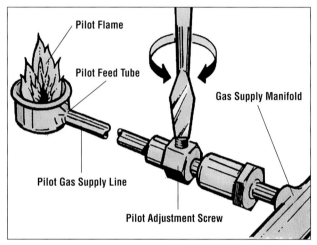

To adjust the pilot flame, turn the adjustment screw on the gas line, as directed by the range manufacturer.

If the appliance has a thermocouple, the problem may be a faulty thermocouple. The thermocouple, which operates as a safety device, turns the gas supply off when the pilot light goes out. It consists of a heat sensor connected to a solenoid; when the sensor is not heated by the pilot flame, the solenoid closes the gas supply line. When a thermocouple fails, the pilot light won't stay lighted. A burned out or broken thermocouple should be replaced. To replace a thermocouple:

Step 1: Unscrew the copper lead and the connection nut inside the threaded connection to the gas line.

Step 2: Under the mounting bracket at the thermocouple tube, unscrew the bracket nut that holds the tube in place.

Step 3: Insert a new thermocouple into the hole in the bracket, steel tube facing up and copper lead down.

Step 4: Under the bracket, screw the bracket nut over the tube. Push the connection nut to the threaded connection where the copper lead connects to the gas line. Make sure the connection is clean and dry.

Step 5: Screw the nut tightly into place, but do not overtighten it. Both the bracket nut and the connection nut should be only a little tighter than if hand-tightened.

....

Motors

Major appliance motors are usually dependable and long-wearing. You can prolong their life and increase their efficiency by keeping them clean and well lubricated. Use motor-driven appliances sensibly. Don't overload them, don't abuse them, and don't ignore problems until they become serious.

There are several basic rules for operating motor-driven appliances:

• Always connect an appliance to an adequate power source; a 220–240-volt appliance must be connected to a 220–240-volt outlet. If the outlet for a major appliance is not grounded, use a grounded adapter plug to ground the appliance.

• Never use a small appliance that's wet, and never operate any appliance while your hands are wet. If a large appliance, such as a washer or dryer, gets wet, do not operate it or try to unplug it. Have the motor examined by a professional before you use the appliance again.

• Never overload an appliance. Overloading causes inefficient operation and motor overheating, and can cause excessive wear. If a motor turns off because it's overloaded, reduce the load before restarting the appliance.

Regular maintenance can forestall many motor problems. To prevent overheating and jamming, vacuum the motor housing periodically to remove dirt and lint. Make sure ventilation to the motor is adequate.

If the motor has belts, examine them periodically for wear and damage. Damaged belts should be replaced. To quiet a squeaky belt, spray it with fan belt dressing, available at automotive and hardware stores and some home centers. Also check the tension of all belts, about halfway between the motor shaft and the nearest pulley. The belt should give about ½ inch when you press on it. If it's too loose, increase the tension by tightening the adjustment bolt. If it's too tight, decrease the tension by loosening the bolt. If pulleys are misaligned, carefully bend them back into alignment, or call a professional service person. Procedures for specific appliances are detailed later in this chapter. Here's a look at three types of motors used in appliances.

Universal Motors

Universal motors consist of a rotor called an armature, with coils of wire wound around it, and a rotating

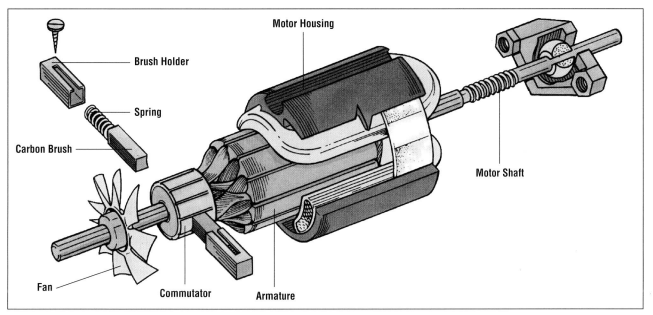

A universal motor has an armature and a rotating commutator, mounted on a motor shaft. Carbon brushes make the electrical contact; worn brushes are the most common problem.

cylinder called a commutator, with alternating strips of conducting and nonconducting material. The armature and the commutator are both mounted on the motor shaft. On each side of the commutator, a carbon brush carries current from the circuit. When the carbon brushes press against the commutator, the armature is magnetized and rotates. Most universal motors also have a cooling fan at the end of the shaft. Universal motors are used in many small and medium-size appliances. They provide strong power at both low and high speeds. Universal motors can operate on either AC or DC current. Their speed is controlled by a rheostat, a tapped-field control, a rectifier, or a governor, or by physical movement of the carbon brushes away from the armature.

Most universal motors are permanently lubricated and sealed by the manufacturer and require no further attention. Some universal motors, however, have covered lubrication ports, usually marked "oil," at the ends of the motor shaft. This type of motor should be oiled every six months, or according to the manufacturer's instructions. Lift each port's lid and apply a drop or two of No. 30 nondetergent motor oil (not all-purpose oil). Do not over-lubricate.

Many universal motor malfunctions are caused by wearing down of the carbon brushes, the soft blocks of carbon that complete the electrical contact to the motor's commutator. When these brushes become worn, the motor will spark, and electrical contact may be incomplete. You can solve both problems by replacing the brushes.

Brushes can be checked visually or tested with a continuity tester. Here's how:

Step 1: To sight-check the carbon brushes, remove the screws that hold the brushes and brush springs into the brush holders at the sides of the commutator. The screws will pop out of the screw holes; turn the motor over to tap out the brushes. The ends of the brushes should be curved to fit the commutator; if they're worn down, new brushes are needed.

Step 2: To check carbon brushes with a continuity tester, remove the motor lead wires from the circuit. Tag the wires as you disconnect them so that you'll be able to reconnect them properly. Hook the tester clip to one motor lead and touch the probe to the other lead; the tester should light or buzz. Slowly rotate the motor shaft, keeping the tester in position. If the tester doesn't light or buzz, or if it flickers or stutters when you turn the motor shaft, the brushes should be replaced. If the springs behind the brushes are damaged, they should be replaced as well.

Step 3: Replace worn carbon brushes and damaged springs with new ones made specifically for the motor. The model information (number and make) is stamped on a metal plate fastened to the motor, or embossed on the metal housing of the motor. If you can't find the model information, take the worn brushes and springs with you to an appliance-parts store to make sure you get the right kind. Insert the new springs and brushes in the brush holders, replace the brush assemblies, and secure the new brushes with the mounting screws that held the old brushes.

Don't attempt other repairs to a universal motor. If a serious malfunction occurs, buy a new motor or take the faulty motor to a professional for repairs. Most large universal motors are fastened to plate-type mountings. To remove the motor, disconnect the wires and remove the holding bolts and any belts that are present. If the faulty motor is in a small appliance, take the entire appliance to the repair shop. It may sometimes be less expensive to buy a new appliance than to have the old one repaired.

Split-Phase Motors

Split-phase motors consist of a rotor turning inside a stator that has two wire coils: a starting winding and a running winding. Current flows through both windings when the motor is starting up, but when the rotor has reached about 75 to 80 percent of its top speed, the starting winding is turned off and only the running winding receives current. Split-phase motors operate on AC current. They are fairly powerful, and are used in appliances such as washing machines, dryers, and dishwashers.

These motors require no maintenance except cleaning and lubrication. Split-phase motors have a special auxiliary winding—the starting winding. Don't try to make any repairs yourself. When a motor malfunctions, buy a new motor or take the faulty motor to a professional service person, whichever is less expensive. You can save the expense of a service call by removing the old motor from its mounting and installing the repaired or new motor yourself.

Capacitor-Start Motors

A capacitor-start motor is a shaded-pole motor with a capacitor (an energy-storing device) wired into the starting winding. The capacitor stores current and releases it in bursts to provide extra starting power. When the motor reaches about 75 percent of its top speed, the starting winding is turned off. Capacitor-start motors operate on AC current. They are very powerful and are used in appliances that require a high starting torque or turning power, such as air conditioners and furnaces.

Capacitor-start motors require regular cleaning, as detailed on page 154, to keep them free of lint and oil. Ventilation to the motor must be adequate. If the motor has oil ports, lift each port's lid and apply a drop or two of No. 30 nondetergent motor oil (not all-purpose oil). Do not over-lubricate.

Capacitor-start motors are usually hard to get at and have a capacitor and special auxiliary windings. Don't try to make any repairs yourself. When a motor malfunctions, call a professional service person.

Caution: Capacitors store electricity, even after the power to the appliance is turned off. When working with a capacitor-start motor, you must discharge the capacitor with a 20,000-ohm, 2-watt wire-wound resistor, as detailed for each appliance.

Repairing Gas Ranges and Ovens

Gas ranges and ovens operate fairly simply, and they're usually easy to repair, mainly because the components are designed for quick disassembly. Most of the malfunctions that affect gas ranges involve the supply and ignition of gas in the burners and the oven.

Caution: Before doing any work on a gas range or oven, make sure it's unplugged, or turn off the electric power to the unit by removing a fuse or tripping a circuit breaker at the main entrance panel or at a separate panel. If there is a grounding wire to the range, disconnect it. Also close the gas supply valve to shut off the unit's gas supply.

Disassembling a Gas Range

A gas range cabinet comes apart very easily. Here's how:

Step 1: Take out the screws that hold the panels, and pull off the control knobs. On the control panel the knobs are friction-fit; pull them straight off. Some knobs may have setscrews in the base of the knobs; back out these screws and pull off the knobs.

Step 2: Remove the back service panel on the control panel by backing out a series of screws around the edge of the panel. To remove the front panel, take off the control knobs and remove a series of screws that hold the decorative panel to the frame. These screws may be hidden by molding or trim; pry off the molding or trim with a screwdriver, or take out several screws.

Step 3: To gain access to the burner assemblies, remove the burner grates and then the top of the range. The entire range top should either lift up and

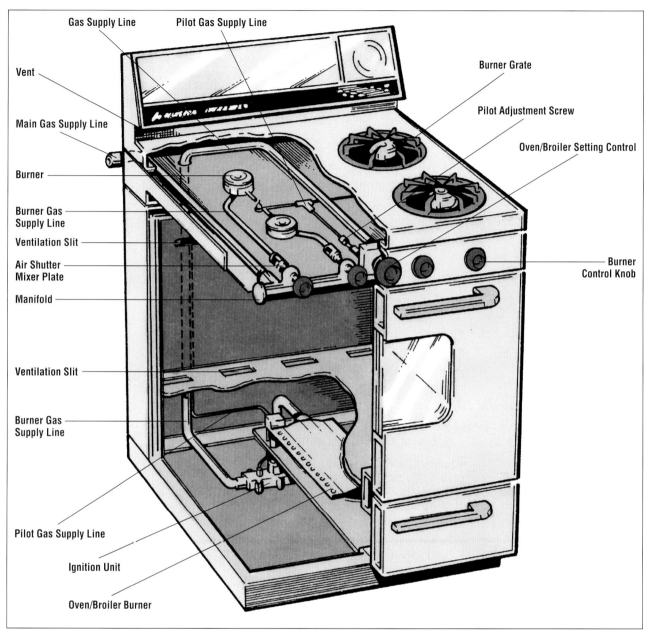

Gas Supply Line
Pilot Gas Supply Line
Vent
Burner Grate
Pilot Adjustment Screw
Main Gas Supply Line
Oven/Broiler Setting Control
Burner
Burner Gas Supply Line
Ventilation Slit
Air Shutter Mixer Plate
Manifold
Burner Control Knob
Ventilation Slit
Burner Gas Supply Line
Pilot Gas Supply Line
Ignition Unit
Oven/Broiler Burner

Gas ranges and ovens use gas burners to heat and cook food. Most malfunctions involve the supply and ignition of gas in the burners.

off the range or open up and back on hinges. The oven door can usually be removed by pulling it straight up off the hinges on both sides of the door. Some hinges have a latch that must be unlocked before the door can be removed.

Step 4: If the surface light of the range burns out, remove retaining screws and panels as necessary to gain access to the bulb. Replace the burned-out bulb with a new one of the same type and wattage; check the ends of the old bulb for this information. Then replace any retaining panels.

Step 5: If the oven light burns out, unscrew it and remove it from the oven. Replace the burned-out bulb with a new one of the same wattage, made for oven use.

Testing and Replacing the Door Gasket

If the oven won't heat to the desired temperature or heats unevenly, the problem could be a defective door gasket. The best way to test for this is to pass your hand around the door, being careful not to touch it, while the

GAS RANGE TROUBLESHOOTING CHART		
Problem	**Possible Cause**	**Solution**
No burners light	1. No gas.	1. Make sure gas valve is open. If open, call gas company.
	2. If range has electric ignition, no power.	2. Check power cord, plug, and outlet. Check for blown fuses or tripped circuit breakers at main entrance panel or at separate entrance panel; restore circuit.
One burner won't light	1. No gas to burner.	1. Test other burners; if they light, clean burner assembly.
	2. Pilot light out.	2. Relight pilot.
	3. Electric ignition faulty.	3. Call a professional.
	4. Defective gas valve.	4. Call gas company.
Pilot won't stay lit	1. Pilot light set too low.	1. Adjust pilot light.
	2. Gas feed tube blocked.	2. Clean feed tube.
Burners pop when lighted	1. Conduction tube misaligned.	1. Reposition conduction tubes on holding bracket.
	2. Pilot light set too low.	2. Adjust pilot light.
Light won't go on	1. Bulb burned out.	1. Replace bulb.
Oven won't heat	1. No gas to range.	1. Make sure gas valve is open. If open, call gas company.
	2. Defective gas valve.	2. Call gas company.
	3. Pilot light out.	3. Relight pilot.
	4. Pilot light set too low.	4. Adjust pilot light.
	5. Electric ignition system faulty.	5. Call a professional.
	6. Thermostat faulty.	6. Test thermostat; if faulty, replace. If thermostat inaccurate, recalibrate; if no result, call a professional.
	7. Timer faulty.	7. Clean timer terminals; set timer to "manual" and turn clock on control panel 24 hours ahead. If no result, call a professional.
Oven heat uneven	1. Door gasket faulty.	1. Make sure door is closed tightly and hinges operate smoothly; if gasket damaged, replace, or call a professional.
Burner won't simmer	1. Simmer nut needs adjustment.	1. Adjust simmer nut on burner.
Flame yellow	1. Not enough air in gas mixture.	1. Adjust air shutter.
Flame noisy	1. Too much air in gas mixture.	1. Adjust air shutter.
Flame too high	1. Too much air in gas mixture.	1. Adjust air shutter.
Soot forms on burner	1. Air shutter clogged.	1. Clean air shutter.
	2. Air shutter needs adjustment.	2. Adjust air shutter.

oven is turned on. If you can feel heat escaping, the gasket needs replacement. Replace it with a new gasket made for the range.

On most ovens, the gasket is located on the frame of the oven, and the door closes against it. This gasket is generally friction-fit in a channel and can be replaced. In other units, the oven door has two sections, and the gasket is not mounted on the door frame, but is installed between the front and back sections of the door. Don't try to replace this type of gasket; call a professional service person. To replace a frame-mounted gasket:

Step 1: Pull the old gasket out of the channel. On some oven door frames the gasket is held in place with screws. To get at the screws, bend back the exposed edge of the gasket.

Step 2: Clean the channel and the door frame with a solution of mild household detergent and water.

Step 3: To install the new gasket, start the replacement at the top of the door frame and work down the sides, easing the gasket around corners. Finish the installation along the bottom, butting the ends of the gasket firmly together.

Gas Smell

Leave the house immediately; do not try to turn off the gas, or turn any lights on or off. Go to a telephone and call the gas company or the fire department immediately to report a leak. Do not reenter your home.

Cleaning the Burners

Clogged burners are a very common problem with gas ranges because foods spilled on the burners block the gas ports and prevent ignition. On some gas ranges you can remove the top ring of the burner to expose the ports. To clean a burner:

Step 1: Turn off the power supply, both gas and electric, to the range. Then remove the burner.

Step 2: Soak the burner in a solution of mild household detergent and water. Clean it with a soft cloth.

Step 3: Clear the gas ports with a pin or needle, rinse the burner, and let it dry. *Caution: Do not use a toothpick or matchstick to clean the gas ports. If the tip of the wood gets stuck in the burner ports, it could cause a serious blockage.*

Step 4: When the burner is completely dry, replace it, and turn on the power and the gas supply.

Repairing the Oven Setting Control

When the oven setting control malfunctions, the oven won't heat. To repair an oven setting control:

Step 1: Remove the control knob.

Step 2: Remove the back service panel or the front panel, if necessary. Remove other control knobs as needed to remove the panel. The oven setting control is located directly in back of the control knob and is usually held to the control panel by two screws.

Step 3: Testing the control with a VOM is not recommended, because the results will not always be conclusive. If you suspect that the setting control is faulty, the best procedure is to substitute a control that you know is working, or you could simply replace the faulty control with a new one made for the oven.

Step 4: Disconnect the electrical lead wires from the control terminal and lift out the control. Connect the new control the same way the old one was connected.

Servicing Oven Thermostats

If the oven doesn't heat evenly or doesn't heat at all, the oven thermostat may be malfunctioning. First, determine how much the temperature in the oven is off from the control setting. To do this, put an oven thermometer on a center rack inside the oven and turn the oven on for about 20 minutes, with the thermostat set at any range between 300° and 400°F. If the oven thermometer reads 25° or more lower or higher than the oven control setting, the thermostat should be recalibrated. To calibrate the thermostat:

Step 1: Pull off the thermostat knob on the control panel. Behind the knob are two screws holding a round, notched plate. Loosen these screws, but do not remove them.

Step 2: With a screwdriver, change the notch setting on the notched plate by turning the plate counterclockwise; for every eighth of a turn, the oven temperature goes up about 25°F. To turn the heat down, turn the plate clockwise.

Some thermostats can be adjusted by turning a screw inside the control knob shaft housing. To do so, remove the knob and insert a screwdriver into the shaft so that the screwdriver blade engages a screw slot. Turn the screwdriver counterclockwise about one-eighth of a turn to raise the heat about 25°F. To test a malfunctioning thermostat:

Step 1: Test the thermostat with a VOM set to the RX1 scale (instructions for using the VOM can be found on page 19). The thermostat is located directly on the back of the control knob that regulates the heat. To gain access to the thermostat, remove the back service panel to the control panel.

Step 2: Disconnect one electrical lead wire from a terminal of the thermostat and clip one probe of the VOM to each thermostat terminal. If the thermostat is in working order, the meter will register zero. If the needle jumps to a higher reading, the thermostat is faulty and should be replaced.

Step 3: If necessary, replace the thermostat with a new one of the same type.

To replace the thermostat:

Step 1: Disconnect the terminal wires to the thermostat and pull off the control knob.

Step 2: Remove the retaining screws. On some ranges, there is a wire running from the thermostat into the oven. This wire operates a sensing bulb that controls the thermostat. The sensing bulb is usually held by a bracket; unscrew this bracket to remove the bulb. Then carefully slip out the wire, the bulb, and the thermostat.

Step 3: Install the new thermostat using a reverse procedure.

Replacing the Timer

The range timer is usually located in the control panel on top of the range. If you suspect the timer is faulty, don't try to fix it yourself. Remove it and take it to a professional service person for testing. To remove the timer:

Step 1: Remove the back service panel to the control panel and release the spring clips that hold it in position, or remove the retaining screws.

Step 2: Push the timer forward to release it.

Step 3: Remove the electrical lead wires from the timer housing. If, when disassembling the timer, you notice that the electrical wire terminals look burned, remove these leads and buff the leads and the terminal points with fine steel wool. Burned and/or dirty terminals can cause the timer to malfunction, but a good cleaning can solve this problem.

Step 4: Replace the old timer or install a new one of the same size and type, if this is necessary. Connect the new timer the same way the old one was connected.

Fuel Mixture Adjustments

The flame of gas range burners should be steady and slightly rounded, with a light-blue tip. The flame should be quiet and should respond to adjustments made at the

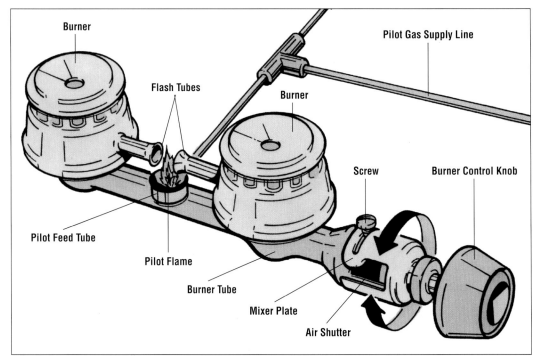

The flame of a gas range burner should be steady and slightly rounded, with a light-blue tip. To adjust the flame, slide the air shutter mixer plate open or closed.

Burner

Flash Tubes

Pilot Gas Supply Line

Burner

Screw

Burner Control Knob

Pilot Feed Tube

Pilot Flame

Burner Tube

Mixer Plate

Air Shutter

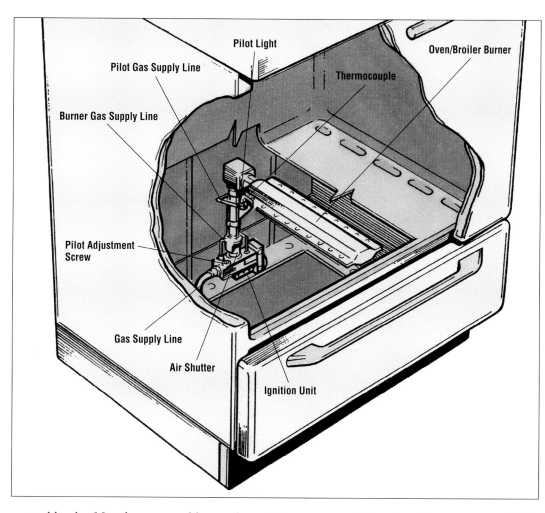

Pilot Light

Pilot Gas Supply Line

Burner Gas Supply Line

Oven/Broiler Burner

Thermocouple

Pilot Adjustment
Screw

Gas Supply Line

Air Shutter

Ignition Unit

The oven pilot is usually located at the back of the oven; turn a screw on the pilot ignition unit to adjust the pilot flame height.

control knobs. Most burner troubles can be quickly solved by adjusting the air shutter mixer plate, which is located at the end of the burner tube near the knob controls. Turn a small screw on the plate, slide the plate open or closed, and tighten the setscrew. If the flame is yellow, it's not receiving enough air. To allow more air in, open the plate slightly. If the flame is high or makes a roaring noise, it's getting too much air and you should close the plate slightly.

Servicing Pilot Lights

One pilot light usually serves all the top burners of a gas range. Some ranges have two pilot lights, one for each side of the range. A correctly adjusted pilot flame is steady and blue, between ¼ and ½ inch high. If the flame goes out repeatedly, or if it's yellow at the tip, it's getting too little air. If there's a space between the flame and the pilot feed tube, it's getting too much air. To correct either condition, turn the pilot adjustment screw on the gas line slightly, as directed by the manufacturer of the range.

When the pilot goes out, relighting it is simple. Instructions for relighting the pilot can be found on pages 153–154.

If the pilot flame is properly adjusted, but the flame doesn't ignite the burners, the problem is probably in the flash tubes that run from the pilot to the burners. These tubes may be blocked by spilled food from the burners. If this is the case, turn off the power to the range and clean out the tubes using a short piece of wire. Push the wire through the opening until the tube is clear. You may have to disconnect the tube to clear it. After cleaning the tube, replace it in the same position.

If the pilot has a switch, the switch may be faulty. Turn off the power to the range and test the switch with a VOM set to the RX1 scale (instructions for using the VOM are given on page 19). Remove the retaining screws that hold the switch in the range cabinet, and disconnect both electrical lead wires to the switch. Clip one probe of the VOM to each switch terminal. If the switch is functioning, the meter will register zero. If the meter reads higher than zero, the switch is faulty and should be replaced. Remove the switch and replace it with a new one of the same type. Connect the new switch the same way the old one was connected.

If the oven doesn't light, the oven pilot may be out or may be set too low. The oven pilot light is usually located toward the back of the oven or under the bottom panel of the oven box. If the range has a drawer unit under the oven, pull out the drawer; this may help you locate the pilot. If the pilot is out, relight it, as described on pages 153–154.

If the flame is set too low, adjust it. Next to the pilot, locate a small boxlike unit with a couple of screws in it. This is the ignition unit. The ignition unit could also be located below the pilot; follow the gas line down until you locate it. Turn one of the screws on the ignition. Experiment, turning the screws a little at a time, until the flame is adjusted properly. It should not be as high as the top pilot flame; leave it as low as possible. On some oven pilots, turn the control to the OFF position and light the pilot; then turn the oven dial to the BROIL position. The pilot will heat the controls to the ignition switch.

Servicing Automatic Shutoff Valves

On some ranges, there is an automatic shutoff valve located in the pilot assembly that shuts off the gas to the burner any time the pilot and the burner are both off. If this unit malfunctions, don't try to fix it yourself; you should call a professional service person for repair or replacement.

An electrically operated shutoff valve used on some gas ranges has two facing valves, an electromagnet, and a manually activated reset button. The thermocouple fitting is next to the pilot valve, as in most burner systems. A small amount of electricity holds the facing valves apart. If the pilot light goes out, no electricity is generated, and the valve closes to turn the gas off. On this type of system, relight the pilot by depressing the reset button and holding a match to the pilot. It should take about a minute to light this pilot. If you aren't able to relight this system, call a professional service person.

Servicing Electric Ignition Systems

Most newer gas ranges and ovens don't have pilot lights. Instead, the gas is ignited by an electric ignition system. In this type of system, an element becomes hot and glows like the filament in a lightbulb when an electric current passes through it. The heat from the filament lights the gas. As a rule, these ignition systems are sealed and cannot be repaired or adjusted. When an electric ignition device fails, don't try to fix it. Call a professional service person for replacement.

Self-Cleaning Ovens

There are two types of self-cleaning ovens, pyrolytic and catalytic. Pyrolytic ovens use very high heat—usually 1,000°F—to incinerate food on the oven's surface, leaving only a fine ash. The smoke produced by the burning is vented from the oven. When the cleaning process is complete, the fine ash left in the oven can be wiped off the surface. Catalytic self-cleaning ovens are coated with a special finish the allows most dirt to burn away at normal cooking temperatures. With these ovens, major food spills and spatters must be cleaned away immediately or the special finish will not work.

Caution: *Never use a commercial oven cleaner to clean either a catalytic or a pyrolytic oven.*

Most problems with pyrolytic ovens occur because procedures are not properly carried out. In most cases, the oven heat selector must be set to the CLEAN position, and the oven door must be firmly closed and sometimes latched. When the oven reaches a predetermined temperature—about 600°F—the door automatically locks shut so that it can't be opened during the cleaning cycle. If you've followed the correct procedures for using a self-cleaning oven, but the oven is not coming clean, call a professional service person.

Before you call, though, make these basic checks:
- Check for a blown fuse or tripped circuit breaker at the entrance panel controlling the unit.
- Make sure the heat selector is set to the CLEAN position, and the timer is set to MANUAL.
- Be sure to allow the prescribed amount of time for the oven to clean itself. If the oven is only partially cleaned, more cleaning time may be required.
- Make sure the oven door is tightly closed and latched.

Repairing Electric Ranges and Ovens

Electric ranges and ovens are generally easy to repair, because there's not much to go wrong and there's not much you can do. Most repairs are actually replacements, a matter of unplugging the old part and plugging in the new. Most of the malfunctions that affect electric ranges involve faulty heating elements.

Caution: *Before doing any work on an electric range or oven, make sure it's unplugged, or turn off the power to the unit by removing one or more fuses or tripping one or more breakers at the main entrance panel or at a separate panel. If the range is fused at a separate panel, this panel may be located adjacent to the main panel or in a basement, crawl space, or other location. If there is a grounding wire to the range, disconnect it. Make sure the power to the unit is off.*

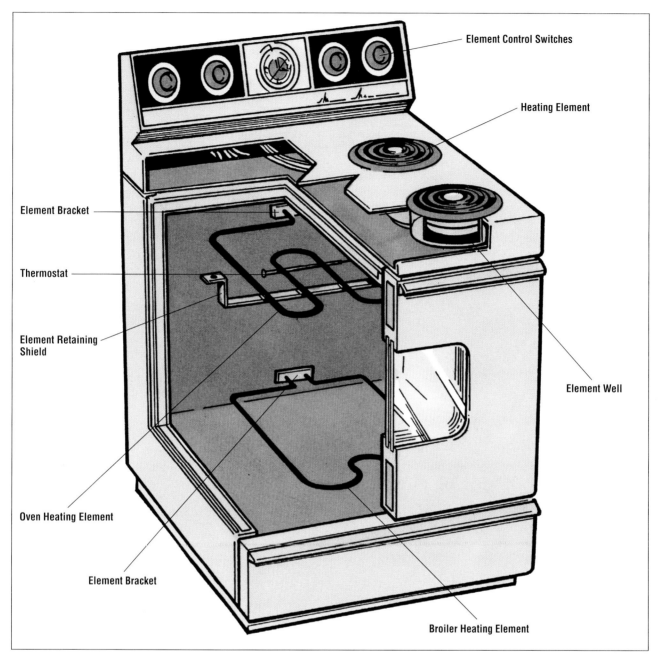

Element Control Switches

Heating Element

Element Bracket

Thermostat

Element Retaining
Shield

Element Well

Oven Heating Element

Element Bracket

Broiler Heating Element

Electric ranges and ovens use Nichrome elements to supply heat. Most malfunctions involve faulty heating elements.

Servicing Fuses

If the range or oven is receiving power but doesn't work, the unit may have its own fuse or circuit breaker assembly. This assembly is usually located under the cooktop of the range. In some units, lift the top of the range to gain access to the fuse assembly; or lift the elements, remove the drip pans, and look on the sides of the cabinets. Inside the oven, look to the back to spot the fuse assembly.

If the unit has this additional fuse or breaker system, components such as the oven light, the range heating elements, the timer, and a self-cleaning feature may be separately fused.

If these components or features fail to work, don't overlook the possibility that the fuses have blown. To replace a blown fuse, unscrew the old fuse and install a new one of the same type and electrical rating. If the unit has circuit breakers, push the breaker or reset button, which is usually located on the control panel.

ELECTRIC RANGE TROUBLESHOOTING CHART

Problem	Possible Cause	Solution
No elements heat	1. No power.	1. Check power cord, plug, and outlet. Check for blown fuses or tripped circuit breakers at main entrance panel or at separate panel, and in range fuse system. Restore circuit.
One element won't heat	1. Element faulty.	1. Test element; if faulty, replace.
	2. Switch faulty.	2. Call a professional.
	3. Terminal block wiring faulty.	3. Call a professional.
Element heats slowly or does not get red-hot	1. Inadequate power supply.	1. Check fuses and switches to make sure 220-volt power is being supplied; half of double-fuse hookup may be blown. If necessary, restore circuit.
	2. Element connections faulty.	2. Clean and tighten element connections.
	3. Element faulty.	3. Test element; if faulty, replace.
Element heats, but food does not cook well	1. Pan not resting flat on element.	1. Use flat-bottomed pan.
Elements burn out often	1. Inadequate power supply.	1. Check fuses and switches to make sure 220-volt power is being supplied; half of double-fuse hookup may be blown. If necessary, restore circuit.
	2. Foil covering pan below element.	2. Make sure drip pans below elements are not covered by aluminum foil.
Light won't go on	1. Bulb burned out.	1. Replace bulb.
Oven won't heat	1. No power.	1. Check power cord, plug, and outlet. Check for blown fuses or tripped circuit breakers at main entrance panel or at separate panel, and in range fuse system. Restore circuit.
	2. Oven element faulty.	2. Test element; if faulty, replace.
	3. Control switch faulty.	3. Call a professional.
	4. Timer faulty.	4. Clean timer terminals; set to "manual" and turn clock on control panel 24 hours ahead. If no result, call a professional.
Broiler doesn't work	1. No power.	1. Check power cord, plug, and outlet. Check for blown fuses or tripped circuit breakers at main entrance panel or at separate panel, and in range fuse system. Restore circuit.
	2. Broiler element faulty.	2. Test element; if faulty, replace.
	3. Control switch faulty.	3. Call a professional.
	4. Timer faulty.	4. Clean timer terminals; set to "manual" and turn clock on control panel 24 hours ahead. If no result, call a professional.

Continued on page 165

ELECTRIC RANGE TROUBLESHOOTING CHART (Continued from page 164)

Problem	Possible Cause	Solution
Oven temperature uneven	1. Door gasket faulty.	1. Make sure door is closed tightly; if gasket damaged, replace or call a professional.
	2. Thermostat faulty.	2. Test thermostat; if faulty, replace. If thermostat inaccurate, recalibrate; if no result, call a professional.
Timer won't work	1. Terminals loose or corroded.	1. Clean and tighten terminals; if no result, call a professional.
Element smokes and smells	1. Food spills; soap residue.	1. Clean element and drip pan with steel-wool soap pad; some odor is normal after cleaning.
Oven sweats	1. Preheating necessary.	1. Preheat oven.
	2. Exhaust vent closed or blocked.	2. Make sure vent is open; clean vent.
	3. Door gasket faulty.	3. Check gasket for leaks; if damaged, replace or call a professional.
	4. Hinges faulty.	4. Check hinges to make sure door shuts tightly; if hinges damaged, call a professional.
	5. Temperature setting too high.	5. Start oven at low temperature; increase to desired temperature.

Replacing Range Heating Elements

When a range heating element burns out, it's easy to replace. But before you disassemble the range to check or replace an element, make sure the range is receiving power. Here's what you can do:

Step 1: Check the power cord, the plug, and the outlet. Then look for blown fuses or tripped circuit breakers at the main entrance panel or at a separate panel.

Step 2: Check the fusing system inside the range. If the circuit is broken, restore it. If the range is receiving power, go on to check the element.

Step 3: Remove the element. In most ranges, each top heating element is connected to a terminal block in the side of the element well. To remove the terminal block, lift the element and remove the metal drip pan that rests below it. The element is held by two retaining screws or is push-fit into the terminal block. To remove a screw-type element, remove the screws holding the wires. To remove a push-type element, pull the element straight out of its connection.

Step 4: Test the element with a VOM set to the RX1 scale, as described on page 19. Disconnect one of the electrical leads to the element and clip one probe of the VOM to each element terminal. If the element is functioning properly, the meter will read between 40 and 125 ohms; if the meter reads extremely high, the element is faulty and should be replaced.

To test a range element without using a VOM, remove a working element from its terminal block and connect it to the malfunctioning element terminal. Don't let the test element overlap the edges of the element well; keep the element inside the well, even if it doesn't fit perfectly. Turn on the power to the range. If the working element heats, the suspected element is bad and should be replaced. If the working element doesn't heat, the terminal block wiring or the switch that controls the element may be faulty. Call a professional service person.

Step 5: Replace a burned-out range element with a new one made specifically for the range. Take the old element to the appliance-parts store; if possible, take the make and model information, too. This data will probably be on a metal tag attached to the back service panel of the range. To install the new element, connect it the same way the old one was connected.

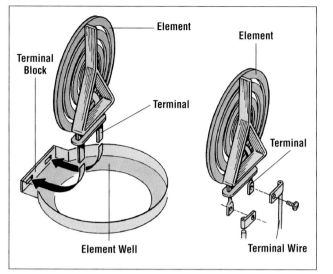

To remove a range heating element, remove the screws holding the terminal wires, or pull the element straight out of its connection.

Replacing Oven and Broiler Heating Elements

Electric oven and broiler elements are often even easier to test and replace than range elements. Here's how:

Step 1: If the oven element doesn't work, first check to see if the range is receiving power. Don't overlook the fusing system inside the range.

Step 2: If the range is receiving power, set the timer on the range to the MANUAL position.

Step 3: If the element still doesn't heat, turn off the power to the range and test it with a VOM set

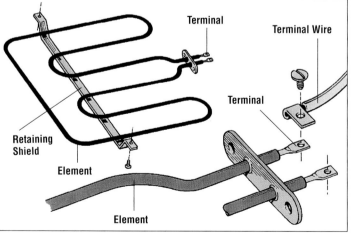

To remove an oven or broiler heating element, remove the screws or pull the plugs that connect it. Remove a retaining shield and lift out the element.

to the RX1 scale (instructions for using the VOM are given on page 19).

Step 4: Remove the screws or plugs that connect the element to the power. Remove the retaining shield, which is usually held by two screws, and remove the element from the brackets that hold it in the oven. The element is usually held in these brackets by screws.

Step 5: Clip the probes of the VOM to each element terminal. If the element is in working order, the meter will read from 15 to 30 ohms. If the meter reads higher than 30 ohms, the element is faulty and should be replaced. If the element tests all right but doesn't work, the problem may be at the terminals. Make sure the terminals are clean and tight at the element connections.

Oven and broiler elements cannot be tested without a VOM. If you don't have a VOM, take the element to a professional service person for testing. The problem is usually a malfunctioning element; however, you aren't risking much by replacing the element without a professional test.

Step 6: Take the burned out element with you to the appliance-parts store to make sure you get the right replacement part; if possible, take the make and model information, too.

To install the new element, place it in the same position as the old one. Connect it the same way the old one was connected, using the same screws to hold it in place.

Just about all the other components of an electric range or oven (including its door gasket, oven controls, and timer) are virtually the same as the components used on gas ranges. Treat them as explained in the previous section.

Repairing Refrigerators and Freezers

Refrigerators and freezers consist of two basic components: a condenser coil and an evaporator coil. A liquid coolant is circulated through these

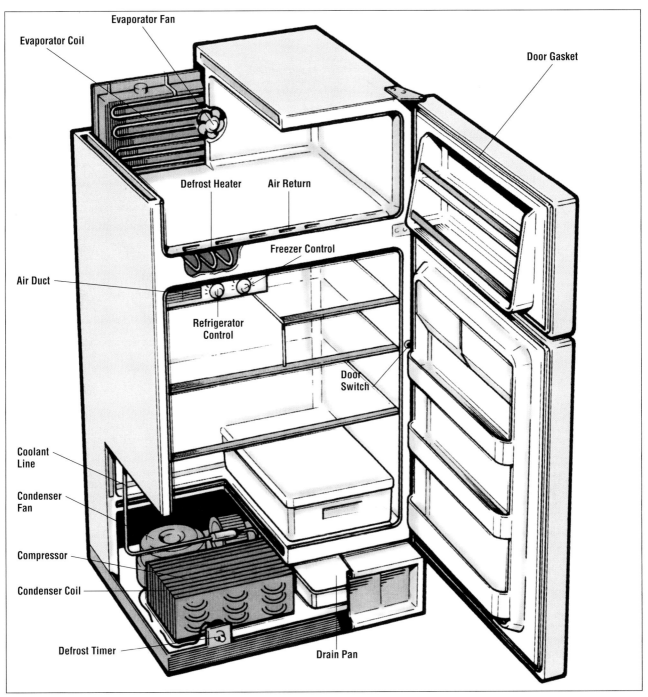

Evaporator Fan

Evaporator Coil

Door Gasket

Defrost Heater   **Air Return**

Freezer Control

Air Duct

Refrigerator Control

Door Switch

Coolant Line

Condenser Fan

Compressor

Condenser Coil

Defrost Timer   **Drain Pan**

In a refrigerator, coolant is cooled in a condenser; from there it flows to the evaporator, where air is cooled by contact with the coil.

coils by a compressor and a motor. The refrigerant liquid is cooled in the condenser; it then flows to the evaporator. At the evaporator, the air in the unit is cooled by contact with the liquid-filled coil. The condenser of a refrigerator or freezer is the coil on the outside of the unit; the evaporator is the coil on the inside. The coolant is circulated through the system by a compressor.

Most newer-model refrigerators and freezers are frost-free. In this type of unit, a heater is automatically turned on by a timer in order to melt the frost inside the unit. Frost is melted by the heater at several different spots in the unit, starting with the coldest and most frosted areas. When the frost is completely melted, the thermostat automatically switches to a cooling cycle in order to maintain the standard freezing temperature. Because this process is automatic, frost does not build up inside the box.

The unit's compressor system, which forces the coolant through the coil system, is driven by a capacitor-type motor. Other basic parts of the cooling/defrosting system include switches, thermostats, heaters, condensers, and fans. A do-it-yourselfer can test and replace many of these refrigerator components. However, there are exceptions, as noted in the procedures below, that are best left to a professional repair person.

Caution: Before doing any work on a refrigerator or freezer, make sure it's unplugged. After unplugging the unit, check to see if the motor/compressor has a capacitor; this component is located in a housing on the top of the motor. Capacitors store electricity, even when the power to the unit is turned off. Before you do any work on a capacitor-type refrigerator or freezer, you must discharge the capacitor, or you could receive a severe shock.

To discharge the capacitor:

Step 1: Unplug the refrigerator or freezer.

Step 2: To gain access to the capacitor, remove the service panel over the back rear portion of the unit or the service panel on the front of the unit below the door, as detailed later for disassembly. The capacitor is located in a housing on the top of the motor/compressor unit; it looks like a large dry cell battery.

Step 3: To discharge the capacitor, use a 20,000-ohm, 2-watt resistor—an inexpensive wire unit available at most electrical supply stores. Fasten the probes of the resistor to the terminals of the capacitor; this discharges the capacitor. If the capacitor has three terminal posts, connect the resistor to one outer terminal and the center terminal, then to the other outside terminal and the center terminal. After discharging the capacitor, you can proceed with the repairs.

Disassembling the Refrigerator

The control components of a refrigerator are usually located in the top or upper section of the unit. The motor, compressor, condenser coil, and condenser fan are located in the bottom section.

To gain access to the components in the upper section of the unit, remove the retaining screws or pry out the clips that hold plastic or metal panels over the parts. These fasteners may be hidden by trim or molding; in this case, pry off the trim or molding with the tip of a screwdriver or a stiff-bladed putty knife.

Protruding controls may also serve as retainers for the various panel sections. In most refrigerators, the shelves can be removed to allow access to some of the panels.

To gain access to the lower section of the refrigerator, remove a service panel held by retaining screws at the back of the unit below the condenser coils. The unit may also have a front access panel below the door. This panel may be held by retaining screws, or it may slip up and off two side brackets. On some models, you can tip the refrigerator over and test and service parts from the bottom. In this case, the refrigerator must be defrosted, unplugged, and emptied before any servicing can be done.

The condenser and evaporator coils and the compressor are sealed units on most refrigerators. If a malfunction occurs within these parts, call a professional service person. Other parts can usually be unscrewed or pried loose from mounting brackets.

Cleaning and Positioning Coils

The condenser and evaporator coils of a refrigerator collect dust and dirt over a period of time. This decreases their efficiency. That's why one of the most important maintenance procedures is to clean these coils with a vacuum cleaner, a soft cloth, and/or a whisk broom. This type of cleaning should be done at least once a year.

Positioning also affects the efficiency of the unit. Refrigerators or freezers with exposed condenser coils on the back panel should be at least two inches from the wall, and the back of the refrigerator or freezer should not be placed against a heat register or a window or door where heat or sun could affect the temperature of the coil. To keep your refrigerator or freezer working properly, make sure it is clean and well positioned at all times.

Testing the Power Cord

If the cord of the unit looks frayed, or if you see burn marks on the prongs of the plug or at the terminal screws—on the terminal block, under the rear access panel of the unit—the cord may be faulty. Test the cord with a VOM set to the RX1 scale (instructions for using the VOM can be found on page 19).

Servicing the Door Gasket

When a refrigerator gasket becomes hard or cracked, its seal is broken, and the unit's efficiency drops sharply. Test the door gasket for leaks by placing a dollar bill between the gasket and the door jamb and closing the

REFRIGERATOR/FREEZER TROUBLESHOOTING CHART

Problem	Possible Cause	Solution
Unit doesn't run	1. No power.	1. Check power cord, plug, and outlet. Check for blown fuses or tripped circuit breakers at main entrance panel; restore circuit.
	2. Controls not set properly.	2. Set controls properly. If no result, test controls; if faulty, replace.
	3. Compressor fan faulty.	3. Call a professional.
	4. Timer faulty.	4. Call a professional.
	5. Compressor faulty.	5. Call a professional.
Fuses blow	1. Circuit overloaded.	1. Put on different circuit.
	2. Voltage low.	2. Call a professional or the power company.
Unit doesn't cool	1. Very hot weather.	1. Set thermostat several degrees lower.
	2. Door gasket faulty.	2. Check gasket for leaks; if faulty, replace.
	3. Condenser coil dirty.	3. Pull unit away from wall and vacuum condenser coil; or remove bottom access panel and clean coil.
	4. Unit needs defrosting.	4. Defrost, reset, and test unit.
	5. Unit in bad location.	5. Move unit at least 2 inches away from wall; keep away from heat registers and windows.
	6. Light stays lit when door is shut.	6. Replace switch.
	7. Wet insulation around unit.	7. Take unit out of service so insulation can dry; locate and mend leak.
	8. Door doesn't close tightly.	8. Level unit so door closes by itself. Check door alignment; if necessary, reset or replace hinges.
	9. Unit overloaded.	9. Store less food in unit.
	10. Condenser fan clogged.	10. Clean fan assembly. If no result, replace if possible; otherwise, call a professional.
	11. Timer faulty.	11. If timer is not complex, test and replace. If timer is complex, disconnect and take to a professional.
	12. Coolant leak.	12. Call a professional.
	13. Defrost heater faulty.	13. Call a professional.
	14. Frost on evaporator coil.	14. Defrost; then defrost frequently.
Frost forms quickly or unit doesn't defrost	1. Controls set incorrectly.	1. Reset thermostat control to higher temperature.
	2. Defrost heater faulty.	2. Test heater; if faulty, replace.

Continued on page 170

REFRIGERATOR/FREEZER TROUBLESHOOTING CHART *(Continued from page 169)*		
Problem	**Possible Cause**	**Solution**
Frost forms quickly or unit doesn't defrost *(continued)*	3. Defrost limit switch faulty.	3. Call a professional.
	4. Door opened too often.	4. Open door less often.
	5. Door gasket faulty.	5. Check gasket for leaks; if faulty, replace.
	6. Door sagging.	6. Level unit so door closes by itself. Check door alignment; if necessary, reset or replace hinges.
	7. Drain clogged (frost-free unit).	7. Defrost freezer; clean drain port.
Noisy operation	1. Unit not level.	1. Level unit from front to back and side to side.
	2. Drain pan vibrating.	2. Reposition pan; if damaged or warped, replace.
Condensation	1. Controls set incorrectly.	1. Set thermostat control to higher temperature.
	2. Door opened too often.	2. Open door less often.
	3. Door gasket faulty.	3. Check gasket for leaks; if faulty, replace.
Water leaks	1. Drains clogged.	1. Defrost and clean drain ports.
	2. Drain hose cracked or split.	2. Replace drain hose.
	3. Drain pan cracked.	3. Replace drain pan.
Unit runs continuously	1. Door gasket faulty.	1. Check gasket for leaks; if faulty, replace.
	2. Controls set incorrectly.	2. Set thermostat control to higher temperature.
	3. Condenser coil dirty.	3. Pull unit away from wall and vacuum condenser coil; or remove bottom access panel and clean coil.
	4. Unit in bad location.	4. Move unit at least 2 inches away from wall; keep away from heat registers and windows.
	5. Door opened too often.	5. Open door less often.
	6. Coolant leak.	6. Call a professional.
Cycles too frequent	1. Condenser coil dirty.	1. Pull unit away from wall and vacuum condenser coil; or remove bottom access panel and clean coil.
	2. Compressor faulty.	2. Call a professional.
Light won't light	1. Bulb burned out.	1. Replace bulb.

door. Pull the bill out. If it offers some resistance, chances are the gasket fits properly. If the bill comes right out, or falls out, the gasket is faulty and should be replaced. Test the gasket at several locations around the door. Before you replace the gasket, check the door hinges for leakage. To replace a gasket:

Step 1: Buy a gasket made specifically for the model refrigerator you own. So-called fit-all gaskets may fit after a fashion, but tailoring them to the door's configuration can be a tough job. If you aren't sure about the model number of your refrigerator, cut out a small section of the gasket and take the sample to an appliance dealer for matching. If the gasket has to be ordered, you can glue the section back into the gap with rubber cement for a make-do repair until the new gasket comes in.

Step 2: Let the new gasket sit about 24 hours in the room with the refrigerator to bring it to the correct temperature and humidity, or soak the gasket in warm water to make it pliable.

Step 3: Begin removing the old gasket. Door gaskets are held by screws, clips, or adhesives, and the gasket may have a retaining strip, which helps shape it and provides a fastening tab or guide. On some units, the gasket may be held in place by the edge of the door panel; the panel is fastened with spring-steel pressure clips, bolts, or screws. To remove the gasket, remove the fasteners that hold it and remove any retaining strips; or remove the fasteners that hold the door panel.

Step 4: Finish removing the fasteners on one side of the door at a time. Do not remove the entire door panel. If the gasket is held by spring clips, be careful not to pry too hard on the clips; they're under tension and could spring out of their mountings. If the gasket is held by adhesive, pry it off with a putty knife.

Step 5: When the old gasket is off, clean the mounting area thoroughly with mild household detergent and water. Remove stubborn adhesive with mineral spirits and fine steel wool, followed by a detergent/water rinse.

Step 6: Start the replacement at one side of the top of the door. Work down the sides to replace the entire gasket. Smooth the gasket evenly into place, easing it around corners. Use gasket cement to secure it if the manufacturer specifies this step. Make sure the gasket lies flat, with no lumps or curled edges.

Step 7: Replace the fasteners, retaining strips, or panel that held the old gasket. After the gasket is in place, tighten or loosen the mounting bolts necessary to adjust the gasket to the door jamb. If the gasket is glued in place, there isn't much you can do but wait for the gasket to conform to the door jamb.

Test the gasket on a freezer door with the same dollar-bill procedure; if the gasket is faulty, replace it with a new gasket made especially for the freezer. Do not remove the freezer door to replace the gasket. Freezer doors are often tensioned with spring devices, which can be very troublesome to replace after the door has been removed, and on some models wiring has to be disassembled as well.

Servicing Door Hinges

A worn or broken door gasket may not be the cause of door leaks. Misaligned and loose door hinges can cause the door to rock or sag slightly, making even a well-fitted gasket ineffective.

Step 1: If the door won't shut tightly, tip the refrigerator slightly backward by propping up the front of the unit or unscrewing the front leveling legs two complete turns. Experiment with this adjustment until the door stays closed, but don't tip the unit very far out of front-to-back level.

Step 2: If leveling doesn't work, tighten the hinge screws. You may have to open the door (especially the freezer door) to turn these screws. On some units, you may have to remove a hinge cap or trim to reach the screws; pry off the cap or trim with a screwdriver. Sagging and looseness can be corrected by shimming the door hinges. Loosen the hinge and place a hinge-shaped cardboard shim between the hinge and the door. Then tighten the hinge again. Sagging may also be caused by a wrongly placed shim. In this case, you can correct the problem by removing the shim. Experiment with the shims; you may be able to eliminate the sagging.

Step 3: If the door is warped, tighten the screws that hold the inner door shell to the outer door shell. You may have to change or adjust the door gasket after making this adjustment.

Step 4: Check the catch. Newer units have a magnetic catch on the door. If the door doesn't latch properly, remove the magnetic strike from the inner door shell and shim it slightly with a piece of thin cardboard. You may have to adjust the gasket to conform with the new shim.

Servicing the Door Switch

On the refrigerator door jamb, locate a small push-button switch. This component operates the light inside the refrigerator. If the switch is malfunctioning, the light in the unit may stay on, and the heat from the lightbulb can cause cooling trouble in the box.

Step 1: Check the bulb to see if it is burned out. If not, depress the push button on the door switch.

Step 2: If the light stays on, remove the switch from the jamb. Remove retaining screws hidden by a plastic trim piece, pry the switch out of the jamb with a screwdriver, or pry off the jamb trim to expose the switch. Then test the switch with a VOM set to the RX1 scale (instructions for using the VOM are given on page 19).

Step 3: Clip one probe of the VOM to each terminal of the switch and press the push button. The meter should read zero. If the needle on the scale moves above zero, replace the switch with a new one of the same type.

Step 4: Connect the new switch the same way the old one was connected.

Servicing the Limit Switch

The limit switch is found only on frost-free refrigerators and freezers. Its function is to keep the defrost heating element from exceeding certain set temperatures. If a refrigerator has lots of frost in the freezer compartment, the problem may be the limit switch. However, other components—the evaporator fan, the defrost timer, and the defrost heater—can cause the same problem. Check these for malfunctions, as detailed below. If these parts are in working condition, the problem is most likely in the limit switch. Don't try to fix the limit switch yourself; call a professional service person for replacement.

Servicing the Thermostat Control

The thermostat control is usually mounted inside the refrigerator. Its visible control knob is turned to regulate the refrigerator/freezer temperature. The workability of this control can be tested in various ways, depending on the problem. To test the thermostat control:

Step 1: If the compressor runs all the time, turn the control knob to the OFF position. If the compressor still runs, unplug the unit, then pull off the control knob and remove the screws holding the thermostat in place. Pull out the thermostat and remove either the red or the

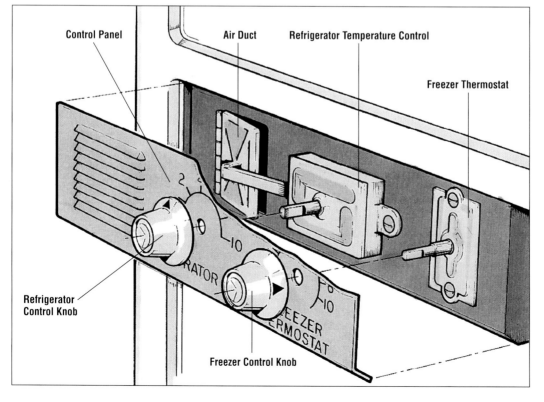

Control Panel · Air Duct · Refrigerator Temperature Control · Freezer Thermostat · Refrigerator Control Knob · Freezer Control Knob

Thermostat controls regulate the temperature of the refrigerator and freezer. Remove the control panel to reach the controls.

blue wire from its terminal. Plug in the unit. If the compressor doesn't run, the thermostat is faulty. Replace it with a new thermostat.

Step 2: If the compressor runs after the wire is removed from its terminal, there is probably a short circuit somewhere in the unit's wiring. In this case, don't try to fix the problem yourself; call a professional service person.

Step 3: If the refrigerator or freezer runs but the box doesn't cool, unplug the unit and remove the thermostat with a screwdriver. Disconnect both wires from the thermostat. Tape the ends of the wires together with electrical tape, and plug in the appliance. If the refrigerator starts and runs normally, the thermostat is faulty. Replace it with a new one of the same type. Connect the new thermostat the same way the old one was connected.

Step 4: If the freezer compartment is normal but the refrigerator box doesn't cool, set the dials that control both compartments to mid-range. Remove these knobs (they're usually friction-fit). Then unscrew the temperature control housing; you'll see an air duct near the control. Replace the knob on the freezer thermostat and turn the control to the OFF position. Open the refrigerator door and look closely at the air duct. If this duct doesn't open wider in about ten minutes, the control is faulty. Replace the control with a new one of the same type. Connect the new control the same way the old one was connected.

Servicing the Evaporator Fan

In some cases, a faulty thermostat may not be the cause of a warm refrigerator or freezer. A warm box may also be caused by a defective fan, a blocked fan, or broken or bent fan blades. If the blades are jammed, try to free them. If they're bent, straighten them with pliers. If this doesn't solve the problem, call a professional service person.

On some refrigerators, the door switch operates the evaporator fan. If the fan seems to be malfunctioning, the door switch could be faulty. Test the switch as detailed on page 172, and replace it if necessary.

Servicing the Defrost Timer

If the compressor doesn't run, it is likely that the defrost timer is malfunctioning. This part is located near the compressor. To test the defrost timer:

Step 1: Unplug the refrigerator.

Step 2: Disconnect the wires from the timer and timer motor. Remove the timer from its brackets by backing out two retaining screws.

Step 3: Test the defrost timer with a VOM set to the RX1 scale (instructions for using the VOM are provided on page 19). Clip one probe of the VOM to each defrost timer—not motor—wire, and turn the timer control screw shaft until it clicks. If the defrost timer is functioning, the meter will read zero. If the needle jumps, the defrost timer is faulty. Replace it with a new one of the same type.

Step 4: Connect the new defrost timer the same way the old one was connected.

To check the defrost timer motor, clip one probe of the VOM to each motor wire, setting the scale to RX100. If the meter reads between about 500 and 3,000 ohms, the motor is functioning properly. If the meter reads higher than 3,000 ohms, the timer motor is faulty. Replace it with a new one of the same type. Connect the new motor the same way the old one was connected.

Servicing the Defrost Heater

This component is a heating element located on the evaporator coil. When the refrigerator or freezer switches to the defrost cycle, the defrost heater is turned on to melt the frost in the compartment. Failure of the defrost heater causes failure to defrost.

Test the element with a VOM set to the RX1 scale (instructions for using the VOM are given on page 19). To gain access to the heating element, remove the compartment's wall panels. Clip one probe of the VOM to each element terminal. The meter should read between 5 and 20 ohms. If it doesn't, the heating element is faulty and should be replaced. Replace the heater with a new one of the same type and electrical rating. Connect the new heater the same way the old one was connected.

Servicing the Condenser Fan

The condenser fan is located under the unit. If the fan is malfunctioning, the refrigerator or freezer won't cool properly, or it will run continuously or not at all.

Test the fan with a VOM set to the RX1 scale. Disconnect the electrical wires to the fan motor and clip one probe of the VOM to each fan motor terminal. If the meter reads from 50 to 200 ohms, the motor is functioning properly. If the meter reads higher than 200 ohms, the fan motor is faulty and you should replace it.

While you're working on the fan motor, make sure the fan blades are clean and unobstructed. If the blades are bent, straighten them with pliers.

Clearing the Drain Ports

The drain ports are located along the bottom of both the freezer and the refrigerator sections of the unit. These holes can become clogged with debris or ice, causing a drainage problem when the unit is defrosting. To clear the ports, use a short section of wire that will fit the holes. Do not use a toothpick, because the wood may break off in the port and become stuck. On some refrigerators, the drain ports are located near the defrost heater at the evaporator coils. A lot of disassembly is required to clean this type of unit. If the refrigerator or freezer is this type, you may be better off calling a professional service person to clear the ports.

On some freezer compartments, the drain is located under the freezer compartment and shaped like a shoehorn. This type of drain can usually be unscrewed so that the drain area can be cleaned.

Servicing the Drain Hose and Pan

The condenser fan is located under the bottom of the refrigerator. During the defrosting cycle, water runs through a small hose into the drain pan and is naturally evaporated. On some refrigerators, the drain hose is rubber instead of metal. This type of hose can become cracked, causing leaks. Examine the hose. If it's damaged, replace it with a new one of the same type. If you spot water on the floor, the drain pan may be tipped on its brackets, or the pan may be cracked or rusted. To eliminate the leak, realign or replace the pan.

Servicing Ice Makers

Freezers with automatic ice makers sometimes malfunction because the water inlet valve strainer that feeds water to the ice maker becomes clogged. To correct this problem, unplug the appliance and disconnect the water supply. Remove the water line where it enters the valve—usually at the bottom edge of the unit. Locate the wire strainer and remove it. Clean the strainer with a stiff brush, using mild household detergent. Reassemble the component in reverse fashion.

Servicing a Refrigerant Leak

Coolant leaks are identifiable by their acrid smell. There is nothing you can do to repair a coolant leak except call a professional service person to deal with the problem.

Servicing the Motor/Compressor

The compressor and motor of a refrigerator or freezer are contained in a sealed unit. If you trace problems to either of these components, do not try to fix the unit yourself. Call a professional service person.

Repairing Dishwashers

The control panels on the latest dishwashers can look intimidating. They're loaded with so many dials, push buttons, and other features that the machine looks too complex to repair. This is actually not the case. With the exception of the control panel, dishwashers haven't changed much in basic design over the last decade. You can repair most dishwasher malfunctions yourself.

Dishwasher parts can be replaced as a unit, which is often easier and less expensive than having a professional service person make repairs. If you aren't sure a part is still usable, remove it from the dishwasher and take it to a professional for testing. You can then decide whether to buy a new part or have the old one repaired on the basis of the repair estimate.

Dishwashers usually run on 115-volt or 120-volt power. The water they use comes directly from the water heater, and wastewater is drained into the sink's drainpipe. The dishwasher is not connected to the cold-water supply. For best dishwashing results, set the temperature control of the water heater to no less than 140°F. Water cooler than this usually doesn't get the dishes clean, unless your dishwasher is a newer model that preheats incoming water. The water shutoff for the dishwasher is typically located below the adjoining sink.

Caution: Because the dishwasher is connected to both the plumbing system and the electrical system, you must consider both systems when working on this appliance. Before doing any work on the dishwasher, make sure the unit is unplugged or the power to the unit is turned off, and remove the fuse or trip the circuit breaker that controls the circuit at the main entrance panel or at a separate panel. Shut off the water supply to the dishwasher at the shutoff in the basement or crawl space under the kitchen.

The repair procedures in this section are complete, but for repairs involving the plumbing system, you may need additional information. For more information on plumbing repairs, see Chapter 7.

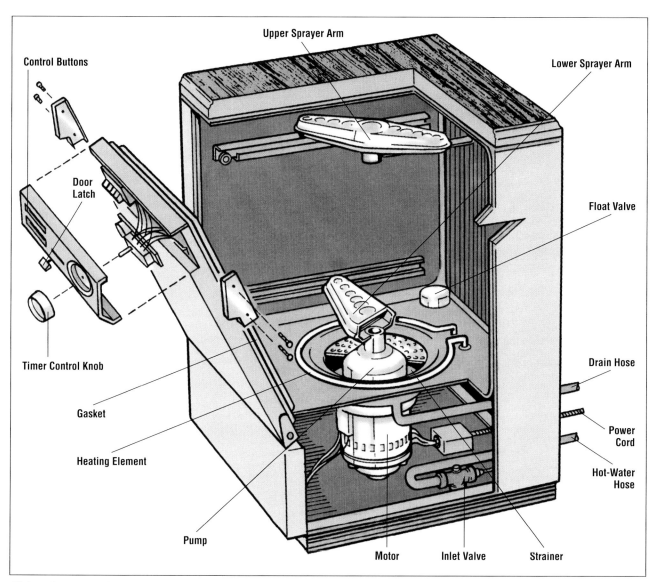

Dishwashers spray hot water into a tub stacked with dishes, then dry the dishes with a blower or heating element. Problems often involve the water supply and drainage systems.

Basic Operating Checks

Here are some operating checks you can make if the dishwasher does not work:

Step 1: Check to make sure it's receiving power. If the unit plugs into a wall outlet, check the cord, the plug, and the outlet to make sure they're functioning properly. Also check the switch that controls the outlet to make sure it's turned on. Most built-in dishwashers are wired directly into a circuit. Check the main entrance panel for a blown fuse or tripped circuit breaker, and restore the circuit. If your home is an older one, the dishwasher may be wired to a separate entrance panel; look for a blown fuse or breaker at this panel, and restore the circuit.

Step 2: If the circuit is receiving power, and the wall outlet is controlled by a switch, the switch may be faulty. Test the switch with a voltage tester. Take off the switch cover plate and place one probe of the tester on one terminal and the other probe on the other terminal. If the tester bulb lights, the switch is functioning. If it doesn't light, the switch is faulty. Replace the switch with a new one of the same type, as detailed in Chapter 4.

Step 3: Make sure the door is tightly closed and latched. The dishwasher will not operate until

MAJOR APPLIANCE REPAIR

DISHWASHER TROUBLESHOOTING CHART

Problem	Possible Cause	Solution
Unit doesn't run	1. No power.	1. Check power cord, plug, and outlet. Check for blown fuses or tripped circuit breakers at main entrance panel; restore circuit.
	2. Motor overload or safety shutoff.	2. Press reset button on control panel.
	3. Controls not properly set.	3. Set controls properly.
	4. Door not latched.	4. Close door so latch engages; if latch faulty, replace.
	5. Timer faulty.	5. Make sure timer is properly set. Test timer; if faulty, replace.
	6. Motor faulty.	6. Check motor leads for proper connections. Remove motor and take to a professional, or replace motor.
Dishes don't get clean	1. Inadequate preparation.	1. Scrape and rinse dishes before loading machine.
	2. Water not hot enough.	2. Set water heater thermostat at 140° to 150°F.
	3. Soap dispenser blocked, clogged, or broken.	3. Leave dispenser exposed when loading. Clean dispenser; if broken, replace.
	4. Wrong type of detergent.	4. Use a detergent recommended for dishwashers.
	5. Detergent ineffective or spoiled.	5. Use new detergent.
	6. Sprayer arm clogged.	6. Clean sprayer arm.
	7. Strainer clogged.	7. Clean strainer.
	8. Pump clogged.	8. Clean pump.
	9. Timer faulty.	9. Make sure timer is properly set. Test timer; if faulty, replace.
Dishes don't get dry	1. Dishes removed too soon after end of cycle.	1. Wait until hot water has had time to evaporate from dishes.
	2. Poor stacking.	2. Stack dishes so there is air space around them.
	3. Water not hot enough.	3. Set water heater thermostat at 140° to 150°F.
	4. Heating element faulty.	4. Test element; if faulty, replace.
	5. Wetting agent gone.	5. Check dispenser; if necessary, refill.
	6. Leaky water inlet valve.	6. Clean water inlet valve; if damaged, replace.
	7. Fan motor faulty.	7. Clean fan assembly; check fan terminals for proper connections. If necessary, replace fan.

Continued on page 177

DISHWASHER TROUBLESHOOTING CHART *(Continued from page 176)*

Problem	Possible Cause	Solution
Dishes have soap spots and film	1. Poor stacking.	1. Stack dishes so there is air space around them.
	2. Not enough detergent.	2. Use amount of detergent recommended by manufacturer.
	3. Wrong type of detergent.	3. Use detergent recommended for dishwashers.
	4. Water not hot enough.	4. Set water heater thermostat at 140° to 150°F.
	5. Inadequate preparation.	5. Scrape and rinse dishes before loading machine.
	6. Water hard.	6. Add rinsing conditioner.
Silverware tarnishes	1. Water contains chemicals.	1. Add rinsing conditioner, or add water softener to water supply.
Dishwasher doesn't fill	1. Float switch stuck.	1. Clean float and float switch; tap lightly with screwdriver handle. If necessary, replace float switch.
	2. Timer faulty.	2. Make sure timer is properly set. Test timer; if faulty, replace.
	3. Water inlet valve screen clogged or dirty.	3. Clean water inlet valve screen.
	4. Water inlet valve solenoid faulty.	4. Tap solenoid lightly with screwdriver handle; if no result, replace water inlet valve.
	5. Drain valve stuck open.	5. Call a professional.
	6. Pressure switch faulty.	6. Replace switch.
	7. Water not turned on.	7. Check valve under dishwasher. Open hot water faucet in kitchen sink; if water doesn't flow, check for problems at water heater.
	8. Water pressure low.	8. Call water company.
Water doesn't drain	1. Impeller jammed.	1. Clean impeller; if faulty, replace.
	2. Drain valve solenoid faulty.	2. Tap solenoid lightly with screwdriver handle; if no result, call a professional.
	3. Drain valve clogged.	3. Clean drain valve.
	4. Drain hose kinked.	4. Straighten drain hose.
	5. Strainer clogged.	5. Clean strainer.
	6. Pump faulty.	6. Clean pump; if no result, replace pump.
	7. Motor faulty.	7. Call a professional.

Continued on page 178

DISHWASHER TROUBLESHOOTING CHART *(Continued from page 177)*

Problem	Possible Cause	Solution
Dishwasher doesn't shut off	1. Timer faulty.	1. Make sure timer is properly set. Test timer; if faulty, replace.
	2. Float switch stuck.	2. Clean float switch; tap switch lightly with screwdriver handle. If no result, replace float switch.
	3. Water inlet valve clogged or stuck open.	3. Disassemble and clean water inlet valve.
Dishwasher runs while door is open	1. Door switch faulty.	1. Replace door switch.
	2. Motor faulty.	2. Call a professional, or remove motor and take to a professional.
Water leaks	1. Poor stacking.	1. Stack dishes so there is air space around them.
	2. Too much detergent.	2. Use amount of detergent recommended by manufacturer.
	3. Door gasket worn or damaged.	3. Replace gasket.
	4. Timer faulty.	4. Make sure timer is properly set. Test timer; if faulty, replace.
	5. Water inlet valve stuck open.	5. Clean water inlet valve; if damaged, replace.
	6. Pump seal faulty.	6. Call a professional.
	7. Hose loose or damaged.	7. Tighten hose connections; if hose damaged, replace.
	8. Door hinges broken or misaligned.	8. Tighten and realign hinges; if necessary, replace hinges.
Noisy operation	1. Poor stacking.	1. Make sure dishes are properly stacked.
	2. Machine out of level.	2. Level unit with shims; check level from front to back and side to side.
	3. Sprayer arms misaligned.	3. Adjust sprayer arms so they don't scrape against screens or racks.
	4. Water level low.	4. Refrain from using washer, shower, and toilets while dishwasher is operating.
Racks stick	1. Door not open.	1. Make sure door is fully open when racks are pulled out.
	2. Racks off tracks.	2. Guide racks into tracks.
	3. Rack guides and glides dirty or misaligned.	3. Adjust and clean rack bearing points.
	4. Rack guides damaged.	4. Replace rack guides.
Dishwasher smells bad	1. Trapped food particles in unit.	1. Clean inside of washer—especially below sprayer—with household detergent; then run through complete cycle. Rinse dishes before stacking in washer.

the latch is properly engaged. To check the latch, close and latch the door, holding the latch tightly in place. Then, still pressing the latch closed, turn the control knob to the ON position. If the dishwasher works, the latch is faulty and should be replaced.

Step 4: Make sure the water is turned on and the water temperature is high enough. A breakdown in the water heater could stop flow of water to the dishwasher. Test the hot water in the kitchen sink or bathroom. If you can draw hot water, the water heater may not be at fault.

Step 5: Make sure the controls on the control panel are properly set. The newer push-button controls can be very sensitive; make sure the buttons are firmly pressed into position.

If you've gone through these five checks without finding the solution, it's time to dig deeper into the dishwasher.

Disassembling the Dishwasher

Access to the working parts of most dishwashers is through the front door of the unit. Many repairs can be made to the machine by simply opening the door and reaching into the various component parts, such as the sprayers, strainers, float switch, racks, and door latch.

To get to the control panel on the door, remove a series of retaining screws around the panel. These screws may be under molding trim strips, which usually snap onto the metal housing. Pry off the strips with a stiff-bladed putty knife or a screwdriver, or remove a setscrew that holds the molding. The control knobs are friction-fit on shafts or are held by small setscrews in the base of the knobs. In some dishwashers, the entire front door panel must be removed to gain access to the control components. This panel is held to the door by a series of retaining screws, usually found around the edge on the inside back of the door.

On many models, once the control panel is removed the door panel can be removed by unscrewing a series of fasteners holding the door panel in place. Sometimes these retaining screws are covered by trim moldings, which must be pried or slipped off. For access to the motor, pump, hoses, inlet valves, and other parts, remove the lower access panel. This can usually be done without removing the entire door. The panel may be held by retaining screws, or it may lift up and off metal hangers.

If the dishwasher is portable, tip the machine over on its back or side before removing the control door or lower access panels. This may give you a more comfortable working position.

Replacing the Door Gasket

If water leaks through the dishwasher door, the gasket is probably faulty. Open the door and examine the gasket. It should be soft and resilient. If it's worn, cracked, or hard, it should be replaced, as detailed on page 171.

Once the gasket is in place, check it for fit against the door frame. It should fit tightly with no cracks or bulges between the gasket and the frame. If necessary, tighten or loosen the retaining screws, or refit the gasket in the clips or the door channel. Then run the machine through a washing sequence and check for leaks. If you spot a leak, and the gasket seems to be properly in place, try adjusting the door latch. The trick is to position the gasket against the frame of the door without flattening

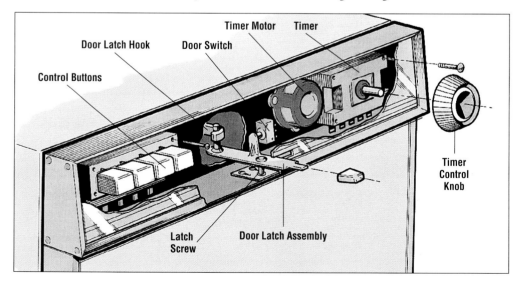

For repairs to the timer, door latch, or switches, remove the control panel. To take it off, remove a series of retaining screws and the control knobs, and lift off the panel.

Control Buttons

Door Latch Hook   Door Switch

Timer Motor   Timer

Timer Control Knob

Latch Screw   Door Latch Assembly

Repairing the Motor

If the dishwasher motor malfunctions, don't try to fix it yourself. Call a professional service person to make repairs or replace the motor. Before you call for service, however, you should check to make sure that the timer is working and that the dishwasher is receiving power.

Repairing Washers

Because washing machines do so many things, they may be harder to diagnose than they are to repair. This is because of the special timing cycles that operate valves and motors that turn water on, spin the tub, drain water, and control the water temperature. But diagnosis is possible: All it takes is common sense and patience.

Caution: Before you do any work on a washer, make sure it's unplugged. Disconnect the grounding wire and the water hoses.

Basic Operating Checks

Here are some initial steps to help you diagnose and fix washer problems.

Step 1: Make sure the washer is receiving power. Check the cord, the plug, and the outlet. If a wall switch controls the outlet, make sure the switch is working. Look for blown fuses or tripped circuit breakers at the main entrance panel. If the unit is receiving power and still won't run, press the reset button on the control panel (if the washer has one).

Step 2: Make sure the control knob is properly set to the ON position and the door is tightly closed. Check the latch to make sure it's free of lint and soap buildup.

Step 3: Make sure that both water faucets are turned on and that the drain and soap-saver return hoses are properly extended, without kinks. If the washer has a water-saver button, make sure the button is depressed; water may not circulate through the filter nozzle if the basket is not full and the button is not depressed.

Step 4: To make sure the water is the proper temperature, check the temperature selector switches on the control panel to make sure they're properly set. Also check the water heater temperature control. It should be set no lower than 120°F.

Cleaning the Washer

Regularly clean the top and door of the washer to prevent the buildup of dirt and detergent. When you wash very linty materials, remove lint from the tub after removing the laundry. Soap deposits may cause laundry to smell bad. To solve this problem, fill the tub with water and add 1 pound of water softener or 1 gallon of white vinegar; then run the machine through the complete wash cycle. If the deposits are really bad, wash the inside of the tub with a solution of household ammonia and mild detergent. Rinse thoroughly and wipe the tub with liquid bleach. *Caution: Rinse the tub thoroughly before wiping it out with bleach. Ammonia and bleach can combine to form a very dangerous gas.*

Finally, run the machine through a complete wash cycle before you put any more laundry in.

Disassembling the Washer

The washer cabinet usually must be disassembled for repairs and some maintenance. The washer is connected to both the electric power outlet and to the water supply. *Caution: Make sure the power cord and water hoses are disconnected before you disassemble the cabinet or tip it over for service.* To disassemble a washer:

Step 1: To remove the control panel, remove retaining screws spaced around the panel. They are usually located under a piece of molding or trim that can be pried off. On some machines, you'll have to remove the back of the control panel, also held by retaining screws, to get at the working parts of the controls. Knobs on the control panel are usually friction-fit. Some knobs are held by small setscrews at the base of the knob. Loosen the setscrews and pull the knobs straight off the shafts.

Step 2: To remove the service panel, remove its retaining screws, then spread an old blanket on the floor to protect the washer's finish. Tip the washer over on its front or side to gain access through the bottom of the machine. The bottom of the machine generally doesn't have a service panel because it is usually open.

Step 3: To remove the top of the cabinet, insert a stiff-bladed putty knife into the joint between the top and side panels and give the knife a rap with your fist. This should release the spring clips so that the top can be removed.

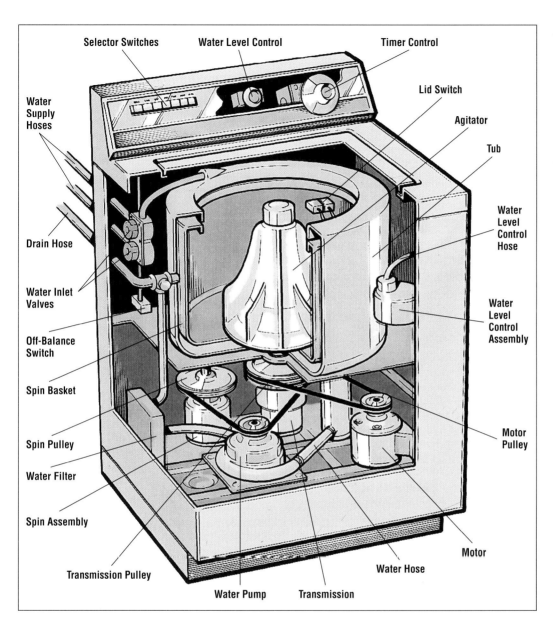

Selector Switches   Water Level Control   Timer Control

Water Supply Hoses

Drain Hose

Water Inlet Valves

Off-Balance Switch

Spin Basket

Spin Pulley

Water Filter

Spin Assembly

Transmission Pulley

Water Pump   Transmission

Water Hose

Motor

Motor Pulley

Lid Switch

Agitator

Tub

Water Level Control Hose

Water Level Control Assembly

A washing machine has a tub and an agitator; various cycles control the water temperature. Problems can occur in either the electrical or the plumbing systems.

Servicing the Lid Switch

The lid switch on a washer often serves as a safety switch. If the switch is not working, or if the switch opening in the lid is clogged with detergent, the machine will not run. To check and repair the lid switch:

Step 1: Unplug the machine. Clean out the lid switch port with a wood manicure stick. Clean off any detergent buildup around the rim of the lid. Sometimes there's enough detergent encrusted on the metal to prevent the lid from closing tightly and keep the washer from operating.

Step 2: If cleaning doesn't help, remove the top of the cabinet to get at the switch. With the switch

exposed, check the screws for looseness. Loose screws can cause the switch to move when the lid is closed or as the machine goes through its cycles. Check the terminals of the switch to make sure they're tight. Tighten the mounting screws after the switch is in alignment.

Step 3: Test the switch with a VOM set to the RX1 scale; procedures for using the VOM are detailed on page 19. Disconnect the power leads to the switch terminals and clip one probe of the VOM to each terminal. Close the lid of the washer. If the meter reads zero, the switch is working. If not, the switch is faulty and should be replaced.

WASHER TROUBLESHOOTING CHART

Problem	Possible Cause	Solution
Washer doesn't run	1. No power.	1. Check power cord, plug, and outlet. Check for blown fuses or tripped circuit breakers at main entrance panel; restore circuit.
	2. Motor overload or safety shutoff.	2. Press reset button on control panel or motor.
	3. Timer faulty.	3. Make sure timer is properly set. Test timer; if faulty, replace.
	4. Lid switch faulty.	4. Remove detergent buildup from orifice; make sure switch is secure and making contact. Test switch; if faulty, replace. Make sure new switch is properly aligned.
	5. Off-balance switch faulty.	5. Test switch; if faulty, replace.
	6. Water pump clogged.	6. Clean out pump, if possible; otherwise, replace pump.
	7. Motor binding.	7. Remove motor and take to a professional.
Fuses blow	1. Too much detergent.	1. Suds can cause problem; reduce amount of detergent used.
	2. Motor overload protector faulty.	2. Replace overload protector.
	3. Machine overloaded.	3. Reduce size of load; load properly to reduce drag on tub.
	4. Motor faulty.	4. Remove motor and take to a professional.
Tub doesn't fill	1. Supply hoses kinked or clogged.	1. Straighten hoses; clean water inlet valve screens.
	2. Water level switch faulty.	2. Remove switch and take to a professional for testing; if faulty, replace.
	3. Water inlet valve solenoids faulty.	3. Clean water inlet valves; tap solenoids lightly with screwdriver handle; if no result, replace water inlet valves.
Tub fills at wrong cycle	1. Water inlet valve solenoids faulty.	1. Clean water inlet valves; tap solenoids lightly with screwdriver handle; if no result, replace water inlet valves.
	2. Water level switch faulty.	2. Remove switch and take to a professional for testing; if faulty, replace.
	3. Pump valve stuck.	3. Remove pump and clean.
Water doesn't shut off	1. Hose to water level switch disconnected or faulty.	1. Reconnect or replace hose.
	2. Water inlet valve faulty.	2. Clean inlet valve; if problem persists, replace valve.

Continued on page 187

WASHER TROUBLESHOOTING CHART *(Continued from page 186)*

Problem	Possible Cause	Solution
Tub won't empty	1. Drain hose kinked.	1. Straighten drain hose.
	2. Pump jammed or clogged.	2. Remove and clean pump; if necessary, replace.
	3. Motor belt slipping or broken.	3. Adjust or replace belt.
	4. Pump pulley loose or worn.	4. Tighten setscrews holding pulley; if necessary, replace pulley.
	5. Pump impeller faulty.	5. Replace pump.
Water too hot or too cold	1. Temperature selector switch set wrong.	1. Make sure water temperature switches on control panel are set properly.
	2. Water heater temperature set wrong.	2. Check water temperature thermostat on water heater; if necessary, reset.
	3. Supply hoses reversed.	3. Switch water hoses at faucets; "hot" hose may be connected to "cold" inlet.
	4. Mixing valve faulty.	4. Check solenoid on valve; if faulty, replace valve.
	5. Temperature selector switch faulty.	5. Test switch; if faulty, replace.
	6. Timer faulty.	6. Make sure timer is properly set. Test timer; if faulty, replace.
Tub fills slowly	1. Water inlet valve screens clogged.	1. Clean water inlet valve screens.
	2. Fill spout clogged.	2. Clean fill spout.
	3. Water pressure low.	3. Call water company.
High water level or overflow	1. Flow valve washer faulty or wrong size.	1. Replace flow valve washer.
	2. Water pressure too high.	2. Call water company; reduce flow by closing water faucets slightly.
	3. Water level control switch faulty.	3. Check and repair hose connected to switch. Remove switch and take to a professional for testing; if faulty, replace.
Tub spins in wash cycle	1. Timer contacts bad.	1. Test timer; if faulty, replace.
	2. Timer improperly wired.	2. Call a professional.
Oil leaks on floor	1. Drain plug faulty.	1. Replace gasket on drain plug.
	2. Support gasket faulty.	2. Call a professional.
	3. Gasket between washer housing and base faulty.	3. Call a professional.
	4. Oil pump faulty.	4. Call a professional.
	5. Vent tube leaking.	5. Solder tube shut, or call a professional.
Wash tangled	1. Not enough water.	1. See "Tub doesn't fill."
	2. Improper loading.	2. Follow manufacturer's loading instructions.

Continued on page 188

WASHER TROUBLESHOOTING CHART (Continued from page 187)

Problem	Possible Cause	Solution
Wash tangled (continued)	3. Extended washing time.	3. Follow manufacturer's control setting instructions.
	4. Agitator pulsator clearance not properly set.	4. Call a professional.
Wash smells bad	1. Soap deposits.	1. Fill tub with water and add 1 pound water softener or 1 gallon white vinegar; run machine through complete cycle. Or wash inside of tub with ammonia-detergent solution, rinse with water, rinse again with household bleach, and cycle as above.
Excessive washer vibration	1. Machine not level.	1. Adjust leveling legs; check for level front to back and side to side.
	2. Tub unbalanced.	2. Follow manufacturer's loading instructions.
	3. Oversudsing.	3. Reduce amount of detergent used.
	4. Tub faulty.	4. Replace tub, or replace washer.
	5. Snubber plate on water pump dirty.	5. Clean plate.
	6. Tub bolts loose.	6. Tighten nut that holds tub, replace tub, or replace washer.
	7. Cross brace damaged.	7. Call a professional.
	8. Supports loose.	8. Call a professional.
Washer rips laundry	1. Machine overloaded.	1. Follow manufacturer's loading instructions.
	2. Agitator rough or cracked.	2. Inspect agitator for rough spots and cracks; if necessary, replace.
	3. Rough spot in tub.	3. Smooth rough spot, replace tub, or replace washer.
Water leaks	1. Oversudsing.	1. Reduce amount of detergent used.
	2. Fill nozzle out of alignment.	2. Align fill nozzle so it squirts into tub.
	3. Overflow nozzle out of alignment.	3. Align overflow so it squirts into drain.
	4. Fill tub faulty.	4. Replace fill tub.
	5. Lid seal faulty.	5. Replace lid seal.
	6. Hose connections loose or faulty.	6. Tighten hose connections; if hoses faulty, replace.
	7. Bolts on pump impeller loose.	7. Tighten bolts.
	8. Hole in tub.	8. Replace tub, or replace washer.
	9. Pump gasket faulty.	9. Replace gasket, if possible; otherwise, replace pump.

Step 4: If necessary, replace the lid switch with a new one of the same type. Connect the new switch in exactly the same way the old one was connected.

Step 5: If the switch still doesn't work, it is probably misaligned. Realign the switch by repositioning the screws holding it in place, testing the switch as you go until it works properly.

Servicing the Temperature Selector Switch

This control panel switch regulates the temperature of the water in the tub. It also plays a role in controlling the fill cycle. If you suspect this switch is faulty, remove it and take it to a professional service person for testing (the test takes special equipment). Or, hook a test wire across the switch terminals; if water flows, the switch is faulty. If the switch is faulty, replace it with a new one of the same type. Connect the new switch the same way the old one was connected.

If there's a problem with both water temperature and tub filling cycles, both the temperature switch and the timer may be faulty. Test both components and replace them as necessary. Procedures for testing the timer can be found below.

Servicing the Water Level Control Switch

This is another control panel switch, usually located next to the temperature switch. There is a small hose connected to this switch, and sometimes this hose becomes loose and falls off the connection. When this happens, the water in the tub usually overflows. To solve this problem, cut about ½ inch off the end of the hose and use a push fit to reconnect it to the switch.

The switch itself can also malfunction, resulting in tub overflow and other water-level trouble in the tub. If you suspect this switch is faulty, remove it by backing out the screws holding it in place. Take it to a professional service person for testing. If the switch is faulty, replace it with a new one of the same size and type. Connect the new switch the same way the old one was connected.

Servicing the Timer

Most washing machine timers are very complicated. The timer controls most of the operations of the washer: water level, tub filling and emptying, length of cycles,

and cycle setting sequences. For this reason, any repairs to the timer should be made by a professional service person. However, there are a couple of checks you can make when you suspect the timer is faulty—you may be able to install a new timer yourself.

Step 1: Unplug the washer. To access the timer, remove the control knobs and the panel that covers the controls. This may be a front panel, or access may be through a panel at the back of the unit. Carefully examine the wires that connect the timer to the other parts of the washer. If the wires are loose or disconnected, try pushing them into position; they usually fit into their terminals like plugs. Use long-nosed pliers to avoid breaking the wire connections—never pull a wire by hand.

Step 2: To test the timer, use a VOM set to the RX1 scale; procedures for using the VOM are detailed on page 19. Disconnect the power leads to the timer and clip one probe of the VOM to each lead. The VOM should read zero if the timer is working. Since the timer is a multiple switch, turn it through its cycle and test each pair of terminals in turn. The meter should read zero at all of these points. If one or more readings are above zero, the timer is faulty and should be replaced.

Step 3: To replace the timer, unscrew and disconnect the old one. Install a new timer made specifically for the washing machine. If there are many wires on the timer, have a helper hold the new timer next to the old one as you work. Disconnect the old wires one at a time, connecting each corresponding new wire as you work, to make sure the connections are properly made. Or, draw a diagram showing the connections before removing the old timer. After all the wires are connected, check the connections again for correctness and screw the timer assembly into place.

Servicing Water Inlet Valves

If the washer won't fill or fills very slowly, if it overfills, or if the water is the wrong temperature, the water inlet valves could be faulty. These components are easy to locate and very easy to replace, at little cost. When you suspect an inlet valve is faulty, first check to make sure the water faucets are fully turned on and properly connected to the hot and cold inlets of the valves. Then check the screens in the valves; if they're clogged, clean

If an inlet valve is faulty, check the water connection and the valve screens. Try gently tapping the solenoids; if this doesn't work, replace the inlet valve assembly.

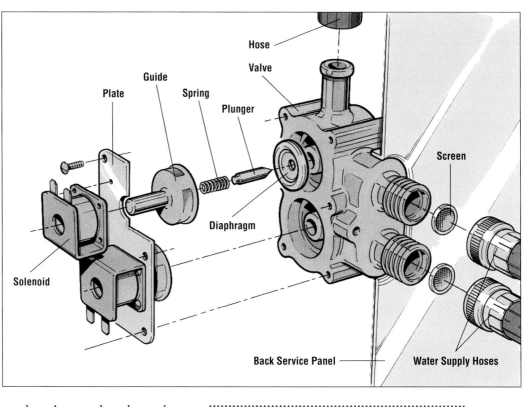

or replace them. If water doesn't enter the tub, set the temperature control to the HOT setting. If there is no water, set the control to the WARM setting. If all that comes out is cold water, the hot-water inlet valve is faulty. Reverse the procedure to test the cold-water valve, setting the control first on COLD and then on WARM. If the tub overfills, unplug the washer. If water still flows into the tub, the valve is stuck open. In any of these cases, the valves should probably be replaced. To check the valve assembly:

Step 1: Remove the back service panel and disconnect the hot-water and cold-water hoses to the valves.

Step 2: Remove the hoses connected to the valves inside the cabinet. Also disconnect the wires from the terminals. Back out the screws holding the valves to the machine. The inlet valves have solenoids inside the housing. These can be tested, but chances are the valves are simply worn out.

Step 3: Tap the solenoids with a screwdriver handle. If this doesn't work, replace the entire inlet valve assembly. Repairs usually cost more than a new part. Make sure the replacement valve assembly is exactly the same type as the old one. Install it in reverse order of the way you disconnected the old one.

Servicing the Tub and Agitator

The washing machine tub, or basket, generally doesn't cause problems. However, at times it may cause damage to the laundry, make a lot of noise, vibrate, or stop completely.

If laundry is torn during the wash cycle, feel around the tub. If you find a rough spot, you may be able to smooth it with an emery board. Sand the spot lightly. If this doesn't work—or if you have to cut to bare metal to remove the roughness—the tub should be replaced. In this case, it's probably much wiser to replace the entire washer.

The agitator—the finned part that fits on the tub shaft—can also tear laundry if the fins are cracked or broken. You may be able to solve the problem temporarily by pinching off the splinters with pliers and lightly filing the plastic smooth, but this is just a stopgap measure; the agitator should be replaced. Replace a damaged agitator with a new one of the same type. To do this, unscrew the cap on top of the agitator. With the cap off, pull straight up on the agitator; it should lift off. If it doesn't move, rap its side with a hammer. If it still won't lift off, drive wedges under the bottom rim of the agitator to dislodge it. Then set the new agitator into place and replace the agitator cap.

Damage to the snubber, a padlike device sometimes located under the agitator cap, can cause the machine to

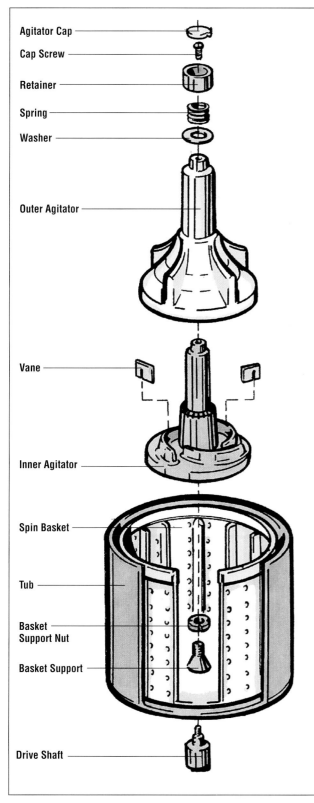

Agitator Cap

Cap Screw

Retainer

Spring

Washer

Outer Agitator

Vane

Inner Agitator

Spin Basket

Tub

Basket
Support Nut

Basket Support

Drive Shaft

Replace a damaged agitator with a new one of the same type. Unscrew the cap on top of the agitator and pull straight up; the agitator should lift off.

vibrate excessively. The snubber may have a suspension spring in it. Lift off the agitator cap and examine the snubber. If the spring is broken, or if the pad is visibly worn, replace the entire snubber. Snubbers might also be found at the splash guard at the top of the tub, under the transmission, or as part of the water pump housing. Look around until you see it.

If the machine doesn't have a snubber, listen for noise at the suspension unit between the tub and the machine cabinet. The suspension unit has fins or pads that may need replacement. In some cases, the entire unit may have to be replaced. Another noise point is the basket support nut. Tighten the nut or, if you can't tighten it, replace it.

Sudden tub stops can be caused by a broken motor belt, but they are usually due to poor tub loading. Check to see if wet laundry is wadded around the bottom of the tub shaft, or under the basket or agitator assembly. Remove the basket or agitator in order to remove the laundry easily.

Troubleshooting Water Leaks

Water leaks in a washer are often difficult to trace. There are many possibilities to look for. The problem could be a loose connection, a broken hose, a cracked component, or a defective seal. It could also be a hole in the tub. If a hole in the tub is the problem, it's usually best to replace the washer.

Most leaks can be eliminated by tightening water connections and replacing deteriorated components. To stop a leak:

Step 1: Check the lid seal. If faulty, replace with a new gasket, as detailed on page 171.

Step 2: Check the hoses at faucet connections. Tighten connections or replace hoses.

Step 3: Check the hoses at water valve connections. Tighten connections or replace hoses.

Step 4: Check the drain hoses. Tighten connections or replace hoses.

Step 5: Check the inlet nozzles. Tighten connections or replace nozzles.

Step 6: Check the splash guard. Tighten connections or replace.

Step 7: Check any plastic valve. Tighten connections or replace.

Step 8: Check the outlet hose to drain. Tighten connections or replace hose.

Step 9: Check the water pump, using the procedures that follow.

Servicing the Water Pump

Of all washing machine parts, the water pump probably takes the most punishment, because it is constantly in use. When the pump fails, you can hear or see the trouble: a loud rumbling inside the machine, or a failure of the water to drain out of the tub. Here's what you can do to fix the problem:

Step 1: Check the drain hoses to make sure they are draining properly. Remove the water supply hoses from the back of the washer. With long-nosed pliers, extract the filter screens from the valve ports in the washer or from the hoses themselves. Wash the screens thoroughly. Then replace them and reattach the hoses. If the machine still rumbles or doesn't drain, examine the pump.

Step 2: To access the pump, first bail and sponge out any water in the machine's tub. Then tip the washer over on its front, using a heavy blanket or pad to protect the washer's finish. Remove the back service panel. The pump is usually located along the bottom of the machine, but with the unit tipped on its front it's easier to remove the pump through the back than through the bottom of the washer.

Step 3: Locate the pump. It has two large hoses attached to it with spring or strap clips. If the clips are the spring type, pinch the ends of the clips together with pliers to release them, and slide the clips down the hoses. If the clips are the strap type, unscrew the metal collar to loosen the clamp. Disconnect the hoses by pulling them off the connections. If the hoses are kinked or crimped at these connections, straighten them as best you can and reconnect them. Then try the machine again to see if this kinking was causing the problem. If the machine still doesn't drain, you'll have to remove the water pump.

Step 4: To remove the pump, loosen the bolt that holds the drive belt taut and move the washer motor on the bracket to loosen the belt. Move the motor out of the way and unbolt the pump; it's usually held by two or three hex-head bolts located on the bottom of the pump housing. As you loosen the last mounting bolt, support the pump with your hand. Then lift the pump out of the washer.

Step 5: You should take the pump apart if you can, because the trouble could be lint, dirt, or pieces

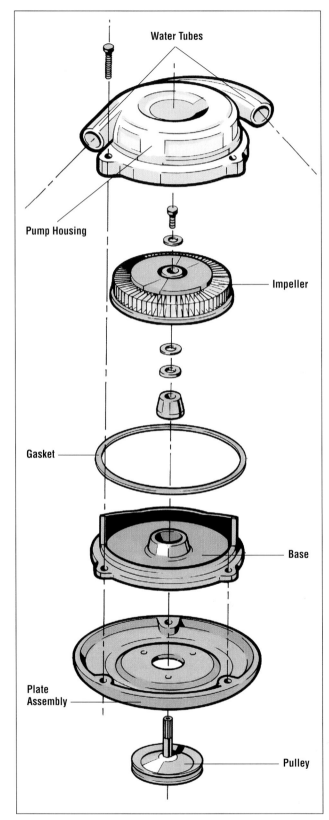

Take the pump apart and clean away all debris inside the pump. Also clear away debris from the water tubes.

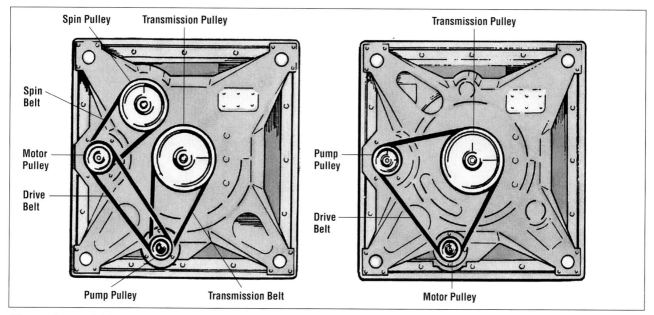

Spin Pulley   Transmission Pulley

Transmission Pulley

Spin
Belt

Motor
Pulley

Drive
Belt

Pump
Pulley

Drive
Belt

Pump Pulley   Transmission Belt

Motor Pulley

Worn or damaged drive belts can cause noisy operation or stop the washer completely. Two common belt arrangements are shown here.

of cloth or paper clogging the pump impeller. Clean away all debris inside the pump and clear any debris out of the water tubes. Then reassemble the pump. Hook up the pump again and test it. If cleaning the pump doesn't put it back into working order, or if the pump housing can't be removed, replace the pump with a new one of the same kind.

Step 6: To install the new pump, set it into position and connect the mounting bolts to the pump housing. Move the motor back into position. Tighten the drive belt on the motor by prying it taut with a hammer handle or pry bar; it should give about ½ inch when you press on it at the center point between the two pulleys.

Step 7: Reconnect the hoses leading to the pump.

Replacing Drive Belts and Tightening Pulleys

The drive belt (or belts) of a washing machine may become worn or damaged, causing noisy operation or stopping the washer entirely. A damaged drive belt is easy to replace. Remove the back panel of the washer to gain access to the belt. To remove the belt:

Step 1: Loosen the bolt on the motor bracket and move the motor to put slack in the belt.

Step 2: Remove the old belt and stretch a new one into place on the pulleys.

Step 3: To put tension on the new belt, use a hammer handle or a short pry bar to push the motor into position while you tighten the bolt in the adjustable bracket. The belt should have about ½ inch deflection when you press on it at the center point, midway between the pulleys. If the belt is too loose, it will slip on the pulleys, causing the machine to malfunction. If the belt is too tight, it will wear very quickly and will probably become so hot that it will start to smoke or smell.

Loose pulleys can also cause problems. Most pulleys are fastened to shafts with setscrews around the hub of the pulley. These screws must be tight or else the pulley or belt will slip. The resulting malfunction may seem to be caused by a faulty motor, but it can be corrected by tightening the pulleys and adjusting the belt. For this reason, always check the belts and pulleys before working on the motor.

Servicing the Motor

In most cases, motor malfunctions should be handled by a professional; do not try to fix the motor yourself. If the motor is a universal motor, however, you can change worn carbon brushes when sparking occurs, as detailed on pages 155–156. To save the expense of a service call, remove the motor from the washer and take it to a professional service person, then reinstall the repaired or new motor yourself. To access the motor, remove the back panel of the washer. The motor is mounted on an adjustable bracket.

There is one other motor problem you can repair yourself. Washer motors usually have an overload protector clipped to the motor. When this component fails, the motor won't work. Before you take the motor in for service, test the protector with a VOM set to the RX1 scale; procedures for using the VOM are detailed on page 19. Disconnect one electrical lead wire to the protector and clip one probe of the VOM to each protector terminal. The meter should read zero. If the needle jumps higher, the protector is faulty and should be replaced. Pry up the protector with a screwdriver and replace it with a new one made specifically for the motor or washer. Connect the new protector the same way the old one was connected.

Repairing Dryers

A dryer is simply a large drum into which wet laundry is loaded. A motor with pulleys—connected by a series of belts—turns the drum. Air heated by a gas heater or electric heating element is blown through the drum to dry the laundry. The temperature and speed of the drum are controlled by a series of thermostats operated from a timer device on the control panel of the dryer. As a safety device, a dryer usually has a door switch that activates the working parts. Unless the door is properly closed, the dryer won't work, regardless of the settings on the control panel. Many dryers are equipped with a reset button on the control panel. If the motor won't run, let the dryer cool for about ten minutes. Then push the reset button. If there are no problems with the motor, switches, or electrical system, this should restart the dryer.

Caution: Before doing any work on the dryer, make sure it's unplugged. Disconnect the grounding wire. If it is a gas-fueled dryer, close the gas-supply valve to shut off the unit's gas supply.

Disassembling the Dryer

Except for the power cord and the exhaust vent, the components that make up the dryer are contained in a sheet metal box. Each component acts independently of the others, but all are interrelated in some way. There are several different ways to disassemble the cabinet for tests and repairs, depending on the manufacturer and model of the machine. Basic disassembly procedures are simple.

Some knobs may be held to their shafts with setscrews. Unscrew the fasteners and pull the knobs

straight out. To get at most parts, however, only remove the back panel. Don't disassemble the rest of the cabinet until you're sure you can't make the tests, replacements, or repairs from the back. If the light in the dryer burns out, remove it from the dryer. You may need to remove retaining screws and panels to access it. Replace the burned-out bulb with a new one of the same type and wattage; check the ends of the old bulb for this information. Then replace any retaining panels.

Step 1: To remove the back panel, remove a series of screws or bolts that hold the panel to the top and sides of the cabinet.

Step 2: To remove the lower front panel, pull it away from the bottom of the cabinet. Lift the lower panel up and away. Remove the springs under each side of the lower panel.

Step 3: To remove the top panel, wedge a stiff-bladed putty knife under the rim of the top and pry the top off. The putty knife helps release several spring fasteners at the top of the cabinet sides and front.

Step 4: To remove the dryer's control panel, remove the screws that hold it to the cabinet top or front. These screws may be under a piece of metal or plastic trim; pry off or unscrew the trim. Most knobs are friction-fit; pull them straight out.

Caution: When testing or repairing the electrical parts of a gas dryer, remember that the dryer is hooked to a gas pipe. Turn off the shutoff valve on the supply pipe before disconnecting the gas supply line or moving the dryer and before doing any electrical work.

Cleaning the Dryer

Besides drying clothes, dryers also remove lint. This fine, fuzzy material can cause trouble because it blocks dryer lint traps, clogs vents, and fills blowers. Lint can also gather around and in the tracks of the drum rollers, or in and under the pulleys and the drive belt. The result is poor clothes drying or—sometimes—no drying. To avoid lint problems, clean out the dryer's lint trap system every time you use the dryer.

To clean the lint screen, remove it from the unit. The screen may be located near or under the door sill, or in the top of the dryer near the control panel. It can usually be removed by pulling it up and out of its housing. Remove the accumulated lint to clear the screen; then replace the screen.

The exhaust vent also collects lint. Vent maintenance involves cleaning the lint from a screen in the dryer's vent exhaust collar and/or at the end of the exhaust vent

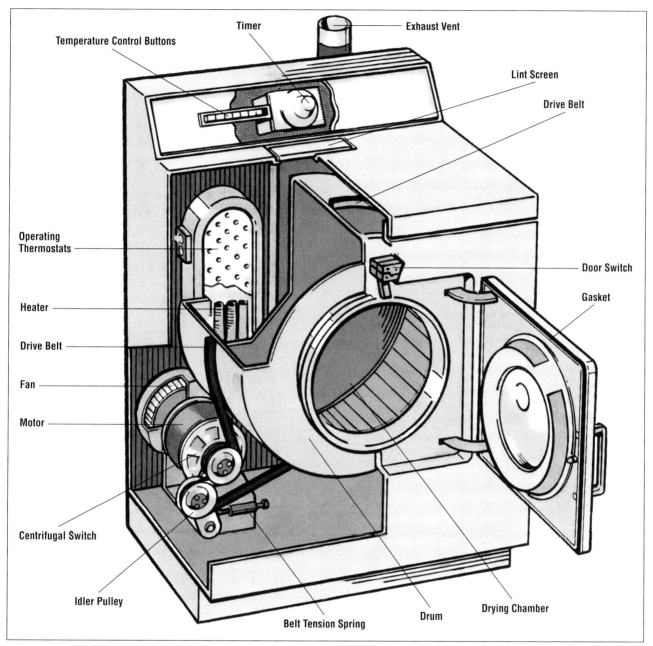

Timer
Temperature Control Buttons
Exhaust Vent
Lint Screen
Drive Belt
Operating Thermostats
Door Switch
Gasket
Heater
Drive Belt
Fan
Motor
Centrifugal Switch
Idler Pulley
Belt Tension Spring
Drum
Drying Chamber

A dryer consists of a large drum into which wet laundry is loaded. A motor with pulleys turns the drum, and heated air is blown through the drum.

where it sticks out through a basement window or through an exterior wall. To clean the screen, remove the clamp that holds the vent to the collar, or back out the screws that hold the vent to the collar, or pull the vent straight off an extended collar. Clean the screen thoroughly and replace it in the vent assembly.

To clean the vent itself, bend the end of a wire hanger into a fairly tight hook. Insert the wire into the vent and use it to pull out any lint deposits. Also check the vent run to make sure that the vent piping or tubing isn't loose at the joints, or—in the case of flexible plastic venting—isn't sagging between hanging brackets. Breaks or sags cause undue strain on the dryer's blower system, and can cause drying problems. If the vent pipe or tubing has become clogged with lint, remove the lint by pushing a garden hose or a drain-and-trap auger through the vent to a convenient joint. Disassemble the joint to remove the debris. With this procedure, it isn't necessary to disassemble the entire vent to find the blockage.

DRYER TROUBLESHOOTING CHART

Problem	Possible Cause	Solution
Dryer doesn't run	1. No power.	1. Check power cord, plug, and outlet. Check for blown fuses or tripped circuit breakers at main entrance panel or at separate panel; restore circuit.
	2. Motor overload or safety shutoff.	2. Press reset button on control panel.
	3. Controls not properly set.	3. Set controls properly.
	4. Door not closed.	4. Close door to activate drum.
	5. Wiring loose or broken.	5. Clean or tighten terminal connections at power inlet.
	6. Door switch faulty.	6. Remove lint and dirt from switch orifice; make sure switch is making contact. Test switch; if faulty, replace.
	7. Door hinges broken or misaligned.	7. Repair hinges so that switch makes contact; if hinges damaged, replace.
	8. Timer faulty.	8. Make sure timer is properly set. Test timer; if faulty, replace.
	9. On/off switch faulty.	9. Make sure switch is properly set. Test switch; if faulty, replace.
	10. Motor faulty.	10. Check motor leads for proper connections. Remove motor and take it to a professional, or replace motor.
	11. Centrifugal switch faulty.	11. If accessible, check switch terminal connections. If inaccessible, call a professional. Or remove switch or entire motor and take to a professional.
Fuses blow	1. Grounding faulty.	1. Call a professional.
	2. Motor bearings worn.	2. Call a professional, or remove motor and take to a professional.
Dryer doesn't heat	1. Inadequate power supply.	1. Check fuses and switches to make sure 220-volt power is being supplied; half of double-fuse hookup may be blown. If necessary, restore circuit.
	2. Lint blockage.	2. Clean lint screen; clean duct.
	3. Thermostat faulty.	3. Lightly tap thermostat housing to jar contacts loose. Test thermostat; if faulty, replace.
	4. Timer faulty.	4. Make sure timer is properly set. Test timer; if faulty, replace.
	5. Overload protector faulty.	5. Test protector; if faulty, replace. If switch is located inside motor, call a professional.

Continued on page 197

Problem	Possible Cause	Solution
Dryer doesn't heat *(continued)*	6. Centrifugal switch faulty.	6. If accessible, check switch terminal connections. If inaccessible, call a professional. Or remove switch or entire motor and take to a professional.
	7. Electric heating element faulty (electric units).	7. Test heating element; if faulty, replace.
	8. Gas heater faulty (gas units).	8. Check to make sure pilot is lit; if necessary, relight. Adjust air shutter of gas burner.
	9. Thermocouple faulty (gas units).	9. Replace thermocouple.
	10. Electric ignition faulty (gas units).	10. Call a professional.
	11. No gas (gas units).	11. Call gas company.
	12. Motor faulty.	12. Check motor leads for proper connections. Remove motor and take to a professional, or replace motor.
Drying slow or inadequate	1. Machine overloaded.	1. Reduce size of load.
	2. Clogged lint screen.	2. Clean lint screen.
	3. Clothes not adequately wrung out.	3. Make sure spin cycle on washer is spinning clothes dry.
	4. Vent blocked.	4. Clean vent. Make sure vent is not sagging, bent, broken at joints, clogged, or loose where it joins dryer's vent collar.
	5. Door seal defective.	5. Check door for air leaks. Check and tighten gasket screws; if gasket faulty, replace.
	6. Blower faulty.	6. Clean blower assembly; check and tighten blower bolts.
	7. Thermostat faulty.	7. Lightly tap thermostat housing to jar contacts loose. Test thermostat; if faulty, replace.
	8. Timer faulty.	8. Make sure timer is properly set. Test timer; if faulty, replace.
	9. Electric heating element faulty.	9. Test heating element; if faulty, replace.
	10. Belt sticking, worn, or broken.	10. Clean belt and pulleys. Check belt; if worn or damaged, replace.
	11. Drum seal faulty.	11. Check drum seals at front and back of drum; if faulty, call a professional.
	12. Exhaust fan clogged or jammed.	12. Clean fan assembly. Check for frozen bearings by turning; if necessary, lubricate.

Continued on page 198

DRYER TROUBLESHOOTING CHART (Continued from page 197)

Problem	Possible Cause	Solution
Drum doesn't turn	1. Belt misaligned or broken.	1. Adjust or replace belt.
	2. Drum bearings need lubrication.	2. Lubricate bearings.
	3. Exhaust fan needs lubrication.	3. Lubricate fan assembly.
Light won't go on	1. Bulb burned out.	1. Replace bulb.
	2. Door switch faulty.	2. Test switch; if faulty, replace.
Motor runs when door is open	1. Door switch faulty.	1. Remove lint and dirt from orifice; make sure switch is making contact. Test switch; if faulty, replace.
Noisy operation	1. Metal or plastic object in drum.	1. Remove foreign objects from drum. Noise from buttons and clips on clothing is normal.
	2. Duct clogged or out of position.	2. Clean duct; if necessary, reposition.
	3. Belt sticking, worn, or broken.	3. Clean belt and pulleys. Check belt; if worn or damaged, replace.
	4. Pulleys misaligned.	4. Realign pulleys.
	5. Rollers sticking or damaged.	5. Lubricate or replace rollers.
	6. Exhaust fan needs lubrication.	6. Lubricate fan assembly.
	7. Motor bearings worn or need lubrication.	7. Lubricate motor shaft ends. Call a professional, or remove motor and take to a professional, or replace motor.
	8. Centrifugal switch faulty.	8. If accessible, check switch terminal connections. If inaccessible, call a professional. Or remove switch or entire motor and take to a professional.

Servicing the Door Gasket

The door of the dryer is sealed with one or more gaskets to keep the hot air in the dryer from escaping and prevent the cool air in the laundry area from being sucked into the dryer. A deteriorated or damaged gasket greatly lowers the efficiency of the dryer. To check the gasket, hold a sheet of tissue paper near the rim of the door while the machine is running. If the door leaks, the paper will flutter. If the gasket or seal leaks, looks worn or warped, has chunks of material missing, or feels hard and nonresilient, it should be replaced with a new gasket of the same type.

Servicing the Door Switch

The door switch is critical to the dryer's operation. If the switch is not working, the dryer will not run unless there's a special grounding problem somewhere in the system. If such a grounding problem occurs, the dryer will run even when the door is open. In this case, call a professional service person.

If the dryer has a door latch, make sure the latch is free of dirt or lint and properly adjusted before you make any switch tests or replacements. Sometimes a misaligned latch prevents the door from being closed tightly, preventing the switch from being activated.

The switch on the dryer may be accessible from the outside door, or you may have to remove the top of the dryer to access it. The switch is a simple assembly, with two lead wires running to it. Test the switch with a VOM set to the RX1 scale; procedures for using the VOM are detailed on page 19. Disconnect the switch leads and clip one probe of the VOM to each switch terminal. Press the switch closed with your finger. The VOM should read zero. If the needle jumps, the switch is faulty and should be replaced with a new one of the same type.

The switch is held to the dryer with setscrews; remove these screws and disconnect the leads to the switch. Install a new switch and connect the leads. Then position the switch and tighten the setscrews to hold it in place.

Servicing the Start Switch

This switch, located on the control panel, is usually the push-button type. Start switches don't fail often, but it does happen. To check the start switch, remove the control panel and test the switch with a VOM set to the RX1 scale; procedures for using the VOM are detailed on page 19. Disconnect the leads from the switch terminals and clip one VOM probe to each terminal. Press the switch button. If the meter reads zero, the switch is working. If the needle jumps to a high reading, the switch is faulty and should be replaced. Replace the switch with a new one of the same type, connecting the new switch the same way the old one was connected.

Servicing the Thermostat

Thermostats, the dryer temperature control switches, are controlled by the temperature inside the dryer or by the heat of the motor. One or more thermostats on the panel can be adjusted to control the temperature in the dryer. Operating thermostats sometimes stick, causing control problems. These thermostats are usually positioned near the exhaust duct bulkhead or the fan housing of the dryer. Remove the back panel of the dryer to get at them. Before you make any checks, try tapping the housing of the thermostats lightly with the handle of a screwdriver. This may jar the contacts loose. Temperature control switches are located behind the dryer control panel, and the panel must be removed for switch testing or replacement. To test and replace the thermostat:

Step 1: To check the control panel thermostat, make sure power is off to the dryer. Test the thermostat with a VOM set to the RX1 scale (instructions for using the VOM are given on page 19). Clip one probe of the VOM to each thermostat terminal. If the meter reads zero, the thermostat is working. If the needle jumps to a high reading, the thermostat is faulty and should be replaced.

Step 2: If necessary, replace the thermostat with a new one of the same type. Connect the new thermostat the same way the old one was connected.

Step 3: To check an operating thermostat, first make absolutely certain that the power to the dryer has been turned off and the dryer is cool. Then disconnect the leads to one side of the thermostat. Test an operating thermostat with a VOM set to the RX1 scale; clip one probe to each terminal of the thermostat. Disconnect the leads to one side of the thermostat so that the meter won't give a false reading. If the meter reads zero, the thermostat is working. If the needle jumps to a high reading, the thermostat is faulty and should be replaced.

Servicing the Timer

The dryer timer, located in back of the control panel, controls several things: the drying time of the clothes in the drum, the flow of electricity to the heating element, and the flow of power to the timer motor and the drum motor in the dryer cabinet. Timers are driven by synchronous motors. Although the contact part of the timer can be cleaned and adjusted on some dryers, this is a job for a professional repair person. Timer motor repairs should also be handled by a professional, but you can replace a faulty timer yourself. To test and replace a dryer timer:

Step 1: To access the timer, remove the front of the control panel. On some dryers, the timer can be removed without removing the panel. In either case, pull the timer knob off the shaft and slip off the pointer. The pointer is usually keyed to the shaft by two flat surfaces to keep the pointer from slipping when it's turned.

Step 2: Test the timer with a VOM set to the RX1 scale (instructions for using the VOM are detailed on page 19). Turn the timer to the NORMAL DRY setting and disconnect one of the timer power leads. Some timers may have several wires connected to them: The power leads are usually larger than the other wires, and this size difference can be spotted under close examination. Clip one probe of the meter to each timer terminal. If the meter reads zero, the timer is working. If the needle jumps to a high reading, the timer is faulty and should be replaced. Replace the timer with a new one of the same size and type.

Step 3: To replace the timer, have a helper hold the new timer close to the old one, especially if there are several wires to be changed. Disconnect the old wires one at a time, connecting each corresponding new wire as you work, to make sure the connections are properly made. Or, draw a diagram detailing the proper connections. After all the wires are connected, check the connections again for accuracy.

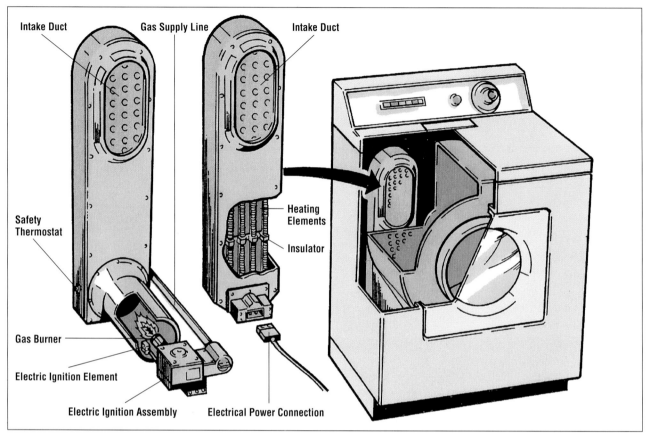

Intake Duct   Gas Supply Line   Intake Duct

Safety Thermostat

Heating Elements

Insulator

Gas Burner

Electric Ignition Element

Electric Ignition Assembly   Electrical Power Connection

In a gas dryer, heat is provided by a gas heater, controlled by an air shutter. Electric dryers have self-contained electric heating elements.

Troubleshooting the Gas Heater

In a gas dryer, heat is provided by a gas heater that is controlled by an air shutter. The gas heater is generally the source of no-heat or drying problems. You can often correct such problems by adjusting the air shutter on the gas burner, which is located along the bottom of the dryer.

To adjust the shutter, take out the screws and remove the panel that covers the gas flame. Turn on the dryer so the flame is burning. If the flame has a deep blue color and you hear air whistling around the burner, the air/gas mixture is receiving too much air. If the flame has a yellow tip, the mixture is not receiving enough air. Turn the thumbscrew or loosen the two screws slightly to increase or decrease the flow of air to the burner. Keep turning until the flame is a light blue color, without any yellow, and the whistling stops.

Newer gas dryers use an electric ignition device rather than a pilot light to light the gas heater. In this electric ignition system, an element becomes hot and glows like the filament in a lightbulb. These electric systems are always sealed; you can't adjust or repair

them. If an electric ignition device fails, call a professional service person for replacement.

Servicing the Electric Heating Elements

Electric heating elements, found in electric dryers, are self-contained units located in the back of the dryer. A defective heating element is frequently the source of no-heat or drying problems. Remove the back service panel to gain access to the elements.

The heating elements are located inside the heater ducts. If you think a heating element is faulty, test it with a VOM set to the RX1 scale (instructions for using the VOM are given on page 19). Disconnect the leads from the power terminals and clip one probe of the VOM to each terminal. The meter should read about 12 ohms. If the reading is higher than 20 ohms, the heater is faulty and should be replaced. Replace a faulty heater with a new one of the same type and electrical rating. A heater connected to a 115-volt line usually has an 8.4-ohm resistance; a heater connected to a 220-volt line usually has 11 ohms resistance.

The heater may also malfunction because it's grounded. To test for this, set the VOM to the RX1 scale and remove the leads to the heater. Clip one probe of the VOM to a heater terminal and touch the other probe to the heater housing. The meter needle should jump to a fairly high reading. If the needle flicks back and forth at a low reading, the heater is probably grounded and should be replaced. To replace the heater:

Step 1: Remove the back of the dryer. If necessary, also remove the cabinet top.

Step 2: Disconnect the leads and remove the screws that hold the duct in position. Then lift the entire heater unit out of the dryer.

Step 3: Remove the screws that hold the heating element in the duct.

Step 4: Slip the new heating element into the heating duct the same way the old one came out. Be careful not to damage the resistance coils. Replace the screws that hold the heating element in the duct, reconnect the leads, and screw the unit back into position.

Servicing the Fan

The most common dryer fan problem is lint clogging the air passages through the heater and through the dryer drum. To clear a clogged air passage, remove the back service panel of the dryer and back out the screws holding the air duct in place. Then reach into the duct and remove all the lint and dirt possible. Reassemble the parts.

Also inspect the fan for a loose screw connection where the motor shaft is set on the dryer's drum. Remove the back service panel, tighten the screw, and replace the panel.

Servicing the Drum Belt

The drum of the dryer is usually turned by a motor-and-belt assembly. There are two very clear signs that the belt is malfunctioning: You can easily spin the drum by hand, or you hear a heavy thumping sound coming from the drum when the dryer is running. To test and replace the drum belt:

Step 1: Locate the belt by removing the back or front service panel. Depending on the type of dryer you own, you may have to prop up the drum to keep it from sagging. Don't let the drum hang; the bolts that hold it in the cabinet could be damaged. Don't remove any more parts than necessary.

Step 2: Identify the belt. The old belt may be threaded around the idler pulley and motor drive shaft. Draw a diagram showing how the pulley is installed so you'll be able to replace it properly. If the old belt is worn or frayed, but not broken, leave it around the drum as a pattern for positioning the new belt; cut the old belt and remove it when the new belt is in position.

Step 3: Remove the old belt from the pulleys and stretch the replacement belt into place. The new belt must extend around the dryer drum and the pulleys. The trick is to align the belt on the drum with the pulleys—the ribs on the new belt go against the drum.

Step 4: Once the belt is aligned, turn the drum by hand, if possible, to make sure the belt is tracking. You may have to reassemble part of the cabinet to do this.

Some older dryers have a V-belt pulley drum drive. With this system, two or three pulleys of different sizes set the speed of the drum. To change this type of belt, decrease the tension on the idler pulley and install the new belt in the V-grooves of all pulleys. Then place the idler pulley back into position.

With any dryer, make absolutely sure that you replace the old belt with a new one made especially for the dryer. Any difference in belts can change the speed of the drum and cause problems with other dryer components.

Servicing the Drum Bearing

With the back service panel off, check the drum bearing around the dryer drum shaft. You may have to remove the dryer belt to reach it. If the bearing looks worn and dirty, or if it's loose, it should be replaced with a new bearing made for the dryer.

A screw in the center of the drum connects the shaft to the drum. Remove this assembly and then lift off the drum pulley. Support the drum to prevent it from sagging. The bearing fits around the drum shaft and is slip-fit. Pull off the old bearing and install the new one, securing it the same way the old one was held. On some dryers, the bearing and shaft are held by a U-bolt, and there are two tapered blocks supporting the bearing and shaft. Remove the bearing by first removing the U-bolt and blocks.

When reassembling the bearing unit, make sure the parts go back together the way they came apart. If the part is assembled with shims, the shims should be placed between the bearing and the support channels. Do not

When replacing a belt, you may have to prop up the drum to keep it from sagging. Don't let the drum hang; the bolts that hold it could be ruined.

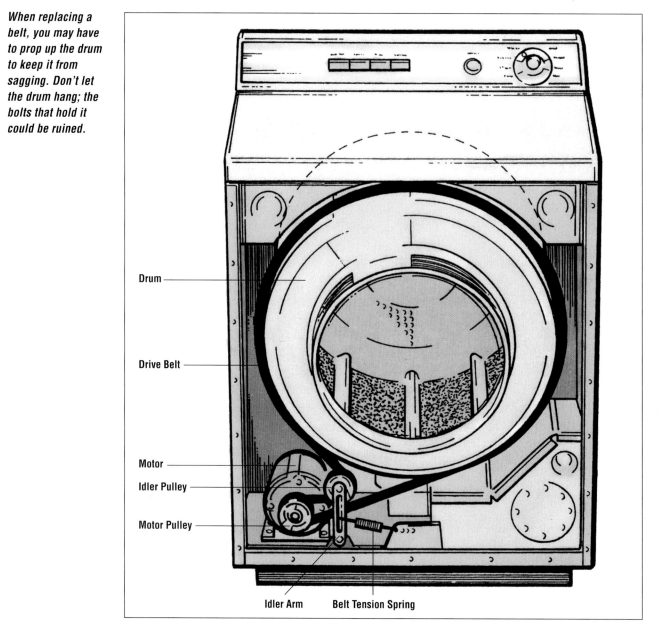

Drum

Drive Belt

Motor

Idler Pulley

Motor Pulley

Idler Arm   Belt Tension Spring

overtighten the screws holding the parts; overtightening could cause damage to the bearing. If the bearing has a lubrication wick, saturate it with auto transmission oil.

Servicing the Drum Rollers

The front of the dryer's drum is usually supported by two rollers. These wheels are either metal with a rubber rim or pressed nylon. If the rollers squeak but appear to be in good condition, apply a few drops of 20-weight nondetergent motor oil (not all-purpose oil) to them. If the rollers are worn, you can replace them if the roller assembly is not riveted. To replace drum rollers:

Step 1: Remove the front of the cabinet. Rollers are usually held on a metal shaft by a spring clip.

Step 2: Remove the rollers by prying the spring clip off with a screwdriver. Under the clip are a washer, the rollers, and another washer. You might have to remove a small nut at the back of the shaft and remove the shaft itself to reach the rollers. Remove the rollers from the shaft and clean away built-up lint and dirt before installing the new roller. This dirt and lint buildup could cause the drum to turn slowly, which prevents proper drying and strains other dryer components.

Step 3: Install the new rollers on the shaft with the washers in the same position.

Servicing the Motor

Motor malfunctions usually call for service by a professional. There are three main causes of motor failure: lack of lubrication, a defective motor switch, or worn or frozen bearings. A humming sound can be related to a burned-out motor or a defective switch. Check these trouble spots before you call a professional service person or take the motor to a repair shop. To check a dryer motor:

Step 1: Remove the back access panel. Then reach behind the drum, motor pulley, and idler arm pulley. If these areas are clogged with dirt and lint, undue strain on the motor may be causing the humming noise. Worn or broken belts can also cause a humming noise. Check the belts for wear and damage and replace them if necessary, as detailed on page 201. If the belts look all right, you may be able to stop the noise by spraying them with fan belt dressing, available at automotive and hardware stores and home centers.

Step 2: Turn the dryer on. The noise you hear may be the whirl of the spinning drum, not the motor. Some noise is normal.

Step 3: Force a little 20-weight nondetergent motor oil (not all-purpose oil) around the ends of the motor shaft. This lubrication may stop the humming noise. If this doesn't solve the problem, remove the motor and take it to a professional service person.

The centrifugal switch on the dryer motor may be located on top of the motor. Humming, no motor power, and no heat can be caused by a faulty centrifugal switch. If the switch is externally mounted, check the terminals of the switch to make sure they are tight and not burned. If you spot trouble, remove the switch and take it to a professional service person for testing. A faulty switch will probably have to be replaced. Some centrifugal switches are located inside the motor housing; you won't be able to remove the switch in this case. Remove the entire motor and take it to a professional for repairs.

If the motor hums, but won't run the pulley on the end of the motor shaft, try turning the pulley by hand. *Caution: Before turning the pulley, make sure the power to the dryer is turned off.*

If you can't turn the pulley, or if the pulley is very hard to turn, the bearings in the motor may be worn. Remove the motor and take it to a professional service person for repairs, or replace the motor. Replacement may be cheaper than repair.

Some motors have overload protectors that turn off the motor when excess strain is put on it. Often, dryers are equipped with a reset button on the control panel. If the motor won't run, let the dryer cool for about ten minutes. Then press this reset button. If the dryer still doesn't operate, check for an overload protector on the motor.

Test the overload protector with a VOM set to the RX1 scale (instructions for using the VOM are given on page 19). Disconnect one lead wire to the protector and clip one probe of the VOM to each protector terminal. If the meter reads zero, the protector is working. If the needle jumps to a high reading, the overload protector is faulty and should be replaced. Remove the protector by prying it off or unscrewing it from the motor housing. Replace it with a new one of the same size and type, connecting the new protector the same way the old one was connected.

CHAPTER 6

SMALL APPLIANCE REPAIR

Small appliances can make life easier and more enjoyable. They help us prepare our meals, clean and light our homes, and get ready for the day. Unfortunately, if an appliance doesn't function as it should, our first reaction may be to toss the offending appliance in the garbage and buy a new one.

This chapter offers an economical and ecological option: Repair it! In many cases, the problems are easily solved, and the satisfaction that comes from repair can make life more fun.

Page 205 of this chapter includes a troubleshooting chart of problems and solutions common to all small appliances. In addition, each small appliance in this chapter has its own troubleshooting chart that can help you quickly narrow down the causes of—and cures for—specific symptoms.

The decision to fix or toss a small appliance is based on more than economics. The food blender that needs a new motor may have been a wedding gift from a close friend, so you may choose to fix the blender this time. However, the problem may be a warning sign that other components will soon fail. If so, you may decide to toss the blender and replace it with a newer model. A popular rule is to spend no more than 60 percent of replacement value on the repair. When estimating cost of repair, be sure to include labor cost! Of course, you can't estimate your labor cost to be the same as an experienced and equipped appliance-repair shop, but you should calculate your labor at $10 an hour or more.

In any case, this chapter will show you how to easily diagnose common small appliance problems so you can quickly make the best decision: fix or toss.

Understanding Small Appliances

Electricity furnishes the energy that powers small appliances and other electrical devices. Current flows to the device through the hot (typically black) wire and returns through the neutral (typically white) wire. The power that moves the current is called voltage. In most household systems, the hot wire has about 120 volts and the white wire has zero volts. The difference in voltage between the two wires moves the electric current and powers your appliance.

There are three types of small, portable, or household appliances. Some appliances, such as toasters and coffee makers, heat something. Other appliances, like food processors and vacuum cleaners, move something. A few appliances, such as hair dryers, do both.

Heating Appliances

Heating appliances convert electrical energy into heat, which is used to toast bread, warm coffee, dry hair, or perform other helpful tasks. This heat is developed by passing current through a special wire called an element. Since the element makes it difficult for electricity to pass through it, some of its energy turns into heat. The electricity uses so much of its energy to overcome the resistance of a toaster element, for instance, that it glows bright red, thus toasting the bread.

Common heating appliances covered in this chapter include toasters, toaster ovens, drip coffee makers, and percolator coffee makers. Heating appliances that work on the same principles include clothing irons; electric fry pans, woks, griddles, and waffle irons; convection ovens; deep fryers; slow cookers; food dehydrators; rice cookers; steam cookers; indoor grills; espresso and cappuccino machines; iced tea makers; and popcorn poppers. Once you've learned how to troubleshoot and repair the most popular heating appliances, it will be easy to repair any of them.

Motor Appliances

Motor appliances convert electrical energy into movement. This power cuts and blends foods, opens cans, grinds waste, picks up dirt, and moves air. A motor converts electrical energy into magnetic energy that rotates a shaft. The end of this shaft may have a blade or other attachment that does the actual work.

Motor appliances that are covered in this chapter include food mixers and blenders, electric can openers, garbage disposers, and upright and canister vacuum cleaners. Other motor appliances with similar operation include juicers, coffee grinders, ice cream makers, electric knives, knife sharpeners, electric pencil sharpeners, electric clocks, fans, humidifiers, and foil-head and rotary-head electric shavers.

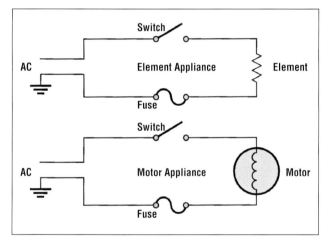

Circuits for heating and motor appliances.

Combination Appliances

Some small appliances both heat and move. The most popular is the electric bread maker. It mixes dough, then bakes it into bread. Bread makers also include diagnostic electronics that assist the owner in troubleshooting and repair, so they are not included in this chapter. Other combination appliances include hair dryers and stirring popcorn poppers.

Troubleshooting Small Appliances

Nearly all small appliances are powered by 120-volt electricity. This means that many of the problems that can occur with toasters can also occur with garbage disposers and hair dryers. These problems are caused by circuit breakers or fuses, switches and plugs, or grounded or loose wires. You'll find a general troubleshooting chart for all small appliances below. In this chapter, you'll learn how to easily solve these common problems. For additional safety information, see Chapter 1.

Appliance Cords

An appliance cord delivers electricity to an appliance. An appliance cord is typically constructed of two or three wires and a plug. Attach the appliance end of the cord with metal connectors or fasteners like electrical nuts.

Wires

Wires used in appliance cords are of different diameters, or gauges. The thicker the wire, the lower the gauge number. That is, a 12-gauge wire is thinner than a 10-gauge wire. Most small appliances use cord wires of copper strands insulated with heat-resistant plastic. An appliance that requires less amperage to operate, such as a lamp, will typically have a two-wire cord of 18- or 16-

TROUBLESHOOTING ALL SMALL APPLIANCES	
Problem	**Solution**
Doesn't work at all	1. Check for power at receptacle. If there is no power, reset breaker or replace fuse.
	2. Check power cord. If faulty, replace.
	3. Check wire connections. If loose or broken, repair or replace wire.
Electrical shock from touching appliance	1. Unplug appliance using insulated tools, then check cord and internal wires. If bare spots or loose ends are touching chassis, repair or replace wires or seek professional service.

Typical appliance cord connection.

gauge wire. Higher-amperage heating appliances will use a two- or three-wire cord of 14- or even 12-gauge wire. Two-strand cords include one hot wire and one neutral wire. A three-strand cord will have one hot wire, one neutral wire, and one ground wire.

Plugs

The plug at the end of an appliance cord receives electricity from the wall receptacle. A two-prong plug is typically used for ungrounded appliances rated at less than 15 amps. Some two-prong plugs are polarized to ensure that the hot and neutral wires are connected correctly. The smaller prong is the hot wire, and the larger one is neutral. Three-prong appliance plugs include one round prong used for grounding and ensuring that the hot and neutral prongs are inserted into the correct receptacle slots. Most small appliances are rated at less than 15 amps. A receptacle with a T-shaped

neutral slot is designed to accommodate 20-amp appliances, though 15-amp cords can be plugged into it.

Connectors

At the other end of the cord, inside the small appliance, the wires are connected to a switch, or controller. The wires may be connected with solder, with electrical twist-on nuts, or with connectors. These connectors physically and electrically connect the power source with the appliance. The connection can be made with crimp connectors, clip or spade connectors, or with U- or O-connectors. Internal appliance wires are typically smaller than those used for cords, which means the gauge numbers are higher.

Repairing Appliance Cords and Wires

To test an appliance cord or wire, first make sure that it is disconnected from any electrical source or capacitor. Then use a continuity tester or multimeter to make sure it can adequately conduct electricity (see page 19). With the tester attached, move the wire to ensure that there is not a break in the strands that can cause intermittent shorts. Also check the quality and pliability of the cord or wire insulation. If there are any breaks or cracks that may eventually expose strands, replace the cord or wire with one of equivalent rating and gauge.

Appliance Controls

Electrical power coming into a small appliance must be controlled: turned on or off or varied based on temperature, time, or function. That's what appliance controls do. Appliance controls include switches, thermostats, rheostats, and timing mechanisms. In many small appliance problems, a controller is the culprit. So,

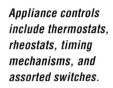

Appliance controls include thermostats, rheostats, timing mechanisms, and assorted switches.

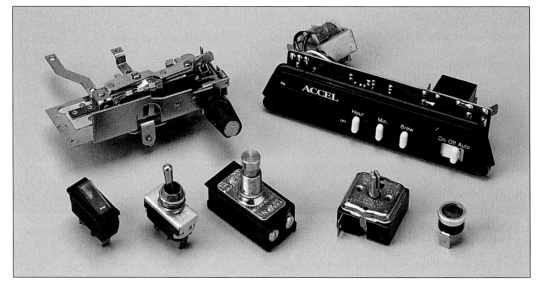

before you begin tearing your toaster or vacuum apart, let's see how small appliance controls work—and what to do when they don't.

Switches

Most small appliance switches are activated by hand to control the flow of current in an appliance. A single-pole switch is pushed or moved to turn power on or off. Multiposition switches allow set amounts of current to flow, such as a multispeed switch for a blender.

Thermostats

A thermostat opens and closes a circuit to furnish current based on temperature. The simplest, a bimetallic thermostat, uses two bonded pieces of metal with different heat ratings. At room temperature, for example, both metals are of identical length and form, allowing contact points in the circuit to touch. Heat flexes one of the two metals and causes them to pull the contacts apart, opening the circuit and stopping current from passing. Thermostats can be used to turn a heating element or a motor on or off. In fact, thermostats are used as overload protectors that open a circuit and turn off a motor if it overheats or overloads.

Rheostats

A rheostat is a variable controller. That is, it variably controls the amount of current flowing to an appliance component. A blender with a speed control that can be turned to increase or decrease motor speed uses a rheostat to do so. Because rheostats can be damaged by moisture, they can easily malfunction. In that case, they must be replaced with a rheostat of the same type and function.

Timing Mechanisms

A timing mechanism controls current flow based on a mechanical or digital timing device similar to a clock. A timing mechanism in your coffee maker can furnish fresh coffee in the morning. In most cases, timing mechanisms turn small appliances on or off. When a timed appliance doesn't turn on, one of the first components to check is the timing mechanism. Some can be repaired, while others must be replaced.

Repairing Appliance Controls

Appliance controls are easily tested with a continuity tester. By placing the clip on the input side and the tester probe on the output side and activating the controller, you can determine whether the control is functioning properly. For variable controllers, it may be easier to use a multimeter that will show you a change in resistance.

Most defective small appliance controls should be replaced rather than repaired. Once you remove the controller from the appliance, take the part, along with the appliance's model and serial numbers, to an appliance-parts dealer to ensure that the appropriate replacement is found. A switch with a higher amp rating or a rheostat with a higher ohm rating can damage your appliance's heating element or motor. It can also be dangerous to the operator.

Where can you find replacement parts for small appliances? First, check your owner's manual to identify the model and part numbers. If you live in or near a metropolitan area, you may have a number of appliance-parts stores from which to purchase. Of course, call them first to determine if they have or can get the type of parts you require. Then take the defective part in for a side-by-side comparison with the replacement part to double-check the match before you purchase it. As a last resort, you can write to the manufacturer. In most cases, they will refer you to an area appliance-parts dealer.

Repairing Toasters

Toasters are categorized as heating appliances. Their function is to develop sufficient heat near a slice of bread to heat and toast it. Breakfast certainly wouldn't be the same without the pop-up toaster.

In many homes, toasters malfunction more than any other small appliance. There are two reasons for this. First, toasters are typically built economically to be a throw-away appliance. Replacement models start at $10. Second, malfunctions are frequently not the fault of the toaster itself but of food particles that interfere with its operation. Excess pieces of bread broken off by carriage movement fall into the base of the toaster and accumulate, obstructing carriage movement, shorting out heating elements, plugging the latch release, and interfering with solenoid operation.

That's why most pop-up toasters have a large crumb tray and door at the bottom of the toaster. By sliding or unlatching this crumb door you can release food particles trapped in the bottom of the toaster. For a toaster that is used daily, this should be done once a week. Simply unplug the toaster, hold it over a trash container, and unlatch the door. Once the primary food particles have fallen out, move the toaster around to release other particles that may be trapped at the edges. Periodically clean out the toaster using a can of compressed air, making sure you don't damage sensitive heating elements or switches.

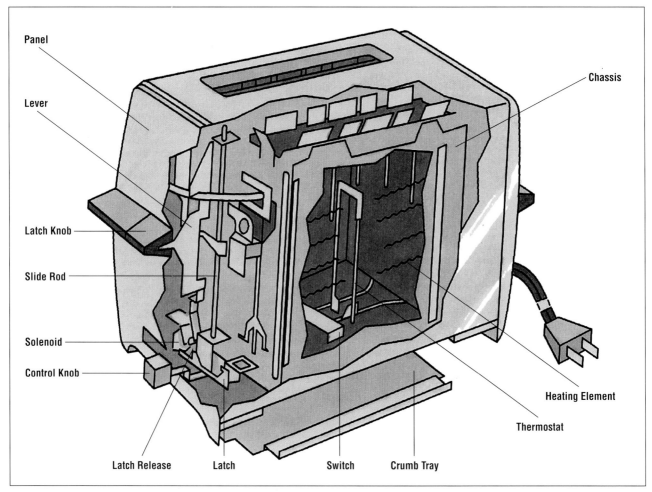

Panel

Lever

Chassis

Latch Knob

Slide Rod

Solenoid

Control Knob

Heating Element

Thermostat

Latch Release   Latch   Switch   Crumb Tray

This cross section of a toaster indicates the various elements that make a toaster work.

How Toasters Work

Most electric pop-up toasters all operate in the same manner. A slice of bread, a frozen waffle, a toaster strudel, or some similar food item is placed through a slot in the top of the toaster and into the carriage. The carriage is lowered into the chassis using the lever at the side of the toaster. When it reaches the bottom, the carriage latches in position and an internal switch is activated to start the heating process. A thermostat determines how long electric current will be sent from the power cord to the heating elements. The person who is operating the toaster sets the thermostat using a control knob or lever calibrated between light and dark. When the desired temperature is reached and the heating process is completed, the solenoid turns the current off, then unlocks the latch and allows the carriage to spring up to its original position. At this time, the toasted food is easily reachable and can be removed by the operator of the appliance.

Repairing a Toaster

Common toaster repairs include servicing the latch assembly, servicing the chassis, recalibrating the thermostat, and servicing the solenoid.

Servicing the Latch Assembly

The carriage and latch are vital components to the operation of pop-up toasters. If they don't work smoothly, bread or other food products cannot be held in position to be heated. To clean and lubricate the latch:

Step 1: To access the latch, remove the end panel by removing levers, knobs, and fasteners. On some models, disassemble the entire case by removing levers, knobs, crumb tray door, and fasteners. Fasteners are usually accessed from the bottom of the toaster, though some models hide them under plates and self-adhesive labels on the side.

Step 2: Once the cover is removed, inspect the latch assembly to determine if there are obvious

TROUBLESHOOTING TOASTERS	
Problem	**Solution**
Doesn't work at all	Refer to Troubleshooting Chart on page 205.
Carriage lowers but doesn't latch or latches stiffly	Check latch and slide rod. If damaged or obstructed, service the latch assembly.
Bread toasts only on one side	Check elements. If faulty, replace element, chassis, or toaster.
Carriage doesn't pop up and toast burns	Check thermostat calibration. If incorrect, recalibrate thermostat. If thermostat is faulty, replace the thermostat or toaster. Check solenoid switch and solenoid. If faulty, service or replace.
Toast too light or too dark	Check thermostat calibration. If incorrect, recalibrate thermostat.

problems such as a food particle or loose part jamming the assembly. Clean the latch area using a can of compressed air to blow away crumbs.

Step 3: Move the carriage lever up and down to check for smooth operation. If the carriage moves stiffly, carefully lubricate the rod on which the latch lever travels. Use a petroleum lubricant, making sure you don't get any of it on adjacent electrical parts.

Step 4: Check the operation of the latch to ensure that it works smoothly. You may need to carefully bend the latch so it catches properly.

Servicing the Chassis

Most of the mechanism within a toaster is mounted on a frame called the chassis. To repair or replace many internal parts, including the heating elements, you will need to remove the chassis from the toaster shell. Disassemble the toaster by removing levers, knobs, and fasteners, then carefully lift the shell off the chassis. Some toasters will require that you disconnect the power cord internally before you can fully remove the chassis. Depending on the problem your toaster is having, you may want to replace the entire chassis or just one or two components.

Recalibrating a Thermostat

The thermostat in a pop-up toaster performs a vital function in telling the solenoid how long you want the heating elements to toast the bread. If your toaster seems to ignore your setting, the thermostat may be out of adjustment. To recalibrate the toaster:

Step 1: Clean the toaster to ensure that food particles are not jamming the mechanism or shorting out the electronics.

Step 2: To recalibrate the thermostat, make sure the toaster is cool, turn it over on its top, and open the crumb tray cover.

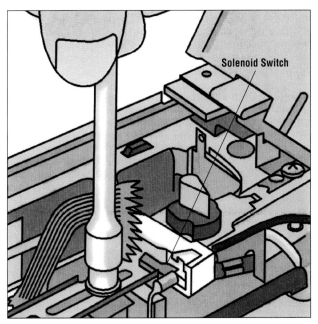

A calibration knob, screw, or nut can be turned to recalibrate the thermostat.

Step 3: On most units, a bracket from the control knob will be visible. On this bracket there will be a calibration knob, screw, or nut that can be turned to recalibrate the thermostat. Moving the bracket toward the solenoid switch typically will shorten the toasting cycle, and moving it away from the solenoid switch will lengthen the cycle. You can shorten the cycle if the toast is too dark or lengthen the cycle if the toast is too light.

Step 4: Close the toaster, plug it in, and toast a piece of bread to determine if the adjustment is correct. If adjusting the thermostat doesn't solve the problem, consider replacing the thermostat or the toaster.

Servicing a Solenoid

The thermostat activates a switch that operates the solenoid. The solenoid releases the latch. So if your toaster burns toast or doesn't want to release the carriage, the solenoid switch or the solenoid itself may be faulty. The solenoid switch is located near the thermostat and can be accessed by opening the crumb tray cover. Test it with a continuity tester. If it is faulty, remove it and replace it with a new switch.

The solenoid is located near the latch at one end of the toaster. To access it, remove the end cover, or the shell. Test the solenoid with a continuity tester and replace if faulty. If either the solenoid or switch is installed with rivets rather than screws, consider replacing the entire chassis or the toaster itself. Riveted parts are difficult to remove and replace without special tools.

Repairing Toaster Ovens

• •

Toaster ovens operate much like toasters. However, a toaster oven is more complex and is typically more expensive to purchase. The higher cost means that repairs are easier to justify. You will probably think twice before tossing a $75 toaster oven into the recycle bin. And because toaster ovens are less compact, they are often easier to work on than pop-up toasters.

Some toaster ovens simply toast bread and related food products horizontally rather than vertically as with pop-up toasters. Other toaster ovens are actually miniature ovens. The differences are identified by the wattage used—broilers require more watts of electrical power to operate—and by the controls. Some toaster ovens allow you to bake and broil foods, offering precise temperature and function control.

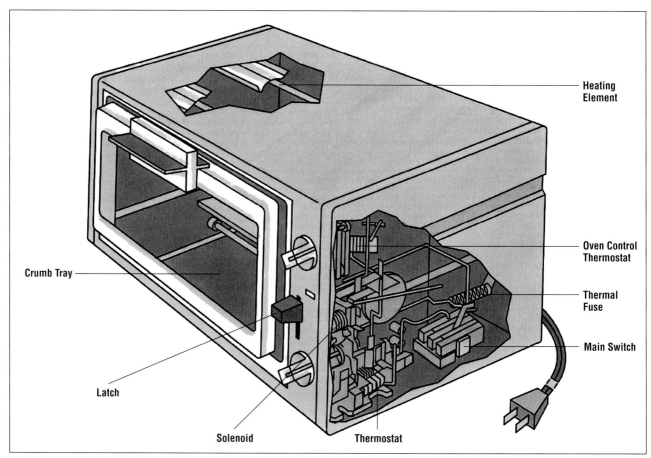

Cross section of a toaster oven.

TROUBLESHOOTING TOASTER OVENS	
Problem	**Solution**
Doesn't work at all	1. Refer to Troubleshooting Chart on page 205.
Doesn't work on toaster function and oven function	1. Check main switch. If faulty, service or replace.
	2. Check thermal fuse. If faulty, service or replace.
Toaster function doesn't turn off unless door is open	1. Check solenoid. If faulty, replace.
	2. Check switch. If faulty, replace or seek professional service.
	3. Check thermostat. If faulty, recalibrate (see pages 208–210 on Repairing Toasters).
Toaster oven stays on when door is opened	1. Check main switch. If faulty, service main switch.
Upper or lower elements don't heat	1. Check upper or lower element. If faulty, replace element.
	2. Check thermostat. If faulty, service thermostat or seek professional service.

How Toaster Ovens Work

To operate a toaster oven, controls are set, the door is opened, food is placed on a shelf, and the door is closed. If set for toasting, a toaster thermostat operates the upper and lower heating elements as selected by the color controller. If set for baking or broiling, the baking thermostat operates the heating elements as selected by the temperature controller and possibly by a timing mechanism.

There are a variety of toaster oven models, each with its own features. However, most operate in the same manner and can be diagnosed and repaired by applying the suggestions on the following pages.

Repairing a Toaster Oven

Typical toaster oven repairs include servicing the main switch, the thermal fuse, the heating element, and the solenoid.

Servicing the Main Switch

The toaster oven's main switch is an important operating part, one that gets extensive use and is a frequent culprit when things go wrong. In many cases, all that's required is cleaning the switch. In others, the switch must be replaced. To access and replace the main switch:

Step 1: Remove the side panel and, if necessary, the power cord.

Step 2: Check the contact points for pitting or discoloration. If they are not making good contact, carefully rub them with very fine sandpaper, then clean them with an electrical contact cleaner spray or isopropyl alcohol on the end of a cotton swab. Be careful not to bend the contact leaves out of alignment.

Step 3: If the contacts are fused or the leaves broken, remove and replace the main switch. Main switches are fastened to the chassis with clips, screws, or rivets.

Servicing the Thermal Fuse

A thermal fuse protects the toaster oven's main switch from damage caused by an electrical overload. If the main switch doesn't work, check the thermal fuse using a continuity tester or multitester. The thermal fuse should show continuity rather than an open circuit. If defective, remove and replace the thermal fuse with one of identical rating. In most models, this means cutting the fuse leads or wires and replacing the fuse unit.

Some toaster ovens use a bimetallic thermostat or thermal cutout to protect the adjacent main switch from damage. Inspect the thermal cutout for debris, distortion, or discoloration. Clean debris away with a can of compressed air. As needed, clean the contact points with emery paper.

Servicing Heating Elements

A heating element is vital to your toaster oven. It may only be on for a few minutes to toast bread, or, in the case of a baking/broiling unit, it may be on for an hour or more at a time. A heating element is simply a high resistance wire that glows as electricity flows through it. Heating elements, then, are easy to test. Here's how:

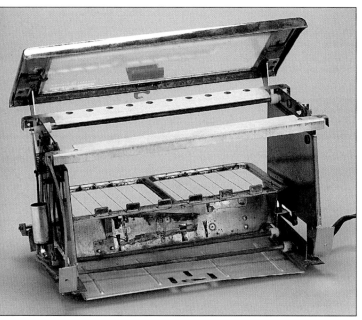

The two dark rods along the base of this toaster are the heating elements.

Step 1: Determine whether or not there is a clear path for electric current by touching a continuity tester or multitester probe to each end of the element.

Step 2: If there is no clear path, remove the heating element. Removing an element may be as easy as unscrewing both ends and any support brackets; however, it may also require that rivets be removed and replaced. Your decision to replace a defective element will then depend on how easy it is to remove as well as the value of the toaster oven.

Step 3: Once the heating element has been removed, replace it with one of identical rating and structure. Be very careful not to distort the shape of the new element as it is installed. Element wires are fragile and can be damaged easily. Higher-wattage elements are of thicker wire, much like the element in your conventional oven.

Servicing a Solenoid

The solenoid turns the electric current to the heating elements on and off. If the heating elements stay on longer than they should and burn your food, or if opening the appliance door turns them off, the solenoid may be defective. To test and replace a solenoid:

Step 1: Look at the unit for visible damage and smell the area around the solenoid for obvious damage to components.

Step 2: Use a continuity tester or multitester to verify your findings.

Step 3: Replace the solenoid. In some units, this is easy. Simply unscrew the brackets and remove the unit. If replacing the unit requires cutting or desoldering, take the unit to an appliance-repair shop for service.

Repairing Coffee Makers

• •

There's nothing more invigorating in the morning than the smell of fresh coffee—nor anything more frustrating than the sight of a coffee maker that isn't functioning as directed.

Fortunately, many repairs to coffee makers are simple to perform and require only basic tools. So, before you toss that coffee maker or defect to a coffee shop, consider how coffee makers work and what to do when they don't.

How Coffee Makers Work

There are two types of coffee makers in common use: those that drip hot water once through the coffee grounds, and those that percolate, or recycle, the water through the grounds many times.

Most drip coffee makers are activated by switches and timers in the control panel, heating water and pumping it up to drop through the coffee basket. The resulting hot coffee falls into a carafe. An element under the carafe keeps the coffee warm.

Percolator coffee makers heat a small amount of water in the base of the unit, forming steam that pushes the hot water up a tube in the center of the percolator. At the top, water falls into the coffee basket and soaks up all that great coffee flavor from the grounds. The resulting hot coffee then drips through holes in the basket base and into the main compartment to be recycled. A thermostat determines when the coffee has brewed sufficiently, then turns the percolating system off. A heating element continues to maintain the coffee at the selected temperature.

Repairing a Coffee Maker

Common repairs to coffee makers include servicing the on/off switch, thermostat, heating element, and warming element.

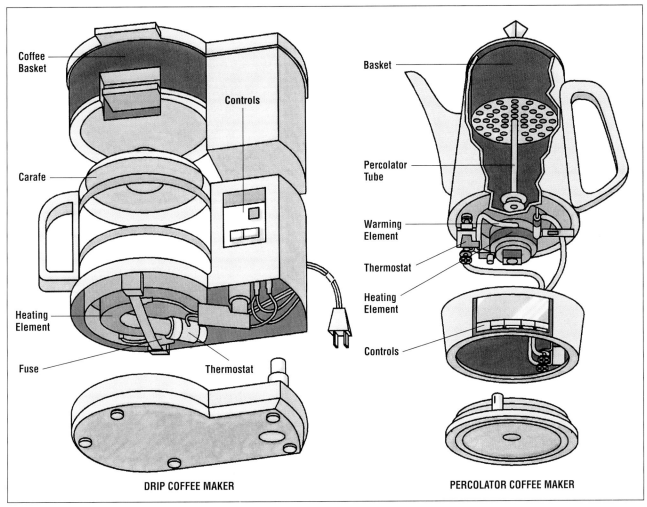

Coffee Basket

Controls

Carafe

Heating Element

Fuse

Thermostat

DRIP COFFEE MAKER

Basket

Percolator Tube

Warming Element

Thermostat

Heating Element

Controls

PERCOLATOR COFFEE MAKER

Cross section of a drip and a percolator coffee maker.

Servicing an On/Off Switch

A coffee maker's switch is a simple device that controls current to the heating unit and pump. Fortunately, this key controller is easy to test and to replace. Here's how:

Step 1: Make sure the coffee maker is unplugged.

Step 2: Remove the base or shell to access the back of the switch.

Step 3: Place test probes across the terminals and activate the switch. The circuit should be closed and show continuity as indicated by the switch positions.

The same test of continuity can be used to test other controllers, such as timers. All operate as switches, conducting electricity in some settings and not in others.

Servicing a Drip Coffee Maker's Thermostat

A thermostat in a drip coffee maker controls electricity to operate the heating element. It can cause problems if

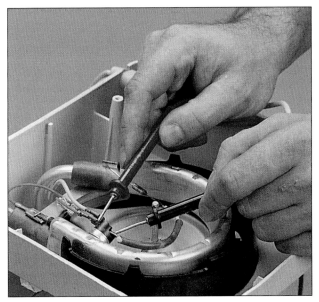

Testing a drip coffee maker's thermostat.

TROUBLESHOOTING DRIP COFFEE MAKERS

Problem	Solution
Doesn't work at all	1. Refer to Troubleshooting Chart on page 205.
	2. Check fuse or thermostat. If faulty, replace.
	3. Check heating element. If faulty, replace.
	4. Check on/off switch. If faulty, replace.
Sputters and brews coffee slowly	1. Check steam pump tubes. If clogged, clean or replace tubes.
Coffee maker leaks	1. Check reservoir or steam pump tubes. If cracked, seek professional repair or replace the coffee maker.

TROUBLESHOOTING PERCOLATOR COFFEE MAKERS

Problem	Solution
Doesn't work at all	1. Refer to Troubleshooting Chart on page 205.
	2. Check fuse or brewing element. If faulty, service fuse or element, seek professional repair, or replace coffee maker.
Heats water but doesn't perk coffee	1. Check steam tube or basket. If clogged, clean or replace.
	2. Check thermostat. If faulty, replace.
Perked coffee boils and reperks	1. Check thermostat. If faulty, replace.
	2. Check heating element. If faulty, replace.
Coffee doesn't stay hot	1. Check warming element. If faulty, replace.
Coffee maker leaks	1. Check seals or gaskets. If worn, seek professional repair or replace coffee maker.

it doesn't work correctly. To test the thermostat in a drip coffee maker:

Step 1: Unplug the unit, empty excess water from the reservoir, turn the unit over, and remove the base.

Step 2: Use a continuity tester or multitester to check the thermostat, placing a probe at each end.

Step 3: If defective, remove and replace the thermostat with one of the same rating.

Step 4: Also check the continuity of the fuse and replace it if the circuit is open.

Servicing a Percolator Coffee Maker's Thermostat

The thermostat in a percolator coffee maker serves the same function, but looks different from one in a drip system. To test a percolator coffee maker's thermostat:

Step 1: Unplug the coffee maker, make sure the coffee and filter are removed before turning it over,

then remove the base to expose the heating element and thermostat.

Step 2: Test the thermostat's continuity.

Step 3: If the thermostat is an open circuit, replace it. If replacing the thermostat requires unriveting or desoldering it, consider taking it to an appliance-repair shop or replacing the entire coffee maker.

Servicing Heating Elements

A coffee maker's heating element is a critical component. No one wants cold coffee. The heating element in either a drip or percolator coffee maker is accessed through the base of the appliance. To test and replace a heating element:

Step 1: Make sure all liquids and grounds are emptied from the appliance before turning it over to remove the base.

Step 2: Once accessed, the heating element can be tested using a continuity tester or a multitester as you would any conductor. Disconnect the unit from the circuit, then place a probe at each terminal and verify that the element can conduct electricity.

Step 3: If no electricity is being conducted, replace the heating element unit or assembly. With masking tape, mark the location of all wires and components you loosen so you will be able to reconnect them with ease.

Servicing Warming Elements

Once the coffee is brewed, the warming element in the base of the coffee maker keeps it warm. The warming element on some coffee makers remains on all day long, so it may be the first component to fail. In addition, water or brewed coffee may spill and leak into the warming element, shorting it out. Here's how to test and replace a warming element:

Step 1: Remove the coffee maker's base, identify the warming element, and disconnect it from the terminals.

Step 2: Check for continuity using a continuity tester or multitester.

Step 3: Replace the warming element, if necessary.

Repairing Food Mixers

• •

Food mixers can be found in nearly every kitchen. They blend ingredients to make cookies, cakes, muffins, breads, desserts, and other foods. Because of their versatility, they have become a favorite gift item for people setting up a new household.

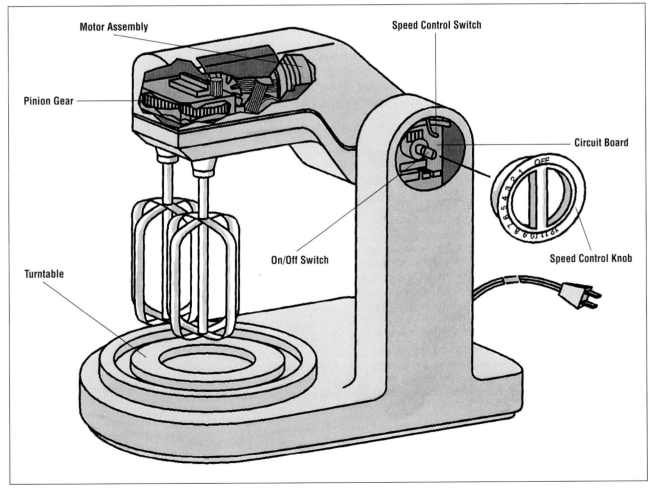

Motor Assembly

Speed Control Switch

Pinion Gear

Circuit Board

On/Off Switch

Speed Control Knob

Turntable

Cross section of a stand mixer.

TROUBLESHOOTING FOOD MIXERS	
Problem	**Solution**
Doesn't work at all	1. Refer to Troubleshooting Chart on page 205.
	2. Check switch. If faulty, service switch.
	3. Check motor fuse. If defective, replace fuse.
Mixer doesn't function at all speeds	1. Check speed control. If faulty, service or replace.
Motor hums, but beaters don't turn	1. Check motor. If seized, replace.
Mixer vibrates excessively	1. Check beaters. If shafts are bent or ends are worn, replace beaters.
	2. Check gears. If broken or misaligned, service gears.
	3. Check motor. If shaft is bent or motor is sparking, replace motor.

How Food Mixers Work

Food mixers are motorized small appliances. That is, rather than heating something, they move something. In this case, they move or mix food ingredients. Obviously, the motor is a primary component of the food mixer. So are the gears. Gears translate the motor's rotation to the opposing rotation of the beaters. A speed controller varies the electrical current delivered to the motor, thus allowing the speed of the beaters to be controlled.

There are two types of food mixers: portable (or hand) mixers, and stationary (or stand) mixers. Portable mixers are lightweight, with small motors for easier mixing and blending jobs. Stand mixers use larger motors and components to manage bigger jobs, such as kneading dough or mixing large batches of ingredients.

Repairing a Food Mixer

Easy repairs to food mixers include servicing a switch, repairing speed controls, and servicing gears. The following sections will show you how.

Servicing a Switch

Switches are simple components that can easily stop the operation of a small appliance. If your mixer doesn't operate and you've checked the plug and cord, test the switch next. To test and replace a switch:

Step 1: Carefully remove the housing around the switch to expose the back side of the switch.

Step 2: Check the terminals on the switch to ensure that the wires from the appliance are fully attached to the switch.

Step 3: Mark the terminal wires for position and disconnect them.

Step 4: Use a continuity tester or multitester to determine if the switch is faulty. If it is, replace it and reconnect the terminal wires.

Servicing Speed Controls

Food mixer speed is controlled by varying the current to the motor. Smaller hand mixers use a speed switch that includes a number of electrical contacts, each increasing current to the motor. Larger units use a variable resistor to control current. Continuity testers or multitesters are useful for checking the operation of either type of speed control. In some cases, contacts can be cleaned to improve function. However, in many cases, problems caused by speed controls can only be solved by replacing the controller.

How to Service Gears

Food mixers work so well because they rotate the beaters in opposing directions to blend the ingredients. This opposing rotation is produced by the gears.

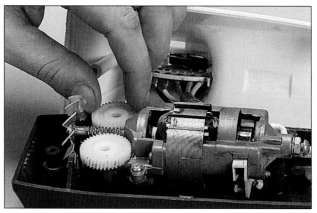

Inspect and lubricate the gears; make sure excess lubricant does not touch the motor or electrical components.

In most food mixers, a worm gear attached to the motor shaft turns two or more pinion gears. The pinion gears, in turn, rotate the beaters. As gears are a physical component rather than an electrical one, servicing them is different. To inspect and lubricate gears:

Step 1: Make sure the appliance is unplugged.

Step 2: Remove the upper housing to expose the gears. In most cases, gears that are causing problems can be checked for damage and then lubricated.

Step 3: Inspect and lubricate the worm gear as well as the pinion gears, making sure that excess lubricant does not touch the motor or any electrical components.

Step 4: Remove any loose shavings or pieces in the housing before reassembling.

Replacing a Fuse

If your food mixer's motor doesn't operate, the motor's fuse may be blown. To test and replace a fuse:

Step 1: Remove the upper housing to gain access to the motor.

Step 2: Find the fuse and disconnect it from the motor.

Step 3: Place a continuity tester or multitester probe at each end to check for continuity. If there is none, the fuse is blown and must be replaced with one of the same amperage rating.

Step 4: Because the fuse's purpose is to save the motor from electrical damage, check the speed controller and other electrical components in the appliance to determine the cause of the blown fuse. Otherwise, the new fuse will blow as soon as the motor is turned on.

Replacing the Motor

If a small appliance is properly designed, the motor should be one of the last components to fail. It is also one of the last components to check. Unless you have the proper tools, you should replace the motor rather than attempt to repair it. Or you can take the motor to a professional service person for repair. To test and replace a motor:

Step 1: Test the motor for continuity as you would any other electrical component.

Step 2: If it fails the test, mark and remove wires attached to it and disconnect the motor from the housing.

Step 3: Make sure the new motor is an exact replacement in size and rating to ensure that it fits the housing and the task.

Disassembling a hand mixer to access the motor.

Repairing Food Blenders

A food blender is a popular and useful kitchen appliance. Foods and liquids placed in it are blended or chopped based on the speed set by the operator. Today's food blender can chop ice, make peanut butter, grate cheese, and perform many other useful functions.

How Food Blenders Work

The kitchen food blender is a motorized small appliance. A blade inside a jar is connected to a motor shaft. By varying current to the motor, the blade's speed is controlled.

Preventive maintenance can reduce the repairs needed to keep a food blender running for many years.

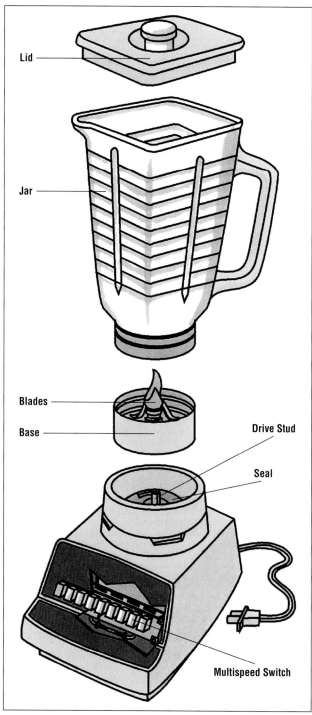

Cross section of a blender.

The two most important steps an operator can take are not to overload the blender and to keep the seals tight.

The multispeed switch in the blender sends current to the motor based on which control buttons are selected or how far the rheostat is turned. More current means a higher motor speed. Placing hard foods in the blender jar and trying to chop them with a low motor speed can cause the motor to burn out.

Because the jar holds liquids, yet must be disassembled for cleaning, it has seals to keep liquids from escaping. In addition, the blender housing has a seal around the coupling to make sure liquids don't leak into the vulnerable motor. Keeping these seals tight and ensuring that liquids don't overflow the jar can help keep a blender operating smoothly.

Repairing a Food Blender

Food blender repairs include servicing a multispeed switch, replacing a fuse, servicing a motor, tightening a drive stud, and servicing a blade assembly.

How to Service a Blender's Multispeed Switch

It's easy to see why the multispeed switch is a critical component to the operation of your food blender. Because of its high use and complexity, it is a frequent culprit when things go wrong. To service the multispeed switch:

Step 1: Remove the blender base.

Removing a blender's multispeed switch and testing it.

Step 2: The multispeed switch will be attached to the base with clips or screws accessed from underneath the base's faceplate or from inside the base. Visually inspect the switch before removing it; in many cases, the problem is a loose terminal. Otherwise, a blackened terminal or wire may identify where the problem has occurred.

TROUBLESHOOTING FOOD BLENDERS	
Problem	**Solution**
Doesn't work at all	1. Refer to Troubleshooting Chart on page 205.
	2. Check motor fuse. If blown, replace.
Runs intermittently	1. Check wire connections. If faulty, repair.
	2. Check motor. If faulty, replace.
Doesn't run at some speeds	1. Check multispeed switch. If faulty, clean or replace switch.
	2. Check wire connections. If faulty, repair.
Motor runs, but blade doesn't turn	1. Check drive stud. If loose, tighten. If damaged, replace.
	2. Check blade. If dirty, clean and lubricate. If damaged, repair or replace.
Jar leaks	1. Check base. If loose, tighten base into jar.
	2. Check seal. If damaged, replace seal, blade assembly, or jar.

Step 3: Check the multispeed switch with a continuity tester or multitester.

Step 4: Because of its exposed location on the front of the blender, the switch is susceptible to damage from liquids. Use a can of compressed air or an electrical contact cleaner to clean the switch. If necessary, replace it.

Replacing a Blender's Fuse

Fortunately, most blenders include an in-line fuse that protects the motor from overload. If excessive current is sent to the motor, the fuse will blow. To determine if the fuse is working:

Step 1: Remove the blender base and locate the fuse in the wire from the multispeed switch to the motor.

Step 2: Disconnect the wire and use a continuity tester or multitester to check the fuse. If the circuit is open, the fuse is blown.

Step 3: Replace the faulty in-line fuse with one of identical rating.

Servicing a Blender's Motor

The motor will typically withstand many years of use (though not much abuse). Unfortunately, if the motor needs to be replaced, it may be less expensive to buy a new blender.

Motor operation is easy to test. Because there is a circuit running from the appliance cord, through the multispeed controls, to the motor, and back to the cord,

an ohmmeter (part of your multitester) can test the circuit. To test a blender's motor:

Step 1: Place a probe on each cord prong.

Step 2: Select a speed-control button or turn the speed controller slightly, then read the resistance on the meter.

Step 3: Next, rotate the drive stud clockwise one turn. If the resistance reading (in ohms) changes, the motor needs service. Take it to an appliance-repair service or replace the appliance, depending on cost.

Tightening a Blender's Drive Stud

If the motor operates well, but the blade in the blender jar doesn't turn as it should, the problem may be the drive stud. The most frequent cause is a loose drive stud. To tighten the drive stud:

Step 1: Remove the base and turn the blender over. The other end of the drive shaft will protrude from the bottom side of the motor.

Step 2: Grip the drive shaft with a wrench or pliers, then turn the blender on its side to attach a wrench to the drive stud.

Step 3: Hold the drive shaft steady as you turn the drive stud clockwise (as seen from above the blender).

The other cause of drive stud problems is the rounding of its corners, requiring a new drive stud. To replace a worn drive stud, reverse the instructions for tightening a drive stud, install the new part, and tighten it.

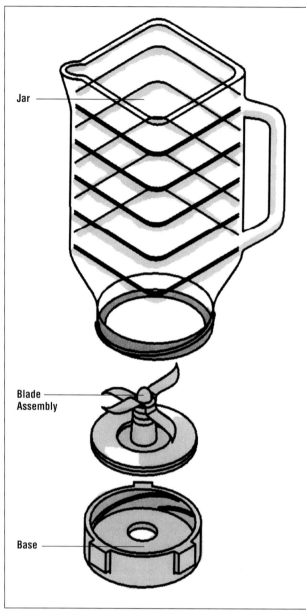

A blender's blade assembly blends or chops food in the jar.

How to Service a Blade Assembly

The blender's blade assembly is simple in function. It is rotated by the drive stud, which blends or chops food within the jar.

The most common problem is caused by the jar leaking liquids. The solution is to tighten the base. If this doesn't solve the problem, inspect and, if necessary, replace the gasket.

If the drive stud is turning but the blade assembly isn't, inspect the assembly socket into which the drive stud fits. It may be worn and require replacement. This is a common problem on blenders with metal drive studs and plastic blade-assembly sockets.

Repairing Electric Can Openers

anned foods bring ease and convenience to meal preparation. In seconds, an electric can opener will present a variety of prepared fruits, vegetables, and even main dishes stored in cans. Some models also open bottles, or sharpen knives.

Of course, trying to open a can with a defective can opener will tempt you to order take-out food. Fortunately, electric can openers are simple appliances that can be easily maintained and repaired.

How Electric Can Openers Work

The electric can opener is activated by an operating lever. The lever is lifted, and the edge of a can is placed between the feed gear and cutter. A magnet grips the top of the can.

When pressed down, the lever activates a switch that turns the motor on. The motor passes power through gears to turn the small feed gear and rotate the can. As it is rotated, the cutter cuts through the edge of the lid. When the can is removed, the lid stays attached to the magnet.

Many problems with electric can openers can be resolved before they occur by periodic cleaning and lubrication of the drive wheel and cutter. Unplug the can opener from the wall receptacle, clean the parts with a toothbrush and mild detergent, wipe clean, and lubricate with a light oil or white lubricant. Wipe away excess lubricant to ensure it doesn't transfer to food or other components.

Repairing a Can Opener

Can openers are simple to repair. Typical repairs include servicing a switch, a gear, a grindstone, or a motor.

Servicing an Electric Can Opener's Switch

An electric can opener is turned on and off with a contact switch activated by the appliance's operating lever. A defective switch may prevent the appliance from working at all. Here's how to service the switch:

Step 1: Remove the can opener's cover so you can watch how it activates.

Step 2: Press the lever down to make sure it makes contact with the switch. If not, check for and

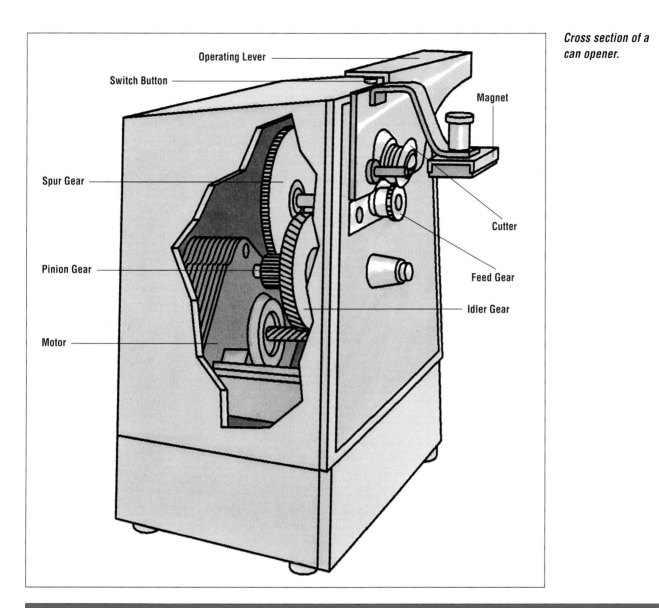

Cross section of a can opener.

Operating Lever
Switch Button
Magnet
Spur Gear
Pinion Gear
Cutter
Motor
Feed Gear
Idler Gear

TROUBLESHOOTING ELECTRIC CAN OPENERS	
Problem	**Solution**
Doesn't work at all	1. Refer to Troubleshooting Chart on page 205.
	2. Check switch. If faulty, service switch.
	3. Check motor fuse. If faulty, service fuse.
	4. Check motor. If faulty, replace or seek professional service.
Motor operates slowly as can is opened	1. Check blade. If not sharp, service grindstone or replace blade.
Can drops off can opener	1. Check feed gear. If it wobbles, service gear.
Feed gear turns when can isn't engaged	1. Check feed gear. If dirty, clean feed gear. If worn, service gear.
	2. Check idler gear. If worn, service gear.

remove any obstruction, or realign the lever so that it makes contact.

Step 3: If the switch still doesn't work, unplug it and test it with a continuity tester or multitester.

Step 4: If the contacts are corroded, use emery paper clamped in pliers to clean them. If a contact is broken or the switch is defective, replace it.

Step 5: Remove and mark all wires, unfasten the switch, and remove it from the housing. Replace it with a switch identified as a replacement part for your appliance.

Servicing an Electric Can Opener's Gears

Gears translate the motor's power into torque that turns a can. This requires a feed gear at the edge of the can and at least one other larger gear inside the appliance. To check and replace gears:

Step 1: Inspect the feed gear and clean or replace if worn or broken.

Step 2: Check internal gears by opening the appliance case and carefully removing gears. Teeth may be missing or warped, or the gears may simply need lubrication with a white lubricant. If the gears need to be replaced, make sure the replacement gears match exactly in every measure, including width, circumference, and number of teeth.

Step 3: If a replacement to a broken gear cannot be found, consider using a plastic or metal glue, as required, to repair the break. When done, carefully reassemble the gears and case, then test the appliance.

Servicing an Electric Can Opener's Grindstone

Some electric can openers will include a built-in grindstone that sharpens the blade as it is being used. Other electric can openers also serve as knife sharpeners, using their motors to power one or more small grindstones for the job.

The most common cause of problems with these grindstones is that stone shavings and other debris obstruct operation. This situation can cause the motor to burn out or the motor's fuse to blow. The best way to avoid this problem is to periodically clean the grindstone and the area around it.

Once worn or damaged, the grindstone must be replaced with one of the same size. Some models use a screw or clip to retain the stone on the shaft. Others will require that the stone and shaft be replaced at the same time. Depending on the grindstone's function on your can opener, you may elect to disconnect or not use it.

Servicing an Electric Can Opener's Motor

Electric can openers and other small appliances that don't require extensive power use a shaded pole motor. It has fewer parts than a universal motor and is less costly. To test and replace an electric can opener's motor:

Step 1: Unplug the appliance, open it up, and find the fuse on the motor.

Step 2: Place one continuity tester probe to one side of the fuse and the second probe on the other side of the fuse. If the continuity light doesn't illuminate, the fuse is blown and must be replaced.

Step 3: Attach a continuity tester or multitester across the two wires on the field coil winding. If the circuit is open, replace the motor as a unit. You can get one of the exact size and rating from an appliance-parts store.

Step 4: Always check the bearings for wear that will cause the shaft to wobble. Remove the rotor to check for damage or excessive wear.

Repairing Garbage Disposers

• •

Garbage disposers are handy kitchen appliances that some consider a luxury and others deem a necessity. Disposers can quickly liquefy waste from food preparation or leftovers. When inoperative, they can also be a frustration, requiring that all food within be removed before repair.

Fortunately, with minimal maintenance, a garbage disposer can last many years without major repair. Simple maintenance includes ensuring that a disposer's enemies—grease, large items, hard items, fibrous foods—be eliminated from its diet.

Also make sure that water is running while the disposer is operating so that ground-up kitchen waste can be swept down the drain and not solidify inside the appliance.

How Garbage Disposers Work

A garbage disposer is a motorized small appliance. The motor turns a flywheel to which impellers are loosely attached. Food waste within the chamber is repeatedly hit and cut by these rotating impellers, grinding it into

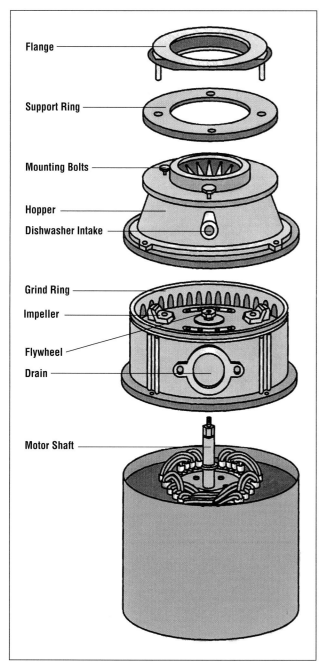

Flange
Support Ring
Mounting Bolts
Hopper
Dishwasher Intake
Grind Ring
Impeller
Flywheel
Drain
Motor Shaft

Cross section of a garbage disposer.

small particles that can be flushed through the drain pipe and into the septic system.

Some garbage disposers include an intake line for a dishwasher. The entire unit is attached to the sink using a flange, ring, and mounting bolts.

Repairing a Garbage Disposer

Common garbage disposer repairs include servicing a flywheel, hoses and seals, and a worn impeller. Here are step-by-step instructions for these repairs.

Servicing a Garbage Disposer's Flywheel

The flywheel in a garbage disposer rotates to spin the impellers that shred the food waste. If the flywheel doesn't turn, the disposer doesn't do its job. A stuck flywheel can also burn out a motor if left on too long. Fortunately, a flywheel is typically easy to free. To free the flywheel:

Step 1: Check the bottom side of the disposer for a six-sided (hex) hole.

Step 2: If it has one, look for a hex wrench in a pouch on or near the disposer. The hex wrench is used to rotate the motor shaft and flywheel without having to access the inside of the garbage disposer. If you don't find one, check your toolbox or purchase one.

Step 3: Simply insert the hex wrench in the hex hole and rotate it in a circle in both directions to free the flywheel.

If there is no hex hole, insert a shortened broom handle through the drain hole, resting one end at the side of an impeller. Gradually apply leverage to move the impeller in one direction or the other to free up the flywheel.

Servicing Hoses and Seals

A common complaint about garbage disposers is that they leak water into the cabinet below. By studying the leaked water and its location, you can often determine its source.

TROUBLESHOOTING GARBAGE DISPOSERS	
Problem	**Solution**
Doesn't work at all	Refer to Troubleshooting Chart on page 205.
Disposer does not turn	Check flywheel. If jammed, service flywheel.
Disposer leaks water	Check hoses and seals. If loose or worn, tighten or replace.
Disposer turns but doesn't grind up waste	Check impellers. If worn, replace.

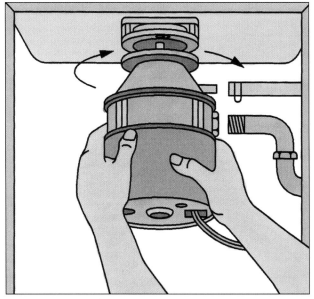

If leakage is from underneath the garbage disposer, remove the disposer from the drain system.

Standing water with discoloration from food means the drain pipe or the dishwasher intake is leaking. If the water is at all warm, it is probably from the dishwasher. If the standing water is clear, it may have come from the sink before the water entered the disposer. To assess a leak and replace the seal:

Step 1: Place a hand at various locations around the disposer. You can sometimes pinpoint the source by feeling water run across your hand.

Step 2: If the leakage is from underneath the garbage disposer, it is probably leaking through the flywheel seal and into the motor. In this case, you will need to remove the garbage disposer from the drain system. Disassemble the unit and replace the seal—or take it in for service.

Servicing Worn Impellers

To remove a garbage disposer to sharpen impellers:

Step 1: Unplug the garbage disposer, remembering to trip the circuit breaker first or remove the fuse at the main electrical box if the disposer is wired directly into the house.

Step 2: Remove all hose fittings leading into or away from the disposer. Some garbage disposers can then be removed by twisting to free them from the support ring. Others require that the unit be unscrewed from the ring. Remember that a garbage disposer is a relatively heavy small appliance, so freeing it will suddenly put its full weight in your hands.

Step 3: To service worn impellers on many models, you must remove the flywheel. Lock the flywheel in place with a screwdriver, then loosen the flywheel lock nut.

Step 4: Once the flywheel is removed, the impellers can be removed or sharpened in place. If the impellers cannot be sharpened, the flywheel assembly will need to be replaced.

Repairing Vacuum Cleaners

• •

Vacuum cleaners typically last 8 to 12 years, depending on their quality, frequency of use, and general maintenance. By maintaining and repairing your vacuum cleaner as needed you can extend its service life and reduce its actual cost.

There are two common types of vacuum cleaners: upright and canister. The upright vacuum cleaner has the motor and beater bar in the same unit. A canister vacuum cleaner has the motor and storage bag in the canister and the beater bar in a separate power head, with the two units connected by a hose.

How Upright Vacuum Cleaners Work

An upright vacuum cleaner uses a motor and fan to pull dirt from a surface and deposit it in a bag. Dirt is loosened and swept into the vacuum with a rotating brush called the beater bar. The upright vacuum cleaner is guided by the operator using the handle on which the bag and controls are mounted. Operation is simple. Maintenance and repairs are easy to perform.

How Canister Vacuum Cleaners Work

A canister vacuum cleaner places the majority of its weight (vacuum motor, filters, bag, and cord winder) in a separate unit to make the power head lighter.

With a long hose, the canister can be placed in the middle of the room and the power head moved more easily. This design allows larger and more powerful motors to be used.

As with the upright, the canister vacuum cleaner loosens dirt with the beater bar, located in the power head and driven by a smaller motor. Dirt is pulled through the hose by the main motor in the canister.

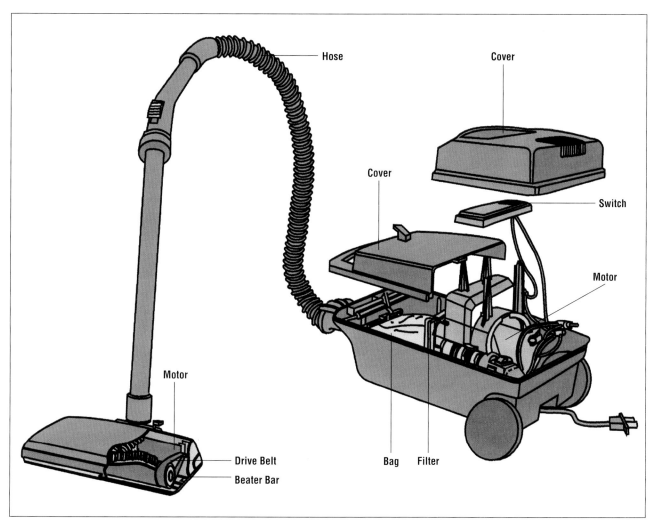

Labels on the diagram:
Hose
Cover
Cover
Switch
Motor
Motor
Drive Belt
Beater Bar
Bag   Filter

Cross section of a canister vacuum.

Wheels on the canister make it easily portable. Because the fan in a canister vacuum is more isolated than the fan in an upright vacuum, it is generally less susceptible to damage.

Repairing a Vacuum Cleaner

This section offers easy instructions for servicing an upright vacuum cleaner's on/off switch, beater bar, drive belt, dirt fan, and motor. It also covers the repair of an on/off switch, power-head wire connection, beater bar, motor, and cord reel for a canister vacuum.

Uprights: Servicing an On/Off Switch

Because of its repeated use, a vacuum cleaner's on/off switch can malfunction. Fortunately, on most models the switch is easy to access and test. Some are fastened in place with rivets, but most use screws. To test and replace the switch:

Step 1: Make sure the vacuum is unplugged, then remove the cover plate to expose the back side of the switch. The switch may be on the handle or on the housing.

Step 2: Check the wires to make sure they are completely attached to the switch.

Step 3: Use a continuity tester or multitester to make sure that there is an open circuit when the switch is off and a closed circuit when it is on.

Step 4: If there is a problem with the circuit, or if the switch doesn't test correctly, remove and replace the switch with one designed to be a replacement.

Uprights: Servicing a Beater Bar

The beater bar in an upright vacuum cleaner is the first contact your upright vacuum has with dirt. It's also one of the first components to need servicing.

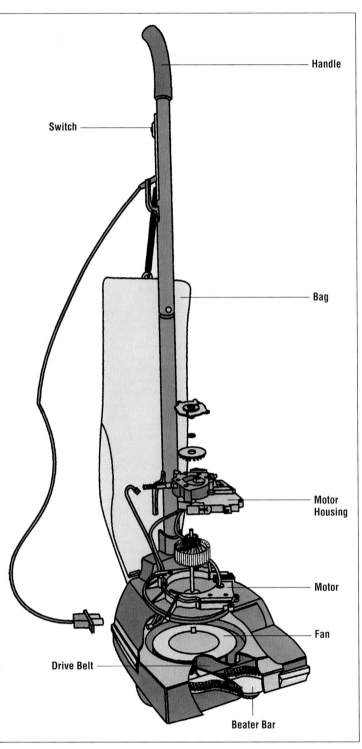

Cross section of an upright vacuum.

Step 1: To inspect the beater bar, turn the vacuum upside down. The beater bar will be at the front edge of the housing.

Step 2: Remove the clips at each end, remove the drive belt, and lift the beater bar from the housing.

Step 3: To disassemble the beater bar, remove the end cap and flange; pull the brush from the casing.

Step 4: If worn, replace the brush. If broken, replace the cap, flange, or case. If necessary, replace the entire beater bar.

Uprights: Servicing a Drive Belt

The drive belt in an upright vacuum cleaner passes power from the motor to the beater bar. The drive belt should be checked once a month to ensure that it is in good condition. Some beater bars have an adjustment that allows the drive belt to be tightened or loosened. To replace the drive belt:

Step 1: Remove one end of the beater bar (see Servicing a Beater Bar on pages 225–226) from the vacuum housing.

Step 2: Loosen the drive belt from the motor pulley and remove it from around the beater bar.

Step 3: Slip the replacement drive belt over the beater bar and around the motor pulley.

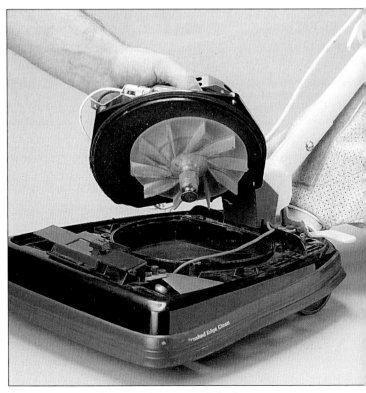

Servicing an upright vacuum's motor and dirt fan.

The beater bar is a round roller with an offset row of brush fibers. The brushes can wear down, the roller can be damaged, the end cap can come off and be lost, or the drive belt can come loose. To remove and replace the beater bar:

TROUBLESHOOTING VACUUM CLEANERS (UPRIGHT AND CANISTER)	
Problem	**Solution**
Doesn't work at all	1. Refer to Troubleshooting Chart on page 205.
	2. Check motor. If faulty, service motor.
Stops soon after unit is turned on	1. Check bag and filter. If full or dirty, replace bag and clean or replace filter.
	2. Check wire connections. If disconnected, connect. If worn, replace.
Motor overheats	1. Check fan. If dirty or jammed, service fan.
	2. Check motor. If faulty, service motor.
Doesn't clean as it should	1. Check bag. If full, replace bag.
	2. Check filter. If clogged, clean or replace filter.
	3. Check hose. If clogged, unblock hose with broom or mop handle.
	4. Check beater bar. If clogged, remove debris. If worn, replace beater bar.
	5. Check drive belt. If loose or broken, service drive belt.
Excessive noise when operating	1. Check fan. If faulty, service fan.
	2. Check drive belt. If loose or broken, service drive belt.
Power cord doesn't rewind in cord reel (canister type)	1. Check cord reel. If faulty, service cord reel.

Step 4: Reinstall the beater bar and adjust the drive belt as necessary.

Uprights: Servicing a Dirt Fan

The dirt fan in an upright vacuum cleaner is located underneath the motor. It pulls dirt swept back by the beater bar up into the vacuum bag. In most cases, the dirt fan doesn't need replacement, only periodic maintenance. Here's what you need to do.

Step 1: Remove the motor cover and dismount the motor from the vacuum frame. The fan will be on the underside of the motor.

Step 2: Clean the fan's blades and base with a moist cloth. Inspect the blades for damage caused by vacuuming solid objects.

Step 3: Unscrew or unbolt the dirt fan from the motor shaft to inspect and clean the back side.

Step 4: Check whether the motor shaft needs lubrication.

Step 5: If the dirt fan needs replacement, make sure the new part is an identical replacement. Take the old unit to an appliance-parts store to verify the replacement.

Uprights: Servicing a Motor

Most upright vacuum cleaners are designed for reasonably long life. However, some will last longer than others. Much depends on the quality of the motor. If a

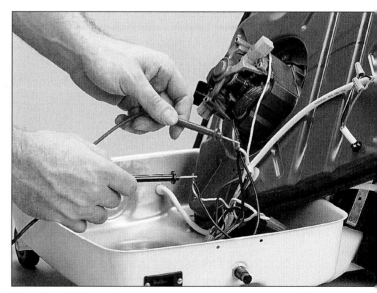

Test the upright vacuum's motor brushes with a continuity tester or multitester if you suspect a defective motor.

vacuum's motor stops working unexpectedly, check the power cord, the fan (for jams), and the on/off switch. It's also possible that you have a defective motor. Here's how to find out:

Step 1: If you suspect that the motor is defective, first test the motor's brushes with a continuity tester or multitester.

Step 2: Turn the motor shaft or beater bar by hand. The motor should maintain continuity.

Step 3: If not, replace the brushes or take the vacuum to an appliance-repair shop to have it done. If the motor is unrepairable, consider replacing the entire upright vacuum, as the cost of a new motor is a major investment.

Canisters: Servicing an On/Off Switch

Like the switches on most small appliances, the on/off switch on a canister vacuum cleaner gets a lot of use. Considering the ease of repair and its low replacement cost, this switch is one of the first components to check if a vacuum doesn't turn on or off correctly. To test and replace the switch:

Step 1: Open or remove the canister housing to access the back side of the switch.

Step 2: Use a continuity tester or multitester to ensure that there is an open circuit when the switch is in the OFF position and a closed circuit when the switch is in the ON position.

Step 3: Also check the wiring and terminals to ensure that they are connected properly.

Step 4: If the switch doesn't test correctly, remove it and replace it. Some switches are fastened to the housing with screws, others with clips or friction snaps. A few are riveted in place.

Canisters: Servicing the Power-Head Wire Connection

An advantage of the canister vacuum is that the part that is pushed and pulled across the floor is lighter than with a single-unit upright vacuum. A disadvantage is that power must be delivered first to the canister, then to the separate power head.

The wire connection between the two units is often a source of problems, even in better-quality canister vacuum cleaners. The reason is that there are four sections to the connecting wire: from canister to hose, from one end of the hose to the other, from one end of the power-head tube to the other, and within the power head itself. The end of each section of wire has a connector. If the connection is not made sufficiently, the power head doesn't operate or operates intermittently.

In most cases, servicing the power-head wire connection simply requires that each connector be checked and tightened as needed. If a specific connector frequently makes a poor connection, you can clean the male and female connections with a small piece of emery paper and a can of compressed air.

Broken wires or worn insulators can sometimes be reconnected and wrapped with electrical tape. However, the wire may be located inside the hose, requiring that the hose be replaced as well.

Canisters: Servicing the Beater Bar

The beater bar on a canister vacuum cleaner is serviced in almost the same manner as one on an upright unit (see pages 225–226). Here's how:

Step 1: Remove the clips at each end of the beater bar, and pull it and the drive belt from the power-head case. In many cases, all you have to do is clean the brush and the two ends. Remove any excess pet hair or carpet fibers that get wound into them.

Step 2: If needed, remove the beater bar end cap and flange to remove the brush from the shaft and clean or replace it.

Step 3: Also check the drive belt and replace it if it is worn or damaged.

Step 4: When reinstalling the beater bar, make sure there is sufficient tension on the drive belt to rotate the bar by pulling on the belt. If the belt is loose, adjust it following the instructions in the owner's manual—or use common sense.

Canisters: Servicing a Motor

The motor for a canister vacuum cleaner is easy to access on most models. To test and replace the motor's brushes:

Step 1: Open the canister's top cover and remove the motor cover to expose the motor itself.

Step 2: Place the probes of a continuity tester or multitester on the two wires that lead to the motor from the on/off switch.

Step 3: Rotate the motor shaft a few revolutions by hand. The motor should test as a closed circuit with some resistance. If an ohmmeter indicates no resistance or infinite resistance, the motor is probably damaged.

Step 4: Check the motor's brushes in the same manner, if they are accessible. Replace the brushes if needed.

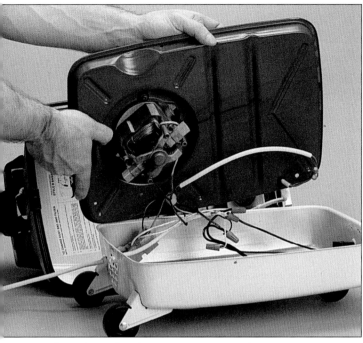

Open the canister's top cover to access the motor.

For other motor repairs, take the appliance to an appliance-repair service or motor-repair shop. If the motor needs replacing, evaluate the overall condition of the vacuum and consider replacing the entire appliance.

Canisters: Servicing a Cord Reel

The cord reel on a canister vacuum cleaner is a gadget that simply makes storage of the cord easier. It doesn't clean anything. The cord reel unit is usually located at the rear of the canister.

An internal spring offers sufficient tension to retract the cord onto the reel. The cord reel winds the cord in a circle, so the internal end of the cord must also move in a circle. At the same time, it must be electrically connected to the motor.

To make this work, the cord is attached to a rotating contact called a commutator block. It is a circular conductor of electricity that passes current from the internal end of the cord to a stationary block. If the blocks become dirty or corroded, they will not pass current to the motor. To remove and clean or replace the cord reel:

Step 1: Open the top cover of the canister. Another sealing cover will protect the cord reel—and probably the motor as well—from the vacuum chamber.

Step 2: Depending on whether you're cleaning or replacing the cord reel, you may need to

remove it from the housing. To do so, find the clips or fasteners holding it into place and undo them. If necessary, cut the two wires leading from the cord reel to the motor. In some cases, you may be able to make adjustments and repairs without cutting the motor wires.

Step 3: Clean the cord reel of dirt, then clean the commutator and stationary block with some isopropyl alcohol on a soft rag. If pitted, the blocks should be lightly sanded and wiped clean.

Step 4: Adjust the spring as needed and reinstall the unit in reverse order, replacing any cut wires.

Repairing Hair Dryers

Hair dryers combine both types of small appliances: those that heat and those that move something. Therefore a hair dryer includes both a heating element and a fan motor.

Most people don't bother to fix even the simplest problems on their hair dryers because they are generally inexpensive to replace. It's easier to toss them and buy new ones. In the long run, however, it may be more efficient to purchase a better-quality hair dryer and make most of the repairs yourself.

How Hair Dryers Work

Personal hair dryers come in a variety of shapes and sizes, but they all contain the same components and work in the same way. The typical hair dryer includes an on/off switch, a fan-speed switch, a fan and motor, a heat switch, a heating element, and a thermal cutout switch. The heating switch controls the amount of current delivered to the heating element, thus controlling the heat delivered by the hair dryer. The fan-speed switch controls the speed of the fan motor and fan, thus controlling the force of the air delivered by the hair dryer. The thermal cutout switch, a safety feature, shuts off the heating element if it gets too hot.

Repairing a Hair Dryer

Common hair dryer repairs include servicing the switch, fan, heating element, and thermal cutout.

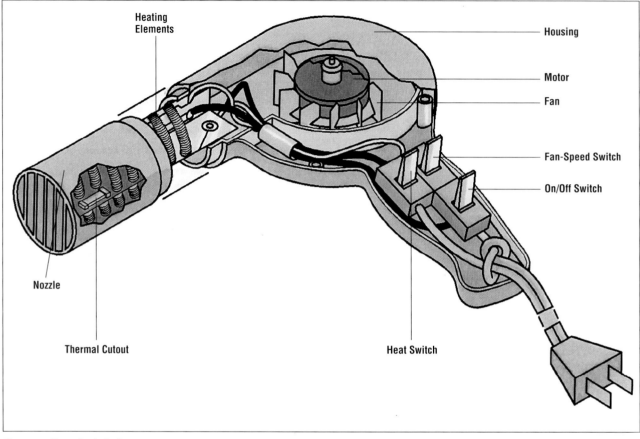

Cross section of a hair dryer.

Servicing a Hair Dryer Switch

On/off, fan-speed, and heat switches all work in the same way. They control the current going to the hair dryer, the fan, or the elements.

Some switches have only two positions: on or off, high or low. Others have three or more. However, they are all tested and replaced in the same way. Here's how to test a hair dryer switch:

Step 1: Unplug the appliance and carefully unscrew and remove the housing. Screws are typically recessed near the motor vent.

Step 2: Switches will be mounted in the handle or main housing between the electrical cord and the fan motor and heating element (see diagram above for reference). Remove the switch and disconnect it.

TROUBLESHOOTING HAIR DRYERS	
Problem	**Solution**
Doesn't work at all	1. Refer to Troubleshooting Chart on page 205.
	2. Check thermal cutout. If faulty, service thermal cutout.
Fan doesn't work on all settings	1. Check fan switch. If faulty, service switch.
Heat doesn't work on all settings	1. Check heat switch. If faulty, service switch.
Fan works, but heat doesn't	1. Check heat switch. If faulty, service switch.
	2. Check elements. If faulty, service elements.
Heat works, but fan doesn't	1. Check fan-speed switch. If faulty, service switch.
	2. Check fan. If faulty, service fan.

Step 3: Using a continuity tester or multitester, make sure the switch functions as it should. That is, an on/off switch will indicate an open circuit (continuity light off) in the OFF position, and a closed circuit (continuity light on) in the ON position.

Fan-speed switches and heating element switches will show continuity in all settings.

How to Service a Hair Dryer Fan

The fan in a hair dryer pulls air in through a vent and pushes it out the nozzle. The fan-speed switch feeds it electrical current.

Hair dryer fans are generally quite durable. The primary causes of problems are hair and moisture—two elements found in abundance in a bathroom.

Hair, lint, and other debris can clog up the screen filter on the air intake. To clean it, use compressed air or a soft-bristle toothbrush, as shown.

Moisture can damage any motor by shorting out components. To test and repair a hair dryer fan and motor:

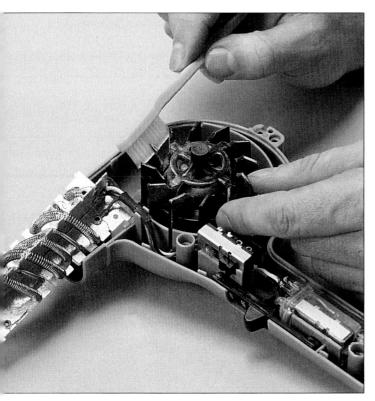

You can clean built-up debris from a screen filter by using a soft-bristle toothbrush.

Step 1: Remove housing screws and lift off the housing.

Step 2: Remove and inspect the fan blades, repairing or replacing as necessary.

Step 3: Test the motor using a continuity tester to ensure that current has a closed path (continuity light on) through the motor. If not, remove and replace the motor with one of an identical rating in watts and size.

If a replacement motor cannot be found, or if it costs more than half the price of a new hair dryer, consider replacing the entire hair dryer.

Servicing a Hair Dryer's Heating Element

The heating element in a hair dryer is a continuous high-resistance wire wound around a nonconducting frame. It is installed in the appliance nozzle or output vent. When electrical current is applied to it, the element heats up. The adjacent fan forces air past the element, warming it before it exits the nozzle. To test a hair dryer element if you suspect a problem:

Step 1: Remove the housing of the hair dryer and the element shield.

Step 2: Find the two wires leading to the element. Visually inspect the wires and the element coils for any obvious breaks or debris.

Step 3: Use a continuity tester or multitester to check for continuity. The circuit between the two lead wires should be closed (continuity light on). If not, check the thermal cutout.

Step 4: If the thermal cutout functions properly, replace the heating element with an exact replacement part.

Servicing a Thermal Cutout

A thermal cutout is located in the element assembly of most electrical hair dryers. The purpose of a bimetallic thermostat is to shut the hair dryer element off if it gets too hot. To test the thermal cutout:

Step 1: Open the housing and gain access to the element assembly (see above).

Step 2: Find and inspect the thermal cutout for debris, distortion, or discoloration.

Step 3: Clean the contact points with emery paper. Loosen debris with a few short blasts of compressed air held at sufficient distance to avoid damage to the sensitive element wires.

CHAPTER 7

PLUMBING

Few things strike such terror in our hearts as the word "plumbing." Plumbing, for most of us, is a mysterious system that works in ways known only to people who belong to the union— people who never seem to be available when you need them the most. Fortunately, plumbing works according to the basic laws of nature—gravity, pressure, water seeking its own level—and if you know this, you can understand its "mysteries" in no time. In reality, there is little mystery about how your plumbing system works, but there is often a great deal of misunderstanding. Once you know the basics, you can take care of many plumbing problems yourself. You can also save yourself time, trouble, and money!

How the Plumbing System Works

The plumbing in your home is one system composed of two complementary but entirely separate subsystems. One subsystem brings fresh water in, and the other subsystem takes wastewater out. Naturally, if you and your family are to stay healthy, you must avoid any cross-connection between the supply and disposal lines.

Understanding the Water Supply System

The water that comes into your home is under pressure. It enters your home under enough pressure to allow it to travel upstairs, around corners, or wherever else it's needed.

In urban and suburban areas, the community water department pumps water into the water system. If you have your own well, you probably have a pump to bring water into your home under pressure. Before you actually use the water for drinking, bathing, washing clothes and dishes, and so on, the water probably passes through a meter that registers the number of gallons or

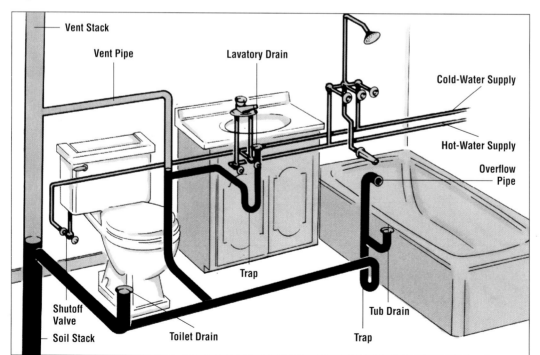

Vent Stack
Vent Pipe
Lavatory Drain
Cold-Water Supply
Hot-Water Supply
Overflow Pipe
Trap
Shutoff Valve
Soil Stack
Toilet Drain
Trap
Tub Drain
Trap

Your home's supply and drainage systems must always be two distinct subsystems, with no overlapping. At the fixtures (bridges between the two systems), the air admitted by the vent stack and vent pipes keeps the traps sealed and prevents sewer gases from backing up through the drains.

cubic feet you use. The water meter may be somewhere on your property outside the house, or it may be inside, at the point where the supply pipe enters the building. The outside type of meter has a metal cover over it that you can lift to access the meter.

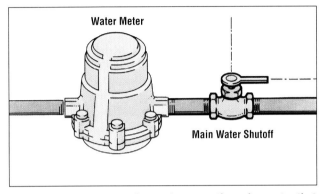
Water Meter

Main Water Shutoff

As water comes into your home, it passes through a meter that registers the amount you use. The main water shutoff, or stop, valve is generally located close to the meter.

Even if you never look at the water meter itself, you should be familiar with one device that's generally located close to the meter. This is the main shutoff, or stop, valve. In a plumbing emergency, it's vital that you quickly close the main shutoff valve. When a pipe bursts, for example, it can flood your house in no time, but you can minimize damage by closing the main shutoff valve to shut off all the water coming into the house. The shutoff may be a stop-and-waste valve, which drains the water from the pipes as well as shutting off the supply. If the emergency is confined to a sink, tub, or toilet, however, you may not want to turn off your entire water supply. Therefore, most fixtures should have individual stop valves.

Once the water has passed through the main supply line to your individual supply line, water meter, and main shutoff valve, it travels to the different fixtures in the house for your use. Water from the main supply is immediately ready for your cold-water needs.

The hot-water supply, however, requires another step. One pipe carries water from the cold-water system to your water heater. From the heater, a hot-water line carries the heated water to all the fixtures, outlets, and appliances that require hot water. You can adjust the water temperature by raising or lowering the temperature setting on the water heater. A thermostat on the heater maintains the temperature you select by turning the device's heating elements on and off as required. The normal temperature setting for a home water heater is between 140° and 160°F, but 120°F is usually adequate and is also more economical. Some automatic dishwashers require higher-temperature

water, though many of these have a water heater within them that boosts the temperature another 20 degrees.

The water pressure in your home is like any other good thing; too much of it can be very bad. Residential water pressure that reaches or exceeds 70 to 80 psi (pounds per square inch) can cause your pipes to bang and your faucets to leak. It can also break pipe joints and connections. At the very least, excessive pressure wastes water.

You can measure the average water pressure in your home by attaching a pressure gauge to the cold-water faucet nearest the main shutoff valve. Be sure to test the pressure at several different times during the day to find an average. Water pressure does fluctuate, but it shouldn't fluctuate greatly or else you'll have an uncomfortable time trying to take a shower. As you perform this test, make sure no water is running from any other outlet in your home besides the one to which the gauge is attached.

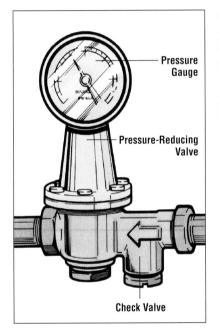
Pressure Gauge

Pressure-Reducing Valve

Check Valve

If you must reduce the water pressure in your home, a pressure-reducing valve can be installed in the supply pipe coming into the house.

If the gauge registers 70 to 80 psi or more, you should install a pressure-reducing valve. This is a fairly inexpensive device that a do-it-yourselfer should be able to install easily. Most of these valves work best when installed on a horizontal pipe; the valve can be connected into the supply line with joint fittings without much difficulty. Once the valve is installed, you can set it to the water pressure that best suits your needs. The valve will lower the pressure and maintain it at that setting.

Decreasing excessive water pressure is easy. Increasing inadequate water pressure is much harder, and requires the help of a plumber.

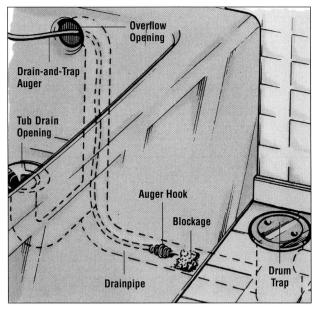

A clog near the tub's drain can be attacked from several places—the overflow opening (as shown), the tub drain opening, or the drum trap. Start working at the tub drain. If you can't remove the obstruction there, move on to the overflow, and then the drum trap.

For floor drains, such as those in basements and showers, a garden hose can be effective in unclogging drains, especially if the clog is not close to the opening. Attach the hose to a faucet, feed the hose into the drain as far as it will go, and jam rags around the hose at the opening. Then turn the water on full-force for a few moments.

If you suspect a clog is in the main drainpipe, locate the main clean-out. This is a Y-shaped fitting near the bottom of your home's soil stack, or where the drain leaves the building. Set a large pail or container under the clean-out and spread plenty of papers and rags around the site to soak up the backed-up water. Using a pipe wrench, slowly unscrew the clean-out plug counterclockwise, trying to control the flow of water that will seep from the clean-out. Once the flow has stopped and you've cleaned up the flooded site, insert the auger to remove the debris.

If you still haven't located the blockage, another place you can try is the house trap. This is a U-shaped fitting installed underground. You can locate it by finding two adjacent clean-out plugs in the floor, if the main drain runs under the floor. Again, place papers and rags around the site before opening the clean-out nearest to the sewer outside. If the clog is in the house trap or between the trap and the main clean-out, you should be able to remove it. But if the water starts to flow out of the trap as you unscrew it, check quickly beyond the house trap with an auger. If you can remove the clog rapidly, do so. Otherwise, replace the trap plug and call in a professional to do the job.

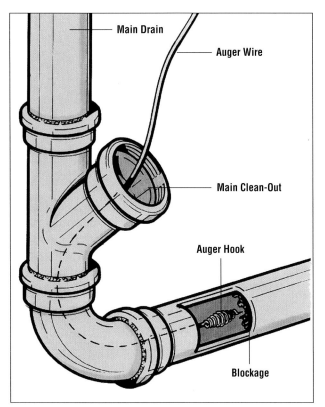

A clog in the main drain can be reached from the main clean-out; this is a Y-shaped fitting near the bottom of your home's soil stack or where the drain leaves the building.

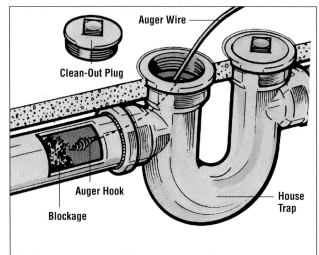

The house trap is a U-shaped fitting installed underground. You can locate it by finding two adjacent clean-out plugs in the basement floor. A blockage between the trap and the main clean-out can be reached by removing the plug closest to the main clean-out.

If the clog is between the house trap and the main clean-out, insert the wire from the auger into the trap in the direction of the main clean-out. If the blockage is not in the trap but is in the drain itself, remove the adjacent clean-out plug and try to reach the blockage from there with the auger.

There is one type of drain clog that will not respond satisfactorily to a plunger or an auger. This is when the main drain outside the building or a floor drain in the basement gets stopped up from tree roots that have grown in at the joints. The most effective solution in this case is a power auger or electric rooter, which is inserted into the pipe and cuts away roots from the pipe walls as it moves along.

You can rent a power auger at a tool-rental firm. Feed the auger cable into the clean-out opening closest to the blockage. When the device's cutting head encounters roots, you should be able to feel the cable strain. Keep feeding the cable slowly until you feel a breakthrough; then go over the area once again. Remove the cable slowly and run water from a garden hose through the pipe to wash away the root cuttings. Before you return the power auger to the rental firm, replace the clean-out plug and flush a toilet several times. When you're sure the drain is clear of tree roots, clean the cable and return the machine.

Stopping Faucet Drips

A dripping faucet is the most common plumbing problem as well as one of the easiest to repair. Yet many people try to ignore it, and leave the dripping faucet unrepaired. That costs money! A steady drip can waste $50 or more in water in a short time. Multiply that figure by the number of faucet drips in your home, and you can calculate how much of your money is literally going down the drain. The waste from a dripping hot-water faucet is even more because you're also paying to heat the water before it goes down the drain.

What's the solution? A drip is caused by seepage from the water supply. Remember that the water supply enters your house or apartment under pressure. Therefore, there must be a watertight seal holding back the incoming water when the faucet handle is in the OFF position. That seal is usually created by a washer pressed tightly against the faucet seat. Obviously, when the washer or the seat is not functioning properly, a little water can seep through and drip out of the faucet spout. To stop the drip, all you usually have to do is replace the washer or repair the seat.

The first thing to do when fixing a faucet drip is to turn off the water supply. You should be able to turn off the supply at a nearby shutoff; but if your house is not equipped with shutoffs for individual fixtures, you'll have to go to the main shutoff and turn off the entire water supply throughout your home.

Compression-Type Faucets

No matter what the faucet looks like, whether it has separate handles for hot and cold water or just one that operates both hot and cold, it operates according to certain basic principles. Here's how to disassemble a faucet and stop a drip:

Step 1: Shut off the water supply and remove the faucet handle held to the main body of the faucet by unscrewing a tiny screw on the top or at the back of the handle. Some screws are hidden by a metal or plastic button or disc that snaps out or is threaded. Once you get the button out, you'll see the top-mounted handle screw. If necessary, use penetrating oil to help loosen it.

Step 2: Remove the handle and look at the faucet assembly. Remove the packing nut with either a large pair of slip-joint pliers or an adjustable wrench, being careful not to scar the metal. Twist out the stem or spindle by turning it in the same direction you would to turn on the faucet.

Step 3: Remove the screw that holds the washer. Use penetrating oil, if necessary, to loosen the screw. Examine the screw and stem, replacing as needed.

Step 4: Replace the old washer with an exact replace-ment. Washers that *almost* fit will *almost* stop the

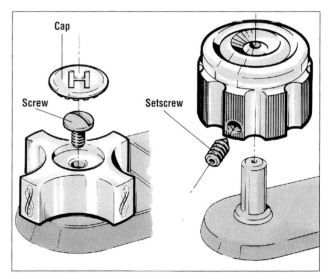

Some faucets are secured by a screw on top, which may be hidden by a snap-out or threaded cap (left); others are secured by a setscrew (right).

drip. Also note whether the old washer is beveled or flat and replace it with one that is identical. Note that washers designed only for cold water expand greatly when they get hot, thereby closing the opening and slowing the flow of hot water. Some washers will work for either, but you should make sure the ones you buy are exact replacements.

Step 5: Fasten the new washer to the stem and reinstall the assembly in the faucet. Turn the stem clockwise. With the stem in place, put the packing nut back on. Be careful not to scar the metal with the wrench.

Step 6: Reinstall the handle and replace the button or disc. Turn the water supply back on and check for leaks.

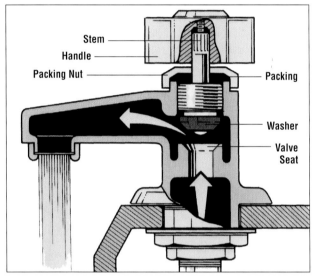

A typical compression-type stem faucet is closed by a washer when the handle is turned. Most leaks are caused by faulty washers.

Other Types of Faucets

Instead of washers, some faucets use rubber diaphragms to control the flow of water. If you have this type of faucet, you may have to remove the faucet stem from the faucet body with a pair of pliers. Be sure to wrap the top of the stem with tape to protect it from the teeth of the pliers. The rubber diaphragm covers the bottom of the stem, and you may have to pry it off with a screwdriver. Make sure the replacement diaphragm fits snugly over the base of the stem before you reassemble the faucet.

Another type of faucet uses a rubber seat ring that acts like a washer. To remove it from the stem, hold the end of the faucet stem with pliers while you unscrew the threaded center piece that holds the seat ring in place.

Remove the sleeve to insert the new seat ring, but be sure the seat ring's lettering faces the threaded part of the stem.

Cartridge-type stem faucets may have a spring and a rubber washer. To replace these, lift the cartridge out of the faucet body and remove the washer and spring. Insert the new spring and washer, and carefully align the cartridge so it fits correctly into the slots in the faucet body when reassembling it.

There are also faucets with washers that have the faucet seat built into the stem itself. This type of assembly lifts off the base in a removable sleeve, which contains the valve seat. Unscrew the stem nut from the base of the stem and remove the metal washer and the washer retainer, which contains a rubber washer. Insert the new washer—bevel side up—into the washer retainer.

One type of faucet doesn't have washers at all. It works by means of two metal discs. Turning the faucet on aligns holes in the discs and allows water to flow through the faucet. If something goes wrong with this type of faucet, the valve assembly usually must be replaced.

Repairing a Faucet Valve Seat

If a faucet still drips after you've replaced a washer, there may be something wrong with the faucet valve seat. A defective washer may have allowed the metal stem to grind against the seat and leave it uneven, or else chemicals in the water may have built up a residue that now prevents the washer from fitting tightly against the valve seat.

What do you do to repair a bad faucet seat? Of course, you can replace the entire faucet. An easier solution, however, would be to use a valve seat grinder, or dresser, an inexpensive tool that will even out a worn seat. But be careful not to use the tool too long or with too much force, because the seat is made of soft metal, and you can grind too much of it away quite easily.

To use this tool, remove the faucet stem and insert the seat grinder down to the valve seat in the faucet body. Using moderate pressure, turn the tool clockwise a few times. Then clean the valve seat with a cloth to remove any metal shavings.

Another option is to replace the seat. Removal of the old valve seat is fairly simple if you have the right tool, called a seat wrench. Insert the seat wrench into the seat and turn it counterclockwise. Once you get the old seat out, be sure the replacement seat you buy is an exact duplicate. If the valve seat is impossible to remove, insert a seat sleeve that slides into place in the old seat and provides a tight seal.

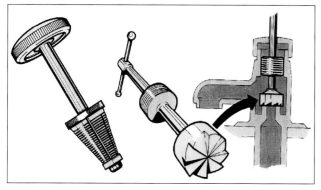

Shown are two types of seat grinders, or dressers, for evening out a worn valve seat.

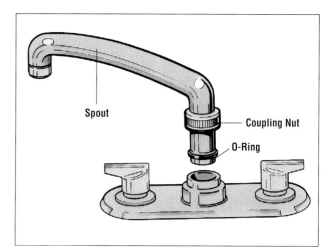

Spout — Coupling Nut — O-Ring

Some kitchen faucets contain one or more O-rings to prevent water from oozing out around the spout. Worn O-rings can be replaced easily.

Stopping Faucet Leaks

A drip occurs when the faucet is turned off; a faucet leak occurs when the water is running. If you see water coming out around the handle, you have a faucet leak.

The first thing to do is make sure the faucet's packing nut is tight, but be careful not to scratch the nut with pliers or a wrench. If you find that a loose nut is not causing the leak, you should replace the packing. Faucet packing can be a solid piece of packing. It can consist of one or more rubber O-rings, or it can resemble string or soft wire wrapped around the stem under the packing nut. To replace the packing:

Step 1: Shut off the water supply and remove the faucet handle.

Step 2: Loosen the packing nut and slip both the nut and the old packing up off the stem.

Step 3: Install the new packing. If you use the stringlike packing material, wrap a few turns around the stem. Packing that resembles soft wire is wrapped around the stem only once. Before you finish reassembling the faucet, smear a light coat of petroleum jelly on the threads of the stem and on the threads of the packing nut.

Kitchen faucets have one or more O-rings to prevent water from oozing out around the spout. If the ring wears out, you'll see water at the base of the spout every time you turn on the water. To replace an O-ring:

Step 1: Shut off the water supply and remove the threaded coupling nut that holds the spout in place by turning it counterclockwise. Be sure to wrap the nut with tape to prevent it from being scratched by pliers or a wrench.

Step 2: With the coupling nut removed, work the spout up and out of its socket, where you will find the ring(s).

Step 3: Replace any defective ring(s) with new rings of the exact same size. Reassemble the faucet.

Single-lever faucets are easy to fix too, but there are so many different types that you must buy a specific repair kit for the faucet you have. Generally, a faucet company makes repair kits for its products and includes detailed instructions and diagrams with the replacement parts. The hardest part of repairing a single-lever faucet may be tracking down the hardware dealer or plumbing-supply store that carries the appropriate kit. Once you have the kit, however, you should have little difficulty eliminating the leak. Make sure the water supply is shut off before disassembling the faucet, and follow the kit's instructions carefully.

Silencing Noisy Faucets

Faucets can scream, whistle, or chatter when you turn them on or off. There are several possible causes for these ear-shattering phenomena. If your house is newly built, you may have pipes that are too small to allow the water to pass through them properly. Similarly, pipes in older homes can become restricted by the formation of scale, indicated by a noisy faucet. In either case, you must replace the pipes to get rid of the noise.

Most likely, however, your noisy faucet is caused by a washer that is either the wrong size or is not held securely to the stem. Turn off the water supply before starting on this or any other faucet repair job. Replacing the washer or tightening it should eliminate the noise. If the faucet still makes noise, check the washer seat. The seat can become partially closed with residue, and the restricted water flow can cause whistling or chattering. If this is the case, clean the seat.

A terrible squealing noise when you turn the faucet handle means that the metal threads of the stem are binding against the faucet's threads. Remove the stem and coat both sets of threads with petroleum jelly. The lubrication should stop the noise and make the handle easier to turn. Of course, if the stem threads or faucet body threads have become worn, the resulting play between them causes vibration and noise in the faucet. In this case, you'll need more than just lubrication to quiet the faucet. Install a new stem and see if the noise stops. If not, the faucet body threads are worn, and the only solution is a completely new faucet. Fortunately, the stem usually wears first. But even if you must replace the entire faucet, the job is fairly easy.

Replacing a Faucet

Replacing a faucet requires a little more work than just changing a washer or putting in a new faucet valve seat. Fortunately, new faucet units are made for do-it-yourself installation, with easy-to-follow instructions included. A new faucet can work wonders for the appearance of your fixtures, and also will eliminate all the leaks, drips, and other problems you may have had with your old faucet.

Make sure whatever unit you choose will cover the old faucet's mounting holes. If you have an unusual sink, look for an adjustable faucet unit that's made to fit many types of sinks. Once you select the faucet model you want, follow these steps to install it properly.

Step 1: Turn off the hot-water and cold-water supplies to the sink faucets.

Step 2: Disconnect the old faucets from their water supply lines under the sink. The connections will probably be threaded compression fittings that are held by locknuts. Loosen the nuts with an adjustable wrench or basin wrench, and disconnect the water supply pipes from the faucets.

Step 3: If the old assembly has a spray head and hose, remove the spray head mounting nut under the sink. Also disconnect the hose from its spout connection.

Step 4: Clean the sink around the faucet mounting area, then remove the old faucet assembly from the sink.

Step 5: Before you install the new faucet, apply plumbers' putty around its base. If gaskets are supplied with the faucet for this purpose, putty is not necessary.

Step 6: If the new faucet has a spray hose, attach the hose. Run the spray hose down through its

opening in the faucet assembly, through its opening in the sink, and up through the sink's center opening. Then attach the hose to the supply stub on the faucet.

Step 7: Install the new faucet assembly into the mounting holes in the sink. With the new faucet assembly in position, place the washers and nuts on the assembly's mounting studs under the sink and hand-tighten them, making sure the assembly is in proper position and any gaskets are correctly aligned. Then further tighten the nuts with a basin wrench.

Step 8: Align the original water supply lines with the flexible supply tubes coming from the new faucet, and connect them with compression couplings. Make sure the hot-water and cold-water lines are connected to the proper supply tubes on the faucet assembly. When you attach the lines, be sure to use two wrenches. One holds the fitting, and the other turns the nut on the water supply line.

Step 9: Turn on the hot-water and cold-water supplies to the fixture. Run both hot and cold water full-

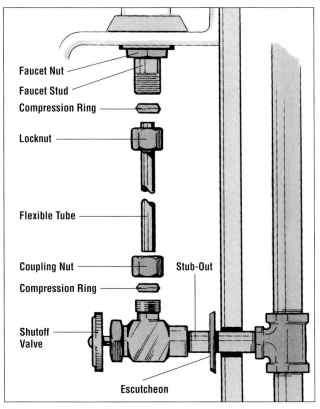

The faucet is secured to the sink by a nut under the basin. The water supply line is usually connected to the faucet with a threaded compression fitting.

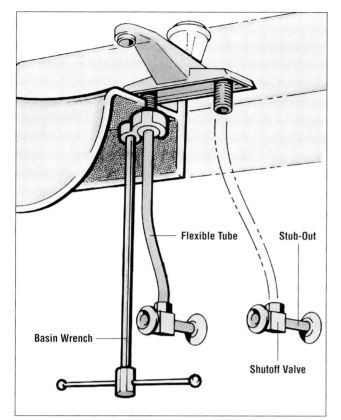

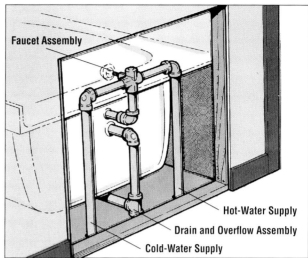

Faucet Assembly

Hot-Water Supply
Drain and Overflow Assembly
Cold-Water Supply

Replacing tub faucets can be complicated because the connections are behind a wall. There may, however, be an access panel so you can reach the connections.

Flexible Tube

Stub-Out

Basin Wrench

Shutoff Valve

Because there is very little room under the sink, you will probably need a basin wrench to tighten the coupling nuts.

force to clear the supply lines and to check the fixture for leaks. If there's any evidence of leakage, go back over the procedure to check for loose or improper connections.

A bathroom lavatory faucet can be replaced using the same procedures. One difference may be the presence of a pop-up drain that's connected by a linkage to a knob or plunger on the old faucet assembly. There should be one or two places in the linkage where it can be easily disconnected from the faucet before removing the original unit from the basin. Instructions provided with the new faucet will tell you exactly how to connect the new drain assembly. Be sure to reconnect the drain linkage when installing the new faucet.

Shower and tub faucets are usually more complicated because the connections are made not under a sink, but behind a wall. There should be an access panel so that you can get at the pipes without ripping the wall apart. If you find that you must cut into the wall, however, be sure to add an access panel for future pipe and faucet repairs.

Once you get to the tub faucet connections behind the wall, the job is no harder than working on your kitchen sink. Shut off the water supply, remove the

faucet handle on the tub side, and then disconnect the old faucet unit from the back. If there's an old shower head pipe, unscrew it from its pipe inside the wall; do the same thing with the tub spout. Now you're ready to install all the new parts. Just follow the directions that are included with the new assembly.

Repairing a Spray Hose

Many modern sink faucets are fitted with spray hose units, and these units occasionally leak or malfunction. The assembly has a diverter valve within the spout body, a flexible hose connected to the spout under the sink, and a spray head with an activating lever and an aerator assembly. The spray head body and lever is a sealed unit, so if it malfunctions or fails, the unit must be replaced with another identical unit. Other parts of the spray system, however, can be repaired.

The aerator portion of the spray head is similar to a regular faucet aerator. If aeration is inadequate or water squirts off at various angles, the aerator screen has become clogged with sediment or mineral deposits, and must be cleaned. To repair an aerator:

Step 1: Remove the aerator and disassemble it.

Step 2: Backflush the screens and the perforated disc with a strong stream of water, being careful not to let the parts get washed down the drain.

Step 3: Dry the parts and brush them gently with a fine-bristled but fairly stiff brush. Mineral deposits can sometimes be removed by soaking the parts in vinegar, or you may be able to scrape the deposits away with a penknife.

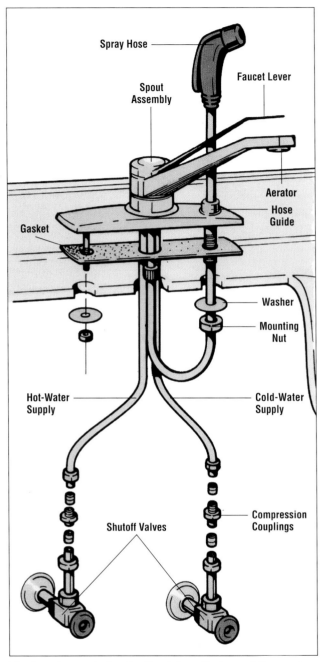

Spray Hose

Spout
Assembly

Faucet Lever

Gasket

Aerator

Hose
Guide

Washer

Mounting
Nut

Hot-Water
Supply

Cold-Water
Supply

Compression
Couplings

Shutoff Valves

The hose is attached under the sink, at the base of the spout assembly. The entire spray assembly can be removed from the top of the sink by unscrewing it and pulling it out through the hose guide.

Step 4: Reassemble the aerator, making sure that you get all of the parts positioned in the proper order and direction.

Water dripping off the flexible hose beneath the sink indicates a leak at the hose-to-spout connection, the hose-to-spray-head connection, or somewhere in the hose itself. To repair the hose:

Step 1: Dry the hose thoroughly and check the head connection. If the leak is at this point, tighten the connection, disassemble and make repairs, or replace the head and hose assembly.

Step 2: Check the spout connection under the sink. Tightening may stop a leak here.

Step 3: If the leak continues, disconnect the hose, apply plumbers' joint compound or wrap plumbers' joint tape around the threads, and reconnect it. The easiest way to spot a leak in the hose is to inspect it inch by inch under a strong light while water is running through it. Look particularly for tiny cracks, chafes, or indications of some mechanical damage. Temporary repairs can be made by wrapping a slightly damaged section of hose with vinyl electrical tape, but replacement of the hose will be necessary eventually.

Uneven water flow, low pressure when the pressure at other faucets seems all right, or troublesome switching back and forth from spray head to sink spout can be caused by a malfunctioning diverter valve or by a restricted hose. To check the diverter valve:

Step 1: Remove the spray head at the coupling and disconnect the coupling from the hose by prying off the snap-ring retainer.

Step 2: Turn on the water and let a strong stream of water flow into the hose. If a strong stream of water flows out of the open end of the hose, then you know the diverter valve is the source of the trouble. A weak stream flowing from the open end of the hose may indicate a blockage in the hose itself. Running the water full-force for a brief time may clear the hose.

Step 3: If the above steps don't locate the problem, remove the hose from the spout attachment, stretch it out straight, and sight through it toward a strong light source. If the hose appears to be clear, the problem lies in the diverter valve. If the hose is blocked, clear it with a wire coat hanger or a length of wire.

Step 4: As needed, replace the hose. If you can't get an exact replacement, adapters are available for connecting other types and sizes.

To service the diverter valve:

Step 1: Remove the sink spout by loosening the screw on top, unscrewing the threaded spout ring or nut, and lifting the spout out of its socket to expose the valve. Some valves are just set in place and can be lifted straight out by gripping them with a pair of pliers; others are secured by a screw. If there is a screw, turn it enough to free the valve. If possible, disassemble the valve.

Step 2: Flush all the parts with water, and clean all the surfaces and apertures with a toothpick. Don't use metal tools, as they could damage the unit.

Step 3: Reassemble and reinstall the valve, then test the unit. If it still operates poorly, you will probably have to replace the valve. The replacement must be exact, so take the faucet manufacturer's name and the unit model number, or the old valve, with you when you buy a new valve.

Fixing a Shower Head

Shower heads are subject to several problems. Leaks can occur where the head connects to the shower arm or at the connection between the shower-head body and the swivel ball. If the arm connection leaks:

Step 1: Unscrew the entire shower head from the pipe, using a pair of strap wrenches if necessary. If you use a different type of wrench, tape the pipe to avoid scratching it.

Step 2: Clean the arm threads and coat them with plumbers' joint compound or a wrap of plumbers' joint tape.

Step 3: Screw the head back on and hand-tighten it. Remove any excess compound or tape.

If the leak is at the swivel:

Step 1: Unscrew the shower-head body from the swivel-ball ring.

Step 2: Find the O-ring or a similar seal inside. Replace it and screw the shower head back into place.

Problems can also be caused by grit or sediment lodged in the head or by a buildup of scale or mineral deposits. The solution is to remove the shower-head body at the swivel ball, take it completely apart, and start cleaning. It may be necessary to soak some parts in vinegar and scrape others, but be careful not to scratch or gouge anything. If the shower head is of the adjustable-spray type, examine all of the moving parts carefully for signs of excessive wear. If the adjustment handle binds or does not work smoothly, or if the internal cam is fouled up, usually the only solution is to replace the entire head.

Replacing a Trap

Directly beneath the drain outlet of every kitchen sink and every bathroom lavatory is the trap. This element is vital not only to the proper functioning of the drainage system, but to your health and safety as well. Each trap contains, and maintains, a plug of water within its curved section that seals against the entrance of harmful sewer gases. If the trap leaks, this water barrier may disappear and create a hazardous situation. All traps must be kept in proper working order and good condition. Restrictions and clogging are immediately noticeable because the drainage flow is slowed or stopped. Clearing the blockage takes care of the problem. Leakage or seepage can often go undetected for a while, so check your traps from time to time and make quick repairs if anything seems wrong.

Trap assemblies have several parts. The short piece of pipe that extends downward from the drain outlet flange in the sink or lavatory is called the tailpiece. The curved section of pipe connected to the tailpiece is the trap itself. The trap may be either one piece or two coupled sections. The piece of pipe extending from the end of the trap to the drainpipe outlet in the wall or floor is the drain extension. All of these pieces may be made of rather thin metal that is subject to corrosion, seal failure, and mechanical damage. Damage can also result from reaming with a plumbers' auger. Whatever the reason for failure, a malfunctioning trap should be repaired immediately.

Sometimes the problem is simply that the slip nuts holding the trap assembly to the drain and the drainpipe have loosened. Tightening them may solve the problem. But if the metal has corroded through, if the slip-nut threads are damaged, or if other damage has occurred, the only solution is replacement. Trap assemblies and parts to fit just about any possible installation requirement are readily available at most hardware and

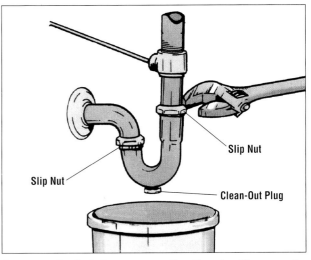

To remove the drain trap, unscrew the slip nuts with a wrench and slide them out of the way.

all plumbing-supply stores. Chrome-plated thin-wall brass traps are popular, especially where appearance is important. Polypropylene (PP) plastic traps, notable for their ruggedness and longevity, will outperform all other types. ABS plastic traps are also in use, but they become deformed and eventually fail when forced to handle frequent passage of boiling water and caustic household chemicals. In addition, they may not be allowed by your local plumbing code.

Whatever the material, there are typically two trap diameters: 1½-inch traps for kitchen sinks, and 1¼-inch traps for lavatories. Take the old trap with you when you buy the new one; if possible, also take the old tailpiece and drain extension. In most cases, trap replacement is simple. Here's how:

Step 1: If the trap is equipped with a clean-out plug on the bottom of the curved section, remove the plug with a wrench and let the water in the trap drain into a bucket. Otherwise, unscrew the slip nuts and slide them out of the way.

Step 2: If the trap is a swivel type, the curved trap section(s) will come free. However, keep the trap upright as you remove it, and pour the water out after the part is free. If the trap is fixed and does not swivel, remove the tailpiece slip nut at the drain flange and the slip nut at the top of the trap, and shove the tailpiece down into the trap itself. Then twist the trap clockwise until you can drain the water in the trap, pull the tailpiece free, and unscrew the trap from the drain extension or drainpipe.

Step 3: Buy a trap of the proper diameter, a new tailpiece, a drain extension, or other fittings as necessary. A swivel trap is the easiest to work with, because it can be easily adjusted for angled or misaligned drainpipe/fixture installations. A clean-out plug on a trap is handy so that the trap can be taken apart for cleaning if necessary.

Step 4: Replace the new parts in appropriate order, making sure you have the slip nuts and compression seals, or large washers, lined up on the proper pipe sections. Couple the parts together loosely with the slip nuts, make the final adjustments for correct pipe alignment, and tighten the nuts down snug, but not too tight. Plumbers' joint compound or tape is not usually necessary, but you can use either.

Step 5: Run water into the new trap immediately, both to check for leaks and to fill the trap with water to provide that important barrier against sewer gases.

Repairing Toilets

The toilet is one of the most important fixtures in your home. Although toilets are sturdy and reliable components of the plumbing system, it's a rare homeowner or apartment-dweller who never has any problems with a toilet. Clogging is perhaps the most common toilet trouble, but it is far from the only one. The tank, for example, can make all sorts of strange noises, or water can run continuously. Fortunately, most toilet troubles can be fixed by a do-it-yourself plumber.

Replacing a Toilet Seat

The easiest toilet repair task is replacing the lid and seat. There are so many styles of replacement seats available that you should have no trouble finding one to match any bathroom color scheme or motif. Most modern toilets are manufactured in two standard sizes, and replacement seats are made to fit them.

Once you have the right size seat, remove the old one. Remove the two nuts on the hinge and lift your old toilet seat up and out. A common problem is that the nuts

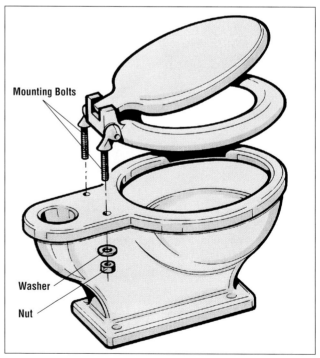

A new toilet seat can be installed by inserting the two bolts, slipping on the washers, and tightening the nuts. Be careful not to overtighten the nuts or the seat might be hard to remove later.

SINK, TUB, AND DRAIN TROUBLESHOOTING CHART

Problem	Possible Cause	Solution
Water in tank runs constantly	1. Float ball or rod is misaligned.	1. Bend float rod carefully to move ball so it will not rub against side of tank.
	2. Float ball contains water.	2. Empty or replace float ball.
	3. Float ball not rising high enough.	3. Carefully bend float rod down, but only slightly.
	4. Tank ball not sealing properly at bottom of tank.	4. Remove any corrosion from lip of valve seat. Replace tank ball if worn. Adjust lift wire and guide.
	5. Ballcock valve does not shut off water.	5. Replace washers in ballcock assembly or, if necessary, replace entire assembly.
Toilet does not flush or flushes inadequately	1. Drain is clogged.	1. Remove blockage in drain.
	2. Not enough water in tank.	2. Raise water level in tank by bending float rod up slightly.
	3. Tank ball falls back before enough water leaves tank.	3. Move guide up so tank ball can rise higher.
	4. Leak where tank joins toilet bowl.	4. Tighten nuts on spud pipe; replace spud washers, if necessary.
	5. Ports around bowl rim clogged.	5. Ream out residue from ports.
Tank whines while filling	1. Ballcock valve not operating properly.	1. Replace washers or install new ballcock assembly.
	2. Water supply is restricted.	2. Check shutoff to make sure it's completely open. Check for scale or corrosion at entry into tank and on valve.
Moisture around fixture	1. Condensation.	1. Install foam liner, tank cover, drip catcher, or temperature valve.
	2. Leak at flange wax seal.	2. Remove toilet and install new wax ring seal.
	3. Leak at bowl-tank connection.	3. Tighten spud pipe nuts; replace worn spud washers, if necessary.
	4. Leak at water inlet connection.	4. Tighten locknut and coupling nut; replace washers and gasket, if necessary.
	5. Crack in bowl or tank.	5. Replace bowl, tank, or entire fixture.

securing the toilet seat may be rusted or corroded. The nuts on some toilet seats are recessed and practically inaccessible, making the job even more difficult.

What's the solution? If you can get to the fasteners relatively easily, apply some penetrating oil to help loosen them. Give the oil plenty of time to soak in. Use a wrench, or, if you can't reach the nuts with a regular wrench, a deep socket wrench. Be sure you don't use too much force; if the wrench slips off a stubborn nut, it could strike and crack the tank or the bowl or anything else it happens to hit.

If all else fails, you'll have to cut off the bolts with a hacksaw. To protect the bowl's finish, apply tape to the bowl at the spots the hacksaw blade is likely to rub against. Then insert the blade under the hinge, and saw through the bolts. Be extremely cautious in using the saw—a careless slip with a hacksaw can crack the fixture just as easily as a blow with a wrench.

With the nuts removed or the bolts cut, you can remove the old seat without further difficulty. Clean the area before installing the new seat. The new one can be installed by inserting the bolts and tightening the nuts.

Be careful not to overtighten the nuts, as you may want to replace this seat someday as well. If you live in a rented apartment and install a new seat that you paid for yourself, be sure to keep the old one. When you're ready to leave, you can replace the new one with the original and take the new seat with you.

If the toilet lid and seat are still in good condition, but the small rubber bumpers on the bottom are in bad shape, you can buy replacement bumpers at the hardware store. Some bumpers screw in; others must be nailed or glued into place. Whichever type you have, try to install the new ones in holes that are close enough to conceal the original holes.

Clearing a Clogged Toilet

You can generally clear a clogged toilet with a plunger, otherwise known as the plumbers' friend. Make sure that there's enough water in the toilet bowl to cover the rubber suction cup, then work the handle of the plunger up and down. If there isn't enough water in the bowl, do *not* flush the toilet; flushing a clogged toilet will just cause the bowl to overflow. Instead, bring a pan or pot of water from another source to supply the water you need to cover the plunger cup. There are two types of plungers, and the one with a bulb-type head is especially effective for toilets. Some types have a fold-out head that's designed for toilet use.

Usually, whatever is blocking the toilet drain is not very far away. If the plunger's action doesn't dislodge the clog, you can try to hook the blockage and pull it free. A wire coat hanger can sometimes do the job, but it is really a substitute for the closet or toilet auger. The

auger, discussed on page 237 of this chapter, has a long sleeve or tube to guide the snake and auger hook into the trap. A crank on the end enables you to turn the hook in the drain or trap. Here's how to use it:

Step 1: Insert the auger into the toilet trap and turn the crank until it feels tight. This means that the snake has twisted its way to and into the blockage.

Step 2: When you pull in the auger, you should be able to remove whatever is clogging the toilet. If you aren't successful, try the closet auger several more times. In some cases, you may have to resort to pushing a regular plumbers' snake through the blockage.

Step 3: When all else fails, the toilet may have to be removed from the floor and turned upside down so you can get at the blockage. This is not what anyone would call an easy job, so you should give the simpler methods as good a try as you can before you remove the toilet. But removing the toilet is not beyond the capabilities of the average do-it-yourselfer, and this procedure is explained in the forthcoming section "Replacing a Toilet," found on page 252.

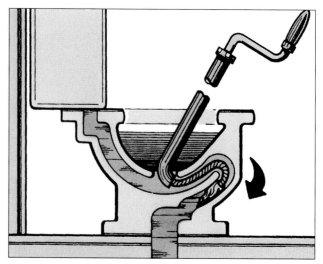

The closet auger has a long sleeve to guide the snake and auger hook into the trap. A crank enables you to turn the hook and dislodge the blockage.

Toilet Tank Problems

Compared with a clogged toilet, tank troubles can seem relatively insignificant. Yet strange noises or continuous water running can be more than annoying. They can also be costing you money in wasted water. Fortunately, you can eliminate most tank troubles quickly and easily.

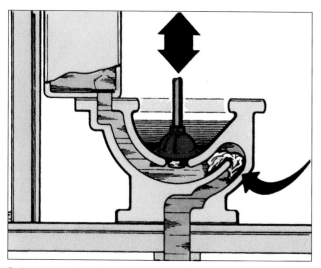

Before using the plunger, make sure there's enough water in the toilet bowl to cover the suction cup. Pump the plunger to dislodge the clog.

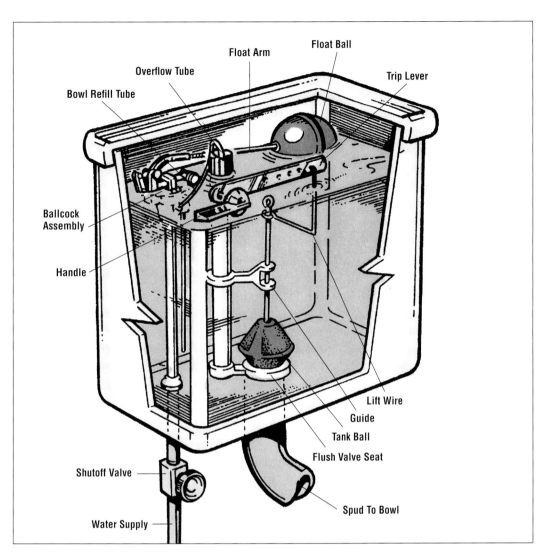

Float Arm

Float Ball

Overflow Tube

Trip Lever

Bowl Refill Tube

Ballcock Assembly

Handle

Lift Wire

Guide

Tank Ball

Flush Valve Seat

Shutoff Valve

Spud To Bowl

Water Supply

Toilet tank troubles are both common and annoying, and they could be costing you money in wasted water. Most problems, however, can be eliminated quickly and easily. This is a cross section of a typical toilet tank and its components.

Once you know how the toilet works, you can start to look for the source of toilet tank problems. Lift the lid off your toilet tank, and you should be able to follow this procedure quite easily.

When you trip the handle on the tank to flush the toilet, a trip lever is raised inside the tank. This lever lifts wires, which, in turn, raise the tank ball or rubber flap at the bottom of the tank. When the flush valve opening is clear, the water in the tank rushes out past the raised tank ball and into the toilet bowl below. This raises the level of water in the bowl above the level of water in the toilet trap.

While the water is rushing out of the tank, the float ball, which floats on top of the water in the tank, drops down. This pulls down on the float arm, raising the valve plunger in the ballcock assembly and allowing fresh water to flow into the tank. Since water seeks its own level, the water from the tank pushes the bowl water out into the drain, causing a siphoning action that

cleans everything out of the bowl. When all the water is gone from the toilet bowl and air is drawn into the trap, the siphoning stops. Meanwhile, the tank ball falls back into place, closing the flush valve opening.

As the water level rises in the tank, the float ball rises until the float arm is high enough to lower the valve plunger in the ballcock assembly and shut off the incoming water. If the water fails to shut off, there is an overflow tube that carries excess water down into the bowl to prevent the tank from overflowing. If water flows continuously out of the tank to the bowl and down the drain:

Step 1: Lift up on the float arm. If the water stops, you know the problem is that the float ball doesn't rise far enough to lower the valve plunger in the ballcock assembly. One reason could be that the float ball is rubbing against the side of the tank. If this is the case, bend the float arm slightly to move the ball away from the tank side.

249

over the water inlet pipe under the tank in this order: coupling nut, friction washer, cone washer, and retaining or mounting nut.

Step 3: Install the new unit inside the tank, fitting the threaded shank down through the hole over the water supply pipe and making sure the gasket fits into the hole. Start tightening the retaining or mounting nut under the tank onto the threaded shank; hand-tighten it only. Push the washers into place and hand-tighten the coupling nut under the tank; be careful not to overtighten it.

Step 4: Inside the tank, attach one end of the refill tube to the tank's overflow pipe and place the other end on the stem of the replacement unit.

Step 5: Open the water supply valve to fill the tank. The water level in the tank can be adjusted by a knob on the new valve unit.

Solving Common Toilet Problems

What can you do if too little water comes from the tank to flush the toilet bowl clean?

Step 1: Check the water level in the tank. It's probably too low. If the water level doesn't reach within 1½ inches of the top of the overflow tube, bend the float arm up slightly to let more water enter the tank.

Step 2: If the water level is correct but there's still not enough water coming from the tank to clean the bowl properly, the problem may be the tank ball on the flush valve seat at the bottom of the tank. The ball is probably dropping too soon because the guide is set too low. Raise the guide, but make sure it stays in line with the lift wire. If the guide and the wire are out of alignment, the tank ball will not drop straight into the valve seat opening, and the toilet will run continuously.

Step 3: Look for other causes of inadequate flushing. The small ports around the underside of the toilet bowl's rim can get clogged with residue from chemicals in the water and prevent a sufficient amount of tank water from running out into the bowl. A small mirror can help you examine the holes, and a piece of wire coat hanger or an offset Phillips screwdriver—if one is available—can ream out any clogged debris.

Here's another common problem among toilets. Toilet tanks can sweat and drip onto your floors just as pipes can. There are jackets designed specifically to fit

over the tank and absorb the moisture. There are also drip pans that fit under the tank to catch the dripping condensation so that it doesn't damage your bathroom floor. A device called a temperator valve is another way to combat tank sweating. The valve provides a regulated mixture of hot and cold water, which lessens the difference between the temperature inside the tank and the temperature of the surrounding air. It is this difference in temperature that causes condensation, or sweating. Consider installing a temperator valve if the water in the tank is usually below 50°F.

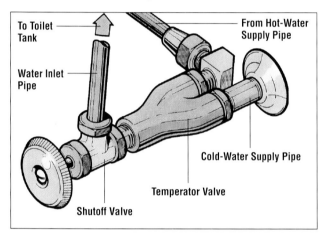

The temperator valve, which requires both hot-water and cold-water supply connections, can reduce toilet tank sweating.

A temperator valve requires you to hook up a hot-water line to the valve, which may be quite inconvenient if there is no such line relatively close to the toilet. Moreover, the temperator valve does not prevent the water inside the tank from cooling between flushings; thus, condensation can still occur even on a temperator-equipped toilet.

A leak may be due to loose connections or defective washers on the spud pipe or where the water inlet pipe and ballcock assembly are attached to the tank. Replace any worn gaskets or washers and tighten all of the nuts, then test with bluing in the water.

It is also possible that water is seeping out from *under* the toilet bowl. The wax ring seal that joins the bowl to the drain outlet may be defective. If this is the case, the bowl must be removed, and a new gasket installed. If the leak is due to a crack in the tank or bowl, the whole toilet must be replaced.

Replacing a Toilet

Removing and replacing a toilet is not a task to be undertaken without good reason, but it is certainly not beyond your capabilities. When you can't unclog the toilet by less drastic means, removing it is the answer.

Maybe you want a more modern toilet, maybe the bowl or the tank is cracked, or maybe the fixture leaks around its base. All of these situations call for removing and reinstalling the old toilet or installing a new fixture.

Although there's nothing difficult about removing and replacing a toilet, local plumbing code may prohibit anyone but a licensed plumber from doing the job. Check the code for your community to make sure it is okay for you to undertake the task. To replace a toilet:

Step 1: Measure the rough-in distance—the distance from the wall behind the bowl to the center of the toilet floor drain. Measure from the wall to the center of either of the two hold-down bolts, one on each side of the toilet, that hold the fixture to the floor. If there are two bolts on each side, measure to the center of the rear bolt.

Step 2: Select the replacement toilet unit using the rough-in distance so that it will fit properly in your bathroom. You can replace your old toilet with a more modern fixture, but you must make sure that the new unit will fit into the space between the drainpipe and the wall. You can install a smaller unit, but you cannot put a larger toilet into a space that was occupied by a smaller fixture.

Step 3: Shut off the water supply to the toilet tank, then remove all the water from both the tank and the bowl. Trip the flush handle to eliminate most of the water from the tank. Then soak up whatever water is left with a sponge. Bail out the water in the bowl with a small container, and then use a sponge to dry out the bowl completely.

Step 4: If the tank is connected to the wall, remove the hanger bolts inside the tank that secure the tank to the wall. Then remove the pair of bolts at the bottom of the tank that connect the tank to the bowl. Remove the tank and set it out of the way.

Step 5: Remove the caps over the hold-down bolts at the base of the bowl if there are any. Most of these caps are made of ceramic to match the bowl. Some types are held on by plumbers' joint compound and can be pried off with a putty knife; others are threaded and can be unscrewed. After removing the caps, brush away the dried compound before proceeding.

Step 6: Remove the hold-down nuts or bolts. These may be extremely stubborn, but some penetrating oil should make removal much easier. Save the washers and bolts if you will be reinstalling the bowl. Once the hold-down nuts or bolts are out, there's nothing else holding the bowl to the floor. *Caution: To prevent sewer gas from backing up the drain, you should plug the opening while you work. Tie a cord around an old towel so it won't fall through the opening, and jam this plug into the drain.*

Step 7: Remove the bowl. Because the bowl and the tank can crack from just one sharp blow to the porcelain, spread out an old piece of carpeting on which you can lay the fixtures. You should also have a bucket and sponge handy to soak up the water you couldn't bail out earlier. With your work surface prepared, rock the bowl gently back and forth to loosen it, and then lift it straight up. It weighs about 60 or 70 pounds. Set the bowl on the piece of carpeting.

Step 8: Inspect the uncovered drain. If necessary, clear the drain, as detailed in the section "Clearing Clogged Drains" beginning on page 235. Once the pipe is clear, you can proceed with the replacement of the toilet.

Step 9: Putting in a new toilet and reinstalling the old one are done in the same way. With a putty knife, scrape away all the old putty or other

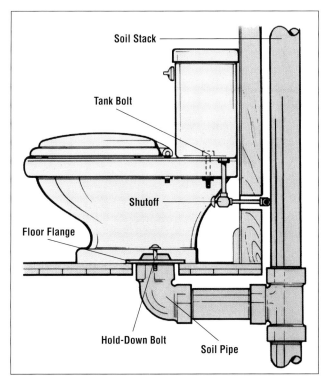

Typical installation of a two-piece floor-mounted toilet.

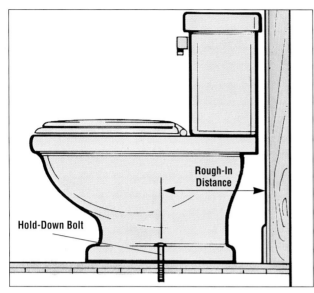

The rough-in distance can be measured with the toilet in place by measuring from the wall to the center of the hold-down bolt, or to the center of the rear bolt if the fixture is held by two pairs of bolts.

sealing material from both the bottom of the bowl and the floor flange. Inspect the floor where the toilet was. If the floor has rotted, it will have to be rebuilt before the toilet can be installed. Depending on how bad the damage is, the rebuilding may involve the floor, the subfloor, and even the joists. In this case, have a carpenter rebuild the damaged area before you install the toilet. Also inspect the flange and the bolts that come up from the flange. If the flange is damaged or the bolts are stripped, replace the faulty part or parts before you go any further.

Step 10: Install a new sealer ring on the water outlet opening on the bottom of the new bowl. With the fixture upside down, set the sealer ring into place on the bottom of the bowl. If the floor flange is recessed, you'll need a gasket with a plastic sleeve in the ring. This sleeve should face toward you as you position it, since it will go into the soil pipe.

Step 11: Apply a uniform layer of toilet-bowl setting compound about ⅛ inch thick around the edge of the bowl at the base. This compound is available at hardware stores and plumbing-supply stores.

Step 12: Remove the plug from the drain or soil pipe. Turn the bowl right side up and place it down over the flange, guiding the bolts into place. Press down firmly, and give the bowl a slight twist to make sure the wax ring seats properly against the flange. Place a level across the bowl to make sure that it is level. Move the bowl as needed to level it, but don't disturb or break the seal of the wax ring or the toilet will leak.

Step 13: Hand-tighten the nuts to hold the bowl to the floor. Do not overtighten the nuts, or else the fixture may crack. Coat the hold-down nuts and bolts with toilet bowl setting compound and reinstall the caps.

Step 14: If the tank and bowl are separate fixtures, you should now attach the tank. Rebolt a wall-mounted tank, or reinstall the bolts and washers that connect a bowl-supported tank. Replace any damaged parts. If the tank and bowl are connected with a spud pipe, apply pipe joint compound to the threads of the spud slip nuts and tighten them in place.

Step 15: Reconnect the water supply inlet pipe to the tank, make sure the ballcock assembly is properly attached, and turn the water back on.

Solving Pipe Problems

Most plumbing problems occur at or near fixtures such as sinks, tubs, and toilets. Less often the pipes themselves can leak, sweat, freeze, or bang. Here's how to deal with these difficulties.

Stopping Leaks in Pipes and Joints

There are all kinds of plumbing leaks. Some can flood your home, while others are not nearly so damaging. Your approach to stopping a leak depends on the type of leak it happens to be.

If the leak is at a joint, tighten or remake the joint. If the leak is in a pipe, remove the section that is leaking and replace it with a new section. Unfortunately, this is more easily said than done. When you turn a threaded galvanized steel pipe, for instance, to unscrew it from its fitting at one end, you tighten the pipe into its fitting at the other end. With copper pipe, the new section must be sweat-soldered in place. Most pipe replacement jobs are best left to a plumber, but as a do-it-yourselfer you may consider an alternative: the pipe patch.

You'll find patch kits for plumbing leaks at the hardware store, or you can make your own with a piece

PIPE TROUBLESHOOTING CHART		
Problem	**Possible Cause**	**Solution**
Leaking pipe	1. Joint not watertight.	1. Tighten threaded joint, if possible. Apply epoxy paste to joint. Have a plumber disassemble and resolder sweat-soldered joint in copper pipe or tubing or cut out and replace joint in plastic pipe.
	2. Hole in pipe.	2. Repair by patching hole, using best available method, or replace section of pipe. If section is inaccessible, a plumber can disconnect it from system and route new section of pipe.
	3. Burst pipe.	3. Immediately turn off water at main shutoff. Repair or replace pipe or joint. Avoid electrical shock due to contact between electrical devices or equipment and water.
Pipe drips, but there is no leak	1. Condensation.	1. Apply insulation to pipe.
Noise in pipes—hot water only	1. Steam causing rumbling in hot-water pipes.	1. Turn down thermostat setting on water heater or replace thermostat.
	2. Pipe creaks against surroundings from expansion and contraction.	2. Rehang pipe on slip hangers or in larger notches or holes.
Water makes sucking noise when draining	1. Improper venting.	1. Clean roof vent. If there is no vent, add antisiphon trap.
Hammering noise when water is shut off	1. Air chambers waterlogged.	1. Shut off and drain supply line to allow air to reenter air chambers.
	2. No air chamber.	2. Install air chamber.
Banging noise while water is running	1. Loose pipe.	1. Track down loose pipe and brace, cushion, or strap it.
No water supply	1. Frozen pipes.	1. Open faucets. Start at closest point to faucet and work back.
	2. Main shutoff valve closed.	2. Open main shutoff valve.
	3. Broken or closed main.	3. Call water department.
	4. Well pump failure.	4. Check and repair pump.

of heavy rubber from an old inner tube and a C-clamp. Another possibility is to use a hose clamp with the rubber patch. Factory-made kits contain a rubber pad that goes over the hole in the pipe and metal plates that compress the rubber pad over the hole. A quick and easy way to stop a leak, the patch kit can even be used on a permanent basis if the pipe is otherwise sound.

Other quick and easy temporary measures for stopping pipe leaks include wrapping waterproof tape over the bad spot and rubbing the hole with a stick of special compound. Applying epoxy paste to the leak or inserting a self-tapping plug into the hole are other alternatives. When using waterproof tape, be sure to dry the pipe thoroughly before you start wrapping. Start the tape about two to three inches from the hole and extend it the same distance beyond. For tiny leaks in pipes, use a compound stick available at most hardware stores. Simply rub the stick over the hole to stop the leak. It can even stop small leaks while the water is still running in the pipe. Epoxy paste can be applied only to dry pipes, and the water must be turned off.

The problem with all of these solutions is that a pipe that's bad enough to spring one leak often starts leaking in other places too. You may fix one spot only to see the

In a basement or crawl space, galvanized steel pipes are typically suspended from the joists by perforated pipe straps. A long run of suspended pipe may move within the straps, strike against something, and create a racket. A block of wood strategically wedged along the run can eliminate the pipe's movement and the resulting noise. If you secure a pipe, don't anchor it so tightly that it can't expand and contract with changes in temperature. If you place a bracket on a pipe, install a rubber buffer between the pipe and the bracket. You can make such buffers from garden hose, foam rubber, rubber cut from old inner tubes, or even kitchen sponges.

You may find that supply pipes and drainpipes that run right next to each other are striking one another and creating a clatter. One solution to this problem is to solder the two pipes together. Another solution is to wedge a piece of rubber between them. If the vibration and noises are caused by water pressure that's too high, try reducing the water pressure.

If the knocking sound occurs only when you turn on the hot water, it means that the water heater is set too high. The noise is steam rumbling through the hot-water system. Turning the heat setting down may silence the pipes.

A pipe that's too small to begin with, or that has become clogged with scale or mineral deposits, can be a big noise problem. It's almost impossible to clean clogged supply pipes, and you must replace pipe that's too small if you want to stop the noise. You can diminish the sound level of clogged pipes considerably by wrapping them with sound-damping insulation.

Drainpipes rarely clatter, but they can make a sucking noise as the water leaves the sink or basin. This sound means that a vent is restricted, or perhaps that there's no vent at all attached to the drain. In either case, you have a potentially serious plumbing problem on your hands because a nonfunctioning or nonexistent vent can eliminate the water seal and allow sewer gas to back up into your home. If possible, run a plumbers' snake through the vent from the fixture or from the roof vent to eliminate any clogging. If there is no vent on the drain, install an antisiphon trap to quiet the noise and to prevent any problem with sewer gas. An antisiphon trap is available at a hardware or plumbing-supply store.

Water Hammer

Water hammer is a specific plumbing noise, not a generic name for pipe clatter. It occurs when you shut off the water suddenly, and the fast-moving water rushing through the pipe is brought to a quick halt, creating a sort of shock wave and a hammering noise. Plumbing that's properly installed has air chambers, or

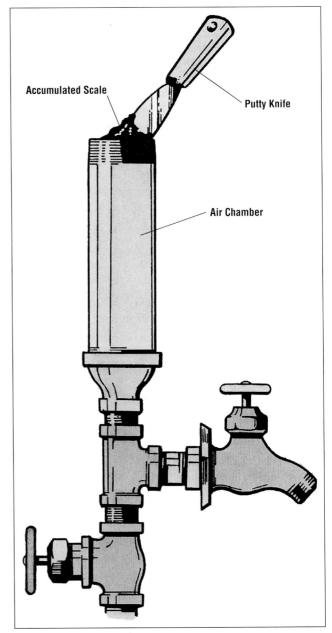

An air chamber will not drain properly if it is clogged. Remove its cap and ream out the accumulated scale inside the chamber.

"cushions," that compress when the shock wave hits, softening the blow and preventing this hammering. The chambers can fail, though, because water under pressure gradually absorbs the air. If you formerly experienced no hammering and then it suddenly starts, most likely your plumbing system's air chambers have become waterlogged.

You can cure water hammer by turning off the water behind the waterlogged chamber, opening the offending faucet, and permitting the faucet to drain thoroughly.

Once all the water drains from the chamber, air will fill it again and restore the cushion. If the air chamber is located below the outlet, you may have to drain the main supply lines to allow the chamber to fill with air again.

The air chamber will not drain properly if it's clogged with scale or residue from chemicals or minerals in the water. The chamber always should be larger than the supply pipe to preclude such clogging. Since the chamber is simply a capped length of pipe, however, all you have to do to clear it is remove the cap and ream out the scale.

What do you do if there are no air chambers built into your plumbing system? You must do something, because water hammer pressures may eventually cause damage—failure of fittings or burst pipes. Because water hammer is most often caused by water pressure that's too high, the first step is to reduce the water pressure if possible. Sometimes this isn't feasible, because a reduction in pressure may result in only a dribble of water at an upper-floor faucet if one on the first floor is turned on. Where the idea is a workable one, you can reduce pressure by installing a pressure-reducing valve in the supply line that comes into the house. The same purpose is served by installing a globe valve at the head of the affected pipeline. But this too may result in pressure too low for proper operation when other faucets are open.

If pressure reduction is not feasible or is ineffective, install the necessary air chambers to prevent water hammer. If you have no room to make the installation without tearing into a wall, go to a plumbing-supply dealer and find out about the substitute devices that are designed for such problem areas. Many of these devices have a valve that makes it easy for air to reenter the system.

CHAPTER 8

HEATING AND COOLING SYSTEMS

Most of us take heating and cooling for granted. We expect our heating systems to keep us warm during the winter, and we depend on air conditioning to keep us cool during the summer. When the house is cold in winter or hot in summer, the natural reaction is to call for professional service. Fortunately, there is an alternative. You can cut service costs drastically and keep your heating and cooling systems working efficiently by doing maintenance and simple repairs yourself.

Heating and cooling systems can be intimidating, but they are based on simple, easily understood principles. Adjustments can often be made without much difficulty, and if you take care of your furnace and air conditioner properly, they'll reward you with dependable service.

Realize, too, that there's more to heating and cooling than just the machines that heat or cool a home and the network of ducts or pipes that distribute heating and cooling energy. Almost as important are the components that conserve this energy, most notably weather stripping and insulation. The latter part of this chapter tells how you can evaluate and, if necessary, upgrade these vital elements.

How Heating and Cooling Systems Work

• •

All climate-control devices or systems have three basic components: a source of warmed or cooled air, a means of distributing the air to the rooms being heated or cooled, and a control used to regulate the system (thermostat). The sources of warm air (furnace) and cool air (air conditioner) in a house often use the same distribution and control systems. If your house has central air conditioning, cool air probably flows through the same ducts that heat does and is regulated by the same thermostat. When a heating or cooling system malfunctions, any of these three basic components may be causing the problem.

Both heating and air conditioning work on the principle that heat always moves from a warm object to a cooler one, just as water flows from a higher to a lower

level. Furnaces and heaters put heat into the air to make your home warmer; air conditioners remove heat to make your home cooler.

All heating and cooling units burn fuel. Air conditioners use electricity. Some of the most popular home heating systems use natural gas or fuel oil; other systems use electricity. The heat pump—an electrically powered climate control unit—both heats and cools air. In summer it extracts heat from the air inside your home; in winter it extracts heat from the air outside and uses this heat to warm the air inside.

When the furnace is turned on, it consumes the fuel that powers it: gas, oil, or electricity. As fuel is consumed, heat is produced and channeled to the rooms and living areas of your home through ducts, pipes, or wires, and it is blown out of registers, radiators, or heating panels. Some systems use the heat they produce to heat water, which in turn heats the air in your home. These systems use a boiler to store and heat the water supply, which is then circulated as steam or water through pipes embedded in the wall, floor, or ceiling, or connected to radiators.

When an air conditioner is turned on, electrical power is used to cool a gas in a coil to its liquid state. Warm air in your home is cooled by contact with the cooling coil, and this cooled air is channeled to the rooms of your home through ducts and out registers, or—in the case of room air conditioners—directly from the unit itself.

Heating and cooling system sources are discussed in more detail later in this chapter (see page 264).

Distribution Systems

Once air is warmed or cooled at the heat/cold source, it must be distributed to the various rooms of your home. This can be accomplished with forced-air, gravity, or radiant heating systems.

Forced-Air Systems

A forced-air system distributes the heat produced by the furnace or the coolness produced by a central air conditioner. It does so by means of an electrically powered fan, called a blower, which forces the air through a system of metal ducts to the rooms in your home. As the warm air from the furnace flows into the rooms, colder air in the rooms flows down through another set of ducts, called the cold-air return system, to the furnace to be warmed. This system is adjustable: You can increase or decrease the amount of air flowing

through your home. Central air conditioning systems use the same forced-air system, including the blower, to distribute cool air to the rooms and to bring warmer air back to be cooled.

Problems with forced-air systems usually involve blower malfunctions. The blower may also be noisy, and it adds the cost of electrical power to the cost of furnace fuel. But because it employs a blower, a forced-air system is an effective way to channel airborne heat or cool air throughout a house.

Gravity Systems

Gravity systems are based on the principle that hot air rises and cold air sinks. Gravity systems, therefore, cannot be used to distribute cool air from an air conditioner. In a gravity system, the furnace is located near or below the floor. The warmed air rises and flows through ducts to registers in the floor throughout the house. If the furnace is located on the main floor of the house, the heat registers are usually positioned high on the walls, because the registers must always be higher than the furnace. The warmed air rises toward the ceiling. As the air cools, it sinks, enters the return air ducts, and flows back to the furnace to be reheated.

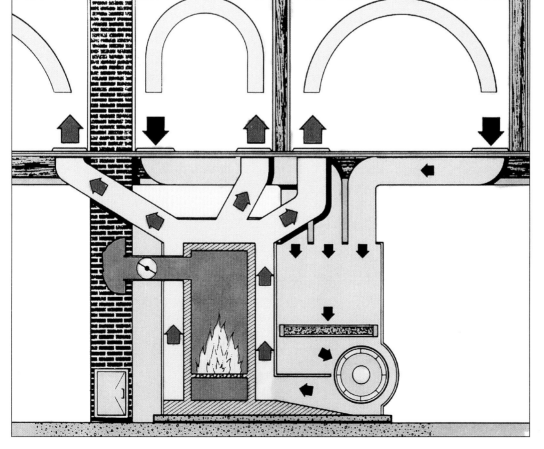

Forced-air heating systems use a fan to move warm air.

A gravity system relies on warm air rising naturally.

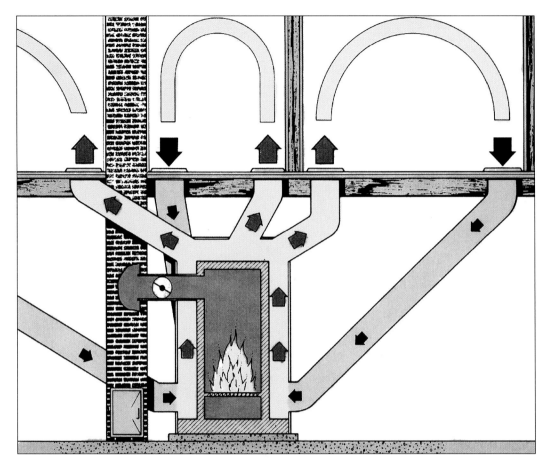

The big advantage to gravity heating is that it uses no mechanical distribution device. The furnace needs no blower to circulate the heat. Gravity systems use no electric current, and the movement of the heated air is silent. There are disadvantages, though. Gravity-moved air doesn't move with much force and thus cannot usually be filtered. The gravity system doesn't work well if the heated air must travel long distances, and the slow movement of the heated air allows for greater heat loss before the air reaches the rooms of your home. Gravity heating systems are not adjustable and cannot warm a home as evenly as most forced-air systems.

Some wall heaters are of the gravity type, with a return air vent at the bottom and a vent for the hot air to go out at the top. These units are used in warmer climates, where heating demands are not extreme.

Radiant Heating

Radiant systems function by warming the walls, floors, or ceilings of rooms, or, more commonly, by warming radiators or convectors in the rooms. These objects then warm the air in the room. The heat source is usually hot water, heated by the furnace and circulated as steam or water through pipes embedded in the wall, floor, or

ceiling, or connected to radiators. Some systems use electric heating panels to generate heat, which is radiated into rooms. Like gravity wall heaters, these panels are usually installed in warm climates. Radiant systems cannot be used to distribute cool air from an air conditioner.

Radiators and convectors, the most common means of radiant heat distribution in older homes, are used with steam and hot-water heating systems. Steam systems depend on gravity; steam rises into the radiators. Hot-water systems may depend on gravity or on a circulator pump to circulate heated water from the boiler to the radiators or convectors. A system that uses a pump, or circulator, is called a hydronic system.

Modern radiant heating systems are often built into houses constructed on a concrete slab foundation. A network of hot-water pipes is laid under the surface of the concrete slab. When the concrete is warmed by the pipes, it warms the air that contacts the floor surface. The slab need not get very hot; it will eventually contact and heat the air throughout the house.

Radiant systems—especially gravity systems—are prone to several problems. The pipes used to distribute the heated water can become clogged with mineral

A radiant heating system functions by warming walls, floors, or ceilings, which then warm the surrounding air.

deposits, or they may become slanted at the wrong angle. The boiler, in which water is heated at the heat source, may also malfunction. Steam and hot-water systems are seldom installed in new homes.

Controls

The thermostat, a heat-sensitive switch, is the basic control that regulates the temperature of your home. It responds to changes in the temperature of the air where it is located and turns the furnace or air conditioner on or off as needed to maintain the temperature at a set level, called the set point. The key component of the thermostat is a bimetallic element that expands or

The thermostat regulates the temperature of your home. The key component in older systems is a bimetallic element that expands or contracts as the temperature changes. Newer systems use solid-state sensors.

contracts as the temperature increases or decreases in the house.

Older thermostats have two exposed contacts. As the temperature drops, a bimetallic strip bends, making first one electrical contact and then another. The system is fully activated when the second contact closes, turning on the heating system and the anticipator on the thermostat. The anticipator heats the bimetallic element, causing it to bend and break the second electrical contact. The first contact is not yet broken, however, and the heater keeps running until the temperature rises above the setting on the thermostat.

More modern thermostats have coiled bimetallic strip elements, and the contacts are sealed behind glass to protect them from dirt. As the temperature drops, the bimetallic elements start to uncoil. The force exerted by the uncoiling of the elements separates a stationary steel bar from a magnet at the end of the coil. The magnet comes down close to the glass-enclosed contact, pulls up on the contact arm inside the tube, and causes the contacts to close, completing the electrical circuit and turning on the heater and the anticipator. As the air in the room heats up, the coil starts to rewind and breaks the hold of the magnet on the contact arm. The arm drops, breaks the circuit, and turns off the system. At this point, the magnet moves back up to the stationary bar, keeping the contacts open and the heater turned off until the room cools down again.

The latest heat and air conditioning controls use solid-state electronics for controlling the air temperature. They are typically more accurate and more responsive than older systems. However, repair to solid-state controls usually means replacement.

Maintenance Procedures

Heating and cooling systems are relatively trouble-free and easy to maintain. Efficient operation is a function of good regular maintenance. No matter what type of system you have, there are several things you can do to keep it in top condition. You'll need a few tools and materials: screwdrivers, flashlight, pliers, wrenches, hammer, level, newspaper, rags, brushes, and a vacuum cleaner. A few specialized materials are required: motor oil, fan-belt dressing, refractory cement, and duct tape. These materials are available at hardware stores and at some home-improvement centers.

HEATING AND COOLING SYSTEMS

When a heating or cooling system malfunctions, any one of its three components—heat/cold source, distribution system, or thermostat—may be causing the problem. If the furnace or air conditioner doesn't run, the malfunction is probably at the source. The furnace or air conditioner may have lost power. Fuel may not be reaching the unit. If the fuel is gas or oil, it may not be igniting. If the furnace or air conditioner turns on but the warm or cool air isn't reaching the rooms of your home, the problem is likely to be the blower or the distribution system. And a faulty control, or thermostat, could keep the system from turning on or could cause it to turn on and off repeatedly. Whatever the problem, start with the simplest procedures. In most cases, all it takes is patience and commonsense.

Before you start work on a heating or cooling system, take these preliminary steps:

- Check to make sure the unit is receiving power. Look for blown fuses or tripped circuit breakers at the main entrance panel. Some furnaces have a separate power entrance, usually located at a different panel near the main entrance panel. Some furnaces have fuses mounted in or on the unit.
- If the unit has a reset button, marked RESET, near the motor housing, wait 30 minutes to let the motor cool, then press the button. If the unit still doesn't start, wait 30 minutes and press the reset button again. Repeat at least once more.
- If the unit has a separate power switch, make sure the switch is turned on.
- Check to make sure the thermostat is properly set. If necessary, raise (or, for an air conditioner, lower) the setting five degrees.
- If the unit uses gas, check to make sure the gas supply is turned on. If the unit uses oil, check to make sure there is an adequate supply of oil.
- If the unit uses gas, make sure the pilot light is lit.

There are also several important safety factors to remember:

- Before doing any work on any type of heating or cooling system, make sure all power to the system is turned off. At the main electrical entrance panel, trip the circuit breaker or remove the fuse that controls the power to the unit. If you're not sure which circuit the system is on, remove the main fuse or trip the main circuit breaker to cut off all power to the house. Some furnaces have a separate power entrance, usually at a different panel near the main entrance panel. If a separate panel is present, remove the fuse or trip the breaker there.
- If the fuse blows or the circuit trips repeatedly when the furnace or air conditioner turns on, there is a problem in the electrical system. In this case, do not try to fix the furnace. Call a professional service person.
- If the unit uses gas and there is a smell of gas in your home, do not try to shut off the gas or turn any lights on or off. Get out of the house, leaving the door open, and go to a telephone; call the gas company or the fire department immediately to report a leak. Do not reenter your home.
- To keep your heating and cooling systems in top shape, have them professionally serviced once a year. The best time to have a furnace serviced is at the end of the heating season. Because this is the off-season, you can often get a discount, and service is likely to be prompt. Have your air conditioner checked at the same time.

Dirt is the biggest enemy of your home's heating and cooling system. It can waste fuel and drastically lower efficiency. Dirt affects all three basic components of the system, so cleaning is the most important part of regular maintenance. Lubrication and belt adjustment at the furnace are also important. To keep your system working properly, use the following general procedures. Specific procedures for each type of system are detailed later in this chapter.

Maintaining the Source

The heat/cold source is the most complicated part of the heating and cooling system, and it's the part most likely to suffer from neglect. Problems in the heat/cold source may also lead to distribution problems. Whatever heat/cold source your system uses, give it regular attention to prevent problems.

Cleaning a Furnace

Three parts of the furnace should be cleaned: the filter system, the blower, and the motor. The furnace filter should be replaced or cleaned at the beginning of the heating season and about once a month during periods of continuous use. To check the filter, take it out and hold it up to the light. If it looks clogged, replace it regardless of the length of time it has been used. Replace it with a new filter of the same type and size. Filters are available at hardware stores and home-improvement centers.

A disposable furnace filter consists of a fiber mesh in a cardboard frame. The size of the filter is printed on the edge of the frame. An arrow on the edge of the frame indicates the correct direction of airflow through the filter. Air flows from the return-air duct toward the blower, so the arrow on the filter should point away from the return-air duct and toward the blower. A

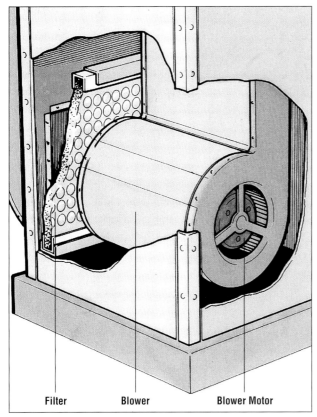

Filter   Blower   Blower Motor

Three parts of the air-moving system should be kept clean: the filter, the blower, and the blower motor.

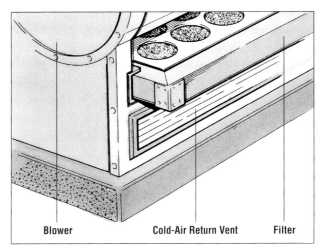

Blower   Cold-Air Return Vent   Filter

Replace a clogged furnace filter with a new one of the same type. The arrow on the filter, indicating air flow, should point away from the return-air duct and toward the blower.

permanent filter is usually sprayed with a special filter-coating chemical, available at hardware stores and home centers. Clean this type of filter according to the manufacturer's instructions, which are usually attached to the furnace housing. To replace a filter:

Step 1: Look for a metal panel on the front of the furnace below the return-air duct, between the duct and the blower system. The panel may be marked FILTER, or it may form the lid or the front of a boxlike projection on the furnace housing.

Step 2: Slip the panel off its holding hooks or unscrew the panel from the box or furnace housing. On some heating units, the filters are exposed; just slip the filter up and out of the U-shaped tracks that hold it in place.

Step 3: Inspect and replace or clean the filter, depending on the type.

Step 4: Clean the blower assembly, the belts and pulleys to the blower, and the motor housing. Cleaning the blower is critical if the furnace has a squirrel-cage fan, because the openings in this type of blower often become clogged with dirt.

Step 5: To clean the blower, turn off the power to the furnace. Remove the panel that covers the filter to gain access to the blower, or remove a panel on the front of the furnace. This panel may be slip-fit on hooks or may be held by a series of retaining screws. Access to the inside of the blower is usually gained by sliding out the fan unit, which is held on a track by screws. If the power cord to the fan assembly is not long enough to permit the fan unit to slide all the way out, disconnect the cord. Mark the wire

Use an old toothbrush to clean each fan blade on the blower. Then, with the hose of a vacuum cleaner, remove all the dirt loosened by the brushing.

connections first so you'll be able to reassemble the unit correctly. With a toothbrush, clean each fan blade and the spaces between the blades. Then, with the hose of a vacuum cleaner, remove all the dirt and debris loosened by the brushing.

Step 6: Vacuum the belts and pulleys. Wipe the motor housing clean to prevent heat buildup in the motor.

Cleaning a Central Air Conditioner

A furnace used in conjunction with a central air conditioning system should be cleaned as detailed on page 264. In addition, the evaporator and the condenser, usually located outside the house, should be cleaned annually. These procedures are detailed later in the chapter in the section on central air conditioning (see page 294–295).

Lubrication of the Heating and Cooling Motor

To keep the motor running cool, make sure it's clean. Most motors are permanently lubricated and sealed by the manufacturer. They require no further attention. Some motors, however, have covered oil ports above the bearings, near the motor shaft. If the motor has oil ports, it should be lubricated annually. Apply two or three drops of 10-weight nondetergent motor oil (not all-purpose oil) to each port. Do not overlubricate. If the blower shaft has oil ports, it too should be lubricated annually, following the same procedure. You'll probably have to remove an access plate to get at the ports. If the blower has grease cups instead of oil ports, remove the screw caps that cover the cups and fill the cups with bearing lubricant, available at automotive and hardware stores.

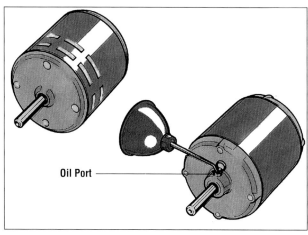

If the fan motor has oil ports, it should be lubricated annually. Apply two or three drops of oil to each port.

Belt Adjustment and Replacement

On furnaces that have a blower, inspect the belts on the blower and motor when you clean and lubricate the furnace. If the belts are worn or frayed, replace them with new ones of the same type and size. To replace a worn belt:

Step 1: Loosen the mounting bolts on the motor and slide the motor forward toward the blower unit. This releases the worn belt.

Step 2: Remove the old belt and stretch a new one into place on the pulleys. Then slide the motor back and tighten the motor mounting bolts to increase the tension.

Step 3: Adjust the bolts so that there's about ½-inch deflection when you press on the belt at its center point between the two pulleys.

If a belt squeaks when the blower is running, spray it with fan-belt dressing, available at automotive and hardware stores and at some home centers.

Maintaining the Distribution System

Whatever the heat/cold source, warm or cool air must travel to the various rooms of your home. When the distribution system is dirty or supply and return registers are blocked, the heat or coolness generated by the furnace or air conditioner cannot reach your living spaces. A dirty system is very inefficient and wastes energy. To keep your system operating at top efficiency, clean it regularly and make sure supply and return registers are not blocked by draperies, furniture, or rugs.

Forced-Air and Gravity Systems

These two systems use the same type of ducting to distribute heated or cooled air. To maintain the ducting, vacuum supply and return registers thoroughly at least once a month during the heating season. If your home has floor registers, lift the register grilles and clean the ducting below them with a brush and vacuum. Cold-air returns are especially prone to dirt buildup, because air is sucked into them from the rooms back to the furnace. In forced-air systems, the blower and the motor should also be cleaned and lubricated regularly, as detailed on page 264.

Radiant Systems

The efficiency of radiator or convector systems—either steam or hot water—depends on free circulation to the radiators or convectors. In both systems, the supply pipes and the radiators/convectors must slope toward the boiler. Check the slope of radiators and pipes with a level. Correct the tilt as necessary to restore proper operation. Lack of heat in a radiator or convector can be caused by air trapped in it. To remove air from a hot-water radiator or convector, open the air vent until the hissing stops and a few drops of water squirt out. Then close the vent. Steam radiators typically have a bullet-shaped valve that releases air with each heating cycle. If a radiator isn't heating properly, try clearing the orifice at the top of this valve with a straight pin or a paper clip. In steam systems, the boiler should be flushed once a month; in hot-water systems, once a season. All these procedures are detailed later in this chapter in the sections on steam and hot-water systems.

Maintenance is usually not possible for radiant systems with distribution pipes embedded in floors, walls, or ceilings.

Maintaining and Repairing the Thermostat

A thermostat is a highly sensitive control instrument, responding to even the slightest changes in temperature. While it has fewer parts to malfunction than the other components of your heating and cooling system, it can be a source of problems. A thermostat cover that's improperly installed or inadvertently bumped can cause the heater or air conditioner to fail to start. Or the thermostat base may slip out of level, causing it to operate incorrectly. A far more common problem, however, is dirt. Dirt can affect the thermostat's calibration and interfere with its operation. If a thermostat set for 70°F, for example, is really maintaining the temperature at 73°F, the additional

energy used can increase your fuel bill by as much as seven percent. To prevent this, check your thermostat for accuracy every year before the heating season begins.

Other problems with a thermostat can often be traced to switches on the base and wires near the bimetallic element that loosen and become corroded. Tighten loose connections with a screwdriver, and use a cotton swab to clean away corrosion.

Cleaning and Checking a Thermometer's Calibration

To check a thermostat's accuracy and clean it if necessary:

Step 1: Tape a glass tube thermometer to the wall a few inches away from the thermostat. Pad the thermometer to prevent it from touching the wall. Make sure that neither the thermometer nor the thermostat is affected by any outside temperature influences. In some homes, the hole in the wall behind the

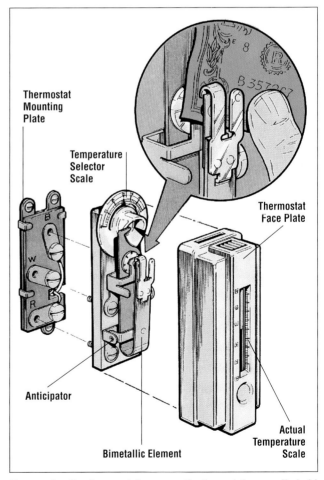

To examine the thermostat, remove the face plate, usually held by a snap or friction catch. Clean exposed contact points by pulling a new dollar bill between them.

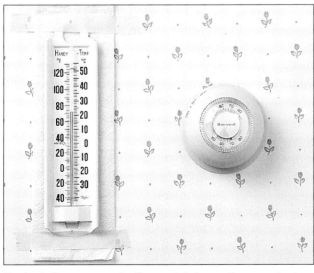

To check the accuracy of a thermostat, tape a thermometer to the wall a few inches away and compare the readings.

thermostat, through which the wires come, is too large, allowing cold air to reach the thermostat and affect its reading.

Step 2: Wait about 15 minutes for the mercury to stabilize. Then compare the reading on the thermometer with the reading of the thermostat needle.

Step 3: If the variation is more than a degree, check to see if the thermostat is dirty. To examine the thermostat, remove the face plate, usually held by a snap or a friction catch. Blow away any dust inside it with your own breath or with a plastic squeeze bottle used as a bellows. Do not use a vacuum cleaner; its suction is too great. If the thermostat has accessible contact points, rub a new dollar bill between them to clean these spots. Do not use sandpaper or emery cloth. If the element is coiled, use a soft brush for cleaning.

Step 4: If the thermostat has a mercury vial inside, use a level to make sure the unit is straight. If it isn't, loosen the mounting screws and adjust the thermostat until it is level. Then retighten the screws.

Step 5: After cleaning the thermostat, check it again with a glass thermometer, as detailed in Steps 1 and 2. If the thermostat is still not calibrated properly, it should be replaced.

Replacing a Thermostat

Replace a faulty thermostat with a new one of the same voltage. The thermostat must be compatible with the heating system. *Caution: Before replacing the thermostat, remove the fuse or trip the circuit breaker to turn off the power to the circuit that controls it. If you aren't sure which circuit controls the thermostat, remove the main fuse or trip the main circuit breaker to turn off all the power to the house.* To replace a thermostat:

Step 1: Remove the old thermostat. Take the face plate off the old unit and look for the mounting screws. Remove the screws to release the thermostat from the wall. Remove the wires from the back of the old thermostat by turning the connection screws counterclockwise. Be careful not to let the loose wires fall down between the walls.

Step 2: Clean the exposed wires by scraping them with a knife until the wire ends shine. Attach the wires to the new thermostat. The new thermostat must have the same electrical rating as the old one.

Step 3: Once the wires are attached to the replacement thermostat, push the wires back into the wall and tape up the opening to prevent cold air inside the walls from affecting the thermostat.

Step 4: Install the mounting screws to secure the new thermostat to the wall. If the thermostat has a

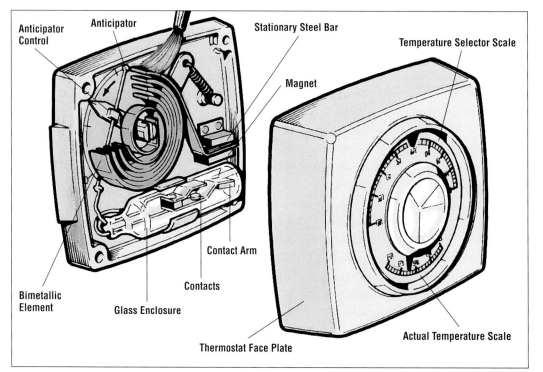

Anticipator Control
Anticipator
Stationary Steel Bar
Temperature Selector Scale
Magnet
Bimetallic Element
Glass Enclosure
Contacts
Contact Arm
Thermostat Face Plate
Actual Temperature Scale

Many thermostats have coiled bimetallic strip elements, and the contacts are sealed. Pull off the face plate and clean the coil with a soft brush.

mercury tube, set the unit against a level during installation; mercury tube thermostats must be exactly level.

Step 5: Snap the face plate back into place. Make sure the new thermostat turns the heating/cooling system on and off when the temperature setting is adjusted.

Improving Heating and Cooling Efficiency

Although regular maintenance and repair of a central heating and air conditioning system can save you money, the system will operate even more efficiently if your home is sealed against the weather. Make sure the structure is properly insulated, weather stripped, and caulked. Install storm windows and doors to prevent heat loss in the winter and heat gain during the summer. This will be discussed in greater detail later in this chapter (see page 299).

For maximum energy-efficiency, follow these simple procedures:

- Protect the thermostat from anything that would cause it to give a false reading. If the thermostat is in a draft, misplaced on a cold outside wall, or too close to a heat-producing appliance or register, its accuracy will be compromised.
- If you won't be home for a few days, turn the thermostat to its lowest setting. If there's no danger of pipes freezing, turn the heating system off completely.
- Install a thermostat timer to save fuel and money. The timer can be set to automatically raise and lower the temperature during peak and off hours. Installation instructions are usually included with the timer.
- Close the draperies over large windows and glass doors to form a barrier against heat loss during the winter and heat gain during the summer. Insulated draperies or shades increase efficiency.
- If your home has rooms that are seldom or never used, close the vents in these rooms and shut the doors.
- Avoid constant thermostat adjustments, as they can waste fuel. When coming into the house after the thermostat has been turned down, don't set it higher than the desired temperature. Setting the thermostat up very high generally will not cause the temperature to reach the desired level any faster.
- One heating adjustment you should make, however, is a reduction in the thermostat setting before you go to bed every night. Cutting back for several hours can make a big difference in fuel consumption.
- Reduce the thermostat setting when you have a large

group of people in your home. People generate heat, and a party can quickly raise the temperature.
- Keep the fireplace damper closed except when you have a fire going. Otherwise, updrafts will suck heated air out through the chimney.
- Maintain proper humidity. A house that's too dry can feel uncomfortably cold even when the temperature setting is correct.

The following are some additional tips for efficient air conditioning:

- Aim the vents of room air conditioners upward for better air circulation; cold air naturally settles downward. On central air conditioning systems, adjust the registers so that the air is blowing up.
- Make sure the outside portion of the air conditioning system, whether a room unit or a central system, is not in direct sunlight or blocked from free airflow.
- If you have room units, close all heating system vents so that the cool air isn't wasted.

Troubleshooting Heating Plants

There are several types of heating plants in common use. They include oil, gas, and electric furnaces; gas or electric wall or baseboard heaters; and heat pumps. These plants all have their own problems, depending on how they're designed and how they work. In any system, the method of distributing the heat is as important as the means of generating it. Specific procedures are provided below for maintaining and repairing each type of heat source, followed by information about the systems they use to distribute heat.

Gas Furnaces and Heaters

Although natural gas is more expensive than fuel oil in some parts of the country, it is often the preferred source for heat. Natural gas burns cleaner than fuel oil, and most natural-gas furnaces present fewer operational difficulties than oil burners do. In fact, the problems that affect natural-gas furnaces usually have little to do with the fuel source. Instead, they typically involve the furnace's thermocouple, the pilot light, or some component of the electrical system. Gas furnaces and heaters have control shutoffs to prevent gas leaks, but they are not fail-safe. If there is a smell of gas in your

GAS FURNACE AND HEATER TROUBLESHOOTING CHART

Problem	Possible Cause	Solution
Furnace won't run	1. No power.	1. Check for blown fuses or tripped circuit breakers at main entrance panel or at separate entrance panel; restore circuit.
	2. Switch off.	2. Turn on separate power switch on or near furnace.
	3. Motor overload.	3. Wait 30 minutes; press reset button. Repeat if necessary.
	4. Pilot light out.	4. Relight pilot.
	5. No gas.	5. Make sure gas valve to furnace is fully open.
Not enough heat	1. Thermostat set too low.	1. Raise thermostat setting five degrees.
	2. Filter dirty.	2. Clean or replace filter.
	3. Blower clogged.	3. Clean blower assembly.
	4. Registers closed or blocked.	4. Make sure all registers are open; make sure they are not blocked by rugs, drapes, or furniture.
	5. System out of balance.	5. Balance system; see section on forced-air systems.
	6. Blower belt loose or broken.	6. Adjust or replace belt.
	7. Burner dirty.	7. Call a professional.
Pilot won't light	1. Pilot opening blocked.	1. Clean pilot opening.
	2. No gas.	2. Make sure pilot light button is fully depressed; make sure gas valve to furnace is fully open.
Pilot won't stay lit	1. Loose or faulty thermocouple.	1. Tighten thermocouple nut slightly; if no results, replace thermocouple.
	2. Pilot flame set too low.	2. Adjust pilot so flame is about two inches long.
	3. Electric pilot faulty.	3. Call a professional.
Furnace turns on and off repeatedly	1. Filter dirty.	1. Clean or replace filter.
	2. Motor and/or blower needs lubrication.	2. If motor and blower have oil ports, lubricate.
	3. Blower clogged.	3. Clean blower assembly.
Blower won't stop running	1. Blower control set wrong.	1. Reset thermostat from ON to AUTO.
	2. Limit switch set wrong.	2. Reset limit switch for stop/start cycling.
	3. Limit control needs adjustment.	3. Call a professional.

Continued on page 271

Problem	Possible Cause	Solution
Furnace noisy	1. Access panels loose.	1. Mount and fasten access panels correctly.
	2. Belts sticking, worn, or damaged.	2. Spray squeaking drive belts with belt dressing; replace worn or damaged belts.
	3. Blower belt too loose or too tight.	3. Adjust belt.
	4. Motor and/or blower needs lubrication.	4. If motor and blower have oil ports, lubricate.
	5. Burner dirty.	5. Call a professional.

house, do not turn any lights on or off, and do not try to shut off the gas leading to the furnace. Get out of the house, leaving the door open, and go to a telephone; call the gas company or the fire department immediately to report a leak. Do not reenter your home. *Caution: Before doing any work on the furnace, make sure the power to the furnace is turned off.*

Disassembling a Gas Furnace or Heater

On some units, a plug-type door covers the pilot light assembly. To gain access to the pilot burner, pull the door out of the furnace housing. On other units, remove the panel that covers the pilot and gas burners.

The pilot light controls, reset buttons, gas valves, and thermocouple are usually contained in an assembly at the front of the furnace. The furnace limit switch is located on the plenum or main duct junction on the upper housing of the furnace.

Pilot Light

The pilot light can go out because of drafts. Instructions for relighting the pilot are usually fastened to the furnace. Follow the manufacturer's instructions exactly. If instructions for relighting the pilot are not provided, follow this general procedure.

Step 1: Find the pilot light assembly. It typically has a gas valve with ON, OFF, and PILOT settings.

Step 2: Turn the valve to OFF and wait three minutes.

Step 3: Switch the valve to the PILOT setting. Hold a lighted match to the pilot opening while you push the reset button on the pilot control panel. Keep this button depressed until the pilot flame is burning brightly; then set the valve to the ON position.

Step 4: If the pilot flame won't stay lit, the opening may be clogged. Turn the gas valve off and clean the opening with a piece of fine wire. If it won't stay lit after several attempts to light it, the problem may be a faulty thermocouple. Replace a faulty thermocouple as detailed below. If the pilot flame still won't stay lit, call a professional service person.

Some furnaces have an electrical system to ignite the gas; in these systems there is no pilot light. Instead, an electric element heats up and ignites the burners. If this electric ignition system malfunctions, call a professional service person.

Thermocouple

The thermocouple is a gas furnace component located near the pilot light burner. It is a safety device that shuts off the gas if the pilot light goes out or the electric igniter fails. If the pilot light won't stay lit, the thermocouple may be faulty and should be adjusted or replaced.

To adjust the thermocouple, you must tighten the thermocouple nut with a wrench. Take care not to apply too much pressure to the nut—just tighten it slightly. Then try lighting the pilot. If the pilot won't stay lit, replace the thermocouple with a new one of the same type. To replace a thermocouple:

Step 1: Unscrew the copper lead and the connection nut inside the threaded connection to the gas line.

Step 2: Under the mounting bracket at the thermocouple tube, unscrew the bracket nut that holds the tube in place.

Step 3: Insert a new thermocouple into the hole in the bracket. Be sure the steel tube is up and the copper lead is down.

Step 4: Under the bracket, screw the bracket nut over the tube.

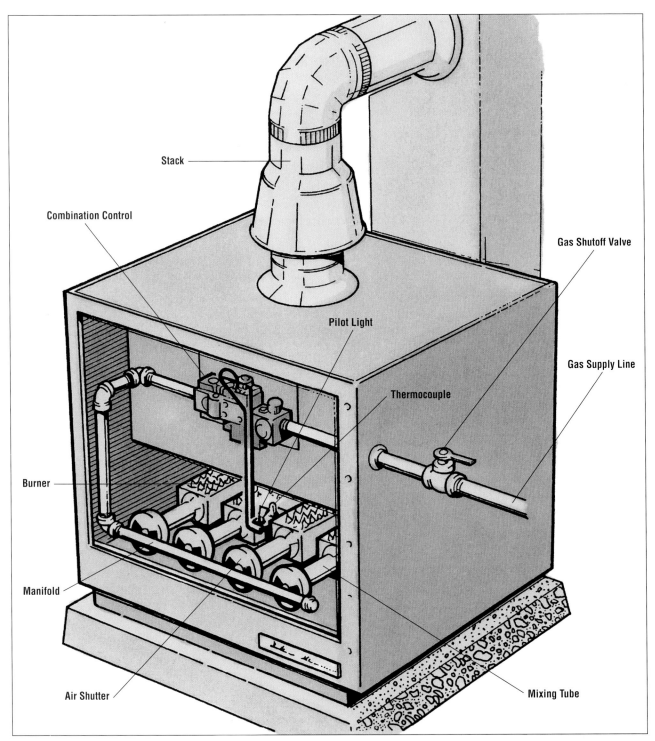

Stack

Combination Control

Gas Shutoff Valve

Pilot Light

Gas Supply Line

Thermocouple

Burner

Manifold

Air Shutter

Mixing Tube

Most natural gas furnaces have few operational difficulties. Problems typically involve the pilot light, the thermocouple, or some part of the electrical system.

Step 5: Push the connection nut to the threaded connection where the copper lead connects to the gas line. Make sure the connection is clean and dry.

Step 6: Screw the nut tightly into place, but do not overtighten it. Both the bracket nut and the connection nut should be only a little tighter than if hand-tightened.

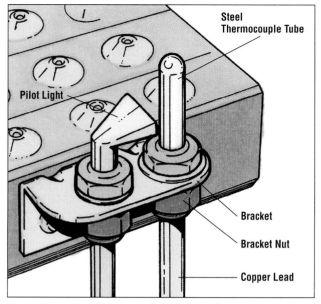

The thermocouple is installed next to the pilot light. A bracket holds it in place, steel tube up and copper lead down.

Limit Switch

The limit switch is a safety control switch, located on the furnace just below the plenum. If the plenum gets too hot, the limit switch shuts off the burner. It also shuts off the blower when the temperature drops to a certain level after the burner has shut off. If the blower runs continuously, either the blower control on the thermostat has been set to the ON position or the limit control switch needs adjustment. Check the thermostat first. If the blower control has been set to ON, change it to AUTO; if the blower control is already on AUTO, the limit switch needs adjusting.

Remove the control's cover. Under it is a toothed dial with one side marked LIMIT; don't touch this side. The other side of the control is marked FAN. There are two pointers on the fan side; the blower goes on at the upper pointer setting and turns off at the lower pointer setting. The pointers should be set about 25 degrees apart. Set the upper pointer at about 115°F and the lower one at about 90°F.

Burner Adjustment

The flames on the gas burner should be full and steady, with no sputtering and no trace of yellow. To adjust the flame height on the main burners, call a professional service person. To adjust the height of the pilot flame, turn the flame adjustment screw until the flame is from 1½ to 2 inches high. The adjustment screw is located near the gas valve on the pilot assembly, if the control has this adjustment feature.

Gas Leaks

If you suspect leaks around the furnace unit, stir up a mixture of liquid detergent and water. Paint this mixture on the gas supply line along its connections and valves; the soapy water will bubble at any point where there's a leak. If you find a leak, try tightening the leaking connection with a pipe wrench, but be careful not to overtighten the connection. If the pipe connections or valves still leak, call a professional service person.

....

Oil Furnaces

Oil-fired burners are used in many parts of the country as the basic heat source for warm-air, hot-water, and steam heating systems. Most of the home oil systems in use today are called pressure burners. In this type of system, oil is sprayed into a combustion chamber at high pressure, propelled by a blower, and ignited by an electric spark. The oil continues to burn as the mist is sprayed. There are few repairs that you can do yourself with this type of system, so an oil furnace should be inspected by a professional service person once a year.

While there aren't many repairs you can undertake yourself, good regular maintenance can help eliminate many problems. Regular maintenance should include these steps:

- During the heating season, check the smoke from the chimney. If the smoke is black, the furnace is not burning the oil completely, and fuel is being wasted. Call a professional service person for adjustments.
- Clean the blower at the beginning of the heating season and again about midway through the season.
- Clean the soot from the stack control about midway through the heating season.
- If the blower motor has grease or oil fittings, lubricate the fittings midway through the heating season with cup grease or 10-weight nondetergent motor oil (not all-purpose oil), available at hardware stores.
- Clean the thermostat before each heating season.

Caution: Before doing any work on the furnace, make sure the power to the furnace is turned off.

Disassembling an Oil Furnace

An oil furnace is a complex assembly. The maintenance and repair work for this type of furnace is limited to simple parts—the filters, the blower, the motor belts, the switches, and the thermostat. Electrodes, oil nozzle, air tubes, transformer, pump, and other components require special tools and testing equipment and are best left to a professional for service.

Remove the access panel covering the burner blower by removing the retaining screws around the rim of the housing. You can access the air blower and filter through a metal panel on one side of the furnace. The panel is held by either hooks or retaining bolts; slip the panel up and off the hooks or remove the bolts and lift the panel off. Most furnaces have switches and reset buttons located on the motor or in a switch box outside the

furnace housing. These are usually identified with stampings or labels, such as DISCONNECT SWITCH, RESET, and so on. The stack control sensor, a safety device that monitors burner operation, is positioned in the stack and held with a series of retaining bolts.

OIL FURNACE TROUBLESHOOTING CHART		
Problem	**Possible Cause**	**Solution**
Furnace won't run	1. No power.	1. Check for blown fuses or tripped circuit breakers at main entrance panel or at separate entrance panel; restore circuit.
	2. Switch off.	2. Turn on separate power switch on or near furnace.
	3. Motor overload.	3. Wait 30 minutes; press reset button. Repeat if necessary.
	4. No fuel.	4. Check tank; if necessary, refill tank.
	5. Fuel line blockage.	5. Clean oil filter and oil pump strainer. If problem persists, call a professional.
Burner won't fire	1. No fuel.	1. Check tank; if necessary, refill tank.
	2. No ignition spark.	2. Press reset button on stack control, once; if necessary, clean stack control. If no result, call a professional. If furnace has electric-eye safety, clean safety; if no result, call a professional.
Not enough heat	1. Thermostat set too low.	1. Raise thermostat setting five degrees.
	2. Air filter dirty.	2. Clean or replace air filter.
	3. Blower clogged.	3. Clean blower assembly.
	4. Registers closed or blocked.	4. Make sure all registers are open; make sure they are not blocked by rugs, drapes, or furniture.
	5. System out of balance.	5. Balance system; see section on forced-air system.
	6. Blower belt loose or broken.	6. Adjust or replace belt.
	7. Burner dirty.	7. Call a professional.
Furnace turns on and off repeatedly	1. Air filter dirty.	1. Clean or replace air filter.
	2. Oil filter dirty.	2. Clean or replace oil filter.
	3. Motor and/or blower needs lubrication.	3. If motor and blower have oil ports, lubricate.
	4. Blower clogged.	4. Clean blower assembly.
	5. Stack control faulty.	5. Call a professional.
Blower won't stop running	1. Blower control set wrong.	1. Reset thermostat from ON to AUTO.
	2. Limit switch set wrong.	2. Reset limit switch.

Continued on page 275

OIL FURNACE TROUBLESHOOTING CHART *(Continued from page 274)*

Problem	Possible Cause	Solution
Furnace noisy	1. Access panels loose.	1. Mount and fasten access panels correctly.
	2. Belts sticking, worn, or damaged.	2. Spray squeaking belts with fan belt dressing; replace worn or damaged belts.
	3. Blower belt too loose or too tight.	3. Adjust belt.
	4. Motor and/or blower needs lubrication.	4. If motor and blower have oil ports, lubricate.
	5. Burner dirty.	5. Call a professional.

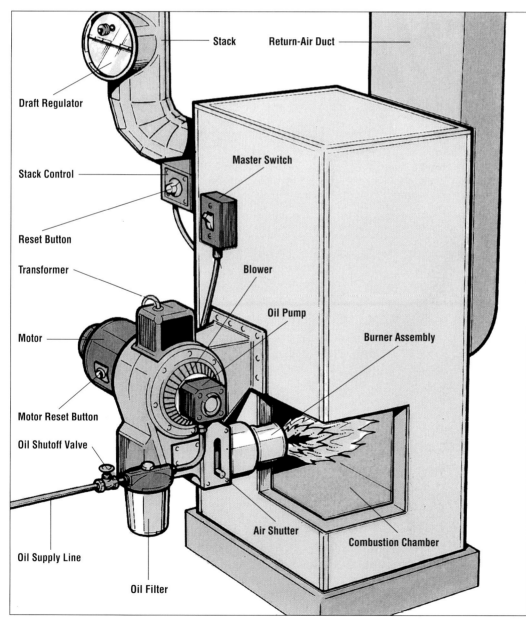

Stack

Return-Air Duct

Draft Regulator

Master Switch

Stack Control

Reset Button

Transformer

Blower

Oil Pump

Motor

Burner Assembly

Motor Reset Button

Oil Shutoff Valve

Air Shutter

Combustion Chamber

Oil Supply Line

Oil Filter

Most oil furnaces in use today are called pressure burners. In this type of system, oil is sprayed into a combustion chamber at high pressure.

Oil Filters

The oil filter should be changed or cleaned at the start of the heating season and about midway through the season. To clean or replace the filter:

Step 1: Close the oil shutoff valve between the fuel tank and the filter.

Step 2: Unscrew the bottom or cup of the filter housing and remove the filter.

Step 3: If the filter is disposable, insert a new one of the same size and type. If the furnace has a permanent filter, wash the filter in kerosene every 45 to 60 days and replace it in the housing. ***Caution:*** *Kerosene is flammable; be very careful when cleaning a permanent oil filter.*

Step 4: Replace the old filter gaskets with new gaskets.

Step 5: Screw in the bottom of the housing and open the oil shutoff valve.

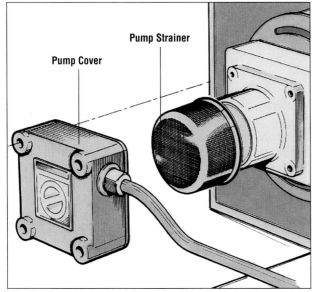

Clean the pump strainer after cleaning the oil filter. To reach the strainer, unbolt the cover of the pump housing, and lift off the cover.

Some oil furnaces have a pump strainer, which is located on the pump attached to the burner/blower unit. Clean this strainer at the same time as you clean the oil filter. Here's how:

Step 1: Unbolt the cover of the pump housing (where the oil line enters the burner) and lift off the cover.

Step 2: Remove the thin gasket around the rim. Find and remove the strainer, a cylindrical or cup-shaped wire mesh screen.

Step 3: Soak the strainer in kerosene for several minutes to loosen any built-up sludge. Carefully clean the strainer with an old, soft toothbrush.

Step 4: Inspect the strainer. If it's torn or badly bent, replace it with a new pump strainer of the same type.

Step 5: Set the strainer into place on the pump, place a new gasket on the rim, and bolt the cover of the pump housing back on.

Switches

Some oil furnaces have two master switches. One is located near the burner unit, and the other is near the furnace housing or even at a distance from the furnace. Make sure these master switches are both turned to the ON position.

Stack Control

The stack control, located in the stack, is a safety device that monitors the operation of the oil burner. If the burner fails to ignite, the stack control shuts off the motor. Frequently, however, a furnace shutdown is caused by a malfunctioning stack control rather than by the burner. If the burner fails to ignite, first check the fuel tank and refill it if necessary. If the tank doesn't need to be refilled, press the reset button on the stack control. If the burner doesn't ignite after you've pressed the button once, clean the control, as detailed below. Then press the reset button again. If the burner still doesn't operate, call a professional service person.

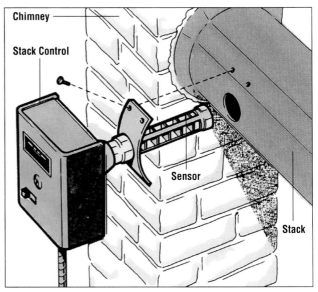

Clean the stack control every month. To remove the control, turn off the power to the furnace, then back out the bolts that hold it in the stack.

The stack control gradually becomes coated with soot during the heating season. To keep it working properly, clean the control every month, or as soon as it becomes soot-covered. To clean the stack control:

Step 1: Turn off the power to the furnace.

Step 2: Remove the bolts that hold the control in the stack. Pull out the sensor and its housing.

Step 3: With a brush dipped in soapy water, remove all soot from the control. Wipe the control dry with a soft cloth.

Step 4: Before replacing the control, clean the stack. Spread newspaper to protect the floor, and disassemble the stack. As you work, remove soot and debris from each section by tapping it firmly on the newspaper-covered floor.

Step 5: After cleaning the sections, reassemble them in reverse order. Make sure that the stack sections are properly aligned and firmly connected.

Step 6: Finally, reposition the stack control in the stack and reseal the connection to the chimney with refractory cement.

Some oil furnaces have an electric-eye safety switch instead of a stack control. This switch serves the same function as the stack control. If the burner has an electric-eye safety, remove the access cover over the photocell; it is held by hooks or retaining screws. Wipe the cover clean to remove accumulated soot. Reassemble the switch, replace the cover, and turn the power back on. If the burner still doesn't ignite, call a professional service person.

If the stack control or electric-eye safety switch is especially dirty, the furnace may not be properly set to burn the fuel completely. In this case, call a professional service person for adjustment. ***Caution:*** *Do not attempt to replace these controls yourself. Call a professional service person.*

Draft Regulator

The draft regulator, located on the stack, is closed when the burner is off, but opens automatically to let air into the chimney when the burner is turned on. Accumulated soot and rattling are signs that the draft regulator needs to be adjusted.

Too much air in the chimney wastes heat; too little air wastes fuel by failing to burn it completely. To increase the airflow, screw the counterweight inward. To decrease airflow, turn the counterweight outward. The draft regulator should be adjusted by a professional service person as part of regular annual maintenance.

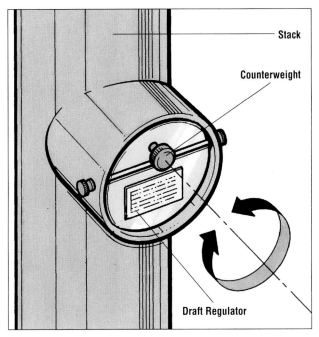

The draft regulator on the stack opens automatically when the burner is running. To increase the airflow, screw the counterweight inward.

Limit Switch

The limit switch is a safety control switch and is located on the furnace just below the plenum. If the plenum gets too hot, the limit switch shuts off the burner. It also shuts off the blower when the temperature drops to a certain level after the burner has shut off. If the blower runs continuously, either the blower control on the thermostat has been set to the ON position, or the limit control switch needs adjustment. Here's what you can do to determine the problem:

Step 1: Check the thermostat. If the blower control has been set to ON, change it to AUTO; if the blower control is already on AUTO, the limit switch needs adjusting.

Step 2: Remove the control's cover and find the toothed dial underneath. One side is marked LIMIT; don't touch this side. The other side of the control is marked FAN. There are two pointers on the fan side; the blower turns on at the upper pointer setting and shuts off at the lower pointer setting. The pointers should be set about 25 degrees apart. Set the upper pointer at about 115°F and the lower one at about 90°F.

Burner Adjustments

Do not try to adjust the burner of an oil furnace; call a professional service person.

Electric Furnaces and Heaters

In most regions, electric heat is expensive, whether the unit consists of a central furnace, a boiler system, or baseboard or wall units to heat individual rooms. Although an electric heating system does have advantages, its operating cost generally makes it less desirable than any of the other furnace systems available today. The high cost means that minimizing heat loss caused by improperly installed ducts or inadequate insulation is even more important than with other types of systems.

The big advantage of electric heating is that no combustion takes place. Electric heat is cleaner than fuel-burning types of heat.

Moreover, since no flue is required to carry off undesirable combustion materials, no heat is lost through such venting, as it is in gas and oil systems. The only moving parts in an electric heating system are in the blower assembly.

ELECTRIC FURNACE TROUBLESHOOTING CHART		
Problem	**Possible Cause**	**Solution**
Furnace won't run	1. No power.	1. Check for blown fuses or tripped circuit breakers at main entrance panel, at separate entrance panel, and on or in furnace; restore circuit.
	2. Switch off.	2. Turn on separate power switch on or near furnace.
	3. Motor overload.	3. Wait 30 minutes; press reset button. Repeat if necessary.
Not enough heat	1. Thermostat set too low.	1. Raise thermostat setting five degrees.
	2. Filter dirty.	2. Clean or replace filter.
	3. Blower clogged.	3. Clean blower assembly.
	4. Registers closed or blocked.	4. Make sure all registers are open; make sure they are not blocked by rugs, drapes, or furniture.
	5. System out of balance.	5. Balance system; see section on forced-air systems.
	6. Blower belt loose or broken.	6. Adjust or replace belt.
	7. Element faulty.	7. Call a professional.
Furnace turns on and off repeatedly	1. Filter dirty.	1. Clean or replace filter.
	2. Motor and/or blower needs lubrication.	2. If motor and blower have oil ports, lubricate.
	3. Blower clogged.	3. Clean blower assembly.
Blower won't stop running	1. Blower control set wrong.	1. Reset thermostat from ON to AUTO.
	2. Relays faulty.	2. Call a professional.
Furnace noisy	1. Access panels loose.	1. Mount and fasten access panels correctly.
	2. Belts sticking, worn, or damaged.	2. Spray squeaking belts with fan belt dressing; replace worn or damaged belts.
	3. Blower belt too loose or too tight.	3. Adjust belt.
	4. Motor and/or blower needs lubrication.	4. If motor and blower have oil ports, lubricate.

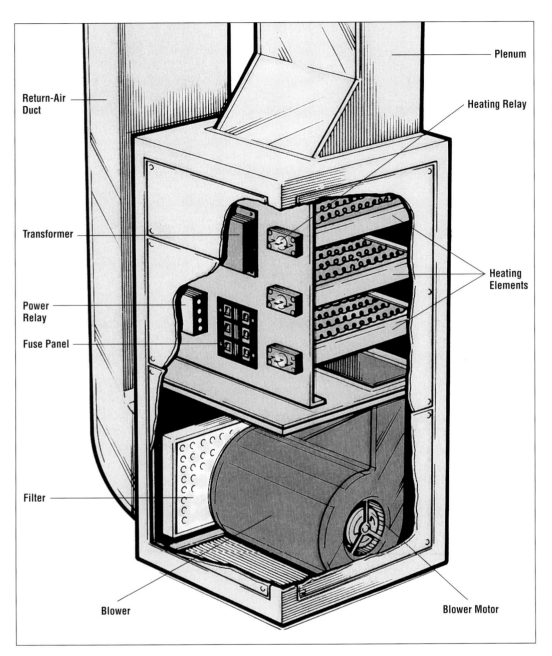

Return-Air Duct

Transformer

Power Relay

Fuse Panel

Filter

Blower

Plenum

Heating Relay

Heating Elements

Blower Motor

Electric furnaces use heating elements, controlled by relays, to warm the air. The elements are fused on a separate panel.

For maximum energy efficiency, have a professional service person clean and adjust your electric furnace every year before the beginning of the heating season. *Caution: Before doing any work on the furnace, make sure the power to the furnace is turned off. Do not attempt any repairs to the heating elements, electrical connections, relays, transformers, or similar components of an electric furnace; repairs to these components must be made by a professional service person.*

Disassembling an Electric Furnace

The controls of an electric furnace may be mounted on the surface of the housing or installed behind an access panel on the front of the furnace. The access panel may be slip-fit on hooks, or it may be fastened to the furnace housing with a series of sheet-metal screws. To remove the access panel to the blower, filter, and blower motor, slip the panel up off hooks or remove a series of sheet-metal screws.

Fuses

Electric furnaces are fused at the main electrical service entrance to the building. Many electric furnaces are on separate circuits, sometimes located in a separate fuse box away from the main panel. The heating elements of the furnace are also fused, and these fuses are located on

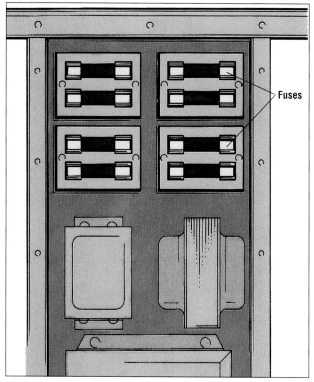

The heating elements on an electric furnace are fused on a separate panel located on or inside the furnace housing.

a panel on or inside the furnace housing. If changing the fuses or resetting the breakers does not restore power to the furnace, call a professional service person. Do not attempt to repair heating elements, the transformer, heating relays, or power relays. Repairs to these components must be made by a professional service person.

Heat Pumps

A heat pump not only heats your home during the winter, it also cools it during the summer. It does not burn fuel to produce heat, nor does the electricity it consumes go through an element. The heat pump functions on the same principle as refrigerators and air conditioners. A liquid absorbs heat as it turns into a gas and releases heat as it returns to a liquid state.

During the summer, the heat pump operates as a standard central air conditioner: It removes heat from the house and vents it to the outside. A liquid refrigerant is pumped through an evaporator coil of tubing. The liquid expands as it moves through the coil, changing to its gaseous state as it absorbs heat from the air surrounding the coil. A blower then pushes air around the cooled coil through ducts and into the house. The gas, now carrying considerable heat, moves through a

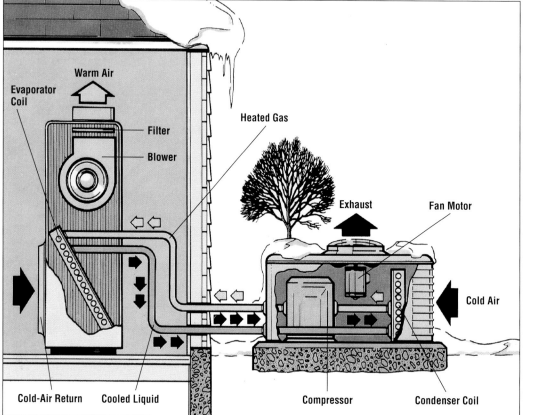

In cold weather, the heat pump extracts heat from the cold air outside and releases it inside the house. This process is reversed for cooling during warm weather.

compressor and begins the liquefying process. It then moves to a condenser coil outside the house, where the compressed gas releases its heat and returns to a liquid state.

During the winter, the heat pump reverses this process, extracting heat from the cold air outside and releasing it inside the house. The heat pump is very efficient when the outside temperature is around 45°F to 50°F, but it becomes less efficient as the temperature drops. When the outside temperature is very low, an auxiliary electric heater must be used to supplement the heat pump's output. Like standard electric heating systems, this auxiliary unit is more expensive to operate. Thus, in areas where the winter temperature is consistently below freezing, the heat pump is not practical. It has few advantages over conventional heating systems in areas where air conditioning is not necessary, but is very efficient in warm to hot climates.

Heat pump maintenance is important. Small problems that are not addressed can lead to very expensive compressor problems. Since maintaining a heat pump is more technical than caring for the average heating system, you should call a professional service person when the pump malfunctions. You can, however, keep the system free of dirt by keeping the filter clean and removing any other obstacles to the flow of air. *Caution: Before doing any work on the heat pump, make sure the power to the pump is turned off.*

General Maintenance

Replace filters and clean and lubricate the components of the heat pump regularly. Use the procedure for electric furnaces that is detailed on page 279.

Outdoor Maintenance

Heat pumps, like central air conditioners, have an outdoor unit that contains a compressor, a coil, a fan, and other components. To function properly, this unit should be kept free of debris such as leaves and dirt. The unit should be level on its concrete support pad.

HEAT PUMP TROUBLESHOOTING CHART		
Problem	**Possible Cause**	**Solution**
Pump won't run	1. No power.	1. Check for blown fuses or tripped circuit breakers at main entrance panel or at separate entrance panel; restore circuit.
	2. Switch off.	2. Make sure switch is turned on.
	3. Pump overloaded.	3. Wait 30 minutes; press reset button on outside cabinet. Repeat if necessary.
	4. Coil blocked with dirt or ice.	4. Remove debris from around coil.
	5. Reversing valve stuck.	5. Set on emergency heat and call a professional.
Ice on coil	1. Coil blocked with dirt.	1. Remove debris from around coil.
	2. Reversing valve stuck.	2. Set on emergency heat and call a professional.
Not enough heat	1. Thermostat set too low.	1. Raise thermostat setting five to ten degrees.
	2. Filter dirty.	2. Clean or replace filter.
	3. Problems in distribution system.	3. See sections on electric furnaces and forced-air systems.
	4. Problems in auxiliary heater.	4. See section on electric furnaces.
Pump goes on and off repeatedly	1. Coil blocked with dirt.	1. Remove dirt and debris from around coil.
	2. Filter dirty.	2. Clean or replace filter.
	3. Problems in distribution system.	3. See sections on electric furnaces and forced-air systems.

Clean pine needles, leaves, and dirt out of updraft fans by removing the grille, which is held to the frame by a series of retaining screws. Make sure the power to the unit is off before this type of cleaning is done. A vacuum cleaner hose can sometimes be inserted between the fan blades to remove debris from the sides and bottom of the unit. At the beginning of each heating season, set a carpenters' level across the top of the metal cabinet and check the level from side to side and from front to back. If the unit is no longer level on the pad, lift the pad back to level by prying it up with a pry bar or a piece of 2×4, and build up the ground under it with stone or crushed rock. Also check the piping insulation for deterioration. If this insulation is faulty, replace it with new insulation, available at heating-supply stores. Installation instructions are usually provided by the manufacturer.

Power Interruption

If a heat pump has been off for more than an hour because of a blown fuse, a tripped circuit breaker, or a utility power failure, the unit should not be operated for about six to eight hours—especially if the temperature is 50°F or lower. The reason for this is that the lubricant in the pump's oil reservoir may be too cool to circulate properly and may cause damage to the valves of the unit. Instead, set the pump on emergency heat. This turns the pump off and keeps it from running. Leave the pump in this mode for about six to eight hours, then switch the pump to its normal heating setting. If little or no heat is generated at this point, call a professional service person for repairs.

Troubleshooting Distribution Systems

The way heat is distributed is as important as how it's generated. Whatever type of system you have, regular maintenance is essential to make the best use of the heat your furnace provides. Forced-air systems are the most common. Radiant heat is also widely used. Gravity systems, the simplest of the three types, are not as efficient as forced-air and radiant heat and are not used much today. To maintain the ducts, registers, and returns of a gravity system, follow the procedures detailed for forced-air systems.

A forced-air distribution system uses a blower to distribute warmed air and return cold air to the furnace so it can be rewarmed and distributed again.

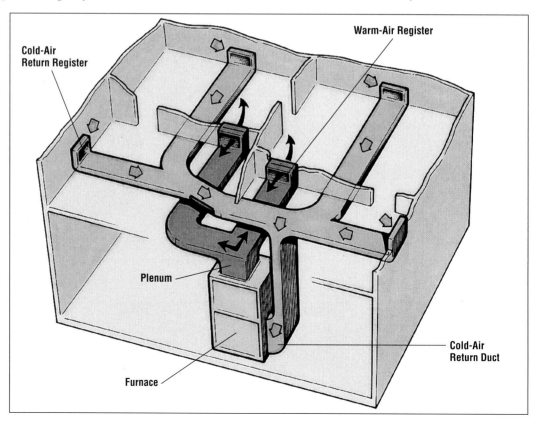

Cold-Air Return Register

Warm-Air Register

Plenum

Furnace

Cold-Air Return Duct

FORCED-AIR SYSTEM TROUBLESHOOTING CHART

Problem	Possible Cause	Solution
Motor won't run	1. No power.	1. Check for blown fuses or tripped circuit breakers at main entrance panel, at separate entrance panel, and on furnace; restore circuit. Also see charts for specific furnaces.
	2. Switch off.	2. Turn on separate power switch on or near furnace.
	3. Motor overload.	3. Wait 30 minutes; press reset button. Repeat if necessary.
Not enough heat	1. Thermostat set too low.	1. Raise thermostat setting five degrees.
	2. Filter dirty.	2. Clean or replace filter.
	3. Blower clogged.	3. Clean blower assembly.
	4. Registers closed or blocked.	4. Make sure all registers are open; make sure they are not blocked by rugs, drapes, or furniture.
	5. Blower running too slow.	5. Increase blower speed.
	6. Blower loose.	6. Tighten nut that holds blower to drive shaft.
	7. Blower belt misaligned or broken.	7. Adjust or replace belt.
	8. Duct joints loose.	8. Trace ducts and wrap leaking joints with duct tape.
	9. Ducts losing heat.	9. Insulate ducts.
Uneven heating	1. System out of balance.	1. Balance system.
Blower won't stop running	1. Blower control set wrong.	1. Reset thermostat from ON to AUTO.
	2. Limit switch set wrong (gas or oil furnace).	2. Reset limit switch; see sections on gas and oil furnaces.
	3. Limit control needs adjustment.	3. Call a professional.
System noisy	1. Access panels loose.	1. Mount and fasten access panels correctly.
	2. Blower running too fast.	2. Decrease blower speed.
	3. Belts sticking, worn, or damaged.	3. Spray squeaking drive belts with belt dressing; replace worn belts.
	4. Blower belt too loose or too tight.	4. Adjust belt.
	5. Blower/motor pulleys loose or misaligned.	5. Tighten pulleys on shafts, and/or realign pulleys.
	6. Blower/motor needs lubrication.	6. Lubricate blower/motor.
	7. Ducting loose.	7. Make sure ducts are tightly fastened to framing with duct hangers; wrap joints with duct tape.

Forced-Air System

Fueled by gas, electricity, or oil, a forced-air distribution system is just what the name implies. Air is forced from the furnace through ducts to registers in various rooms. Besides warming the air, the blower system that distributes the warmed air also returns the cold air to the furnace so it can be rewarmed and distributed to the rooms again. A forced-air system is also efficient for distributing cool air from a central air conditioner with the same ducts, registers, and blower. There is little that can go wrong with a forced-air system. The big problems typically include noise and blockage of airflow, usually caused by dirt or by furniture or draperies blocking the registers. Forced-air systems should be cleaned and maintained as detailed on page 264 of this chapter. Also, see the troubleshooting procedures in the chart on page 283.

Disassembling a Forced-Air System

Floor registers are slip-fit into ducts, or are held by retaining screws on the frame of the register. Wall and ceiling registers are also held in place by retaining screws on the frame of the register. Duct joints are usually slip-fit and held with sheet-metal screws or duct tape. The ducts are supported by wire or metal strap hangers nailed or screwed to wooden framing members such as studs and rafters. All of these parts are easy to disassemble. Lay them out in order as you work so you'll be able to reassemble them properly.

Filters and Blowers

Refer to the previous sections on specific furnaces for cleaning and adjustment details.

Balancing the System

Forced-air systems often go out of balance, causing some rooms to be too hot or too cold. The furnace is usually not to blame; the problem is caused by ducts and registers that are not properly set. You should balance the system while the furnace is turned on. To balance a forced-air system:

Step 1: Open all the ducts and registers in the system. There may be dampers in various ducts that need to be turned to open the ducts. The damper is open when it's turned parallel with the top and bottom of the ducting.

Step 2: Gather six or seven thermometers and get them all to have about the same temperature reading. You can do this by laying the thermometers out together for about 30 minutes and then noting any discrepancies.

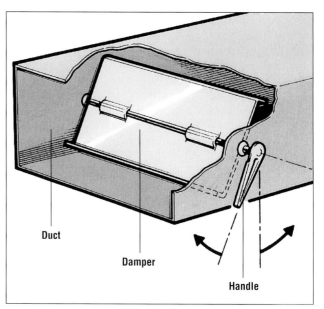

The ducts throughout the house often have dampers. The damper is open when it's turned parallel with the top and bottom of the duct.

Step 3: Tape the thermometers on the walls of each room so each thermometer is about 36 inches up from the floor, away from the hot-air register or cold-air return. Then wait one hour.

Step 4: Take a thermometer reading in each room when the heat is on. If one room shows a higher temperature than an adjoining room, close the damper or register slightly in the hotter room.

Step 5: Follow this procedure for each room, opening and closing dampers and registers until the same temperature is maintained in each room, or the temperature balance you want is reached. The thermostat to the furnace should be kept at the same reading while you balance the system.

Adjusting Blower Speed

An increase in blower speed can sometimes improve the flow of warm air through your home. A decrease can make the system quieter. You can increase or decrease the blower speed by slightly adjusting the pulley on the blower drive motor. To increase the speed:

Step 1: Slightly loosen the setscrew that holds the pulley to the drive shaft.

Step 2: Move or turn the pulley clockwise on the shaft one turn, then tighten the setscrew. If more speed is desired, turn the pulley clockwise two turns.

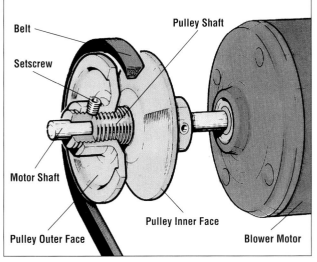

Belt

Pulley Shaft

Setscrew

Motor Shaft

Pulley Inner Face

Pulley Outer Face

Blower Motor

To adjust the blower speed, loosen the setscrew that holds the pulley to the drive shaft, and turn the pulley on the shaft.

To decrease blower speed:

Step 1: Loosen the setscrew that holds the pulley to the drive shaft.

Step 2: Move or turn the pulley counterclockwise on the drive shaft one turn, then tighten the setscrew. If less speed is desired, turn the pulley counterclockwise two turns.

The motor and blower pulley may also get out of alignment. This causes the blower to be noisy and cuts down on the efficiency of your distribution system. To check alignment:

Step 1: Place a carpenters' square against the outside of the motor and blower pulleys. The pulleys should be in a straight line and at right angles to the motor shaft.

Step 2: If the pulleys are not lined up at right angles to the motor housing, loosen the setscrew holding

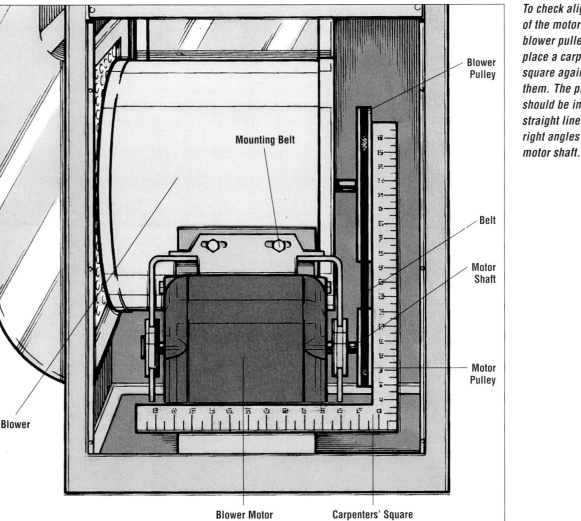

Mounting Belt

Blower Pulley

Belt

Motor Shaft

Motor Pulley

Blower

Blower Motor

Carpenters' Square

To check alignment of the motor and blower pulleys, place a carpenters' square against them. The pulleys should be in a straight line, at right angles to the motor shaft.

the motor pulley and move the pulley backward or forward as needed to align it properly. If the setscrew is jammed or rusted and won't loosen, or if the pulleys are out of alignment, loosen the mounting bolts on the motor and slide the motor backward or forward until the pulleys are properly aligned.

Noise Problems

Air forced through the ducts of the forced-air system can cause vibration and noise if the ducts are not firmly connected. The best way to stop this noise is to add duct hangers to the ducting system.

The hangers are usually wrapped around or across the ducting and nailed or screwed to the stud or rafter framing. At the elbows of the ducts, where air moving through the ducts changes direction, the duct sections can become loose or separated. Push loose sections back together and tape the joints firmly with duct tape to stop vibrations.

Noise can also be caused by inadequate lubrication, worn or damaged belts, or blower speed too high. Correct these problems as detailed on page 284 of this chapter.

Heat Loss From Ducts

If ducts run through cold basements or exterior crawl spaces, wrap the ducts with fiberglass insulation. Spiral insulation around the ducting and secure it with duct tape, wire, or heavy cord. Or, you can wrap the ducts with aluminum-faced insulating tape, sold in wide rolls and available at heating-supply stores.

Motors and Belts

Refer to page 266 for information on how to service motors and belts for specific types of furnaces.

Steam Systems

Steam heat is not installed in modern homes, but it is such a durable heating system that many homes and apartment buildings are still heated by steam. Basically, a steam heat system works by gravity. A boiler in the basement of the building, usually powered by an oil or gas burner, heats water until it turns to steam. The steam rises in pipes, going up to radiators and warming the air in the rooms throughout your home. The steam condenses as it cools, and the water flows back to the boiler.

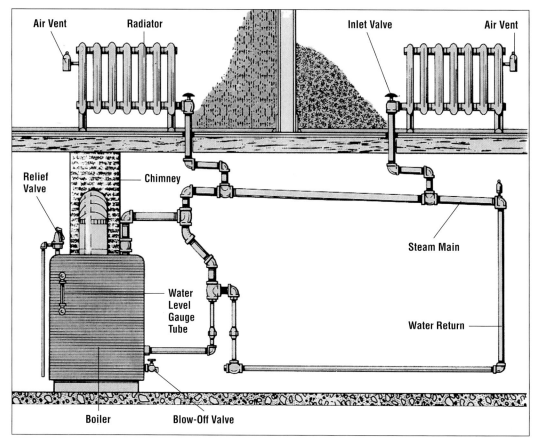

Air Vent   Radiator   Inlet Valve   Air Vent

Relief Valve   Chimney

Steam Main

Water Level Gauge Tube

Water Return

Boiler   Blow-Off Valve

A steam heat system works by gravity. A boiler in the basement heats water until it turns to steam; the steam rises to the radiators and warms the air in the rooms of your house.

STEAM SYSTEM TROUBLESHOOTING CHART		
Problem	**Possible Cause**	**Solution**
System won't run	1. Problems in boiler/furnace assembly.	1. See sections on specific furnaces.
Not enough heat (entire system)	1. Thermostat set too low.	1. Raise thermostat five degrees.
	2. Boiler water level low.	2. Check boiler; if necessary, let boiler cool and refill half full.
	3. Problems in boiler/furnace assembly.	3. See sections on specific furnaces.
	4. Rust or scale in boiler and/or pipes.	4. Flush boiler system; add antiscale preparation. If problem persists, call a professional.
	5. Problem in boiler.	5. Call a professional.
Not enough heat (individual radiator)	1. Radiator or pipes not sloping properly.	1. Check slope; prop radiator or adjust supply pipes to slope toward boiler.
	2. Inlet valve closed or partially open.	2. Open inlet valve completely.
	3. Air trapped in radiator.	3. Clear or replace air vent.
	4. Radiator blocked.	4. Make sure radiators are not blocked by rugs, drapes, or furniture.
Uneven heat	1. Air vents not sized or adjusted properly.	1. Adjust air vents so that those far away from boiler are open more than those close to the boiler.
Leaks	1. Loose pipe connection.	1. Tighten pipe connection.
	2. Worn stem packing or washer on inlet valve.	2. Replace stem packing or washer on inlet valve.
Water level gauge unreadable	1. Rust or scale in system.	1. Flush boiler system; add antiscale preparation. If problem persists, call a professional.
Pipes or radiators noisy	1. Water trapped in system.	1. Check slope; prop radiators or adjust supply pipes to slope toward the boiler.

Slope

The steam system is a simple one, but for it to work properly, all pipes and radiators must slope back toward the boiler. If the water can't run back to the boiler, it collects and blocks the path of the steam. When this happens, you will hear hammering noises in the system, and one or more individual radiators may not function.

Correcting malfunctions caused by inadequate slope is easy. Place blocks of wood under the legs of the affected radiators to correct the angle of slope. If you suspect that the return pipes are at fault, check their angle of slope with a level. These pipes may become incorrectly tilted when the building settles. If you can get at the pipes, you can solve the problem by supporting the pipe with pipe straps to reestablish the proper slope.

Water Level

If the heat throughout the system is inadequate, either the boiler isn't heating or the water level is too low. If the boiler isn't heating, the furnace may malfunction. Specific procedures for oil, gas, and electric heating systems are detailed earlier in this chapter.

The second possibility, a low water level in the system's boiler, is easier to handle. The level of water in the boiler should be maintained at about half full, and there should be an air space, or "chest," between the surface of the water and the top of the tank. Without the chest, the boiler can't work up a full head of steam, and the water overfills the return lines and may trip the relief valve. To correct, keep the water level at half full. If the water level in the boiler is consistently low, check the pipes for leaks. If you spot a leak at a pipe connection, tighten the connection with a pipe wrench. If the connection still leaks, call a professional service person.

Radiators

If an individual radiator is cold and both it and the pipes leading to it are tilted properly, check the radiator's inlet valve. This valve must be opened completely for the radiator to function properly. If some radiators get warmer than others, air vents may be at fault. Some air vents are adjustable. Turning a screw to a lower setting reduces the flow of heat into the radiator; conversely, raising the setting lets more air out, bringing in more heat.

If your radiators' air vents aren't adjustable, consider replacing them with units that are. Some hardware stores stock standard, bullet-style air vents in a range of sizes. If a radiator gets too hot, replace its vent with a smaller one; for cold radiators, go up a size or two.

Leaks

Leaks around inlet valves, radiators, and pipes are plumbing problems, and you may not be able to correct them without professional help. There are special additives that you can put into the boiler's water supply to stop leaks. Pipe leaks are frequently due to loose connections; connections can be tightened with a wrench. Leaks around inlet valves are caused by deterioration of the stem packing or the washer in the valve; to correct this problem, the valve must be disassembled.

Radiator inlet valves are similar to faucets. The valve has a packing nut, a valve body or stem, and a washer assembly. To replace the valve packing or the washer:

Step 1: Shut off the boiler and let it cool. It isn't necessary to shut off the water supply; as the steam in the system cools, it will condense and flow back out of the radiator to the boiler.

Step 2: Remove the screw that holds the handle to the valve. Unscrew the packing nut, remove the handle, and back out the valve stem or body. At the bottom of the stem is a washer, held by a screw. Remove the screw and the washer.

Step 3: Replace the washer with a new one of the same size and type. The packing nut may have a washer or may be filled with packing string. Replace the washer or install new packing as you reassemble the valve.

Step 4: Tighten all connections and turn the system back on.

For detailed instructions on faucet repairs, see Chapter 7 (pages 235–245).

Flushing the System

Once a month, the entire heating system should be flushed to keep the pipes clear and the steam flowing freely. To flush the system, open the blow-off valve and let the water run off into a bucket until it runs clear. If the water remains rusty, or if the entire system is operating at less than optimum efficiency, the pipes are probably clogged with rust and scale. If you see any rust in the water level gauge tube, shut off the boiler and let it cool; then flush the system by draining and refilling it several times. Finally, add a commercial radiator preparation formulated to curb the buildup of rust and scale. These products are available at heating-supply stores.

Boiler/Furnace Assembly

The boiler of a steam-heat system uses a gas or oil burner or an electric heating element to heat the water in the system. If there is no heat in the system, follow the procedures detailed previously for gas, oil, or electric furnaces, as appropriate. If problems occur in the boiler itself, follow the procedures listed above or call a professional service person.

Hot-Water Systems

Because water retains heat, it is used to store and distribute heat in home systems. There are two types of hot-water systems: the gravity system and the hydronic or forced hot-water type. Like steam systems, hot-water heating systems can be powered by gas, oil, or electricity.

Gravity systems depend on the upward flow of hot water to circulate heated water from the boiler through a system of pipes to radiators in the rooms of your home. The better radiators for hot-water systems are called convectors. These units employ a series of fans to disperse the heat.

The heat from the water in the radiators or convectors is transferred first to the metal radiators and then to the air. As the water loses its heat, it sinks and flows back to the boiler through return pipes. Most gravity systems heat the water to no more than about 180°F, and the cooled water that goes back to the boiler rarely falls below 120°F. Open gravity systems have an overflow outlet to let water escape; this prevents a buildup of excess pressure in the system. Closed systems have a sealed expansion tank; when water pressure builds up in the system, the excess water flows into the expansion tank to prevent damage to the pipes or the boiler. Hydronic hot-water systems are much like closed gravity systems, except that a hydronic system uses a motor-driven circulating pump to move the water. As a

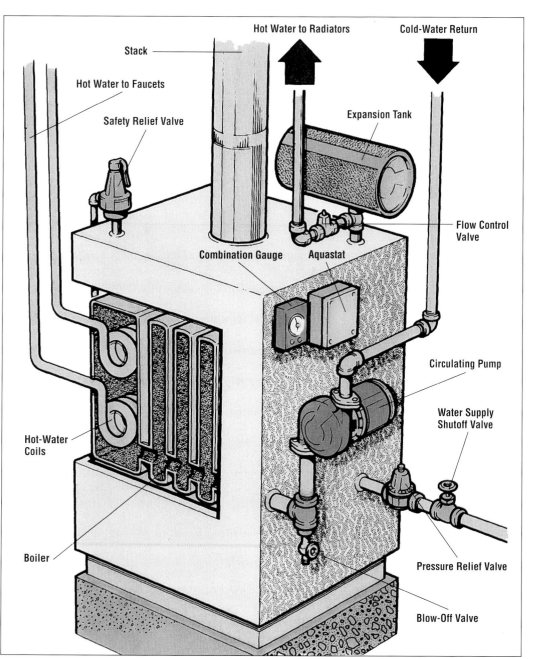

Stack

Hot Water to Faucets

Safety Relief Valve

Hot Water to Radiators

Cold-Water Return

Expansion Tank

Flow Control Valve

Combination Gauge

Aquastat

Circulating Pump

Water Supply Shutoff Valve

Hot-Water Coils

Boiler

Pressure Relief Valve

Blow-Off Valve

Hydronic hot-water systems use a motor-driven circulating pump to move the hot water; the water moves rapidly and arrives at the radiator with little heat loss.

result, water in a hydronic system moves more rapidly and arrives at the room radiator with less heat loss than water in a gravity system.

Slope

Like steam systems, hot-water systems depend on proper slope. All pipes and radiators must slope back toward the boiler. Hammering noises and failure to heat indicate incorrect slope. To correct these malfunctions, check the slope of radiators and pipes and prop radiators or fasten pipes so that all components are properly tilted. To correct malfunctions caused by inadequate

slope, refer to instructions for correcting slope in steam systems on page 287.

Water Level

The water level in the hot-water system's boiler should be maintained, as with steam systems, at about half full. There should be an air space between the surface of the water and the top of the tank. A water level that is too low can cause inadequate heating. In most cases, an automatic filling system keeps the boiler filled with the proper amount of water. However, if the water level of the system is consistently low, check the pipes for leaks.

power failure. It may also be necessary to drain the system to make repairs. To drain the pipes:

Step 1: Turn off the power to the boiler at the main electrical entrance panel. To do this, remove the fuse or trip the circuit breaker that controls the circuit. Let the water cool until it's just warm.

Step 2: When the water has cooled, turn off the water supply valve and attach a length of garden hose to the boiler drain. The hose should be lower than the boiler; position it in a laundry sink or at a floor drain.

Step 3: Open the drain valve and the air vents on all of the convectors or radiators. The water from the system will flow out through the hose. Give the valve plenty of time to drain.

Step 4: To refill the system, close the air vents on all the convectors or radiators and shut the drain valve. Turn on the water supply to the boiler. If the boiler has an automatic shutoff, refilling is automatic. If the boiler doesn't have automatic shutoff, fill it until the combination valve gauge reads 20 pounds of pressure per square inch.

Step 5: Release air from all the convectors in the system so they'll heat properly. The gauge on the boiler should read 12 pounds per square inch. If the pressure on the gauge shows less than 12 pounds per square inch of pressure, add more water. If the pressure is above 12 pounds per square inch, drain off some of the water.

Troubleshooting Cooling Systems

There are two types of home cooling systems—central air conditioning and individual room air conditioners. Both systems use the same components—a condenser, which uses electricity to cool a refrigerant liquid in a coil, and an evaporator, which cools the air in your home. Heat pumps, when operated in their cooling cycle, function as central air conditioners. Procedures for heat-pump maintenance and repairs are detailed on page 282 of this chapter.

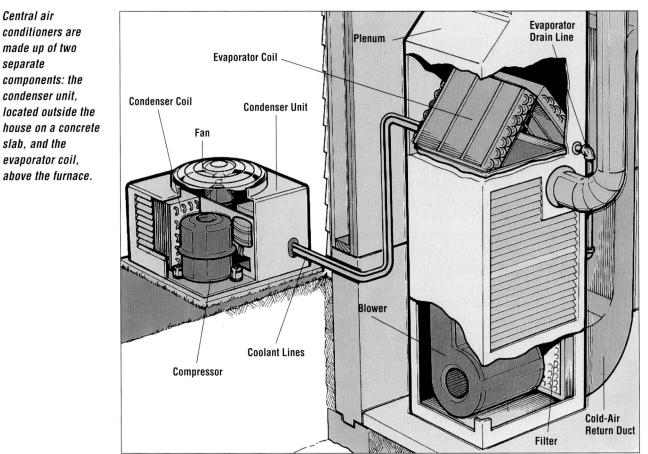

Central air conditioners are made up of two separate components: the condenser unit, located outside the house on a concrete slab, and the evaporator coil, above the furnace.

Plenum

Evaporator Drain Line

Evaporator Coil

Condenser Coil

Condenser Unit

Fan

Blower

Coolant Lines

Compressor

Cold-Air Return Duct

Filter

CENTRAL AIR CONDITIONER TROUBLESHOOTING CHART

Problem	Possible Cause	Solution
Condenser doesn't run	1. No power.	1. Check for blown fuses or tripped circuit breakers at main entrance panel or at separate entrance panel; restore circuit.
	2. Thermostat set too high.	2. Lower thermostat setting five degrees.
	3. Motor faulty.	3. Call a professional.
	4. Compressor faulty.	4. Call a professional.
Uneven cooling	1. Distribution system out of balance.	1. Balance system; see section on forced-air systems.
Inadequate cooling	1. Thermostat set too high.	1. Lower thermostat setting five degrees.
	2. Evaporator dirty.	2. Clean evaporator.
	3. Unit too small.	3. Replace with larger unit; call a professional.
	4. Problem in distribution system.	4. See section on forced-air systems.
Unit doesn't cool	1. Thermostat set too high.	1. Lower thermostat setting five degrees.
	2. Condenser dirty.	2. Clean condenser coil and fins; if necessary, straighten fins.
	3. Condenser unit blocked.	3. Remove debris blocking condenser; cut down weeds, grass, and vines.
	4. Evaporator dirty.	4. Clean evaporator.
	5. Problem in distribution system.	5. See section on forced-air systems.
	6. Compressor faulty.	6. Call a professional.
	7. Not enough refrigerant in system.	7. Call a professional.
Condenser unit turns on and off repeatedly	1. Condenser dirty.	1. Clean condenser coil and fins.
	2. Condenser unit blocked.	2. Remove debris blocking condenser; cut down weeds, grass, and vines.
	3. Evaporator dirty.	3. Clean evaporator.
	4. Problem in distribution system.	4. See section on forced-air systems.

Central Air Conditioning

Central air conditioners have two separate components: the condenser and the evaporator. The condenser unit is usually located outside the house on a concrete slab. The evaporator coil is mounted in the plenum or main duct junction above the furnace. Two coolant lines run from the condenser unit to the evaporator. When the air conditioner is turned on, the liquid refrigerant in the condenser coil cools. The cooled liquid flows to the evaporator coil through the first connection line. At the evaporator, warm air in your home is cooled by contact with the liquid-filled coil. As the warm air around it

becomes cooler, the liquid in the coil becomes warmer and is transformed to its gaseous state. The gas flows through a second connection line back to the condenser unit, where it is pressurized and cooled again to its liquid state. As it cools, the gas gives off heat, which is vented out of the unit by a fan located at the top or back of the condenser.

Most central air conditioners are connected to a home's forced-air distribution system. Thus, the same motor, blower, and ductwork used for heating are used to distribute cool air from the air conditioning system. When a central air conditioner is operating, hot air inside the house flows to the furnace through the return-air duct. The hot air is moved by the blower across the cooled evaporator coil in the plenum, and is then delivered through ducts to cool the house. When the air conditioner works but the house doesn't cool, the problem is probably in the distribution system. In this case, refer to the section on troubleshooting forced-air systems on page 284.

Both the evaporator and the condenser are sealed. Therefore, a professional service person should be called for almost any maintenance other than routine cleaning. Central air conditioners should be professionally inspected and adjusted before the beginning of every cooling season. However, don't let your maintenance end with this annual checkup. While there aren't many repairs you can make yourself, there are specific maintenance procedures you can follow to keep your system operating at peak efficiency. *Caution: Before doing any work on an air conditioning system, make sure the power to the system, both to the condenser and to the evaporator assembly, is turned off.*

Evaporator

The evaporator is located directly above the furnace in the plenum. The evaporator may not be accessible, but if it is, you should clean it once a year. If the plenum has foil-wrapped insulation at its front, you can clean the evaporator; if the plenum is a sealed sheet-metal box, do not attempt to open it. To clean an accessible evaporator:

Step 1: Turn off the power to the air conditioner.

Step 2: Remove the foil-wrapped insulation at the front of the plenum; it's probably taped in place. Remove the tape carefully, because you'll have to replace it later. Behind the insulation is the access plate, which is held in place by several screws. Remove the screws and lift off the plate.

Step 3: Clean the entire underside of the evaporator unit with a stiff brush. A large hand mirror can help you see what you're doing. If you can't reach all the way back to clean the entire area, slide the evaporator out a little. The evaporator can be slid out even if it has rigid pipes connected to it, but be careful not to bend the pipes.

Step 4: Clean the tray below the evaporator unit. This tray carries condensation away from the evaporator. Pour a tablespoon of household bleach into the weep hole in the tray to prevent fungus growth. In extremely humid weather, check the condensate drain and pan every other day. If there's much moisture in the pan, the weep hole from the pan to the drain line may be clogged. Open the weep hole with a piece of wire.

Step 5: Put the unit back into place, reinstall the plate, and tape the insulation back over it.

Step 6: Turn on the air conditioner and check for air leaks. Seal any leaks with duct tape.

Condenser

In most systems, the condenser unit is located outside the house and is prone to accumulated dirt and debris from trees, lawn mowing, and airborne dust. The condenser has a fan that moves air across the condenser coil. You must clean the coil on the intake side, so before you turn off the power to the air conditioner, check to see which direction the air moves across the coils. To clean the condenser:

Clean the fins on the condenser with a soft brush to remove accumulated dirt; you may have to remove a protective grille to reach the fins.

Step 1: Turn off the power to the air conditioner.

Step 2: Cut down any grass, weeds, or vines that have grown around the condenser unit because they could be obstructing the flow of air.

Step 3: Clean the condenser with a commercial coil cleaner, available at refrigerator-supply stores. Instructions for use are included. Flush the coil clean with a spray bottle—not a hose—and let it dry.

Step 4: Clean the fins with a soft brush to remove accumulated dirt. You may have to remove a protective grille to reach them. Do not clean

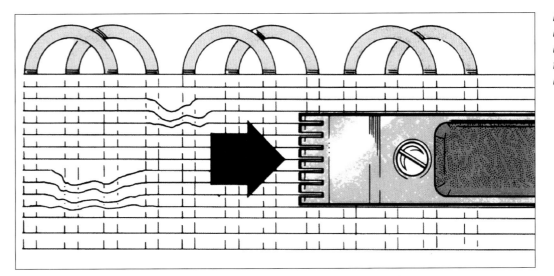

If the fins on a condenser are bent, carefully straighten them with a fin comb.

the fins with a garden hose, as water could turn the dirt into mud and compact it between the fins. Clean the fins very carefully: They're made of light-gauge aluminum and are easily damaged. If the fins are bent, straighten them with a fin comb, sold at most appliance-parts stores. A fin comb is designed to slide into spaces between the fins. Use it carefully to avoid damaging the fins.

Step 5: Check the concrete pad on which the condenser rests to make sure it's level. Set a carpenters' level front to back and side to side on top of the unit. If the pad has settled, lift the pad with a pry bar or a piece of 2×4; then force gravel or rocks under the concrete to level it.

During the fall and winter, outside condenser units should be protected from the elements to prevent leaf blockage and ice damage. Cover the condenser unit with a commercial condenser cover made to fit the shape of the unit, or you can use heavy plastic sheeting secured with sturdy cord.

Refrigerant

The coolant used in most air conditioning systems is a refrigerant called Freon. If the system does not contain the proper amount of Freon, little or no cooling will take place. If you suspect a Freon problem, call a professional service person to recharge the system. *Caution: Do not try to charge your system's Freon lines. Freon is volatile and can be dangerous!*

There is one repair to the system's coolant lines that you can make. Examine the lines running from the condenser outside the evaporator inside the house. If the insulation is damaged or worn, it will cut down on the cooling efficiency of the unit and, therefore, should be replaced. Replace damaged or worn coolant-line insulation with new insulation of the same type as soon as possible.

Distribution System

In most cases, circulation problems and noisy operation are caused by problems in your home's heating and cooling distribution system. For instructions on correcting distribution problems, see the section on troubleshooting forced-air systems on page 284 of this chapter.

Room Air Conditioners

Room air conditioners, also called window units, work the same way central air conditioners do. They are smaller than central systems, and they can be more expensive to operate. Depending on its size, a room unit may cool only the room in which it's located, or it may be able to cool adjoining rooms as well.

Both the condenser and the evaporator are contained in one housing. The condenser coil faces outside, and the evaporator faces inside. Sandwiched between the coils are a compressor, two fans, a motor, and thermostat controls. Dirt is the biggest enemy of window air conditioners; it can lower the efficiency of the evaporator coil, block the operation of the fan that blows out the cool air, clog filters, and block drain ports.

The coils, the compressor, and the motor of a room air conditioner are sealed components, so any repairs to them should be left to a professional service person. You can make minor repairs, and regular maintenance will keep your unit running well. When extensive repairs are needed, you can also save the cost of a service call by removing the air conditioner from its mounting and taking it to the repair shop.

Both of the major components of a room air conditioner are contained in one housing. The condenser coil faces outside, and the evaporator faces inside.

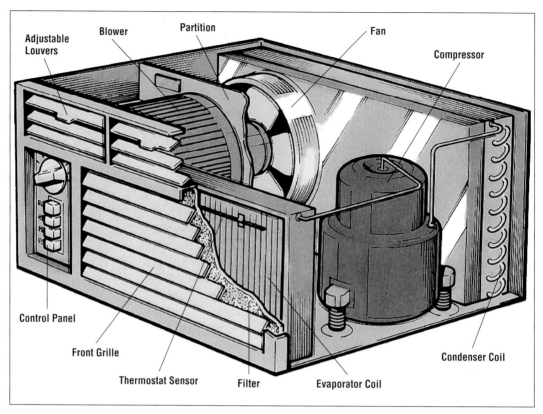

During the winter, room air conditioners should be protected from the elements. Either remove the unit from its mounting and store it, or cover the outside portion of the unit with a commercial room air conditioner cover or with heavy plastic sheeting, held in place with duct tape. Air conditioner covers are available at hardware stores, home centers, and appliance stores. *Caution: Before doing any work on an air conditioner, make sure it's unplugged. Room air conditioners have either one or two capacitors, located behind the control panel and near the fan. Capacitors store electricity, even when the power to the unit is turned off. Before you do any work on an air conditioner, unplug it and discharge the capacitor or you could receive a severe shock.* To safely discharge the capacitor:

Step 1: Unplug the air conditioner or turn off the power to the circuit.

Step 2: Gain access to the capacitor(s) by removing the unit's control panel. The capacitor is located behind the control panel and near the fan and looks like a large dry-cell battery.

Step 3: Discharge the capacitor using a 20,000-ohm/ 2-watt resistor, an inexpensive wire unit available at most electrical-supply stores. Carefully fasten the clips of the resistor to the terminals of the capacitor. This discharges the capacitor. If the capacitor has three terminal

posts, connect the resistor to one outer terminal and to the center terminal. Then connect it to the other outside terminal and the center terminal. After discharging the capacitor, you can proceed with the necessary repairs.

Disassembling a Room Air Conditioner

You can access the filter, controls, thermostat, and evaporator coil of a room air conditioner through the front grille, which is held to the housing of the unit by retaining screws or spring clips. To disassemble the control panel, remove the control knobs and lift off the panel. The knobs may be friction-fit on shafts. Pull them straight out and off the shafts. Or the knobs may have tiny setscrews at the base of the knob. Loosen these screws and pull off the knobs. The escutcheon plate of each knob is screwed to the frame of the appliance. On some models, the working parts of the air conditioner can be removed from the housing shell by removing a series of screws. On others, the sides and tops of the cabinet can be disassembled. But for most repairs, only the grille and the control panel must be removed.

Filter

At the beginning of every cooling season, and once a month during the season, remove the front grille and clean or replace the filter. If you live in a very dusty area,

ROOM A/C TROUBLESHOOTING CHART

Problem	Possible Cause	Solution
Unit doesn't run	1. No power.	1. Check power cord, plug, and outlet. Check for blown fuse or tripped circuit breaker at main entrance panel; restore circuit.
	2. Motor overload or safety shutoff.	2. Wait 30 minutes; press reset button. Repeat if necessary.
	3. Switch faulty.	3. Check terminals and insulation; if burns are evident, replace switch. If switch looks all right, call a professional.
Fuses blow	1. Circuit overloaded.	1. Put on different circuit.
	2. Voltage low.	2. Call a professional or the power company.
Cooling inadequate	1. Thermostat set too high.	1. Lower thermostat setting five degrees.
	2. Filter dirty.	2. Clean or replace filter.
	3. Coils dirty.	3. Clean coils.
	4. Condenser blocked from outside.	4. Make sure outside of unit is not blocked.
	5. Motor faulty.	5. Call a professional.
	6. Compressor faulty.	6. Call a professional.
	7. Coolant leak.	7. Call a professional.
Fan runs, but unit doesn't cool	1. Thermostat set too high.	1. Lower thermostat setting five degrees.
	2. Thermostat faulty.	2. Test thermostat; if faulty, replace, or call a professional.
	3. Coils dirty.	3. Clean coils.
	4. Motor faulty.	4. Call a professional.
	5. Compressor faulty.	5. Call a professional.
Unit cools, but fan doesn't run	1. Control switch set wrong.	1. Reset switch; try different settings.
	2. Fan clogged.	2. Clean and tighten fan blades.
	3. Fan blades bent.	3. Straighten fan blades.
	4. Fan motor faulty.	4. Replace fan motor or call a professional.
Unit turns on and off repeatedly	1. Coils dirty.	1. Clean coils.
	2. Filter dirty.	2. Clean or replace filter.

clean or replace the filter more often. Most room air conditioners have a washable filter that looks like sponge rubber. Clean the filter with a solution of mild household detergent and water; rinse well. Let the filter dry completely before reinstalling it. Some units have a throwaway filter, similar to a furnace filter. When this type of filter becomes dirty, replace it with a new one of the same type.

Power Cord

The power cord that connects the air conditioner to the wall outlet may become worn and fail to supply

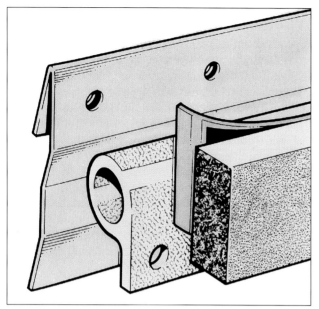

Three of the most popular types of weather stripping include spring metal (left), tubular gasket (center), and self-adhesive foam strips (right).

- Spring-metal strips (V-shaped or single) are available in bronze, copper, stainless steel, and aluminum finishes. Most manufacturers package spring-metal weather stripping in rolls, and they include the brads necessary for installation. Although this kind of weather stripping seems like a simple installation, it does require patience.
- Self-sticking spring metal has a peel-and-stick backing. These are like the standard spring-metal strips just described, but they are far easier to install.
- Felt is one of the old standbys and is very economical. It comes in a variety of widths, thicknesses, qualities, and colors (brown, gray, and black). Felt strips are usually nailed in place, but they are also available with a pressure-sensitive adhesive backing.
- Serrated metal is felt- or vinyl-backed weather stripping that combines the sturdiness of metal with the application ease of felt. Most manufacturers package their serrated-metal weather stripping in rolls that include brads for installation.
- Tubular gasket weather stripping is made of extremely flexible vinyl. Tubular gasket weather stripping is usually applied outside where it easily conforms to uneven places. Available in white and gray, it cannot be painted because paint causes the tube to stiffen and lose its flexibility.
- Foam-filled tubular gasket weather stripping includes a foam core in the tubular part of the gasket just described. The foam provides extra insulating qualities and extra strength. Moreover, the foam-filled

tubular gasket will hold its shape better than the hollow-tube type. It should not be painted.
- Interlocking metal weather stripping requires two separate pieces along each edge. One part fits inside the other to form the seal. One piece goes on the door while the other is attached to the jamb. Since installation generally requires cutting (rabbeting), interlocking metal weather stripping may well be beyond the capabilities of the average homeowner. In addition, should the pieces get bent, they would no longer seal and could, in fact, do damage to surrounding surfaces. Therefore, no step-by-step installation instructions are provided for this type of weather stripping. If you already have interlocking metal weather stripping installed, keep it working right by straightening any bent pieces with a screwdriver, pliers, or putty knife.

Interlocking metal weather stripping can provide a secure seal as long as the separate pieces fit together as they should. Installation is tricky, and maintenance requires careful examination for bent pieces.

- Casement window gaskets are specially made vinyl channels that slip over the lip of the casement frame. No adhesives or tools—except scissors for cutting the gasket to the proper length—are needed. This weather stripping is generally available only in shades of gray.
- Jalousie gaskets are clear, vinyl tracks that can be cut to fit over the edges of jalousie louvers. They snap in place for a friction fit.
- Door sweeps fill any gap at the threshold under a door. Door sweeps come in wood and felt, wood and foam, metal and vinyl, and in a spring-operated version that is mounted on the outside of a door that opens inward.

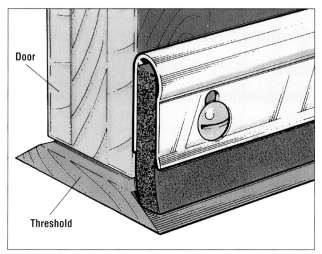

A door sweep can create a tight seal when a gap exists between the bottom of the door and the threshold. Door sweeps can be made of wood and felt, wood and foam, or metal and vinyl. All are effective in sealing out drafts.

Weather-Stripping Windows

Double-hung wood windows almost always require weather stripping, although if the top sash is never opened, you can solve an air leak problem by caulking to seal any cracks. You may find it advantageous to use more than one type of weather stripping to complete the job. Be sure to follow the correct installation procedures for each type of weather stripping.

Double-hung windows require weather stripping that surrounds both sashes.

Spring-metal weather stripping is available in V-shaped strips (middle, left), or flat strips (middle, right). Felt strips (top, left) are economical to use but aren't as long-lasting as other types of weather stripping. Serrated-metal strips (top, right) are sturdier than felt but can be difficult to install. Tubular gasket weather stripping is available with a hollow tube (bottom, left) or foam-filled tube (bottom, right).

Spring-metal weather stripping fits into the tracks around the windows. Each strip should be about 2 inches longer than the sash so that the end of the strip is exposed when the windows are closed. To install spring-metal weather stripping:

Step 1: Position the vertical strips so that the flared flange faces toward the outside. The center strip should be mounted to the upper sash with the flare aimed down, while the other horizontal strips are mounted to the top of the upper sash and the bottom of the lower sash with the flared flange facing out. Cut the spring-metal weather stripping to allow for the window pulley mechanisms.

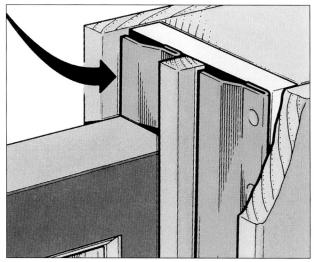

Position the flange on spring metal so that the flared edge faces outside.

Step 2: Cut the spring-metal strips to size using tin snips.

Step 3: Attach the strips to the window frame. Position the strip properly and note any hinges, locks, or other hardware that might interfere. Trim away the metal where needed. Then trim the ends of the strip at an angle or miter where vertical and horizontal strips meet. Tap in one nail at the top and one nail at the bottom of the strip. Do not

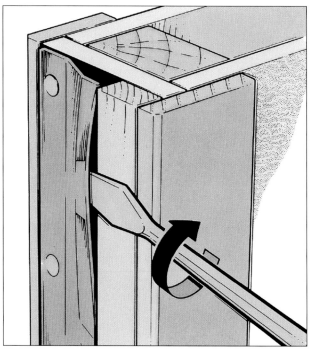

Flare the edge of a spring-metal strip with a screwdriver to render a snug fit.

put in more nails and do not drive the top and bottom nails all the way in. Since some vertical strips do not come with nail holes, you may have to make pilot holes with an ice pick or awl.

Step 4: Check to make sure the strips are straight and properly positioned. Then drive a nail in the center of the strip—but again only partway. Add more nails between the starter nails. To avoid damaging the strip, never drive any of the nails all the way in with the hammer. Instead, drive the nails flush with a nail set.

Step 5: Flare out the edge of the strip with a screwdriver to render a snug fit.

Pressure-sensitive types of weather stripping can be used only on the friction-free parts of a wooden window such as the lower sash or the top of the upper sash. If the strips were installed snugly against the gap between upper and lower sashes, the movement of the window would pull it loose. To install pressure-sensitive foam weather stripping:

Apply pressure-sensitive types only on the friction-free parts of a wooden window.

Step 1: Clean the entire surface to which the weather stripping is to be attached. Use a detergent solution and make certain that no dirt or grease remains. If pressure-sensitive weather stripping had been installed previously, use a solvent to remove any old adhesive. Dry the surface.

Step 2: Use scissors to cut the strip to fit, but do not remove the backing paper yet. Start at one end and slowly peel the paper backing as you push the sticky foam strips into place. If the backing proves stubborn at the beginning, stretch the foam until the seal between the backing and the foam breaks.

To install self-sticking spring-metal weather stripping on wooden windows:

Step 1: Measure and cut the strips to fit the window, then clean the surface where the strips are to be placed.

Step 2: Put the strips in place without removing the backing paper, and mark the spots for trimming (for example, indicate hardware points and where vertical and horizontal strips meet).

Step 3: Peel off the backing at one end and press the strip in place, peeling and pressing as you work toward the other end.

Felt strips are somewhat unsightly for sealing gaps on wooden windows. There are places where felt can be used to good advantage, however. Attach felt strips to the bottom of the lower sash, the top of the upper sash, and to the interior side of the upper sash. The strips will then function as horizontal gaskets. To weather-strip with felt strips:

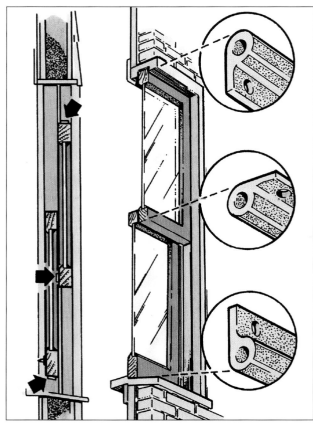

Felt strips (left) *can be placed on the bottom of the lower sash, on top of the upper sash, and to the interior side of the upper sash. Tubular gaskets* (right) *should be installed only on window exteriors.*

Step 1: Measure the felt and cut the strip from the roll with scissors. Keep in mind that felt strips can go around corners. Push the material snugly against the gap.

Step 2: Nail the ends of each strip first, but do not drive these nails flush; leave room to pry them out. Start at one end and drive a tack every 2 to 3 inches, pulling the felt tight as you go. If you find slack when you reach the other end, remove the nail, pull to tighten, and trim off any excess.

Note: If possible, do this job on a warm day. The adhesive forms a better bond if applied when the temperature is at least 60°F.

To install pressure-sensitive felt, follow the same steps as you would to attach pressure-sensitive foam.

Tubular types of weather stripping are also unsightly. They are best used when installed on the outside of the window. If the window is easily accessible from outside the house, then tubular weather stripping is worth considering. It can also be used to improve existing weather stripping. To install tubular and foam-filled gaskets:

Step 1: Begin by measuring the strips and cutting them to size with scissors. Cutting all the strips for a window at one time will save you trips up and down the ladder later on.

Step 2: Position each strip carefully and drive a nail into one end. Space nails every 2 to 3 inches, pulling the weather stripping tight before you drive each nail.

Most metal windows are grooved around the edges so that the metal flanges will interlock and preclude the need for weather stripping. Sometimes, though, gaps do exist, and you must apply weather stripping in such instances.

Generally, the only kind of weather stripping that can be applied to metal windows is the pressure-sensitive type. Screws would go through the metal and impede movement of the window. To install pressure-sensitive, adhesive-backed foam weather stripping:

Step 1: Apply the weather stripping to the top of the upper sash (if it is movable) and to the bottom of the lower sash. These are usually the only spots where metal windows allow for air movement.

Step 2: If you find any other gaps, attach a vinyl tubular gasket to the area with a special adhesive formulated to hold vinyl to metal.

Sliding windows, those in which the sash moves laterally, come in both wood and metal frames. Weather-strip the wooden frames much as you would a double-hung window turned sideways. If only one sash moves, weather-strip it and caulk the stationary sash. For metal frames, follow the instructions for weather-stripping standard metal windows.

Special gaskets are designed for sealing gaps in jalousie and casement windows. To weather-strip jalousies, measure the edge of the glass louver, cut the gasket to size with scissors, and snap the gasket in place. To weather-strip casement windows, measure the edges of the frame, cut strips of gasket to size, miter the ends of the gasket strips where they will intersect, and slip the strips in place over the lip of the frame.

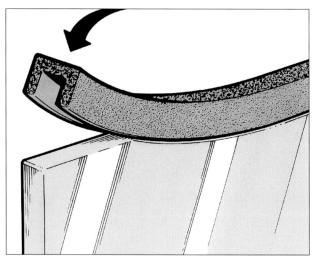

To weather-strip jalousie windows, cut the special gasket to size and snap it into place along the edge of the glass.

Weather-Stripping Doors

All four edges around doors can permit air to leak in and out of your house. In fact, the average door has more gaps than a loose-fitting window. Doors, moreover, don't run in grooves as windows do, so any crack area around a door is likely to be far greater than the area around a window.

Before you start weather-stripping, inspect the door to be sure it fits properly in the frame opening. Close the door and observe it from the inside. Look to see that the distance between the door and the frame is uniform all along both sides and at the top. The distance does not have to be precisely the same all the way around, but if the door rests crooked in the frame, weather stripping may make it impossible to open or close. Naturally, if there is great variance in the opening between the door and frame, it will be difficult to fit weather stripping snugly at all points, and gaps will result.

The cause of most door problems is usually the hinges. Therefore, the first thing to do is open the door and tighten all the hinge screws. Even slightly loose screws can cause the door to sag. If the screw holes have been reamed out and are now too big to hold the screws, you can use larger screws as long as they will still fit in the hinge's countersunk holes. If even the larger screws won't work, pack the holes with toothpicks dipped in glue, and use a knife to cut off the toothpicks even with the surface. Now the screws have new wood in which to bite.

Sometimes the door must be planed off to prevent binding. If so, you can usually plane the top with the door still in place. Always move the plane toward the center of the door to avoid splintering off the edges. If you must plane wood off the sides, take the door off its hinges, plane the hinge side, and always move toward the edges.

Spring metal is quite popular for door weather-stripping. It works effectively when installed properly, and it is not visible with the door closed. In the packages designated as door kits, most manufacturers include the triangular piece that fits next to the striker plate on the jamb. To install spring-metal weather stripping around doors:

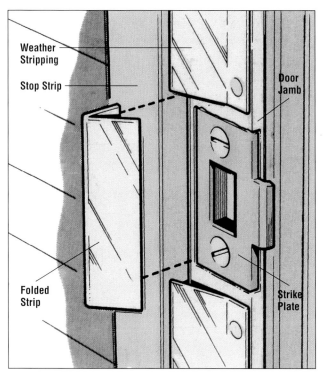

Install spring-metal weather stripping with the flared side facing out. On the latch side, attach the folded strip to the edge next to the strike plate; then fasten strips above and below the strike plate.

Step 1: Measure and cut the spring-metal strips to size.

Step 2: Position the side strips so that the flared flange almost touches the door stop. Trim away the metal where needed to accommodate any hinges, locks, or other hardware.

Step 3: Tap in one nail at the top and one nail at the bottom of each side strip. Do not put in any more nails, and don't drive the top and bottom nails in all the way. If the strips do not have prepunched holes, make pilot holes with an ice pick or awl. Check to make sure that the side strips are straight and properly positioned.

Step 4: Drive a nail in the center of a side strip, but again only partway in. Then add nails spaced at regular intervals between the ends. To avoid damaging the strip, never drive any of the nails all the way in with the hammer. Instead, drive the nails flush with a nail set. Repeat the procedure for the other side strip.

Step 5: Put the top strip in last and miter it to fit. Flare out the edge of each strip with a screwdriver to render a snug fit.

Self-sticking spring metal can be used in the same places as regular spring metal. To install self-sticking spring-metal weather stripping around doors:

Step 1: Measure and cut the strips to fit, and clean the surface where strips are to be placed.

Step 2: Put the strips in place without removing the backing paper. Mark the spots for trimming (for example, hardware points and where vertical and horizontal strips meet).

Step 3: Peel off the backing at one end and press the strip in place, peeling and pressing as you work toward the other end.

Pressure-sensitive foam weather stripping is easy to install around most doors. The foams are effective, but they have a shorter life span than other weather-stripping materials. To install pressure-sensitive foam weather stripping around doors:

Step 1: Select a warm day to do the work, if possible. The adhesive forms a better bond if applied on a day when the temperature is at least 60°F.

Step 2: Clean the entire surface to which the weather stripping is to be attached. Use a detergent solution and make certain that no dirt or grease remains. If pressure-sensitive weather stripping had been previously installed, use a solvent to remove any old adhesive. Dry the surface.

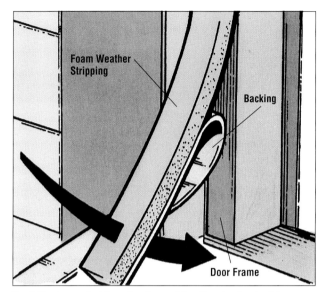

Seal the top and sides of a door with adhesive-backed foam weather stripping. To install the foam, peel off the backing and stick the strip down.

Step 3: Use scissors to cut the strip to fit, but don't remove the backing paper yet.

Step 4: Start at one end and slowly peel the paper backing as you push the sticky foam strips into place. If the backing proves stubborn at the beginning, stretch the foam until the seal between the backing and foam breaks.

Step 5: Attach the strips on the hinge side to the door jamb.

Step 6: Attach the other two strips to the door stop. If the corner of the door catches the weather stripping as you close it, trim the top piece of foam on the hinge side.

Serrated-metal weather stripping, usually with a felt-strip insert running the length of the serrated groove, also can be used to seal air gaps around doors. To install this type of weather stripping material, measure the length of strips required, and then use tin snips or heavy-duty scissors to cut the serrated-metal material to the proper lengths. Nail each strip at both ends, add a nail to the center of each strip, and drive additional nails every two to three inches along the rest of the strip.

The gap at the bottom of the door is treated differently from the gaps on the sides and along the top. The hump on the floor along the bottom of the door is called the threshold. A threshold can be made of either wood or metal. Many of the metal types feature a flexible vinyl insert that creates a tight seal when the door closes against it. Other thresholds consist of one

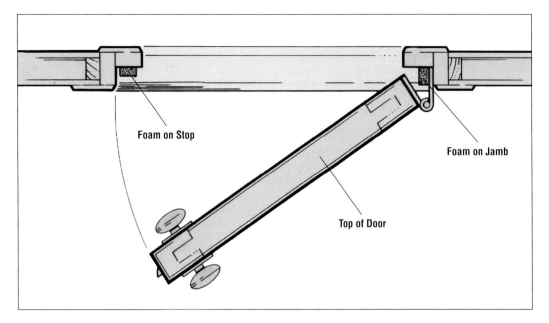

Foam on Stop

Foam on Jamb

Top of Door

unit on the floor and a mating piece on the bottom of the door. These two pieces interlock to form a weathertight barrier.

In most cases, the threshold with a flexible vinyl insert is the best one for a novice weather-stripper to install. Interlock systems are quite effective when properly installed, but they require a perfect fit or they will not work satisfactorily.

Wooden thresholds often wear down to the point where they must be replaced. This is an easy installation, and there are many types of replacement thresholds from which to choose. Most are aluminum and come in standard door widths; however, if your door is not

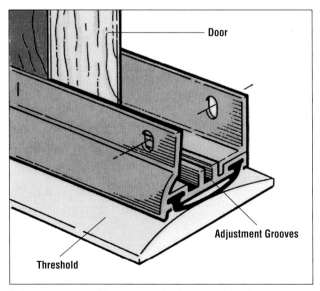

Door

Adjustment Grooves

Threshold

A bottom sweep slides on over the bottom of the door; adjustment grooves adapt it to any door thickness.

standard width, you can trim the aluminum threshold with a hacksaw. To install a replacement threshold:

Step 1: Remove the old threshold. If it is wood, there are two ways to remove it. In most cases, you can pry it up after removing the door stops with a small, flat pry bar or putty knife, but you must work carefully and slowly. If the jamb itself rests on the threshold, saw through the old threshold at each end. Use a backsaw placed right against the jamb, and saw down through the threshold, being careful not to scar the floor. Once you make the cuts, the threshold should be easy to pry up. If prying fails to do the job, use a chisel and hammer to split the piece. Metal thresholds are frequently held down by screws concealed under the vinyl inserts. Once you remove the screws, the threshold will come up easily.

Step 2: Install the replacement threshold by driving screws through the metal unit and into the floor. If the idea of an aluminum threshold doesn't appeal to you, you can cut a replacement from wood, using the original one as a pattern.

Step 3: Install a door sweep to seal the gap. Most sweeps are attached to the inside of the door with nails or screws. Cut the sweep to size and close the door. Tack both ends of the sweep to the door, then install the remaining nails or screws. If you are using screws, drill pilot holes first.

Some types of sweeps slip under the door and wrap around the bottom. Still another type fits on the outside, with a section of it flipping upward to miss the threshold when the door is opened. When the door is closed, this section flips back down to provide a seal against the threshold. You can adjust this type of door sweep so it renders a snug fit.

Most door sweeps are attached to the inside of the door with nails or screws. Cut the sweep to size, close the door, and install the sweep.

Insulating

Inadequate insulation lets heating or cooling energy escape through your walls and ceilings. To keep this energy in, wrap the entire living area of your house in the proper amount of insulating material.

What areas should be insulated? Insulation should go between the floor and either a crawl space or unfinished basement, between the ceiling and an unfinished attic, between the attic and the roof if the attic is finished, and inside all exterior walls including those adjacent to an unheated garage. The goal is to envelop the entire living area in insulating material.

Insulation requirements are defined in terms of the R-value. A material's R-value means its resistance to heat passing through it. The higher its R-value, the greater the material's insulating qualities.

The insulation materials available to the homeowner include a variety of R-values. But since these materials also vary in terms of installation ease and flammability, selection is not merely a matter of picking the one with the highest R-value. To make an intelligent choice, you should be familiar with all the properties of the most common insulating materials.

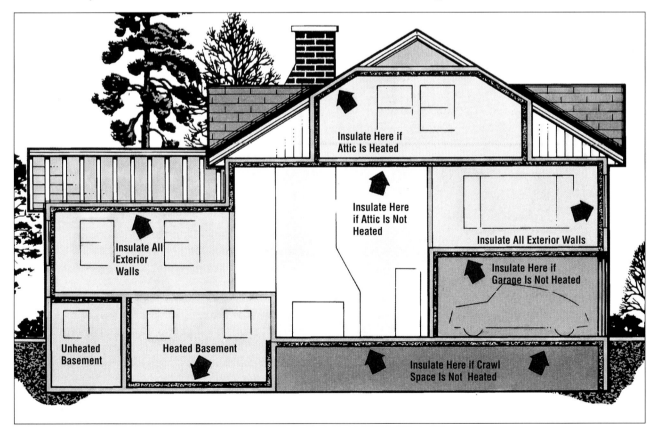

Insulation should go between the floor and either the unheated crawl space or basement, between the ceiling and unheated attic (between the attic and roof if the attic is heated), and inside all exterior walls (including those adjacent to an unheated garage).

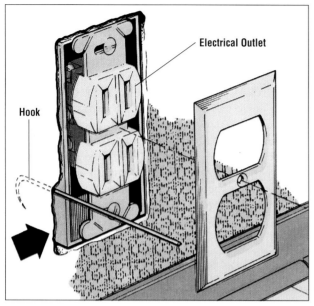

To check wall insulation, widen the opening around an electrical outlet. Pull out some of the insulation with a wire hook.

Take the cover plate off the outlet and see if there is enough space to the side of the junction box to allow you to inspect the insulation with a flashlight. If not, widen the crack on the side opposite where the metal box is attached to the stud. Use a utility knife to widen a crack in wallboard; use a cold chisel if the wall is plaster. Be careful, though, to widen only as much as the cover plate can hide. Then inspect the insulation with a flashlight. If you don't know the type of insulating material used, pull out a sample with a wire coat hanger.

Insulating an Attic

Now that you know what insulation you need and the type and quantity of the material already there, you're ready to install the new material.

The easiest place to insulate in most homes is the attic. Fortunately, the attic is also the place where proper insulation has the most pronounced effect. In the winter, most of the home's lost heat goes out through the attic. In the summer, the uninsulated attic acts as a heat collector, making the air conditioning system work harder than it should.

If you find that there is no insulation whatsoever in your attic, follow these steps for installing batts or blankets. You'll find that batts are generally easier to install than blankets in most attics. To determine how much insulation you need:

Step 1: Measure the length and width of the attic and multiply the length by the width to arrive at the total square footage.

Step 2: Measure the distance between the joists. Most are on 16-inch centers (16 inches from the center of one to the center of the next), but some are on 24-inch centers. Buy batts or blankets of the correct width to fit between joists.

Step 3: Calculate insulation requirements. For 16-inch centers, multiply the square footage by .90 to give you the number of square feet of insulation required. For 24-inch centers, multiply by .94.

You must install a vapor barrier in attics that have no insulation. The easiest way to lay down a vapor barrier is to install batts or blankets of insulation that already have a vapor barrier attached.

Before you begin installation, cut pieces of plywood to use as movable flooring, and carry up wide planks to serve as walkways. If you step onto the ceiling material, you probably would break right through it, but the joists will support your weight. If the attic is inadequately lighted, rig up a lighting system so you can see what you're doing. A drop light suspended from a nail or hook should be sufficient. If you are installing fiberglass or rock wool, you must protect yourself with gloves, safety goggles, and a breathing mask. A hard hat is also a good idea to protect your head from protruding nails and low rafters. To lay down the insulating material:

Step 1: Start under the eaves and push the end of the blanket or batt in place with a long stick. Be sure to put the vapor barrier side on the bottom. Press the insulation down firmly between the joists.

Step 2: Continue until you reach the center of the room. Then work from the opposite end of the joists out to the center.

Step 3: Use a sharp knife with a serrated edge to cut insulating material to fit around pipes and other obstructions. The material is easier to cut when compressed with a scrap piece of board. Trim the insulation to fit around any vents, recessed lighting fixtures, exhaust fan motors, or any heat-producing equipment that protrudes into the attic. Allow 3 inches of clearance. Do not pull on any electrical wiring to move it out of the way.

If you choose to insulate your uninsulated attic with loose fill, first staple the polyethylene between joists to serve as a vapor barrier. To calculate total material needs, measure the square footage of the attic and consult an insulation dealer. The dealer has a chart showing the maximum net coverage per bag at various thicknesses and the R-value for each thickness. The bags

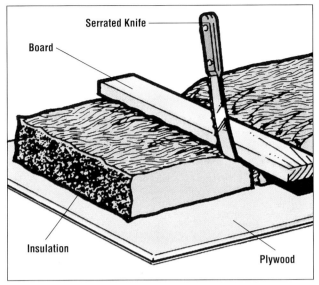

Use a sharp knife with a serrated edge to cut insulation. Cutting is easier when you compress the material with a scrap piece of board.

metal retainers made from tin cans will keep loose-fill insulation away from other problem areas. Pour the insulation into the spaces between the joists. Then spread and level the material with a garden rake. If you want the joists to be covered with the loose fill, work from all sides back toward the attic access hole. Finally, staple a batt of insulation material to the access cover.

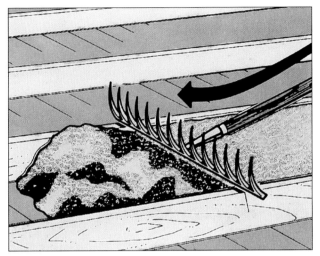

Pour loose fill into the spaces between the joists, and then spread and level the insulating material with a rake.

in which the loose fill is packaged also supply the same information. Be careful not to cover vents and heat-producing gadgets that stick up in the attic. Strips of insulating batts do a good job of guarding vents, while

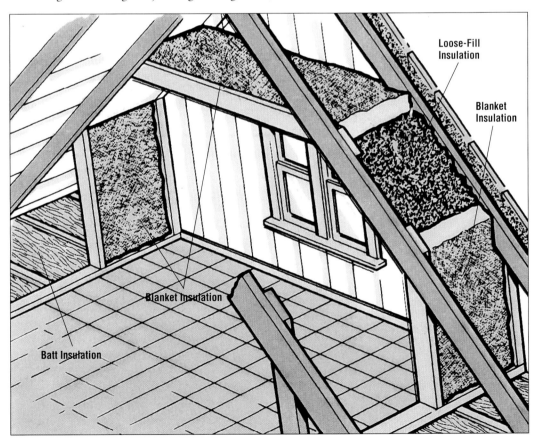

You may need a combination of batts, blankets, and loose fill to insulate an attic used for living space.

You can use batts, blankets, or loose fill to add material to existing but inadequate insulation. Follow the same installation procedure outlined for an uninsulated attic but lay down unfaced batts or blankets instead of the versions with a vapor barrier attached. If you add loose fill, do not apply a vapor barrier over the existing insulation.

Hand-pack insulation around pipes and wires that come up through the floor of the attic, closing the holes around these elements.

If you decide to heat your attic, remove the existing insulation from between the joists before installing the finished attic floor. Add insulation under the eaves as necessary. Remember that insulation should only go between heated and unheated areas, and keep in mind that the vapor barrier always faces the heated area.

Staple insulation blankets between knee-wall studs and rafters before you cover them with paneling or wallboard. You might choose to use loose fill in sloping sections of the ceiling.

Insulating Walls

After the attic, the next most important places to insulate are the exterior walls. If you live in an older home and you have access from the attic to the cavities between the wall studs, you can merely pour loose-fill insulation in the holes after probing to make sure that the cavities are closed at the bottom.

If you don't have this type of construction, you or a contractor will have to cut holes in the walls about every 16 inches and blow the insulation in with a special machine that can be rented. Additionally, if your exterior walls have fire stops (2×4s nailed horizontally between the studs), you'll need a second row of holes just below the fire stops.

Drill holes either from the inside or from the outside of the home. If the inside walls have decorative molding, you may be able to remove the molding, make holes behind it, and then cover the holes with the molding. If you have a brick home or one with metal siding, then you should drill from inside; most other exteriors can be cut into and patched. Clapboard siding, for example, can often be pried up without damage and replaced after the insulating is done. To install blown wall insulation from the exterior:

Step 1: Insert a piece of sheet metal or a flat, wide-blade scraper under the piece of siding to be removed. The sheet metal or scraper will protect the siding from the pry bar that is wedged in under the siding.

Step 2: Pry gently until the siding comes up about a ½ inch. Then remove the pry bar and push the

siding back in place. Use a mallet if the siding won't go down.

Step 3: Pull out any nails you find sticking up and repeat prying every 16 inches to remove all nails. If a piece of siding is difficult to remove, look for a nail you missed or a paint seal holding the siding from above. Wood shingles have hidden nails except at the top. If so, pry away the overlap.

Step 4: Once the top row of shingles is exposed, you can usually pry them up without breaking any shingles. A flat spade slipped under the shingles provides good prying leverage. After the shingles are pried up slightly, the nail heads will be up far enough so that you can pull them out.

Step 5: If necessary, remove more than one row of shingles to find the right spots for the insulation access holes. For prying up shingles from obstructed lower areas, purchase a shingle nail remover. Shingles can also be removed with the shingle nail remover tool.

Step 6: Remove the facing material to expose the building paper. Make a horizontal cut along the top of the paper, all the way across the wall. Then make vertical cuts at each end, and fold the building paper down. You are now ready to position the holes between each pair of studs. You should be able to spot the studs by noting the nails in the sheathing. Be sure to make the holes large enough to accommodate the nozzle of the insulation blower.

Step 7: Before filling each cavity, make sure that the hole is open all the way down. To check, you can lower a weight on a string. If you encounter an obstruction, you'll need to drill another hole below.

Step 8: To install insulation, follow the instructions that come with the insulation blower.

Step 9: Once all cavities are filled with insulation, plug the holes with plastic inserts that snap in and lock. You can also nail tin can lids or sheet-metal squares over the holes.

Step 10: Staple the building paper back in place and replace the siding, using existing nail holes where possible.

When you must drill from inside, use a magnetic stud finder to locate the studs. Then drill or saw holes at the top of the wall big enough to accept the nozzle of the insulation blower. Drop a weight on a string to be sure

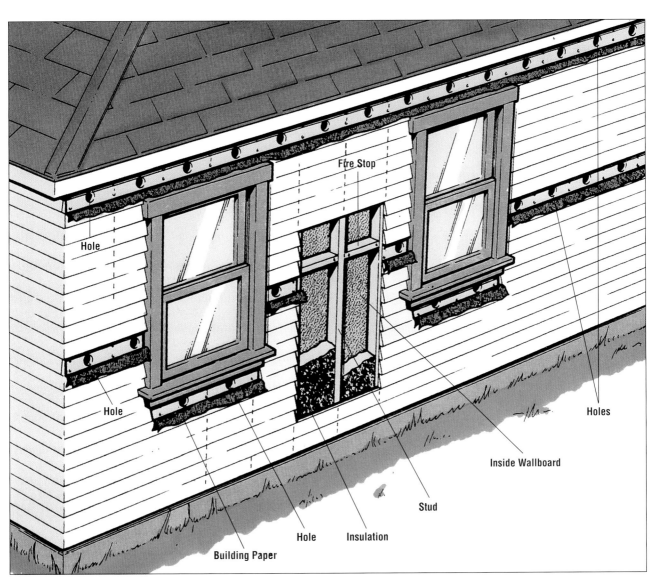

If you cannot insulate your exterior walls from the attic, you'll have to cut holes in the walls about every 16 inches and blow the insulation in. If the walls have fire stops, you'll need a second row of holes just below the horizontal 2×4s.

the cavities are unobstructed, and blow in the insulation according to the instructions supplied with your rental unit.

After the insulation is in place, you must patch all the holes. Usually the holes are so large that they need backing to prevent the patching compound from falling into the cavity. If the loose-fill insulation does not provide enough backing, insert scraps from insulation batts into the holes and plaster over the openings with spackling compound. After the compound is dry, it must be primed and painted.

Insulating Floors

Exposed joists in an unheated crawl space or basement can be filled with a layer of insulation installed under the floor of your home. The best insulation to use is batts because they are the easiest to handle. Estimate your material needs the same way you would if you were insulating the attic (see page 310).

Installing batts under a floor can be difficult, but you have several options to make installation easier. Strips of wood lath can be nailed across the joists about every 16 inches; chicken wire strips can be stapled across the joists (leave room between strips to work in the batts); heavy-gauge wires can be cut slightly longer than 16 inches and wedged between joists; or wire can be laced back and forth and held with nails. Whatever method you choose, you must support the batts so they don't sag. Airspace between batts and subflooring can provide insulation if batts are snug.

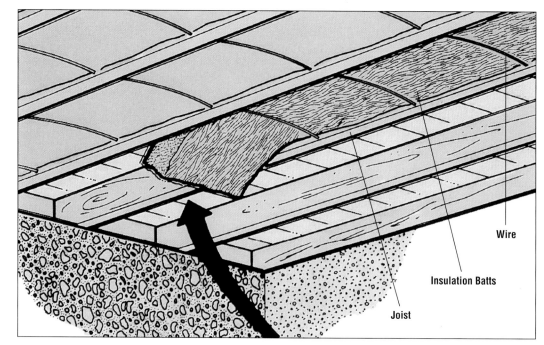

Insulation batts are easy to install between the exposed joists of an unheated crawl space or basement; heavy-gauge wire will hold the batts in place. Alternatively, you can support the batts with strips of wood lath or chicken wire.

Wire

Insulation Batts

Joist

If ground moisture is a problem, be sure to provide a ground vapor barrier. If the moisture problem still exists after you install the vapor barrier, cover the bottom of the joists with low-grade plywood or staple a plastic vapor barrier in place.

Some homes have an insulated basement or insulation on the foundation to provide what is called a heated crawl space. The heated crawl space doesn't necessarily mean that heat is actually piped down there. The insulation around the foundation is designed to prevent heated air that reaches the crawl space from escaping.

Naturally, a basement or crawl space with insulation around the foundation does not provide nearly as effective a barrier to heat loss as does insulation under the floor. A heated basement, on the other hand, should be insulated around the foundation, while its ceiling should not. The warm air that rises from the heated basement will help warm the rest of the house.

If you have an unfinished basement, you can choose from two practical insulation alternatives. You can install studs to which you staple or friction-fit insulating blankets, or you can attach furring strips to which you apply rigid sheets of insulating material, covered over and made fire resistant. The latter method is easier in most instances, since the rigid insulation sheets can merely be glued to the wall with special mastics. Check your local building code to determine what types of wall covering are acceptable over this type of insulation.

With either method, be sure to cover the box joists and headers with insulating blankets stapled to the subfloor above and the framing below. The box joist is

the joist that runs parallel to all other joists between the subfloor and the basement walls. The headers are the spaces between and at the end of all the other joists.

If you have a heated crawl space in which the walls will never be finished, you need only fasten insulating blankets at the top of the wall and pile bricks to hold the blankets against the wall at the floor. Wider blankets can make the installation quicker, but a narrow crawl space is not going to be easy to insulate no matter what. Here's the procedure:

Step 1: Starting on a box joist side of the wall, lay a plastic vapor barrier strip on the ground along that wall. Leave about 2 inches at each end to run up the wall. Use duct tape to secure the ends.

Step 2: Starting at a corner, staple the blankets to the box joist, trimming the blankets at ground level. Butt the next strip to the first and trim it, working all the way across. Trim the last panel to fit. Lay the next strip of vapor barrier, letting the two overlap by about 6 inches.

Step 3: Attach a blanket strip in the corner of the wall with headers. Trim to accommodate the joists, but don't trim at ground level. Instead, place a brick on the ground to hold the blanket. Then run the blanket out to the middle of the room. At the opposite corner, attach another strip in the same manner and run it out to meet the first strip. Trim both at the center and use bricks to hold each end down.

314

Step 4: Work your way down each wall, overlapping vapor barrier strips as you go and trimming and attaching the blankets at the top. At floor level, however, extend the blankets toward the center no more than about 2 feet. When you reach the other box joist side, finish the wall and run corner blankets to the center.

A home built on a slab should have rigid insulation attached to the foundation all around its perimeter. This insulation will make a significant difference in the temperature of the slab floor.

Since the insulating material should extend down below the frost line, the installation may require digging. After the rigid insulating sheets are attached to the foundation with the specific mastic recommended by the insulation manufacturer, they should then be finished over with stucco, plaster, or other code-approved material.

When converting a garage or porch to living space, you can insulate the concrete floors quite effectively with rigid sheets. If there was no vapor barrier installed under the slab when it was poured, you should apply a vapor-repellent coating.

Apply rigid sheets to the floor using the recommended mastic. Nail furring strips on top of the rigid insulation sheets, using masonry nails and a

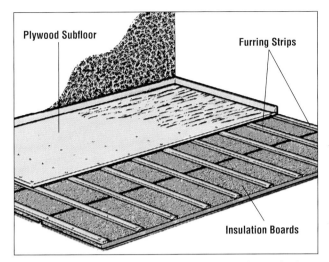

Nail furring strips on top of the rigid insulation sheets, laying the furring strips on 16-inch centers to accommodate the subflooring. Naturally, if there is no vapor barrier under the slab, you should apply a vapor-repellent coating to the slab before attaching the rigid insulating sheets.

proper-size hammer. Be sure to wear safety goggles. Lay the furring strips on 16-inch centers to accommodate the subflooring. Finally, nail ½-inch exterior-grade plywood to the furring strips and apply your desired flooring.

CHAPTER 9

OUTSIDE JOBS

The outside of your home is the first thing visitors see. To make a good impression, you should keep your yard and house looking their best, season after season. This chapter tells you how. Outside jobs are more than just a matter of keeping up appearances, however. It is necessary to keep your house and yard in top condition for practical purposes as well. A lawn that's neglected soon goes to seed and begins to erode. Ignore a roof leak and it will soon wreak havoc inside your house.

Fortunately, most outside jobs are neither expensive nor difficult. All that is required is a few tools and materials, some know-how, and a few weekend mornings when the weather is pleasant. Outside jobs can actually be fun!

Yard Work

Though you'll probably have to mow and water throughout the summer, spring and fall are the best times to catch up on yard work. Your first task may be to get your landscaping into an easily maintainable condition. After that, you only need to keep after matters from time to time.

Minimizing Yard Maintenance

A yard will take some maintenance to remain presentable. If you plan ahead, you can keep yard work to a minimum and still have a good-looking, healthy lawn.

Mowing and Edging

Mowing in itself is not a problem unless there are slopes or other tough-to-mow areas. If there are steep slopes, you could plant a ground cover, terrace with rocks or stones, or change the slope. There are no easy solutions, but once you have done something to cover the hard-to-mow area, the mowing problem is licked. Depending on the size of your lawn, you may be able to eliminate all mowing by using a ground cover instead of grass. Growing ground covers include ivy, ajuga, sedum, and other such plants, while inert ground covers include pebbles, bark, or gravel.

Another difficulty you might encounter with mowing is edging—trimming the places where the grass ends. You can install mowing strips where the lawn meets a flower bed or where it runs to a wall. Mowing strips are strips that are flush with the lawn and wide enough for the mower wheels to ride on. You can make these from bricks, concrete blocks, railroad ties, or landscaping ties. Be sure to put a good bed of sand or gravel under the mowing strip to ensure that it doesn't sink into the lawn. If flower beds are a big part of the yard, corrugated edging strips help prevent grass from getting into the beds.

Watering

The best answer to watering problems is to install an automated underground sprinkler system. Short of that, be selective in the sprinkler you get. Moving sprinklers are better than sprinklers that emit a steady spray. Let the shape and size of your yard guide you in selecting a sprinkler. Buy one that will adjust to odd shapes without too much waste, but also get one that will cover as much area as possible without your having to move it. To accomplish this, you may need to have more than one sprinkler. Water only when there is a need. Overwatering or everyday shallow watering isn't as good as deep-watering when needed.

Weeds

Some homeowners never win the battle with weeds. In flower beds, cover empty spaces with mulch or inert ground cover. Mulch also retains moisture and does other good things for the beds. For the lawn, herbicides kill weeds. They will also kill other plants, including grass, unless you are careful and use the right type for your lawn. One of the most effective ways to control weeds is to feed your lawn with a quality fertilizer distributed with a spreader, give it plenty of water, and mow regularly. A healthy lawn will choke out weeds, and keeping them cut won't allow them to seed. Add some hand-pulling to that, and you should be able to get rid of weeds altogether.

One of the most effective ways to control weeds is to feed your lawn with a quality fertilizer distributed with a spreader.

Insects

Battling insects requires identifying the insect, choosing a proper insecticide, and using it at the time that will be most effective. The use of combination fertilizer-insecticides will do a good preventive job, although you will need specific formulations for some bugs. Picture charts of insects for identification purposes, along with insecticides, are available at stores that sell garden and lawn supplies.

Leaves

There isn't much you can do about leaves if you have trees that shed each fall. If you are going to plant new trees, you can do a little research to find out which trees are native to your area and will serve your purpose but have less of a leaf problem. Some trees, such as mimosas, not only drop leaves, but also shed beans, flowers, and sap at different times of the year. If you have a big leaf problem, buy a power lawn vacuum or a leaf blower.

Other Ways to Reduce Maintenance Time

In addition to the five biggest problems already discussed, here are some more things to consider:
- Treat the lawn as a unit: Don't break it up into separate sections with fences, flower beds, or anything else that would break up the unity of the yard.
- Don't try to grow grass where it won't grow, such as in areas that receive little sunlight.

- Determine what type of grass grows best in your area.
- Plant trees native to the area. You can get other species to grow, but they might require more time and effort.
- Plant for the future. Remember that trees will spread as they grow, so don't plant them too close together.

Planting a Lawn

A healthy, green lawn makes your home look attractive, but there are other important benefits as well. Healthy grass helps fight air pollution, provides some oxygen, prevents soil erosion, and reduces noise pollution. A super lawn takes super care. An occasional mowing is not all that is required to provide that well-manicured look.

The type of grass that grows best in your area varies with the climate, moisture, and soil. You can and should talk to experts, but one of the best ways to select a suitable grass is to pick out several healthy-looking lawns in the neighborhood and ask the owners what they did to achieve such results. Find out which species of grass is most successful and how much trouble it is to maintain. The owners will be flattered, and you will most likely learn a great deal.

Planting a New Lawn

After you select the type of grass you want, learn which time of year is the best for planting in your region. If the ground hasn't been graded yet, have it done or do it yourself. The ground should slope gradually away from the house in all directions. After grading, check for low places by turning on a sprinkler and looking for spots where water collects.

Check the soil; it should have the proper pH. The only way to find out about the soil's pH is to test it. Most county agents and many seed stores will test your soil at little or no cost to you. Lime should be added to soil that is too acidic, and gypsum to soil that is too alkaline. The soil should also be crumbly. Squeeze a handful tightly in your fist and release it. If the blob falls apart, the soil is too sandy. If it looks like a mud ball, it contains too much clay. The soil should hold its shape initially but should break apart easily if pressed. Make whatever soil additions are indicated by the tests, and then till the soil. You can rent a tiller if you don't want to buy one. When tilling, avoid making the soil too fine. Marble-size lumps are better than fine dirt. Wet the soil to pack it down and then wait 24 hours.

Spread the grass seed at the rate recommended for the specific variety of seed you are planting. If you spread the seed too thick, the young seedlings will compete for nutrients and most will die. Rake the

When tilling the soil, avoid making the soil too fine. Marble-size lumps are better than fine dirt.

ground lightly to cover the seeds partially with soil, then go over the ground once with a roller to press the seeds into the soil. Don't try to bury them.

Feed the lawn as soon as you finish the seeding if this is recommended by the company that packaged the seed. Follow the directions on the bag to fertilize as recommended for your variety of grass.

Water the lawn as soon as you finish fertilizing. During the next two weeks, water two or three times a day, keeping the top layer of soil damp at all times. When the seedlings are up, revert to regular morning waterings.

Wait until the sprigs are two inches tall before mowing. Mowing will help to spread the root system and make the lawn thicker. Mow weekly until you note the proper thickness, then mow as needed.

Never use a weed killer on a new lawn. Pull the bigger weeds and mow the rest. As your lawn thickens, many of the weeds will be choked out. You can use a weed killer the second year your lawn is in.

Redoing an Established Lawn

The maintenance of a lawn depends on the species of grass planted, the soil condition, and the climate. A lawn specialist or county agent can tell you what type of fertilizer you should have and how often you should apply it, as well as how much water you should be using. All fertilizer is numbered, for example, 5–10–5, 24–3–3,

10–10–10. The numbers stand for chemical contents of the products. The first number is for the amount of nitrogen, the second number is for the amount of phosphoric acid, and the third is for the amount of potash. Here's a memory aid for remembering what each of these numbers mean: "Up." "Down." "All Around." The first number makes the grass grow up and green. The second number makes the roots grow down and healthy. The third number increases the root growth all around. So, if you want your grass to be extremely green, choose a fertilizer with a high first number. If you are just starting a new lawn or reshuffling the old one, you want a high second number to encourage root growth. If you want a root growth that is healthy and even across the lawn, you want a fertilizer with a high third number.

If your existing lawn is in poor condition, try to renovate it. If at least 50 percent of the area is still covered with grass, plant new seed in the bad spots. First, get rid of all weeds and apply a chemical weed killer according to the manufacturer's directions. Next, mow the grass very close to the ground. Rake the yard to remove all grass clippings and leaves, and also to loosen the surface of the soil. Test the soil as described above. Finally, seed the bare spots following the same planting procedures detailed previously.

Planting a Shrub

What do you want a shrub to do? Screen an unsightly view? Help stop erosion? Accent the design of your home? Buy the type of shrub that will do the job best. A nursery will help you make this decision. There are hundreds of shrub and bush varieties from which to choose.

Most nurseries and garden centers certify that their shrubs and bushes are free from insects, disease, and other growth problems. Get this in writing so the plant will be replaced if it dies through no fault of yours. If you spot cankers, leaf rot, spots, insects, or other problems, don't buy the shrub.

After you've selected the shrub, dig a hole about eight inches wider and six inches deeper than the balled roots of the plant. Carefully place the root ball into the hole. If the ball is wrapped in burlap, cut and remove the string that holds the burlap to the plant. If the ball is in a plastic or metal container, remove it by lightly tapping down on the container while you hold onto the base of the plant. The container should drop right off.

Spread out the plant's root system in the hole, and cover the roots with topsoil or a good, rich soil mixture. Then lightly pack the soil down and against the base of the plant.

Plant the shrub in a hole about eight inches wider and six inches deeper than the balled roots of the plant.

Deep-water the roots. The soil must be kept damp until you see growth on the plant. The dealer who sold you the plant should be able to tell you the best watering schedule.

If you are planting a hedge, you can plant it in a trench instead of in individual holes. The trench should be deep enough and wide enough to accept the root system without crowding it. If you want the hedge to grow to about six feet high, the hedge plants should be spaced about 20 inches apart. If you want the hedge to grow higher, space the plants about three feet apart.

Pruning Trees

Although it seems wasteful to trim away perfectly healthy foliage, trees should be pruned for several good reasons. Pruning gives trees a more desirable shape, strengthens them by improving their structure, removes dead limbs and diseased portions, and increases the production of foliage, flowers, and fruit. Think of pruning as the equivalent of getting a haircut.

Begin by sharpening all pruning tools; dull tools lead to ragged cuts, and ragged cuts can lead to problems. Be sure, too, that you select the right size and type of tool

Prune any stalks that are broken or dead. In fall, when the plant is dormant, prune the stalks back about a third of their length; this will promote better growth.

Before pruning a tree, sharpen all pruning tools. Dull tools lead to ragged cuts, which can cause problems.

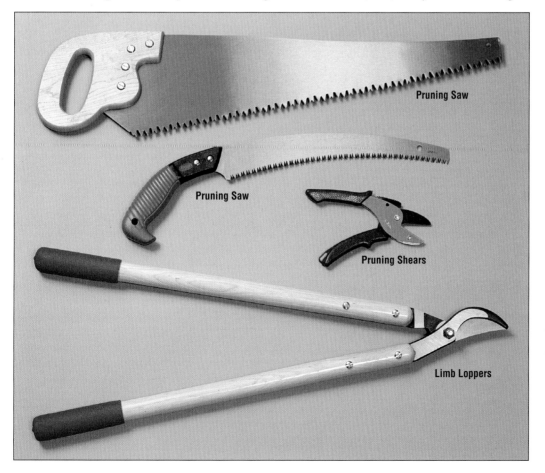

Pruning Saw

Pruning Saw

Pruning Shears

Limb Loppers

for trees. A tool that is too large or too small can make ragged cuts.

Make all cuts as close as possible to the base of the piece being removed without damaging the larger limb to which it is attached. Try to do as much pruning as possible while standing on the ground. When you must work from a ladder, never try to reach very far; instead, move the ladder frequently and make certain that it is always on solid ground. Position yourself and your ladder so that the limbs you prune fall free and nowhere near you. If you are cutting away large limbs, make certain that there is no chance of them falling against electric power lines. Finally, seal all cuts with wound compound.

Winter is the best time for pruning trees because that is when most trees are dormant. Naturally, trees that exude sap during the winter should not be pruned until the following spring. Because their root systems have usually been greatly reduced, newly transplanted trees should always be pruned no matter what season it happens to be.

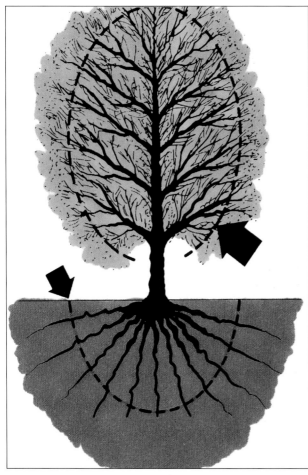

The root systems of newly transplanted trees have usually been greatly reduced, so prune the branches back, too.

In spring, prune most trees lightly for shaping purposes. Remove broken limbs any time of the year, but prune dead limbs in the fall.

If heavy pruning (as much as a third of the tree) is needed, don't perform all the pruning during a single season. Do it in stages over a two- or three-year period.

Fences

Sun, wind, snow, rot, and below-ground frost subject fences to a terrific beating. The following pages tell how to keep your fences mended and how to build new ones the right way. As you work with fences, keep nature in mind. Wood is vulnerable to nature's punishments, especially rotting. This means you should always repair or construct fencing with the most rot-resistant lumber you can afford. Here are the most common choices:

- Pressure-treated lumber has been saturated with preservatives and lasts almost indefinitely, even with wood that has been buried in the ground. Pressure-treated wood is costly.
- Cedar and redwood also stand up well underground and are also costly.
- Creosote and asphalt roofing compound can be painted on just about any wood for an underground coating that stands up almost as well as pressure-treated, cedar, or redwood lumber. Creosote has a medicinal smell and can't be painted over. With roofing compound, apply three coats, leaving lots of time between coats for drying. Both methods are inexpensive but take time to apply.
- Copper naphthenate is odorless and nontoxic but imparts a greenish cast to the wood. It's moderate in price. Apply at least two coats.
- Exterior paints and stains work well above ground but are almost useless below or on parts of fences in frequent contact with water.

Repairing Fences

The components of a wooden fence include vertical posts, rails that run horizontally from post to post, and screening material such as boards or pickets. Examine your fence, no matter what its type, and you can probably identify each of these elements.

Rot is a wooden fence's biggest enemy. Posts that weren't properly treated or set in concrete typically rot away at ground level. Bottom rails and the bottoms of screening can suffer too, especially if vegetation has been rubbing against them and trapping water. Carefully inspect fences at least once a year, paying particular attention to these areas. When you find a problem, resolve to correct it before the damage spreads. One weak post, for example, could pull down the entire fence.

Rails

A rail that's pulled loose from one or more of its posts may or may not be salvageable, depending on how badly rotted the joint is. You may be able to mend the break with a 2×4 scrap or a couple of metal T-braces, or you may have to replace the entire rail. To repair a rail:

Step 1: Before you make a repair, saturate the damaged areas liberally with copper naphthenate wood preservative. This keeps the rot from spreading. If you choose to use a 2×4, soak it with preservative too.

Step 2: To make a cleat that supports the rail, make sure the rail is level, then fit the 2×4 snugly underneath and nail the 2×4 to the post with galvanized nails. Drive a couple of nails down through the rail into the cleat.

Step 3: Carefully caulk the top and sides of the repair to keep out moisture.

One way to mend a broken fence rail is to shore it up with a 2×4 scrap and secure it with galvanized nails.

Galvanized steel T-braces, available at most hardware and home stores, are somewhat less conspicuous and make a more lasting repair.

Step 1: Level the rail, and drill pilot holes into the post and rail.

Step 2: Secure the T-braces to the rail with galvanized screws.

Step 3: Caulk the joint.

Step 4: Paint the braces to match the fences.

For a less conspicuous and more lasting repair, use a galvanized T-brace; the screws should be galvanized, too.

If the entire rail needs to be replaced, dismantle that section of fence and rebuild it as explained beginning on page 324 in "Building a New Fence."

Screening

Replacing broken or rotted screening takes only a few hours and simple carpentry skills. To replace rotted screening:

Step 1: Measure an unbroken piece to get the correct length and width for the new piece or pieces you'll need. Use lumber the same width as the old screening or rip boards to the proper width with a handsaw or power saw. Check all cuts with a carpenters' square before you make them.

Step 2: If you're replacing pickets or other curved-top screening, set the cut board against an unbroken picket and trace the top onto the new board. Make these cuts with a saber, coping, or keyhole saw. If yours is a painted fence, give the new screening a coat of top-quality exterior primer. If the fence is natural wood, stain the new boards to match.

Step 3: Remove the broken pieces by hammering and prying them away from the rails. Pull out any nails left in the rails.

Step 4: Set the new board or picket against the rails, align it, and nail it firmly into place with galvanized 8d nails.

Step 5: Paint the new pieces to match the rest of the fence.

Posts

When a post begins to wobble, determine the cause before you make the repair. If the post is rotted or broken you may be able to repair it with a pair of splints, or you may have to replace the entire post. If the post seems intact but has come loose in its hole, a pair of stakes or, better yet, a new concrete base, can steady the post. To stake a post:

Step 1: Select a pair of 2×4s long enough to reach below the frost line for your region and that extend at least 18 inches above the ground. Use only pressure-treated lumber, cedar, or clear all-heart redwood.

Step 2: Bevel-cut one end of each 2×4 and drive them into the ground along opposite sides of the post.

Step 3: Bore two holes through both 2×4s and the post and bolt everything together with galvanized carriage bolts.

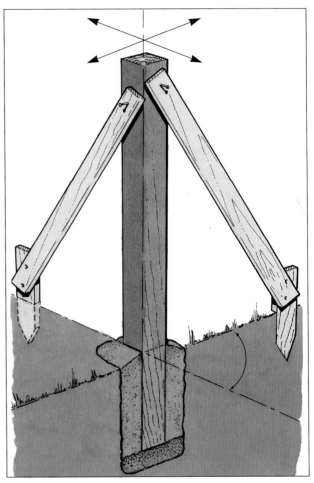

For a more permanent cure, dig out around the post, plumb it with temporary braces, and pour concrete around the post's base.

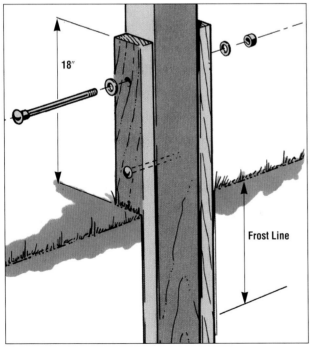

A pair of stakes can steady a wobbly post. Drive them into the ground on either side of the post and bolt them to it.

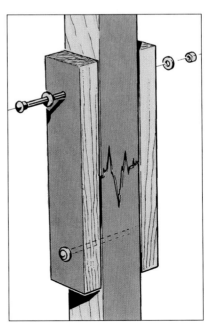

If a post has broken off above ground, repair it with 2×4 splints bolted to the post.

An alternative that will probably last longer is to dig out around the post, plumb it with temporary braces, and pour concrete around the base of the post. To learn about setting posts in concrete, see "Building a New Fence" beginning on page 324.

If a post has broken off below ground level, dismantle the fence, set a new post, and reassemble everything. For an above-ground break, however, you may be able to make a repair with a couple of pressure-treated or rot-resistant 2 × 4s. Cut each to a length of about 18 inches and nail or clamp them to opposite sides of the post. Check to be sure the post is plumb, bore holes through the splints and post on either side of the break, and secure them with steel carriage bolts.

Gates

When a gate sags or won't close properly, the first thing you should do is check its hinges. If they're bent, replace them with heavier versions. If the hinge screws are

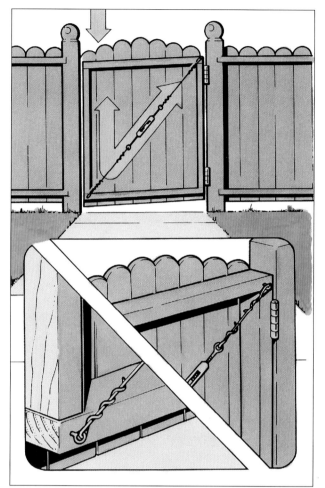

To square up a gate, drive screw eyes into opposite corners, run wire and a turnbuckle between them, and tighten the turnbuckle.

pulling loose, remove them and plug the holes by gluing in short pieces of dowel. Then drill new holes and install longer screws or carriage bolts. All hardware should be galvanized steel.

With a gate that's sagging only slightly, you may be able to straighten it up by shimming under the bottom hinge. Prop up the gate in its open position, remove the screws from the post side of the hinge, and cut a thin piece of cedar shake to fit into the hinge mortise. Reattach the screw by driving longer screws through the shim.

Sometimes a gate sags because its own weight has pulled it out of alignment with the fence. One quick way to square up a gate is to drive a screw eye into the upper corner of the gate on the hinge side and another into the lower corner on the gate side. Run wire and a heavy-duty turnbuckle from one screw eye to the other and tighten the turnbuckle until the gate frame is square.

Straighten a slightly sagging gate by removing screws from the bottom hinge and shimming it with a cedar shingle.

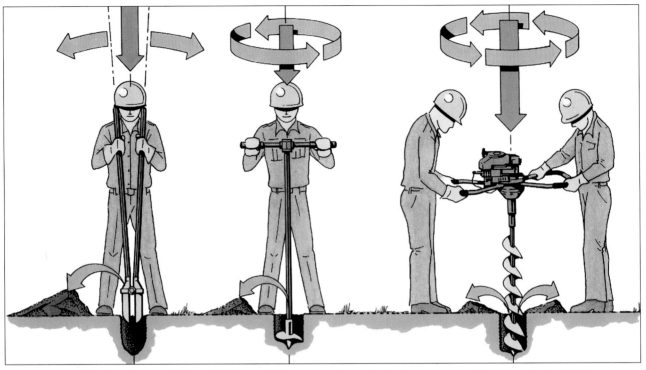

Dig postholes with a hand-operated clamshell digger (left) or auger digger (center), or a power-driven auger (right). All are available at tool rental outlets.

Building a New Fence

The hardest part of building a new fence is digging the holes for the posts. For this you'll need a posthole digger. Hand-operated clamshell and auger diggers work fine in sandy, rock-free soil. If your soil is rocky or you have a lot of holes to dig, rent a power-driven auger.

For best results, use pressure-treated, ground-contact lumber, cedar, or redwood. With the latter, no finishing is necessary; the fence can be left to weather naturally. If you must, you can use untreated wood for screening and top rails, and for bottom rails that are at least four inches above the ground. You'll need 4×4s for fence posts, 2×4s for rails, and 1×4s or 1×6s for screening. To build a fence:

Step 1: Lay out the approximate fence line, making sure you're not on your neighbor's property.

Step 2: Establish the exact location of the first end or corner post. Dig a hole there that's 18 to 24 inches deep. For a fence that's five or six feet high, dig down 24 inches.

Step 3: Pour about three inches of gravel into the bottom of the hole, to improve drainage, then set the post into the hole.

Step 4: Level the post. Then brace it in two directions with wooden stakes.

Step 5: Prepare premixed concrete, stir it well, and pour it into the hole around the post. Slice the concrete mix periodically with a spade as you pour to eliminate any air pockets. At the top of the hole, mound concrete around the base of the post to shed water.

Step 6: After the first post is set, determine exactly where you want the opposite end or corner

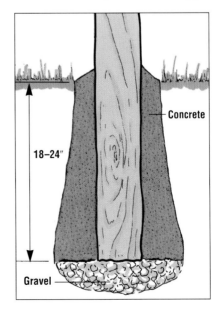

18–24"

Concrete

Gravel

Before plumbing a post, pour about three inches of gravel into the hole to aid drainage. Pack concrete or soil around the post.

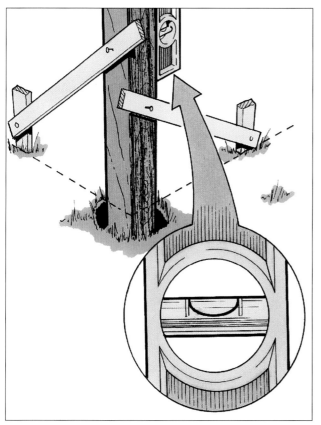

Posts must be absolutely plumb (vertical). To plumb a post, set it in its hole, hold a level to one side, and adjust the post until the level's bubble is exactly centered. Do the same on an adjacent side of the post, then brace it with outriggers.

post. Set this post the same way you set the first one. Only end, corner, and gate posts need to be set in concrete. Intermediate posts usually can be set in soil.

Step 7: To set intermediate posts, measure the height of each end post above grade level to ensure that both are the same height. Drive a nail partway into each post, facing the direction of the fence line, just above ground level. Tie a piece of twine to one nail, stretch it to the other post, and secure it to the other nail. Using the string as a guide, drive stakes to locate the intermediate postholes. Posts are usually spaced eight or ten feet apart. Remove the string and nails after you've driven the stakes.

Step 8: Dig holes for the intermediate posts.

Step 9: Pour about three inches of gravel into each hole. Set a post into each hole and use the twine as a guide for checking the post's height. If necessary, make height adjustments by

varying the depth of gravel in each hole or shimming up the posts with stones.

Step 10: Set and plumb each post, then fill in around its base with about six inches of gravel. Fill up the rest of the hole with soil, shoveling in about four inches at a time and compacting each layer with a scrap of 2×4.

Step 11: Cut 2×4 rails to fit flat along the tops of the posts. The rails can extend from post to post, or a rail can span two sections. Measure and cut each rail individually, to allow for slight variations in fence-post spacing. Butt the ends of the rails tightly together. Then, beginning at one end of the fence line, nail the rails into place, using two 10d galvanized common nails at the ends of each rail.

Step 12: Measure and cut a 2×4 bottom rail to fit snugly between each pair of posts. Position the rails flat between the posts, anywhere from slightly above grade level to 12 inches up. Toenail the bottom rails into place with a 10d galvanized nail driven through the fence post and into the end of the rail on each side. Use a level to keep the rails even.

Step 13: Measure and cut the fence boards. The boards should be of uniform length, as long as the distance from the bottom of the bottom rail to the top of the top rail, as measured at one of

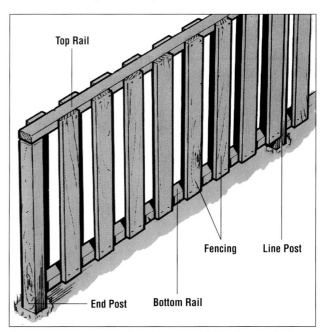

Once posts are set, construction goes quickly. Cut and install top rails first, then bottom rails. Finally, nail up fencing boards.

the posts. Starting at one end, nail the boards to one side of the rails, with a space equal to a single board width between each; use a board as a spacer as you work. Secure each board to the rails with two 8d galvanized nails at the top and two at the bottom. Nail the tops first, flush with the top, then nail the bottoms, pulling or pushing the bottom rail into alignment as you go. If your fence will have boards on both sides, nail up all the boards on one side first, then nail alternate boards to the other side of the rails, positioning the boards to cover the spaces left by the boards on the opposite side of the fence.

Other Outside Jobs

Your home is built to withstand wear and weather, and if you don't look at the outside too closely, it's easy to assume that everything is in good shape—until one day it's too late, and all the little problems have become big ones. To prevent this kind of structural deterioration, make a periodic inspection tour around the outside of your home, so that you can find the damage and repair it before it's serious. Depending on what components your home has, look for damage in siding, porch flooring, garage doors, roofing, flashing, vent pipes, gutters, and chimneys. You can forestall more serious problems by taking care of minor repairs immediately.

Replacing Damaged Siding

When clapboards or shakes are rotten or broken, your home's siding can no longer do the job it's meant to do. Damaged siding lets air, water, dirt, and insects through to the inside. It also allows decay and further damage in the wood around it.

Clapboards

When you notice a bad spot in your home's siding, repair it as soon as you can. The damaged board or shake is the only part that must be replaced, and the job goes fairly quickly. Replace the old board with a new one of the same size and shape. To repair damaged clapboards:

Step 1: Wedge the board away from the house by driving wedges up under the damaged board to pull it out from the sheathing below. Look for the nails in this section of clapboard and pull

them out. If you can't remove them with a claw hammer or pliers, use a hacksaw to cut them off flush with the sheathing. To release the top of the board, drive wedges under the clapboard that overlaps the damaged board and remove the nails from the top of the board.

Step 2: Cut through the board on each side of the damaged area, using a backsaw or a hacksaw. If you don't have enough room to use a saw conveniently, use a hacksaw blade with one end wrapped with electrical tape to protect your hand. Cut all the way through the board to include the damaged area. If necessary, move the wedges to make room for the saw, but leave the wedges under the clapboard. When the board is completely cut through on both sides of the damage, the damaged section should pull down and out fairly easily. If it won't come out, break it up with a hammer and chisel, and remove it in pieces. Be careful not to damage the surrounding boards.

Step 3: Cut the new clapboard to fit the opening and test it for fit. It should slide right into place, with its top edge under the board above and its bottom edge over the board below. Plane the edges for an exact fit, if necessary.

Step 4: When the new board fits well, paint it with a primer coat. Make sure both sides and all edges are covered. Also paint the raw edges of the opening, where the old siding was cut out. Let the paint dry completely.

Step 5: Set the new board into the opening and adjust it so that it fits perfectly. Nail the board into place

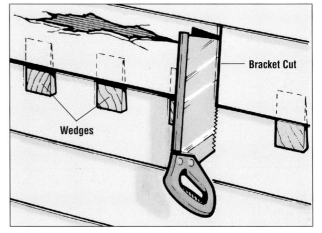

Bracket Cut

Wedges

To remove a damaged clapboard, drive wedges to pull it away from the house and pry out the nails. Then cut out the damaged section with a backsaw.

with 16d nails, driven through the bottom and through the board above into the top edge. Caulk the edges of the patch with acrylic latex caulk. When the caulk is dry, paint the new siding to match the rest of the house.

Slide the new clapboard into the gap, with its top edge under the board above and its bottom edge over the board below.

Shakes or Shingles

Damaged shakes or shingles are replaced the same way clapboards are. If they're natural unstained cedar, however, it's a good idea to take your replacement shakes from an inconspicuous area of the house and to use the new shingles on that spot. This trick eliminates a new-looking unweathered patch in the repair area.

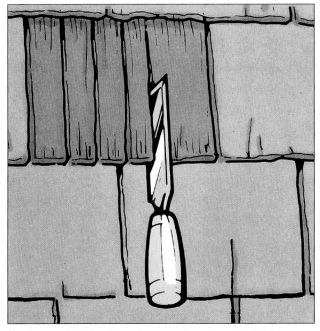

If a damaged shake doesn't come out easily, split it into several pieces with a hammer and chisel. Remove the pieces and pull out the nails.

Wedge each damaged shake or shingle out, driving wedges under the damaged shake and under the shakes that overlap it. Pull out or cut off all nails, as above. Then remove the damaged shake. If it doesn't come out easily, split it into several pieces with a hammer and chisel and remove the pieces. Insert the new shake and nail it into place with 16d aluminum nails; do not use steel nails. If the shake doesn't have predrilled nail holes, drill pilot holes for the nails to keep the wood from splitting.

Replacing Damaged Porch Flooring

Many older homes and even some new ones have wooden porches. Wooden porches are subject to heavy wear and damage. If you live in an older home, the porch floor may be the first thing to go. When porch flooring breaks or wears out, more than the looks of the porch are involved. A weak spot in the floor is dangerous and can lead to further damage. Unless the whole floor is weakened, you can easily replace the damaged boards.

Porch flooring is nailed directly to the joists of the framing. To repair damaged porch flooring:

Step 1: Look at the boards to see where the joists are, indicated by a line of nails along each joist. Using a carpenters' square, draw an outline around the damaged area from board edge to board edge, from the inside of a joist to the inside of another joist. If the boards are damaged where they cross a joist, draw the outline out to the joists on either side of the damaged area. The boards in this outlined area will need to be replaced.

Step 2: Bore a hole inside two diagonally opposite corners of the outline, using a ¾-inch bit. Position each hole so that it touches the marked outline on both sides but does not touch the sound boards outside the repair area.

Step 3: Cut across the damaged boards from hole to hole. You should have to cut only across the boards; the long edges are joined by tongue-and-groove edges and should pull apart. Carefully pry out the damaged boards with a pry bar. At the outside board edges, be very careful not to damage the tongue or the groove of the sound board outside the outline. You may have to use a chisel to remove the last pieces of the old boards.

Step 4: Cut new tongue-and-groove flooring strips the same width and thickness as the old ones, to replace the old ones. Test them for fit in the opening; they should fit exactly in the gap left by the old boards. On the last board, you'll have to cut off the bottom part of the groove to make the board fit flat. Cut the groove piece off with a hammer and a sharp chisel, being careful not to damage the rest of the board. Then sand the raw surface lightly.

Step 5: Brace the boards at each end by installing 2×4 cleats along the inside faces of the joists at the sides of the hole. Cut a piece of 2×4 as long as the hole for each joist. Paint all of the patching materials with wood preservative before installation, covering all surfaces. Let the preservative dry as directed, then nail the 2×4 cleats flat to the side joists, with their top edges exactly flush.

Step 6: If the old boards were rotten, you should take steps to prevent further decay. Cover the ground under the porch with heavy plastic, lapping the plastic about six inches up at the sides. Set a few stones or bricks on the plastic to hold it in place. For the most effective rot prevention, paint all exposed wood under the porch with a coat of wood preservative. These preventive measures will keep your porch strong and healthy for years to come.

Step 7: With the cleats in place, set the new floorboards into the opening, one by one, with their ends

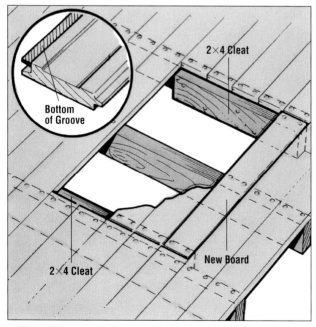

Nail a 2×4 cleat to each outside joist and set the new boards into the opening. You'll have to cut off the bottom of the groove on the last board.

resting on the cleats along the joists. Set the first board in tongue first, and insert each board to lock its tongue into the groove of the previous board. Nail each end of each board to the cleat with two or three 16d finishing nails. At the last board, lock the tongue in and set the groove side flat over the tongue of the adjoining board. It won't lock to the joining board, but with the bottom of the groove removed, it will fit into place. When all the nails are in place, countersink them with a nail set, and fill the cracks and cover the nail heads with water putty. Do not use wood plastic; it isn't strong enough. Water putty dries rock-hard.

Step 8: To finish the job, let the water putty dry and then sand the patch lightly. Paint the patched area with a primer coat of porch and floor enamel, and let the paint dry. Then repaint the porch as needed.

Repairing a Garage Door

Overhead garage doors, whether they roll up in sections or swing up in one piece, operate on spring tension. The door moves on metal tracks on the garage walls, and a heavy spring or springs provide the power. In most cases when the door doesn't work easily, repairs are fairly simple. To repair a garage door:

Step 1: Check the metal tracks inside the garage. Look at the mounting brackets that hold the tracks to the walls. If they're loose, tighten the bolts or screws at the brackets. Working inside the garage with the garage door closed, examine the tracks for dents, crimps, or flat spots. If there are any damaged spots, pound them out with a rubber mallet, or with a hammer and a block of scrap wood. If the tracks are badly damaged, they should be replaced. This is probably a job for a carpenter, not a do-it-yourselfer.

Step 2: Check the tracks with a level to make sure they're properly aligned. Horizontal tracks should slant slightly down toward the back of the garage; with roll-up doors, the vertical sections of track should be exactly plumb. Both tracks must be at the same height on the garage walls. If the tracks are not properly aligned, loosen but do not remove the screws or bolts that hold the mounting brackets, and tap the tracks carefully into position. Recheck the tracks with the level to make sure they're in the right position; then tighten the screws or bolts at the mounting brackets.

Step 3: Clean the tracks with concentrated household cleaner to remove dirt and hardened grease. Clean the rollers thoroughly, and wipe both tracks and rollers dry.

Step 4: Lubricate both the tracks and the rollers using garage door lubricant spray or powdered graphite in the tracks, and household oil or silicone spray on the rollers. If there are any pulleys, lubricate them with the same lubricant you used on the rollers.

Step 5: Check for loose hardware, and tighten as needed. On swing-up doors, check the plates where the spring is mounted to be sure the screws are tight, and tighten any loose screws. On roll-up doors, check the hinges that hold the sections of the door together; tighten any loose screws, and replace any damaged hinges. Sagging at one side of the door can often be corrected by servicing the hinges. If a screw hole is enlarged, replace the screw with a longer one of the same diameter, and use a hollow fiber plug, dipped in carpenters' glue, with the new screw. If the wood is cracked at a hinge, remove the hinge and fill the cracks and the screw holes with wood filler. Let the filler dry and then replace the hinge. If possible, move the hinge onto solid wood.

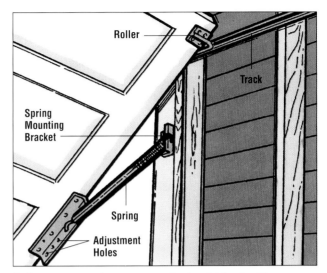

Swing-up garage doors move on horizontal tracks. The power spring is mounted on the door frame and hooked to the door.

Roll-up garage doors have tracks that curve from vertical to horizontal; both parts must be aligned. Make sure the door sections are securely hinged.

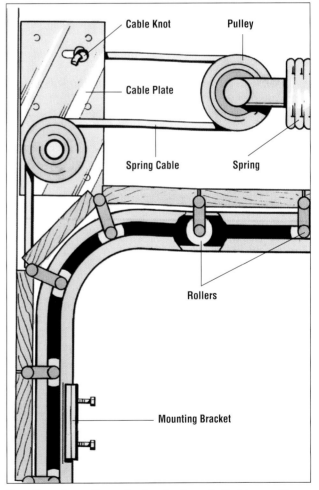

On roll-up doors, the spring tension is controlled by a cable on a pulley. To adjust the tension, pull the cable and reknot the end to shorten or lengthen the cable.

roof pitches meet; this is called valley flashing. When flashing is badly damaged, or when a leak is severe, you need a professional repair job. In many cases, however, you can repair the damage yourself. Use ladders and safety ropes to get at the roof, as detailed previously. Make sure the roof is dry.

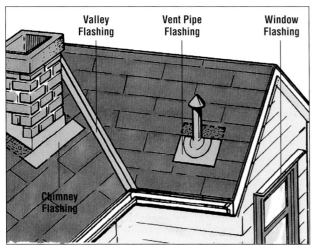

Metal flashing is used to seal out water around the chimney, at vent pipes, along the valleys where two roof pitches meet, and sometimes over exposed windows. Inspect flashing yearly.

To prevent leaks at the flashing, inspect it every spring. If you see thin spots or gaps along a flashing joint, spread roof cement over the entire joint, applying it generously with a trowel. The flashing edge should be covered completely. At the chimney, examine the flashing carefully. Chimney flashing is installed in two parts: the base, which covers the bottom of the chimney and extends onto the roof; and the cap, which is mortared into the chimney bricks. If the mortar holding the cap flashing is crumbling, or if the flashing has pulled loose, you'll have to resecure the flashing. To resecure the flashing around a chimney:

Step 1: Pull the lip of the cap flashing out of the mortar joint, only as far as it comes easily. Do not yank the entire flashing out or pull it completely away from the chimney. The less you have to separate it, the easier it will be to fix.

Step 2: With the flashing out of the mortar joint, clean out the old mortar with a hammer and chisel, wearing safety goggles to protect your eyes. Then, being careful not to damage the flashing, wire-brush the joint to clean out the debris.

Step 3: Use cement mortar mix to fill the open joint, mixing the mortar as directed. Wet the joint with a paintbrush dipped in water. With a small trowel, fill the joint firmly with mortar.

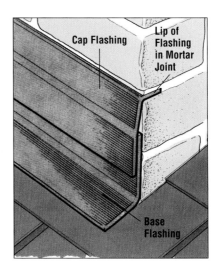

Chimney flashing has two parts, the base and the cap. The lip of the cap is embedded in mortar between the chimney bricks.

Step 4: When the joint is full, press the lip of the flashing into the mortar, in the same position it was in before. Press the flashing in firmly, but don't push too far or it may pop back out and you'll have to start all over again. Let the mortar dry as directed.

Step 5: When the joint is completely cured, caulk all around the joint and over the lip of the cap flashing with butyl rubber caulk.

At vent pipes or metal chimneys, make sure the joint at the base of the pipe or chimney is sealed. If you can see gaps at the roof line, caulk around the base of the pipe or chimney with roof cement in a caulking gun. Vent pipes on pitched roofs usually have a protective collar; if the collar is loose, tap it back into place, and then caulk the collar-base joint with roof caulk.

Valley flashings are not always repairable. If you see a strip of metal all along the joint where two roof pitches

In a closed valley, the flashing is covered by shingles; no exposed metal is visible. This type should be professionally repaired.

meet, the valley is open. If the joint is shingled over, it's closed. Open valleys are easy to get at because you can see the damage and repair it. Because closed valleys aren't visible from the roof, the only sign of damage is usually a leak directly under the valley. This kind of valley should be repaired by a professional roofer. To repair an open valley:

Step 1: Inspect the valley for holes all along the joint. You can patch small holes with the same type of sheet metal the valley is made of. Most valleys use either aluminum or copper. Do not use a different metal to patch the valley, as this would cause corrosion.

Step 2: Clean the surface of the valley with a wire brush.

Step 3: Cut a sheet-metal patch about 2 inches bigger all around than the hole.

Step 4: Spread a thick coating of roof cement on the damaged area and press the patch into place, bending it to the shape of the valley.

Step 5: Spread more roof cement over the edges of the patch to seal out water.

In an open valley, the flashing strip is exposed; a strip of metal is visible along the joint where two roof pitches meet. Repair this type yourself.

If you can't see any holes along an open valley, but you know it has leaked, look for loose shingles along the edges of the valley. Working from the bottom up, reset any loose shingles with roof cement, then apply more roof cement to cover the shingle edges all along the valley. If you can't find any loose shingles, the problem may be that the valley is too narrow, and simply isn't adequate to seal the joint. This situation should be handled by a professional roofer because the entire valley will have to be replaced.

Reflashing a Vent Pipe

Vent pipes and appliance chimneys are sealed with metal flashing to prevent leaks, but the flashing may eventually need replacement. Pitched-roof vents are usually flashed with a flat metal sheet cut to fit around the pipe, and a protective collar that fits around its base. Flat-roof flashing usually covers the entire vent, with a flat base and a pipe casing that slides on over the chimney. Replacing either type of flashing is fairly easy. Make sure your replacement flashing is exactly the same type and diameter as the old one. Follow the roof safety procedures detailed earlier in this chapter. ***Caution:*** *Wear work gloves when working with metal flashing because the edges of the flashing are sharp.*

On a pitched roof, the base of the flashing is covered with shingles on the side above the chimney, and left exposed on the side below it. To reflash a vent pipe on a pitched roof:

Step 1: Remove the shingles on the up-roof side of the chimney. Lift the shingles with a pry bar, but be careful not to damage them, as you will have to replace them to cover the new flashing. If you break a shingle, you'll need a new one to replace it.

Step 2: Remove the flashing by inserting the blade of the pry bar under its edge, and lever the bar on a block of scrap wood to lift the flashing.

Step 3: Lift the flashing up over the vent pipe, being careful not to knock the pipe out of place. Then pull out any nails left around the pipe, and fill the holes with roof cement.

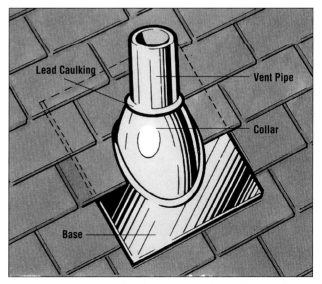

Pitched-roof vent pipe flashing consists of a flat base and protective collar that fits around the pipe.

Step 4: Set the new flashing over the pipe, with its protective collar aligned the same way the old one was. Nail down the flashing with 6d galvanized roofing nails, and cover the nail heads with roof cement. Apply more roof cement to seal the base of the protective collar.

Step 5: Replace the shingles over the top of the flashing. Starting with the bottom row and working up, nail each shingle into place at the top. Use two 6d galvanized roofing nails for small shingles, four nails for large ones. As you work, cover the nail heads with roof cement. Slide the top edges of the top row of shingles under the overlapping bottom edges of the row above.

To reflash a vent pipe on a flat roof:

Step 1: If there's gravel on the roof, sweep it away from the vent pipe to clear a 4-foot-square area.

Step 2: Locate the edge of the flashing base and use a sharp utility knife to cut a slit through the roofing felt along one side of it.

Step 3: Insert the blade of a pry bar into the slit and under the edge of the flashing. Lever the bar over a block of scrap wood, working along the slit in the roofing, to release the flashing. Cut around the remaining three sides to free the flashing completely.

Step 4: Lift the old flashing out and over the pipe.

Step 5: Set the new flashing on top of the roof to determine how to fill the hole. For each layer of roofing that you can see in the hole, cut a patch of 15-pound roofing felt. Use the base of the old flashing as a pattern to cut the felt. On each piece of roofing felt, mark the location of the vent pipe, and cut a hole at that point so that the patch will fit snugly over the pipe.

Step 6: Spread a thick layer of roof cement on the bottom of the hole, set the first patch over the pipe, and press it firmly into the hole. Then spread more roof cement on top of it. Fill the entire hole this way, building up layers of roofing felt and roof cement, until the top patch is level with the surface of the roof. Spread a thick layer of roof cement over the top patch, and fill any gaps around the vent pipe with more cement. *Caution: Wear work gloves when working with metal flashing to protect your hands from the sharp edges of the flashing.*

Step 7: Set the new flashing carefully into place over the vent pipe and press it down firmly, so that the vent pipe is encased in the flashing pipe and the base is aligned in exactly the same way the old flashing was.

Step 8: Nail down the flashing with 6d galvanized roofing nails, and cover the nail heads with roof cement. Using pliers, fold the top edge of the casing pipe down over the top edge of the vent pipe to seal the new flashing.

Step 9: Cover the base of the flashing with two more layers of roofing felt, the first layer 3 inches larger and the second 6 inches larger all around than the flashing. As you did with the first patches, cut a hole in the center of each piece so that it will fit over the vent pipe. Spread another thick layer of roof cement over the base of the flashing, extending it 3 inches onto the roof all around. Set the smaller piece of roofing felt over the pipe and press it into place. Cover this piece of felt with another layer of roof cement, again extending it 3 inches onto the roof all around, and set the larger patch into place. Press this final patch down and nail it into place with 6d galvanized roofing nails, about 1 inch apart, and cover the nail heads with roof cement.

Step 10: If you removed gravel from the patch area, you can now spread it back over the bare spot, but this isn't necessary.

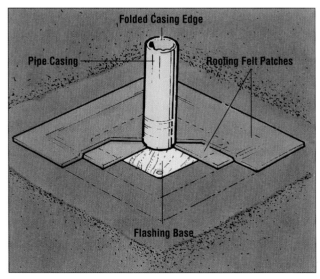

Flat-roof vent pipe flashing has a casing pipe that covers the entire pipe; the edge of the casing folds down to seal it. The base is covered by roofing.

Maintaining and Repairing Gutter Systems

Good drainage is very important to your home's structural well-being. Gutters and downspouts, the main components of your drainage system, must be kept clear to prevent storm water from overflowing or backing up. Blocked gutters can cause erosion around the house, damage to the exterior walls, basement leaks, and—eventually—uneven settling of the foundation. To prevent these drainage problems, regularly maintain your gutters and downspouts, and repair them at the first sign of trouble. When you work on your gutters, follow the roof safety procedures outlined earlier in this chapter.

At the minimum, clean your gutters twice a year, in late spring and late fall. If you live in a wooded area, clean them more frequently. A plastic scoop is an ideal gutter-cleaning tool. Wear work gloves to protect your hands. To clean the gutters:

Step 1: Shovel out leaves and other debris with the plastic scoop. Work from a ladder that's tall enough to let you reach the gutters comfortably. As you work, move the ladder frequently. Don't lean or bend to reach to either side or you might lose your balance.

Step 2: After cleaning out all the loose debris, flush the gutters with a garden hose.

Step 3: Check the downspouts by flushing them with the hose. If a downspout is clogged, you can break up the clog with a plumbers' snake fed down through the opening in the gutter. Clear out any remaining debris with the hose.

Clean gutters at least twice a year to prevent clogging. Shovel out leaves and other debris with a plastic scoop.

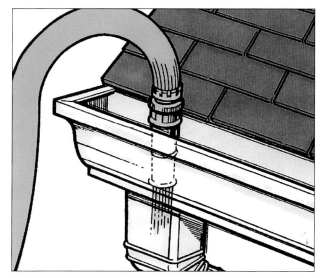

To keep downspouts clear, flush them with a hose. If necessary, remove clogs with a plumbers' snake. Use a wire leaf strainer at each downspout.

To keep the downspouts clear, use a wire leaf strainer at each one. Insert a leaf strainer into each downspout opening along the gutters, then push it in just far enough to hold it steady. The strainer will prevent sticks and other debris from entering the downspout and clogging it.

Many homeowners use plastic or metal screening leaf guards on their gutters to keep leaves from building up. Leaf guards are not effective against leaf fragments, leaf cases, and other small debris that can go right through the screening. Gutters covered by leaf guards must still be cleaned regularly, and leaf guards may make the cleaning much more difficult.

After cleaning out the gutters, let them dry thoroughly, and inspect them for signs of damage. Rust spots and holes can be mended with scrap wire screening and asphalt roof cement. First, wire-brush the damaged area to remove dirt and loosen rust. Clean the area well with a rag soaked in mineral spirits. If the hole is small, or if the metal isn't rusted all the way through, a screening patch isn't needed; just spread roof cement over the damaged area. To repair an open hole in a gutter:

Step 1: Cut a piece of scrap wire screening, ½ inch to 1 inch bigger all around than the hole.

Step 2: Spread roof cement around the hole, and press the patch down into it. Spread a thin layer of cement over the screening. Let the patch dry.

Step 3: If the holes of the screening are still open, spread another layer of cement over the patch to close it completely.

brush to do the cleaning. Chimney brushes are available at larger hardware stores.

Step 3: Fasten the bag or brush securely to a rope. Working from the roof, lower the bag or brush down the chimney until it hits the bottom. Lower and raise the brush several times to dislodge caked soot. If you're using a bag, start at one corner of the chimney. Lower the bag, pull it up, and repeat, lowering and raising it several times. Move the bag around the perimeter of the opening, moving it about a foot each time, and repeat this procedure until you've cleaned the entire chimney area.

Step 4: If the fireplace has an outside door, open it and remove the soot that's fallen through. Wait an hour or so for the dust to settle, then remove the plastic sheet or plywood from the fireplace opening.

Step 5: Use a large hand mirror and a flashlight to inspect the chimney. Look for any obstructions. If there are any, repeat the cleaning procedure described before. If there are no obstructions, reach over the damper to the smoke shelf. Gently clean away the debris.

Step 6: Use a shop vacuum to clean out the fireplace and the smoke shelf.

Exterior Painting

Y ou'll never realize just how big your house is until you start to paint it. House painting is a job that consumes time, energy, patience, and money. On the other hand, exterior painting is really no more difficult than interior painting (see Chapter 3), and most of the same tools and techniques apply. Perhaps the most persuasive argument for doing it yourself is that hiring the work out can easily cost you up to four times as much as doing it yourself.

Selecting Exterior Paint

One of the major differences between indoor and outdoor painting is that with outdoor painting there is a wider range of exterior surfaces to consider. These surfaces include clapboard and aluminum siding, wood shingles, tar shingles, cedar shakes, brick, concrete block, stucco, and old paint. On many older homes, you'll find a combination of these surfaces. Fortunately, there is also a paint for every type of surface and some paints that are suitable for more than one surface.

Like interior paints, exterior paints are available in either water-thinned or solvent-thinned formulas and in

Estimating Exterior Paint

T he size of the house, the condition of the surfaces, the type of coating you select, and the method of application are all factors that will determine the amount of paint you need to buy.

Narrow lap siding, shingles or shakes, masonry, or stucco exterior walls can take 10 to 50 percent more paint than smooth, flat walls take.

Airless sprayers, which apply the equivalent of two coats of paint at one time, may require twice as much paint as brushes, rollers, or pads for the same surface dimensions.

You can get more standard, premixed paint if you run out. Or, if you buy too much, many stores will give credit or refunds for unopened gallons. With custom-colored paints, however, it may be difficult to get a precise match if you run short. Calculate your needs carefully, then buy an extra gallon for insurance.

To determine how much paint the house needs, measure its perimeter and multiply that figure by the height, excluding gable ends. Take the measurements with a steel tape or reel out a ball of twine around the house and mark and measure the twine. If you will use a different trim paint, subtract 21 square feet for every door and 15 square feet for typical windows. Divide the final figure by the square-foot coverage specified on the paint can to figure the number of gallons you'll need for one coat.

If your house has gables, you can estimate by just adding 2 feet to the height when making your calculations. For more precision, measure the width of the gable wall and multiply that figure by its height. Divide the final figure by 2 to determine the gable's square-foot dimensions.

For trim paint, the rule of thumb is 1 gallon for every 6 gallons of wall paint. To be more accurate, you'll have to figure the areas of doors, windows, and shutters. For gutters, a linear foot is about equal to a square foot, so for 50 feet of gutter, buy sufficient paint to cover 50 square feet.

SELECTING THE RIGHT EXTERIOR COATING

Most of the coatings listed below can be applied with an airless sprayer as well as a brush, roller, or painting pad. But if you want to spray, read the labels carefully or ask your paint dealer if you're buying a sprayable coating. Latex paints require only water to thin them enough for spraying. With alkyds, oils, and other types of paints, you'll have to purchase the appropriate solvents to dilute them.

Type	Characteristics/Use	Application
Acrylic	A type of latex; water-thinned and water cleanup. Fast-drying and suitable for any building material, including masonry and primed metal.	Brush, roller, pad, spray. Comparable to regular latex paint.
Alkyd	Similar to oil-based paints, but dries faster. Solvent thinned, solvent cleanup. Use over oil and alkyd coatings.	Brush, roller, pad, spray. Smooths out more readily than latex, but more difficult to apply.
Latex	Most popular exterior paint. Excellent durability. Water-thinned, water cleanup. Mildew-proof; may even be applied over damp surfaces. Do not use over oil paints unless specified by the manufacturer.	Brush, roller, pad, spray. Except when spraying, don't thin; apply thickly with little spreadout.
Oil	Extremely durable, but dries slowly. Solvents must be used for cleanup. Least popular.	Brush, roller, pad, spray on very dry surfaces. Insects and rain are dangers because of lengthy drying time.
Marine	Excellent durability on wood, some metals. Expensive. Solvent cleanup.	Brush recommended due to thick, gooey consistency.
Masonry	May be latex, alkyd, epoxy, Portland cement, or rubber. Some contain their own primers.	Brush, roller. Latex types easiest to apply.
Metal	Water-thinned or solvent-thinned, usually with rust-resistant ingredients.	Brush, roller, pad, spray. Prime bare metals first.
Primers	Seals raw wood, bare metal. Also use over old, worn finishes. Provides good bonding for top coating. Use primer formulated for top coat.	Brush, roller, pad, spray. Easier than top-coat painting. Porous surfaces may drink up lots of primer.
Porch/Deck	Alkyd, latex, epoxy, rubber, oil, or polyurethane types. Synthetics dry quickly; oil-base types dry slowly, but are very durable. Limited color selection.	Brush, roller, pad, or wax applicator. For floors, pour on, smooth out. For decks, dip applicator and apply.
Shingle	Alkyd-, oil-, or latex-base. For wood siding shingles. Permits escape of moisture behind shingles.	Brush, roller, pad, spray. Do not use on creosote-treated wood less than eight years old.
Stains	Water- or solvent-thinned; both types durable. Choice of transparent, semi-transparent, solid-stain pigmentation. May contain preservatives.	Brush, roller, pad, spray.
Preservatives	Moisture-, rot-, and insect-resistant for decks, fences, wood siding, and shingles.	Dipping, brush, spray.
Varnish	Acrylic for metal; moisture-cured urethane, alkyd, or spar types for exterior wood.	Brush, roller, or pad. Limited durability; one to two years. Won't dramatically alter natural appearance and color of woods.

- **Mildew.** This moldy growth appears where dampness and shade prevail. And if you paint over it, it's likely to come right through the new paint. Use a fungicide such as chlorine bleach or a commercial solution to kill patches of mildew before repainting.
- **Running Sags.** A wavy, irregular surface results from improper brushing. To correct it after the paint is dry, sand and repaint, smoothing out the new coat to a consistent thickness.
- **Paint Won't Dry.** This is perhaps the best reason to buy good, high-quality paint. Prolonged tackiness is an indication of inferior paint. If you apply the paint too thickly or during high humidity, it will stay tacky for a long time. Good paint, on the other hand, dries quickly. If you think you may have an inferior paint, experiment on an inconspicuous portion of the house first.

Removing Old Paint

If you're lucky, all your house may need before repainting is a good healthy bath. Wash it down with a hose and go over stubborn dirt with a scrub brush and warm, soapy water.

If you're not so lucky, then you just have to face the fact that a time-consuming and dirty job lies between you and a new coat of paint. Do the job well and your paint job will not only look better, it will last for five to eight years on the average.

Start by examining the outside of the house thoroughly, not just the walls, but under the eaves, around windows and doors, and along the foundation. Look for split shingles and siding, popped nails, peeling or blistering paint, mildew, and rust stains. Once you've identified the areas that need attention, roll up your sleeves and make the repairs.

Scraping

Use a wire brush and a wide-blade putty knife to remove small areas of defective paint. Scrub under the laps of clapboard siding as well as on downspouts and gutters.

For speedier work on metal, a wire brush attachment on an electric drill will remove rust and paint with less effort.

For more extensive paint removal, invest in a sharp pull scraper—a tool with a replaceable blade that's capable of stripping old paint all the way down to bare wood with a single scrape. Hold the scraper so that the blade is perpendicular to the wood, apply moderate to firm pressure, and drag it along the surface. Keep the blade flat against the wood so that it doesn't gouge the surface.

Remove small areas of defective paint with a wire brush and/or a wide-blade putty knife. Scrub under the laps of clapboard siding and on downspouts and gutters.

Sanding

For feathering the edges of scraped spots here and there, you can just wrap a piece of sandpaper around a wood block. For larger areas, it's less tiring and more effective to use an electric orbital sander. Move it up and down or back and forth across the surface to remove old paint and feather rough edges at the same time. Don't use an electric disc sander or a belt sander. Both can leave swirls or dips in the wood that will show through a new coat of paint.

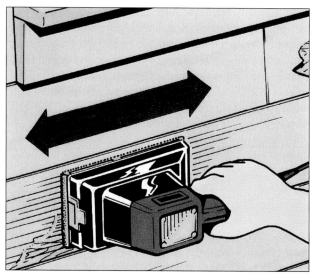

Move an electric orbital sander up and down or back and forth to remove old paint and feather rough edges.

Melting

For particularly heavy deposits of paint, heat may be more effective than muscle. One way to apply heat is with an electric paint remover, a device with a platelike heating element that "cooks" the paint and has a built-in scraper to pull it off. Wear gloves and hold the heating element against the surface until the paint sizzles. Pull the remover firmly over the surface. The attached scraper will pull off the cooked paint as you go.

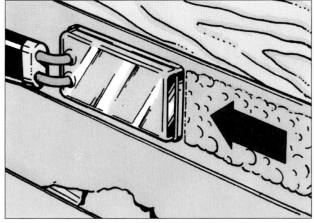

Another way to remove old paint is with an electric paint remover—a device with a platelike heating element that softens the paint and has a built-in scraper.

You can also carefully burn off old paint with a propane torch fitted with a spreader tip that produces a thin, fan-shaped flame that burns off wide bands of paint. Hold the torch in one hand, a wide-blade scraper in the other. The heat from the flame will blister and loosen the paint so you can remove it with the scraper. Again, wear gloves to protect your hands from falling flakes of melting paint. Keep a fire extinguisher nearby and take every precaution against accidentally setting the house on fire.

Use liquid paint removers only as a last resort. They work well, but they're expensive, especially on big jobs. Also, they can slop onto perfectly good paint, giving you one more problem to deal with.

Priming

Once you have removed all the loose paint, it will be necessary to apply an appropriate primer to some of the distressed areas. This is especially true if your paint-removal system has exposed raw wood or bare metal. The kind of primer you use depends on the kind of paint you'll be using later. For latex paint, use latex primers; for solvent-thinned paints, use solvent-based primers; and for metals, use metal primers. Not only do these coatings provide extra protection against the elements,

they also form a firm foundation for finishing paints. Also, priming is always required when you're working on new wood.

Other Prep Work

Even if you're fortunate enough to be able to skip spot-scraping, sanding, and repriming, there are still some prepainting chores to attend to. They're much less laborious than removing peeling paint, but no less vital to a successful job.

Airborne dirt that has affixed itself to the outside of your home should be washed off so that the new coating bonds well to the old. Rust stains on siding, overhangs, and foundations need to be removed. Leaks in gutters and downspouts have to be repaired. Loose caulking should be replaced, along with split shingles. Cracks in siding must be filled, sanded, and primed. Mildew has to be scrubbed off, and steps must be taken to eliminate its return.

Also, to make painting easier, storm windows, screens, shutters, awnings, wall-mounted light fixtures, the mailbox, and even the street address numbers should be taken down, cleaned, and painted separately. You may even want to remove downspouts, as it's sometimes difficult to get a paintbrush behind them. Be sure to turn the power supply off before dismantling light fixtures.

To make painting easier, remove light fixtures and other accessories.

You can typically complete all of these preparations in a single day or over a weekend. If you're painting with latex, you can start the following day. If you're using a solvent-based paint, remember that it does not adhere well to moist surfaces. Wait several days until all the washed surfaces are absolutely dry before applying a new coat of paint.

Washing

Not only will this process get the outside of your house clean and provide a dirt-free foundation for the new coating, it will also help you find surface flaws that have to be dealt with.

Depending on just how dirty the outside of the house is and on its size, there are two ways to approach this job. If you live in an average-size house, use a garden hose with a car-wash brush attachment to bathe the big areas. For caked-on dirt, use a scrub brush or a sponge and a pail of warm water with a good, strong household detergent in it. Work from the top down, naturally, and rinse all areas where you scrubbed with soapy water.

To remove caked-on dirt, use a scrub brush or a sponge and a pail of warm water with a good, strong household detergent in it. Work from the top down and rinse all areas where you scrubbed with soapy water.

For bigger houses or for faster work on smaller ones, rent a high-pressure spray cleaner. This device attaches to your home's water-supply system and puts out a jet of water at a pressure of about 600 pounds per square inch. It is equipped with a hand-held wand tipped with a trigger-activated nozzle. The pressure is high enough to dislodge not only stubborn dirt, mildew, stains, and dried-on sea-spray salt, it's enough to remove peeling paint. In fact, if the jet nozzle is held too close to the surface it can even peel off perfectly sound paint, split open shingles, and drill a hole in siding. So follow the manufacturer's directions and wear goggles and protective clothing.

You can use the spray while working from a ladder—although scaffolding is better—but practice at ground level first; the force of the spray against the house could knock you off a ladder if you're not careful. Some of these machines come with separate containers you can fill with cleaning solutions or antimildew solutions. Sprayers are so powerful that ordinarily you probably won't need to use a cleaning solution; if you do, remember to rinse the surface with clean water afterward.

Nailing

The house bath may well reveal the location of nails that have popped out of the siding or rusting nail heads that have left streaks of rust on the exterior walls. If so, use a nail set and a hammer to reset them. First, use sandpaper or steel wool to clean the nail heads. On clapboard siding, use the nail set to recess the nail head about ⅛ inch below the surface of the wood. Dab on a coat of rust-inhibiting primer (unless the nail is aluminum or non-rusting galvanized steel), and let it dry. Then fill the nail hole with spackle or putty. When the filler is dry, give it a coat of primer. For flathead nails, which cannot be recessed, sand the heads until they're shiny, and coat with a primer.

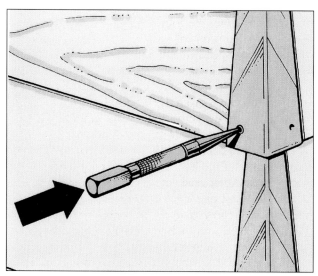

Reset popped nails with a nail set and hammer, then protect them with rust-inhibiting primer.

For rusting nail heads and rust stains, go over both siding and nail heads with sandpaper or steel wool. If the rust is just on the surface, this should remove it. If it does, then follow up with a coat of primer. If the rust stain doesn't come off with a light sanding, it has soaked into the wood too deeply to remove without damaging the wood itself. In that case, your only option is to sand the nail head, apply a primer to it and the rust stain, and then paint over it.

Covering Shrubs

Trees, bushes, and ornamental shrubs can also get in the way of your painting. Prune any branches that overhang the house or brush up against walls. For evergreen trees and tall bushes growing close to the house, wrap them with canvas drop cloths. Then, tie one end of a rope around the trunk at least halfway up. Pull the top of the tree out and away from the house, and tie the other end of the rope to a stake placed farther out in the yard. Cover smaller shrubs, flower beds, sidewalks, and driveways with drop cloths to protect them from paint drips and spills.

Painting Siding

With the surface preparations out of the way, you're almost ready to brush, roll, or spray on a new coat of paint. First, because paint colors tend to vary slightly from batch to batch, mix all the paint together in one or two large containers. You don't want a color change in the middle of a wall! Leftover paint should go back in the original paint cans and be resealed.

Plan to paint from top to bottom so you don't have to worry about dripping paint on freshly-painted areas. Do the walls first, then the trim.

Plan your painting day so that you follow the sun, working in the shade after the sun has dried off the early-morning moisture. Try not to let the setting sun catch you in the middle of a wall at the end of the day. If you have to stop, try to finish painting an entire course of siding all the way across the house. Otherwise, you may leave lap marks in the middle of the course.

Also, plan to paint high places in horizontal sections across the top of the wall. Never lean away from an extension ladder or reach more than an arm's length to either side. Paint one high section, move the ladder, and paint another, creating a painted band as you go. Repeat the process all the way across the wall. Then, lower the ladder to work on a lower section.

As explained in Chapters 1 and 3, an extension ladder can be perilous. Make sure it's on firm footing about one-quarter of its length out from the foundation of the house. Also make sure it doesn't tilt to the left or right. Always check both extension hooks to ensure they are firmly locked on the supporting rungs. The two sections of the ladder should overlap at least three rungs. When moving the ladder, watch out for power lines.

Here's another tip: Hang your paint bucket on a rung with an S-shaped bucket hook so you can hang on to the ladder with one hand while painting with the other.

If your house has dormers, you may have to paint them from the roof instead of the ladder. If so, the ladder should reach at least 3 feet above the edge of the roof so you can step onto the roof without standing on the top rungs of the ladder.

To paint clapboard siding, use at least a 4-inch brush. To begin, dip the tips of the bristles in the paint and coat the underside edges of four or five clapboards to a length of 3 feet or so. With a fully loaded brush, paint the face of each board, using fairly short strokes to cover the surface. To finish, level the paint with smooth, broad, horizontal strokes.

Begin by painting the undersides of four or five clapboards.

Next, paint the face of each board, using short strokes to cover the surface.

347

To finish, level the paint with smooth, broad, horizontal strokes.

Paint shingles and shakes in the same way, except apply the paint with vertical strokes. Painting pad applicators, specially designed for shingle painting, are easier to use than a brush. They have a carpet of short nylon bristles embedded in a foam rubber pad attached to the applicator. For edge painting on shingles, just dip the edge of the pad in a paint tray. For the face of the shingles, load the face of the pad, place it against the face of the shingle, apply some pressure and pull it downward. These pads can also be used horizontally on wide clapboard siding.

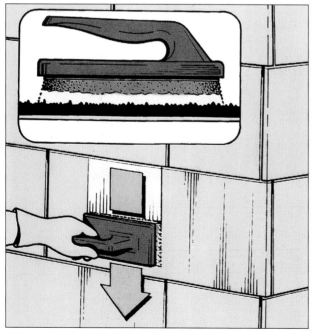

Painting pad applicators, specially designed for shingle painting, are easier to use than a brush.

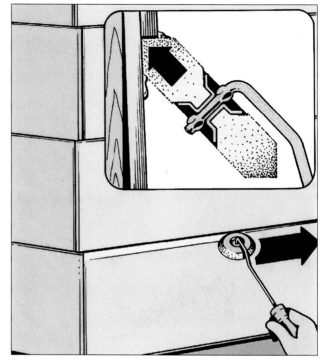

A corner roller makes short work of the undersides of shingles or clapboards.

A corner roller is another time-saving tool. Use it to apply paint to the undersides of either shingles or clapboards.

When painting either clapboard or shingles, pay special attention around door and window casings. At the top of each casing you'll find a drip cap or metal flashing that tucks up under the siding. Paint a tight seal between metal and wood. At the sides of the casings, jab

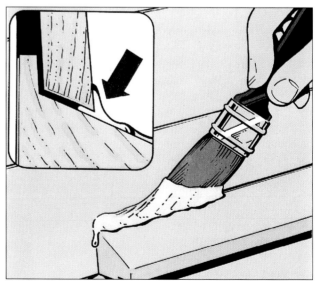

Paint a tight seal between the drip cap and siding atop windows and doors.

At the sides of window and door casings, jab your brush into joints, then smooth out the paint.

your brush into joints, then smooth out the paint to seal them. At casings and for the undersides of siding laps, you may prefer to use a corner roller.

Before dismounting and moving the ladder, check your work for drips, runs, thin areas, and missed spots.

Painting Trim

Painting exterior trim means that you're making progress and the job is winding down. Unfortunately, painting trim is a slow process that consumes a considerable amount of time, even if you apply the same color used on the siding.

Diligence and patience in dealing with these details pays off. If done carefully and thoroughly, trim painting will keep your house looking fresh and protect it from the elements for a long time. Here are some tips on making the job easier:

When painting trim, work from the top down; gables, dormers, eaves and gutters, second-story windows, porch railings, porches and stairs, and finally, foundations. If you don't want to bother with masking tape around window panes, use a paint shield and then go back later and scrape off spatters and drips.

If you've replaced the caulking around doors, windows, and joints, make sure it's dry before painting over it. And use enough paint to form a tight seal

between the siding and the trim to keep out moisture, wind, and insects.

Paint exterior windows, sashes, sills, and jambs in the same order as interior ones, working from the muntins and sashes out to the frames. Pay close attention to the sills. They bear the brunt of rain, snow, and accumulated dirt. If they look particularly weather-beaten, take the time to give them two or even three coats of paint, including the underside edges.

Paint double-hung windows in the sequence shown, moving the top and bottom sashes for access to all surfaces.

Screens and storm windows should be removed and painted separately. If the screens have holes, this is a good time to mend them or replace the screening. If the screening is sound, but needs painting, coat it first (using a pad applicator), then paint the frame. Don't forget to do both sides and all edges of screens and storms.

Doors are easier to paint if you remove the knobs, latch plates, and the door knocker. If you can, remove the entire door, lay it flat, and paint one side at a time, working on recessed panels first, then raised areas. Sand the bottom and top edges and apply a thin coat of paint to keep out moisture and prevent rot. While the door is open or off its hinges, paint the jambs and the frame and give the wooden threshold a coat of urethane varnish. Do not paint the hinges.

Gutters and downspouts made of galvanized metal should be scraped with a wire brush to remove loose paint and then primed and painted again. On downspouts, paint in the direction of the flutes, usually up and down, to prevent runs, drips, and sags. Because some downspouts are flat on all four sides and are attached closely to the house, you may even want to take them down to paint them. Consider simultaneously coating the inside of gutters with an asphalt-based paint, which waterproofs them and seals tiny holes and joints.

On ornamental metal work and porch railings, use a lamb's wool applicator instead of a trim brush. The mitten applicator, which can be used on either hand and is cleanable and reusable, allows you to grasp a railing support as you would a broom handle, smearing on the paint as you move your hand from top to bottom.

Paint all the risers on stairs at the same time, then the treads. If the stairs must be used while the paint is still wet, paint alternate treads. When they're dry, paint the other ones.

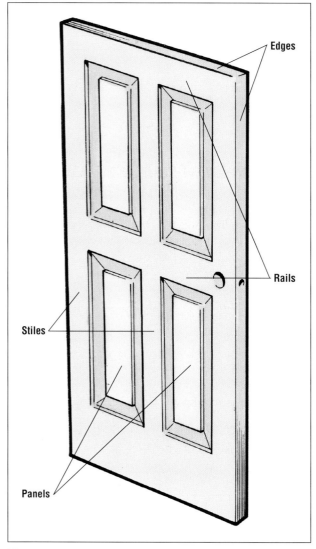

When painting an exterior door, paint the panels first, then the rails, the stiles, and finally the edges, working from top to bottom.

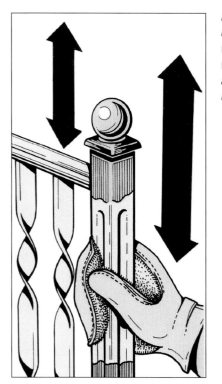

For railing and ornamental metal work, use a lamb's wool mitten applicator instead of a trim brush.

CHAPTER 10

SMALL ENGINE REPAIR

Small gas engines serve us in many ways. They power lawn mowers, tillers, cultivators, trimmers, edgers, snowblowers, chain saws, pumps, generators, air compressors, and other useful home tools. They also power our fun: outboard boats, snowmobiles, motorcycles, all-terrain vehicles, ultralight aircraft, and other toys.

To keep them operating efficiently, an owner of these tools and toys should know about small engines: how they work and what to do when they don't. The purpose of this chapter is to help you understand, service, and troubleshoot small two-stroke gasoline engines.

Understanding Small Engines

The purpose of a small gas engine is to convert chemical energy (gasoline) into mechanical energy. This energy can be used in many ways to make our lives easier and more fun. Here's a brief description of how small gas engines work.

A gasoline engine is an internal combustion engine. That is, gasoline is combined with air and a spark to ignite within the engine. To produce power, the engine

Lawn mowers are typically powered with a vertical-shaft two-stroke engine.

must intake fuel and air, compress the mixture, add a spark for ignition, then exhaust the resulting fumes. These four steps comprise the power cycle of a small engine.

Understanding Two-Stroke Engines

A two-stroke gas engine is simple in operation. There are two strokes, or movements, for each power cycle: the intake/compression stroke and the ignition/exhaust stroke. Technically, these engines are two-stroke cycle engines. Commonly, they are called two-stroke engines. A two-stroke engine has fewer moving parts, is lower in cost, and is typically easier to work on than a four-stroke engine. Four-stroke engines are used in tractors, automobiles, and other larger equipment.

Two-stroke engines are easily recognized by the high-pitched sound they make when operating. A small two-stroke engine may only have three moving parts: the piston, the connecting rod, and the crankshaft. Let's see how a two-stroke engine works.

Intake/Compression

Two-stroke gas-powered engines require only two strokes or one rotation to produce a power cycle. The first stroke is called the intake/compression stroke because it takes in the fuel-air mixture and compresses the mixture.

First, rotation of the crankshaft moves a connecting rod that pushes the piston up the cylinder. The moving piston covers the intake and exhaust ports along the side of the cylinder, closing off the intake of the fuel-air mixture. The piston simultaneously compresses the mixture within the cylinder to make it more flammable. A two-stroke engine requires compression of at least 60 pounds per square inch (psi) to operate.

As compression occurs above the piston, a vacuum is formed below the piston. To equalize pressure, the fuel-

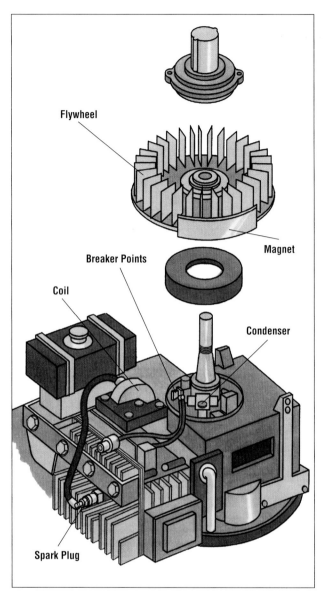

Typical components of an ignition system on a two-stroke engine.

Flywheel

Breaker Points

Coil

Magnet

Condenser

Spark Plug

- **Magneto-Powered Ignition System:** A magneto uses magnetism to supply electricity in ignitions where there is no battery. The magneto is turned by the crankshaft, which rotates when the manual recoil starter is pulled. The three types of magneto ignition systems are mechanical-breaker, capacitor-discharge, and transistor-controlled.
- **Battery-Powered Ignition System:** If your small engine includes a battery for starting, the ignition coil will also use it to supply spark to the spark plugs. A battery stores electrical energy until needed. Battery ignition systems also use mechanical-breaker, capacitor-discharge, and transistor-controlled ignitions.

- **Mechanical-Breaker Ignitions:** High-voltage electricity must be sent to the spark plug at the appropriate time. In mechanical-breaker ignitions, this job is performed through the contact points and a condenser.
- **Points:** As the crankshaft rotates, a cam opens and closes a set of contact points. These points function as an on/off switch: Closed is on, and open is off.
- **Condenser:** Because the spark moving across points can damage their surfaces, the condenser stores voltage to reduce arcing between points.
- **Capacitor-Discharge Ignitions (CDI):** A capacitor is a large condenser. A CDI stores and delivers voltage to the coil using magnets, diodes, and a capacitor.
- **Transistor-Controlled Ignitions (TCI):** Transistors are electronic controllers. A TCI uses transistors, resistors, and diodes to control the timing of the spark.
- **Coil:** An ignition coil is simply two coils of wire wrapped around an iron core. The coil changes low voltage (6 or 12 volts) into the high voltage (15,000 to 30,000 volts) needed by the spark plug.
- **Spark Plug:** A spark plug is an insulated electrode that is screwed into the top of the engine cylinder. High-voltage timed electricity from the magneto travels by wire to the spark plug. The base of the plug has an air gap of about 0.030 inch (30 thousandths of an inch), which the current must jump.
- **Wires:** The primary wire from the coil to the breaker point and secondary wire from the coil to the spark plug(s) deliver electricity to the ignition components.
- **Distributor:** A distributor is an ignition system for engines with more than one cylinder and spark plug. It distributes the spark to the appropriate cylinder using a rotor, cap, and individual spark plug wires.

Combustion

The combustion system of a small gas engine is where the work gets done. Components of the combustion system include the cylinder block, cylinder head, camshaft, valves, piston, connecting rod, crankshaft, timing gears, and flywheel. To better understand small gas engines, let's look at how this vital system works.

- **Cylinder Block:** The largest single part in a small gas engine is the cylinder block. It is a piece of metal in which the cylinder hole is bored or placed.
- **Cylinder Head:** The cylinder head is the top, or ceiling, of the cylinder and is attached to the block with bolts. Depending on the type of engine, the head may or may not include valves.
- **Piston:** A piston is the movable floor in the combustion chamber. Its upward movement compresses the fuel-air mixture. After combustion, its downward movement rotates the crankshaft.

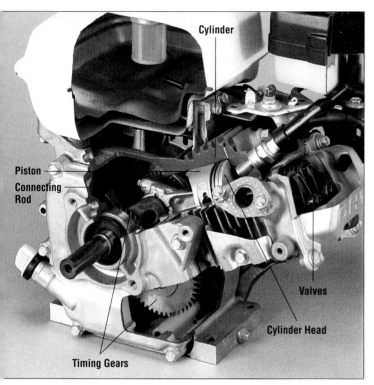

Some of the components of a two-stroke engine's combustion system.

- **Crankshaft:** An engine's crankshaft is a metal shaft with an offset section onto which the connecting rod is attached. Rotation of the crankshaft moves the piston up in the cylinder. Movement of the piston down in the cylinder then rotates the crankshaft.
- **Connecting Rod:** Between the piston and the crankshaft is a connecting rod. At the larger end of the connecting rod is a bearing that allows rotation around the moving crankshaft. The small end is attached to the piston pin.
- **Valves:** Valves simply open and close passages. A reed valve in a two-stroke engine is activated by changes in air pressure.
- **Flywheel:** At the end of the crankshaft is a circular weighted wheel called a flywheel. The flywheel delivers the engine's power to devices (wheels, blades, etc.) and helps keep the crankshaft turning smoothly.

Cooling and Lubrication

Combustion and friction produce heat. Heat and friction—if not controlled—can quickly damage an engine's components. Small gas engines are typically cooled by air. Friction is reduced using movable bearings and lubricants.

- **Air-Cooling Fins:** For simplicity, most smaller gas engines are cooled by air. Metal fins around the

outside of the combustion chamber help dissipate the internal heat.
- **Friction:** Friction is resistance that occurs when one surface rubs against another. Friction causes wear. In an engine with many moving parts, friction is reduced with bearings and lubricants.
- **Bearings:** A bearing is a replaceable part that takes the brunt of the friction. A friction bearing relies on lubricants to minimize friction. A nonfriction bearing uses hard steel rollers or balls to prevent wear, though it too requires some lubrication.
- **Lubricants:** Lubricants such as oil and grease reduce surface friction by coating parts with a film. Lubricants in two-stroke engines are applied to surfaces by mixing oil with fuel.
- **Viscosity:** An oil's viscosity is its resistance to flow. The thicker a lubricating oil or grease is, the higher its viscosity number.
- **Filters:** Friction happens. Moving parts wear, even with the best lubricants. The resulting metal as well as carbon from the combustion process must be cleaned from the oil to ensure long lubrication. Some small engines use oil filters to remove contaminants from the circulating oil.

Servicing Small Engines

• •

Purchasing a small engine-driven implement can make a dent in your budget. Tools and toys powered by small engines can cost anywhere from $100 to $10,000. That's why it's a good idea to invest in periodic servicing of your small engine. Replacing an engine every couple of years is an annoying and needless expense.

This section will give you detailed and illustrated information on how to service two-stroke gas engines. Following these procedures could help you put more money in the bank and less into your mechanic's pocket.

Benefits of Regular Service

Servicing your small engine tool or toy on a regular basis offers many advantages over the Wait-'til-It-Breaks Maintenance Program. First, by establishing a service schedule, you will gain confidence that whenever you need the unit it will be ready for use. Second, by performing a number of service functions together, you will save time. You can pick up all needed parts and lubricants in one trip to the parts store. Then you need to disassemble a component only once to perform numerous service procedures rather than taking it apart many times. Third, regular service gives you a chance to visually inspect the entire engine and related components for damage, wear, and other potential problems.

How, Where, and When to Service

Knowing how to service is as important as knowing when. The following pages offer procedures and illustrations to show you how to service your small engine.

Some service procedures can be performed wherever you store your tool or toy: in a garage, storage shed, or tool shed. If the unit is heavy, you can build a ramp up to a sturdy table that is at a handy height for working. Or you can use a ratchet winch to lift the engine. Units weighing less than 40 pounds may be lifted to a workbench or table as long as you lift with your legs rather than with your back. Get help if you need it, and make sure that the unit will remain sturdily in place as you service it. Remember to always put safety first!

Servicing a small engine is easy once you know what to do and when to do it. A service chart can help you determine common service requirements as well as track what service has been done. Your engine-powered unit may have a service chart in the owner's manual or service manual. Typical recommendations include changing engine oil every 25 hours of use and tuning up the engine at least once a year.

The purpose of ongoing service, also known as preventive maintenance, is to keep your engine-driven tool or toy in good operating condition. Ongoing service procedures include air cleaner service, crankcase breather service, cooling system service, muffler service, lubrication, and tune-up.

Lubrication service means making sure that all moving parts have sufficient lubrication (oil and/or grease) to minimize wear. Lubrication service procedures include mixing oil with fuel in two-stroke engines, and lubricating other moving parts.

A tune-up consists of the adjustment and/or replacement of parts critical to smooth and efficient engine operation. Those parts include components in all engine systems: fuel, exhaust, ignition, combustion, cooling, and lubrication. Ignition tune-ups are more important for mechanical-breaker ignitions than they are for self-contained solid-state ignitions. Regular tune-ups will keep your small engine running smoothly and reduce the need for repairs.

In addition, you should check other systems and make adjustments as needed to keep them operating smoothly. This includes adjusting the throttle, choke, and governor linkage, and cleaning off debris.

Engine-driven tools and toys usually come with an owner's manual. While some manufacturers' manuals are more complete and better written than others, most manuals include basic information on safe operation and service. Unfortunately, product manuals are often written to reduce the manufacturer's liability for accidental misuse rather than to help the owner service the product. In addition, manuals for engine-driven products typically show how to service the nonengine components: the grass catcher, wheel adjustments, blades, chains, and other parts. Service information for the engine may be minimal or nonexistent in the owner's manual.

What can you do about this lack of information? Fortunately, there are numerous after-market publishers of service manuals for specific models of small engines. If you don't have an owner's manual, you can contact the manufacturer directly to purchase one; manufacturers also sell service manuals. Most manufacturers keep product manuals for up to 20 years. If they only have one original copy left, you can often request a photocopy for a small charge.

Servicing Fuel Systems

The function of a small engine fuel system is to store and deliver fuel to the combustion chamber. Maintaining a fuel system includes servicing the fuel filter, air cleaner, fuel tank, and fuel lines; adjusting the carburetor; and adjusting the governor. Of course, not all small engines have all of these components.

This fuel tank has two filters: one at the opening and one at the entry to the fuel line.

Servicing Fuel Filters

Some small engines have a fuel strainer in the bottom of the fuel tank. Others have a removable fuel strainer in the fuel line. Still other small engines use disposable in-line fuel filters made of pleated paper. To clean sediment from a tank:

Step 1: Drain or siphon all fuel from the tank.

Step 2: With a flashlight, find the lowest point in the tank: the sediment reservoir. Clean all sediment from the reservoir indentation.

Step 3: Wipe sediment from the end of the filter element.

Step 4: Wipe the inside of the tank with a clean rag.

Step 5: Refill the fuel tank.

To clean sediment from a fuel strainer:

Step 1: Find and close the shutoff valve on the fuel line.

Step 2: Loosen the lock nut on the bowl retainer and remove the sediment bowl.

Step 3: Empty and clean the sediment bowl. Clean the filter screen. Refill the sediment bowl with fresh fuel.

Step 4: Reinstall the sediment bowl and bowl retainer, tightening the lock nut.

Step 5: Open the shutoff valve.

To replace an in-line fuel filter:

Step 1: Find and close the shutoff valve on the fuel line or use a clothespin to pinch the fuel line closed.

Step 2: Disconnect the fuel filter from the fuel line.

Step 3: Replace the in-line fuel filter with an exact replacement part.

Step 4: Open the shutoff valve.

Servicing Air Cleaners

The purpose of an air cleaner on a small engine is to keep large particles from clogging the carburetor. The two types of air cleaners used on small engines are oil bath and dry. To service an air cleaner:

Step 1: Remove the cover of the air cleaner, typically by unscrewing a nut on top of the cleaner.

Step 2: If it's an oil cleaner, remove all oil and contaminants from the center channel of the cleaner, wipe it clean, then replace oil to the indicated level. A dry cleaner cannot be cleaned and therefore must be replaced.

Step 3: Replace the air cleaner cover and make sure all fasteners are securely tightened.

Servicing Fuel Tanks and Lines

Fuel systems with pumps use nonpressurized fuel tanks. Outboard engines typically use pressurized tanks. Fuel lines are usually made of neoprene. To service a fuel tank and line:

Step 1: Remove the cap from the fuel tank.

Step 2: Using a flashlight, check for sediment in the fuel tank. If sediment is found, clean the tank and replace the fuel (see left). Replace the fuel cap when done.

Step 3: Check the fuel line and siphon bulb, if there is one, by squeezing them and inspecting for cracks. If damaged, replace with a line or a bulb of the same inside diameter. Make sure it is approved for use with fuel.

Adjusting Carburetors

A carburetor mixes fuel and air in the correct proportion for use by the engine. The three types of carburetors commonly used in small engines are natural draft, updraft, and downdraft. These names describe the direction that air flows from the inlet to the engine manifold. To maintain your small engine, you will want to make sure the carburetor's speed and mixture are correctly adjusted.

There are many types and models of carburetors used on small gas engines. Some have more available adjustments than others. Depending on the design, some carburetors are set at the factory and don't include adjusting screws. For example, a carburetor may allow adjustment of high speed, idle speed, and idle mixture while another only allows high and idle speed adjustments. To adjust the typical three-adjustment carburetor:

To set the correct idle speed, turn the idle adjustment screw with a screwdriver.

Step 1: With the engine running, open the throttle wide. Turn the high-speed adjustment needle forward and backward until the highest speed setting is found.

Step 2: Move the throttle to the slowest running speed. Adjust the idle-speed needle until the recommended idle speed is found.

Step 3: Once the idle speed has been set, adjust the idle mixture until the engine runs smoothly.

Adjusting Governors

A governor is a device that controls the speed of the engine as the load changes. As the load slows the engine down, the governor opens the throttle to return the engine to a set speed. Governors are commonly used on engine-powered electrical generators where constant speed is important. Two types of governors are installed on small engines: mechanical and air-vane.

A mechanical governor responds to the centrifugal force created by the engine's revolution.

A mechanical—also known as a counterbalance or flyweight—governor uses the centrifugal force of the engine's rotation to measure the load on the engine. This measurement is matched to the setting of an adjustment nut. If the load on the engine falls below the setting, a spring opens the throttle and speeds the engine up. An air-vane governor uses the air from the rotating flywheel to determine the speed of the engine. *Caution: An incorrectly adjusted governor can cause the small engine to operate at excessively high speeds and damage or destroy it.*

An air-vane governor responds to the air movement created by the rotating flywheel.

Unfortunately, there is no universal adjustment sequence for small engine governors. Much depends on the type of governor, whether the crankshaft is horizontal or vertical, the complexity and pivot points of the linkage, and the intended operating range. Because of these factors, refer to an owner's manual or service manual for your specific engine and application to adjust the governor.

Servicing Ignition Systems

An ignition system in a small engine produces and delivers the high-voltage spark that ignites the fuel-air mixture to cause the combustion. Some small engines require a battery to supply electrical power and the ignition spark. Others develop the ignition spark using a magneto.

A small engine ignition includes the ignition controller (mechanical-breaker, capacitor-discharge, or transistor-controlled), spark plugs, flywheel, and wiring. Servicing the ignition system of your small engine depends on which types of components it has. The following pages include step-by-step instructions for servicing ignition systems found in modern small engines.

Servicing Nonbattery Ignition Systems

A magneto applies magnetism to supply electricity in ignitions where there is no battery. The magneto is turned by the crankshaft, which rotates when the manual recoil starter is pulled. The steps to servicing a non-battery ignition system are:

Step 1: Service magneto.

Step 2: Service ignition controller.

Step 3: Service spark plug(s).

Step 4: Service flywheel.

To service a magneto:

Step 1: Remove the magneto cap and clean surfaces with a small, clean paintbrush. Wipe any excess oil away.

Step 2: Service the ignition controller (mechanical-breaker, capacitor-discharge, or transistor-controlled) as described on the following pages.

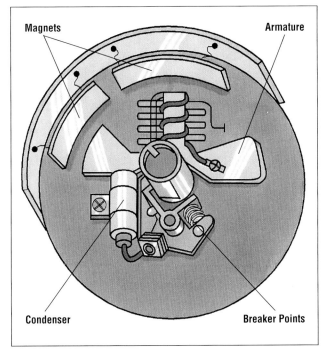

Parts of a typical flywheel magneto.

Servicing Battery Ignition Systems

A battery is a device containing electrical cells that produce and store direct current. Batteries used to start and operate small engines typically store 6 volts or 12 volts. Twelve-volt batteries are more commonly used to operate small engines. The steps to servicing a battery ignition system are:

Step 1: Service battery and charging system.

Step 2: Service ignition controller.

Step 3: Service spark plug(s).

Step 4: Service flywheel.

To service a battery and charging system:

Step 1: Use a voltage tester to verify that the battery is storing sufficient voltage. Each cell develops approximately 2 volts (1.9 to 2.1 volts). A 6-volt battery testing lower than 5.7 volts or a 12-volt battery lower than 11.4 volts should be recharged to rated voltage or higher.

Step 2: If the battery is conventional (has three or six caps on top), use a hydrometer to check the density of the liquid electrolyte in each cell. The density or specific gravity should be between 1.26 and 1.28 at room temperature. If it's below 1.25, recharge the battery. The difference in specific gravity between any two cells should be no more than 0.05. Note that a sealed maintenance-free battery cannot be tested in this way.

Step 3: Clean battery terminals using a small amount of baking soda and a stiff wire brush. Clean battery cables the same way.

Step 4: Inspect the cable insulation for corrosion and breaks; replace as needed.

Servicing Mechanical-Breaker Ignitions

For many years, mechanical-breaker ignition systems were the most popular of all ignition systems. The high voltage electricity from the coil is turned on and off using contact points and a condenser. The spark must be correctly timed to reach the spark plug at the exact moment when the piston is at the top of its travel and the fuel-air mixture is fully compressed. To service a mechanical-breaker ignition:

Step 1: Remove the cover from the stator plate to expose the breaker points and condenser.

Step 2: Manually turn the crankshaft until the high point of the cam lobe opens the contact points. Inspect the points for uneven wear or damage. If necessary, replace the breaker points and condenser.

Step 3: Slightly loosen the points setscrew and place the appropriate thickness gauge between the two contacts. (Check your owner's or service manual for the correct gap.) Move the points setscrew until the thickness gauge is touching both contacts but can be withdrawn without moving them.

Step 4: Tighten the points setscrew.

Step 5: Check the points gap with the thickness gauge again. Tightening the setscrew may have changed the gap.

Step 6: Clean the points with lint-free paper to remove any oil left by the thickness gauge.

Note: Some mechanical-breaker ignitions can be set using a dwell meter. If you have a dwell meter, refer to the unit's operating instructions and the ignition specifications to determine what dwell angle setting is correct and how to set it.

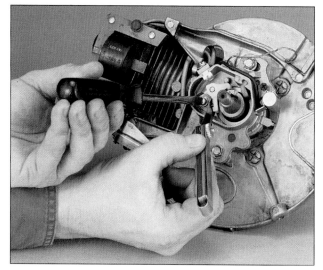

To adjust a mechanical-breaker ignition, loosen the points setscrew and use a thickness gauge to check the gap between the breaker contacts.

Timing Mechanical-Breaker Ignitions

To work efficiently, the spark must be delivered to the combustion chamber at the exact moment that the piston is at or near TDC (top dead center). To time the ignition spark:

Step 1: Loosen the adjustment nut(s) on the stator so it can be turned.

Step 2: Disconnect the coil lead wire from the points.

Step 3: Connect a lead of the continuity tester light or ohmmeter to the breaker point terminal and the other to the housing or a ground location.

Step 4: Rotate the stator until the light or ohmmeter indicates that the points have opened the circuit (light off or resistance high).

Step 5: Tighten the adjustment nut(s) on the stator without moving it.

Step 6: Reconnect the coil lead wire to the points.

Servicing Capacitor-Discharge Ignitions

Capacitor-discharge ignitions (CDIs) store and deliver voltage to the coil by way of magnets, diodes, and a capacitor. The mechanical points of a breaker point ignition are replaced with electronics. The only moving

parts are the magnets on the flywheel. That's why this system is sometimes called a breakerless ignition.

Because there are no breaker points on this system, there is no requirement for timing. However, the trigger module performs the same function as points. There must be a specific gap between the trigger module and the flywheel projection. Refer to your owner's or service manual for specific steps to setting this gap. The typical steps to setting the trigger module gap on a CDI system are the following:

Capacitor-discharge ignitions and transistor-controlled ignitions look the same. Check the engine's owner's manual for specific information on servicing and repair.

Step 1: Remove the lead from the spark plug to prevent starting. Ground the spark plug lead by attaching it to the shroud.

Step 2: Rotate the flywheel so the projection is aligned with the trigger module.

Step 3: Loosen the trigger module adjustment screw(s) and insert a thickness gauge of the correct thickness (typically 0.005 to 0.015 inch) in the gap.

Step 4: Move the trigger module until it touches the thickness gauge, making sure the projection and module surfaces are parallel.

Step 5: Tighten the trigger module adjustment screw(s) and replace the spark plug lead.

Servicing Transistor-Controlled Ignitions

A transistor-controlled ignition (TCI) uses transistors, resistors, and diodes to control the timing of the spark to the engine. Because it has no moving parts, it too is called a breakerless or solid-state ignition. Most TCIs require no service. However, to ensure long-term performance, perform the following inspection on a regular basis.

The TCI controls a voltage of up to 30,000 volts for delivery to the spark plug. Be extremely careful when working around the TCI, as you can injure yourself or the ignition system with high voltage. To service a transistor-controlled ignition unit:

Step 1: Remove the lead from the spark plug to prevent starting. Ground the spark plug lead by attaching it to the shroud.

Step 2: Check the TCI unit to make sure it has not been damaged. Sensitive electronic components are mounted on a printed circuit board within the box and can be damaged by force or by excessive heat.

Step 3: Check all leads to and from the TCI unit to make sure they are tightly connected and that insulation is not cut or frayed.

Step 4: Visually inspect the magnet and ignition coil mounted next to the flywheel. Look for damage to the end of the magnet or the edge of the flywheel.

Servicing Spark Plugs

The spark plug in a small gas engine must withstand high voltage, high heat, and millions of ignitions during its life. A new spark plug requires about 5,000 volts of electricity to jump the gap. A used spark plug may require twice as much voltage to function. So servicing the spark plug is important to your engine's operation. To service a spark plug:

Step 1: Disconnect the lead wire from the top of the spark plug.

Step 2: Using the appropriate spark plug wrench, loosen the plug from the cylinder head. Before removing the plug, clean debris from around the spark plug base.

Step 3: Note the electrode's appearance. Excessive buildup can mean incorrect fuel-air mixture, incorrect carburetor adjustment, weak spark voltage, or poor air cleaner maintenance, among other causes.

Step 4: Clean the spark plug surface with a soft cloth and the electrode with a wire brush or spark

plug cleaning unit. If the electrode is worn or damaged, replace the spark plug with one of the same size and heat range to avoid any damage to the engine.

Step 5: Using a feeler gauge, set the gap on the spark plug electrode to the manufacturer's recommendations.

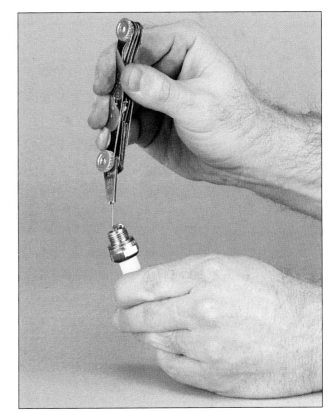

To check the spark plug gap, insert a feeler gauge between the electrodes. When the gap is correct, there should be a slight drag on the feeler gauge as it is removed.

Servicing Flywheels

The flywheel on a small gas engine is a simple part that requires little service. The most important part of servicing a flywheel is to inspect it for damage periodically. To service a flywheel:

Step 1: Remove the lead from the spark plug (to ensure that the engine doesn't start), then rotate the flywheel by hand and inspect it for wobble and obvious damage. Check edges and cooling fins, looking for cracks and missing pieces that can make the flywheel—and the engine—rotate out of balance.

Step 2: To inspect the inside of the flywheel, use a flywheel puller or a knock-off tool to remove the flywheel from the end of the crankshaft.

You may need a special tool called a flywheel puller to remove the flywheel.

Step 3: Inspect the magnets on the inside of the flywheel, if so equipped. Wipe all surfaces clean, removing rust, oil, and debris.

Servicing Lubrication Systems

Friction causes wear; it's a law of physics. Small gas engines can wear out prematurely if moving parts aren't lubricated. In the following pages, you'll learn how to reduce wear on your small engine and increase its useful life by servicing the lubrication system. Topics include the fuel-oil mixture for two-stroke engines and performing other lubrication services.

Always use the type and viscosity grade of oil recommended by the engine manufacturer. Lubricating oils and additives designed for four-stroke engines are not suitable for two-stroke engines.

Mixing Fuel-Oil for Two-Stroke Engines

Two-stroke engines are efficient. They only require a single rotation of the crankshaft to develop power. This simplicity requires economy in all engine systems, including lubrication. A two-stroke engine is lubricated by mixing oil with the gasoline. This fuel-oil mixture can be purchased as such, or you can mix it yourself. To make a two-stroke engine fuel-oil mixture:

Step 1: Check the manufacturer's recommendations for the specific ratio and grade of oil and fuel to be mixed.

Step 2: In a vented gas can used only for mixing, pour a specified amount and type of gasoline.

Step 3: Add the correct amount of recommended oil for the fuel-oil ratio. A gallon contains 128 ounces. A fuel-oil ratio of 50:1 means 50 ounces of fuel should have 1 ounce of oil added, or you should add about 2.5 ounces of recommended lubricating oil to every gallon of recommended gasoline. A 25:1 fuel-oil ratio requires about 5 ounces of oil per gallon of fuel. Also pour in any additives recommended by the manufacturer.

Step 4: Make sure all caps are securely fastened to the mixing gas can, and shake it to thoroughly mix the fuel and oil.

Step 5: Carefully pour the resulting fuel-oil mixture into the engine's fuel tank.

Step 6: Whether you purchase fuel-oil mixed or mix it yourself, rotate the fuel tank in a circle a few times to remix the fuel and oil before each use.

Lubrication Service

Some small engines require additional lubrication, depending on their design and the tasks they perform. A riding lawn mower, for example, may require lubrication of the axles and steering box. Though this manual can't cover all possible lubrication service procedures, it can offer procedures that are easily adaptable to most small engines.

Lubrication service is the application of lubricating greases. Greases are simply petroleum products with higher viscosity or thickness than oils. A lubricating grease may have a grade as low as 60 (about twice as thick as 30 grade oil) to over 100. Common viscosities for lubricating greases are 80 and 90 grade. At these viscosities, lubricants have the density of toothpaste. Special tools called lube guns are used to apply lubricating greases. Professional repair shops use pressurized lube guns; the engine owner can apply lubricating greases with a ratchet lube gun. The greases are sold in tubes that fit into the lube gun. To apply lubricating grease to small engine components:

Step 1: Check the owner's manual for specific information on lubrication: where and with what.

Step 2: Apply the recommended grade of lubricating grease. Some components have fittings to which the end of the lube gun is attached. Others require that the top of a reservoir is opened and fluid added to a specific FULL point. Still other components require that a lubricant such as white grease be spread on the part by hand.

Step 3: Clean up any excess greases or oils before starting the engine.

Caution: Make sure that lubricating greases do not touch electrical parts. Lubricants can conduct electricity, shorting out the system and potentially causing a fire.

Servicing Cooling Systems

An internal combustion engine can develop an internal temperature as high as 4500°F (2200°C) during the power stroke. Obviously, a small engine's cooling system is critical to smooth operation as well as long engine life. A defective cooling system can ruin an otherwise good engine in minutes. Fortunately, small engines have simple cooling systems that require little maintenance to operate for many years.

A small two-stroke engine is typically air-cooled.

Servicing Air-Cooled Engines

Most small, single-cylinder engines are cooled by a stream of air developed by fan blades on the flywheel. The air stream is deflected around the cylinder and cylinder head by a metal or plastic cover called a shroud. Additional engine heat is dissipated through cooling fins

Cooling Fins

Shroud

Flywheel

On an air-cooled engine, the shroud directs the airflow from the flywheel across the cylinder and head to keep them cool.

around the cylinder. Servicing air-cooled systems is generally very easy. To service an air-cooled system:

Step 1: Periodically remove the shroud from around the engine flywheel and inspect the inside for debris.

Step 2: With the shroud removed, visually inspect the flywheel blades for debris and damage.

Step 3: Visually inspect cooling fins on the cylinder and cylinder head. Use a wooden stick or clean paintbrush to clear away any debris. When the engine is cool, wipe the surfaces of the cooling fins, cylinder, and cylinder head with a cloth. Remember that even the tip of a cooling fin can have a surface temperature of over 100°F (38°C).

Step 4: Replace the shroud over the flywheel and cylinder. Make sure the flywheel blades aren't striking the shroud.

Servicing Exhaust Systems

Exhaust systems require little maintenance. The function of an exhaust system is to get rid of the exhaust gases from the internal combustion process going on in the engine. Depending on what type of implement the small engine is powering, the exhaust system may have a spark arrestor or a muffler that requires periodic service.

Servicing Spark Arrestors

A spark arrestor on a small engine does just that: It arrests—or stops—sparks from leaving the combustion chamber and entering the outside atmosphere. Spark arrestors are especially important on equipment, such as chain saws and trail bikes, that is used around combustible trees and brush. In fact, spark arrestors are required equipment on some small engines in many states.

A spark arrestor is simply a screen on the exhaust port of a small engine. It is designed to stop sparks from exiting the engine. To service a spark arrestor:

Step 1: Make sure the engine is fully cooled and the ignition switch is off.

Step 2: Find the spark arrestor on the side of the engine. It is a screen or a short tube located wherever the exhaust gases exit the engine. Visually inspect the spark arrestor for blockage or damage. If any is found, remove the spark arrestor and clean or replace it.

Step 3: Tighten all nuts on the spark arrestor bracket and the exhaust system.

A spark arrestor consists of a screen inside the engine's muffler. Some spark arrestors are separate units outside the muffler.

Servicing Mufflers

Mufflers are designed to reduce noise levels on small gas engines. Operating a small engine for any length of time without a muffler will sell you on the value of this device!

Fortunately, exhaust mufflers require no regular servicing beyond a visual inspection. To service a muffler:

Step 1: Make sure the engine is fully cooled and the ignition switch is off.

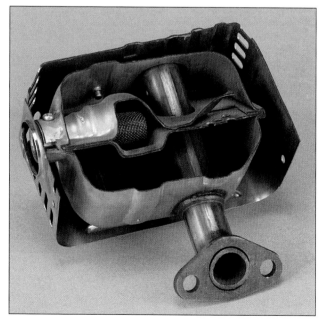

This cross section shows the internal construction of a muffler, including the baffles that reduce the engine's noise.

Step 2: Find the muffler on the side of the engine where the exhaust gases exit. Use the end of a screwdriver to lightly strike the muffler at various locations, checking for rust damage or loose nuts. Also check the end of the muffler to ensure that there is no obstruction to exiting gases.

Step 3: Tighten all nuts on the muffler bracket and the exhaust system.

Servicing Controls

Small engines are used to power a wide variety of tools and toys. Controls make engines and their driven devices go faster or slower, turn on or off, change gearing, and make other operating adjustments. Servicing small engines requires servicing these controls as well.

In most cases, servicing controls means adjusting or lubricating them. Some controls are electrical (switches) while others are mechanical (throttles and gear selectors).

Adjusting Controls

Adjusting controls on a small engine typically requires the owner's manual or a service manual for the specific model. That's because control adjustments are frequently unique to that model. However, if you don't have an owner's manual, mechanical controls can be adjusted following commonsense procedures. To adjust a throttle control:

Step 1: Make sure the engine is off and cooled before working on it.

Step 2: Inspect the control cable for kinks, bare spots, or other visible damage. At the same time, wipe oils and debris from the control cable and lever.

Step 3: Inspect both ends of the control cable, checking the connection to the throttle lever as well as to the carburetor or governor. Make sure both ends are securely fastened.

Step 4: Move the throttle lever back and forth as you watch the movement of the carburetor connection. If full lever movement doesn't fully move the carburetor throttle, adjust the cable as required. In some cases, a fastener on or near the carburetor holds the throttle casing in place while allowing the throttle wire to move. Move the casing as needed and tighten the fastener.

Step 5: Lubricate the control as required (see next section) before reassembly.

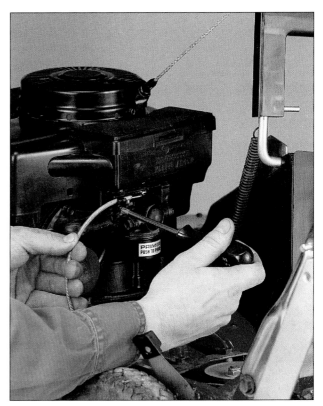

To adjust a throttle control, you may need to loosen the screw that holds the throttle casing and move the casing.

Lubricating Controls

Mechanical controls on engine-driven devices require periodic lubrication to minimize binding and wear. To lubricate a cable control:

Step 1: Disconnect one end of the control wire to allow free movement within the cable. Apply spray or grease lubricant to the wire, making sure lubricant doesn't reach other parts. Wipe away excess lubricant.

Step 2: Check the control for correct action. If adjustment is required, follow the procedures for adjusting controls (see previous section).

Troubleshooting Small Engines

The following chart offers symptoms and solutions for problems encountered by small two-stroke air-cooled engines.

SMALL ENGINE REPAIR

SMALL ENGINE TROUBLESHOOTING CHART

Problem	Possible Cause	Solution
Engine fails to start or is hard to start	1. No fuel in tank.	1. Fill tank with recommended fuel.
	2. Fuel shutoff valve closed.	2. Open shutoff valve.
	3. Fuel line plugged or kinked.	3. Clean or replace fuel line.
	4. Fuel tank suction tube screen plugged.	4. Clean screen; if ball is stuck, clean or replace tube.
	5. Water in fuel tank.	5. Drain and clean fuel tank; refill with recommended fuel.
	6. Weak or no voltage at spark plug.	6. Check breaker points, coil, condenser, and lead; adjust or replace as necessary.
	7. Spark will not jump gap.	7. Check spark plug condition and gap; clean or replace plug; check ignition coil and replace as necessary.
	8. Engine flooded with fuel.	8. Open choke and close fuel tank valve; then crank engine until excess fuel is forced from exhaust.
	9. Choke partly open.	9. Close choke completely; if necessary, adjust choke cable.
	10. Carburetor needs adjustment.	10. Adjust needle valve and idle mixture to recommended settings.
	11. Throttle closed.	11. Open throttle to FAST or RUN position; check for binding throttle linkage or disconnected governor linkage.
	12. Plugged exhaust ports.	12. Remove muffler and clean exhaust ports.
	13. Bent or broken reed valve.	13. Replace reed valve or reed valve assembly.
	14. Leaking oil seal or gaskets.	14. Install new oil seal or gasket set.
	15. Low or no compression.	15. Check head gasket; if blown, replace gasket. Check piston rings; if worn or broken, replace piston rings. Check valves; if sticking, burned, or warped, recondition or replace valves.
	16. Carburetor or fuel tank vent blocked with dirt.	16. Clean out vent holes.
	17. Faulty magneto.	17. Check timing and point gap and, if necessary, repair or replace magneto.
Engine misfires under load	1. Weak or irregular spark.	1. Check ignition system, coil, and leads; replace as needed.
	2. Worn or fouled spark plug.	2. Replace with new spark plug, setting gap to recommended setting.
	3. Air cleaner plugged.	3. Service air cleaner.
	4. Choke partly closed.	4. Open choke; if necessary, adjust choke cable.

Continued on page 367

SMALL ENGINE TROUBLESHOOTING CHART *(Continued from page 366)*

Problem	Possible Cause	Solution
Engine misfires under load (continued)	5. Carburetor mixture too lean.	5. Adjust needle valve for richer mixture.
	6. Carburetor or fuel tank vent blocked with dirt.	6. Clean out vent holes.
	7. Fuel not reaching carburetor.	7. Remove and clean fuel tank; clean or replace fuel line and fuel screen.
	8. Ignition shutoff not in full ON position.	8. Move or adjust shutoff to full ON position.
	9. Engine running too hot.	9. Remove debris from cooling fins. Check oil level; if low, add oil as needed.
	10. Too much or too little oil mixed with gasoline.	10. Drain fuel tank and refill with correct fuel/oil mixture.
	11. Plugged exhaust system.	11. Clean exhaust ports; remove and clean or replace muffler.
	12. Low compression.	12. Recondition or replace valves and valve seats; replace worn piston rings.
	13. Weak valve springs.	13. Install new valve springs.
	14. Reed valve bent.	14. Replace reed and reed valve assembly.
	15. Crankshaft seals or gaskets leaking.	15. Replace faulty seals or gaskets.
	16. Pitted ignition breaker points.	16. Replace pitted breaker points.
	17. Faulty condenser.	17. Replace condenser.
Engine overheats	1. Insufficient oil in fuel mixture.	1. Drain fuel tank and refill with recommended fuel/oil mixture.
	2. Air cooling fins blocked with dirt.	2. Clean areas between cooling fins.
	3. Shroud not in place or screen plugged.	3. Clean shroud and replace it in correct position; clean screen.
	4. Carburetor set too lean.	4. Adjust needle valve for richer fuel/air mixture.
	5. Ignition system out of time.	5. Retime ignition to correct firing point.
	6. Valves out of adjustment.	6. Adjust valves to recommended specifications.
Engine surges, will not hold steady speed	1. Carburetor or fuel tank vents are plugged.	1. Clean vent holes.
	2. Float level set too low.	2. Adjust carburetor float to correct level.
	3. Fuel tank screen or fuel line partly plugged.	3. Clean fuel tank, screen, fuel line, float needle, and seat.
	4. Needle valve not properly adjusted.	4. Adjust needle valve.
	5. Governor linkage binding.	5. Clean and repair governor.
	6. Throttle or shaft binding.	6. Clean and adjust throttle and shaft.
	7. Throttle or governor springs unhooked, or in wrong position.	7. Connect or replace broken throttle or governor spring in correct position.

Continued on page 368

SMALL ENGINE TROUBLESHOOTING CHART *(Continued from page 367)*

Problem	Possible Cause	Solution
Engine surges, will not hold steady speed (continued)	8. Carburetor not adjusted properly.	8. Adjust carburetor to recommended specifications.
	9. Carburetor internal parts dirty.	9. Clean or replace carburetor.
	10. Water in fuel.	10. Drain tank, carburetor, and fuel lines; replace with recommended fuel.
Engine functioning well but driven device doesn't work properly	1. Driven device doesn't move.	1. Check belts, chains, and shafts; adjust or replace as needed.
	2. Driven device moves slower than normal.	2. Check belts, chains, and shafts; adjust as needed.
	3. Blade or tines don't cut properly.	3. Sharpen or replace blade or tines; lubricate as needed.
	4. Wheels don't turn properly.	4. Tighten wheels on shaft; check for wear and replace as needed.
	5. Belt or chain slips.	5. Check adjustment bolt or screw; replace if damaged or stripped.
	6. Chain broken.	6. Replace chain link or chain.
Engine lacks power	1. Choke partially closed.	1. Open choke.
	2. Improper carburetor adjustment.	2. Adjust carburetor.
	3. Magneto improperly timed.	3. Time magneto.
	4. Worn rings or piston.	4. Replace rings or piston.
	5. Air cleaner fouled.	5. Clean air cleaner.
	6. Valves leaking.	6. Recondition valves.
	7. Reed valves fouled or sluggish.	7. Clean or replace reed valves.
	8. Incorrect fuel/oil mixture.	8. Drain tank and fill with recommended fuel/oil mixture.
	9. Crankcase seal leaks.	9. Replace worn crankcase seals.
Engine rattles or knocks	1. Piston hitting carbon deposit in upper cylinder.	1. Remove cylinder head or pot and clean carbon from surfaces.
	2. Loose blade, pulley, gear, or clutch on crankshaft.	2. Tighten or replace loose end of part.
	3. Worn cylinder.	3. Repair or replace cylinder.
	4. Magneto improperly timed.	4. Time magneto.
	5. Loose connecting rod cap.	5. Tighten connecting rod bolts and bend up locking lugs.
	6. Worn connecting rod or crankshaft.	6. Replace connecting rod and, if necessary, crankshaft.
	7. Worn main bearings.	7. Replace main bearings and, if necessary, crankshaft.
	8. Loose flywheel.	8. Replace flywheel key and tighten flywheel to correct torque.

Continued on page 369

SMALL ENGINE TROUBLESHOOTING CHART *(Continued from page 368)*		
Problem	**Possible Cause**	**Solution**
Engine rattles or knocks (continued)	9. Blade, pulley, gear, or clutch out of balance.	9. Balance or replace unbalanced part.
	10. Engine loose on mountings.	10. Tighten mounting bolts.
	11. Bent crankshaft.	11. Install new crankshaft.
	12. Flywheel fan blades broken off.	12. Replace flywheel.

Disassembly
  dishwashers, 179
  dryers, 194
  electric furnaces, 279
  faucets, 239–240
  forced-air heating systems, 284
  gas furnaces, 271
  gas heaters, 271
  gas ranges, 156–157
  of major appliances, 147–148
  oil furnaces, 273–274
  refrigerators, 168
  room air conditioners, 296
  washers, 184
Dishwashers, 174–184
  detergent dispensers, 182
  door gaskets, 179–180
  door latches, 180
  drain valves, 181
  float switches, 180
  heating elements, 181
  inlet valves, 183
  motors, 184
  sprayer arms, 182
  strainers, 182
  troubleshooting, 176–178
  water inlet valves, 181
  water pumps, 183
Doorbells, 132–134
  troubleshooting, 133
Doors, 62–67
  dishwashers, 180
  dryers, 198
  folding, 64–65
  garage, 143–145, 328–330
  interior, 63–65
  locksets, 65–67
  openers, 143–145
  overhead, 328
  painting, 82–83, 350
  prehung, 63–64
  refrigerators, 171–172
  roll-up, 328, 329
  sweeps, 300, 306–307
  swing-up, 328, 329
  thresholds, 306
  unsticking, 62–63
  weather stripping, 304–307
Drain-and-trap augers, 20, 21, 237

Drains
  basements, 238
  bathtubs, 237, 238
  chemical openers, 237
  clogged, 235, 237–239
  floors, 238
  main, 238
  pop-up, 243
Drawer pulls, 104
Drills, 12–13
  bits, 13
Dryers, 194–203
  air shutters, 200
  cleaning, 194–195
  drum bearings, 201–202
  drum belts, 201
  drum rollers, 202–203
  electric heating elements, 200–201
  exhaust vents, 194
  fans in, 201
  gas heaters in, 200
  lint traps, 194
  start switches, 199
  thermostats, 199
  timers, 199
  troubleshooting, 196–198
  vents, 194, 195
Drywall, 24, 37
  installing, 44–46
  joints, 44, 45–46
  nails, 24
  placing, 44–45
  repairing holes in, 72–73
  taping, 45–46

E

Electrical systems
  branch and feeder circuits, 116–117, 119, 120
  ceiling fans, 134
  circuit breakers, 31–32, 114, 115–116, 119–120
  discharging, 32
  doorbells, 132–134
  fluorescent lights, 126–128
  function, 113–119
  fuses, 31–32, 114, 115–116, 119–120
  garage door openers, 143–145
  grounding, 32, 118–119
  incandescent light fixtures, 124–125

Electrical systems (*continued*)
    intercom systems, 138–141
    lamp rewiring, 121–124
    main disconnects, 114
    meters, 113–114
    outlet polarity, 120–121
    overload protection, 115–116
    power outages, 120
    receptacles, 32, 130–131
    restoring circuits, 119–120
    safety, 31–32, 117–119
    security systems, 134–138
    service equipment, 114
    sound systems, 141–142
    switches, 32, 128–130
    transformers, 132, 133
Electrical tools, 18–20
Energy conservation, 299–315
    insulating, 307–315
    weather stripping, 299–307
Engines, small
    air cleaners, 357
    carburetors, 357–358
    combustion systems, 354–355
    controls, 365
    cooling systems, 355, 363–364
    exhaust systems, 353, 364–365
    fuel filters, 357
    fuel tanks, 357
    governors, 358
    ignition/exhaust strokes, 352–353
    ignition systems, 353–354, 358–362
    intake/compression strokes, 351–352
    lubrication systems, 355, 362–363
    mufflers, 364–365
    spark arrestors, 364
    troubleshooting, 365–369
    two-stroke, 351–353
Epoxy, 28, 29–30, 255
    paints, 70, 84
Escutcheons, 104
Estimating needs for
    ceramic tiles, 40
    job times, 69
    painting, 69, 340
    paneling, 37
    wall coverings, 92
Evaporators, 167, 173
Expansion bolts, 28, 34–35

F

Fans
    ceiling, 134
    condensers, 173–174
    refrigerators/freezers, 173
Fasteners, 24–30
    adhesives, 28–30
    anchors, 34, 35
    bolts, 28
    corrugated, 25
    in major appliances, 146
    nails, 24–25, 50
    screws, 25–28
    for wall hanging, 34–35
Fastening tools, 13–15
Faucets
    bathtubs, 243
    cartridge-types, 240
    compression-type, 239–240
    dripping, 239–240
    leaking, 241
    noisy, 241–242
    outside, 257
    showers, 243
    single-lever, 241
    valve seats, 240
Fences
    gates, 323
    installing, 324–326
    posts, 322–323, 324
    rails, 321
    repair, 320–323
    screening, 321–322
Files, 21–22
Fillister-head screws, 25
Filters
    air conditioners, 296–297
    fuel, 357
    furnaces, 264–265, 276, 284
    small engines, 353
Finishing nails, 24, 37, 38
Fixtures, 235
    fluorescent lights, 126–128
    incandescent lights, 124–125
    plumbing, 233
    recaulking, 40
Flashing
    chimney, 333–335

Flashing *(continued)*
    roof, 333–335
    valley, 334, 335
    vent pipe, 335–336
Flat files, 22
Flathead screws, 25
Flooring nails, 50
Floors
    hardwood, 53–54
    insulating, 313–315
    painting, 84
    paint spatters on, 86
    porch, 327–328
    primer for, 53
    sheet, 52
    squeaks in, 50–51
    stripping, 53–54
    tiled, 51–52
Food mixers, 205, 215–217
    fuses, 217
    gears, 216–217
    speed controls, 216
    switches, 216
    troubleshooting, 216
Force cups, 21
Freezers. *See* Refrigerators and Freezers.
Freon, 295
Fry pans, electric, 204
Furnaces, 260. *See also* Heating systems.
    assembly, 288
    belt adjustments, 266
    blowers, 264
    burner adjustments, 273, 277
    cleaning, 264–266
    draft regulators, 277
    electric, 278–280
    filters, 264, 276
    fuses, 279–280
    gas, 269, 271–273
    limit switches, 273
    motors, 264
    oil, 273–277
    pressure burners, 275
    stack controls, 276–277
    switches, 276
    thermocouples, 271–272
    troubleshooting, 270–271, 274–275, 278
Furniture, wood, 100–112
    black spots, 106

Furniture, wood *(continued)*
    blisters, 101
    blushing, 106
    burns in, 110–111
    cleaning, 111, 112
    construction, 100
    dents in, 108
    dings on, 108
    discolorations, 105–106
    finishes, 100, 105, 112
    gouges in, 108–110
    hardware, 104–105
    ink stains, 106
    patching sticks, 107, 108
    refinishing, 105–112
    repairing, 101–105
    reviving, 111
    scratches on, 107–108
    spot refinishing, 107
    stains in, 105–106
    stripping, 112
    surface damage, 107–111
    veneer repair, 101–104
    wax spots, 106
    white spots, 105–106
Furring, 37, 47–48
    double, 38
Fuses, 31–32, 114, 115–116, 119–120, 175, 219
    cartridges, 116
    electric ranges, 163, 165
    furnaces, 279–280
    plugs, 116
    thermal, 211

G

Garbage disposers, 222–224
    flywheels, 223
    hoses, 223–224
    impellers, 224
    seals, 223–224
    troubleshooting, 223
Gardening. *See* Yard work.
Gaskets, 150–151
    channel-mounted, 150, 151
    dishwashers, 179–180
    dryer doors, 198
    flush-mounted, 150, 151
    jalousie, 300

Gaskets (continued)
  range doors, 157, 159
  refrigerator doors, 168, 171
  universal, 150
  window, 300
Gas leaks, 273
Gas smell, 159, 269, 273
Gates, 323
Glaziers' points, 55, 56
Glue. See Adhesives.
Graphite powder, 50
Groove-joint pliers, 14
Ground-fault circuit interrupter, 148
Grounding
  in electrical systems, 32, 118–119
  in major appliances, 148, 198
  in small appliances, 206
Grout, 38, 39–40, 42
  flexible, 40
  sealer, 41
Gutter systems, 337–338
  painting, 350

H

Hair dryers, 205, 229–231
  fans, 231
  heating elements, 231
  switches, 230–231
  thermal cutouts, 231
  troubleshooting, 230
Hammers, 14
Hand drills, 12
Hardware
  cover-up, 104–105
  furniture, 104–105
Heat
  cables, 257
  pumps, 260, 280–282
  tape, 257
Heaters
  electric, 278–280
  freezer defrost, 173
  gas, 269–270, 271–273
  gas dryers, 200
  water, 174, 233
Heating elements, 152, 211–212, 214–215, 231
Heating systems, 260–292
  aquastats, 291

Heating systems (continued)
  balancing, 284
  blowers, 261, 284
  circulators, 291
  combination gauges in, 291
  controls, 263
  convectors, 262, 266, 291
  distribution systems, 261–263, 266–267, 282–292
  draining, 291–292
  ducts, 286
  expansion tanks, 290–291
  filters, 284
  flushing, 288, 291–292
  forced-air, 261, 266, 282, 283, 284
  gravity, 261–262, 266, 282, 288
  hot-water, 262, 288–292
  hydronic, 262, 288–289
  improving efficiency in, 269
  leaks in, 288, 291
  maintenance procedures, 263–269
  noise problems, 286
  radiant, 262–263, 266–267, 282
  radiators, 262, 266, 267, 286, 288, 291
  slope in, 287, 289
  steam, 262, 286–288
  thermostats, 263
  troubleshooting, 269–282
  water levels, 287–288, 289–290
Heat pumps, 292
Hinges
  door, 62, 63
  furniture, 104
  gate, 323
  refrigerator door, 171–172
  shimming, 62, 63
  stiles, 64
Hollow-wall bolts, 28
Hose clamps, 255

I

Installation
  ceiling fans, 134
  ceiling tiles, 47
  doorbells, 132–134
  drywall, 44–46
  fluorescent lights, 126–128
  folding doors, 64–65
  garage door openers, 143–145

Installation (*continued*)
  intercom systems, 138–141
  interior doors, 63–65
  locksets, 65–67
  molding, 36–37
  security systems, 134–138
  sound systems, 141–142
  suspended ceilings, 48–49
  wall tiles, 40–42
Insulation
  adding, 309
  attic, 310–312
  floor, 313–315
  R-value, 307
  types, 308–309
  vapor barriers, 309, 310, 312
  wall, 312–313
Intercom systems, 138–141
Interior decorating, 68–112
Irons, clothing, 204

J

Joint compound, 45
Juicers, 205

K

Keyhole saws, 12
Kilowatt hours, 113

L

Lacquer, 100, 105, 106, 111
Ladders, 30–31
Lag screws, 27–28
Lamps
  rewiring, 121–124
  troubleshooting, 123
Landscape
  shrubs, 318–319
  tree pruning, 319–320
Lawns. *See also* Yard work.
  planting, 317–318
  reseeding, 318
Levels, 11
Lights
  fluorescent, 126–128
  incandescent, 124–125

Lights (*continued*)
  troubleshooting, 127
Locking pliers, 14
Locks
  door, 65–67
  furniture, 104
Lumber, 22–24
  fencing, 320
  preservatives, 320
  pressure-treated, 320

M

Machine bolts, 28
Machine screws, 27
Maintenance
  central air conditioning, 294–295
  furnaces, 264–266
  gutter systems, 337–338
  heating distribution systems, 266–267
  heating systems, 263–269
  heat pumps, 280–282
  thermostats, 267–269
  yards, 316–320
Masonry bolts, 28
Masonry nails, 24–25
Materials, 22–24
Measuring tools, 10–11
Meters, water, 232–233
Mildew, 40
Miter boxes, 36
Miter squares, 11
Moldings
  cove, 48
  installing, 36–37
  quarter-round, 35–37
  removal, 35–36
  shoe, 35–37
Motors, 154–156, 217
  belts, 154
  capacitor-type, 156, 168
  cooling, 266
  heating, 266
  nonreversible, 181
  reversible, 183
  shaded pole, 222
  split-phase, 156
  synchronous, 153, 199
  timer, 199

Motors (continued)
    universal, 154–156, 222
Multitesters, 19
Murals, wall, 93
Muriatic acid, 70, 84

N

Nails, 24–25
    popped, 71–72
    roofing, 332
Needle-nose pliers, 14

O

Open end wrenches, 14
Oval-head screws, 25
Oxalic acid, 106

P

Paint and painting, 68–87
    acoustic, 70, 71
    acrylic, 68–69, 341
    airless sprayers, 77–79
    alkyd, 69, 70, 341, 342
    alligatoring, 343
    baseboards, 82
    beading, 82
    blistering, 343
    brick, 340
    brushes, 16–18, 75–76, 79, 82, 85, 86, 87
    cabinets, 83–84
    cement, 70, 84
    chalking, 343
    clapboard, 340
    cleaning up, 84–86
    concrete, 340
    cutting in, 82
    deck, 84, 341
    deglossing, 74
    doors, 82–83, 350
    dripless, 70
    epoxy, 70, 84
    equipment, 75–79
    exterior, 320, 340–350
    floors, 84
    gloss, 68, 69, 74, 342
    gutters, 350

Paint and painting (continued)
    interior, 68–87
    ladders, 30–31
    latex, 16, 68–69, 70, 84, 341, 342
    marine, 341
    masking, 75
    masonry, 69, 70, 84, 341
    melting, 345
    metal, 70, 341
    mildew, 344
    milk, 105
    oil-base, 68, 84, 341
    one-coat, 70, 71
    opacity, 69
    peeling, 343
    planning, 68–71
    polyurethane, 84
    polyvinyl, 68
    porch, 84
    preparation for, 71–75, 344–347
    priming, 69, 71, 345
    problems, 84, 343–344
    raw wood, 69, 71
    removal, 344
    resin content, 68
    rollers, 18, 76–77, 80–81, 86, 348
    rubber-base, 70
    safety precautions, 78, 79
    sanding, 344
    scraping, 75, 344
    second coats, 69
    shingles and shakes, 340
    shutters, 82–83
    siding, 347–349
    solvents, 69, 70, 78, 85, 340
    spatters and drips, 85–86
    special effects, 86–87
    stenciling, 87
    striping, 86–87
    textured, 70, 86
    thinning, 69
    in tight spots, 81
    tools, 16–18
    trays, 18, 76–77, 85
    trim, 69, 81–83, 349–350
    troubleshooting, 342
    over wallpaper, 69
    walls and ceilings, 79–81
    washability, 69

Paint and painting (*continued*)
    water-based, 16, 68–69, 340
    water-resistance, 70
    windows, 82, 349
    woodwork, 69, 81–83
    wrinkling, 343
Paneling, 37–38
Partitions, framing, 42–44
Picture hangers, 34–35
Pilot lights, 153–154, 161–162, 269, 271
Pipes, plumbing
    frozen, 256–257
    insulation, 257
    leaks, 254–256
    noisy, 257–259
    sweating, 256
    troubleshooting, 255
    water hammer, 258–259
Plane face hammers, 14
Planes, wood, 63
Plaster
    of paris, 73, 74
    walls, 73–74
Pliers, 14
Plugs
    appliance, 206
    female and male, 150
    power, 149–150
    two-prong, 206
Plumbers' friend, 21, 235, 248
Plumbers' snakes, 21
Plumbing, 232–259
    drain-waste-vent systems, 234
    faucet drips, 239–240
    faucet leaks, 241
    noisy faucets, 241–242
    pipe problems, 254–259
    shower head repairs, 245
    systems, 232–235
    toilets, 246–254
    tools, 20–21
    traps, 234, 238, 239, 245–246
    troubleshooting, 236–237
    vents, 234
    water supply systems, 232–233
Plungers, 21, 235
    bulb-type, 248
    fold-out, 248
Plywood, 23–24, 37

Porches, flooring, 327–328
Power
    augers, 239
    cords, 149–150, 168, 297–298
    drills, 12–13
Pruning, 319–320
Putty, 55, 56
    sticks, 109
    water, 109
    wood-tone, 109

R

Radiators, 262, 266, 267, 286, 288, 291
Ranges, electric, 162–166
    fuses in, 163
    heating elements, 165–166
    troubleshooting, 164–165
Ranges, gas, 156–166
    automatic shutoff valves, 162
    burners, 159
    door gaskets, 157, 159
    electronic ignition systems, 162
    fuel mixture, 160–161
    oven setting controls, 159
    oven thermostats, 159–160
    pilot lights, 161–162
    self-cleaning ovens, 162
    timers, 160
    troubleshooting, 158
Refinishing furniture, 105–112
Refrigerators and Freezers, 166–174
    cleaning coils, 168
    compressors, 174
    condenser fans, 173–174
    defrost heaters, 173
    defrost timers, 173
    door gaskets, 168, 171
    door hinges, 171–172
    door switches, 172
    drain hoses, 174
    drain ports in, 174
    evaporator fans, 173
    frost-free, 167–168, 172
    ice makers, 174
    limit switches, 172
    refrigerants in, 174
    thermostats, 172–173
    troubleshooting, 169–170

Repair

air conditioner fans, 298–299
appliance controls, 207
blenders, 217–220
carpet burns, 52–53
ceiling tiles, 46
coffee makers, 212–215
dishwashers, 174–184
doorbells, 132–134
drains, 235, 237–239
dryers, 194–203
electrical, 119–145
electrical outlets, 130–131
electric can openers, 220–222
electric ranges and ovens, 162–166
faucet valve seats, 240
fences, 320–323
floor squeaks, 50–51
floor tiles, 51–52
food mixers, 215–217
furnace limit switches, 273
furniture, 101–105
furniture hardware, 104–105
garage doors, 328–330
garbage disposers, 222–224
gas ranges and ovens, 156–166
gutter systems, 337–338
hair dryers, 229–231
hardwood floors, 53–54
incandescent light fixtures, 124–125
lamps, 121–124
major appliances, 146–147
oven setting controls, 159
plaster cracks, 73–74
receptacles, 130–131
refrigerator door hinges, 171–172
refrigerators and freezers, 166–174
roof flashing, 333–335
roof leaks, 330–336
sheet flooring, 52
shower heads, 245
small appliances, 204–231
small engines, 351–369
spray hoses, 243–245
stair squeaks, 51
sticking doors, 62–63
thermocouples, 154
thermostats, 267–269
toaster ovens, 210–212

Repair (continued)

toasters, 207–210
toilet ballcock assembly, 250–252
universal motors, 155–156
vacuum cleaners, 224–229
Venetian blinds, 60–62
wall coverings, 89–91
wall cracks and holes, 72–74
wall switches, 128–130
wall tiles, 38–40
washers, 184–194
window glass, 55–56
window screens, 56–59
window shades, 59–60

Replacement

air conditioner thermostats, 298
carbon brushes, 155–156
door thresholds, 306
dryer drum rollers, 202–203
electric range heating elements, 165–166
faucets, 242–243
furnace belts, 266
gaskets, 150–151
gas range door gaskets, 157, 159
gas range thermostats, 160
gas range timers, 160
incandescent light fixtures, 124–125
plumbing traps, 245–246
porch flooring, 327–328
siding, 326–327
thermocouples, 154
thermostats, 268–269
toilets, 252–254
toilet seats, 246–248
universal motors, 155–156
vacuum beater bars, 226
wall tiles, 38–42
washer drive belts, 193
window glass, 55–56

Resin, penetrating, 100, 105
Resistors, 168
Rheostats, 151, 206, 207
Ripsaws, 12
Rollers, paint, 18, 76–77, 80–81, 86
Roofing compound, 320
Roofing nails, 24
Roofs

flashing, 333–335
flat, 332–333

Roofs *(continued)*
    gutter systems, 337–338
    leaking, 330–336
    shingle, 331–332
    vent pipes, 334
    wood, 333
Round-head screws, 25

S

Saber saws, 12
Safety
    electrical, 31–32, 117–119
    fire, 32
    gas range, 156
    gas smell, 159
    glasses, 30
    ladder, 30–31
    painting, 78, 79
    small engine, 32–33
    with tools, 30
    ventilation in, 32–33, 78
Sanders, 53
Sandpaper, 21–22
Saws, 11–12
Screens, window, 56–59
Screw clamps, 15
Screwdrivers, 14
Screws, 25–28
    sizes, 25
    types, 25, 50
Seat wrenches, 240
Second-cut files, 22
Security systems, 134–138
    troubleshooting, 137
Septic tanks, 234
Servicing
    blender blade assembly, 220
    blender drive stud, 219
    can opener gears, 222
    condenser fans, 173–174
    controls, small engine, 365
    cooling systems, small engine, 363–364
    defrost heaters, 173
    defrost timers, 173
    detergent dispensers, 182
    dishwasher door latches, 180
    dishwasher door switches, 180
    dishwasher drain valves, 181

Servicing *(continued)*
    dishwasher heating elements, 181
    dishwasher sprayer arms, 182
    dishwasher timers, 180–181
    dishwasher water inlet valves, 181
    dishwasher water pumps, 183
    diverter valves, 244–245
    dryer door gaskets, 198
    dryer door switches, 198
    dryer drum belts, 201
    dryer drum rollers, 202–203
    dryer electric heating elements, 200–201
    dryer fans, 201
    dryer motors, 203
    dryer start switches, 199
    dryer thermostats, 199
    dryer timers, 199
    electric ignition systems, 162, 200
    evaporator fans, 173
    exhaust systems, small engine, 364–365
    food mixer speed controls, 216
    food mixer switches, 216
    fuel systems, small engine, 356–358
    garbage disposer flywheels, 223
    garbage disposer hoses/seals, 223–224
    garbage disposer impellers, 224
    gas range thermostats, 159–160
    gears, 216–217
    hair dryer fans, 231
    hair dryer heating elements, 231
    ice makers, 174
    ignition systems, small engine, 358–362
    lubrication systems, small engine, 362–363
    pilot lights, 161–162
    refrigerant leaks, 174
    refrigerator door hinges, 171–172
    refrigerator door switch, 172
    refrigerator drain hoses, 174
    refrigerator gaskets, 168, 171
    small engines, 355–365
    vacuum beater bars, 225–226, 228
    vacuum dirt fans, 227
    vacuum drive belts, 226–227
    vacuum power-head connections, 228
    washer lid switches, 185
    washer motors, 193–194
    washer temperature selector switches, 189
    washer timers, 189
    washer tubs/agitators, 190–191

Servicing *(continued)*
    washer water inlet valves, 189–190
    washer water level control switches, 189
    washer water pumps, 192–193
Sewer gas, 232, 234
Sewer lines, 234
Shades, window, 59–60
Sheet-metal screws, 26–27
Shellac, 100, 105, 106, 109, 110, 111
Shelves, hanging, 34–35
Shingles/shakes, 326–327
    painting, 348
    ridge, 331
    roof, 331–332
Shutters, painting, 82–83
Siding
    clapboard, 326–327
    painting, 347–349
    replacement, 326–327
Sinks, 235
    clogged, 235, 237–239
Slats, window blind, 61–62
Slip-joint pliers, 14, 20
Smooth files, 22
Socket wrenches, 14, 20
Solenoids, 151, 154, 181, 208, 210, 212
Sound systems, 141–142
Spackling compound, 72, 74
Splining, 57, 59
    tool, 59
Sprayers, airless painting, 77–79
Spring clamps, 15
Spudwrenches, 21
Squares, 11
Steel wool, 21–22
Stenciling, 87
Stereo systems, 141–142
Stopped-slot screws, 25
Stove bolts, 28
Stoves. *See* Ranges.
Straight-slot screws, 25
Strain-relief device, 149
Strap clamps, 15
Striping, paint, 87
Strippers, paper, 91
Studs, 34
Switches, 206, 207
    blenders, 218–219

Switches *(continued)*
    coffee makers, 213
    control devices, 152
    dimmers, 129
    dishwasher controls, 180–181
    dishwasher doors, 180
    dryer doors, 198
    dryer start, 199
    electrical, 32
    electric can openers, 220, 222
    failure of, 152
    fan-speed, 230
    fire sensor, 136
    float, 180
    freezers, 172
    hair dryers, 230–231
    heat, 230
    lever-action, 129
    limit, 172, 273, 277
    multiposition, 207
    multispeed, 218–219
    on/off, 213, 225, 228, 230
    pilot lights, 161
    push-button, 129, 151
    refrigerator doors, 172
    relay, 143
    reset, 163
    reversing, 143
    rheostat, 151
    rocker, 151
    rotary, 153
    safety, 277
    secondary, 151
    selector, 298
    single-pole, 129, 130, 207
    slide, 151
    solenoids, 151
    solid-state, 135, 137
    tamper, 136
    thermostats, 151, 152
    three-way, 130
    throw, 151
    timers, 151, 153
    toggle, 129, 151
    wall, 128–130
    washer lids, 185
    washer temperature selectors, 189
    washer water level controls, 189

INDEX

T

Tape
"drip," 256
heat, 257
masking, 75, 85
measures, 10
for painting, 75, 85
veneer edging, 103
waterproof, 255
window foil, 136
Thermocouples, 153–154, 269, 271–272
Thermostats, 151, 152, 206, 233, 260
air conditioners, 298
bimetallic, 207, 231, 263
calibration, 159–160, 209–210, 267–268
coffee makers, 213–214
dryers, 199
gas ranges, 159–160
heating, 263, 267–269
refrigerators/freezers, 172–173
replacement, 268–269
Tiles
ceiling, 46–49
ceramic, 38–42
edging caps, 41
floor, 51–52
grouting, 39–40, 42
installing new, 40–42
nippers/cutters, 41
paint spatters on, 86
replacing, 38–42
sealants, 40
wall, 38–42
Timers, 151, 153, 207
defrost, 173
dishwashers, 180–181
dryers, 199
gas ranges, 160
washers, 189
Toaster ovens, 204, 210–212
heating elements, 211–212
main switches, 211
thermal fuses, 211
troubleshooting, 211
Toasters, 204, 207–210
latch assembly, 208–209
thermostats, 209–210
troubleshooting, 209

Toenailing, 44
Toggle bolts, 28, 35
Toilets, 235, 246–254
ballcock assembly, 250–252
clogged, 21, 248
replacing, 252–254
running, 248–250
seats, 246–248
self-traps, 234
sweating, 252
tank problems, 248–250
troubleshooting, 247
Tools
awls, 57
clamps, 14–15, 58
crimper, 149
drills, 12–13
electrical, 18–20
fastening, 13–15
hammers, 14
measuring, 10–11
painting, 16–18, 75–79
paper stripper, 91
planes, 63
pliers, 14
plumbing, 20–21
polarity checker, 121
pruning, 319
saws, 11–12
screwdrivers, 14
small engines, 21
splining, 59
tile nippers/cutters, 41
wall covering, 88–89
wall scraper, 92
wire strippers, 122
wrenches, 14, 20–21
Trays, paint, 18, 76–77, 85
Troubleshooting
blenders, 219
central air conditioners, 293
coffee makers, 214
cooling systems, 292–299
dishwashers, 176–178
dishwasher dish racks, 182
dishwasher leaks, 183
distribution systems, 282–292
doorbells, 133
dryers, 196–198

Troubleshooting (continued)
    electric can openers, 221
    electric ranges, 164–165
    fluorescent lights, 127
    food mixers, 216
    forced-air heating systems, 283
    furnaces, 270–271, 274–275, 278
    garage door openers, 145
    garbage disposers, 223
    gas ranges, 158
    hair dryers, 230
    heating plants, 269–282
    heat pumps, 280–282
    hot-water heating systems, 290
    intercom systems, 140
    lamps, 123
    painting, 342
    pipes, 255
    plumbing, 236–237
    refrigerators/freezers, 169–170
    room air conditioners, 297
    security systems, 137
    small appliances, 205–207
    small engines, 365–369
    steam heating systems, 287
    toaster ovens, 211
    toasters, 209
    toilets, 247
    vacuum cleaners, 227
    washers, 186–188
    washer water leaks, 191
Try squares, 11

V

Vacuum cleaners, 205, 224–229
    beater bars, 225–226, 228
    canisters, 228–229
    cord reel, 229
    dirt fans, 227
    drive belts, 226–227
    power-head connections, 228
    switches, 225, 228
    troubleshooting, 227
    uprights, 224–228
Valves
    blow-off, 291
    dishwasher drain, 181, 183
    dishwasher water inlet, 181

Valves (continued)
    diverter, 243, 244
    gas shutoff, 162
    pressure-reducing, 233
    safety, 290
    stop-and-waste, 233
    temperator, 252
    water inlet, 189–190, 288
    water stop, 233
Varnish, 54, 100, 105, 111, 341
Veneer
    cracked, 102–103
    missing, 103
    repair, 101–104
    wood, 23, 101–103
Voltage, 113
Voltage testers, 18
Volt-ohm meter, 19
Volt-ohm meters, 151

W

Wainscoting, painting, 82
Wallboard, 24
Wall coverings, 88–99
    adhesives, 88, 90, 94, 98, 99
    blisters in, 89–91
    butt seams, 95, 96, 98
    color variations, 88
    cork, 93
    in corners, 96–97
    cutting in, 97–98
    double cutting in, 90, 96–97
    durability, 88
    estimating need for, 92
    fabric, 99
    flocked, 88, 93
    foil, 88, 93, 99
    grass cloth, 88, 93
    lapped seams, 95, 96, 98
    paper strippers, 91
    patterns, 88
    prepasted, 88, 93–94
    printed, 93
    removing, 91–92
    repairing, 89–91
    seams in, 90, 95–96
    selecting, 88–89, 93
    silk-screened, 88